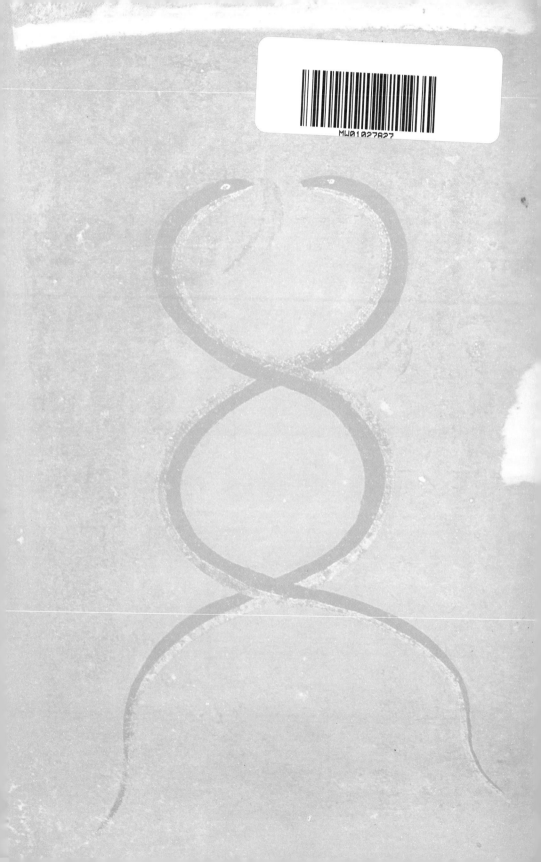

MW0102782?

INVADING THE SACRED

INVADING THE SACRED
An Analysis of Hinduism Studies in America

Editors:
Krishnan Ramaswamy
Antonio de Nicolas
Aditi Banerjee

Rupa & Co

Copyright © Krishnan Ramaswamy,
Antonio de Nicolas and Aditi Banerjee 2007

Published 2007 by
Rupa • Co
7/16, Ansari Road, Daryaganj,
New Delhi 110 002

Sales Centres:

Allahabad Bangalore Chandigarh
Chennai Hyderabad Jaipur Kathmandu
Kolkata Mumbai Pune

All rights reserved.
No part of this publication may be reproduced,
stored in a retrieval system, or transmitted, in any form or by any means,
electronic, mechanical, photocopying, recording or otherwise,
without the prior permission of the publishers.

Typeset in 10.5 pt. Sabon by
Mindways Design
1410 Chiranjiv Tower,
43 Nehru Place
New Delhi 110 019

Printed in India by
Gopsons Papers Ltd.
A-14 Sector 60
Noida 201 301

Contents

Foreword

Non-white and non-Christian cultures will increasingly have a significant impact on the affairs of the humankind in this millennium. Here, India will be a global player of considerable political and economic impact. As a result, the need to explicate what it means to be an Indian (and what the 'Indianness' of the Indian culture consists of) will soon become the task of the entire intelligentsia in India. In this process, they will confront the challenge of responding to what the West has so far thought and written about India. A response is required because the theoretical and textual study of the Indian culture has been undertaken mostly by the West in the last three hundred years. What is more, it will also be a challenge because the study of India has largely occurred within the cultural framework of America and Europe.

In fulfilling this task, the Indian intelligentsia of tomorrow will have to solve a puzzle: what were the earlier generations of Indian thinkers busy with, in the course of the last two to three thousand years? The standard textbook story, which has schooled multiple generations including mine, goes as follows: caste system dominates India, strange and grotesque deities are worshipped in strange and grotesque ways, women are discriminated against, the practice of widow-burning exists and corruption is rampant.

If these properties characterize India of today and yesterday, the puzzle about what the earlier generation of Indian thinkers were doing turns into a very painful realization: while the intellectuals of European culture were busy challenging and changing the world, most thinkers in Indian culture were apparently busy sustaining and defending undesirable and immoral practices. Of course there is our Buddha and our Gandhi but that is apparently all we have: exactly one Buddha and exactly one Gandhi. If this portrayal is true, the Indians have but one task, to modernize India, and the Indian culture but one goal: to become like the West as quickly as possible.

However, what if this portrayal is false? What if these basically Western descriptions of India are wrong? In that case, the questions about what India has to offer the world and what the Indian thinkers were doing become important. For the first time, the current knowledge of India will be subject to a kind of test that has never occurred before.

Why 'for the first time'? The answer is obvious: the prevailing knowledge of India among the English-educated elite was generated primarily when India was colonized. Subsequent to the Indian independence, India suffered from poverty and backwardness. In tomorrow's world, the Indian intellectuals will be able to speak back with a newly found confidence and they will challenge European and American descriptions of India. That is, for the first time, they will test the Western knowledge of India and not just accept it as God's own truth. This has not happened before; it will happen for the first time.

Generations of Indian intellectuals have accepted these descriptions as more or less true. The future generations will not be so accommodating though: they will test these answers for their truth. I say this with confidence because I find that more and more people in India are gravitating towards this kind of research. These are not of mere academic interest to such people, whose numbers steadily increase. Many of them realize that Western explanations of their religions and culture trivialize their lived experiences; by distorting, such explanations transform these, and this denies Indians access to their own experiences. It can thus be said to rob them of their inner lives. But that is not all. More than most, they realize that answers to these and allied questions about the nature of Indian culture have the potential to ignite an intellectual revolution on a world scale.

The essays and critiques of Western scholarship on India's religions contained in this book must be seen as the early signs of this awakening, and of this questioning. It is thus an important chronicle of the beginnings of a shift. Some of the essays are critical surveys of what is still being purveyed as factual and veridical knowledge about India and Hinduism. These are often startling and shocking to the Indian reader, but serve the useful purpose of benchmarking the state of current Western 'knowledge' about India. Others are critiques of the application of European ideas like psychoanalysis to Indian culture. But all of them, at various levels, must ask the question—is the Western academia producing knowledge about India?

The latter half of the book chronicles how key sections of the academic establishment in America have responded to these challenges, and tries to understand how they processed it as a threat rather than as a long overdue call for a dialog. The book suggests that the answers to some of these questions may lie in American culture and its European roots. In many ways, therefore, the book is an attempt to reverse the gaze on the West, and is sure to make for provocative reading.

S.N. Balagangadhara
University of Ghent,
Belgium

Preface

I

The relations between the academic community and the Hindu community in North America have recently come to be characterized by a sharp debate, which has also spilled over into journalism and on to the Internet. It was prompted by the reservations expressed by a significant number of Hindus in North America over the way Hinduism is portrayed in the Western academia and by the vigorous response of the academic community to such criticism.

As an academic, who is also a Hindu; or conversely, as a Hindu, who is also an academic, I (along with some of my other colleagues) stand at the volatile point of intersection between these two communities. This makes my role in the debate particularly fraught but also, by the same token, also particularly sought at times. I was requested a couple of years ago by Mark Silk, Professor of Religion in Public Life at Trinity College, to address the issue through an article in *Religion in the News*.[1] I am thankful to him for having provided me with the opportunity. That was in 2004. Now, after an interval of three years, I have been invited to write this preface to a book which documents an important segment of this ongoing controversy. It seems only fair that I should accept this request as well. It enables me to examine the issue once more and to tease out my thoughts on the issues further in this already tense narrative. This book singes with the sparks that flew as the psychoanalytic approach to the study of religion became the lightning rod of the grievances of the Hindus, particularly those residing in the United States, against a cross-section of the academic community in North America devoted to the study of Hinduism. It documents the way these

---

[1]See Arvind Sharma, "Hindus and Scholars", Religion in the News (7:1 (2004) pp. 16-17, 27.

grievances were articulated and ventilated, as well as the response from the world of the Western academia and, to a certain extent, from the media, as the issue came to a head.

II

It seems to me that the issue first needs to be viewed on the broadest canvas possible, namely, that of history, before one turns to the details.

Such a historical perspective is best developed by utilizing the distinction regularly drawn in the study of religion between the insider and the outsider, notwithstanding some problems of definition involved in invoking this distinction. From the point of view of this distinction, the study of religion, in the intellectual history of humanity, seems to exhibit a fourfold typology in terms of the modalities of transmission involved, in the context of the various religious traditions over the past few centuries: (1) insider to insider; (2) outsider to outsider; (3) outsider to insider and (4) insider to outsider.[2] The various religions flourished in relative isolation in the pre-modern era. Historians do warn us that perceptions of such isolation may be somewhat exaggerated, but no one has seriously challenged the view that the main channel of the intellectual communication of a religious tradition was from *insider to insider* during this period. This state of affairs began to change with the rise of the West and the onset of the modern era. During this phase, as the West became familiar with the religions of the Americas, Africa, and Asia, one main mode of transmission about these religions became that from *outsider to outsider*. Western scholars, outsiders to these various religious traditions, began sharing their knowledge about them with *other* Westerners, who were as much of an outsider to the religious traditions they were receiving information about, as those who were providing it. However, as the Western domination of the world became institutionalized in the form of colonialism, the West began to control the intellectual discourse in its colonies and the insiders to these traditions began to be profoundly affected, even in their self-understanding of their own religious traditions, by Western accounts.[3] Thus another dimension was added to the channeling of religious communication—

---

[2]Arvind Sharma, "Insider and Outsider in the Study of Religion", Eastern Anthropologist 38(1985):331-33.

from *outsider to insider*. This age of European imperialism had run its course by the end of the Second World War, and, with the liberation of the former colonies, the direction of the discourse took yet another turn. The members of the various non-Western religious traditions began to challenge their colonial descriptions in the post-colonial world. Now the insiders themselves began to claim the right to tell the outsiders about their faith, thus reversing the flow of information from outsider to insider, to *insider to outsider*.

It could be argued that this book reflects the state of discourse about Hinduism at this cusp of insider to outsider.

III

If the perspective presented above possesses some measure of verisimilitude, then we are now at a turning-point in the relationship among the interlocutors in the study of religion. Historical changes, however, are not linear, even when their direction is discernible. Historical changes are more like the changes in ocean flows caused by tides. It is sometimes not apparent that the tide has begun to turn, even when it has. And even as the tide advances there are backflows, which tend to confuse the onlooker. Such a tidal shift generates eddies and undercurrents. The going is not as smooth as at high tide, when the scene takes on a serene aspect and the ocean seems to bare its bosom to the moon, as Wordsworth might say.

This metaphor, if not off the mark, may serve to both illustrate and explain the messiness of the present situation. However, although it might make it more understandable, it does not make it easier to deal with, for many issues seem to demand our attention all at the same time.

One is thus forced to be selective, one hopes without being arbitrary. In the rest of this preface I would like to identify four such issues which stare us in the face. I hope these issues will resonate with the readers independently of whether they belong to the academic community or the Hindu community. I shall employ a rubric to encapsulate the key point of each of the four issues I wish to foreground, and hope that

---

[3]See Arvind Sharma, "Towards a Post-Colonial Comparative Religion? Comparing Hinduism and Islam as Orientalist Constructions", in Thomas A. Idinopulos, Brian C. Wilson and J.C. Hanges, eds., *Comparing Religions: Possibilities and Perils* (Leiden, Boston: Brill, 2006) pp. 221-233.

these, perhaps initially cryptic, expressions become increasingly less so as we proceed. These four encapsulating expressions are the following:

- The response threshold
- Cognitive versus non-cognitive approaches
- Bias and error
- The genetic fallacy

IV
The Response Threshold

We owe this expression to Prof. Eric J. Sharpe. He writes:

A "response threshold" is crossed when it becomes possible for the believer to advance his or her own interpretation against that of the scholar. In classical comparative religion this was hardly a problem, since most of the scholar's time was spent investigating the religions of the past and often of the very remote past. Interpretations might be challenged, but only by other specialists working according to Western canons and conventions. Today, by contrast, a greater proportion of study is devoted to contemporary, or at least recent, forms of living traditions. The study of religion often shades into a dialogue of religions, in which the views of both partners are (at least in theory) equally important. The response threshold implies the right of the present-day devotee to advance a distinctive interpretation of his or her own tradition—often at variance with that of Western scholarship—and to be taken entirely seriously in so doing.[4]

What one is thus experiencing now in the academic world is the crossing of the response threshold by the Hindu community in North America. This Hindu community in North America has now reached the demographic critical mass, when its reactions can no longer be disregarded. As teachers of religion we have perhaps already had our own more innocuous experience of the response threshold being crossed by our students, when we have fielded questions by students who belong to the very faith we are teaching.

This raises the question: How are we to react when members of the *faith* community, and not just members of the *student* community

---

[4]Eric J. Sharpe, "Study of Religion: Methodological Issues", in Mircea Eliade, editor-in-chief, *The Encyclopedia of Religion* (New York: Macmillan Publishing Company, 1987) Vol. 4, p. 25.

or colleagues in the *academic* community, cross the response threshold? The answer to this question is now in the process of being formulated before our very eyes and the reaction to this book will provide one answer to the question.

V
Cognitive Versus Non-Cognitive Approaches

It is clear from the documentation provided in the book that the protest is not always about *facts* which may be adjudicated on the basis of evidence but often about *interpretations,* especially psychoanalytic ones, which do not seem susceptible to such verification. The main achievements of modern science proceeded from the falsifiability of its hypotheses but such does not seem to be the case here. We thus need to distinguish clearly between cognitive and non-cognitive approaches to the study of religion. This distinction is crucial. "When we assert what we take to be a fact (or deny what is alleged to be a fact), we are using language cognitively. 'The population of China is one billion,' 'This is a hot summer,' 'Two plus two make four,' 'He is not here' are cognitive utterances. Indeed, we can define a cognitive (or informative or indicative) sentence as one that is either true or false."[5] Thus the statement that the god Ganeśa in Hinduism is depicted with an elephant's trunk represents an example of the cognitive use of language. "There are, however, other types of utterances which are neither true nor false because they fulfill a different function from that of endeavoring to describe facts."[6] When it is proposed that the trunk of Ganeśa connotes a limp phallus, this statement cannot be said to be true or false in the sense of his possessing a trunk but should we ask whether such a claim is cognitive or non-cognitive, the "query at once divides into two: (1) Are such sentences intended by their users to be construed cognitively? (2) Is their logical character such that they can, in fact, regardless of intention, be either true or false."[7] Once the presentation of the tradition, which happens to be non-cognitive in nature, is attacked by the followers of the tradition, the non-cognitive approach may be far more open to frisson than if a cognitive approach were being employed.

---

[5]John H. Hick, *Philosophy of Religion* (fourth edition) (Englewood Cliffs, New Jersey: Prentice Hall, 1990) p. 89.
[6]Ibid.
[7]Ibid.

If, for instance, some scholar was attacked for claiming that the worship of Ganeśa is a relatively late arrival in the Hindu pantheon,[8] then the charge could be met by pointing to existing historical evidence, which is not possible if a scholar is accused of misinterpreting Hindu mythology in the light, not of the tradition, but in terms of the scholar's own educated imagination. Here we have another version of the personalist epistemology insinuated by the phenomenological method in the study of religion, except that the person involved in this case turns out to be the scholar studying the tradition rather than a member of the tradition! One could perhaps appeal to the verdict of the "academic community" on the point, just as one might determine the stance of a "faith community." The fact, however, that the approach is non-cognitive, which is to say non-falsifiable either historically or phenomenologically, does seem to suggest that a new set of criteria might be required to assess it. It makes the study of religion less of a science to that extent, and more of an art. This fact also complicates the claims to academic freedom, for how is one to adjudicate the charge of the community that, in a particular instance, an exercise in academic freedom has turned into an exercise in academic licence and that the exercise in academic licence, in its own turn, has turned into an exercise in academic licentiousness?

The current controversy thus enables us to identify a new challenge: How to adjudicate differences of opinion, sometimes sharp, between the academic and faith communities, with criteria acceptable to both? The insiders, after all, cannot be excluded indefinitely.

VI
Bias and Error

In this book, the critics of the academics claim in essence that the academics are either biased or in gross error when dealing with some aspects of Hinduism. However, fallibility is a human condition—no one is either infallible or capable of achieving Archimedean objectivity. Both common sense and humanity demand that some procedures be devised in our field for distinguishing between random human error and error caused by bias (conscious or unconscious). Only a person guilty of the latter should reasonably be put in the dock, as it were.

---

[8]A.L. Basham, *The Wonder That Was India* (New Delhi: Rupa, 1999[1954]) p. 314.

The task might appear insurmountable on the face of it, but there is good news. Statistics as science is concerned with, and indeed has, evolved ways of distinguishing between *random* error and *systemic* error (or bias) through the process known as hypothesis-testing.[9] It is a pity that for all the rage statistics is enjoying, no one has been willing to give to the discussion of Orientalism this scientific turn. What one needs is a data bank of examples of (alleged) biases and errors pertaining to a work, and individual scholar, or a field of scholarship. This will make it at least *theoretically* possible to identify both orientalist as well as chauvinistic excesses in current discourse perpetrated by "outsiders" and "insiders" respectively.

The current situation thus enables us to identify a third new challenge: the need for creating a data base for which the following acronym is proposed: ASBESTOS (Archives for the Study of Bias and Error in the Study and Teaching of Religions). Pandora's box will perhaps not be opened, as it might otherwise, if it is kept statistically sealed.

VII
The Genetic Fallacy

Members of both the Hindu and the academic community have expressed deep distress at the *ad hominem* nature of the attacks leveled on or by the members of the two communities. This book, to which this preface is being written, itself attests unabashedly to such a state of affairs. The Hindu community wonders if the academic community can ever evoke Hinduism without condescension and the academic community wonders if the Hindu community can evoke Hinduism without sentimentality.

The concept of genetic fallacy provides us with the intellectual basis for dispensing with *ad hominem* attacks. Scholars have long insisted that the truth or falsity of a proposition can only be determined by examining the proposition on its own merits, irrespective of the source. One scientist offers the following telling if homespun illustration of the genetic fallacy: the theory of relativity is false because Einstein was not a good husband or a mere clerk. Character assassination can kill the person (metaphorically speaking) but not the proposition.

---

[9]See David S. Moore and George P. McCabe, *Introduction to the Practice of Statistics* (fourth edition) (New York: W.H. Freeman & Co., 2002) Chapter 6 and passim.

This is not to say that a person's background has no bearing on the discussion, for, after all, an expert's statement may not always be treated the same way as that of one who is not. But such background only affects the *credibility* of the proposition, not its *falsity*. After all, experts can also commit mistakes.

As the book is primarily concerned with psychoanalysis and its application to Hinduism, it may not be out of place to cite the following comments of Erich Fromm on the genetic fallacy (sometimes alluded to as the psychogenetic fallacy in certain contexts):

Freud himself states that the fact that an idea satisfies a wish does not mean *necessarily* that the idea is false. Since psychoanalysts have sometimes made this erroneous conclusion, I want to stress this remark of Freud's. Indeed, there are many true ideas as well as false ones which man has arrived at because he wishes the idea to be true. Most great discoveries are born out of interest in finding something to be true. While the presence of such interest may make the observer suspicious, it can never disprove the validity of a concept or statement. The criterion of validity does not lie in the psychological analysis of motivation but in the examination of evidence for or against a hypothesis within the logical framework of the hypothesis.[10]

Thus both communities might wish to steer clear of the genetic fallacy.

The controversy recorded in this book has generated much heat. But where there is heat there is also the possibility of light. Perhaps it will shine forth all the more if now the focus is turned towards resolving the pedagogical and epistemological issues raised by it, as it will then move the debate on to a plane where reasonable people might still differ but will have reasons clearer to all for doing so.

Arvind Sharma
McGill University,
Canada

---

[10]Erich Fromm, *Psychoanalysis and Religion* (New Haven & London: Yale University Press, 1967) p. 12 note 1.

About the Contributors

Aditi Banerjee received a B.A. in International Relations, magna cum laude, from Tufts University, and a J.D. from Yale Law School. She is a practicing attorney in New York. Her publications include: *The Hyphenated Hindus,* in *Outlook India*; *Hindu-American: Both Sides of the Hyphen*, in *Silicon India*; and *Hindu Pride*, in *Buddhists, Hindus, and Sikhs in America* (Jon Butler et al. eds., Oxford University Press.) She is interested in the preservation and revival of the traditional ways of knowledge rooted in Sanatana Dharma.

Antonio T. de Nicolas, Ph.D. is Professor Emeritus of Philosophy at the State University of New York, Stony Brook. He was educated in Spain, India and the United States receiving his Ph.D. in Philosophy from Fordham University, New York. He is presently a director of the Biocultural Research Institute in Florida. He is the author of several books on Philosophy and Hinduism such as *Avatara: The humanization of Philosophy through the Bhagavad Gita, Meditations through the Rig Veda and Habits of Mind: An introduction to Clinical Philosophy.*

Alan Roland, Ph.D. is a practicing psychoanalyst who has worked extensively with Indians and Japanese abroad and in New York City. He is on the faculty of the National Psychological Association for Psychoanalysis. He is the author of *Cultural Pluralism and Psychoanalysis: The Asian and North American Experience.*

Arvind Sharma Ph.D. is Birks Professor of Comparative Religion at McGill University, Canada and a distinguished scholar of Religion, Philosophy and Ethics. His publications include *Are Human Rights Western?: A Contribution to the Dialogue of Civilizations, The Rope and the Snake: A Metaphorical Exploration of Advaita Vedanta, Hinduism and Human Rights: A Conceptual Approach (Law in India)* and *Women Saints in World Religions.*

S.N. Balagangadhara, Ph.D. is Director of the Research Centre Vergelijkende Cultuurwetenschap (Comparative Science of Cultures) in Ghent University, Belgium. He is the author of *The Heathen in His Blindness: Asia, the West and the Dynamic of Religion*, a seminal work on the nature of religion. His central area of inquiry is to develop a description of Western culture against the background of Indian culture. Prof. Balagangadhara was recently co-chair of the Hinduism Unit of the American Academy of Religion (AAR).

Pandita Indrani Rampersad, Ph.D. (Mass Communication and Journalism), is a fourth generation born Person of Indian Origin from Trinidad, West Indies. She is a teacher, journalist, and a Hindu priest (ordained by the Arya Samaj and the first female Hindu priest to be formally recognized by the government and institutionalized religion in Trinidad, West Indies). She is an activist in Hindu, Women and Minority Issues. She chose India for her higher education, studying at the Benares Hindu University and the University of Pune.

Kalavai Venkat is a practicing agnostic Hindu with degrees in Business Administration and Physics. He is a consultant providing solutions to large corporations. His areas of specialization are Tamil literature, historiography and the impact of Abrahamic religions on Indian civilization. He also volunteers as a teacher of Tamil and Hinduism in the Indian community in the Bay Area. He resides with his wife and children in the Bay Area in California.

Krishnan Ramaswamy, Ph.D. is a scientist with a background in psychometric research. His areas of research include clinical outcomes trials in major mental and neurological illnesses. He is active in rural education projects in India, particularly among disadvantaged children. He works with the Infinity Foundation and is a student of the Vedas, Vedanta, Sanskrit and Panini, and has had a lifelong interest in bhakti poetry from various regions of India, particularly Maharashtra.

Vishal Agarwal is a Biomedical Materials Engineer with graduate degrees in Materials Engineering and Business Administration. He resides with his wife and children in Minnesota, where he works for a leading biomedical device company. He is an ardent student of religion, archaeology and the history of ancient India and has numerous contributions to his credit in peer-reviewed publications. He is currently engaged in creating electronic versions of important Hindu scriptures.

Ramesh N. Rao, Ph.D. is Professor and Chair, Communication Studies and Theatre Department, Longwood University, Farmville, Virginia. He is the author of several papers on India and its portrayals in the Media.

Sankrant Sanu is a software entrepreneur who lives in Redmond, WA and India. Following several years of working at Microsoft, he left in 1999 to co-found Paramark, a software company. A prolific writer on issues regarding India, Sankrant is a strong advocate of Indian pluralism. He is an alumnus of the University of Texas at Austin and IIT Kanpur. His interests are varied—from spirituality to skiing, from computers to playing the congas. More recently, he has been volunteering as a Hindi teacher for youths in Redmond, and drawing up a blueprint for rural education in India.

Yuvraj Krishan, MA, LL.B. is a scholar of Indian History, Religion, Philosophy and Art. He has published over 150 research papers on these topics in renowned journals in India and abroad. He has a long and distinguished record of service under the Government of India – in the Railways, Indian Administrative Service and the Audits & Accounts Department from where he retired as Deputy Comptroller and Auditor General of India in 1980. He has published several books, including *The Buddha Image: Its Origin and Development*; *The Doctrine of Karma in Brahmanical, Buddhist, Jaina Traditions*; and *Understanding Partition*.

Yvette C. Rosser, Ph.D. is an author, scholar and educationist. Her Master's thesis (at the Department of Asian Studies at the University of Texas) examined the treatment of India in the social studies curriculum. Her Ph.D. dissertation studied the politics of history in South Asia. She has authored several books and papers, including *Indoctrinating Minds: Politics of Education in Bangladesh* (2004). Rosser is co-founder of the "G M Syed Memorial Committee" and is also on the advisory board of the Baacha Khan Research Centre in Baacha Khan Markaz, Peshawar; and founder of the Badshah Khan Peace Initiative (BKPI).

Chapter 1

Why This Book is Important

Indeed, hateful speech and false information can create a climate in which . . . violence is to be expected . . . So how long will it be before a crazed gunman attacks a crowded Hindu temple in America, believing, . . . that Hindus are possessed by demons? How many children will grow up believing Hinduism is a 'filthy' religion, or that Hindus worship the devil? When they grow up, how will such children treat their Hindu co-workers and neighbors? Will they give them the respect due to a fellow citizen and human being?[1]

Jeffery D. Long, Chair, Department of Religious Studies
Elizabethtown College

This book is a chronicle of an important attempt to start a *new kind* of dialog in India-related cultural and post-colonial studies. Unlike the debates internal to the academy which privilege Western theories, institutions and networks of influence, this dialog brings practitioners of Indian traditions as *equals* at the table. Each side (the 'outsiders' and the 'insiders', respectively) has its limitations and blind spots in examining the traditions, and each is burdened by its baggage. Yet each view has merits and deserves to be considered with due respect.

The debate challenges Western portrayals of India, her religions and problems. With some variations, these portrayals have had, in a relatively unchanging way, the following features familiar to many of us from much of international media and colonial and missionary literature: Indian culture is defined by a series of abuses, such as caste, sati, dowry murders, violence, religious conflict, instability, immorality, grotesque deities and so forth. The problems in India are not seen as historical and economic in origin, but as essences of the traditions, cultures and civilization of India, making it a 'chaotic and even desperate country'. In other words, India's problems are in its DNA. India's own ongoing responses and solutions to these problems are rarely taken seriously— even though Indian history is filled with self-correcting reform movements from *within* and this process is actively at work today. In its most insidious form, this view implies that unless Indians are rescued from their culture by external intervention, they are doomed. Indians simply lack the agency to chart their own destiny and are in need of foreign care in their own best interest. What is startling is that these ideas which formed the keystone of moral rationalizations offered by the British for colonialism and exploitation continue to enjoy wide academic respectability in the West today. What has changed over time, as other scholars have noted, "is the intellectual jargon that clothes these 'analyses'".[2]

The first goal of this book is to explain how and why such images of India and its culture and civilization are produced, sustained and propagated today. It shows that these chaotic and selective images of India are *not only* the product of the personal biases and prejudices of journalists, TV producers, religious bigots or individual researchers, but also of entrenched *institutionalized mechanisms*. Starting in well-respected, ostensibly 'research based' but culturally parochial halls of American and Western academe, these images filter down into mainstream Western culture where they acquire an incredible force in shaping how India is seen.

The starting point of this book is a searching analysis of how elements of the American academy, notably the powerful American Academy of Religion (AAR), like to imagine India and Hinduism. In contrast to how American Business Schools view India—as a place of opportunity, problems and problem-solving creativity—these scholars project a generally negative, chaotic and backward view of India.

Americans in general are a deeply religious people who see the world through the lenses of religion, primarily some variant of Judeo Christianity. Western representations of India are inseparable from depictions of India's religions, particularly Hinduism. Many postcolonial scholars of Indian origin have tried unsuccessfully to wish this link away. The problems of India are seen by Americans as inseparable from the problems of Hinduism. Attempts by secular Indians to distance themselves from Hinduism have led to an academic vacuum about

Indian traditions which has been filled by external voices which often have their own agendas.

The research and writings of religion scholars go beyond the discipline's boundaries, penetrating the mainstream media, and directly impact the American public perception of India via museum displays, films and textbooks. The study of religion informs a variety of disciplines, including Asian Studies, International Studies, Women's Studies, Sociology, Anthropology, History, Literature, Journalism, Education and Politics. Western theories of Hinduism have produced fantastic caricatures of Hindus that could be dramatized by Hollywood movies, satirical TV sitcoms, or animated sci-fi cartoons. In this hierarchical structure, AAR's Religions in South Asia group can be identified as a key source of Western academic influence over India-related studies.

Input from these scholars can also have an impact on US foreign policy. For instance, a recent conference at the University of Chicago featured Wendy Doniger, Martha Nussbaum, Amartya Sen, among others, talking about generic 'Hindu groups' as being the most serious threat to India's democracy. Indeed, in the conference announcement, Nussbaum claims that Americans are wrong to be focusing on Islamic fundamentalism as a threat to democracy. She alleges that "Thinking about India is instructive to Americans, who in an age of terrorism can easily over-simplify pictures of the forces that threaten democracy . . . **In India, the threat to democratic ideals comes not from a Muslim threat, but from Hindu groups.**"[3] [Emphasis added]. The worrisome trajectory of such statements is to put Hinduism and Hindu-Americans on US government scanners and congressional hearings as threats to democracy.

Unlike in India, the academic study of religion in the USA is a major discipline involving over 8,000 university professors, most of who are members of the AAR. Within this organized hierarchy, the study of Hinduism is an important and influential discipline. This book argues that the discipline has been shaped by the use of preconceived Eurocentric categories that are assumed to be *universal* by Western syndicated research. Most internal criticism or 'peer-review' comes from among scholars who are interrelated in different ways, and it largely excludes practitioners of Hinduism. The producers and distributors of this specialized knowledge comprise a sort of closed, culturally insular cartel, which has disastrous consequences for original thinking about India and Hinduism.[4] Because much of this scholarship seems to portray Hindu culture and therefore Indian culture as pathological, exotic and abusive; a diaspora intellectual named Rajiv Malhotra has coined the term Hinduphobia to describe this phenomenon, which he has studied in great detail. This selective, questionable academic 'research' and its conclusions filter into American classrooms, textbooks and media. Thus the average American learns as much about India and Hinduism from the received wisdom of the academy as she does from any other source.

This book is about a recent intellectual challenge to this state of affairs, and the responses and counter-attacks from the academic Religious Studies establishment in America. As a result of this debate, Indian-Americans and others have started to systematically critique the misrepresentation of their traditions with the hope of widening the range of ideas presented in the academy. This generated a groundswell of support among Indians worldwide and appreciative participation by many academic scholars. At the same time, however, it has brought anger from many entrenched academicians who see the *status quo* of power being threatened.

Section I is a summarization of Rajiv Malhotra's[5] path-breaking paper critiquing the academic study of Hinduism, an event which many academicians have recognized as a 'tipping point' in opening up a serious debate.[6] The problems he exposes and the evidence he cites are extensive and worrisome. The evidence shows serious problems with the training and competence of academic scholars of Hinduism, and raises questions about parochial lenses and sloppy methodology. Most troubling are the questions he raises about the rigorousness of peer-review, and about whether scholars are in fact free to publish critiques of powerful living academics without fear or favor. Malhotra has argued that these mechanisms of quality control and self-correction which the academy relies upon have corroded into ineffectiveness in the case of Hinduism studies. These issues should deeply concern anyone who cares about the health of our academic programs.

Section I gives many examples of how India and Hinduism are distorted by these scholars. Imagine the psychological damage on a young Indian who is made to read a text that says that Ganesha's trunk symbolizes a 'limp phallus'. Or the impression left on the average American student who learns that Shiva temples are 'notorious for ritual rape and murder'. How authentic are books claiming that Sri Ramakrishna Paramahansa (an Indian saint widely revered by both Hindus and non-Hindus) was a conflicted homosexual and a pedophile who sexually abused Swami Vivekananda? How responsible is it to include a poem in the American school system (funded by a US Federal grant to *promote* multiculturalism in America) which accuses Lord

Rama of *causing* the oppression of Indian minorities and women? What is the harm caused by award-winning scholarship according to which the Hindu Goddess is 'the mother with a penis'? Many Indian-Americans have started to challenge the educational material according to which these are the *defining* characteristics of their identity. They are concerned because such material is being taught to students at an impressionable age, often to the exclusion of the practitioners' points of view. Similar negative caricatures are not presented by educators about other religions in America, making this Hinduphobia even starker. Indeed such 'scholarly' works are being used by American Christian groups to describe Hinduism as a 'dirty dignity destroying religion' and as a 'pig-pen from the east'.[7]

What we found particularly useful and stimulating was that in addition to presenting powerful evidence, Malhotra consistently tries to 'reverse the gaze' on the scholarly establishment, by using various hermeneutic techniques grounded in Eurocentric traditions and postmodernism as well as Indic thought. This incidentally, has made the academic targets of his study profoundly uncomfortable, and has caused them to lash out in response. Nevertheless this technique has very interesting possibilities—it certainly makes for provocative and insightful analyses that are worthy of further research.

Section II contains various other scholarly and thoughtful essays, many of which resulted from Malhotra's attempts to start a critique of academic Hinduphobia. Included are essays and summarization of papers from noted academic scholars like Prof S.N. Balagangadhara, Dr Alan Roland, Prof Somnath Bhattacharya, Yuvraj Krishna and Yvette Rosser, among others. These essays by experts in various fields highlight serious problems with the use of Eurocentric lenses and methodologies to Indic thought and culture and also raise questions about the level of scholarly training in the academy. This section is capped by two masterful, evidence-based critiques of specific instances of academic bias, by non-academic diaspora scholars. The intellectual rigor and scholarliness of these latter works demonstrate that the health of the academy would be enhanced by greater scrutiny from the 'outside'—i.e., views of practitioner-scholars who are currently excluded by academic fiat from the discourse.

Section III chronicles what transpired in the wake of all this intellectual ferment. It describes both the community activism by the Indian-American community and the actions and reactions of many scholars from the academic establishment. It is a fascinating drama of how the debate got started, derailed, started again, and still continues today. The diaspora and a few courageous members of the academia attempted to start a serious, no-holds barred debate *on the merits of the issues* raised. But on the other side of this are many Western scholars who insist that they know Indian culture perhaps even better than Indians themselves. They come armed with advanced degrees, prizes and endorsements from prestigious America universities, and they hold powerful posts in some of the best-funded institutions of higher education in the world. They claim that adequate self-criticism already exists in the form of internal peer-reviews and they resist opening up the debate to non-academics. They see such criticisms from 'outsiders' as *attacks* from unqualified people who are 'emotional' and 'dangerous' rather than 'rational'. What is particularly fascinating is that *all* attempts at debate by diaspora members have been branded as 'Hindutva' or 'saffron' or 'fundamentalism' without any basis. It seems that the mere act of defiance against the American institutional establishment can bring down wrathful condemnation.

Section IV examines how this debate played out in the American mainstream media—such as in *Washington Post* and *New York Times*—as well as niche publications like the diaspora press and alumni magazines. It provides an account of well-entrenched stereotypes and tropes as well as of attempts to challenge them. It highlights an important aspect of this cross-cultural dynamics—the huge asymmetries of power that exist between Eurocentric academics and their critics in access to venues where views can be articulated fairly and openly.

We wish to be clear that the entire blame of biased and selective portrayals of Hinduism and Indian Culture cannot be laid at the doorstep of the American Academy of Religion or even of biased scholars within it. Indians themselves have contributed to the problem in significant ways. While American universities have major programs for studying world religions and cultures, Indian universities do *not* offer similar programs. Indeed, the discipline of Religious Studies does not even exist in most universities in India due to the peculiar myth that positive knowledge about, and intellectual involvement with, religion breeds communalism. Many Americans are shocked to learn that there is a deep prejudice among India's intellectually colonized intelligentsia according to which secularism implies the exclusion from, or even the condemnation of, Indic religions in civic society—which is the exact opposite of the respectful place given by American secular civic society to its majority Judeo-Christian traditions.

While the intellectually rigorous discourse of traditional Indian religious scholarship continues to limp along in ashrams, *mattas*, Jain *apasaras* and *gurudwaras*, in order to engage in a serious *academic* study of Hinduism, Indians have to go to American, British or Australian universities because there are hardly any opportunities available for such study within India. In other words, unlike all other major world religions, Hinduism does not have its own *home team*, by which we mean a committed group of academic scholars who are both practitioners of the faith and well-respected in the academy at the highest levels. Judaism, Christianity, Islam, Buddhism and Sikhism each have their respective home teams in the academy—in fact, multiple homes representing different denominations of these religions. Even China has recently established numerous well-funded Confucius Institutes around the world that teach Chinese civilizational approaches to human issues on par with Western models.

Malhotra has pointed out that while Chinese, Japanese, Tibetan, Korean, Arab, and even various European cultures—such as Irish, Italian and French, for instance—have actively funded and managed the American academic representation of their cultural identities, Indian-Americans have not done so to a comparable extent. They have been content with building temples, while their cultural portrayal in the education system and in the media has been abandoned to the tender mercies of the dominant Western traditions. The results have hardly been fair and balanced. In a world where perception and reality are interlinked, this is worrisome for Indians worldwide. Authenticity of representation and full participation in shaping the understanding of one's culture has implications beyond the fields of anthropology, cultural and religious studies.

For one, Indian-American, and especially Hindu-American children are often the target of cultural and racial bias in the classroom. By and large the civilizational achievements of India in science and technology in its long history, or its contributions to modern American lifestyles like yoga, vegetarianism, non-violent political protest and the like are largely ignored in the classroom setting. In other words, the positive contributions of India and its cultures are made invisible. (For the Chinese, after years of effort this is changing). When academically licensed misportrayal of the oppressiveness, weirdness and dangerous-ness of Indian culture and religions is added to this mix, it has a powerful impact on Hindu-American children, many of who try to hide their religious identity. Many of them become disaffected with their families and communities. The pride that Christian-American children take in their civilzational contributions to the world is lacking in many Indians, and this leads to emotional pain and self-alienation.

Furthermore, as numerous American historians point out, the *control* of 'others' depictions by white Americans has led to their ethnic cleansing, incarceration, enslavement, invasions and genocides. Native Americans, Blacks, Jews, Gypsies, Cubans, Mexicans, Chinese, Filipinos, Japanese, Vietnamese and now Iraqis have suffered brutalities that were legitimized by depictions of them as primitive/exotic, irrational, heathen, savage and dangerous and as lacking in human values.[8] Malhotra has raised the alarming possibility that the failure of Indian-Americans to translate their personal success into respect for their cultures and traditions is a condition paralleling Jews in Europe not so long ago, and that in an economic downturn, they could become scapegoats in America.

The view from the business world and from top business schools is increasingly upbeat. It sees Indians as problem-solvers and the Indian economy as a positive engine for the world. This is exemplified by books like Gurcharan Das' *India Unbound*, or Tom Friedman's *The World is Flat*. Numerous articles in business periodicals like *Forbes*, *Fortune* and *Businessweek* also see India this way. While keenly aware of numerous Indian problems, this view does not see them as being *inherent pathologies* of Indian civilization and therefore unchangeable. Rather, these problems are the result of historical and economic forces, and Indians are seen as having the necessary civilizational creativity, will and wherewithal to address them. This view is counteracted by academic Hinduphobia.

For instance, the diplomat and public intellectual, Simon Anholt[9] observes that while India is shining in business and especially IT, there are many other factors determining its image and credibility. This image, in turn, will either facilitate or hamper India's quest for economic growth in a globally competitive world, and its ability to provide more than a billion people with a humane future. He is also acutely aware of an important dichotomy in how the world, especially the West, views India:

> A country is like a brand because it has a reputation, **and because that reputation partly determines its success in the international domain.** The ability of each country to compete against others for tourists, for investment, for consumers, for the attention and respect of the media and of other countries is significantly determined by

the power and quality of its image . . . What seems certain is that India's brand new **image is a fragile one,** based on a couple of prominent sectors and a handful of globally successful entrepreneurs: . . . but it isn't yet clear how 'Capitalist India' fits together in the public imagination with the 'Indo-chic' of music, fashion and movies, and with the 'Traditional India' image of a vast, mysterious, culturally rich but **chaotic and even desperate country.** A clear, single, visionary national strategy is badly needed— but one that is, of course, rooted in truth and not in wishful thinking.[10] [Emphasis added]

Anholt's point is that unless Indian's take charge of engaging with the world concerning how their country and its culture are portrayed, the economic future of *all Indians* may be at stake. India's reputation in the world is still fragile, and there is a perceived dark side to her culture. While we are firmly in favor of acknowledging and tackling India's numerous problems, we also understand that not all problems are 'cultural' as the outside world perceives them. Nevertheless this perception—which is at least partly shaped by Eurocentric academic wisdom about India's religious and cultural milieu—can undermine India's future. This is not just an unacknowledged problem for Hinduism, but for India as well. As Anholt notes,

Just like any other country, India needs to consider perceptions alongside reality, and recognise their almost equivalent importance in today's globalised world. India's brand image **may not be complete, up-to-date or even very fair,** but so much in the modern world depends on what people believe to be true, that a good twenty-first century government must learn to be as good at branding the country as building the country.[11] [Emphasis added]

Anholt is dead right when he says that unfair perceptions can have serious economic consequences for India. Even the most successful and admired Indians can be affected in surprising ways. For instance, in the recent acquisition of Arcelor by Mittal Steel, the culture, race and religion of Mittal Steel's principals, specifically its chairman Lakshmi Narayan Mittal, played an important role. The *New York Times* reported that Arcelor's principals initially ridiculed the idea of a merger with 'a company of Indians' and it was only after shareholders threatened to revolt that they backtracked. The *Times* also reported that the offer by Mittal was originally mocked as 'monkey money from an Indian'. Mittal was viewed as **"Attila the Hun attacking from the east, taking over an iconic company from the west."**[12] Arcelor even turned to a shadowy Russian conglomerate—on the publicly declared grounds that they were Europeans, (and therefore civilized)—to act as a White knight to prevent takeover by the Indians. A bidding war ensued. No one knows how much of the final price Mittal paid for Arcelor was the 'Hindoo premium', or the indirect tax for being from a backward and oppressive culture.

This book is also about another major development of our times: the use of the Internet to bypass old channels of information flow that tend to be controlled by established power structures. Sulekha.com was merely one of many web portals catering to Indian interests on the Internet, until the diaspora challenge to the academic scholars arrived at its doorstep in 2002. This controversy became the focal point of an energetic and often learned debate on Sulekha, converting it into an important forum for a large number of immigrants and others disenfranchised by the existing discourse. The articles on Sulekha have also been used as reading material in several courses in Hinduism Studies, South Asian Studies, History, Cultural Studies and Anthropology.

These debates and controversies have had effects on both sides. On the side of the American academics, there are the unacknowledged and informal beginnings of a re-evaluation and introspection. For Indian-Americans, the debate has lent a voice—as students whose tuitions help to fund the education system; as philanthropists being solicited for donations to colleges; and as a community being profiled in absentia by the scholars. Indian-Americans have also been inspired by this public debate to launch a variety of new organizations to represent them on relevant issues in America. Indian-Americans now demand participation in these debates as equals. This will influence Indians' self-images in the twenty-first century.

We hope that this book will make a contribution to understanding what happens when those who know Indian culture best sit on the sidelines and allow its portrayal to be controlled *exclusively by others i.e. by the dominant culture*. It should provoke Indians to question the Western representation of India that has become the canonical self-representation of many Indians. We hope the book will appeal to intellectuals in India, especially students of History, Sociology, Postcolonial Studies, International Relations and Indology. We also hope that the book gives a gripping account of the political dynamics unleashed when the Hindu 'other' wants to be included as an equal in the intellectual discourse.

This comic is intended to be satirical, and any resemblance herein to actual events or persons living or dead is purely coincidental.

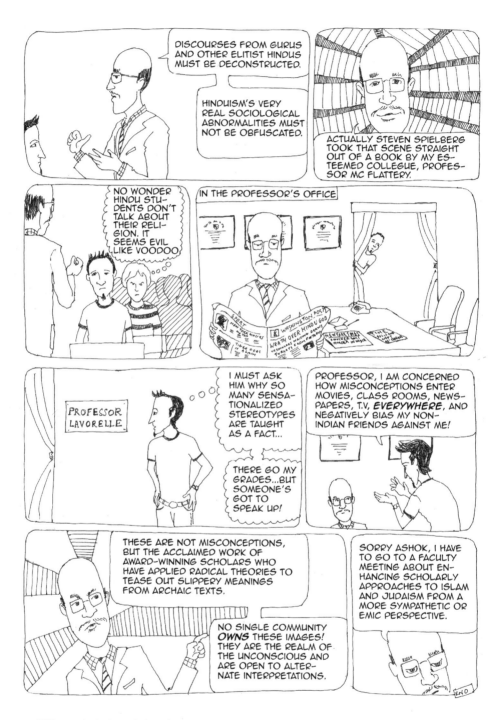

This comic is intended to be satirical, and any resemblance herein to actual events or persons living or dead is purely coincidental.

I
EXPOSING ACADEMIC HINDUPHOBIA

◆

By Pandita Indrani Rampersad, PhD

The *Bhagavad Gita* is not as nice a book as some Americans think . . . Throughout the *Mahabharata* . . . Krishna goads human beings into all sorts of murderous and self-destructive behaviors such as war . . . The *Gita* is a dishonest book; it justifies war.

Wendy Doniger, in *Philadelphia Inquirer*[1]

There is generally, therefore, an inverse ratio between the worship of goddesses and the granting of rights to human women. Nor are the goddesses by and large compassionate; they are generally *a pretty bloodthirsty lot*. Goddesses are not the solution.

Wendy Doniger, in *Washington Post*[2]

This comic is intended to be satirical, and any resemblance herein to actual events or persons living or dead is purely coincidental.

This comic is intended to be satirical, and any resemblance herein to actual events or persons living or dead is purely coincidental.

Chapter 2

Religious Studies: Projecting One's Shadow on the 'Other'

This section paraphrases *RISA Lila-1: Wendy's Child Syndrome,* a seminal essay by Rajiv Malhotra, published in September 2002 on an Indian-American web magazine.[3] The essay critiqued a selection of scholarly literature associated with the American Academy of Religion summarized prior criticisms of established scholars.[4] Its main contribution was to make the academic materials more easily accessible and to encourage non-academicians to participate in the debate. Being online allowed the essay to reach a global audience quickly and informally and encouraged rich interactivity as never before in the diaspora. The essay revealed explicit examples of Hinduphobia in the work of certain scholars in Religious Studies and related academic fields.[5] It also examined the training and expertise of several Western scholars, particularly their ability to translate Indian languages into English.[6] The essay also examined the use of psychoanalysis and other Eurocentric theories to analyze specifically Indic categories and conditions.

The objective here is to analyze and critique a specific genre of American scholarship that uses Freudian theories to interpret Indian culture. A central point made by the essay is that **there are no true outsiders**—because those who stand outside Hinduism remain firmly inside their own ideologies, institutions and cultures. Academic objectivity is presumed to exist based on peer-reviews, but sometimes there are 'cartels' wherein a few powerful academicians exert excessive, influence in the field, resulting in an unfair power equation. The views of 'insiders' (in this case practising Hindus, including Western-educated ones) are marginalized by interpretations from 'outsiders' (Ivory Tower scholars holding Eurocentric and sometimes markedly anti-Hindu ideological stances).

Chapter 3 shows how *award-winning* scholars declared Sri Ramakrishna (hereafter referred to simply as 'Ramakrishna'), the nineteenth century Hindu saint, to be a sexually disturbed and abusive homosexual. A closed coterie of scholars claims to have 'academically proved and established' that Ramakrishna was a child molester, who also forced homosexual activities on Swami Vivekananda. Further, this new 'discovery' claimed that Ramakrishna's mystical experiences, and those of Hindu mystics in general, are pathological sexual conditions in need of psychoanalysis. However, very serious questions have been raised about the 'evidence' used to make these startling claims. The chapter follows the work of Swami Tyagananda who casts serious doubt on whether the sources referenced by the scholars were being adequately cross-checked during the peer-review process.

Chapter 4 shows how other *award-winning* scholarship from America describes the Hindu Goddess in ways that would resemble a sex maniac and demonic person. She is seen as over-sexed and violent—her sexuality being the focus of scholarly analyses and she allegedly inspires or somehow causes violence. These scholars are busy capturing obscure data in the backwaters of rural India in their attempts to ascribe diverse mental pathologies in the Goddess. They also attempt to link Hindu religious icons with various pathologies and problems in India.

Chapter 5 shows how some well-placed scholars have concluded that Ganesha's trunk symbolizes a 'limp phallus'; his broken tusk is a symbol for the castration-complex of Indian men; and his large belly and love of sweets are proof of the Hindu male's enormous appetite for oral sex. Shiva is interpreted as a womanizer whose temples encourage 'ritual rape', prostitution and murder, and his worship is linked to violence and destruction. Such academic works have received *awards from the most prestigious American institutions of scholarship*, and such views about Hinduism have started to gain respectability in mainstream America.

Chapter 6 exposes scholarship which claims that Hindu mothers do not love and bond with their children to the same extent that White women do. Those critics from outside the academy who have dared to speak up have been condemned as 'hijackers' of the scholarship.

Chapter 7 gives examples where one of today's pre-eminent American interpreters of Sanskrit texts, Wendy Doniger, is harshly criticized by a few scholars. Her translations (and mistranslations) are widely relied upon by other scholars, and are widely disseminated as prescribed readings in American colleges and among the public as popular paperbacks.

Chapter 8 shows how this group of scholars dismisses Tantra as a hypocritical philosophical and spiritual mask hiding its true character as pornography and a system of exploitation of the lower castes.

Many inauthentic translations and interpretations by pre-eminent Indologists have been popularized into standard meanings today. Such scholars dismiss the translations and interpretations of contemporary Tantric practitioners as inauthentic and are contemptuous of practicing Hindus participating in the discourse about their own traditions. Indeed, practicing Hindus are treated as inferior to the scholars and are excluded from the discourse about their traditions. The American Academy of Religion (AAR) needs to investigate this serious issue and its multi-faceted ethics committees could serve as ombudsmen to ensure that the communities' voices have a fair representation.

The group of scholars who are the focus of this book has concluded that, in order to understand modern India, Hindu society at large needs to be psychoanalyzed for its sexual deviance and pathologies. *RISA Lila-1* raised the concern that, historically, pogroms, incarceration, slavery, oppression, and genocides of ethnic peoples— such as of Native Americans, Blacks, Jews, Gypsies, Cubans, Mexicans, Vietnamese, Filipinos, Chinese, and Japanese—have often followed depictions of them by White Americans, first as primitive/exotic, then as dangerous 'savages' threatening civilization or 'our way of life', and finally as lacking in human values and therefore unworthy in 'civilized' society.[7]

Many scholars in this group are interconnected, and follow the lead of the powerful and influential academician, Wendy Doniger. **By focusing its analysis on this specific group of scholars, *RISA Lila-1* was adapting an established practice in Indian logic, termed *prathama-malla-nyaya*, where the exemplar of a particular line of argument is taken on, and if demolished, the whole school or argument is debunked. It is in this context that the critiques in the next few chapters must be seen. The scholarly works chosen are indeed emblematic of this genre. In order to draw attention to this troubling and degrading phenomenon of pathologizing Hinduism, we not only present evidence from the work of these scholars (tongue-in-cheek termed 'Wendy's Children' after their powerful mentor),[8] but we also try to understand** how these scholars manufactured their uniformly negative views of Hinduism.

Later, this section presents two new theoretical models: one called the *Chakra Hermeneutics* model for understanding how a diversity of approaches to Hinduism is possible; and the other called *Wendy's Child Syndrome* to reverse the gaze upon this group of scholars by applying Chakra Hermeneutics.

The key issues are about distortions and are *not* a denial of Hinduism's eclectic and diverse views on sexuality that make it very open-minded. (For instance, Hinduism does not discriminate against homosexuality the way Abrahamic religions do. Nor is Hinduism prudish about sexuality in the human or divine realms.)

In the wake of *RISA Lila-1*, numerous groundbreaking essays and critiques began to appear, written by individuals with an interest in India Studies—including Prof. S.N. Balagangadhara, Sankrant Sanu, Prof. Ramesh Rao, Dr. Alex Alexander, David Freedholm, Prof. Ramdas Lamb, Dr. Yvette C. Rosser, Vishal Agarwal, Prof. Somnath Bhattacharyya, Swami Tyagananda, Dr. Sunthar Visuvalingam, and Madhu Kishwar, among others.[9] Several of these articles appear in Section II or in the Appendices, or are extensively referenced in this book.

Asymmetries of Power

The majority of the scholars in academic Hinduism Studies are from outside the Hindu traditions, while at the same time they are 'insiders' to other religious and political ideologies and cultural identities. McKim Marriot explains how this leads scholars to unconsciously superimpose their own ideologies and identities onto their work. In his book, *India Through Hindu Categories,* he writes: "The assertion that all social sciences are cultural (and therefore 'emic') amounts to denying the privileged position claimed for an imaginary 'etic' social science, which is really derived from the investigator's emics".[10] This is exactly what *RISA Lila-1* pointed out—there are no truly neutral outsiders. While they may stand outside Hinduism they remain firmly inside their own cultures.

The views of Hindu practitioners are seen as being less reliable and legitimate than scholarly perspectives. As will be seen, a divergent view or critique from Hindu practitioners, is sometimes perceived by academicians as a personal 'attack' against them.

The result of personal and career bonds among the small number of specialists in a given topic is unhealthy to the integrity of the peer-review process. Personality cults develop around certain scholars who are in academic positions of power in Hinduism Studies and whose work is propagated uncritically by their students. The powerful scholar in turn nurtures and protects his/her students.[11]

In this atmosphere of patronage, it is questionable whether junior scholars can openly and fundamentally question the quality of the work of living senior scholars. In much the same gullible way that the mainstream American media did not investigate the Bush administration's claims that the WMDs (weapons of mass destruction) in Iraq are a 'smoking gun in the form of a mushroom cloud', so too, disappointingly, neither the mainstream media nor scholars in the field have bothered to investigate the detailed allegations of Hinduphobia enumerated in this book.

The theoretical model called 'Wendy's Child Syndrome' (presented later in this section) reverses the gaze back on the scholars of India. The primary symptom of the syndrome is the use of Freudian analysis and other fashionable Eurocentric theories to deconstruct and reconstruct the 'Hindu other', and in the process caricature and trivialize Indian personalities, practices, scriptures and deities. Contrary to their scholarly commitment to intellectual freedom and openness, many academicians have responded to this investigative research with a surprising degree of intolerance and hostility, while thankfully, there were others who privately encouraged it.[12]

Freudian Psychoanalysis of Non-Western Cultures

The validity of applying Freudian psychoanalysis to non-Western religions is questionable. Even though it has been largely rejected within contemporary Western academia, psychoanalysis has become a very fashionable methodology to study Indian culture. Sudhir Kakar, one of India's best known psychologists and academicians anticipated this challenge when he wrote back in 1982:

> Psychoanalysis . . . has been insufficiently aware of its underlying paradigm and its deep roots in Western culture. The implicit model of man that underlies the psychoanalytic meta-theory is certainly not universal; the psychoanalytic notion of the person as an autonomous, bounded, abstract individual is a peculiarly Western notion. In contrast, the holistic model of man that underlies Indian mystical approaches and propels their practices is rooted in the very different Indian cultural tradition which, in some ways, lies at an opposite civilizational pole.[13]

Kakar has criticized psychoanalysts for not questioning traditional Western paradigms and thus allowing them to paint the rest of the world with the 'lever of psychopathology'. He calls this a "reductionist, 'nothing-but' approach in which mystic states as well as other Indian cultural phenomena are reduced to psychopathology". He criticizes scholars who treat Indian culture and society as a 'patient'.

Applied psychoanalysis is a method used to analyze myths, religion, folklore, and culture. Kakar finds it unfortunate that "the constraints which apply to the psychoanalytic treatment situation, namely, the analyst's attitudes of respect and objectivity towards the patient, are largely absent in . . . works of 'applied' psychoanalysis."

Freud's fascination with 'taboo totems' influenced many social scientists to use psychoanalysis to interpret their ethnographic studies. Their ethnographies would 'confirm' or 'falsify' Freud's notions such as the Oedipus complex. The work of the renowned Western anthropologist Margaret Mead and that of Bronislaw Malinowski were sometimes used to 'disprove' or 'prove' Freud's theories.

Many have wondered whether psychoanalysis is applicable and appropriate to use in areas that have nothing to do with the psycho-clinical research on which it is based. Indian societies have not been subjected to the scientific data-gathering required in order to apply such theories. This is especially so when the analysts are amateurs, untrained in the discipline of Psychology and/or lack knowledge in Indian cultural nuances.

Institutions of Knowledge Production and Distribution

As with any large academic field, Religious Studies in the US is highly organized and features prestigious journals, academic chairs, and extensive programs of study. The American Academy of Religion (AAR) is the primary organization for academic scholars of Religious Studies in the United States. RISA (Religions in South Asia) is the unit within the AAR for scholars who study and teach about religions in the Indian subcontinent. For the most part, the controversies described herein emerged out of the Indian diaspora's debates with RISA scholars and **the issues cannot automatically be generalized to apply to other areas of the academy.**[14]

The AAR traces its origins back to 1909, when an organization was formed for professors and scholars of Biblical Studies whose 'purpose was to stimulate scholarship and teaching in [the Christian] religion'.

In 1922, the name was changed to the National Association of Biblical Instructors (NABI, meaning 'prophet' in Hebrew); thus its early history was clearly Bible-centric. In 1963, stimulated by 'changes in the study of religion'[15] NABI became the American Academy of Religion. The 'American Academy of Religion has over 8,000 members who teach in some 1,500 colleges, universities, seminaries, and schools in North America and abroad.'[16] Since its inception, the Religious Studies organizations that evolved into the AAR have maintained close relations with the Society of Biblical Literature (SBL), founded in 1880. For many decades the two have held their annual conferences jointly. While SBL members primarily study and promote *insiders'* views of Judeo-Christianity,[17] AAR members are not supposed to promote any particular viewpoint, and are required instead to pursue the study of religions through a neutral lens. Notably, the stated mission of the AAR is to promote objectivity, whether from within, or outside of, any particular religious tradition. With a growing membership, the AAR has developed enormous clout over the direction of Religious Studies and the humanities at large.

Wendy Doniger, the Mircea Eliade Prof. essor of History and Religion at the University of Chicago, is one of the most influential persons in the study of religion.[18] Partly as a result of Malhotra's essay, Doniger and other scholars have come under the scrutiny of Hindus in North America—for their practice of dredging-for-dirt and using disheveled, questionable approaches to translations and interpretations of traditional Hindu texts. Many white Americans with personal spiritual connections to Hinduism have also taken note of this fabulously contrived, out-of-context eroticizing of Indian culture.

Professor Doniger is a high-profile scholar in the field. She is former president of the American Academy of Religion and a past president of the influential Association of Asian Studies (AAS). Currently, she is the director of the Martin Marty Center for Advanced Study of Religion at the University of Chicago, and chairs many academic bodies. She has two PhDs, one from Harvard and one from Oxford, and is a prolific author.

Doniger's former students have been successfully placed in academic jobs and chairs, carrying forward the torch of her theories and research principles regarding Hinduism. Her former graduate students are found throughout the field of Hinduism Studies, providing tremendous intellectual influence.[19] She is notorious for her racy, bawdy interpretations of Hindu texts. A BBC-linked site wryly describes her:

> Professor Wendy Doniger is known for being rude, crude and very lewd in the hallowed portals of Sanskrit Academics. All her special works have revolved around the subject of sex in Sanskrit texts.[20]

Through the years, she "has heartily enjoyed building her 'franchise'[21] with notions of her own immortality". In a 2000 issue of the *Criterion*, she declared triumphantly that her former students had given her a sort of immortality, because they "have provided [her] with a *parampara*[22] (or spiritual lineage) more enduring than [her] own books, let alone [her] flesh".[23]

More importantly, the influence of Doniger's Freudian approach to Indian society is not relegated to the confines of the Ivory Tower; indeed, it has had a pervasive and pernicious impact across mainstream America. She and her protégés—the *chelas* in her *parampara*, many of whom have approvingly been called Wendy's Children—contribute many articles on India and Hinduism to widely used resources. These include Microsoft's *Encarta*, and other encyclopedias and reference works, as well as textbooks used in Asian Studies courses across the US. Therefore, as *RISA Lila-1* pointed out, if one wishes to get to the bottom of *how and why* the American mainstream misunderstands and misinterprets India, the University of Chicago is certainly one of the primary knowledge production factories to investigate.

Further, Freudian speculation about Ganesha having an Oedipal complex) has made its way into American museums as 'fact'. One of the foremost art museums in the US is the famous Walters Art Gallery in Baltimore. Its display on Asian Art features some rare and precious art objects of Asia. Each display item has an explanation next to it that is also in the museum's coffee table book referenced below. These explanations are important, because many school tours visit the museum, and through art, the kids learn about Asian culture. The large eleventh century Ganesha carving in the collection has a write-up, and the following are excerpts from it: *"Ganesa, is a son of the great god Siva, and many of his abilities are comic or absurd extensions of the lofty dichotomies of his father."* And it then goes on to say: *"Ganesa's potbelly and his childlike love for sweets mock Siva's practice of austerities, and his limp trunk will forever be a poor match for Siva's erect phallus."*[24]

Furthermore, anthropologists, like Stanley Kurtz,[25] have concluded that nursing Hindu mothers do not bond with their babies the way white women do and that Hindus lack a sense of individuality because of their inability to perceive separation in space or time. Additionally, Doniger sees the classic, widely revered and time-honored Indian epic *Mahabharata* as Krishna engaging in genocide.

While most Hindu saints and gurus are unconcerned about these academic matters, Kakar notes that there have been 'a few eminent mystics . . . unable to resist the temptation of taking contemptuous swipes' at the psychoanalytic paradigm. He cites the Indian yogi, Sri Aurobindo, who found it "difficult to take psychoanalysis seriously" seeing it "as a science [that] was still in its infancy—inconsiderate, awkward and rudimentary at one and the same time". The poetic Indian sage further commented, "One cannot discover the meaning of the lotus by analyzing the secrets of the mud in which it grows."

Recently, a significant number of Hindu-Americans and members of the academy have called into question the off-color, ingeniously refashioned scholarly works made by some academicians. The Hindu intellectuals who persist in analytically questioning this scholarship have been profiled and targeted as 'fundamentalists' and 'attackers' by RISA scholars and some journalists. This dismissive, dehumanizing process potentially sets Hindu-Americans up for a denial of their basic human rights.

During the past decade, many Hindu-Americans have participated in panels at conferences, moderated online discussion groups, and published critical essays in order to better understand these issues. They have documented an entrenched bias in Hinduism Studies. As later chapters of this book will show, this ongoing research has provoked incendiary reactions on several academic Internet forums. After reading the 'official' though skewed and rather ribald narratives about their religious traditions, Hindus approached the gates of academia with their keyboards buzzing. Those in the Ivory Towers raised their bridges and filled the moats against the savage barbarians. The battle lines were drawn.

The Paradigm is Shifting[26]

RISA Lila-1 galvanized many members of the diaspora and academic scholars to start paying attention to the issues, and some of them wrote letters and articles on this relevant topic—a selection of which is featured in this book. Ironically, in the process they were transformed from objects of 'clinical' study by academicians to objects of academic scorn and phobia. Instead of being seen as a treasured resource, and as a source for professional research, the Hindu/Indian 'others' morphed into dangerous academic adversaries threatening the purity and elitism of the Ivory Tower.

Chapter 3

Targeting Sri Ramakrishna

This chapter and the ones that immediately follow, quote directly and explicitly from the writings of the scholars under review, and give equally direct rejoinders. Many readers who are not used to academic writings about Indian culture and religion find such language shocking. They have suggested that we should avoid being so explicit, and that such an analysis might even be in bad taste. However, we offer the following reasons for this open style:
1. Our children have to face such educational materials, so we should be courageous to deal with it, in order to ensure more authentic portrayals.
2. Without explicitly citing exact quotes and examples, such scholarship seems unbelievable to many lay persons. When a milder and indirect approach has been applied to critiquing such work, many readers have regarded it as our opinions not based on fact. They have rightfully demanded hard evidence, which is why we have adopted the direct approach.
3. Just about every facet of Hindu sacredness is under direct and systematic attacks by these scholars. Hindu deities (including Ganesha, Devi, Shiva, etc.), Hindu pre-eminent gurus and Hindu society itself are depicted as pathological and dangerous. Therefore, it is essential to be equally direct in documenting this bias.
4. The freedom to analyze and understand the 'other' psychologically must go both ways. Just as the academic scholars have their intellectual freedom to depict our sacredness through their lenses, their critics have similar rights.

Under the guidance of Wendy Doniger at the University of Chicago, Jeffrey Kripal did his PhD dissertation on the eighteenth-century Hindu mystic, Sri Ramakrishna. During his research, Kripal visited the Ramakrishna Mission in West Bengal. Several people at the Ramakrishna

Mission recall enthusiastically helping him during his research. One of the sisters of the Mission said, "He seemed to be such a nice and endearing young man that anybody would trust his intentions."[27] Consequently, many at the Mission helped him with his work. However, contrary to what most people would consider to be academic ethics and common decency, Kripal did not afford anyone in the Mission an opportunity to make sure that there were no factual or linguistic inaccuracies in the dissertation he was preparing. Later, Kripal himself acknowledged that the well-known American scholar of Religious Studies, Gerald Larson, had admonished him for not vetting the manuscript with the Ramakrishna Mission before publishing it.[28]

The scholars at the Ramakrishna Mission learned about Kripal's rather sensational conclusions only years later, after Kripal's book had come out and had won great acclaim. The book, *Kali's Child*, was based on his PhD dissertation.[29] **It won the First Book Award from the American Academy of Religion**, an organization in which Doniger and her colleagues hold powerful positions. Kripal soon landed a job at Harvard, which was followed by a prestigious academic chair at Rice University at a very early stage in his career. **The popular and prestigious reference source, *Encyclopedia Britannica*, listed Kripal's book as its top choice for learning about Ramakrishna**—indicating the immense impact such factually questionable portrayals can have. This goes to show that even a shoddily researched and hastily peer-reviewed work, if accepted and promoted by the academic establishment, can swiftly become authoritative. This is dangerous, especially when the readership consists largely of persons who are ignorant about the tradition, and, worse still, when the readers have Biblical or race-based stereotypes passed on through mythic images of folkloric 'others.'

Kripal's work hinges on his translations of old Bengali texts along with the application of Freudian psychology. It has been shown that much of his thesis was based on *mistranslations* of Bengali writings about the life of Ramakrishna and sweepingly ignorant misinterpretations of Bengali culture. This was independently established by several Bengali language experts.[30] It was reported that the sole Bengali language expert on Kripal's thesis committee was absent when the dissertation was accepted. Significantly, none of the scholars on the AAR committee who glorified this book by awarding it the prestigious First Book Award, were fluent speakers of Bengali. Yet, accuracy of translation was considered to be a defining aspect of this particular 'prize-worthy' product. The exotic 'other' was up for grabs and not entitled to the same agency or voice that the scholars would have afforded to a similarly important Western icon.

Different Standards for Different Religions

It is difficult to imagine that such a PhD dissertation, if it were based on sources in Aramaic or Hebrew, would emerge full-blown in the field of Biblical Studies or early Christianity without an independent and thorough cross-checking of sources. It certainly would not be showered with praise and awards. Such a controversial interpretation of an aspect of Western culture by a non-Westerner would *not* have passed review without being subjected to serious counter-arguments. The standards that prevail in writing about Judeo-Christian culture are more rigorous and demand a greater burden of proof before a scholar can overthrow long-established views with his/her convoluted interpretations. The issue is thus not with any particular conclusion which a scholar might reach, but about the *processes* employed, and the lack of rigorous quality control, especially given the possibility of reinforcing stereotypes and biases about a minority culture. The non-White 'other' was too easily available in the mythic imagination of these scholars and they used and abused it with impunity.

Neither Kripal nor Doniger are trained as psychologists. Numerous experts in psychology have raised serious issues about Kripal's understanding and application of psychological theory.[31] Would an equivalent dissertation in Biblical Studies, based on amateur Freudian psychoanalysis, be supported and valorized to a similar extent in the mainstream academy, if, for instance, its core thesis was to *prove* incest in the Bible or a lesbian Mary? Yet, scholars associated with RISA, by their celebratory support of Kripal's interpretations, passed sweeping and unfounded pedophiliac judgments on Ramakrishna, without even a modicum of representation from the opposing points of view—which just happen to be the perspectives of those who knew about Ramakrishna's life best. No wonder the *RISA Lila-1* article deliberately provoked controversy by asking, "Is this fashionable hermeneutics of eroticization of Indian spirituality simply another form of Eurocentrism being projected upon the 'other'?" Some critics have expressed the opinion that instead of winning a prize, this research should have been reviewed as a possible violation of academic due process and ethical norms, especially after it was challenged on grounds of extensive mistranslations and its arbitrary and questionable usages of Freudian methodology.

It is especially troubling that forthright challenges from within academia are discouraged for political reasons.[32] Another disingenuous tactic used to discourage criticism is to pose the scholar as the victim of violent and obscurantist forces.[33]

The Ramakrishna Mission was at first reluctant to battle the academic establishment concerning these misportrayals, though eventually one of its scholarly monks, Swami Tyagananda, began addressing the matter seriously. This, however, happened only after Kripal's thesis had already begun to tarnish Ramakrishna's reputation in mainstream society, including American universities. This inspired Swami Tyagananda to write a 130-page rebuttal to *Kali's Child* that moves point-by-point through a list of many serious errors in Kripal's work.[34] Kripal turned down suggestions to include a summary of Tyagananda's rebuttal at the end of the new edition of his book, in spite of the fact that such a move would have restored some semblance of objectivity to it.[35]

The Making of a Best-Seller

The section below gives just a brief summary of some of Kripal's glaring errors of scholarship, followed by an explanation of why this sort of scholarship is dangerous on many different levels, especially since it gets legitimized and popularized by the politics in the academy.

1. *Lack of required language skills:*

Swami Tyagananda and other Bengali scholars who have had extensive discussions with Kripal are in little doubt that he simply does not know the Bengali language even though he claims to have read the documents cited by him about Sri Ramakrishna's life. Swami Tyagananda pointed out that when spoken to in Bengali, Kripal didn't understand, and when asked something directly about Bengali culture he could not respond. Swami Tyagananda elaborates:

> Kripal's conclusions come via faulty translations, a willful distortion and manipulation of sources, combined with a remarkable ignorance of Bengali culture. The derisive, non-scholarly tone with which he discussed Ramakrishna did not help either . . . Kripal's ignorance of Bengali culture jumps right off the page. Many of the author's misrepresentations are due to a simple lack of familiarity with Bengali attitudes and customs . . . [Furthermore,] it's painfully clear that he also has little knowledge of Sanskrit.[36]

Prof. Narasingha Sil[37] is a historian and native Bengali speaker who does not consider himself religious, and is in no way associated with the Ramakrishna Mission. In fact, his works about Ramakrishna and Vivekananda are considered controversial by religious scholars associated with the Ramakrishna Mission. In his independent assessment, Sil wrote,

> Jeffrey [Kripal] is very adept at using Bengali-English dictionaries and picking the most appropriate synonyms of words (disregarding the primary, secondary, tertiary meanings) he feels could make his point... [He] is unable to converse in Bengali (but very prompt at using dictionaries)... In order to fit the square peg of a Tantrika Ramakrishna into the round hole of a homosexual Paramahansa, Kripal manufactures evidence by distorting the meaning of sources.[38]

2. *Misinterpreting Tantra:*

Kripal's bizarre central thesis is summarized in his own words:

> Ramakrishna was a conflicted, unwilling, homoerotic Tantrika[39] [...] Tantra's heterosexual assumptions seriously violated the structure of his own homosexual desires. His female Tantric guru and temple boss may have forced themselves . . . on the saint . . . but Ramakrishna remained . . . a lover not of sexually aggressive women or even of older men but of young, beautiful boys.[40]

Kripal authoritatively asserts that his interpretation of Tantra as 'sexy, seedy and strange' is authentic and that long-standing Indian and Western philosophical interpretations of Tantra are a cover-up. Responding to this charge, Swami Tyagananda replies,

> What is Kripal's understanding of the word, Tantrika? He says it is a term associated with 'magical power, strangeness, seediness, and sex'.[41] He dismisses the 'philosophical expositions' of Tantra as inauthentic because they are 'designed to rid Tantra of everything that smacked of superstition, magic, or scandal'.[42]

Given this predisposition, Kripal insists, "Ramakrishna's mystical experiences were constituted by mystico-erotic energies that he neither fully accepted nor understood."[43]

3. *Superimposing psychological pathologies upon Ramakrishna, without basis:*

Kripal posits with supreme confidence, but with no evidence whatsoever, some rather sweeping assertions about Ramakrishna by superimposing generalizations out of a superficial vocabulary on psychology. Kripal's theories are reminiscent of self-help pop-psychology:

> The literature on sexual trauma suggests that individuals who have experienced abuse often become adept at altering their state of consciousness . . . lose control of their bodily, and especially their gastrointestinal functions, experience visions and states of possession, become hypersensitive to idiosyncratic stimuli (like latrines), symbolically re-enact the traumatic events, live in a state of hyperarousal . . . become hypersexual in their language or behavior, develop hostile feelings towards mother figures, fear adult sexuality, and often attempt suicide. This list reads like a summary of Ramakrishna's religious life.[44]

However, as Swami Tyagananda notes,

> None of the symptoms enumerated in the 'literature on sexual trauma' is present in Ramakrishna's life. But since Kripal has approached his subject with a predetermined verdict, he resorts to specious reasoning in order to come up with the judgment he has in mind. Ramakrishna has 'pronounced homosexual tendencies', ergo he must have suffered childhood sexual trauma, ergo he must re-enact the traumatic events. This exercise in weak-link logic is reminiscent of kangaroo courts where the prisoner is convicted first and then the 'evidence' is manufactured at a more convenient time.[45]

4. *Mistranslating lap as genitals, and later calling it a 'defiled sexual space':*

In the first edition of his book, *Kali's Child*, Kripal translates the Bengali word for lap, *kol*, as meaning 'on the genitals'. In the second edition, he changes it somewhat, "It is clear that Ramakrishna saw 'the lap' as normally defiled sexual space."[46] A bewildered Tyagananda replies, asking Why does the author consider the lap (kol) to be 'normally defiled'? In Indian culture—and Bengali culture in particular—the lap has an extremely positive and warm maternal association. For instance, the national anthem of Bangladesh, written by Tagore, contains the following line: "Takhon khela dhula sakal phele, O Ma, tomar, kole chute ashi." Translation: "After the day's play is over, O Mother, I run back to your lap."[47]

Thus, as Sil noted above, Kripal appears to be essentializing important Bengali words into connotations that go well beyond the primary, secondary or tertiary meanings of the words, simply to suit his thesis. Similarly, Kripal justifies his translation of 'head' as phallus in Hindu texts because, according to his simplistic understanding: "The head in the mystical physiology of yoga and Tantra [is] the ultimate goal of one's semen and so an appropriate symbol for the phallus."[48]

5. *Mistranslating 'touching softly' as sodomy:*

Based on his mistranslation of 'softly touching' to mean sodomy, Kripal claims that Ramakrishna was "uncontrollably rubbing sandal-paste on the penises of boys."[49] Tyagananda rebuffs, "I must admit that when I read Kripal's interpretation of 'touching softly' (aste aste aparsha korchhen) as attempted sodomy I could only laugh." In Indian culture, elders lovingly pat and caress children out of affection. There is nothing sexual in it. Perhaps the scholar is superimposing attitudes towards children based on his experiences of his own culture's coldness and/or perversions.

6. *Mistranslating* tribhanga *as cocked hips:*

The Bengali text used by Kripal refers to the term *tribhanga*, the characteristic three-curved pose that is seen in Indian sculpture and Indian classical dance. *Tribhanga* literally translates from the Sanskrit to mean three bends. This is also Krishna's common pose with his body bent in three places—at the knee, waist and elbow—with flute in hand. A common expression used for Lord Krishna in Bhakti poetry is 'tribhangi-laal'. However, Kripal translates this pose as 'cocked hips' and uses it in his grossly inept translations/interpretations: "Stunned by the cocked hips of the boy, Ramakrishna falls into *samadhi*."[50] This is Kripal's *scholarly proof* that Ramakrishna's mystical states were homoerotic. Since Krishna is commonly depicted as bent in three places, with flute in hand, would it not follow from Kripal's psychoanalytic interpretation that any Krishna devotee's love for this beatific form is a sign of the devotee's sexual or homosexual arousal by the Lord's cocked hips?

7. *Mistranslating* vyakulata *to give it a sexual spin:*

The Bengali word *vyakulata* is translated by Kripal to mean erotic torment or anxious desire instead of the appropriate word, longing. Tyagananda writes, "There is nothing in the word to suggest *desire*, which, typically, for Kripal, carries a sexual connotation. [...] To load the Bengali words heavily with sexual innuendo is to completely distort the meaning of the text." Yet, Kripal mistranslates this word to make the claim, "Ramakrishna's anxious desire was often directed to his young male disciples."[51]

8. *Mistranslating* uddipana *to give it erotic meaning:*

Another Bengali word distorted by Kripal is *uddipana*. According to Tyagananda, the word's meaning is enkindling or lighting up. But Kripal arbitrarily gives it the meaning of homoerotic excitation: "Ramakrishna turns to the youth and says, 'Please don't leave today. When I look at you, I get all excited'."[52]

9. *Kripal lets his imagination runs wild:*

Apart from the above mistranslations and mischaracterizations of both esoteric and mundane aspects of Indian and Bengali culture, Kripal also slips into creating and inventing scenes. Referring to Ramakrishna's important meeting with a *sanyasin* of the Naga sect, Kripal assumes that there was a lot happening for which there is no record whatsoever. Kripal's erotic visualizations define his discourse as he writes,

> [W]hat it must have been like for Ramakrishna, a homosexually oriented man, to be shut away for days in a small hut with another, stark-naked man. Vedanta instruction or not, it was this man's nudity, and more especially, his penis, that normally caught Ramakrishna's attention. How could it not?[53]

Based on the facts that have been presented thus far, it appears that there are a lot more complex and convoluted things going on in Kripal's mind than there were in that simple, rustic hut, as Tyagananda notes.

10. *Special effects thrown in:*

To spice up his research with erotic special effects, Kripal inserts the phrase 'his nearly naked body' while referring to a boy in the *Lilaprasanga*. However, Swami Tyagananda writes that after carefully examining the entire *Lilaprasanga* text, "Nowhere in the *Lilaprasanga* is there even a mention of the boy's nakedness." Similarly, since Kripal wants to make the claim that the temple manager sexually forced himself upon Ramakrishna, he dramatizes it by retranslating the manager of the temple to 'boss'. There are many other amusing and outlandish remarks Kripal interjects that prove that he did not perform rigorous research or expend due diligence to genuinely understand his subject matter. For instance, Tyagananda explains, "Kripal may be at his most laughable when he tells us that Ramakrishna's practice of

Vedanta consisted of only taking the monastic vows and eating rice in the portico of the *Dakshineswar* temple."[54]

11. *Suppressing the facts:*

The massive archive on the life of Ramakrishna has more than enough material to provide authentic accounts of his life and the theory and practice of his teachings. However, this would run counter to the conclusions upon which Kripal premises his work, so, according to Tyagananda, 'He simply ignores the evidence that contradicts his theory. Picking and choosing his way through the materials, searching for phrases and scenarios that support his thesis, Kripal indulges in the outright suppression of information that would provide an entirely different perspective. Isn't this just a convenient form of 'censorship'?"[55]

It is said that Kripal's soft spoken and charming demeanor at first endeared him to many Indians, who later found it hard to believe that he would blatantly falsify the facts. Tyagananda points to the following as just one example of catching him red-handed doing just that:

> Kripal says that he has never argued something as simplistic as that Ramakrishna was a pederast [sexual lover of young boys] . . . While Kripal may not have used those words in his book, that was certainly his conviction which guided his interpretations. How else can one explain his letter (14 August 1996) written to the secretary of the Ramakrishna Vedanta Society, Boston, in which he wrote that it was quite "obvious" that "Ramakrishna's mystical states were accompanied, and **likely generated, by some ethically problematic acts, among them pedophilia**".[56] (Emphasis added)

12. *The Kangaroo Court Trial of Sri Ramakrishna*[57]:

Tyagananda summarizes the methods that Kripal uses in the name of scholarship:

> Since Kripal wants to associate Ramakrishna with boys, no matter what, we shouldn't be surprised that he first suspects, then assumes, then presents as a fact that Ramakrishna was sexually abused as a child. That there is absolutely no evidence for this makes no difference to Dr. Kripal; we have the effect—Ramakrishna's 'homoerotic impulses'—so now the cause must be found. Aha! Certainly he must have been sexually abused as a child. The spiritual ecstasies that Ramakrishna experienced as a child are thus reinterpreted as 'troubling trances'.[58] The only one 'troubled' by

them is Kripal who feels compelled to find sexual abuse somewhere in there.

Legitimized by a staged peer-review process, and by dodging all the critical analyses, Jeffrey Kripal triumphantly proclaims in the introduction to the second edition, that "The case of Ramakrishna's homosexuality . . . seems to be closed . . . *Kali's Child* has been lauded by scholars . . . for being right."[59] [Emphasis added] Tyagananda responded to this claim, "One wonders if any of those praising the book have ever read its citations. Have any of those scholars who have given the book so much acclaim actually read the Bengali sources that he quotes? How many of them can actually read Bengali *well*, if at all?"

Huston Smith, perhaps the most widely read Western scholar of Religious Studies, severely criticized *Kali's Child* in the *Harvard Divinity Bulletin*, calling Kripal's type of scholarship 'colonialism updated'.[60] Many individuals in the Indian diaspora are not prepared to believe that bias-afflicted academics can have the final word about their traditions.

13. *Evasive dismissal of criticism by psychoanalyzing the critics:*

Kripal, instead of responding to the point-by-point critique with his own evidence, attacked his critics and their alleged motives. The RISA establishment has not held him accountable for this tactic. Tyagananda rejects Kripal's attempts to put the spotlight on Hindus' alleged narrow-mindedness and sees this as a ploy to shift attention away from his bad scholarship:

> To say, therefore, that those who reject Kripal's thesis are doing so from their own homophobia is to completely miss the point . . . To sum up: The problem I address in my critique is not the sexualized reading per se. The problem has nothing to do with homosexuality. The problem is with the evidence, and in particular the massive distortion and misuse thereof in Prof. Kripal's book. Where there is adequate evidence, let there be homoerotic, hetero-erotic, or otherwise erotic readings of the lives and motivations of saints— and scholars! But let not the evidence be manufactured.[61]

Tyagananda continues,

> To make the facile claim that the criticism leveled against *Kali's Child* was due to [the critics'] homophobia is to deflect from the real issue of shoddy and deceptive scholarship . . . Kripal, in

discussing the angry reaction to his book received in India and among Ramakrishna devotees, views their outrage as an expression of their fear of homosexuality . . . Now with pious admonitions rising like the full swell of a church choir, Kripal pleads: 'I can only encourage them not to walk down this path, as so much of our humanity (and divinity) lies in a decidedly different direction.'[62]

First Kripal twists the data on Sri Ramakrishna to fit into the pattern of psychopathology and homoerotica. Then he accuses his critics of homophobia, when in fact they were pointing out his shoddy methodology and erroneous conclusions. It is rather disingenuous to accuse Hindus of being anti-modern 'puritans,' 'irrational' and homophobic, thereby implicating an entire civilization as obscurantist. It is a handy way to play the victim role and not have to face the critics.

Psychological Profile of the Scholar

RISA Lila-1 employs an innovative device that reverses the gaze upon the scholars. It applies the same psychological techniques on scholars that they use to analyze 'others'. For instance, it utilizes 'psychoanalysis'

> in the reverse direction, as an American minority gazing at the dominant white culture, and in Kripal's case gazing at the fascinating process by which non-whites assume whiteness to gain upward mobility [and] social capital. This exercise may make some of the objects of this reverse psychoanalysis angry even though my case is well backed by the evidence cited, whereas Kripal used a postmodern approach that eschews responsibility.[63]

One may use the data provided by the scholars themselves to accomplish this. At the 2000 AAR conference, Kripal mentioned that his father was a dark-complexioned man whose family was of Roma ('Gypsy') extraction and had lived in Central Europe for many generations. (Roma are the target of racial bias in much of Europe to this day.) His father had married a woman of Germanic descent. Kripal explained that his Indian-sounding name comes from his father but that he and others in the academy pronounce it differently than the way the common Indian name is pronounced—he pronounces it as 'cry-pal' whereas Indians would pronounce it 'Kri-paal'. Kripal confirmed this and **wrote publicly** about his ethnicity:

> My Czech surname also happens to be popular in northern India, where it is usually associated with the Sikh tradition (in a new twist

on the story, **this summer I learned that family oral tradition traces
our roots back to East European gypsies, who immigrated from—
where else?—India**). [Emphasis added.][64] 'Jeffrey J. Kripal,' then,
strikes the Indian eye as an unusual amalgamation of Western-
Christian (Jeffrey) and Indian-Sikh (Kripal) traditions.[65]

Malhotra wonders whether a thorough psychoanalysis of Kripal's
Oedipal struggle to distance himself from his father, and to be White,
might illuminate Kripal's compulsion to prove his alienation from Indic
traditions.

Prof. Sil also interprets Kripal's psychosexual psychology:

We learn that prior to joining graduate school at Chicago, Jeffrey
was training to be a monk or a minister at a Catholic seminary,
where he was 'forced to explore the interfaces between sexuality
and spirituality' and he felt 'more than tortured by [his] own
psychosexual pathologies.' By 'psychosexual pathology' Kripal
means, as he put parenthetically, anorexia nervosa. This means,
as is well known, a pathological condition in which the patient
cannot retain any food (or feces, if we choose to go by a Kripal-
like psychoanalytic symbolism which he applied to Ramakrishna)
in the body. He also writes that he felt his readings in Christian
bridal mysticism somewhat unholy because of its apparent
homoeroticism. However, upon further cogitations (or perhaps,
meditations) on the subject Kripal 'came to a rather surprising
conclusion in regard to [his] own mystico-erotic tradition:
heterosexuality is heretical.' He then tells readers that his 'religious
life was quite literally killing [him]'—his 'body weight had sunk
well below the normal'. It was at this juncture that the future
biographer of Ramakrishna turned his attention to stuff Hindu and
chanced upon the Bengali priest of Dakshineswar.[66]

RISA Lila-1 identified areas of Kripal's personal psychology that
may be relevant in interpreting his work, including:

(i) his self-acknowledged homophobia generated by his apprehension
of homoeroticism, resulting in his fear or confusion over his own
trans-gendered repulsions and tendencies, and

(ii) his complex about being half Roma, and perhaps a subconscious
push to prove his separation from the Indian part of his roots, in
order to claim a full-fledged white American pedigree.

This raises a very important issue about objectivity and reflexivity
in the representation of Hindu themes in the academy.

RISA Lila-1 raises the issue of how many in this scholarly cult allow their personal psychoses to color their scholarship: "It is quite common for Western scholars to play out their private lives through their scholarship about 'others', in ways that create both positive and negative results and, when misused, can be self-serving, insensitive and quite low-brow". Indeed, an examination of additional examples provided by the article does strongly suggest that for many RISA academics, objectivity and scholarly rigor are easily sacrificed.[67]

Conclusions Concerning Kripal's Craft

Besides the numerous serious errors in translation that the academy failed to investigate, three methodological problems have become evident with the award-winning book, *Kali's Child*:

1. Scholars in psychology departments do not rely upon Freudian methods to dish out serious allegations against a person. Such applications, by religion scholars who are untrained in psychology, to targets that are far removed from their familiar American culture, run the risk of the blind leading the blind.
2. Freud himself seems to have questioned the propriety of applying his methods to third parties via native informants or posthumously. The analyst was required to directly engage the subject of inquiry.[68]
3. Freud never had access to non-Western patients, so he never established the validity of his theories in other cultures. This is a point emphasized by Alan Roland, who has researched and published extensively to show that Freudian approaches are not applicable to study Asian cultures.[69] Doniger's school of scholarship universalizes Freudian methodologies and pathologies, and combines them with obscure Indic materials to weave wild theories about Indian culture. Indians advocating Freudian psychoanalysis have simply accepted and mimicked the Western theories *without* independently verified clinical and empirical data to establish their applicability in Indian contexts.

To illustrate that Kripal's work is not an isolated case, but rather the dominant variety of scholarship, one may examine Doniger's psychopathological interpretation of the *Mahabharata* (I.101). For instance, she wrote:

A sage named Mandavya is wrongly supposed to have participated in a robbery and is impaled on a stake. We may see masked homosexual symbolism in the impalement (a homosexual violation) and the cutting off of the long stake (a castration), though we should also notice what the Indian tradition makes of this episode: In a kind of reverse castration, Mandavya feels that he has gained something, has been given a stake that, however shortened, he still seems to regard as an extension of himself, a useful superpenis as it were. The childhood guilt that inspired the episode of anal intercourse gives way to the fantasy of the large penis of the grown man.[70]

As both Edward Said and Ronald Inden[71] have elaborated, the West's 'other' and 'self' are co-constructed intellectually; the construction of one being used to construct the other. Ironically, perhaps, this is why it pains RISA-related academicians to have their pet theories about India refuted—because their self-images rest on neo-Orientalist constructions belying their bellicose claims of having *already* deconstructed all those nineteenth-century Orientalists. India's imagined, exoticized culture offers a prism of creatively construed pathologies, a delightful looking-glass through which imaginative scholars define themselves, enabling their secret fantasies to play out in their descriptions and narratives.

It is not unreasonable to explore whether a certain type of psychosis directs the motivations of the practitioners in this academic field and ultimately drives the work of some academic South Asianists—in the form of the topics and questions selected, the data imagined and filtered, and the interpretations given. This awareness of scholars' self-projection on to the 'other' has solid academic precedence. Anthropologists have long been aware that scholars' private lives get unintentionally superimposed on to their work. As an introductory Anthropology textbook explains,

> In the 1930s some American anthropologists even went so far as to undergo psychoanalysis before fieldwork in an attempt to 'calibrate' the instrument of data collection, a practice quickly abandoned.[72]

Our concern is that personal traumas often determine the tone of scholars' works. Their personal dramas are superimposed on trendy interpretations of Hindu deities and scriptures that are far outside the tradition's own interpretations.[73] Doniger's followers bring too much of their personal baggage with them. Their private psychological predilections are let loose by their privilege to imagine Hindu religious texts and traditions as they please. The resulting interpretations are often less a product of the text than a window into the exoticized mind of the writer/researcher.

Monaghan and Just describe the epistemological problems anthropologists face in their work: "No one comes to fieldwork as a tabula rasa". Scholars are drawn to the field of anthropology, as with other related disciplines such as South Asian Studies and Indology, often by powerful philosophical movements that color their worldviews and interpretations.[74] Ultimately, as many critics have pointed out, Kali's Child offers more insights into the psychoanalytical elements of Wendy's Children than any legitimate insights into the life and work of Ramakrishna.

The self-criticism of contemporary anthropologists about their discipline provides a model of humility, as noted by Monaghan and Just:

> [S]ome anthropologists have argued that 'objectivity' is a false issue. Our bias—that is, our social and historical situation—is what gives us a point of view, and hence constitutes a resource we should openly draw upon in our interpretations. Others contend that any form of representation is an exercise in power and control [...] All the same, isn't it an act of extraordinary hubris for someone to propose to present a definitive account of another people, even when it is based on long-term 'participant observation'? And isn't it problematic that the vast majority of ethnographers are Westerners when the vast majority of their subjects have been non-Western? [Emphasis added]

Scholars of Religious Studies are trained to use a system of tools and methods known as hermeneutics. These are methods that enable new interpretations from a body of knowledge or a text, with the intention of expanding insights about the materials beyond what the practitioners of the given faith have traditionally maintained. But how does one prevent hermeneutics from becoming an arbitrary and ad hoc methodology driven and shaped by a scholar's own psychosis? In what ways are the resulting analyses, mirrors of the scholars' own cultural maps rather than windows into the other culture? What are some checks and balances that would help reduce such risks? The following chapters summarize other cases that show the seriousness of these questions.

Chapter 4

The Hindu Goddess Reinterpreted as a Symbol of Sex and Violence

Sarah Caldwell, another member of RISA, won the prestigious Robert Stoller Award for her scholarship on the Hindu Goddess. Below is a long excerpt from her research paper, 'The Bloodthirsty Tongue and the Self-Feeding Breast: Homosexual Fellatio Fantasy in a South Indian Ritual Tradition', for which she was given an award by her largely Western peers.

> This essay demonstrates that in Kerala, symbolism of the fierce goddess [Kali] does not represent abreactions of the primal scene fantasies of a Kleinian 'phallic mother' or introjection of the father's penis; rather, we will show that themes of eroticism and aggression in the mythology are male transsexual fantasies reflecting intense preoedipal fixation on the mother's body and expressing conflicts over primary feminine identity.[75]

> The essential rituals of the Bhagavati cult all point to the aggressive and fatal erotic drinking of the male by the female, the infamous orgy of blood sacrifice of male 'cocks' at the Kodungallur Bhagavati temple; the male veliccappatu's cutting of his head in a symbolic act of self castration . . . [Kali] is herself, first of all, a phallic being, the mother with a penis . . . she is the bloodied image of the castrating and menstruating (thus castrating) female . . . In this type of analysis the phallic abilities of the goddess disguise castration anxieties ultimately directed toward the father as well as homosexual desire for the father's penis. Following Freud, such analyses stress the father-son polarity of the oedipal conflict as the central trauma seeking expression.[76]

> As Alter and O'Flaherty amply demonstrate, milk and breast-feeding are also symbolically transformed in the male imagination

into semen and phallus . . . The ascetic male who retains the semen becomes like a pregnant female with breasts and swollen belly; the semen rises like cream to his head and produces extraordinary psychic powers . . . Not only are the fluids of milk and semen, symbolic equivalents, but the act of 'milking' or breastfeeding becomes a symbolic equivalent to the draining of semen from the phallus in intercourse.[77] [Emphasis added]

Caldwell uses the English word 'cock' for the rooster, so as to link the ritual with the phallus. Since the Keralites were not mentally imagining this *English* word with its double meaning for both rooster and penis during their ritual, this translation by Caldwell is a clear example of how her psychological predispositions enter into a supposedly 'scholarly' interpretation. She goes so far as to put quotation marks around the word 'cock' in order to emphasize the double meaning that she is aware of, but not the Keralites. In other words this is a projection of the scholar.[78]

In the example cited above, the Goddess becomes shorn of all her numerous, traditionally accepted meanings and a new *primary* meaning is authoritatively adduced by the privileged Western scholar. Thus Kali becomes, without argument, *"first of all,* a phallic being, the mother with a penis . . . she is the bloodied image of the castrating and menstruating (thus castrating) female." [Emphasis added] This genre of essentializing, which precludes all other meanings, is a symptom of Wendy's Child Syndrome as explained in a later chapter.

Caldwell quotes *one* twenty-one year old man in order to 'prove' that homosexual encounters are rampant in Kerala. Many such overplayed 'confessions' are the basis to reach sweeping conclusions.

Fortunat⸴y, criticisms from within the scholarly community of the methods used by scholars such as Caldwell are not entirely lacking. But they do not go far enough in uncovering the problems that lie within these free-floating kinds of analyses. In 1999, Caldwell published another book, *Oh Terrifying Mother: Sexuality, Violence and Worship of the Mother Kali.*[79] In her review of the book, Cynthia Humes wrote,

Caldwell documents numerous themes of sexuality, abuse, and vengeance in Keralite religion and culture. She concludes, 'Mutiyettu actors who are particularly talented at playing the role of Kali might be traumatized individuals whose particular psychological propensities and histories compel them towards this form of performance' (259). I find this unconvincing. As she herself notes, Caldwell did not conduct a detailed study of or even collect the life histories of the individual Mutiyettu actors playing the role of Kali; so there is no direct evidence of even one individual fitting this typology (259). The implications she sees, while tantalizing and truly fascinating, are based on extended digging into and assembling a dispersed array of sensationalist and homoerotic mythological themes, combined with rumored sexual activity. The unlikelihood of the thesis is underscored by the fact that the role of Kali is only open to a handful of individuals, who must wait until the age of over fifty to even assume this coveted starring role, and further, they would need to evidence 'particular talent'.[80]

But how seriously does Caldwell have to take such criticism? Is such criticism serious enough to question the quality of the scholar's work so as to insist that such work be simply disregarded? Or, in the absence of that, should at least some safeguards be put in place to ensure more rigorous quality control over work like this in the future? Unfortunately, Humes is not willing to go that far. In spite of her acknowledging the lack of evidence in Caldwell's sweeping claims, Humes is still able to imagine how Keralite society is indeed highly charged with homosexuality, sexual trauma, and abuse, without citing any credible scholarship. In fact, later in her review, Humes agrees with certain aspects of Caldwell's sexual interpretation of the ritual. She superimposes an entirely different sexual psychosis on the Keralites than does Caldwell, and thus the peer-review becomes merely an argument between different kinds of pathologies of Keralite Hindus.[81]

The above can be seen as the cozy willingness of certain scholars and critics within academia to lower standards of evidence and give the stamp of validity to work that should actually be seriously questioned. "This is the difference between a slap on the wrist and rigorous peer-review".[82] It certainly gives the impression that criticism by RISA insiders is encouraged to remain within certain boundaries, in order to give this kind of lackluster analysis the appearance of peer-reviewed integrity. On the other hand, as we shall see in later chapters, when Indians talk in a similar fashion about White scholars and their culture, they are denounced by the academic establishment as 'attackers'. The right to criticize is a carefully protected privilege.

Autobiography as Scholarship

Cynthia Humes mentions that Caldwell's work (like Kripal's) is largely autobiographical in nature. In the end, they may only amount to creative psychodramas that expose personal pathologies, often hidden deep beneath wounds of past trauma. Humes writes,

> I do not doubt the sincerity of Caldwell's belief that the goddess was somehow 'running my show' or that her personal tragedies had 'meaning and significance beyond my personal lusts, fears, neuroses, and confusions.' (267). Abundant examples of Caldwell's lingering resentment are given free reign, deservedly in some ways toward her now ex-husband but less so toward her disapproving academic guide. This guide (despite his assistance in interviews, and arrangements to have one of his students aid her in settling in, and provision of some obviously helpful advice) she grills for his attempt to influence her research program. She further suspects him of avariciousness toward her grant and, ironically, belittles his suspicion of her possible infidelity (a suspicion that turns out to be justified) (54). These become examples of Obeyesekere's theories of 'progressive orientation', underscoring how **Caldwell's personal confession authorizes her broad psychoanalytic theories** about a remarkably similar projected rage and resentment in the person of Bhadrakali.[83] In so doing, Caldwell preserves and in important ways, I believe, even enlarges the power differential between author and reader that authorizes her participant-observer projections onto her subjects. [Emphasis added]

Taking a page from Humes, many in the diaspora wonder about the extent to which Caldwell's personal trauma of sexual abuse caused her to focus on erotic pathologies and to what extent she was driven by conformity with academic fashion to eroticize Hinduism.

No single form of the Goddess represents all of her forms, and any view of the Goddess is incomplete if it is not seen as a part of a wider and more comprehensive portrayal of her. Therefore, the Westernized over-emphasis on her sensational, sexual and violent aspects is reductionism of the worst kind. This is analogous to a textbook that reduces Bill Clinton's presidency to incidents about Monica Lewinsky. Such a partial approach would be considered unethical, misleading and highly irresponsible.

Scholars often contend that their works are meant exclusively for fellow residents of the Ivory Tower and therefore have few real-world implications for 'outsiders'. However, such works filter into school textbooks, popular culture, media and journalism, thus becoming the accepted lenses through which many aspects of Indian culture are viewed. Such works can't be excused as 'only for academic consumption', because in this Information Age there are hardly any secrets from the public. Moreover, it is amply clear from examining the works of Wendy's Children that these sensationalist writings are not incidental to their work, but comprise the very heart of their claims to original thinking.[84]

Many of these scholars have an interesting love-hate relationship with India. They appropriate the practices, symbols, vocabulary and awareness that may make them seem distinct in their own culture. The enhancement of the scholar's status is often done at the devastating expense of India's native culture, which nurtured them and gave them dignified lives in their own vulnerable years.[85] This raises ethical and moral questions about whether the scholars provide full disclosure to, and obtain informed consent from, their Indian subjects and collaborators about the potential negative stereotyping of their cultures in America.

Psychoanalyzing Popular Hindu Culture

Scholars build upon each other's work, and often expand the intended scope of such works. Thus, Caldwell supported Kripal's work on Sri Ramakrishna, and adds another intriguing dimension. She interprets all complaints from Hindus about Kripal as signs of psychological disorders within the Hindu community, and she strongly recommends psychoanalyzing Hindu society to find out its pathologies. Blatantly equating the critiques of scholars such as Narasingha Sil and Swami Tyagananda with Hindu nationalism, a Hinduphobic Caldwell writes,[86]

> The hostility with which Jeff's book has been attacked in India is due, I believe, not to what Jeff has to say about the real, historical Ramakrishna, but what his thesis implies about Vivekananda, and by extension, contemporary Hindu nationalism. Anyone who has seen Anand Patwardhan's *Father, Son, and Holy War* film series (particularly part 2, 'Hero Pharmacy') understands the deep connections between male sexual prowess, virility, and Hindu nationalist violence that are so explicitly presented therein. Ramakrishna's tantric 'madness' easily fits a South Asian understanding of the behavior of saints; many gurus and saints display anti-social or inverted tendencies (and Ramakrishna's open and active rejection of heterosexuality, even more than his homosexuality, was a deeply antisocial act in Ramakrishna's social world); and the tantric use of sexuality as reversal (both social and spiritual) goes back deep into Hindu tradition, as we all know [...].

To get back to the point, I suggest it is not really the problematic of Ramakrishna that underlies the hate mail Jeff has received. Implications that Vivekananda, who reformulated Ramakrishna's message into the masculine, cleaned-up reformist Hinduism that first presented itself to the world stage in presentable form a century ago, was the passive homosexual object of his guru's lust is deeply threatening. Such an image raises specters of the 'feminine' male of India that was so much a part of colonial discourse, and that pervades contemporary Hindu nationalism.

Extrapolating further, Caldwell claims that these alleged sexual pathologies of Hindus, their saints, and their Goddesses, can be used to understand India's public culture and contemporary politics:

In short we need to be careful to examine what 'homosexuality' means in the rhetorical and personal contexts in which it is being used, and the historical and political background of the discussion of masculinity in South Asia, and not to focus exclusively on the personal domain as is common in Europe and America. We need to psychologize public culture as well as the private sphere. Jeff's book, while providing a nuanced and empathetic account of an individual life, invites us to broaden our lens to understand the reception of that life and its distortion in a century of highly contested religious posturing. With the current election of a BJP-led government, such careful analysis is timely and essential. [Emphasis added]

This kind of theorizing has deeply troubling implications. Academic exercises to psychoanalyze a public culture could serve as a cover for 'ethnic profiling' of the Indian-American diaspora, and be used to foster campaigns of hatred against Indians.

One has to note that Caldwell separates out the 'personal domain as is common in Europe and America,' and offers Euro-Americans individuality and agency; whereas, on the other hand, she denies Indians, and especially Hindus, that same individual agency. In contrast to her approach towards the 'good white people', whom she grants a personal domain, in the case of Indians she suggests psychoanalyzing their culture to expose the 'distorted masculinity' of Hindus, and the 'confused sexuality' of the Hindu male, as symptoms of abusive social orientations and dangerous nationalism. She culminates with a warning regarding today's Indian/Hindu male threat—invoking tragedy, trauma and fear of the 'other'.[87]

By reversing the gaze, one can look at the source of this genre of scholarship as emanating from individuals who are in psychological need of a 'Hindu Other'. Malhotra surmises that their inner-directed psychological and cultural conditioning drives them to the following allegations:

1. Sexual 'madness' in Hindu saints and in the Goddess is common and expected.
2. To hide this pathology from the West, Vivekananda (who was Ramakrishna's 'passive homosexual object') had to repackage Hinduism into a 'presentable' masculine image.
3. The alleged sexual deviance and hyper-masculinity applies not only to particular Hindu individuals but also to the social culture of Hinduism in general.
4. Hence, there is urgency to study contemporary Hindu culture in a sexually explicit, psychopathological fashion. This approach is particularly 'timely and essential' because it enables US foreign policy the option to intervene against such 'human rights abuses' inherent in the 'other'. This ties in well to the demented religious paranoia calls for fundamentalist Christian thought to drive US International Relations.[88]

The academic field of Religious Studies in the US has become inextricably linked with contemporary Indian politics. The nation-state of India and its socio-political system can now be studied as pathology. Kripal legitimizes this fringe scholarship:

> Hindus sometimes find the conclusions of psychoanalysis
> ...offensive to their own self-perceptions and cultural
> understandings; given the psychoanalytical attempt to crack the
> codes of the social and intra-psychic censors and its explicit desire
> to reveal secrets and uncover hidden truths, it would be very
> surprising indeed if they reacted in any other way. In short,
> psychoanalysis is a method that expects to be rejected.
> Psychoanalysis, then, goes well beyond the anthropologist's field
> study and the Sanskritist's text and the historian of religions'
> phenomenological study to answer questions that no interview, text,
> or phenomenological study is willing to ask, much less answer.[89]

Thus Kripal paints his critics as being emotionally and intellectually incapable of self-reflection, thereby evading the real issues that they have raised. The primary reason Hindu intellectuals question psychoanalysis is not because they fear the codes it may crack, but because the basic building blocks and suppositions of psychoanalysis are incongruent with the foundational concepts of dharma. Aurobindo isn't the only Indian intellectual who found psychoanalysis to be infantile. In *The Analyst and the Mystic: Psychoanalytic Reflections on Religion and Mysticism*,[90] Sudhir Kakar reflected on the inapplicability of psychoanalysis in interpreting Hindu ethos, writing about 'the existence of a deep gulf between psychoanalysis and the Indian mystical tradition'. He notes:

> Unlike his Western counterpart, the Indian analyst has...consciously faced and reflected on the conflict between an absorbing intellectual orientation, psychoanalysis—which is the mainstay of his professional identity, and the working of a historical fate which has made the 'mystical' the distinctive *leitmotif* of the dominant Indian cultural tradition and thus the core of his communal identity.

Kakar sees an inherent 'disdain for the mystical tradition' in the psychoanalytical method. The mystic experience, the very core of spirituality, is considered as pathology in need of psychoanalysis controlled by self-appointed white doctors. Kakar explains that psychoanalysis 'arose at a time in the history of European imagination when the older techniques of introspection and self-interrogation had largely withered away'. He quotes George Steiner:

> It (psychoanalysis) provided a secular, though heavily mythological surrogate for an entire range of introspective and elucidatory disciplines extending from private meditation to the meta-privacies of the confessional.[91]

Kakar describes psychoanalysis as "a technique of rational mediation for the scientific era . . . successor to the more ancient introspective techniques which have drawn their sustenance from religion". He explains that during its fledging years:

> psychoanalysis sought to sharply demarcate its boundaries and differentiate itself from the mystical traditions which antedate it so vastly in the history of human consciousness and constantly threatened to engulf it.

Kakar suggests that there is a deep cultural unease—a sense of insecurity felt by early adherents of psychology; there was a commonly felt threat perception about the mystical traditions. He further notes: "The threat posed by the mystical tradition to psychoanalysis must have been ominously heightened by Jung's apostasy into mysticism and his fascination with its Indian varieties". Given the vagaries of history and the imperative of psychoanalysis' evolution as a discipline, coupled with the antipathy of psychoanalysis for mysticism, a profound clash of cultures is embedded in the paradigm. He explains:

> As a set of assumptions, an implicit framework underlying a science, a paradigm guides its adherents toward areas of inquiry that seem 'sensible' and promise to be 'fruitful'. A paradigm, however, also has a built-in blinder to certain other areas which it considers as trivial if not completely nonsensical. Since a scientist's professional identity is intimately bound to the stability and continuity of his normal paradigm, the confrontation with a very different paradigm naturally tends to make the blinder active.[92]

Kripal, given his inadequate training in psychoanalysis, is unaware of these fundamental issues about the psychoanalyst's penchant to reject the mystical, and therefore writes: "Psychoanalysis is a method that expects to be rejected". He then alleges that this is because Hindus fear what it will reveal to the world about them. The issues run much deeper than that. Kripal is, first of all, unable to demonstrate the validity of psychoanalysis in a setting that does not share the historical, traditional, and civilizational paradigms that gave some meaning to Freud's European myths, motifs, and theories. Moreover, given Kripal's utter lack of formal training as a psychoanalyst working directly with Indians, it raises the fundamental question as to "Why he believes he can accomplish the goal of psychoanalyzing Indians he has never met"?[93] This is not just about Kripal's personal shortcomings as a scholar. Even more troubling is why the establishment at RISA believes that researchers like Kripal can produce valid scholarly work in the absence of adequate training and mastery over Indian languages, and over techniques like psychoanalysis, *and* in the absence of rigorous peer review.

This comic is intended to be satirical, and any resemblance herein to actual events or persons living or dead is purely coincidental.

This comic is intended to be satirical, and any resemblance herein to actual events or persons living or dead is purely coincidental.

Chapter 5

Abusing Ganesha and Shiva

Other major Hindu deities have also been targets of Western scholars. In 1985, Paul Courtright, currently in the Department of Religion at Emory University in Atlanta, Georgia, published a book on Ganesha in which he employed particularly Eurocentric categories to analyze Hindu religion and folklore.[94]

Scholarly books on Ganesha may be expected to emphasize stories, rituals, and their spiritual meanings and cultural interpretations. In art books or literature, or in the social sciences, Ganesha is depicted from various perspectives—theoretical, historical, religious and cultural. However, Courtright's book includes another scheme and infers novel meanings using Freudian analysis. Unfortunately, despite the book's many positive qualities, it also includes poorly evidenced and pornographic interpretive descriptions of Ganesha, such as the following excerpts:

> [F]rom a psychoanalytic perspective, there is meaning in the selection of the elephant head. Its trunk is the displaced phallus, a caricature of Siva's linga. It poses no threat because it is too large, flaccid, and in the wrong place to be useful for sexual purposes. ... So Ganesa takes on the attributes of his father but in an inverted form, with an exaggerated limp phallus—ascetic and benign—whereas Siva is 'hard', erotic, and destructive.[95]

> [Ganesa] remains celibate so as not to compete erotically with his father, a notorious womanizer, either incestuously for his mother or for any other woman for that matter.[96]

> Ganesa is like a eunuch guarding the women of the harem. In Indian folklore and practice, eunuchs have served as trusted guardians of the antahpura, the seraglio. "They have the reputation of being homosexuals, with a penchant for oral sex, and are looked upon

as the very dregs of society." (Hiltebeitel 1980, p. 162). [...] Like
the eunuch, Ganesa has the power to bless and curse; that is, to
place and remove obstacles. Although there seem to be no myths
or folktales in which Ganesa explicitly performs oral sex, his
insatiable appetite for sweets may be interpreted as an effort to
satisfy a hunger that seems inappropriate in an otherwise ascetic
disposition, a hunger having clear erotic overtones. Ganesa's broken
tusk, his guardian staff, and displaced head can be interpreted as
symbols of castration . . . This combination of child-ascetic-eunuch
in the symbolism of Ganesa—each an explicit denial of adult male
sexuality—appears to embody a primal Indian male longing to
remain close to the mother and to do so in a way that will both
protect her and yet be acceptable to the father. This means that
the son must retain access to the mother but not attempt to possess
her sexually.[97]

These bizarre interpretations, wholly manufactured by Courtright,
are far outside the tradition and even worse, they caricature and
ridicule Hinduism. Because Courtright was confident that he would
not be held accountable by peers for manufacturing offensive images
about a revered deity of Hinduism, he could candidly admit that he
has no evidence for what he says, and then proceed to pronounce his
flights of fancy as valid, scholarly interpretations. In other instances,
evidence is invented from non-existent textual sources. Such books are
not presented as fiction, or even acknowledged as parochial, limited
interpretations—they are received by the academy as authoritative
scholarly works. They then percolate into the mainstream culture via
textbooks, media images, and explanations of Ganesha in American
art museums.

Courtright's book had an unexpected impact when it became a
catalyst for waking up the diaspora. What brought the Indian-American
community to its feet was the realization that wild ideas from the book
were being presented in museums and other fora as *fact*. Many Indians
wrote articles critical of Courtright's interpretations. One critic wrote
a particularly sarcastic piece, mimicking Doniger's approach but
applying it in the reverse direction to interpret Christian symbols and
narratives. Using evidence similar to Courtright's, this anonymous
writer offered the following tongue-in-cheek analysis:

> Jesus was a filthy and indecent man. He learned some magic tricks
> from the visiting Persian merchants. The Romans often invited him
> to perform at their parties, and in exchange, they offered him wine.
> So he routinely got drunk, tried to be 'a notorious womanizer', and

was a hobo all his life. Since Jesus' mother was a prostitute, she did not want to announce the true identity of his father, and had to make up a story for the illiterate nomads. Therefore, Mary claimed that Jesus was born without physical intercourse. So all his life, Jesus guarded the myth of his mother's virginity and hid the immoral activities of his father and other customers who visited her for sex. The Roman commander played a joke upon Jesus by crucifying him using the cross, symbolizing that the cross was the phallus which his mother must have used for his conception. Thus, his followers today carry a cross as the phallic symbol of his immaculate conception.[98]

The sarcastic scribe then asked, "How would the above be considered if it were written by a non-Christian academic scholar in a country where Christianity is a small minority—just as Hinduism is a small minority in the US?" Even if such a work were produced in scholarly circles—as opposed to satire—the influence and impact that it would command would be minimal. It is unlikely that it would be allowed to become the *standard educational or reference text* for understanding those figures.[99] Multiple scholarly criticisms of such a work [against Christianity], backed by enormous funding from deep-pocket Western foundations and organized religion in the West would bury the book. It is also unlikely that the scholar's career would be enhanced and the scholar rewarded for creatively transcending the bounds of evidence.

You Scratch My Back, I'll Scratch Yours

Doniger wrote a highly appreciative foreword to Courtright's book. Stressing his affinity to her, Courtright wrote in an email to Malhotra, "You are using the term 'child' metaphorically, but I'm honored to be considered part of [Wendy's] kinship group". He seems unconcerned about his intellectual autonomy being compromised by this evident 'back-scratching' relationship among scholars. He returns the favor to Wendy by advertising how 'good' she is for Indic traditions, and how lucky Hindus are to have her to interpret their religion:

> Wendy has been influential in raising the visibility of Indian civilization through a presentation of the liveliness of its mythic tradition and shifting it away from a more bland and pious and negative image that came through a lot of the Orientalist and missionary scholarship that you rightly take issue with.[100]

Historically, scholars whose work is considered offensive to the 'others' have never seen themselves as consciously 'hating' or even disliking the 'others'. The British always remarked how they 'loved' India. Malhotra points out the irony: "Christian proselytizers trying to 'save' heathens do it out of love for them; so do the multinationals who 'love' the countries where they are devastating local farmers and producers; and so do imperialists trying to eradicate indigenous cultures so as to 'civilize' or [provide] 'progress' [for] the poor natives." Such 'love' for the 'other' absolves one of any guilt for one's actions and perpetuates one's presumed superiority. It became known as the 'civilizing mission'.

Hindu Images: Lascivious, Salacious, and Disheveled

In an introductory textbook on Eastern religions that is used extensively in undergraduate courses on World Religions and Asian Studies, *Awakening: An Introduction to the History of Eastern Thought,* Dr. Patrick Bresnan writes 'authoritatively' about Shiva. Note that the sensationalist prose and imagery he employs has now become a commonly accepted depiction of Shiva in academic circles:[101]

> Entering the world of Shiva worship is to enter the world of India at its most awesomely mysterious and bewildering; at least for the non-Indian. In Shiva worship, the Indian creative imagination erupts in a never-ending multiplicity of gods and demons, occult rituals, and stunning sexual symbolism . . . Linga/yoni veneration was not the whole of it . . . Young women, known as devadasis, were commonly connected with Shiva temples, and participated in the rituals, sometimes only in a symbolic fashion; sometimes not. In a degraded form the devadasi became nothing more than temple prostitutes. These extremes were more often to be found among the practitioners of Tantra, that enigmatic antithesis of conservative Hinduism that developed in northeastern India. Some Tantra temples became notorious for all kinds of extreme practices, including ritual rape and ritual murder. In Calcutta, at the Temple of Durga (one of the forms of Shiva's shakti) there was an annual festival at which many pigs, goats, sheep, fowl, and even water buffaloes would be slaughtered and ritually burned before the statue of the goddess.

This sensationalized, extreme story of rape and murder at Shiva temples is described in an *introductory* textbook meant for common use. The imagery of these 'strange and terrible things' gets filtered through the students' Eurocentric lenses, and consciously or unconsciously, remains a part of the students' lifelong mythic view of Indic cultures. Most Americans go through life burdened with these kinds of stereotypes about exotic 'others' and India seems to be at the top of the list for such exotica. Misinformation and ignorance about Hinduism and other non-Abrahamic religions dominate the popular imagination.[102]

This is disturbingly problematic for Hindu minorities around the world. Let us reverse the situation to make the point: A hypothetical book titled *Introduction to the History of Western Thought* that presented a similar discourse about pathologies inherent in Christianity would not be acceptable in college classrooms in India to teach Christianity to Hindu, Muslim, Buddhist, and Sikh students. In that context, an *introductory* text would not delve at length into the Inquisition in Medieval Europe (or in Portuguese Goa) when thousands of women, and even children, were burned at the stake as heretics under the auspices of the Church.[103]

The hypothetical textbook would certainly refrain from blithely informing the students about the historically frequent occurrences of sex, rape and unwanted pregnancies in nunneries or the recently exposed epidemic of pedophilia among Catholic priests and evangelical ministers. Such a book would not include statements such as: "Being the bride of Christ and crucifix-veneration was not the whole of it. In a degraded form, the nuns who were 'married' off to Jesus were little more than church prostitutes, available to the powerful among the priesthood as well as the laity".

Nor would one approve a statement like: "Catholic churches are notorious for all kinds of extreme practices from rape of children to official protection for the rapists over decades". Indeed such a statement *could* be backed by enormous amounts of data. For instance, in the United States alone, hundreds of Christian priests have been implicated in molesting children. Of the nearly 200 dioceses in the country, every single one except a handful has had many such incidents. The victims are in the thousands and the problem stretches back at least a half century.[104] We are not suggesting that such information be taught in schools, but just pointing out the asymmetry, and the Hinduphobia that allows such asymmetry.

Since cannibalism does occur occasionally in Western societies, another equivalent scenario to make our point would be a textbook statement such as: "Young Christian men and women are taught at an early age that eating the flesh and drinking the blood of the god-man Jesus is a good thing. They regularly participate in rituals where human flesh and blood are consumed, sometimes symbolically, sometimes not". Such a selective presentation of Christianity is very unlikely to be found in a classroom in India, in spite of the fact that claims of cannibalism and clerical pedophilia can ostensibly be based on data. Yet, in an introductory college textbook on Hinduism for American students they are nonchalantly—and falsely—informed that Shiva temples 'became notorious for all kinds of extreme practices, including ritual rape and ritual murder'. This does not offer a fair or objective view of Hinduism any more than sensational images of people burning at the stake or clerical pedophilia offers an appropriate introduction to Christianity.

At the introductory stage of an American student's learning, depictions and stories about Hinduism must be carefully put into proper context. For instance, discussions of Shiva/Shakti can explore symbolic ideals such as the transcendent meeting of the male and the female—as the Hindu equivalent of the Chinese yin/yang. It is more accurate for students to understand and remember Shiva as Divinity encompassing both male and female—a primary teaching about Shiva shared across India—rather than being bombarded by exotic obscurities that are not central to the religion's practice.

Since there is rarely enough time in the typical American introductory course on World Religions to build a proper foundation for understanding Indic traditions, the first descriptions about Shiva should be relevant, accurate and culturally sensitive. Otherwise, without providing philosophical meaning and contextualization about Shiva, the deity is reduced to being some kind of deranged pervert. Students who encounter such a treatment of Shiva in a textbook will retain a tainted understanding of Hindus everywhere. Consequently, the spiritual ideas of Shaivism would be lost, consumed by the erotic-exotic images that assume center stage. *RISA Lila-1* points out how this skewed religious imagery can dangerously taint cultural perceptions of India,

> At its best, the [Hindu-Shaivite] tradition is seen as not having anything positive to offer to a serious and open-minded young person. At its worst, Shiva is denigrated as the cause of all sorts of social ills such as rapes, sexual irresponsibility, and violence—in other words, he is depicted as a criminal cult god without saying it in so many words.

The essay also points out yet another common essentialization about Shiva in American and Western textbooks—Shiva as 'Destroyer'.

Shiva as an archetype for *samhara* or *dissolution* has numerous meanings, including the transcendence of human misery by the dissolution of *maya* (illusion)—which is why Shiva is associated with yoga. The common mapping of dissolution = destruction is reductionism; it is sensationalized all-or-nothing, black-or-white hyperbole. As with other Hindu deities, the Goddess Kali's meanings are likewise complex and multifaceted, and depend on the cultural context from which the devotee is viewing Her as well as the level of understanding a given practitioner brings to the experience. Freud could not possibly have the experiential or empirical competence to interpret the multiple meanings of a village woman offering flowers at a humble shrine to Shitala Devi.

In conclusion, the approaches taken by Doniger, Kripal, Caldwell, Courtright, and others indicate that they are obsessed with selectively and rigidly interpreting Hindu images for the purpose of forcibly fitting them onto real and imagined problems of contemporary Indian society. This self-perpetuating, neo-colonial orientation feeds the specious and spurious while starving any real understanding of Hinduism. Add to this that scholars often incorporate their voices into the narrative and the result is a heady brew in which personal traumas and dramas play out in the name of Hinduism. These strip away its multifaceted colors as experienced by its practitioners and replace them with the dull, monochromatic hues of the psychopathologic voyeur.

Chapter 6

Targeting Hindu Mothers and 'Hijackers'

Stanley Kurtz, an anthropologist specializing in Indian Studies, uses psychoanalysis to substantiate his loathsome supposition that Hindu mothers do not have 'a Western-style loving, emotional partnership with their babies':[105]

> The special relationship between the Hindu mother and her son appears here as a variation on a distinctive Hindu pattern rather than as a mere intensification of a style of intimacy found in the West . . . Nursing is not therefore, an occasion through which mother and child cement on an emotional union. The child is frequently fed, yet the mother seldom lingers to mirror the baby's satisfaction. Thus, while the child no doubt develops a strong emotional attachment to the mother as a result of the physical gratification she provides, **the mother does not respond by setting up a Western-style loving, emotional partnership.** [Emphasis added.]

This racially biased and bizarre declaration is utterly false, as anyone who has spent significant time with families in India can attest. It is absurd to say that a Hindu mother does not see nursing her baby as an opportunity to cement emotional union, in the same 'loving, intimate' way that Western women presumably do. Even more amazing is the limited evidence on which such statements are based and astonishingly, that they pass inspection with peer-review processes.[106] This kind of religious, racial and cultural profiling—using academically acceptable but unproven Eurocentric techniques—has become a subtle replacement for what used to be more open and blatant racism. Today, unbelievably, this not-so-hidden form of racism is not only justified, it is accepted as the product of 'objective research findings'!

In another book, *All the Mothers Are One*,[107] Stanley Kurtz constructs a model for the psychology of Hindus based on his studies of Indian social and family structures along with interviews of some devotees of the Goddess Santoshi Ma. Kurtz claims that Durga, one of India's most revered deities, symbolizes the *castrating* Mother Goddess. He interprets Goddess' symbols as pathological—a manufactured 'Durga Complex' to explain his 'findings' about Indians:

> [T]he characteristically Hindu form of conflicts over unconscious incestuous strivings [in which] castration symbolism at the most mature level represents transformative self-willed sacrifice signaling the abandonment of infantile attachments.[108]

Obviously, Kurtz denies Hindus their sense of individuality:

> Their notion of the divine knows neither boundaries of time, place, substance, nor identity. [And therefore] . . . individualism is built into our psychic structure but **not into that of the Hindu**. [Emphasis added.][109]

In addition to finding many technical flaws in Kurtz's methodologies, Humes criticizes his work for using 'a method which in the end borders on racism:'

> Despite arguing for greater sensitivity to cultural difference in psychology, 'those people' over 'there' are actually all alike—but not like 'us' . . . Kurtz's psychology excludes Hindu women . . . they are, after all, 'mommies' whose psychology can be dispensed with in a few words and a note.[110]

Mercifully, someone in the academy actually voiced criticism, but it had little impact on Kurtz's theories. Certain forms of racism are apparently quite acceptable in portions of the scholarly world. Racist statements about Indians and Hindus are apparently not a career limiting move in the largely white establishment. Unlike RISA's self-righteous sweeping generalizations, many anthropologists have deplored this:

> Every time anthropologists have attempted to generate universal rules governing human behaviour, the rules have either been proven empirically wrong or are so trivial as to be uninteresting. This is not to say that some attempts at figuring out what really is universal to human beings haven't been better than others or that we haven't learned a good deal from such attempts. But it is to say that trying to discern patterns in human social life that are broad enough to

include all the variations human cultures have produced, while remaining true to the specific cultural contexts that produce those variations, is a hazardous—if not impossible—undertaking.[111]

Dehumanizing and exoticized images of Hinduism—no matter how ludicrous and fringe they may seem on the surface—must not be taken lightly. History shows that pogroms and genocides have followed similar patterns of cultural denigration. The soon-to-be victims are alleged to be irrational, immoral, lacking a legitimate religion, and even lacking in compassion so that they cannot show 'proper' love towards their babies. In Western mythmaking, it follows that these 'savages' must not be extended the same human rights as 'we' enjoy. (See the first chapter in section III for an account of this.)

Kurtz positions the so-called impersonal practices of nursing mothers as a distinctive Hindu pattern per se, along with cases of 'dowry murders' that have been aggressively investigated in US-based academic programs where entire conferences have been devoted to showing how these phenomena are a particularly 'Hindu problem'. This moribund approach ignores mountains of contemporary scholarship, including that of Veena Oldenburg and others, establishing clearly that it is not a 'Hindu' problem per se, but arose in a colonial context.[112]

Though similar practices regarding women are found historically in all major world religions, introductory classes rarely sum up Judaism, Islam or Christianity with a list of negative attributes. Introductory classes on Hinduism at the university level, often begin with the *Rg Veda* and move on through the *Upanishads* and other texts, and end the year with the dangers of Hindu fundamentalists who killed Mahatma Gandhi. The same can be seen in secondary level World History textbooks, where after a survey of Hindu beliefs and texts, they conclude with a list of 'Hindu problems' such as 'suttee' and poverty caused by Hindu cultural norms. In a comparative context, the Hinduphobia is tangible.

The case is being built that Hinduism is not only inferior but that it causes human rights problems, and the cure lies in its eradication. How does today's scholarship regarding Hindus compare with earlier Eurocentric scholarship about Native Americans, Africans, Jews, Roma, and others, who became victims of various kinds of 'savage wars' and genocide? Malhotra has asked:

> Are certain 'objective' scholars, unconsciously driven by their Eurocentric chauvinism, perhaps to pave the way for a future

genocide of a billion or more Hindus, because of the supposed economic and/or ecological pressures of overpopulation later in this century?

Even in those instances where the scholar might be criticizing genuine social problems, Dave Freedholm, a teacher of World Religions in an American secondary school, explains how Hinduism is not given the same treatment as Christianity:

> When scholars examine the world's religions they usually attempt to distinguish between their 'universal' theological/philosophical foundations and the particular historically and culturally bound social structures of societies that practice those religions. To take Christianity as an example, biblical scholars, using a sophisticated hermeneutics, extract a 'universal' Pauline theology from the social context of Paul's letters that presumed slavery, the subjugation of women, etc. Pauline statements that seem to support this social order are reinterpreted in light of passages that are deemed to reflect more universal values.[113]

Courtright is right in saying that Doniger had raised the visibility of Indian civilization and the liveliness of its mythic tradition. But raised the visibility in what manner? In many respects, the increased visibility is not bringing an increase in light and awareness, but is shedding more darkness by highlighting twisted and tangential trivia. Scholars like Doniger tend to stereotype Hindu thought and traditions, trivializing its rationality, its insights into the human mind, and its spiritual truths into fodder for psychoanalysis and other Eurocentric tools. This succeeds in eliding Hinduism's deeper meanings and caricaturing, if not eradicating, its relevance for today's world.

Courtright praises Doniger's efforts in recruiting young Indian students into her school of thought:

> Wendy has worked hard at Chicago to recruit Indian graduate students (as we have here at Emory) because we are concerned that there is an imbalance between 'insider' and 'outsider'—whatever that means—in the field.[114]

Just because one brings in a diversity of skin tones to the University of Chicago's student body does not mean that a true diversity of 'insider' versus 'outsider' perspectives is represented, or that vigorous, uncomfortable debate is permitted. It is always much easier for a student—of any color or background—to conform to the dominant voices in the discipline. As will be seen in section III, sometimes graduate students are sent ahead as storm-troops to electronically engage the 'enemy', creating a Hinduphobic space for their mentors.

This 'sepoy mentality' was exemplified by an Indian-American graduate student at the University of Chicago[115] who, in 2002, warned his RISA colleagues, 'To watch out for WAVES' (the World Association of Vedic Studies), which he found 'deeply disturbing'. His objection to this conference held by a group that explicitly focuses on the Vedas, was on the grounds that it did not include a discussion of Islam![116] He said the WAVES conference made him feel very angry and he worried that the field of 'Religion in South Asia' can be hijacked by these movements. He added, "It is incumbent upon those who know about them to speak out in no uncertain terms and warn everyone else."

Immediately, the well-known Sanskritist, Professor Gerald Larson, who occupied the Rabindranath Tagore Chair at the University of Indiana for many years, chimed in to support the call. Making no attempt to independently verify the allegations, Larson wrote:

> I am becoming increasingly concerned that the field of the serious study of South Asian religion and culture is being 'highjacked' by a variety of folks with 'off the wall' agendas ranging from crackpot religiosity to the worst kinds of Hindu chauvinism. I, therefore, very much appreciate the comment about the 'WAVES' conference and think these sorts of things need to be exposed and rigorously criticized in the RISA exchanges.[117]

Larson used the metaphor of hijacking to describe his concern that the study of Hinduism was being somehow stolen by Hindus. He seems to blithely ignore that the airplane—in this instance Hindu culture—belongs to Hindus. Certainly, they should be allowed to chart their own course. Even if the professor considers himself and his colleagues to be the only competent pilots, this analysis borders on the paranoid and the absurd. Larson reduces the complex variety of Hindus with their great diversity of views and ideas into extreme camps, caught between 'crackpot religiosity' and the 'worst kind of Hindu chauvinism'.

This is yet another example of how Hindus are being attacked with hyperbolic *ad homines* when they study their faith. Christians, Jews, Muslims and Buddhists routinely participate in theological conferences specific to their respective faiths, without becoming the recipients of similar attacks. Hindu self-study groups are unfortunately dismissed as dangerous 'Savages from the Frontier who threaten Eden'. It is exactly this insistence on Eurocentric hegemonic *control* over Hindu religious studies, and the power to categorize and demonize Hindus, that worries many progressive voices and underscores the need for investigations such as this book.

Chapter 7

Challenges to Wendy Doniger's Sanskrit

Malhotra's article also investigated instances of Doniger's own questionable scholarship. *RISA Lila-1* proposed that a logical criterion is that a translation must be acceptable as authentic by the community whose tradition is in question—in accordance with the key Indian concept known as *purva-paksha*. If the intention of the text's translator is to overrule the practitioners' interpretations then there should be a rigorous burden of proof on the scholar's part. Ultimately, a 'correct' translation is inseparable from the applicable contexts.

RISA Lila-1 was not written as a criticism of the *entire* academic work of Doniger, but only specific parts. But it was troubling that there was not a single comprehensive critical evaluation of Doniger's work, nor any plans to produce such a criticism, despite the enormous importance being given to her work, and the fact that what is at stake is the legitimacy of the insider's view of the world's oldest literary tradition. Doniger's translations of Hindu texts are widely available in paperback publications and serve to inform the layperson's image of Hinduism.

In this regard, Professor Michael Witzel of Harvard University is a rare exception. Witzel has claimed that Wendy Doniger's knowledge of Vedic Sanskrit is severely flawed. Malhotra opined that given Doniger's stature, "Witzel's claim seemed as audacious as saying that the Pope was not a good Catholic." When Witzel was publicly challenged to prove his claim, he published examples of Doniger's 'Sanskrit mistranslations' on the Web.[118] An anonymous source noted:[119]

> Witzel was privately reprimanded for being so critical of the latter-day *'Queen of Hinduism'*. He was blackballed in disregard of his

right to criticize such blatant blunders, especially given the clout and power enjoyed by Wendy. If Gods, Goddesses, and saints can be deconstructed by her, then why should her work be exempt from criticism?

This anonymous scholar led the diaspora to Witzel's critiques that had previously been known only within a small section of Sanskrit scholars. The scholar hoped to bring this to wider public attention in order to broaden the debate. A firestorm erupted from Doniger's camp when *RISA Lila-1* merely summarized one scholar's online criticisms of her translation capabilities. Witzel's criticisms of Doniger's Sanskrit translations are reproduced below so that the readers can decide if such criticisms should be taboo, and whether or not critics are entitled to point out the shortcomings of the powerful without being denounced as blasphemers.

Witzel on Doniger's Translation of the *Rig Veda*

In his online critique, Witzel writes, "Doniger's rendering of even the first two *paadas*" of the *Rig Veda* "is more of a paraphrase than a translation", and her style "is rather a stream of unconnected George-Bush-like anacoluthas".[120] Witzel goes on to illustrate his point by referring to Doniger's translation of a particular verse, "'He will shed tears, sobbing, when he learns'." Witzel points out that in an accurate Sanskrit translation, "There is no sobbing here . . . she simply made that up to give the desired effect."

Witzel's analysis includes not just translations but also interpretations. "It is not just in translation that Doniger fails. Her interpretations are also flawed," he says. He charges that Doniger "denies the possibility of male/female friendship—perhaps a current local cultural bias—but certainly not a *Rigvedic* one." He also reveals that in her translations:

> *Sakhya* is completely misunderstood, as is usual in such cases with Indologists not very conversant with Vedic; it is understood on the basis of Epic/Classical *sakhi* 'friend' and thus the whole point of the apparent saying is missed. A Vedic *sakhi* is not just any friend . . .

Witzel concludes forthrightly, if somewhat harshly, "In this hymn (of 18 stanzas) alone I have counted 43 instances which are wrong or where others would easily disagree."

Witzel on Doniger's Translation of the *Jaiminiya Brahmana*

Regarding Doniger's translation of the *Jaiminiya Brahmana*, Witzel remarks, "And of course, the translation, again is a 're'-translation of others' works [in which she has] merely added a fashionable(?) Freudian coating . . . " Witzel continues,

> The trouble again is that [Doniger] did not follow up the secondary literature well, not even with the help of the students she mentions . . . if the secondary literature had been used—the translation would have turned out much better.

Witzel exposes her predilection for street language colloquialisms, such as 'balls of cowshit, balls of shit' and 'balls of Indra', which Witzel considers to be 'Vedic slang' that is not found in the Sanskrit texts and was simply made up by Doniger. Furthermore, he charges that there are many gaps in the translations where words or whole sentences have been forgotten. Of more concern to Witzel are Doniger's grammatical errors for which he scolds her for 'misunderstanding first-year Sanskrit'. "Difficult sentences," writes Witzel, "are simply left out without telling us so." Witzel concludes:

> Simple question: if *that* much is wrong in just one story (and this is a small selection only!)—what about the rest of this book and her other translations? . . . It might have been better to have used the old translations and to have added her Freudian interpretation to them . . . In sum: The 'translation' simply is UNREALIABLE.[121] [Emphasis original]

Witzel on Doniger's Translation of the *Laws of Manu*

Reviewing Doniger's translation of the *Manusmriti*, a work commonly prescribed in the Western academy, Witzel writes: "I give just one example which shows both wrong (rather, lack of) philological method and lack of simple common sense".[122] (See Endnote for the rather technical example.) Witzel scolds Doniger for using only a small selection of the available variations. She does not invest serious enough energy as per his standard in selecting which variations to use, where and why.

Witzel assesses Doniger's scholarship as lazy and not of the 'standard required by Harvard'. "In view of all of this," he concludes, "I wonder indeed whether D's translation would have been accepted in the Harvard Oriental Series rather than in Penguin Books . . . "

He makes the following overall remarks about the above three examples of mistranslations:

> Note that all 3 translations are RE-translations. Mistakes of the type mentioned above could easily have been avoided if the work of our 19th century predecessors (and contemporaries!) had been consulted more carefully . . . Last point: Looking at the various new translations that have appeared in the past decade or so: Why always to RE-translate something done 'several' times over already—and why not to take up one of the zillion UN-translated Skt. texts?

Witzel is also critical of the favorable proclamations for Doniger's works by her fan club. He writes:

> And a little less hype would also do: 'a landmark translation, the first authoritative translation in this century' (cover); 'to offer to more specialized scholars new interpretations of many difficult verses.' (p. lxi)—I doubt it.

Supporting Witzel, Malhotra writes: "This brief but devastating review of Wendy's scholarship was just the tip of the iceberg of what Witzel could have achieved by way of exposing that the 'Queen' often stands naked—had he not been asked to stop."

There was a feeling expressed in many comments to *RISA Lila-1* that RISA scholars should have taken up these criticisms more seriously, given that RISA and the AAR support critical inquiry with open minds. At the very least, a panel of scholars, whose careers are outside her influence, should have critiqued Doniger's work because of her enormous power in academe. Regretfully, and much to the detriment of the field, no further open-minded analyses occurred.

Hushing up criticisms of powerful scholars' works is not an approach that demonstrates academic rigor and fair-mindedness. Shutting critics up is inconsistent with academic freedom. Unfortunately, the power structure vested in the establishment has thus far prevailed. The messengers are shot and the abuses continue garrulously.[123]

Androgynous One-Legged Goats and Other Unmanifest Beasts

Prof. Antonio de Nicolas[124] offers a humorous review of Doniger's translations:[125]

> Wendy [...] wrote her *Rg Veda* putting my translations next to hers. By giving 'maska lagao'[126] to me, she avoided a bad review . . . The

theoretical headings she uses for the *Rg Veda* are arbitrary . . . the jewel is her translation of 'aja eka pada'. Literally it means 'aja' = unborn, unmanifest, 'eka' = one, 'pada' = foot, measure. It is the unmanifest one foot measure of music present in the geometries of the 'AsaT', meaning, the Rg Vedic world of possibilities where only geometries live without forms. Well, Wendy translates it as 'the one footed goat' because 'aja' in Hebrew means goat. What is a one-footed goat doing in the *Rg Veda*?

Nicholas Kazanas, a European Indologist, examined Doniger's obsession with sexual connotations. Referring to her book, *Women, Androgynes and Other Mythical Beasts,*[127] Kazanas writes that she seems to be obsessed with only one meaning—the most sexual imaginable:[128]

> O'Flaherty [a.k.a. Doniger] seems to see only one function . . . of fertility and sexuality, copulation, defloration, castration and the like: even bhakti 'devotion' is described in stark erotic terms including incest and homosexuality (1980: 87–99: 125–129). Surely, erotic terms could be metaphors for spiritual or mystical experiences as is evidenced in so much literature?

Similarly, *RISA Lila-1* also points out how she intentionally destroys any shades of meaning in deference to her preferred one:

> Doniger claims to be championing the diversity of literary interpretation. In actual fact, given her cartel's power over the legitimizing of her interpretations and turning them into canons of 'theories', the opposite effect has resulted: Her approaches have become more than just trendy speculations and are being propagated as the hard *facts* about Hinduism. In *Asceticism and Eroticism in the Myth of Siva,*[129] problematic translations and glamorous gimmicks help to sell books, such as this alluring description advertising the book in bold font, "One myth tells of how Siva and Parvati make love for a thousand year . . . "

RISA Lila-1 cites as examples three specific terms or concepts that are commonly and fabulously confounded by Doniger. These distortions then get widely disseminated by her supporters.

Tantra Equated with Sex

Tantra has far more complex meanings than simple sexual connotations, yet the standard depiction by the Doniger school suggests that Tantra *equals* sex. At the 2001 AAR meeting in Denver, Hugh Urban[130] presented a paper on a panel called *Embracing Orientalism*. It was titled, *Tantra, American Style: Neo-Orientalism, Globalism, and the Western Appropriation of Tantra*.[131] Malhotra attended the session and resonated with Urban's position, which he summarized as follows:

> Urban emphasized that 'Tantra' is not even an Indic category in the sense in which it is used now. It is a false Western reification, constructed in 19th century America, in order to appropriate it for popular use by a white Christian society starved for such erotica. This new construct became essentialized, and even got resold back into the Indian market very successfully. Certainly, the sexual idea of Tantra is true also, *but* not the *only* truth or even the main idea concerning the practice.

Linga = Phallus

Doniger defines *linga* as 'the phallus, particularly of Siva'.[132] She makes no attempt at nuance or to explain the diversity of interpretations, and the levels of meanings in different contexts or at various stages of practice. Diana Eck of Harvard is rather blunt about the impact of this mis-portrayal, "Christians look at the Hindu worship of the *linga* and see it as phallic worship, while Hindus look at the Christian sacrament of communion and are repulsed by its symbolic cannibalism."[133] Doniger instinctively seems to select the exotic-erotic/lewd-crude end of the range of contextual interpretations. This is why her *Purana Perennis* was criticized by Hans Bakker who felt that the racy, poorly researched but heavily promoted books written by Doniger are: "Fast-food-like publications designed to attract attention, readership and sales, but are devoid of meticulous scholarship or authenticity".[134]

Maithuna Essentialized as Sexual Intercourse

Doniger's glossary[135] over-simplifies other Sanskrit terms by giving them reductionist definitions. For example, the term *maithuna*, like its English equivalent 'intercourse', has social as well as sexual connotations. And in the Tantric sense, it also has spiritual meanings. Doniger, as might be expected, focuses exclusively on the sexual meaning. However, *maithuna* also means intercourse with the world with *all* our senses—to intensely engage the world in order to transcend the duality of separation. It is used as a metaphor for a positive engagement with the world, a sort of radical realism—quite the opposite of the stereotype of Hinduism as a 'world-negating religion'. If Doniger purports to be writing nuanced authoritative works, she should provide all the different levels and contexts of meanings, especially in a book or an essay to be read by students who are learning these terms for the first time.

Chapter 8

De-Spiritualizing Tantra

This chapter concerns a scholarly book, *Kiss of the Yogini: Tantric Sex in its South Asian Context*[136]. Its author, Prof. David Gordon White, a protégé of Wendy Doniger, received his PhD in the History of Religion from the University of Chicago in 1988. In an online discussion with Professor Jeffrey Lidke (a former student of White), Malhotra identified the book's purpose as an effort to undermine the deep roots of Tantra's inherent spirituality. This chapter is based on that online discussion that took place in May 2004.[137]

White had previously authored *The Alchemical Body: Siddha Traditions in Medieval India*, a well-received book that helped him achieve the stature of a highly acclaimed scholar of Tantra and Hinduism Studies. His earlier book was based on original sources and his interpretations were broadly accepted by Tantric practitioners. This authenticity provided political and professional credibility for the author in the academy and the Hindu community. His new book caught many Indian scholars and practitioners of Tantra, and Hindus in general, by surprise. This is a good example of Malhotra's *U-Turn Theory*, which describes how some Western scholars study Indic traditions respectfully, and then later repackage the subject to suit their own personal agendas or the needs of institutions, peer groups or the marketplace. This practice sometimes leads to denigrating Indic practices like Tantra as being a form of abusive mind-control, worthy of being mocked and, inevitably, exoticized.

Malhotra's review of the *Kiss of the Yogini* can be summarized as follows:

1. The book positions Tantra as a system of decadent South Asian sexuality. Furthermore, this decadence was seen as the result of

the social suffering of Indian subaltern (lower caste) people in classical times.

2. Eminent Tantra scholars, such as Abhinavagupta, Kashmir Shaivism's towering eleventh century figure, evidently did not know or did not want to know the 'real' Tantra the book purports to have uncovered. This is yet another example of how the natives, native scholars and actual practitioners are not trusted for their own interpretations, even including eminent thinkers whose works have been studied by Westerners and others, for centuries.

3. The bottom line, according to the *Kiss of the Yogini*, is that Tantra is not a legitimate spiritual process.

4. Doniger wrote a glowing review of the book, further extending its political import. She not only gives it the benefit of doubt without seriously challenging many of its presuppositions, but explicitly blames 'Hindu chauvinists' for repackaging Tantra as spirituality. She alleges that this was done to make Hinduism look good in the face of the British colonialists' Victorian values. Hence, her thesis is designed to help postcolonial Indian scholars to undo colonialism by rejecting the spiritual purpose of Tantra.

5. Those who dare deny this thesis are assumed to be 'Hindu nationalists', 'fascists', 'right-winger' and so forth.

6. Doniger then cites Schweder's popular new theory that native societies do not *own* their culture—a theory that Doniger asserts as true even though it is simply one point of view in an ongoing and controversial debate. Thus she accuses the Hindu diaspora and 'Hindu right-wing chauvinists' of claiming the right to interpret their culture and says that they have no such rights.

7. The implication is clear: No one can dare challenge the White-Wendy scholarship for fear of being branded a BJP[138] chauvinist. And Indians have no special standing as insiders in their culture. What a tragedy for the academy that such a ploy works!

A long-time scholar of Kashmir Shaivism and a Tantra practitioner confided that he finds the book 'disgusting'—in methodology, conclusion and its demeaning tone. He was sure that the "pandits in India, at whose feet David White did his research for twenty years, haven't got a clue". They would "be stunned to see how some scholars", who once respected the pandits "with gifts and *namaskars*, have twisted their translations".

Ziauddin Sardar has attacked similar positions by illustrating how non-Western cultures are 'for sale in the supermarket of postmodern nihilism'.[139] Malhotra asserts that White is similarly introducing a 'new product' in the postmodern 'bazaar of realities'. Doniger does a follow-up to reconfigure it into yet another derivative intellectual product: Displaying her manipulative prowess, she claims that those who profess Tantra to be a spiritual process are somehow associated with a hard-line right-wing political party in India. Thus the choice before Indians is between abandoning Tantra and facing disgrace as fascists—a pretty bleak either/or situation. The middle ground of spirituality without a political agenda is made unavailable as an option. Ironically, this apolitical middle ground has been the hallmark of Hinduism and is a distinguishing feature of considerable relevance in today's world of exclusivist dogmas.

Doniger evades the implications of her political thesis when it's applied to Tibetan Buddhism. The heart of Tibetan Buddhism is Tantra and there is a very intimate relationship and sharing of Tantra between Buddhism and Hinduism. Given Buddhism's respected place today, along with the Dalai Lama's clout among liberals worldwide, Doniger sidesteps this issue because it would open up a political and cultural Pandora's Box. Doniger's School simply chooses the softer target of Hinduism for the moment, even while Tantra is far more central to the legitimacy of the advanced practices of Tibetan Buddhism. Conversely, some scholars on the RISA discussion group have expanded this notion to suggest that the Hindu bhakti tradition should also be interpreted via the same lens, i.e. sexuality pretending to be spiritual.[140]

Using Credibility as Defense

Prof. Jeffrey S. Lidke[141], a former student of David White, and hence someone whom Doniger regards as a grandchild of her lineage, posted a response[142] attempting to dismiss the critique by claiming that Malhotra 'did not know the purva-paksha (i.e. opponent's position)', and that he had 'misrepresented the White-Doniger position'.[143] Lidke approached the debate as a knowledgeable scholar of Tantra who had spent several years reading White's writings. Therefore, 'with no small amount of confidence' he could claim that the above synopsis of White's thesis made two inaccurate claims:

First, that White identifies the purpose of Tantra as 'decadent sexuality'; second, that this 'decadence' arises from sociological causes. Given that the second hinges on the first, both collapse when the first is disproved. Nonetheless, I begin with the second, dependent, claim. It is true that White interprets certain aspects of the rise of Tantra in sociological terms; however it is by no means the case that he reduces Tantra to socio-economic factors. As a student of Eliade and Smith he is an historian of religions and not a sociologist. Ultimately, White does not reduce the origins of Tantra to any thing other than the sphere of religion and it is in this sphere that White identifies the true origin and purpose of Tantra: as those practices, traditions, and peoples who sought power, not power in a Foucaultian sense, but true, ontological power harnessed within the body and its products, particularly sexual fluids. Tantric sex was not, White argues, 'decadent'. Rather, it was a primary means by which yogins and yoginis ultimately became immortal. Much more could be written about this argument, but for now, suffice it to say that White's actual thesis is entirely different from what you wrote, Rajiv.

Lidke simply claimed that White had proven his thesis based on Indian texts. He did not offer specific textual proofs in White's defense, but cited White's 'credibility' as proof enough. White's writings were "among the most highly annotated in the business". They contain:

> Well over a hundred pages of citations from a variety of sources, including hundreds of primary and secondary texts, inscriptions, and field research. No serious scholar of Indology would ever say of White's work that he offers no proof. They may disagree with his final conclusions, but that he bases his argument on solid evidence is indisputable.

Lidke argued that: "White makes no claim to demolish the writings of Kashmir Shaivites." This is challenged by other scholars who note that White dismisses out of hand *central* works like the Kularnava Tantra simply because they do not suit his thesis. Thus Chakravarti points out:

> In fact, White gives up on the *Kulârnava Tantra*, which is one of the most prominent texts that finds its way in his list of titles of Sanskrit works. " . . . in spite of the rhetorical glorification of the Kaula in the original chapter," he says, "[the book] shows itself to be an altogether conventionalist work . . . ," i.e., one belonging to the soft-core variety (p. 254).[144]

Lidke then resorted to a tired old comeback that RISA scholars often use, by claiming that criticism by outsiders is spurious because 'obviously' they didn't read the book. The only defenses that Lidke offered were based on acclaim and association, not content and substance. Besides he claimed that White and Doniger had benign intentions even though their quotes may suggest otherwise. This line of argumentation denies the lay reader the same rights that the scholars themselves claim, i.e. freedom to interpret Indic texts according to contemporary sensibilities and theories, in whatever worlds of meaning they wish, and without reference to the author's intent or *vivaksha*.

Analysis of White's Position

Malhotra posted a three-part response online to argue that his assertions about White *were* well-founded. His posts are summarized below, followed by a brief criticism of White's work by an Australia-based scholar of Tantra.

Tantra's history, according to the White-Doniger thesis, went through two stages. In its early history, Tantra was a system of sexual magical acts that were not spiritual. Doniger explains, "In David Gordon White's account, the distinguishing characteristic of South Asian Tantra in its earliest documented stage is a ritual in which bodily fluids—sexual or menstrual discharge—were swallowed as transformative 'power substances'." So Tantra was a system of practices to achieve magical powers by swallowing sexual fluids. Then came stage two, according to White-Doniger, when, Abhinavagupta, the leading proponent of Tantra and Kashmir Shaivism, reconstructed Tantra into a spiritually contextualized system that was more suitable for Brahmin appropriation. Doniger says, "A significant reform took place in the eleventh century, when certain elite Brahmin Tantric practitioners, led by the great theologian Abhinavagupta in Kashmir, marginalized the ritual of fluid exchange and sublimated it into a wider body of ritual and meditative techniques."

Doniger refers to Abhinavagupta's system as 'soft-core, or High Hindu', whose purpose was to allow double-standards among Brahmins so that they could indulge in forbidden sexual acts and yet publicly not "threaten the purity regulations that were required for high-caste social constructions of the self in India". Thus, Doniger maintains that hypocritical Brahmins allowed themselves to indulge in the 'drinking of female menstrual discharge' because they could depict it in philosophical language as 'a programme of meditation mantras'.

Doniger explains that this 'soft-core' became a mask to cover up the 'hard-core' real Tantra which remained underground: "In this way the earlier, unreconstructed form of Tantra, the hard-core, persisted as a kind of underground river, flowing beneath the new, bowdlerized, dominant form". Doniger's and White's terminology is meant to evoke a certain image which equates Tantra with current pathologies in America—hard core and soft core pornography that are a significant part of American society today. This is an old colonial trope in which the best and brightest of India are compared to the dregs of Western society to help make sense of those weird Indians. Earlier we saw that Kripal equated Sri Ramakrishna's towering spiritual achievements and personal integrity to fantasies of a psychologically maladjusted, socially rejected, and personally conflicted, in-the-closet homosexual. Now we find that Doniger and White equate esoteric techniques of Tantra with something familiar to most Americans in an anti-social sense. Thus it is not to be seen as a powerful and valid cultural and religious alternative to American norms, but something familiar, something dismissible as 'been there, done that', and, moreover, something that is 'sexy, seedy and strange'.

White-Doniger claim that the transition from hard-core to soft-core was a discontinuity—a 'reform' by 'elite Brahmins' that 'sublimated' the past practice of 'sexual fluid exchange'. Obviously, this point-of-view is found not only in Doniger's review and analysis, but it is the central thesis cited in White's book:

> In about the eleventh century, a scholasticizing trend in Kashmirian Hindu circles, led by the great systematic theologian Abhinavagupta, sought to aestheticize the sexual rituals of the Kaula. These theoreticians, whose intended audience was likely composed of conformist householder practitioners, sublimated the end and *raison d'être* of Kaula sexual practice—the production of powerful, transformative sexual fluids—into simple by-products of a higher goal: the cultivation of a divine state of higher consciousness . . . (p.xii.)

White claims that until the eleventh century the heart of Tantra practice had been the 'oral consumption of sexual fluids as power substances', and that it was *never* practiced for the spiritual expansion of consciousness. He alleges that Abhinavagupta re-packaged it as a 'consumer product' for sale to Kashmiris whose 'bobo profile' could be compared to modern New Age seekers.

If such a thesis were true, there would be no spiritual legitimacy in the systems that flowed from Abhinavagupta onwards. Their origin would be merely the repackaging of superstition and sexual magic for a consumer market of 'wily Brahmins' who wanted to indulge secretly in wild sex while pretending it was a spiritual practice. This is quite a bombshell dropped on any serious spiritual practitioner of Kashmir Shaivism, Tantra and many other Hindu-Buddhist systems.

The following counter arguments by Malhotra challenge the primary thesis of White and Doniger:

1. Hinduism was never enforced by centralized institutional authorities—very different from the Abrahamic religions. There is no historical evidence of any such political movement across all of South Asia that dramatically imposed a 'soft-core' system upon the previous 'hard-core' system. The mere emergence of scholarly texts does not necessarily bring any social revolution in the case of Hinduism given the absence of a centralized and authoritarian Church in the mode of the Christian one.

2. Tantra was exported from India to other parts of Asia (such as Tibet) where it was seen by the receiving Asian cultures as a *spiritual* tradition. Therefore, the Indian Brahmins' sociopolitical exploitation that White-Doniger allege would also have to be proven in the case of all other Asian societies that imported Tantra. Since the domicile of Tantra practice has extended well beyond the geography of India, and especially since it has extended into territories where Brahmin social influence was not operative—such as Tibet, among others—the thesis of White-Doniger remains unproven until they examine Tantra outside of India and outside the scope of Hinduism.

3. Such scholarship arbitrarily classifies as 'Hindu' certain 'secular' practices and some obscure texts cited may even have never been practised (and certainly not 'enforced'). There may also have been many entirely unrelated multiple spiritual traditions from which the scholar indulges in a cut-and-paste exercise to fit his thesis.[145]

One of the readers of this online debate was Prof. Jayant Bapat, (incidentally, also a Tantra practitioner) at Monash University, Australia. He found White's arguments both unconvincing and reductionist:[146]

White's main argument is embedded in chapter 8 of his work. In this chapter, he hypothesizes the transformation of the Tantra from a folk based ritual, which involved physically donating bodily substances to the chosen goddesses in order to acquire supernatural powers, to an internalization, aestheticization and semanticization of Kaula practice (a change from doing to knowing) by Brahminic Hinduism. He argues that by doing this, which he terms overcoding, Brahmins were able to marginalize Kaula practices and transform them into a body of ritual and meditative techniques, which permitted the average householders to use them as well. Yogini circles of the folk tradition were internalized, transformed into chakras of Hathayogic practice, Yoginis themselves were semanticized into seed mantras and finally ritual substitutes were introduced for the bodily fluids.

The main theoreticians responsible for this change were Abhinavagupta and his disciple Kshemaraja. White has titled this chapter "The Sublimation of the Yogini" and writes that the language of phonemes and photemes, mantras and yantras made it possible for practitioners of high Hindu Tantra to discuss in abstract terms palatable to the higher tradition, what was and remains at the bottom, a sexual body of practice. In other words, to White, the original Tantra was little but sex and the consumption of bodily fluids in order to acquire supernatural powers.

Bapat finds the core of White's sociological thesis both unconvincing and reductionist:

> However, I take issue with his conclusions. White's assertion that there was "an original Kaula tradition" prevalent only in the folk tradition within India is speculative. As my colleague, John Dupuche, the author of the important new work, *The Kula Ritual*, comments, "it has been only a growing and changing tradition".[147] The branding of Abhinavagupta as someone who packaged the tantric path for the consumption of a leisurely Kashmiri populace shows a singular lack of understanding of the Brahmanic scholarly tradition. An examination of chapter 29 of Abhinavagupta's *Tantraloka* would leave no doubt in anyone's mind that he certainly did not shy away from describing and using bodily fluids.[...] What he fails to see however is the fact that sex and metaphysics, i.e. Abhinavagupta's interpretations, do not have to be diametrically opposed. Drinking of sexual fluids has a ritualistic but also a metaphysical and even philosophical element associated with it. The fluids are certainly not foods.[148]

Malhotra cited four specific examples from Doniger's School that could be seen as assault on a whole spiritual tradition:

1. *Assault on mantras:* Because the Tantrics were not elitist Brahmins and lacked access to complex Sanskrit mantras, Doniger notes that they "derived their mantras of nonsense syllables from the

inarticulate moans that the Goddess made during intercourse . . ." White elaborates that Abhinavagupta adopted the 'ha' sound in mantras because it "is the sound a woman makes while enjoying sexual intercourse—a barely articulated 'ha, ha, ha'".[149] White goes on to interpret the origin of the sounds used in meditation, "In other words, the 'ha' sound of the *visarga* is the semanticization of sex in Abhinavagupta's system."

2. *Assault on bindi:* White's explanation of the meaning of the bindi (the sacred mark worn by most Hindu women today) is that "the image of a drop (bindu) that recurs, across the entire gamut of Tantric theory and practice" was originally referring to a physical drop of menstrual blood, but was later explained using the language of mantras and yantras so as to be seen as abstract symbolism about speech and divine consciousness. This re-packaging, says White, was done for the 'high Hindu' elitist consumer market.

3. *Assault on mudra:* Doniger explains the meaning of the word mudra in the texts: "White argues that mudra . . . refers to 'the technique of urethral suction by means of which the Tantric yogin, having ejaculated into his partner, draws his semen together with her sexual emission back into his penis' (the so-called fountain-pen effect)". In this interpretation mudra signifies the practitioner's/consort's vulva, and, by extension, the fluids from the vulva.

4. *Assault on Srividya:* White culminates his arguments showing that many popular contemporary Hindu systems of symbolism emerged out of this 'intellectual whitewash' done by Abhinavagupta. The Srividya tradition as practised widely today was just that— whitewashed pornography and wild sex practices. It gave a spiritual gloss to hard-core practices by making them seem intellectual and spiritual.

This kind of scholarship also reflects the U-Turn syndrome, wherein the scholarship facilitates appropriations while simultaneously denigrating the source traditions. Significantly, it provides theoretical legitimacy to the ongoing Christianization of meditation techniques in which Hindu and/or Buddhist mantras are removed and substituted with either meaningless words, as in Herb Benson's 'Relaxation Response', or Christian words like 'Christ' or 'Amen'.

Christian appropriators can rationalize that the Hindu mantras are made of meaningless sounds, and additionally, that their appropriation would 'clean' them from sounds of a woman having an orgasm. The White-Doniger thesis is among many that supply this kind of scurrilous 'data' to feed this appropriation. Furthermore, White's theory about the origins of certain Hindu mantras and their sounds might in effect disturb many meditators by evoking images of women having orgasms. Hypothetically, mental health problems could then be blamed on mantras—maybe a rapist would be psychoanalyzed to show that the sound of his Hindu mantra made him commit rape.

The book's political thesis seems to be that Tantra was a secret system used by Brahmins to dupe the lower castes and oppress them. White alleges that whitewashed or soft-core repackaging of Tantra "later came to be seized upon by high-caste Hindu householders throughout medieval South Asia as a window of opportunity to experiment with a double (or triple) religious identity". White claims that this devious upper caste ploy was *a means to do what one said one was* not *doing...*".[150] [Emphasis added]. In other words, the entire tradition was one big hypocrisy. Multiple identities, secret rituals and metaphysical hyperbole enabled Brahmins to exert political control via crafty mechanisms, which White compares with espionage:

> A comparison with the world of espionage is a useful one: only those of the privileged inner circle (the heart of the Tantric mandala) have the highest security clearance (Tantric initiations) and access to the most secret codes (Tantric mantras) and classified documents (Tantric scriptures).[151]

Lower castes emulated these pseudo-spiritual practices 'as a means [of] social uplift'.[152] Therefore, the tradition is not only not spiritual, it is also associated with trickery and social oppression across the vast subcontinent. These kinds of analyses are devastating to the Indic tradition's progressive evolution and the self-concept of Hindus.

Abrahamic religions claim that they are the exclusive custodians of prophecies and canons documenting unique historical events. On the other hand, Indic *adhyatmika* spirituality, or inner science, tends to be non-history-centric and emanates from the enlightenment experiments of luminaries, of which Abhinavagupta is a very prominent example. *Adhyatma-vidya* methodology is similar to scientific empiricism, in that a legitimate spiritual tradition is the result of the actual experiences of spiritual masters and these experiences are *reproducible* by the rest of us in this very life. Therefore, White's allegations of Abhinavagupta's packaging of wild sex for the 'soft-core High Hindu' consumer market are as damaging as allegations would be against a Western empirical scientist that he fabricated laboratory data to substantiate a theory.

White's and Doniger's concepts of Tantra are implicated with 'overcoding', which is, according to the use of the word as found in White's book, a euphemism for duplicity or whitewash. Doniger alleges that Hindus led a hypocritical double life. Doniger writes in her review:

> A system of 'overcoding' permitted high-caste, conformist householder practitioners to have it both ways, to lead a double life by living conventionally while experimenting in secret with Tantric identities. Such people might put on a public face of Hindu orthodoxy.[153]

Is a system of academic *overcoding* at work in such scholarship? Do certain scholars live double lives? According to Malhotra, they publicly position themselves as very Hindu-friendly in certain audiences, such as, (i) with pandits in India on whom they are dependent for translations; (ii) with gullible students from the diaspora to cleverly re-engineer them away from Hindu identities; and (iii) with diaspora parents/philanthropists for fund-raising. This overcoding is a mask to cover up their secretly building 'ideological products' to show patterns of Hindu decadence, violence, immorality and abuse.

Just as these scholars claim to be removing the mask of soft-core practices in order to reveal the underlying'truth' of hard-core sexual practices, so too, Malhotra claims to remove the scholars' pretence of being friends of India/Hinduism and exposes their Hinduphobia. He argues:

> It is no coincidence that academic writings by David White, Sarah Caldwell, Jeffrey Kripal and many others apply the thesis of high-caste Hindu 'double lives' to a massive array of case studies which encompass Sri Ramakrishna, Swami Muktananda, Swami Vivekananda, Sri Aurobindo, and Hindu Goddess, among others. These case studies are filled with 'data' and convoluted logic. After winning awards their thesis *is declared final and closed* and those who dare criticize are attacked as being against intellectual freedom!

He maintains that "they are constructing scenarios of alleged moral 'transgressions' by Hindus that can then be applied to a wider socio-political context". In this context, Kripal wrongly claims that Hindu mystics such as Ramakrishna lack ethics. And, Caldwell, likewise, calls for the use of these transgression theories of Hinduism as a lens with which to study modern Hindu society's human rights problems. These academic theories allege that Hindu spiritual leaders secretly do weird things to women and children, while publicly adopting an abstract philosophical system of practices, under which the rituals and symbolism get presented as spiritual metaphysics. The violence or hedonism or sexism, or whatever else the Hindu rituals are shown to signify, are then projected to interpret modern Hindu society at large. Hinduism gets blamed as the cause of all sorts of issues facing modern India.

Hinduism, like all faiths, has its problematic aspects. Describing the religion multifariously from within an ecumenical orientation is not a problem for most Hindus. What is disturbing to them is that some high profile scholars allege that these abuses are the very essence of Hinduism, and not an aberration. In contrast, Abu Ghraib has not been framed by the media as a crime committed by Western culture *caused* by Biblical legends or original Biblical practices. An equivalent thesis would say that the original Biblical practices are *essentially* about hard-core sadomasochistic oppression and that a subsequent overcoding has been done to make the exploitation of non-Christian infidels and non-White peoples seem soft-core. Such a scholar would then claim to be giving Christians the gift of the 'truth' about their faith by uncovering the *real* Christianity. Those who have dared to do such contrarian scholarship are from the margins—they are unlikely to win important awards and Ivy League chairs.

The charge of Tantra as a system of social exploitation is used by Doniger to frame India's internal conflicts between 'tiers' of society—such as Dalits vs. Brahmins, Dravidians vs. so-called Aryans, women vs. men, minority religions vs. Hindus, and other Indic-specific dyads and contrasts. Malhotra interpreted Doniger's conclusions in the review of *Kiss of the Yogini*, as 'the triumphant tone of the white woman rescuing the native from their culture'. Doniger writes that White hopes by "reconstructing the medieval South Asian Kaula and Tantric traditions that involved sexual practices, [he can] restore the dignity and autonomy of the people who invented them and continue to practice them". This is the Tarzan-Saving-Natives-from-Danger-in-Jungle trope, also known as the Missionaries-Saving-Heathens-from-Blindness trope.

Ironically, the method through which White-Doniger claim to restore 'dignity' is to characterize the 'real' subaltern tradition as hedonistic, grotesque, superstitious sexual escapades and 'magic and sorcery' (as the book's blurb claims) and to characterize the seminal texts of Abhinavagupta as secret cover-ups by high caste Hindus.

Such scholars commonly claim to be saving Hinduism from past distortions when, in fact, they are merely applying a new layer of flashy paint on top of the previously applied explicitly colonial layers.[154] Malhotra was moved to ask:

1. By what authority are White, Doniger, et al 'in charge' of such 'restoration' of Indian traditions?
2. By what justification are they privileged to frame the subject in a particular manner as opposed to the many other alternative frames possible?
3. For whose sake is this 'restoration' being done?
4. What is the track record of their Judeo-Christian controlled intellectual institutions in achieving 'restoration' for other peoples in the past?
5. To whom are they accountable?

There is an obvious inconsistency when White and Doniger are promoting this 'restoration' to some 'imagined original past' in which 'Tantra equals sexual magic', and yet any attempts by Hindus to recover a positively 'imagined past' is severely condemned as being chauvinistic and disingenuous. In sharp contrast: "When Western sponsored scholarship indulges in speculative 'restoration' of so-called 'original' Hinduism there is no outcry of chauvinism"! Malhotra argues:

> The hypocrisy cries out for notice: Why is a return-to-the-past that is supervised by Western institutions a good thing, while on the other hand, internally generated perspectives [by Indians] are 'chauvinistic'? This question gives rise to another: Does the difference have to do with *who* exerts power and for what agenda? In this scenario, when the West controls the agenda, selects the topics and frames the issues, then it's positioned as positive 'restoration,' but when Indians outside Western institutions do the same thing, it is condemned by those in the Western institutions as inauthentic or invalid.

Academic Transgressions Excused in the Name of Saving Civilization

In her review of *Kiss of the Yogini*, Doniger raises some issues concerning White's findings, to wit—that they are based on assumptions that cannot be rigorously proven. She asks: "How do we know that the original, supposedly hard-core school was not also interpreting their texts metaphorically"? She elaborates:

> White's historical argument implies that Tantra was a ritual that became, for the dominant culture, a kind of myth, that from the eleventh century Hindus who continued actually to perform the rituals (hard-core) described them in a code that made it appear that they were merely performing them symbolically (soft-core). The assumption that this transformation has taken place enables White to restore the text that the revisionists had eclipsed, to break the code and reconstruct the pre-transformed text, much as Freud— a constant presence in this book—worked backwards to reconstruct the meaning of the dream before it had been censored, to restore the dream that the censoring superego and the dream work had masked.[155]

Doniger acknowledges that a *mere possibility* of meaning does not imply certainty of meaning. She also points out that White adopts literal meanings inconsistently. Where it suits him, White claims the Indian texts to be literal; but where the acts described would seem to be physically impossible, he does not adopt literal meanings but metaphorical ones. This arbitrariness in selecting when a text is literal and when it is metaphorical gives White and other privileged Indological scholars a powerful, disingenuous weapon. Doniger writes:

> . . . White is not entirely consistent in his literalism. When the texts state that the male participants in the Kaula rites feed the Yoginis semen and blood drawn from their bodies in exchange for the magical power of flight, White argues that the female consorts (standing for the Yoginis) really did consume the fluids and drink the blood, but he does not argue that the male practitioners really flew. And when a text speaks of mixing the Yogini's two milks (her breast-milk and her menstrual discharge) he says it is describing 'an impossible ritual practice', since menstruation stops during lactation, and, in any case, Yoginis never have children and hence never lactate. He concludes, therefore, that this is an instance of powerful 'Tantric transgressivity' best read as a piece of the Tantric 'prescriptive imagination'. Only because this could not be done does White assume it was not done. **But is there any reason to assume that the physically possible act of drinking menstrual blood was done other than that it could be done?** White proves *beyond any doubt* that the early Tantrics *may* well have ingested these fluids, but it is impossible for him to prove that they actually did.

Bending over backwards is not the most comfortable position from which to argue.[156] [Emphasis added]

Thus Doniger ends up with a George Bushism (as Witzel would put it) when she claims that White has *proven* a 'definite maybe'. But then Doniger suddenly exonerates White's intellectual transgressions and justifies his thesis on the basis that she finds it politically expedient, even after showing that his hypothesis is inconsistent and unproven. Doniger now argues that, regardless of its scholarly shortcomings, *Kiss of the Yogini* 'has a political importance that eclipses reservations of this kind'. She writes:

> In arguing for the sexual meaning of the texts, White is flying in the face of the revisionist Hindu hermeneutic tradition that began in the eleventh century, was favored by Hindus educated in the British tradition from the nineteenth century onwards, and prevails in India today. The contemporary Indian view is complicated by a new political twist. Right-wing Hindu groups, in India and in the diaspora, have increasingly asserted their wish, indeed their right, to control scholarship about Hinduism.[157]

Thus Doniger seems to be suggesting, that evidence or no evidence, we should accept White's thesis because it *shows* the devious revisionism practised by Hindus for a long time and because it is useful in deflating and denigrating dangerous Hindus today. Bapat criticizes Doniger severely on this point as well, calling her position *vitandavada* or argumentation that ignores reason in favor of establishing pet theories by repetition. He explains:

> Extrapolating Abhinavagupta's work to level criticism at 19th century Indian scholars and the current Hindutva advocates seems far-fetched. Also, I believe Abhinavagupta as an insider, had every right to interpret whatever he saw into Hindu religiosity. To me, he built Tantra elements together into a metaphysical and rational system of thought. Imputing [facile] sociological motives to an eleventh century scholar needs a thorough recreation of his life and times.[158]

The Dalit Card and Other Expediencies

Tantra practitioners and scholars know that one ancient movement *within* the tradition sought *embodied enlightenment* through sexual means. It had two parallel strands, one focusing primarily on consciousness and the other utilizing bodily techniques. Malhotra refers to the traditions claiming spiritual purposes as 'A,' and the Tantric traditions claiming sexual practice as an objective as 'B'. He writes:

> These two have fought and argued for centuries. What is new in White's thesis is his 'ground-breaking' claim that 'A' is simply a whitewash on top of 'B' as a 'consumer product' to hide the 'transgressions' by Brahmins for a thousand years. He claims that 'A' was merely a strategy to deceive publicly, while privately pursuing sexual acts that were forbidden to Hindus. In other words, there is no legitimacy to the 'A' claims as a spiritual system. White and Doniger claim credit for 'restoring' the glory of 'A' by calling it 'B' beneath the covers. She asserts that all these spiritual claims are soft (porn) to cover up the hard (porn). No real attempt has been made to explore, let alone vindicate, how Abhinavagupta might have reformulated that ancient quest for unity through union, not just sexual, in cogent metaphysical terms.

White alleges that all this was simply a political tool for the upper castes to control the masses. While the upper castes made spiritual claims to cover up their *'sexcapades'* behind the mask of spiritual language, the lower castes dumbly practised Tantra as wild sexual orgies. The spiritual claims were a mechanism by which high-caste people duped and oppressed the Dalits. By invoking the subaltern tribal or Dalit identity, White and Doniger can claim to be exposing aspects of the Tantric tradition that have been used to exploit the oppressed.

Doniger has insulated herself from valid critiques, written by people such as those featured in section II, who possess modern, well-educated and liberal voices. She claims that the contemporary Hindus who are critical of her are 'of the Hindutva persuasion'. She carefully identifies her tormentors, as "followers of the recently ousted Hindu Nationalist BJP, with its repressive and purity-obsessed policies".[159] In short, she dismisses her critics as repressed and obsessed puritans.

She expresses concern about the negative impact on Religious Studies from 'Hindu fundamentalist attacks on Freudian interpretations'. The Hindu attackers, she writes: "argue that none of these [psychoanalytical] characterizations has any scriptural validity according to Hindu tenets or eminent Hindu scholars". Doniger notes: "This position finds some support in Western scholarly traditions [such as] Cantwell Smith [who] argued that no historian of religions should ever make a statement about any religion that some members of that religion would not recognize and accept". She mentions, mockingly that, "This view is still honored by many conscientious scholars who follow the take-a-Hindu-to-dinner, Parliament-of-world-religions approach." She adds, emphatically, "It is not, however, the only approach."

Highlighting the comments used to endorse *Kiss of the Yogini* is revealing. The first endorsement on the back cover is written by Lee Siegel, who invites the reader to look at the book in terms of 'magic and sorcery'—words suggestive of inferior cognition and irrationality in the modern Western context. The typical reader associates these words with black arts, witchcraft, devil worship, and other contraband heresies. It would be unusual for a major mainstream work published by the University of Chicago Press to portray popular Christian practices in terms of magic and sorcery that involve the consumption of bodily fluids, such as blood, or to explain Christian theology as the result of a cover-up by Bishops trying to live double lives. Jeffrey Kripal also applauded the reductionist bias in *Kiss of the Yogini* for reminding us 'once again that South Asian Tantra *really* is about sex, bodily fluids and all'. Such an endorsement is self-serving because it helps Kripal avoid the specific questions raised by Tyagananda, Bhattacharyya, Sil and others, by claiming that even if he was utterly wrong on the specifics of Sri Ramakrishna's life, he is vindicated by White's discovery of the cover-ups and hypocrisy of Hindu culture.

White confidently presumes that "much of the Tantric terminology makes sense only if it is read literally".[160] Malhotra asks a crucial question: "It makes sense to whom?" To contemporary scholars, who reject the spiritual legitimacy of Indian traditions in the first place? Or to contemporary practitioners, who inherently accept the spiritual legitimacy of Indian traditions? An equivalent methodology in the reverse direction, as often asserted by critics of Christianity, is one in which Christian rituals and the doctrine of the Eucharist is reduced to a cannibalistic feast of eating flesh and drinking blood. However, Malhotra notes:

> White quickly and assertively rejects doing this to Christianity by using the argumentation strategy of *reductio ad absurdum*—he rejects this because he says that it would make Christians cannibals. But when it comes to Tantra, he not only accepts what to a

contemporary Hindu would be an absurdity, but insists that this is the *only* way to make sense of it.

He then asks a perplexing question, articulated over and over again within the Hindu-American community: "Why are such unsympathetic academicians, conditioned within biblical traditions, in a position to decide which portions of a text on Hinduism are literal and which ones are not"?

Another critic, the philosopher Sitanshu Chakravarti,[161] has raised questions about several of David White's 'literal' translations. For instance he points out that White reduces the Sanskrit word *dravya* (meaning material, object or thing) as fluids, particularly sexual fluids. All Hindus, not just Tantrikas, use *dravya*s ranging from flowers to sweets to clothes, wood and ghee and sandal paste in their *puja*s and *havan*s—these are all homogenized by White into 'fluids'. Chakravarti cites a few such suspect translations and their page numbers in White's book:

> Last, but not the least, some of the translations of Sanskrit words in White's book are significantly suspect, like 'fluid' for '*dravya* (thing)' p.7 onward ['without clan-generated fluids' for '*kulodbhavair-dravyair-vinā*' p.74—(the splitting of the constituent words are mine)], 'swallow' for '*grihna* (accept)' p.228, 'ritual copulation' for '*mithuna* (couple)' p.77, 'actively engaged in drinking' for '*pānodyatah*' (ready to drink) p.76.[162]

Madhu Khanna's Critique

Malhotra had conversations with a bold critic of such abusive scholarship, Madhu Khanna, a renowned scholar-practitioner of Tantra based in India,[163] and he extensively quoted from her paper, '*Paradigms of Female Sexuality in the Hindu World.*'[164] She describes four different representations of female sexuality in Hinduism and emphasizes that these cannot be reduced to *any one category* to the exclusion of the rest. In describing the Tantric paradigm, she explains the 'non-dual unity of life' as follows, "Tantra concerns itself with the series of relationships between the transcendent and real, the macrocosm and the microcosm, the sacred and the profane, the outer and the inner, and weaves them within the framework of its values."[165]

She explains that each pair of opposites is to be held in mutual tension and neither side of the pair may be collapsed into the other, as that would be a dualistic reduction. This is why both radical realism and pure idealism are considered incorrect ways of understanding Tantra.

Criticizing the reductionist tendency of those stuck in Abrahamic dualities (into which White appears to have slipped), Khanna remarked:

> The Western approach that splits the erotic from the sacred appears short sighted and deficient . . . White uses his profane-only lens to collapse the sacred-profane pair into profanity, with the spiritual aspect of the pair getting postured as a deceptive cover for hedonism by corrupt Brahmins. His core theory is that [Hindu] spirituality is a derivative from profanity and was intended for ulterior motives from the beginning. [Emphasis added]

In many Tantra texts (such as *Kulârnavatantra*), considerable space is devoted to spelling out the rigorous prerequisites for being an *adhikarin*, a person who has the psycho-physiological preparation to be qualified to make sense of the esoteric practices. The practitioner must have internalized the sophisticated system of symbols and cosmology. Khanna explains the rigorous self-discipline of the 'left-hand' Tantra practitioners who must:

> Follow the reverse path where the natural instincts which habitually run riot outwards (*pravritti*), turn inwards (*nivritti*) to the source of creation, and all elements of creation are used as a means for the union with the one consciousness which is the origin of all. This process of inner identification with the supreme takes place in their yoga through the sacralization of the senses and sublimation of sexual energy. The ritual is thus prescribed for the highest rank of disciples who have graduated from the seven lower levels of sadhana. [Emphasis added]. These disciples form an exclusive group and do not reveal themselves in society. Absolute secrecy is maintained and the practices are guarded from the profane and unqualified and are not to be disclosed to the undeserving.[166]

White asserts, "I am a historian of South Asian religions and not a Tantric practitioner. . ."[167] This calls into question his qualifications as a reliable restorer of the tradition. "Would a person who is deaf to certain tones be qualified to restore music played in the past based on simply reading the music scores, and to reject the music as played by maestros as invalid?"[168]

Conclusions

According to many members of the Hindu diaspora, the implication of the White-Doniger thesis for the study of India and Indic traditions has been disastrous. Malhotra summarizes the impact:

1. White gives ammunition to those who attack Hinduism as being a collection of barbaric practices.
2. He reinforces the reduction of Hinduism as fodder for anthropological and psychopathological studies.
3. He tries to undermine Hinduism's spiritual claims and renders its philosophical texts as fake or hypocritical.
4. He feeds Hinduphobia in the minds of mainstream Americans who see everyday Hindu symbols as weird and/or as representing immoral practices.
5. He provides a template with which to legitimize further data hunting-gathering about Hindus' alleged violations of human rights, by claiming to have proven that such violations were the original intent and very purpose behind Hindu practices.
6. He plays into India's caste conflicts by theorizing that Tantric spirituality was a ploy by upper castes to control the masses.
7. He tries to de-legitimize Tantra as a means for Dalit spiritual empowerment.
8. He tries to de-legitimize women's empowerment through Tantra, a unique and major claim in contrast with the Abrahamic religions, and, hence, a perceived threat to male-dominated Abrahamic religions.

One of the more interesting asides about *Kiss of the Yogini* is the fact that Doniger uses the book as an opportunity to discredit any attempts at Hindu constructive theology by attacking it as a project of Hindu nationalists who have "increasingly asserted . . . their right, to control scholarship about Hinduism"; and who think theirs is "the only acceptable view". Her basic view of her opponents is false. Doniger's critics neither insist that the spiritual-only view is the only acceptable one, nor that Indians should be the only ones doing Indic Studies. What they do criticize is the attempt to reduce Hinduism to pornography and to wish away the profound spiritual component in Hinduism. As Bapat and Malhotra have noted, Hindu insiders do have the right to constructive theology, as do people of all faiths. Terming this a 'cover up' or 'fascism' based on speculative findings is clearly intended to delegitimize Hindus' rightful access to such processes.

The debate over White's book has continued with more voices joining in from within the tradition. For instance, Prof Neela Bhattacharya Saxena[169] recently published her sharp criticism in an article titled, 'The Funhouse Mirror of Tantric Studies: A Rejoinder to David Gordon White's *Kiss of the Yogini*'.[170] Taking the points in Malhotra-Lidke online debate further, Saxena calls White's work 'insidious' and 'the hallmark of a new imperial structure'. She cites many of the same sources and arguments that were circulated in the online debates, which goes to show the growing impact of the diaspora/practitioner critics on the academy.[171]

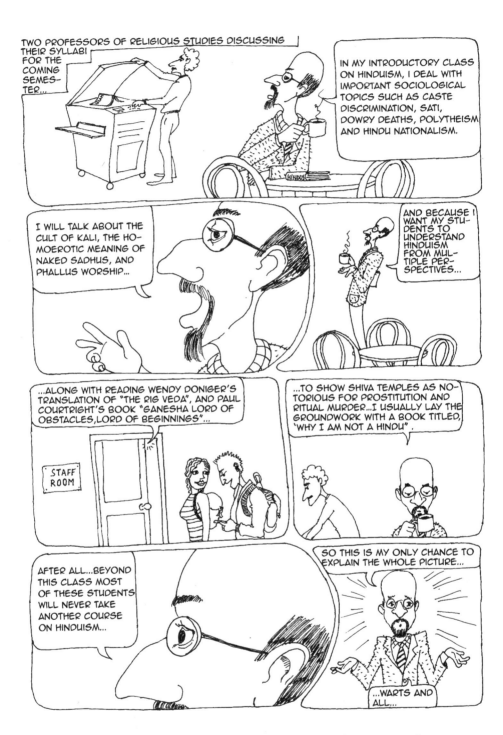

This comic is intended to be satirical, and any resemblance herein to actual events or persons living or dead is purely coincidental.

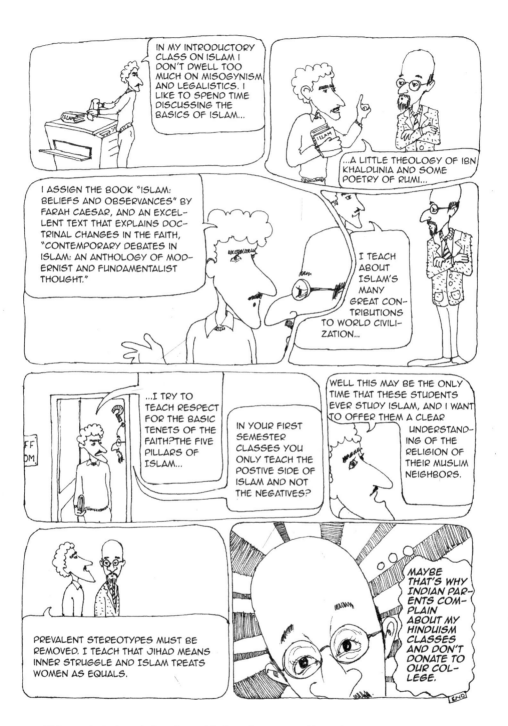

This comic is intended to be satirical, and any resemblance herein to actual events or persons living or dead is purely coincidental.

Chapter 9

Chakra Hermeneutics

This chapter describes a model that uses the Chakra System as a theoretical framework on which to deconstruct the psychological orientations of scholars of Hindu traditions. Malhotra proposed this technique as one way of making sense of contemporary scholarly descriptions of Hinduism that appear unrecognizable to Hindu practitioners:

> The Hindu-Buddhist Chakra framework has seven layers and may be used as a system of hermeneutics. Imagine each chakra as a template of contexts that are usable for multiple purposes. When a phenomenological experience is interpreted or processed from a given chakra, it provides a perspective corresponding to that chakra. The physical locations of the chakras are relevant to yogic or tantric transformative practices, whereas their archetypal meanings are of interest here.

The framework of Chakra Hermeneutics is summarized below.

Chakra Hermeneutics[172]

- *Lowest:* The lower three chakras correspond to basic animal instincts. The lowest or first chakra, near the anus, is about security. The second chakra, located near the genitals, is about pleasure and reproduction. The third chakra, located near the navel, is about self-control and power over others.
- *Middle:* The fourth, fifth and sixth chakras represent positive human qualities, such as love, interconnection and bonding, creativity, altruistic vision, and so forth. These represent the higher human/ divine qualities that all religions espouse, and take us beyond basic animal instincts. Behaviorism or any other strictly mechanistic

worldview, being devoid of spirituality, might not recognize these, and would limit itself to the human needs and desires corresponding to the lower charkas only.

- *Highest:* The seventh, or crown chakra, corresponds to non-dualism and transcendence—moksha, nirvana, self-realization and samadhi. Most Indic *adhyatma-vidya*[173] systems culminate in such a state. In Abrahamic religions, many of the mainstream orthodox worldviews deny this possibility, although mystics, who are often considered fringe or heretical, achieve states compatible with the seventh chakra.[174]

This psychological model may be applied to analyze various scholars. Depending on where a given scholar's psychological state is located in this hierarchy of archetypes, she will experience the world corresponding to the template of the corresponding set of chakras. This means that the same reality may be experienced at many levels—a point that is stressed by Hindu spiritual traditions.

For instance, one may theorize that Wendy's Children appear to reside predominantly at the lower two chakras while conducting their scholarship. In keeping with his own concepts of homophobia and homosexuality, and perhaps a deep insecurity about his Roma heritage, Kripal sees Hinduism from the anal perspective. This is undoubtedly one valid point of view, but by no means *the only* truth. It is certainly not the highest vantage point, nor is it a place where one should remain stuck.

Doniger and Caldwell appear driven partly by their personal sexual histories and partly by career ambitions; they seem to oscillate between the second chakra (genitals and pleasures) and the third chakra (power). This is why their interest in, and depiction of, Hinduism is what it is—ribald and racy and focused on being 'marketable, fast-food style', to modern consumers, as previously noted by Bakker, Kazanas and others. A telling illustration of a lower chakra mindset that marginalizes other possibilities is provided by David White, who in dedicating *Kiss of the Yogini*, thanks his own parents, *not* for their love or moral support or sacrifice over the years, but for contributing sexual fluids to conceive him![175] Doniger would have approved! Larson's call to protect RISA's turf—echoed and amplified by many other cartel bosses—may be seen as an indicator of the Roman gladiator archetype based in the third chakra of power projection.

On the other hand, more elevated and better-integrated RISA scholars see Hinduism from the middle chakras, and are able at least to theorize about the seventh chakra in an authentic manner. They examine the practices and rituals associated with these chakras—love, bhakti, and elimination of *kleshas* (negative conditions)—from the perspective of spiritual advancement. They look at the same things as do Wendy's Children, but with different pairs of eyes.

All of the chakras are interdependent and interconnected. Any experience involves a combination of multiple chakras, and this combination changes from one experience to another. Furthermore, the use of chakras in this *interpretive* manner—as tools of literary and cultural theory—is a novel adaptation because conventionally they are used as *transformational* devices for spiritual advancement.

Malhotra notes that Freud spent his entire career studying European patients with pathologies in the lower chakras, hence his obsession in analyzing them solely in terms of their sexuality. Later, Jung studied Hinduism intensely and practised yoga, based on Patanjali's texts. He claimed to have achieved states of emotional and spiritual consciousness associated with the fourth, fifth, and sixth chakras. This enabled him to break away from Freud (a significant historical development in Western thought) and thus help spiritualize Western science. He also reinterpreted Christian myths and their archetypes using a neo-Hindu worldview.[176] Joseph Campbell and others continued this tradition that was initially respectful of Indic world views. As we will note in section IV, Jung's followers like Joseph Campbell are seen as threats by Doniger from her second and third chakra worldview. She has launched *ad hominem* attacks on Campbell, in an attempt to discredit his ideas.

However, even Jung did not abandon Eurocentrism. Given his enormous influence over prominent Western thinkers for several decades, he helped to radically transform Western thought by appropriating Indic concepts. Malhotra notes that Jung's followers erased the Indian influences on his works. And Jung, too, remapped Indian categories on to Greek-Abrahamic and his own original categories. Till the end, Jung denied the existence of the crown (seventh) chakra because non-duality and transcendence would refute the biblical reinterpretations he had developed. Therefore, by the end of his career, Jung had blocked off any such experiences and "started to impose pathologic glosses on yogic claims about states of consciousness associated with the seventh chakra". He even discouraged his students from practising yoga, calling it dangerous for Westerners, and wanted to develop a special 'new yoga' for Westerners.

Joseph Campbell's *Papers from the Eranos Yearbooks* (in six volumes) show that the participants at Jung's conferences were like a *Who's Who* of Western thinkers. This prolonged series of conferences was a major mechanism for the dissemination of Indic thought into the Western mainstream, with Jung as the presiding deity. Campbell did his own U-Turn from Indic thought after he visited India in 1954, and saw squalor and misery, which lead him to write the book, *Baksheesh and Brahman.*

Mircea Eliade, Doniger's predecessor at the University of Chicago, after whom the chair she holds is named, was a friend and collaborator of Jung. Eliade was intensely interested in Hinduism until his own subsequent U-Turn. Thus, according to Malhotra's Chakra Hermeneutics, many

> Western anthropological and sociological dissections of Indic traditions focus on chakra 3—dealing with power plays between castes, genders, modern political movements, and so forth. The *sanskaras* (archetypes) of gladiators, and hence of many RISA scholars, are also located here. These depictions, just like the views from chakras 1 and 2, are not the crux of what many spiritual texts are trying to convey, but are often a caricature made to serve an agenda.
>
> Using this frame of reference, it would seem that Wendy's Children are scholars operating largely from the anal, genital and navel (power) perspectives. The book, *Kali's Child,* would have been more appropriately named, *An Anal Perspective of Ramakrishna.* The same holds for many of the works of other RISA scholars. The scholarship published by Wendy's Children, based on a worldview resting at the lowest chakras, does not provide students the opportunity of the liberating potential afforded by the higher chakras. They essentialize Hinduism by reducing it to their own self-defined condition at the lowest chakras.[177]

In today's media environment, Islam is often reinterpreted for Western audiences by emphasizing its higher levels of meaning. For instance, readers are often reminded that the word *Jihad* has a connotation of 'inner struggle'—shifting the third chakra view of Jihad to a higher chakra spiritual view. This is being done despite obstacles from within Islam, where such interpretations are questioned by most clergy on the basis that the doctrine of Islam is closed to new interpretations. The Western academic repackaging and facelift of Islam is certainly a good project from the point of view of Islamic progress and inter-religious harmony. Unfortunately, a different standard is being applied to Hinduism, despite the fact that its history and library of texts cry out loudly and clearly in favor of multiple layers of meanings and interpretations. Hindus are also being denied their agency to interpret 'upwards' (in terms of higher chakras) when in fact this should be respected in the same way it is being done with Muslims and Christians.

The different levels of consciousness represented by the chakras, along with the diversity of Hindu contexts, are well suited for interpreting not only the abstract symbolism of lingam, Kali, Tantra, and various ceremonies and rituals, but stories and narratives as well. For instance, when seen from the middle chakras, the head represents the ego, and cutting the head symbolically means getting rid of the ego. But, as Malhotra notes: "Wendy's Children are taught to see the head as the phallus, and cutting is viewed as a message of castration, hence they remain stuck in the anal-genital chakras". All told, it would be more productive if they were to acknowledge that theirs is not a comprehensive view and that it might not even be the most desirable or relevant view for many students.

Collapsing Hindu texts, practices, and symbolism into one Eurocentric lower level chakra perspective is an act of reductionism that does a great deal of violence to the tradition. A.K. Ramanujan's highly-regarded paper[178] on the context-sensitive meanings of Indian thought receives much lip service in the academy, but its purport seems to be missed too often. Malhotra regrets the two-pronged cultural devastation:

> While the higher chakra interpretations are being plagiarized rapidly into all sorts of New Age, Judeo-Christian and 'Western' scientific terminology, academic Hinduism is being reduced to the views from the lowest chakras. It is especially unethical for scholars to apply the lower chakra lens to interpret the higher chakra experiences— seeing mystical experiences as madness, weirdness, or as various sexual pathologies. Therefore, in keeping with Gadamer, Hindus obviously should be allowed to use the Chakra Hermeneutics.

The Myth of Objective Scholarship

As can be seen, many Eurocentric scholars of Hinduism end up virtually reinventing the religion in line with their own agendas, psychoses and cultural conditionings.[179] The Hinduism that they thereby create consists of caricatures, unrecognizable to the people for whom it is a lived reality.

Malhotra shows how Wendy's Child Syndrome emerges out of the following five pathological tendencies:

1. Psychological filters develop over decades through peer consensus and these limit the choices for research topics and what data gets in or out. There is a certain arbitrariness concerning what issues are investigated and a political correctness about the questions asked and not asked. This also applies to choosing the subsets of the Hindu texts relied upon, either salacious or dogmatic. For instance, in the *Manusmriti,* mostly the socially regressive verses are repeatedly highlighted while over a thousand more enlightened ones are ignored.[180]

2. Various contexts are juxtaposed in an ad hoc cut-and-paste manner, and misleading translations are utilized, which are then adamantly defended as authentic and objective scholarship. These heady extrapolations are shielded from criticism by a compromised peer-review process. The conclusions are defended, ironically, not on the intellectual merits, but by invoking freedom of speech.[181]

3. Hindu intellectuals are excluded from the discourse except those Hindus or nominal Hindus who are securely under the control of the academic establishment. Native Hindus are positioned as 'informants'. Representatives of specific *sampradayas* are not invited either as equal participants in the scholarship, or as respondents when conclusions are published about their traditions. This is illustrated by the 'secret trial' of Sri Ramakrishna that was held *in absentia,* after which the case was declared 'closed' by Kripal acting as the accuser, jury and judge.

4. Independent challengers are subject to hyperbolic *ad hominem* attacks, and important scholarly issues are dismissed through repeated fear-mongering allusions to 'saffronized' fascists. That ends the debate and the substantive criticisms are rarely addressed. (Sections III and IV of this volume cover this issue extensively.)

5. A controlled dose of criticism is encouraged from RISA insiders, who have been trained to know where to draw the line. This gives the false impression of peer-review objectivity and integrity. However, those who seek to spotlight academic weaknesses with evidence-based evaluations become objects of intense anger, especially when done in front of the diaspora whose children are sitting in the scholars' classrooms.

A publicly projected, post-modern aura of 'objectivity' has empowered scholars to visualize Hinduism through the lenses of their own personal experiences, cultural biases, feelings, traumas and dramas. For them, all too often, Hinduism is an artifact, a precious curio to be classified and displayed. This is a vision of a luscious antique Hinduism inhabited by the dysfunctional Hindu 'other' trapped in pre-modernity. Because of scholars' unique fixations on a particular scope or slice of Hinduism—textual, or performance, or social—the evolving, interactive aspect of living Hinduism is perceived as threatening.

Educated, Westernized Hindus have recently begun to engage the distortions that they have found in writings about their culture. However, when they raise their voices and take exception, they are attacked as triumphalists. Hinduism is seen as inhabited by homoeroticism, pedophilia and other highly intriguing pathologies. The Hindu 'objects' are of great interest while they are the focus of scholarly analyses, but when they talk back they soon become objects of fear and scorn.

There have been similar criticisms about ethical issues from within the academy. The problem is that these have not been applied rigorously to India Studies or Hinduism Studies. For instance, Monaghan and Just have asked:

> To whom does an ethnographer owe his or her greatest allegiance? Is it to the people studied, to the sovereign government of the country where research takes place, to the agency or foundation that funds the ethnographer's research, to the academic or research institution that employs the ethnographer, or to the community of scholars to which the ethnographer belongs? Should ethnographers be expected only to add to humanity's knowledge of itself or should they be expected to provide more tangible benefits to the people they study or to the world at large? Should ethnographers be held to a higher standard than the one applied to journalists, filmmakers, or photographers who also report on their fellow human beings? These, too, are unresolved questions, subject to lively debate.[182]

Pathologies of Wendy's Child Syndrome

McKim Marriott opined that scholars cannot avoid unintentionally superimposing their own psychological and cultural conditioning onto their works. This happens when they select topics of interest, filter the data, and then view the data through their chosen linguistic and methodological lenses or theories that privilege a given agenda or belief or identity. This conforms to and confirms various *a priori* conceptual formulations.

Malhotra developed his model 'Wendy's Child Syndrome' (WCS) partly in jest in order to make a point in a provocative way. He was convinced that after the articulation of the WCS Theory, scholars would hardly be in a position to resist this inquiry which merely turns the tables around. In his view:

> To fully appreciate the academic portrayals of Hinduism, one must study Wendy Doniger's influence playing out through her followers' subconscious conditioning. Because Wendy wields far greater power in Western academe than does Kali, Wendy's Child is far more important to deconstruct than Kali's Child.

He postulated his theory as follows.

Wendy's Child Syndrome

1. Western women, such as the famous Prof. Doniger herself, who are influenced by the prudish and male chauvinistic myths of the Abrahamic religions, find in their study of Hinduism a way to release their innermost latent *vasanas*[183], but they disguise their autobiography behind a portrayal of the 'other'—in this case superimposing their obsessions upon Hindu deities and saints.[184]
2. American lesbian and gay *vasanas*, also suppressed by Abrahamic condemnation, seek private and public legitimacy, and therefore, interpret Indian texts for this autobiographical purpose.
3. Western women, seeking an alternative to the masculine God in the Abrahamic religions, started a serious study of Hindu Goddess in the 1960s, initially with great respect and devotion. Eventually, though, their lower chakras took control and they U-Turned in two ways: They mapped the Hindu Goddess on to Mother Mary which allowed their ego to preserve its cultural supremacy and continuity of identity. And they used it for Hinduphobic agendas (such as evangelism), finding in the Hindu Goddess nothing more edifying than a symbol of female violence or a symbol of male oppression.
4. Given the Abrahamic God's obsession with his enemy, Satan, the dualism of 'us versus them' is unavoidable. In this zero-sum game, Western women must fight men and displace them by becoming like them, as there is no honored place for the female in Western myths. Hence, this myth also plays out as a theory of 'tutelage' over ethnic women of color, as a sort of White Woman's Burden. It is very fashionable for Indian women to get inducted into this by the lure

of degrees, grants, publishing projects and other rewards. The more ethnically oriented such an Indian candidate appears, the more precious the catch: hence one finds Indian women showing up in saris, bindis and other markers to prove their worth as 'authentic Hindus' wanting to tow the line of the white establishment. Meanwhile, self-assured Hindu women are shunned as a threat to the shifting paradigm, dismissed as not being 'real' Hindus. The Hindu woman of the Western Myth is therefore a straw-woman constructed to fit the needs of the White Woman's Burden. Many Indian women activists, such as Madhu Kishwar (founder and head of Manushi, a prominent activist group in Delhi), bitterly contest Western Feminist portrayals of Indian women. For their audacity these Indian activists get attacked or dismissed.

In other words, Hinduism provides a safe and fertile ground for scholars to experiment playfully with their voyeurism while pretending to be objectively interpreting those far-away, 'far-out' Hindus. While at first glance many such projects may seem harmless, eventually they tend to get appropriated for other more insidious agendas, including the social re-engineering and denigration of Indian culture.

The scholarship of many RISA scholars is afflicted with some combination of the four conditions described above. Malhotra lists nine consequences of this Syndrome.

Implications of Wendy's Child Syndrome

1. Many scholars lack the full knowledge of the cultural context and/or the language skills to be able to legitimately override the native interpretations of a living tradition. Yet this is what they often do.
2. Insiders to the tradition are excluded from participating as equals in their capacity to speak with *adhikara*[185] on behalf of the tradition. Instead, they are reduced to being 'native informants' of various sorts, or else they are brought in under the tutelage, supervision, or authority of Wendy's Children. Those who resist do not advance in their careers. Controlling the membership of the intellectual cartel is crucial to its survival.
3. Many critical terms are simply mistranslated, or else are taken out of context. Words that have a wide range of meanings are collapsed into a simplistic meaning that is usually the most sensational option and fits the thesis of the scholar.
4. There is often complete disregard for understanding the tradition based on any other perspective than the lower chakras. This is because acknowledging the higher levels of interpretations would

validate and legitimize the tradition and make it an attractive alternative for some students. Hence, there is sensational use of sexuality, social abuse, irrationality, etc. to marginalize the seriousness of the deeper tradition.

5. Certain Western scholars have mastered the art of cutting-and-pasting Indian texts and contemporary narratives, superimposing exotic imagery in order to fortify their claims. Onto this lavish landscape they sprinkle content from their imagination and from unrelated areas of Indian culture. The final product is coated with hyper-jargon to make it ridiculous or incomprehensible. It is brand managed through incestuous awards and promotions to capture the dominant market share.

6. Evidences that would refute the nascent thesis are ignored and suppressed. Competing views from within the tradition are dismissively ignored, or the challengers are vehemently attacked.

7. The subject matter to be studied is mapped by the scholar as though it was his or her personal property and therefore it ceases to belong to the community for whom it is a living tradition. As his property, the scholar will defend it fiercely, but at his own will or whim. This tentative loyalty is protected in a very patronizing manner and subject to potential U-Turns in the future.

8. Doctorate degrees, academic papers, academic press books, book awards, and jobs at prestigious institutions are doled out by committees who are part of the knowledge production establishment, and who often suffer from this Syndrome. There is no independent review or audit of RISA's policies and practices.

9. The afflicted scholars emphatically ignore criticism by any one who is not under the umbrella of their power structure. If the criticism persists, they attack the critic, as if to say, 'How dare you talk back this way? You, a mere native informant, or worse, you are an Indian computer geek who grew up practising Hinduism but never studied it at the graduate school level. Don't you know your place?' Any criticism or corrective scholarship that manages to sneak in from outside is not placed in major libraries, or catalogued for online search, nor designated as prescribed reading in colleges. In many instances, it is not even available for purchase at mainstream book retailers. Swami Tyagananda's scholarly response to Kripal's shoddily researched book is a case in point: it has been virtually buried because distribution is controlled by the syndicate.

The Myth of the West

Wendy's Child Syndrome reinforces the broader *Western Myth* by eroticizing the 'other'. It reifies its supremacy while weakening the other culture in the eyes of naïve students and the public. Far from being independent thinkers, scholars afflicted with *Wendy's Child Syndrome* are subconsciously performing their roles within this myth.

[O]ne of the underlying assumptions of Western Indology is a feeling of superiority in relation to India, especially modern India and Indians. This feeling of superiority is expressed in various ways. On one level, there are recurrent attempts to link all fundamental changes in the Indian society and history to Western intervention in some form. The image of ancient India which was foisted on Indians through hegemonic texts emanating from Western schools of Indology had in mind an India that was steeped in philosophical, religious and literary lores and unable to change herself without external influence, be it in the form of Alexander the Great, Roman Ships carrying gold or the Governor-Generals of the British East India Company. On a different level, expressions of Western superiority can be more direct and encompass a wide range of forms: patronizing and/or contemptuous reviews of Indian publications, allusions to personal hardships while working in India, refusal to acknowledge Indians as "agents of knowledge" or even blatant arrogance which makes one wonder if the civilized values of Western Academia have not left its Indology mostly untouched . . .

Western Indology is an essential by-product of the process of establishment of Western dominance in India. Racism—in this case a generic feeling of superiority in relation to the natives—was, quite logically, one of the major theoretical underpinnings of this process. It is but natural that Western Indology should carry within remnants of this feeling of superiority.

Dilip Chakrabarti
Archaeology Department
Cambridge University[186]

Narasingha Sil further elaborates:

I have a vision of the descent of the 'avataras' of the missionaries of yester years who sought to bring the divine light in the land of the benighted pagans and thus make them civilized and Christianized. I see here these 'avataras' as the neo-missionaries hailing from the great secular temples of learning of the powerful and resourceful Western countries and possessing impressive credentials, considerable personal charm and social grace, including, above all, a remarkable gift of packaging, processing, and producing information. Yet, beneath their bonhomie and academic garb (empathy, postmodernist skepticism of positivist knowledge, etc), they are tough customers who mean business, literally as well as metaphorically. This business, alas, echoes the agenda of their simple hearted and minded forbears: to relegate a pagan faith of a distant disturbed land to exoticism and esoterism to affirm its 'otherness' and at the same time, in contrast to the earlier mission of conversion of souls, make a name and also some bucks along the way by aligning the distant 'other' with the normalized and socialized 'others' of their own culture. The 'Lila' of this academic market economy as played out in the hullabaloo surrounding *Kali's Child* thus achieves the twin objectives of discovering the human (in this case homosexual) Ramakrishna and selling him to the campus communities (where acceptance of alternative sexuality, often described as 'queer lifestyle,' have become a badge of respect) throughout the country.

Kali's Child is a product, par excellence, of a relatively new fad— post-Orientalism. The currently fashionable, freely and frivolously used methods of critical literary theory, a product of the West like its adversary Enlightenment rationality, is keen on McDonaldizing (and thus homogenizing) norms and values of the 'other' culture and world views. This agenda is parallel to the political and economic evangelization of the world in the 'mantra' of free market and democracy—a spin off from the imperialistic Christian evangelization of the 'pagan orient'. Hence the penchant for the pathological on the part of the author of *Kali's Child*.[187]

Chapter 10

It's All About Power

The fetishization and relentless celebration of 'difference' and 'otherness' . . . 'the spectacularization of anthropology' . . . cannot easily be distinguished from the process of empire.

—Edward Said[188]

Kripal defended his creative bending of the meaning of Bengali texts by quoting from Gadamer's theories of interpretation. Gadamer's 'fusion of horizons' is a method by which today's scholar can reinterpret classical texts in ways that were not part of the original author's intent and meanings. Such new interpretations are deemed legitimate by this theory. They expand the orthodox meanings with new possibilities. The theory says that the *contemporary horizon* (i.e. Kripal's attitude) fuses with the *past horizon* (i.e. the tradition's view) and *produces a third text* that 'goes beyond its author' and leads to new meanings. This is how Kripal justifies his application of parochial and Eurocentric lenses, to create new meanings.[189]

Malhotra seizes Kripal's method of analysis and wishes to apply it in the pursuit of constructive and progressive Hindu theology:

> Agreeing with his principle, let us ask why, then, are Hindu scholars denigrated when they apply 'probes or techniques of analysis', such as the use of astronomical data in classical Indian texts, to bring about 'fusions of horizons' and 'radically new visions' pertaining to Indic traditions?[190] Are these fresh conclusions 'a bit shocking to someone locked into only one horizon of meaning'—namely, are RISA cohorts boxed-in mentally? Why don't they critically examine these new claims, instead of rushing to condemn such scholarship

as neo-fascist, fundamentalist, Hindu Nationalist and other assorted abuses,[191] without any basis? Or is it that Gadamer's theory of new hermeneutics works only in the direction chosen by the dominant culture, imposing itself to overrule the interpretation indigenous to the colonized culture? [Emphasis added]

[...]

Taking this point further, why are Hindus' own new religious reinterpretations not given credence and *why are such interpretations dismissed as being inauthentic*—often by this very cult of scholars? Do non-white people have the same rights of re-reinterpretation, *without* supervision by the dominant culture, and *not* as mere proxies? Furthermore, why am I attacked when I use a method to deconstruct certain RISA members, when they use the very same methods themselves? Could it be that my conclusions are a bit shocking to someone locked into only one horizon of meaning?

Thus, these asymmetries of power can also lead to Western cultural hegemony rather than greater diversity. Ultimately, who, and on what basis, should determine which interpretations are valid and which are not?

It cannot simply be a matter of prior usage or acceptance by the power structure, for that would perpetuate hegemony and go against the very innovation that Kripal espouses. In practice, how does one avoid *adhikara* (authority) being usurped by a dominant coterie based mainly on power? RISA scholars have evaded debating these methods openly, with their critics. [...]"[192]

Multiple Competing Worldviews

In defending himself in *Evam*, Kripal noted:

I do not honestly believe that the many important differences that have become apparent through this controversy can be fully resolved here or in any other format, as many of us are clearly operating out of radically different worldviews, moral values, and understandings of human sexuality and language.[193]

Kripal here displays a culturally myopic perspective. His principle, stated above, accepts that different views will not get fully reconciled. The problem then is that only a very tiny percentage of the core information and perspectives about Hinduism gets presented in classrooms. Given the *limited time available in classrooms*, it is impossible to explain Hinduism completely. Hence, critical choices are made about the academic lenses through which Hinduism is presented. Malhotra raises a serious question:

> Which of the divergent views available in the marketplace of ideas ends up dominating in the classrooms? This is where the power of the dominant culture—in controlling the distribution of scholarship, media, and classroom teaching—has resulted in Hinduism being reduced to the lower level in the spectrum of meanings.

As an example of resolving this asymmetric power over distribution, Kripal was given the opportunity to respond to Swami Tyagananda in *Evam*, a new journal funded by Malhotra's Infinity Foundation.[194] Kripal concludes his response in *Evam* with: *"Thank you again for giving me a voice"*.[195] However, the diaspora did not receive equivalent access to give their views using the channels of knowledge that are controlled by the academy. Indeed, as *RISA Lila-1* noted, Kripal was not at all open to the idea of giving the Ramakrishna Mission *any* voice in presenting its perspective on his scholarship in the various forums where he had control or influence.

> [Kripal] categorically refused to allow Swami Tyagananda's rejoinder to get published on par with his own work, which would have enabled Tyagananda's work to also get catalogued, indexed and distributed to the same extent as his own. This attitude is driven by 3rd chakra power obsession and is also found in many Christian positions that 'tolerate' other religions, but cannot 'respect' them, because the latter would be tantamount to legitimizing them. This archetype of Abrahamic exclusivism seems to be driving Kripal's decision not to let Tyagananda's views become available on par with his own, while at the same time, Kripal proclaims innovation, openness, and liberalism.

This well-funded, politically acceptable and culturally myopic, syndicated scholarship and its distribution networks, legitimizes and privileges what Gadamer calls *certain* probes or techniques of analysis. It results in skewed and lopsided fusions of horizons. This is not a level playing field of ideas, but one shaped by Eurocentric ethnic and cultural privilege, as well as control of key institutions

> The choice of 'radically new visions' are, therefore, shaped by AAR Awards and other honors, prestigious appointments, and patronage from Wendy's Children and other cartel members. While the production of scholarship is open to all, distribution is what

determines who has influence in shaping the norms. The Khyber Pass of the distribution of Hinduism scholarship in academics consists of journals, university presses, appointment committees, curricula development, and conferences. This is carefully controlled by *sepoys*[196] and *chowkidars*[197] who *work for a small handful of well-entrenched scholar titans.*[198]

Because of this hegemonic control over distribution channels, Doniger's books are amongst the most widely prescribed in the college curricula on Hinduism. She is also the editor of an influential encyclopedia of world religions. And she authored Microsoft's Encarta Encyclopedia, which after being on the market for several years, was analyzed by Sankrant Sanu and shown to be so full of bias and stereotypes, that it was withdrawn by Microsoft.[199]

Too many scholars appear stuck in fixed ideological and cultural camps burdened by intellectual toolboxes that are heavily Eurocentric and devoid of diverse possibilities. The tools they use to analyze Hinduism and Hindus are rigid and monochrome, though wrapped in meta-theoretical, self-reflective rhetoric, sprinkled liberally with lyrical intellectual argot. But, this limited toolbox, no matter how sophisticated it might sound, is untenable and untrustworthy for those who do not believe in finalities of the dominant culture's dogmas.[200]

The Colonizer's Mentality

RISA scholars condemn their Indian-American interrogators using no-holds-barred hyperbolic terms to label and silence them.

They are accustomed to dealing only with certain categories of Indians, and when they meet Indians outside of these boxes, their attempts to apply their standard tools of domination fail, leading them to great frustration. Malhotra notes:

1. Many Western scholars of Indian religions are adept at manipulating and dealing with poor villagers in India, whom they term 'native informants', and from whom they extract research data using their own precontrived filters. This has often been done with the collusion of Indian scholars, NGOs and intermediaries. The native informants feel obliged to dish out what is expected of them by the foreign scholar, who has a lot of grant money to spread around in the data gathering process.

2. In more recent times, these scholars have also had to deal with a second category of Indians—the semi-informed and naïve diaspora youth, called 'heritage students'. Some scholars have been able to adjust their teachings to not seem blatantly anti-Hindu. Given the power and knowledge imbalance, they often adopt deceptively friendly demeanors and portrayals and succeed in fooling the youth into imagining that these scholars genuinely respect their traditions. They convince them that what they teach must be authentic. Duplicity and ambiguity are used as strategic tools by some, because it is widely believed that Hindus are non-confrontational by nature.[201]

The historian, John Keay, describes this classic tool of British colonial entrapment:

> Other foes made their intentions clear by denunciations of one's family or religion, and by ravaging the countryside and plundering the towns. The British, generally so restrained in their language and so disciplined in the field, were very different. **They could make hostility look like friendship and conquest like a favor.** It was difficult to rally support against such tactics.[202] [Emphasis added]

Antonio de Nicolas analyzes RISA's obsessive claims of superior rationality for European people:[203]

> Nothing of what RISA scholars claim of yoga or 'Hindu Religion' has much to do with Indic texts and the practice of religion in India. Notice also, that you are dealing mostly with the University of Chicago. My personal experience with them in philosophy is as bad as yours in religion. [According to these scholars,] Indic texts have no rationality; they are mythical and therefore not historical and therefore false or irrational. Have you asked yourself why? My conclusions come from the way they handled history in ancient times when those same scholars were called Akkhedians, stole writing from the Phoenicians and rewrote history for everyone else so that their dates would make them be the first to hold knowledge, the One (conceptual) God, and mostly revelation, the prophetic voice. Of course we know all this is wrong, but their attitude has not changed. I was told that it was impossible for a Hindu mythic text to be philosophical for it was not historical and therefore irrational. My answer is that to proclaim one single rationality as RATIONAL is sheer irrationality and conceptual imperialism.

Gayatri Chakravorty-Spivak has previously explained this very point about Western historians denying Indians their agency:[204]

> It is almost as if we don't exist. That is to say, colonials, even upper-class colonials, do not exist as agents. It is not as though these historians don't know a lot of people like that when they go for their fieldwork and so on. But when it comes to the work they present we never hear of people . . . you never see anything that puts them on the same level of human agency.

Dilip Chakrabarti observes how the West has bred and bought off a whole generation of elitist Indians, and how this axis operates today:

> After Independence . . . [Indians]—especially those from the "established" families—were no longer apprehensive of choosing History as an academic career. . . To join the mainstream, the historians could do a number of things: expound the ruling political philosophy of the day, develop the art of sycophancy to near-perfection or develop contacts with the elite in bureaucracy, army, politics and business. If one had already belonged to this elite by virtue of birth, so much the better. For the truly successful in this endeavor, the rewards were many, one of them being the easy availability of 'foreign' scholarships/fellowships, grants, etc. not merely for themselves but also for their protégés and the progeny. On the other hand, with the emergence of some specialist centers in the field of South Asian social sciences in the 'foreign' universities, there was no lack of people with different kinds of academic and not-so-academic interest in South Asian history in those places too, and the more clever and successful of them soon developed a tacit patron-client relationship with their Indian counterparts, at least in the major Indian universities and other centers of learning. In some cases, 'institutes' or 'cultural centers' of foreign agencies were set up in Indian metropolises themselves, drawing a large crowd of Indians in search of short-term grants or fellowships, invitations to conferences, or even plain free drinks.[205]

Under the subtitle *We are Not Native Informants Any More!* Malhotra explains how the power structure is shifting:

> The specific kind of Indian that certain RISA scholars are most *uncomfortable* with, is the Indian who is already successful in a Western organization, and especially one who has managed over a large number of Westerners for an extensive period of time. Such a person is not likely to idolize them, or be easily taken for a ride. Any Indian who has succeeded in dealing with Westerners on their

own turf must have enough insight into the Western mind, its strengths and weaknesses, and must be self-confident. Scholars can neither exploit such a person as a 'native informant,' nor patronize him in the same manner as a young NRI[206] student looking for a good grade. For one thing, any such Indian is bound to challenge them, rather than accept their scholarship at face value, and is likely to be skilled at debate and negotiation.

An additional dimension stems from over-specialization, and the systematic exclusion from the peer-review process of experts such as traditional Indian pandits and other indigenous subject matter or language scholars. Within the Western academy, the more specialized a scholar is the less oversight and due diligence is possible, because there are fewer and fewer others who are able to challenge within that ultra-specialized field. This breeds the cults of micro-specialties.

When assertive and knowledgeable Indians show up, the tables are suddenly turned. Malhotra describes three factors that work to preserve this power structure:

1. *Western scholars like to prey upon uneducated Indians:* The Western scholar of the humanities is sometimes unable to deal with the reality that she or he is lower on the West's scale of rational training as compared to successful Indians who are well-educated in science, engineering, medicine, finance, management, entrepreneurship or other areas where analytical skills are critical. This business of depicting the Indian traditions as somehow irrational or backward is unsustainable in front of modern Indians ... It is ironic that some scholars hide behind their 'dense writings' with great pride. Frankly, far too many writings from Religious Studies are poorly structured, loosely argued, and sometimes outright illogical. They have no grounds for their arrogance about intellectual rigor.

2. *The RISA Establishment has neutralized the most threatening Indian dissenters:* Eurocentric scholars are accustomed to exerting power over Indians when they are in PhD programs, when they are seeking jobs in the academy, seeking to be included in conferences or publishing projects, and seeking favorable recommendations for tenure. Many Indians thus get reprogrammed as sepoys. However, when facing a successful Indian who neither wants nor needs their favors, many Eurocentric scholars feel powerless and threatened.

3. *Empowered executive/entrepreneurial Indians are ignorant of this:* Most Indians who have purely by chance encountered the kind of scholarship described in this chapter, and who are successful and assertive professionals independent of the academy, are inadequately informed and unable to deal with the scholars. This is why, from 1995 through 2000, I had to first prepare myself by devoting almost all of my time to reading extensively in a wide variety of humanities subjects. Most scholars are too busy with administrative and other routines, and their own particular line of research, to do this. This academic isolation makes any knowledgeable challenger especially threatening to their sense of superiority.[207]

Many of these scholars of Indian Studies would love to silence the 'threatening' voices that call out their shortcomings. This reminds one of some corporate men who find it hard to respect a female boss. Revisiting the overblown anger of Gerald Larson and his colleagues regarding the alleged 'hijacking' of Hinduism Studies by Hindus, Malhotra observes:

Any attempt by Hindus to claim agency, or to take charge of their *own* affairs—be it looking after their own people without Western guidance, or be it doing scholarship to interpret and reinterpret their dharmas as they choose—is seen as an attack on the Eurocentric person's domination of the world. This includes the Eurocentric person's right to license those neocolonized persons he chooses to appoint under terms and conditions and under supervision ultimately controlled by Eurocentric people.[208] One has to psychoanalyze the strange behavior of many neo-colonialized Indian scholars in this light.

The article '*RISA Lila-1: Wendy's Child Syndrome*' generated a tremendous response. Hundreds of comments were posted on Sulekha and the essay was discussed on numerous scholarly forums, including RISA. The Internet is diminishing the differential between the people on the plains (the Hindu laity) and the elite scholars of Hinduism Studies who inhabit the heights of the highly touted Ivory Towers. Naturally, as with all controversial topics, the responses varied. Importantly, since 2002, the contributions and feedback have continued to flow. The doors of perception are ajar. A paradigm shift is upon us.

II

STORMING THE FORTRESS

♦

I for one have often applauded the dedication of Western scholars who elucidate and expound the intricacies of Indic civilization, their compilation of dictionaries and translations of classics, slanted or distorted as they sometimes might be. But when serious academics publish books that are blatantly insulting to the sensibilities of a billion people, and are also frequently distorted, and write in utter ignorance of how the practitioners currently feel about their deeply religious symbols, then somebody should say, 'Stop this nonsense!' I think that is what Mr. Malhotra has done, and in doing so, he is giving voice to millions of his co-religionists.

If professional Indologists are indifferent to or contemptuous of what Mr. Malhotra has unleashed, I fear the situation could get even worse for the whole world of Indological scholarship. Indeed, if we don't wish this episode to degencrate into an uglier *Kulturkrieg* of even greater proportions, then Indologists would do well to say openly that sometimes they have indeed been insensitive, and that in the future they would be more respectful of the culture about which they write.

—Prof. V.V. Raman, on the Indology list[1]

Chapter 11

The Floodgates of Criticism are Opened

Every inbred organization defends its integrity by citing its so-called 'independent' reviews. But the standard definition of 'independent', as used in business and law, would fail to qualify RISA scholars as being truly independent. Criticism that is controlled and licensed by those who are to be criticized is not entirely legitimate. The denial of agency to Indians who are outside the academy's controls and supervision continues to provide cover to hide questionable practices. Truly independent critics such as those featured in this section become targets of the establishment's wrath. When all other arguments fail to silence these critics, they are attacked personally as being 'anti-social' elements—as we shall see later in section III. This is an entirely arbitrary judgment, without any independent critical analysis or direct representation by those being so condemned.

There are also social/ethical implications of degrading the dignity of American minorities by shaming them for their culture. Rights of individual scholars must be balanced against rights of the cultures and communities they portray, especially minorities that often face intimidation. Scholars should *criticize* but not *define* another's religion.

The article, *RISA Lila-1,* generated an avalanche of critiques of RISA by non-mainstream scholars. This in turn triggered a backlash from several RISA-associated academicians. Their collective brouhaha and resulting paranoia and protectionism exemplify an outdated Orientalist model. While emulating Edward Said by paying lip service to post-Orientalism, hypocritically, many of these scholars refused to allow agency to the living, breathing *other,* who is today also their American neighbor. Perhaps the fight for 'agency' is on behalf of those who are absent, belonging to bygone eras or living in rural India, and unable to talk back. The participation of the living diaspora, whose culture is being represented, has often been seen as an annoyance.

When asked whether his somewhat negative tone could turn off scholars who might otherwise be receptive, Malhotra replied, "The British didn't like Gandhi's *aesthetics*, either." He felt his style had to be commensurate with what it took to get the desired impact, and that it should be compared with the scholars' own styles which are amply on display—against the critics in the Indian diaspora, against the Hindu deities, against the gurus, and so forth. (Section III gives graphic examples of the RISA scholars' verbal abuses of one another and of Indian 'others'.) Many felt that the scholars do not come with 'clean hands' as their own discourse is full of ad hominem attacks.[2]

The essays in this section offer a selection of the numerous voices of reason that chimed in once the door had been flung open.

One of the scholars moved to respond after reading *Risa Lila-1* was Prof. S.N. Balagangadhara of University of Ghent, Belgium.[3] Balu (as he is popularly called) is the author of *The Heathen in His Blindness*, an acclaimed book on the flaws in looking at Indian traditions through the prisms defined by Western scholars based on Abrahamic religions. Balu became actively engaged in arguing against the Doniger School on Sulekha, and has since then deepened his involvement through other forums. He first posted extensive comments in three parts to the Sulekha discussion thread, and these parts are excerpted and presented as chapter 12. (Later, he wrote a further article on Sulekha in which he used Kripal as interlocutor but the points he makes are of general importance to understand how the West studies India. This appears as Appendix-2.)

Chapter 13, titled, 'The Children of Colonial Psychoanalysis' is a summary of an important paper by Christiane Hartnack.[4] It shows how the colonizers used psychoanalysis as a tool to profile Indians, especially Hindus, in a manner that fit the colonial agendas. The similarities between the colonial writings and Doniger's School today are striking.

The article in chapter 14, 'Is the Fight Between Siva and Ganesha an Episode of Oedipal Conflict?' by Yuvraj Krishan, a prolific Indologist from within the tradition, is focused on showing that core Freudian assumptions simply do not apply to Ganesha and Shiva and that Western scholars have stretched the facts to fit their thesis. He references original texts of the tradition to argue his case.

Chapter 15, 'Kripal on the Couch in Calcutta' is a summary of an article by Prof. Somnath Bhattacharyya ('Kali's Child: Psychological

And Hermeneutical Problems'). It exposes the flawed application of Freudian analyses by Doniger's School. Bhattacharyya is a professor of psychology in Calcutta (emeritus) as well as a practising psychologist and well read in the original Bengali texts central to the Kripal scandal.

Sankrant Sanu, an independent scholar who was a Microsoft manager became aware of these biases by visiting Sulekha and immediately started to engage the issues on the comments threads. He discovered that Microsoft's *Encarta* encyclopedia (now the most widely used reference by schoolchildren) had its extensive Hinduism section written by Wendy Doniger. He analyzed the material written by her and wrote a critique of the numerous biases it contained. This became yet another popular Sulekha article and is reprinted as chapter 16. It triggered apologetic inquiries from Microsoft requesting help from the diaspora to rewrite the Hinduism section in order to reflect Microsoft's policy that all religions should be covered in a manner that authentically reflects the given faith community's sentiments and beliefs. In a few months, Doniger's offensive and biased writing was removed by Microsoft and replaced by a more objective one authored by Prof. Arvind Sharma, from McGill University in Montreal. Doniger has said publicly several times that the *Encarta* article was removed because her name was not 'Sharma'—implying a racial bias, rather than her work being unable to withstand Sanu's criticism or her inability to respond to its substance.

Chapter 17 is a reprint of a very detailed point-by-point evaluation of Paul Courtright's book on Ganesha by two dedicated scholars from outside the academia, Vishal Agarwal and Kalavai Venkat. It raises serious questions about the rigorousness of peer-review that occurs within the academia. It also raises very troubling questions about the quality and integrity of Courtright's scholarship, not just about Hinduphobic cultural bias—questions that have so far been ignored both by Courtright and his peers, primarily by claiming victim status for the scholar. It defies Courtright's glib claim that none of his critics have read his book and that his refusal to debate them is because they are ignorant and unqualified in the subject matter. Doniger has also condemned criticisms of Courtright, claiming these are attempts by 'extremists' to *control* the study of Hinduism. Here the reader can review the evidence and judge for herself.

A few others have been selected for inclusion in the Appendices. Dr. Alan Roland is a well-known psychologist who has specialized in clinical work with Indians living in the United States for a few decades and has authored scholarly books based on this work. He criticizes the use of Freudian psychoanalysis in interpreting Indians and Indian cultural symbols, because he is convinced that Freud's models are not valid for Indians. His essay on this issue appeared on Sulekha shortly after *Risa Lila-1*, thanks to Prof. Ramesh Rao who requested Roland to write a rebuttal to Wendy's Children. Appendix-1 is a reprint of Roland's article, titled, 'The Uses (and Misuses) Of Psychoanalysis in South Asian Studies: Mysticism and Child Development'.

Appendix-2 'India and Her Traditions: A Reply to Jeffrey Kripal' is an essay by S.N. Balagangadhara. This is based on Balagangadhara's cogent and direct rejoinder to Jeffrey Kripal. Written in response to Kripal's reply to the questions raised in *Risa Lila-1* it systematically argues *why* Kripal's work does not amount to valid knowledge about Indian culture.

The final article, titled, 'The Butterflies Baulked', is a compilation of reader responses to *RISA Lila-1* by Yvette C. Rosser. It gives a sampling of the over one thousand comments and private emails from supportive voices across cyberspace. These are a good barometer of the quality and quantity of the spontaneous mobilization and intellectual ferment caused by the essay.

Chapter 12

Balagangadhara on the Biblical Underpinnings of 'Secular' Social Sciences

Soon after *RISA Lila-1* appeared, Prof. Balagangadhara, from the Department of the Comparative Science of Cultures in Ghent University, Belgium, posted extensive comments on the Sulekha website. Thus began his prominent role as a key scholar in this debate ever since. Below are excerpts from his remarks made in three parts spread over a few days.[5]

To Rajiv Malhotra and all other seekers, by S.N. Balagangadhara[6]

Deservedly, Rajiv's article has appalled the readers: horror, indignation, anger and bewilderment at the RISA 'lila' . . . I want to raise three issues: (a) how to analyze what Rajiv portrays; (b) depending on that, what an adequate response consists of. Before we do either (this is one of the things I have discovered through my own research during the last two decades), we need to be clear about (c) how we 'should not' analyze the situation that Rajiv has sketched. Given that all three (in their general form) have been my obsessions, I have been reflecting on them deeply, seriously and systematically for some time now. I would like to share some of the results of this reflection with you . . . I will take a (rather slow) run up to tackling the third issue first. And even here, I look at RISA 'lila' as an exemplification of a more general issue or as an expression of a much broader tendency.

Perhaps, it is best to begin in an autobiographical mode. I came to (continental) Europe some 25 years ago, naively thinking that 'cultural difference' is something that 'cosmopolitan' Indians would not experience: after all, I had studied Natural Sciences in India; knew English rather well; was more familiar with the British and European history than I was with that of India (I once had plans to join the IAS by doing exams on these subjects); felt right at home with the Western philosophy ... It took me about four years of living in Europe, without relating to any Indian (or even Asian) community because I did not want to land up in an emotional and social ghetto, to realize that I was wrong: 'cultural differences' were no fictitious invention of anthropologists; it involved more than being a vegetarian or being barefoot at home when the weather was not too cold. This realization was instrumental in shaping my research project: what makes the Indian culture different from that of the West? (I never felt anything other than an Indian amongst the Europeans.) I began to research this issue with some vague hunches and intuitions as my reference points: there was no literature to guide me in my endeavor. Of course, the first fields I went into were Indology and Anthropology. Pretty soon I discovered that neither was of any use. Not only did they fail to provide me with any insights, but they also succeeded in merely enraging me: the kind of rage you feel when you read the analyses of Wendy Doniger or Kripal.

Indology is full of 'insights' like those you have read in Rajiv's article. What has varied over time is the intellectual jargon that clothes these 'analyses'. Going deeper into the history of these disciplines (with respect to India) drove home some lessons very deeply: in both form and content, there was pretty little to differentiate between the Christian missionary reports of the eighteenth to twentieth centuries and the Indological tracts. And that between a Herder and a Goethe on the one hand (the German Romantics who 'praised' India while being derogatory about it at the same time) and a James Mill and an Abbé Dubois on the other, there was not much of a space to draw a dividing line.

Researching further, I discovered that these 'Indological truths' were enshrined in the 'modern' social sciences: whether you read along with a Max Weber on 'The Religions of India' or thought along with a Karl Marx on the 'Asiatic mode of production' or even disagreed with the omnipresent 'Oriental Despotism' of a Karl Wittfogel. Modern psychoanalysis of India, beginning with Carstair's 'The Twice Born' through 'The Oceanic Feeling' of Mussaief-Masson (another Indologist using psychoanalysis to understand Indian religions), had already told our tale: Indian culture was 'narcissistic' (in the sense of 'secondary narcissism') and thus pathological in nature.

My initial reactions to these discoveries parallel the response of many a post on this e-board: horror, rage and a conviction that 'racism' is inherent in these writings. Pretty soon, this conviction about 'racism' of European authors gave way to doubts: Is it possible to convict all European authors of racism? Are we to assume that, in the last 400 years or so, all writers who wrote on India were racists? If yes, how to understand the powerful impact these writers and their theories have had on the Indian authors and Indian social sciences? If no, why did they say pretty similar things? Is one to say that the 'respected' Indian social scientists are no better than brown sahibs? Is Indian social science merely a disguised variant of Indology? So on and so forth.

Today, many of us are familiar with Edward Said and his book 'Orientalism'. In his wake, many buzzwords like 'essentialism', 'Eurocentrism' (though interesting, Blaut is not theoretically well-equipped), 'Orientalist discourse', the 'us-them dichotomy' etc. whiz around. I would be the last to detract from the merits of Said's book: he was one of the earliest writers to have drawn attention to the systematic nature of the Western way of talking about the Orient. Despite this, the concept 'Orientalism' is totally inadequate to analyze the situation underlying RISA lila. Surely, the question is: 'Why is the West Orientalist?' Said's plea ends up denying any possibility of understanding cultural differences or indeed why Orientalism came into being, or what sustains it. To say, as the 'post-colonials' do, that the relation between 'power/knowledge' answers this question is to make a mystique of the dyad of Foucault as though it 'explains' anything. If this buzzword does anything at all, it helps us 'explain' why the 'post-colonials' earn a good living in the States: they talk the talk of their employees, and walk the walk of their patrons. (This is not to deny that there are genuine and committed people among them, or even to deny that they want to address themselves to genuine and urgent issues. It is only to draw attention to the phenomenon of 'post-colonialism'.)

What I am saying is that one should not think that Rajiv paints a 'racist', or 'orientalist' or a 'eurocentric' picture. These words obfuscate the deeper issue, one which is more insidious than any of the above three. It might or might not be the case that Wendy and her children are 'racist'; ditto about their 'eurocentrism' or 'orientalism'. But when **you realize that they are not saying anything that has not been said in the last three hundred years** (despite their fancy jargon), the question becomes: **'why does the western culture systematically portray India in these terms?'**

To say that Western culture is, in toto, racist or 'eurocentric' is to say pretty little: even assuming, counterfactually, that the Western culture is all these things (and that all the Westerners are 'racist', etc), why do these attitudes persist, reproduce themselves and infect the Indians? There is a weightier reason not to tread this path. In fact, it has been a typical characteristic of Western writings on other cultures (including India) to characterize the latter using terms that are only appropriate to describe individual psychologies: X culture is stupid, degenerate, and irrational; Y culture is childish, immature, intuitive, feminine, etc. To simply repeat these mantras after them is to achieve very little understanding.

Rajiv says repeatedly that these writings 'deny agency to the Indian subjects'. I am familiar with this phrase through 'post-colonial' writings. This too is a mantra like many of them, without having the desired effect. And why is that? It might appear to make sense if we merely restrict ourselves to Wendy and her Children's analyses of Ganesha, Shiva or Ramakrishna Paramahamsa. However, it loses all plausibility when we realize that, for instance, social sciences use one and the same 'epistemology' to analyze both the West and India and that despite this, their claims about India reproduce the 'Indological truths.' (Those who do not believe me are invited to dip, for example, into those multiple theories of 'the Indian Caste System': from the sociobiological theories of a Van den Berghe—a sociologist—through the social choice theories of an Olson, jr.—an economist-cum-political scientist. Even a book that wants to criticize the writings that 'deny agency' to the Indians, 'Castes of Mind' of Nicholas Dirks, ends up doing nothing else than 'deny agency to the Indians'.) **Quite clearly, 'the problem' cannot be solved by 'discovering' some or another pet epistemology** (like Ronald Inden does, in appealing to Collingwood). In a way, you could say, we need to do to the West what it has done to us, namely, study it anthropologically. But how to go about doing this and not simply reproduce what generations of thinkers (from the West) have already said about the West?

It is amusing to use Freud to analyze their Freudian analyses of Indian religions; or use Patanjali's Chakras to typify their personalities. But at the end of the day, we are still left with the task of studying and understanding why the Western culture talks about us the way it does. In other words, it would be a 'conceptual blunder' to look either at Wendy or her Children as exponents of racism, eurocentrism or even Orientalism alone. (They might be any or all the three. But that does not really matter.) We need to realize that they are doing two things simultaneously: drawing upon the existing social sciences and also contributing to their further 'development'. I hope to explain the significance of the last sentence in one of my next mails. For the present, let me just say this: our problems do not either begin or end in religious studies or Indology. They are deeper. Much, much deeper. To tackle RISA lila as a separate phenomenon, i.e., to focus either on Wendy or her 'parampara' alone, would be to compound tragedy with conceptual blunder. Not only that. It would prevent us from understanding RISA lila for what it is: a phenomenon that is typical of the Western culture. [...]

In the [above] ... I drew attention to the fact that Wendy and her Children draw from the existing social sciences, while contributing at the same time to their further 'development'. In this post, I will elaborate what this statement means, what it implies, and what it says about the 'Western culture' ... I will only be able to isolate an important thread; within the confines of this post, I cannot 'prove' my claims. (To those interested in 'proofs', I refer them to my book.)

1. Not many would challenge the claim that Christianity has been highly influential in the development of the Western culture. We need to take this statement utterly seriously. It means that many things we 'take for granted', whether in the West or in India, come from the influence that Christianity has exerted. I claim that Christianity expands in two ways. (This is not just typical of Christianity but of all religions. I will talk only of Christianity because I want to talk about the Western culture.) Both of these have been present ever since the inception of Christianity and have mutually reinforced each other. The first is familiar to all of us: 'direct conversion.' People from other cultures and 'religions' are explicitly converted to Christianity and thus the community of Christian believers grows. This is the 'surface' or explicit expansion of Christianity. In India, both in the colonial and modern times, this has been a theme of intense controversy but, according to me, not of very great consequence 'when compared to the second way Christianity also expands'.

2. Funnily enough, the second way in which Christianity expands is also familiar to us: the process of secularization. I claim that Christianity 'secularizes' itself in the form of, as it were, 'de-de-Christianized Christianity'. What this word means is: typically Christian doctrines spread wide and deep (beyond the confines of

the community of Christian believers) in the society dressed up in 'secular' (that is, not in recognizably 'Christian') clothes. We need a very small bit of Western history here in order to understand this point better.

3. Usually, the 'enlightenment period', which is identified as 'the Age of Reason', is alleged to be the apotheosis (or the 'high point') of the process of 'secularization'. What people normally mean by 'secularization' here is the following: the enlightenment thinkers are supposed to have successfully 'fought' against the dominance that religion (i.e. Christianity) had until then exercised over social, political, and economic life. From then on, so goes the standard textbook story, human kind began to look to 'reason' instead of, say, the Church in all matters social, civic, political etc. The spirit of scientific thinking, which dominated that age, has continued to gain ascendancy. As heirs to this period, which put a definitive end to all forms of 'irrational' subservience, we are proud citizens of the modern day world. We are against all forms of despotism and we are believers in democracy; we believe in the role of reason in social life; we recognize the value of human rights; and we should understand that 'religion' is not a matter for state intervention, but a 'private' and personal affair of the individual in question. This, as I say, is the standard textbook story.

4. The problem with this story is simply this: **the enlightenment thinkers have built their formidable reputation (as opponents of 'all organized religion' or even 'religion' tout court) by 'selling' ideas from Protestant Christianity as though they were 'neutral' and 'rational'.** Take for example the claim that 'religion' is not a matter for state intervention and that it is a 'private' affair of the individual in question. (Indian 'secularists' agitatedly jump up and down to 'defend' this idea.) Who thought, do you think, that 'religion' was not a 'private' affair? The Catholic Church, of course. Even to this day, it believes that you 'should' believe what the Church says, and that because the Church mediates between Man and God, what you believe in (as a Christian) is decided by the Catholic Church. The Protestants fought a battle with the Catholics on 'theological' grounds: they argued that 'being a Christian believer' (or what the Christian believes in) is matter between the Maker (i.e. God) and the Individual. It was 'God' (i.e. the Christian God), who judged man; and men 'could not' judge each other in matters of Christian faith. The Church, they argued, could not mediate

between Man and God (according to their interpretation of the Bible); the Catholic Church argued that, using only their reasoning and interpretative abilities, men could not interpret the Word of God (i.e. the Bible). To think so is to be seduced by the Devil, and the only guarantee against the seduction by the Devil and eternal damnation was the Church itself and its interpretation of the Bible. (There is a famous doctrine of the Catholic Church, which says, 'Extra ecclesiam nulla salus': there is no salvation—i.e. being saved from the clutches of the Devil—outside the Church.) To cut the long story short, the Protestants won this theological battle. The enlightenment thinkers repeated this Protestant story, and this has become our 'secularism'.

5. **The same story applies with respect to what is enshrined in the UN charter. The doctrine of Human Rights** (as we know them today) arose in the Middle Ages, when the Franciscans and the Dominicans fought each other. (Both are religious orders within the Catholic Church.) All theories of human rights we know today were elaborated in this struggle that continued nearly for two hundred years. These were 'theological' debates, to understand which one needs to understand Christian theology. (Just take my word for it for now.) When John Locke (a British philosopher) started talking about 'Natural Rights' in the eighteenth century, he was simply regurgitating a theological debate within Christianity.

6. I am not merely making the point that these ideas had their origin in religious contexts. My point is much more than that: I claim that 'we cannot accept these theories without, at the same time, accepting Christian theology as true.' What the Western thinkers have done over the centuries (the Enlightenment period is the best known for being the 'high point' of this process) is to 'dress up' Christian theological ideas (I am blurring the distinction between the divisions within Christianity) in a secular mantle. Not just this or that isolated idea, but theological theories themselves.

7. I am not in the least suggesting that this is some kind of a 'conspiracy'. I am merely explicating what I mean when I say that **Christianity spreads also through the process of 'secularization'. What has been secularized are whole sets of ideas about Man and Society which I call 'Biblical themes'. They are Biblical themes because to accept them is to accept the truth of the Bible. Most of our so-called 'social sciences' assume the truth of these Biblical themes.**

8. I know this sounds unbelievable; but I have started to prove them. I have already shown, for example, that the so-called religious studies presuppose the truth of Christian theology. That is why, when they study the so-called 'religions' from other cultures, their results do not fundamentally differ from a theological treatment of the same religions. In the book I am now writing on ethics, I am able to show the same: the so-called secular ethics are 'secularizations' of Christian ethics. That is why, according to the modern 'secular' ethics, we are either 'immoral' or 'moral cretins'. According to Christianity, only the 'true' religion can provide a foundation for ethical behaviour: the Heathens and the Pagans, because they worship the Devil, are either immoral or intellectually weak. Even in psychology, the notion of the development of 'person' (or 'self') is a non-trivial secularization of the Christian notion of 'soul'. So I can go on, but I will not. Instead of convincing you, such a list might end up generating disbelief.

9. To begin appreciating the plausibility (if not the truth) of my claim, ask yourselves the following question: why are the so-called 'social sciences' different from the natural sciences? I mean to say, why have the social sciences not developed the way natural sciences have? There must have been many geniuses in the social sciences; the mathematical and logical sophistication in some of the social sciences is simply mind-bending; we have computers and we can simulate almost anything. Comparatively speaking, it is not as though the social sciences are starved of funding or personnel. Despite all this, the social sciences are not progressing. Why is this? (When you have, say, a problem in a love-relationship, you do not open a textbook on psychology; you look for a wise friend or an understanding uncle.) There are many answers provided in the history of philosophy and many of you may have your own 'favorite' explanation. Here is my answer: you cannot build a scientific theory based on theological assumptions. What you will get then is not a scientific theory, but an embroidering of theology. I put to you that this is what has happened. **Most of our so-called social sciences are not 'sciences' in any sense of the term: they are merely bad Christian theologies.**

10. If this is true, it also helps us understand why both 'conversion' and the notion of 'secularism' jars Indian sensibilities. Somehow or the other, Nehruvian 'secularism' always connotes a denigration of Indian traditions; if you look at the debates in the EPW and

SEMINAR and journals like that, one thing is very clear: none of the participants really understands what 'secularism' means. In India, 'secularism' is counter posed to 'communalism' whereas 'the secular', in European languages, has only one contrast—'the sacred'. Now, of course, I do not want to make much out of this; but I thought that it would be interesting to draw your attention to this interesting fact.

11. To summarize what I have said so far. Christianity spreads in two ways: through conversion and through secularization. The modern day social sciences embody the assumptions of Christian theology, albeit in a 'secularized' form. That is why when Wendy and her Children draw upon the resources of the existing social sciences, they are drawing upon Christian theology. In this Christian theology, we are worshippers of the Devil. Our gods are demons (followers of the devil). As such, amongst other things, they are perverts: sexually, morally and intellectually. The worshippers of the Devil (which is what we are) are also perverts: why otherwise would we follow the Devil or his minions? Even if Wendy and her Children oppose a straightforward Christian understanding openly (because of their genuine conviction), their conclusions are no different from the simplistic story I have just sketched. How can they be driven to embrace Christian theology, even when they either openly reject it or when they know nothing of it? This will be one of the questions I will take up in my future posts, assuming that people remain interested.

This is the insidious process I talked about: the process of secularization of Christian ideas. I have not been able to do justice to the richness of this process: an inevitable price one pays for condensing complex analyses into short posts. Let the 'simplistic' presentation not lead you to think that the ideas I am proposing are 'simplistic'. They are not.

Chapter 13

The Children of Colonial Psychoanalysis

By Yvette C. Rosser

Since Freud first formulated his theories a century ago, practitioners and enthusiasts have considered psychoanalysis to be more than merely a humane therapeutic treatment for psychiatric disorders. Freudian interpretations have been variously applied to entities as diverse as corporations, nations, and religious traditions. In a study of the use of psychoanalysis in colonial India, Christiane Hartnack[7] wrote: "Beyond healing individuals, [psychoanalysts] also hoped to provide an understanding of complex and threatening cultural phenomena that would be a first step towards the solution of social problems".[8]

Chapter 18 of this volume describes how non-Whites, or people of color, were often depicted as untamed, innocent children, whom white Americans could benevolently train to become civilized and socialized. During different phases of America's history, different peoples were identified as the savage de jour, such as Native Americans, Mexicans, Chinese, and Filipinos, including today's 'illegal aliens'. By the late nineteenth century, such blatant racism was sugarcoated with an icing of 'race sciences'. *Totem and Taboo: Resemblances Between the Mental Lives of Savages and Neurotics* applied psychoanalysis to the fields of archeology, anthropology, and the study of religion. Published by Freud in 1913, it provided yet another quasi-scientific theoretical veneer, lending credibility to such ideas as eugenics.

Freud classified cultures and societies based on developmental schema. Natives or primitives were likened to children through a twofold process. First, different cultures of the world were classified into a hierarchical model of developmental stages of historical and cultural progress. Since Europeans formulated the scale, naturally they placed themselves at the top. Secondly, these societal stages were seen as an externalization of individual, biological development. Therefore, due to their culture's position on the scale, it was scientifically justified to classify any individual belonging to a non-European culture as being inferior to Whites. This assumption was amplified if the nation or culture of the native had been colonized, because that label came with an automatic and morally convenient justification of being in need of Western tutelage.

In the context of *applied psychoanalysis*, when Abrahamic monotheism is placed at the apex of religious hierarchy or cultural potential—as it has been for millennia of Eurocentric thinking—then both dharmic thought and the polytheistic lens through which Hinduism is perceived, by many outsiders, become fertile and exotic fields for psychoanalytic searches dredging for pathologies. William Parsons explained that in European culture, Freudian psychoanalysis worked to "undermine religious tenets [of] . . . our present-day 'Christian civilization' [by using] childhood development and meta-psychological concepts like projection, repression, and the unconscious".[9]

Post-modern deconstruction theories have legitimized analyses that dislocate symbols from their sources, making them available for 'slippery' meanings that are often antithetical to the tradition and irrelevant to mutually understood referents. This 'teasing out' of alternative interpretations is the essence of the post-modern project. Given the arbitrary nature of the choices made by certain scholars, this free-for-all approach has twice empowered a new generation of social science researchers—already empowered by the privilege of being affiliated to powerful western institutions—to experiment with applied psychoanalysis in order to find new and exciting interpretive meanings 'hidden' in Hindu texts—meanings that were not only unintended by the authors, but also mutually exclusive by any authentic measure. However, these alternative strategies of interpretation play well with a Western audience.

Freud's theories have been applied to Indic themes since the early twentieth century. Hartnack explains how two British officers in the colonial army, Owen Berkeley-Hill and C.D. Daly, were inspired by reading Freud's theories in psychoanalytical journals such as *Imago* and the *International Journal of Psychoanalysis*. On this basis, they "attempted to analyze and interpret some of those elements of Indian culture, religion, sexuality and politics that they apparently found strange, puzzling, uncanny or even frightening". Hartnack adds that "psychoanalytical interpretations of Hindu religious rituals" were particularly fascinated by "the imagery of Kali".[10]

Under the subtitle, *Hindu as the White Man's Burden,* Hartnack describes the early use of psychoanalysis in the Indian context. Hartnack mentions Berkeley-Hill's 1921 essay, *The Anal-Erotic Factor in the Religion, Philosophy and Character of the Hindus,* published in the *International Journal of Psychoanalysis:*

> In this work, [Berkeley-Hill] gave a range of examples of what he considered to be a sublimation of, or reaction formations against, anal-erotic impulses among Hindus. According to him, reverence for deities such as Agni, Indra and Surya shows anal-erotic fixations, as these deities are associated with passing enormous amounts of wind. The singing chants of classic Hindu liturgies also appeared to him to be related to the same flatus complex. He further pointed to classic Vedic texts that indicate a preoccupation with control over the sphincter muscles, and discussed hatha yoga in this respect 'breath exercises are really efforts to direct flatus into a most elaborate quasi-philosophical system'.

In other words, the intention of a Hindu, while chanting mantras, is to pass wind as an expression of reverence for Agni, Indra, or Surya— the hot air presumably being indicative of the nature of Hindu devotion. In this colonial version of the use of applied psychoanalysis in the interpretation of Hinduism, breathing exercises such as *pranayama* are relegated to elaborate exercises in passing gas. The earliest use of psychoanalysis to interpret Hinduism focused almost exclusively on flatulence, in all its audible forms. Such early psychoanalytical approaches were Eurocentric, phallocentric, and profoundly naïve.

Freud viewed all human possibility through the lenses of the first (anal) and the second (procreative) chakras. In contrast, Indic thought aims to put the focus on higher chakras that represent more elevated or evolved states of consciousness.[11] Moreover, Freud encouraged the application of these anal-oriented perspectives to entire societies, not just individuals.

In *Civilization and Its Discontents,* Freud wrote about the psychoanalysis of societies classified as primitive by Eurocentric thinkers:

> The diagnosis of communal neuroses is faced with a special difficulty. In an individual neurosis we take as our starting-point the contrast that distinguishes the patient from his environment, which is assumed to be 'normal'. For a group all of whose members are affected by one and the same disorder no such background could exist; it would

have to be found elsewhere . . . But in spite of all these difficulties, we may expect that one day someone will venture to embark upon a pathology of cultural communities.

And indeed, many psychologists and non-psychologists, in particular anthropologists and Religious Studies academicians, have used Freudian analysis to offer facile and parochial explanations of the complexities of Indic civilization. Interestingly, this seems more prevalent in studies of India than in studies of other regions of the world.[12] The psychoanalytic discipline's traditional purpose is a methodology through which a trained analyst and his or her paying patient discuss the patient's problems and work together to ameliorate neuroses by analyzing dreams and childhood experiences. There is a strong, peer-enforced, ethical covenant between the two which the psychoanalyst only violates at great professional peril. However, when a psychoanalyst—trained or untrained—embarks on an ethnographic study of an entire social unit or civilization, rather than an individual, he or she is dealing with many layers of abstraction—each one of which can be manipulated at will. Instead of the analyst working with the patient to achieve optimum mental health, the ethnographer simply records data obtained through paid or unpaid native informants and interprets the alien culture based on ad hoc use of psychoanalytic theories. Such imagined data is exemplified by Kripal,[13] and carelessly woven into Courtright's work on Ganesha.[14] The native informant's role is not as an equal who should be accorded the dignity of being a partner in the search for understanding. Ultimately, the subject has no role in shaping the context, much less a right to critique the final product of the research. The very idea of such ownership is repugnant to most contemporary researchers.

As noted by Susantha Goonatilake in his book, *Anthropologizing Sri Lanka: A Eurocentric Misadventure*, ethnography is of dubious value to the mental health of the informants except in a negative, counter-productive sense that can be damaging to their self-esteem.[15] He points out that it is doubtful if any of the informants will read their own ethnographies because they are usually only published in European languages. Hence, the informers do not even get a chance to talk back. Certainly, there is no chance of giving a rejoinder. Ethnographic psychoanalysis may claim to enhance the understanding of non-Western cultures, but in actuality, it simply imposes Eurocentric constructs to describe the *Other*.[16]

Hinduism as Flatulence

Hartnack's description of early attempts to use psychoanalysis as a tool to interpret Hinduism exposes stark examples of abusive scholarship:

> Berkeley-Hill further claimed that the essence of the notion of *atman* is that in Brahmanism, the flatus complex masquerades as a metaphysical spirit. What he saw as the excessive ritualism of Brahmanism is also an indication of classical pedantic-compulsive, anal-erotic components. To prove this point, he gave detailed descriptions of repetitive elements in Brahmanic rituals, for example eighteen rules for answering the call of nature, and nine for cleaning the teeth. Berkeley-Hill also discussed the enormous units of time in Hindu myths, e.g., thousands of golden ages, millions of years within each *yuga*, and the extremely high numbers associated with deities, such as ten million royal deities. He saw in this propensity to juggle with large arithmetical quantities an expression of the moulding capacities characteristic of early anal activities.

Thus, as explained in Chapter 8, David White's reduction of Tantra to a weird sex-cult of hypocritical Hindus consuming each other's sexual fluids is based on the colonial-era psychoanalytical precedents. It is a genuine coin of the colonial regime.

Similar exoticized and pathologized fascination with Kali and other Hindu images continues to this day, as can be seen through the work of Kripal, Caldwell, Courtright, Doniger, and others. Not surprisingly, quite a few colonialists had serious cases of Kali-phobia. Hartnack wrote:

> Daly pointed out that Kali is worshipped as the all-embracing mother, but that she is also considered to be the goddess of death, destruction, fear, night and chaos, as well as the goddess of cholera and of anti- and asocial groups, such as thieves and prostitutes, the symbol of cemeteries, the destroyer of time—in short, the source of all evil. The iconographic representation from which he derived his conclusions [...] depicts Kali as dancing wildly on the corpse of her husband Shiva, with the head of a giant whom she has just killed in her hand. Everything is dripping with blood. Hacked-off limbs decorate her body. She wears a long necklace of human heads, a belt consisting of human arms with hands, and earrings in the shape of human beings. Because Kali is completely covered in such pictures with phallic symbols, Daly saw in the decoration a symbolization of the gruesome appropriation of this desired object, thus representing the penis envy of ali women. That

explained, in his opinion, the Hindu fear of this overwhelmingly powerful and castrating goddess, whose rage and temper need to be calmed with bloody sacrifices.[17]

This image of the Hindu Goddess as a bloodthirsty, phallic being is faithfully echoed to this day. In Caldwell's description, Kali is "first of all, a phallic being, the mother with a penis . . . she is the bloodied image of the castrating and menstruating (thus castrating) female . . . "[18] Of course Caldwell 'updates' the thesis by attributing newly fashionable homosexual psychopathologies to Hindus who worship the Goddess. Her stated ambition is to "show that themes of eroticism and aggression in the mythology are male transsexual fantasies reflecting intense preoedipal fixation on the mother's body and expressing conflicts over primary feminine identity".[19]

Ultimately, Daly claimed that aspects of the "uncanny and dreadful, such as menstruation and death, are represented in pictures of Kali to an overwhelming extent". Hartnack explained:

> [Daly] interpreted this as an expression of repressed infantile complexes and stated: 'The Hindu race succumbed to a regression on the basis of their abnormal reaction to the castration complex, which appears later than the menstruation complex'.

Hindus are thereby classified as a community dominated by obsessive compulsive traits. Hinduism is seen as a societal neurosis, or perhaps a collective pathology exemplified by the Goddess Kali. Among today's scholars, Doniger brings it home with her sweeping statements to the press about 'bloodthirsty' goddesses and 'inverse ratios' between worship of the Goddess and the status of women in Hindu society. She asserts that worship of the Goddess offers 'no solutions'. Huston Smith was right on when he talked of 'colonialism updated' in the context of *Kali's Child*. Describing this strategically implemented use of psychoanalysis from a particularly colonial point of view, Hartnack wrote:

> Daly pointed out that, whereas with regard to Ireland, one might understand a favorable identification with a lovely virgin, in India the identification was with the dreadful Kali, which seemed perverse to him. He therefore considered the Hindus' behaviour to be beyond even the broadest margins of normality and summarized his analysis of revolutionary tendencies with the following words: 'we have a psychology which differs considerably from the European, its equivalent with us being found only in pathological cases. They

are a race who fail in their rebellion against the father and as a result of this failure adopt a feminine role with feminine character traits. There results, so to speak, a split in the male personality, the aggressive component undergoing repression, which accounts for the childlike and feminine character traits of the Hindu as a whole, and the fact that they thrive only under very firm and kindly administration, but if allowed latitude in their rebellious tendencies are quick to take advantage of it.[20]

Handy political uses of psychology are still uppermost in the minds of many Western researchers in dealing with Indians, as can be seen from Caldwell's call to psychoanalyze Hindu culture as a whole. For Doniger, too, this overwhelming desire to discredit any political identity for Hindus—leads to her eager approval of David White's reductionist thesis on Tantra, not because she finds his evidence entirely convincing— she doesn't—but because of the immense political and civilizational value of degrading uppity Hindus and taking them down a notch or two. Both Daly and Doniger seem to share a common anxiety about putting the Hindus in their proper place, lest their rebellious tendencies threaten the world order and/or academic stability.

Hartnack explains that the dominant view in Europe at the time was a commonly held theory, derived from Enlightenment thought, that the "development of the individual is structured according to the development of mankind". She points out that Freud also adhered to this perspective. Results of this theory were racial sciences, such as eugenics in the nineteenth century, which led to institutional discrimination in America and Europe. This was taken to its insane conclusion by Hitler's one-pointed racist obsession. But it was also exemplified and codified by US immigration laws against non-Whites, specifically Asians, which remained on the books for almost a hundred years. Using this approach to categorize Indians, Daly's racism is sorely apparent, alongside his Kali-phobia. Hartnack described Daly's thought processes about Kali:

> [The] Hindu's retreat before, and subjection to, this castrating and killing super-mother [is] not only an infantile neurotic trait, but also evidence for stagnation and fixation at an early stage of human development. In summary, he argued that *Hindus became psychologically stuck in a dark age, while Europeans had proceeded to a psychologically advanced stage.* [Emphasis added][21]

Scholars whose work have recently been critiqued by the diaspora apply this 1920s' era reasoning to all Hindus, seeing them as stuck in infantilism and incapable of understanding sophisticated jargon. However, in today's politically correct world of public proclamations, scholars are careful to apply this blanket reasoning only to the despised Hindutva-Hindus or to particularly iconic figures such as Sri Ramakrishna—both seen as contributing to a dangerous Hindu revivalism.

While defending Kripal's creative interpretation of homoerotica, Caldwell suggests to her fellow RISA researchers, that they should contextualize the 'distorted masculinity' of Hindu culture, and the 'confused sexuality' of the Hindu male. She sees this mangling of the male as the catalyst that set off a highly contested, socially emasculated politicized century of dangerous nationalistic posturing.[22] Thus what starts as tentative, poorly evidenced, and speculative research is quickly elevated as a way of making sense of those dangerous Indians and their psychologically corrosive culture.

Regarding the article by Berkeley-Hill, *The Anal-Erotic Factor in the Religion, Philosophy and Character of the Hindu*,[23] Hartnack states that "Hindus did not receive [the] article enthusiastically [when] the original English version . . . was read at the Indian Psychoanalytical Society. [In] the memoir of the . . . meetings [...] the participants preferred to delay discussion until the next meeting, but that discussion seems never to have occurred." Perhaps what is most discomfiting to the Donigers, Courtrights and other latter-day Berkeley-Hills is that the Indians of today, particularly in the diaspora, are not shy or beaten down. They would rather debate these alleged 'analyses', and ask inconvenient questions, than defer them for some future debate.

Hartnack goes on to tell how Daly had bragged about having discussed a draft of this article with Freud. According to Daly, Freud found the confirmation of his psychoanalytic theory very interesting, and personally gratifying, and suggested that Daly should emphasize the theory still more. Hartnack adds sardonically, "This constructive critique by Freud hardly led to an improvement in the quality of the article." She disdainfully critiqued Daly for using pathologies to try to explain racial and cultural characteristics that were unfamiliar to him. Hartnack elaborates in terms that could be applied, *mutatis mutandis,* to the particular school of contemporary scholars under review in this book:

> Though some theory is tagged on to it, the essay remains a conglomeration of densely presented images and associations, wild

ideas, and racist attributions. Daly freely converted prevalent psychoanalytical concepts that explained psychopathological defects of individuals into explanations for all those aspects of Indian culture that appear strange to Europeans to substantiate his belief in the European culture's superiority over Hinduism.[24]

This lower chakra view of Hinduism turns the mystical experience into pathology.[25] Since the early decades of the twentieth century, there has been a steady stream of scholars who use psychoanalysis in their interpretation of Indian society in general and Hinduism in particular. This methodology imagines all the mystical and spiritual experiences of Hinduism as nonsensical, and all the gurus, deities and rituals as ridiculous, or even outright dangerous. The basic interpretive view of the Judeo-Christian experience is in total contrast to Hinduism. On the surface, Freudianism may be able to attach a few untenable meanings onto Hindu symbols, but the results are unreliable.

Phallocentric Circles

Freud seriously questioned humanity's dependence upon religion, even though he was proud to be ethnically Jewish. One thing he pathologized in religions was the belief in a supreme being. He felt that the concept of religion in the 'final form' taken by present-day Christian civilization was fatally flawed. He was highly critical of Christianity and saw it as an expression of infantilism.

Though Freud may have had revulsion to religion, the origins of psychoanalysis are deeply rooted in encounters with Biblical religious traditions. The Bible is among the primary sources where Freud extracted his symbols and myths, and from where all of his patients were situated, upon whom he based his prognoses, *Ipso facto*, the entire corpus of his knowledge or experiences of religion and spirituality were extracted from within the Judeo-Christian context.

Although much of Freud's work serves as a critique of religious feelings, psychoanalysis nevertheless employed and carried forward the core themes of the Bible. Judeo-Christian tropes dominate psychoanalytical concepts, as Freud mined Biblical literature to extract analogies for his favorite phobias. The 'primal scene'. which Freud associated with Original Sin, signifies the experience when a child sees the parents engaging in sex, which means, according to Freudian psychoanalysis, that the child will be traumatized for the rest of his or her life, or until properly psychoanalyzed.

In *Why Freud Was Wrong: Sin, Science and Psychoanalysis*, Richard Webster explains how the 'cryptic Judeo-Christian ethos' was the very foundation of what was touted to be a scientific theory. Webster notes that Freud misdiagnosed several of his early patients as traumatic hysteria when they were "actually cases of injury-related brain damage and epilepsy". He called psychoanalysis a "crypto-theological system" which encompassed "a modernized reworking of traditional Judeo-Christian morality, sexual realism, and restraint".[26]

Its very structure was church-like, in that psychoanalytic treatments in Freudian practice were modeled after the Catholic confessional. The psychoanalyst replaces the priest, who is relatively invisible to the patient just like the priest is not visible during confession. The patient confides the traumas he or she has experienced just like the Catholic confides sins. In so doing, the patient is relieved of a burden, and redeemed into good mental health just like the sinners who confess are saved from their sins.

The Primal Scream became another Freudian-based concept that took the confession model to an extreme. In the 1970s, Arthur Janov originated primal therapy in which the client is theorized as withholding a primal wound or pain. Mental health is achieved not through confession, but through blood-curdling screams releasing the primal pain. Primal Scream therapy became popular in America and patients would live in a motel room with the therapist for many days, struggling to contact their primal pain in this manner. But instead, often they fell into near psychosis. In similar fashion, several other post-Freudian therapies became discredited.[27]

For Freud, religion was simply psychology projected onto the external world. Biologically speaking, he traced religion back to the tiny child's helplessness. At the root of all Biblical religions is a longing for the Father, which inevitably involves the Oedipus complex, and all the accompanying symptoms of fear and guilt. Much to the chagrin of the Church, Freud noted similarities between religious ritual observance and the compulsive, ritualistic behavior of the obsessive-compulsive neurotic in a prominent paper he published in 1907 called *Obsessive Actions and Religious Practices*.

Freud brought phallic symbolism intimately into our lives. In *A Mind of Its Own: A Cultural History of the Penis*, David Friedman notes how psychoanalytic interpretations have enduringly placed the penis and associated anxieties at the center of society.[28] Friedman suggests that: "attitudes toward the penis have been instrumental in mapping the course of both Western civilization and world history". He notes that through the centuries, "the penis has been deified, demonized, secularized, racialized, psychoanalyzed, politicized and, finally, medicalized." This extreme cultural focus on the phallus, codified (overcoded?) by Freud, brought concepts such as 'castration anxiety' and 'penis envy' into popular discourse.

The psychoanalytic movement at the turn of the twentieth century has been compared to a religious cult. Freud, who saw himself as a messiah, obsessively promoted his theories. He had visions of grandeur, and his personality and ideas certainly achieved immortality. Freud shared with Karl Marx a belief that religion is an illusion—neither man believed in a soul or life after death.

E.M. Thornton wrote in *The Freudian Fallacy*:

> Freud's concept of the unconscious must be attributed to his cocaine usage. Death wishes, infantile incestuous desires and perversion are not the pre-occupations of the normal mind. Constantly recurring throughout the drug literature are the same words and phrases used by Freud and his followers to describe his concept of the unconscious mind. In both psychoanalysis and this literature the same metaphors of looking down into an abyss occur.[29]

Sometimes a Saint is Only a Saint

In *The Future of an Illusion*, Freud portrays religion as a fantasy that fulfills "the oldest, strongest, and most urgent wishes of mankind". In 1927, Freud sent a copy of his controversial book to his friend Romain Rolland, the renowned French Nobel laureate and humanitarian. Rolland, who was a student of Ramakrishna and Vivekananda, began a thirteen-year correspondence with Freud.

Rolland thought that Freud's book on religion was 'spirited' and that it dealt with an adolescent form of belief that prevailed among the masses. Rolland felt that true religion arose from the mystical experience of oneness with the world, which he called *La Sensation Océanique*. He said that he himself had experienced this oceanic feeling, emphasizing its presence in mystics of all religious traditions. Rolland invited Freud to analyze mysticism as the true source and nature of religious sentiments.[30] Rolland was speaking from the perspective of someone who had actually experienced the higher level chakras. Thus in Roland's assessment, unlike in Kripal's and Doniger's anally fixated Eurocentric perspectives, Sri Ramakrishna was the equal of Jesus Christ or Buddha, and his mystic experiences had tangible validity, rather than just being the misinterpreted result of homo-sexually induced panic attacks or some other jargon dense hyperbole.

Women, Infants, Hindus and the Irish

There were many similarities between the writings of these two colonial officers, who were self-educated in what could be called pop-psychoanalysis. Hartnack notes that they both had a derogatory style and an exclusive focus on negative content. Both consistently failed to note any achievement or positive aspect of Indian culture. Hartnack elaborates:

> Instead, they compared the behaviour of Indians with other dependent people, with women, infants and the Irish, and time and again with European neurotics. They tried to explain group behaviour by attributing it to psychopathological defects of individuals, a procedure quite common in the international psychoanalytical discussion of their time.[31]

Hartnack notes that this work had clear colonial overtones. Several contemporary works use parallel approaches to Indian Studies.

> Both [Daly and Berkeley-Hill] identified themselves fully with British colonialism. Indians were a threat and had thus to be fought, and resistance had to be smashed not only on a military but also on a cultural level. Unlike Orwell, who left Burma in order not to cope with the dual identity of a colonial bureaucrat by day and a questioning and critical human being by night, Daly and Berkeley-Hill worked to abolish these scruples and contribute to a properly functioning colonial world.[32]

One critic in the Hindu diaspora in the USA, when reading an earlier draft of this chapter, asked "Is Doniger's anxious eagerness in accepting Kripal's and White's astounding theses a symptom of the same colonial mindset?" Hartnack continued:

> Contemporary psychoanalytical thought offered Daly and Berkeley-Hill models to legitimize their degradation of, and thus their separation from Indians: If one were not a healthy adult British male, one was in trouble, for all other human beings were looked down upon. There were gradations in this contempt. British women, Anglo-Indians, Irish, Muslims, children, and sick and old people could still be accepted to some extent, as there were some common

denominators between them and the British ideal. But women who did not obey Victorian mores, mentally disturbed British subjects, Hindus and people of color were not only perceived as entirely different and thus inferior, but also considered to be dangerous. They were in the majority and there was the potential of hysteria, violence, revolution, sexual seduction and other supposedly irrational acts, which would be difficult to control. Therefore, it was the white man's responsibility to keep them under surveillance, if not behind iron gates. In this context, psychoanalytical investigations offered structures of explanation, the first step toward a mastery of the perceived threat.[33]

Contemporary professional psychologists, such as Alan Roland and Salman Akhtar,[34] distance themselves from and disapprove of this reductionist, infantilizing approach. Some of the caveats and foibles in what has been called the Wendy's Children genre of scholarship are also found in Freud's work. The psychoanalytic movement at the turn of the century has been compared to that of a religious cult, disdainful of its critics and hyper-attached to a particular hyperbole. Many similarities are in evidence.

In *The Memory Wars: Freud's Legacy in Dispute*, Frederick Crews, professor emeritus at the University of California at Berkeley, describes the coercion of clients by Freud to fulfill the mission of his institute.[35] As a result of this, and other examinations of Freud's methodologies, his data gathering has been shown to have been less than authentic— a charge similar to what has been leveled against some members of the RISA school of thought.

Ninety years ago, the innovative thinkers who challenged Freudianism, such as Wilhelm Reich and Carl Jung, among others, were ex-communicated from the psychoanalytical society.[36] Similarly, in RISA and other associated venues, not much dissent is allowed. In the case of Jung and Freud, there was an on-going disagreement about the concepts of the new orthodoxy that played out very much like an Oedipal relationship. It is striking how similar the approaches are today. Thus Doniger has launched attacks against Jungians like Joseph Campbell because their interpretations of Hindu myth differ from her own.[37]

Freud's work has been criticized by many people through the years. Freud did not take well to criticism. In his critique of psychoanalysis, Frederick Crews uses similar words used by Indian-Americans in these pages, calling Freudian theory hegemonic: "A doctrine plagued by mechanism, reification, and arbitrary universalism."

Today a number of scholars rely on applied psychoanalysis to create new and ever more exciting research, even though they are not competent in psychoanalysis. This methodology has found its way into History, Sociology, Anthropology, and Religious Studies, among other disciplines. As can be witnessed throughout the present book, many of today's South Asian specialists—including historians, anthropologists, and scholars of Humanities and Religious Studies—often employ similar theories that reach parallel conclusions, describing modern Indian-Americans as Daly and Berkeley-Hill describe colonized Indians almost a century ago.

Hindu-Americans who question scholarship written about their religion are perceived as invalid, inferior. They are not considered 'legitimate intellectuals'. Those who write articles on websites such as Sulekha are spoken of as 'dangerous', perhaps capable of irrational acts and as Berkeley-Hill also described Indians a hundred years ago, 'difficult to control'. Some scholars of Hinduism Studies are threatened by this contemporary challenge to their established paradigms. They have furiously begun to psychoanalyze the Hindu diaspora as the first step toward a mastery of the perceived threat. Simultaneously, Hindu-Americans have turned the 'surveillance' inside-out, and are gazing back with their own tools—such as the Chakra Hermeneutics described in Chapter 9—to better understand those who control the narrative about Hindu traditions.

Chapter 14

Is the Fight Between Siva and Ganesa an Episode of Oedipal Conflict?[38]

By Yuvraj Krishan[39]

The *purānic* legend of the combat between Siva and Ganesa, resulting in the decapitation of Ganesa's head and its replacement by the head of an elephant, has been interpreted by Freudian scholars in terms of the Oedipus complex and the castration complex. In this legend Ganesa bars the entry of his father Siva into the chamber of his spouse, Pārvati, and this leads to a conflict between the father and the son. It is this conflict, which is deemed to represent the hostility of the son towards the father and the libidinal or sexual impulse of the son towards the mother: attraction towards the parent of the opposite sex and antagonism towards the parent of the same sex.[40] Beheading is considered a regular symbol for castration,[41] both in dreams and fantasies: the elephant head (of Ganesa) "is a relic of the conflict in the ritual system between father and son and of the marriage of the son to the mother".[42]

Another episode in the mythology of Ganesa, in which he loses one of his tusks, is also interpreted as castration.[43]

Goldman[44] elaborates: "The legend of Ganesa ... is a much clearer example of a story representing the primal oedipal triangle of son, father and mother and the son's attempts to possess the mother to the exclusion of the father, an attempt that leads to violent conflict and the final symbolic castration of the son".

Goldman emphasizes that Pārvati creates the male child Ganesa from the dirt of her body to guard her privacy and to prevent anyone from entering her boudoir without her permission. According to

Goldman, "This is a clear realization of a male child's oedipal fantasy with regard to his unique right of sexual access to his mother."

Another scholar[45] has described this combat a 'father-son conflict with the father as the victorious aggressor', and categorizes this episode as 'This Indian Oedipus' or more precisely an *Indianized* version of the classic oedipal conflict.

In the classical Oedipus tale, the son attacks the father in order to secure sexual possession of the mother: the aggression is directed from son to father and libido from son to mother. In the Indian legend of Ganesa, however, the son is passive and the father (Siva) is aggressive. Hence, it is characterized as "Indian Oedipus Pattern"[46] or 'negative oedipal situation'.[47] It is emphasized that the substitution of an elephant's head on the decapitated trunk of the boy Ganesa is the "substitution of an animal's organ for symbolic or actual genitalia lost through the attack of a father figure . . . " but "the final castration and degradation of Ganesa is not an unequivocal example of a positive oedipal legend".

Loss of one tusk in the case of Ganesa is also considered as evidence of 'displaced castration'.[48] Further: "This makes Ganesa sexually ambiguous or a sexless being who can no longer commit incest with his mother . . . "[49]

Another scholar[50] suggests that the chopping off of Ganesa's head by Siva is castration by the father and the substitution of the phallic nose, the elephant head and trunk used "is a gross-visible sign of his incestuous fixation . . . Ganesa icons with the trunk and single tusk are generally recognized as phallic."[51]

The interpretation of the Siva–Ganesa conflict as an oedipal situation is based on a misunderstanding of the oedipal complex.

At the outset, it is essential to know the significant differences in the legends of Ganesa and Oedipus.

In the legend of Ganesa's conflict with Siva, the father (Siva) is not killed as in the legend of Oedipus; on the other hand, it is the son (Ganesa) who is beheaded, killed, and later revived with an animal's head. It is the father who eliminated the son. Thus, there is a reversal of the direction of aggression or desire, from that in the Oedipus legend, from son to father.

As regards to the loss of one tusk, Ganesa loses his tusk in a combat not with his father Siva but with Parasurāma or Balarāma. In some of the *paurānic* legends, Ganesa is born *ab-initio* with an elephant form but with only one tusk. This will be dealt with in greater detail while discussing the *paurānic* legends.

We shall first deal with the question whether the concept of oedipal conflict is a valid psychological truth and whether it can be applied to the Siva–Ganesa conflict.

While Freud believed that the oedipal situation is universal, "Most anthropologists now question its universality, since there are many cultures in which it does not appear." In fact Horney claims that, "it was neither normal nor universal" and that it is "symptomatic of a neurotic behaviour on the part of the parents."[52] Experimental studies have also discovered that in parental preferences during the oedipal age, "No consistent trends were found that would indicate that the child felt relatively more positive towards the opposite sex than towards the same sex parent".[53] And that "The more masculine boys were found to have had a warm rather nurturant relationship with their father. This pattern does not fit Freud's concept that male identification is basically energised by a threatening stance on the father's part".[54]

In fact, some eminent psychologists have disputed the validity of the Oedipus complex as adumbrated by Freud. Erich Fromm[55] in an analysis of Freud's concept of the Oedipus complex has explained that the attachment of a man to his mother is not sexual in its nature, that it is a longing for a situation in which the child is protected and has no responsibility to bear—it is a paradisiacal existence for the child under the mother's protective custody. He emphasizes that sexuality is fickle and is not characterized by great stability. According to Fromm, Freud's assumption that the child-mother relationship is sexual was his 'great error' and is 'nothing short of absurd'. He further explains the hostile relationship between the father and son as a feature only of a patriarchal society. He goes on to point out that Sophocles had expressed his philosophy or ideas in a trilogy—*Oedipus Rex, Oedipus at Colonus*, and *Antigone* which together gives the whole Oedipus myth. Fromm points out: "If we look at the trilogy as a whole we discover that Sophocles is speaking of the conflict between the patriarchal and the earlier matriarchal world". In other words, Freud built his concept of Oedipus complex on a fragmentary study of Sophocles limited to *Oedipus Rex*.

Again some Indian psychologists[56] have doubted the relevance of the oedipal conflict in Indian social ethics. As regards the suggestion that the Siva-Ganesa conflict represents more precisely negative oedipal complex because of its variations from the classical concept, positive oedipal complex, it is pointed out that according to modern psychology,[57] in negative oedipal complex, or the Reversed Oedipus complex also known as the Inverted Oedipus complex, the son desires the father and regards the mother as a rival; it is not aware of a new category of libidinal situation in which there is a reversal of the flow of aggression: the father suppresses or eliminates the son and the mother desiring the son.

Further, the Oedipus complex is not a bilateral phenomenon; it is unilateral—the sexual instinct of son or daughter towards the parent of the opposite sex. It is only a stage in the development of infantile sexuality and not a feature of adult sexuality. It sets in at the phallic stage of psycho-sexual development of a child between the ages of three and six so that parents do not suffer from the complex.

Again the substitution of the elephant's head over the decapitated trunk in the case of Ganesa is not the substitution, symbolic or actual, of the genitalia lost through the attack of a father figure—Ganesa's genitals were not involved in the conflict with Siva. To identify the elephant's trunk as a genital, as a phallic nose,[58] a displaced phallus is erroneous. Elephant's trunk is his proboscis, a sensory organ of the oral region, the nose and not the organ of reproduction.

An analysis of the *pauranic* legends as to how Ganesa comes to acquire an elephant's head shows that the oedipal conflict explanation is based on tenuous evidence.

In the *Brahmanda Purana* (2.3.42.33) Vinayaka's head is decapitated accidentally—how and when is not stated. Thereafter it was replaced by an elephant's head.

The *Lalitamahatmya*, an apocryphal portion of the *Brahmanda*, states that Ganesa was born with an elephant's head. In other words, it was a congenital deformity.

In the *Brahmavaivarta Purana* (3.12), *Siva Purana* (2.4.13.5) and the *Brhaddharma Purana* (60.39–42) Ganesa, as a baby, loses his head due to the unfavorable gaze of planet Sani or Saturn. To revive the boy, an elephant's head was severed and grafted on the trunk of the baby Ganesa. This was done at the insistence of Parvati for replacement—*Brahmavaivarta* (3.20) and *Brhaddharma* (60.39–42).

Another version of this legend is contained in the *Siva Purana* 2.4.16.34, *Skanda Purana* 3(2) 12.10–23 and the *Mahabhagavata Purana* 35. It is according to these versions that Ganesa lost his human head in a conflict with Siva, when he (Ganesa) barred him (Siva) from entering the apartments of Siva's spouse, Parvati.

The *Skanda Purāna* (7.3.37), however, contains another contradictory explanatipn: Pārvati had made the figure of Ganesa from a paste but it was without a head due to the inadequacy of the paste. Hence, an elephant's head was used to complete the head limb.

Further, in the majority of the legends in the *Skanda Purāna* (1.2.27.4–5, 6. 214.3–10, 6.214.47–50 and 7.1.37.29–30), Pārvati created an elephant-faced figure from her bodily impurities and infused it with life. In other words, Ganesa was elephant-headed *ab initio* and there was no combat with Siva.[59]

According to the *Ganesa Purāna* (2.69.42), Vināyaka assumed the form of an elephant-headed being in the Krtayuga (first time cycle) to kill the demon Devāntaka. Likewise, the *Ganesa Purāna* (2.130.30–31) states that in the *dvāpara* (the third time cycle) Ganesa was born with an elephant's head.

According to the *Varāha Purāna* (20.11.18) Ganesa loses his human head when, out of jealousy for having captivated the mind of Pārvati (Siva's spouse), Siva cursed his son to ugliness with an elephant's head.

It would be evident that there is no unanimity among the *purānas* as to how Ganesa came to acquire an elephant's head.

Only in the three *purānas*, *Siva*, *Skanda*, and *Mahābhāgavata* is there a combat between Ganesa and his father Siva in which Ganesa is beheaded and given an elephant's head in replacement.

The *Varāha Purāna* may be considered to corroborate indirectly the decapitation and replacement legend. Again the *Skanda Purāna* also carries totally different legends regarding the elephantine head of Ganesa and have nothing to do with Ganesa's combat with Siva and the ensuing decapitation. Furthermore, some *paurānic* legends maintain that Ganesa was born with an elephant's head; as such it was not severed and then grafted.

There is thus overwhelming evidence that the legend of combat between Siva and Ganesa leading to the decapitation of the latter's head and its replacement by an elephant's head is not a representative *paurānic* legend.

Consequently, the explanation of the combat in terms of the oedipal conflict is of severely limited value. More importantly, as has been explained earlier, the Siva–Ganesa combat is radically different from the classic oedipal conflict and it is nothing but semantic jugglery to characterize it as an Indian Oedipus conflict.

The Freudian oedipal situation is said to be enacted in the loss of one of the tusks of Ganesa described as 'displaced castration' by modern psychologists. But the *pauranic* legends regarding the loss of one tusk do not support the proposition that the loss was due to an oedipal conflict. Firstly, in the legends, Ganesa does not lose his tusk in a combat with Siva. Secondly, the tusk is lost in an entirely different cycle of legends—the combat between Parasurama and Ganesa when the former tried to enter Siva's (and not Ganesa's mother's) apartment and Ganesa barred his entry (*Brahmavaivarta Purana* 3.43), or in the combat between Ganesa and Balarama (*Padma Purana, Uttarakhanda* 277.25.35), or in the combat between Mahotkata and Ganesa in *Krtayuga* (first time cycle) and the demon Devantaka when the latter tried to pull out the tusks of Mahotkata after he had assumed the form of an elephant-headed being (*Ganesa Purana* 2.70.2). Thus this legend of a combat in which Ganesa loses one of his tusks occurs only in the three *puranas* cited above. In the version in the *Skanda Purana* (1.1.10.37), Ganesa pulls out one of his tusks himself. According to the *Siva Purana* (2.4.17.49) and the *Brhaddharma Purana* 2.60, Ganesa, after decapitation, had his head replaced by an elephant's head. Thus none of the legends ascribe the loss of the tusk to an oedipal conflict between the father (Siva) and the son (Ganesa).

Chapter 15

Kripal on the Couch in Calcutta

By Yvette C. Rosser

As was customary throughout antiquity, primitive people today make free use of phallic symbols, yet it never occurs to them to confuse the phallus, as a ritualistic symbol with the penis. They always take the phallus to mean the creative mana, the power of healing and fertility, 'that which is unusually potent'.

– Carl Jung[60]

This chapter examines an essay written by Prof. Somnath Bhattacharyya called 'Kali's Child: Psychological And Hermeneutical Problems',[61] Bhattacharyya is emeritus professor and former head of the Psychology Department at Calcutta University.[62] He has also been a practising psychoanalyst in Calcutta for over 30 years. He is uniquely qualified to present a substantial critical analysis of Jeffrey Kripal's book, *Kali's Child*, on at least four grounds: He is (i) personally familiar with the primary sources cited in the text, (ii) a long time student of Indian religion and philosophy, (iii) a professional psychotherapist, and (iv) fluent in Bengali.

While examining *Kali's Child* from this vantage, Bhattacharyya was "struck by the numerous irregular and insinuating translations, factual misrepresentations and speculative innuendo". After reading *Vishnu on Freud's Desk*[63] and *Kali's Child*,[64] he was asked to write a rejoinder that was published in the subsequent issue of the *Harvard Divinity School Bulletin*.

In the 12,000-word article that appeared on Sulekha, Bhattacharyya hones in on succinct examples of what he calls Kripal's 'catachrestic' use

of words and phrases selectively chosen to substantiate his overriding
obsession with Ramakrishna's hypothetical homosexuality. His detailed
critique closely examines and contests several of Kripal's translations.
"The curious twists of translation, the typos, the 'honest mistakes' and
unconscious errors that litter the text of *Kali's Child* would literally
force Freud to sit up in his grave and take notice".[65]

Bhattacharyya cites two examples that 'clearly don't require a
gloss'. First, in one of Ramakrishna's parables, a housewife tries to
dissuade her husband from taking to the life of an itinerant begging
monk saying: "Why should you wander about? If you don't have to
knock at ten doors for your stomach's sake, go", Kripal translates the
passage as: "Why sleep in seven beds when you can sleep in one"?

Another example is from a line in 'A song to the Divine Mother':
"Mother hold me to your bosom, covering me with the *aanchal* of your
love". Here is Kripal's translation: "Hold me to your breasts. With
affectionate love, hide me under your skirt, O Ma"! Bhattacharyya
adds parenthetically: "The Western reader may note that *aanchal* refers
to the end of the Indian sari covering the head, shoulders, and upper
trunk". He points out that Kripal's hermeneutical style perpetuates,
"the very patterns of textual misrepresentation and misinterpretation
that he wishes to refute".

Bhattacharyya interrogates the methodologies and motivations
guiding Kripal's radical reinterpretations of the life of Ramakrishna,
providing examples of violations of scholarly discretion that have
resulted in simplistic, culturally disconnected definitions and overly
interpretive, free-association translations—fiction, if you will, but not
history or ethnography. His article brings to the fore two essential
components of the debate:

First, he identifies several psychoanalytical pathologies at work
within the methods Kripal uses to defend himself. For instance, he notes
that Kripal continues to brand Ramakrishna a pedophile even as he
denies ever having consciously done so.

> Kripal explicitly writes about Ramakrishna's 'obvious pedophilia'
> and then, when things get hot [he] becomes amnesic. How does one
> explain that? Clearly deeper and more complex unconscious
> psychological forces are at work here, and any attempt to identify
> them in this short paper would be too inadequate to be regarded
> as meaningful.

Second, he demonstrates how Kripal's understanding of a mystic
such as Ramakrishna is not only a mishmash of psychoanalytic apples

and oranges, but how Ramakrishna's messages and symbols are exponentially more evolved—light years beyond Kripal's cluttered Freudian slips and lower chakra titillations. The two realms hardly intersect. The directions of the gazes are fundamentally and irrevocably opposed. This renders Kripal's obsessive and exclusive focus on Ramakrishna from the lower chakras irrelevant. It would be amusing if it hadn't sadly caused so much sorrow and defamation.

Sometimes scholarly stories and images are created through speculative and uninhibited uses of literary devices such as metonymy and synaesthesia,[66] and other linguistic intertextualizations of the written language. Such alternative interpretations are often re-enforced and propagated through official awards and notoriety, as happened with *Kali's Child.*

Queer Hermeneutics a.k.a. Queermeneutics?

Like many others, Bhattacharyya asks, "Why this bizarre interpretation?" Certainly, it is naïve to solely blame "the author's homosexual inclinations or gay agenda"[67]. However, when "one puts Kripal's obsession for 'sexual abuse' themes and deviant sexuality . . . alongside the recent spate of pedophilic scandals involving the clergy in the USA [One worries] what Kripal's experiences at the Seminary were actually like." In 'Secret Talk: Sexual Identity and Politics of Scholarship", Kripal frankly admits: "that his work proceeded from his personal experiences at a Benedictine Seminary and from his personal desire to heterosexually engage a female divinity". Bhattacharyya notes that even the Projection Defense Mechanism: "with all its complexities, cannot adequately explain . . . the present controversy".

It is disingenuous on the part of Kripal to issue public disclaimers on his gay or non-gay status in order to divert attention from the basic problems of his approach. This turns the issue of responsibility on its head by accusing the critics of homophobia—a classic case of *aufgestellte Mausdrek*—a mouse-turd standing up on end.[68] Consequently, there is a buildup of 'sinister negative transferences' on the 'clean slate that is Jeffery Kripal'. Bhattacharyya's trained eye saw signs of the reaction formation defense mechanism wherein the opposite impulse or behavior is taken up to hide true feelings by behaving in an exact opposite way.

Discussing the manner in which Kripal contradicts himself and appears to be in denial, Bhattacharyya writes:

The real key to this issue lies in what psychoanalysts call 'self-analysis'—a discipline that one has to rigorously undergo before one can start psychoanalyzing others. This practice was initiated by Freud himself and remains a desideratum for all analysts to this day.

[...]

Erik Erickson, in many ways the father of psychohistory, himself warns about the dangers of projections to which the psycho-historian is always prone. He pointed out that any psycho-historian *'projects on the men and the times he studies some unlived portions and often the unrealized selves of his own life.'* [Emphasis added]

Bhattacharyya suggests that the way out of this dilemma is through honest self-analysis. He adds, humorously: "I hope the analyst is analyzable". Certainly, honest self-analysis would help trace the roots of many of these problems. Bhattacharyya quotes from Roland's critique of *Kali's Child:*

Kripal [has a] penchant for facile speculative decoding and turning these into adamant conviction. He thus persists in insisting that Ramakrishna
1. 'was very likely sexually abused by any number of actors who had power over him', that his trance states were related to such abuse, that the direction of the
2. 'saint's desire [was] always directed towards males (deities or male disciples)', [and]
3. 'when a text uses sexual language it often, if not always, reflects real physiological and psychological analogues' and that the materials of his thesis are
4. 'by their very nature offensive.

Bhattacharyya examines the psychoanalytic considerations of several issues found in Kripal's analysis, including sexual abuse, feminine identity, homoeroticism and misogyny. Under the subtitle *Sexual Abuse,* he writes:

Kripal insists that village people must have abused Ramakrishna presumably because he had states of absorption right from his childhood. But Ramakrishna's own descriptions of his childhood suggest quite the contrary, e.g. 'During my younger days the men and women of Kamarpukur were equally fond of me. No one distrusted me. Everybody took me in as one of the family.'

Under the subtitle, *Feminine Identity?* several loopholes in Kripal are pointed out:

> It is easy to talk loosely with Masson about Ramakrishna's transvestite activities, but dressing up in a feminine dress as a part of a legitimate and culturally accepted *sadhana* for a short period of time does not amount to transvestism. Ramakrishna after all also dressed like a Shakta and a Vaishnava during his Shakti and Vaishnava *sadhana* days and like a Muslim during his Islam *sadhana*—and these were male attires—only to try and make his identification with these cults complete. Moreover, contrary to Kripal's thesis, *most transvestites are heterosexual.* [Emphasis added]

He further suggests that Kripal's claims about Ramakrishna's 'secondary trans-sexuality' are also all too facile. He explains:

> The American Psychiatric Association (*Diagnostic and Statistical Manual IV*) defines trans-sexuality as strong and persistent cross-gender identification, and not merely a desire for any perceived cultural advantages of being the other sex. It is a disorder always involving distress to the person, with a feeling of estrangement from the body and a felt need to alter the appearance of the body. If Ramakrishna sometimes talked about his femininity he was also clear about what he meant by it—'Formerly I too used to see many visions, but now in my ecstatic state I don't see so many. I am gradually getting over my feminine nature; I feel nowadays more like a man. Therefore I control my emotions; I don't manifest it outwardly so much'.

The *Kathamrita* often portrays Ramakrishna in a masculine role with 'leonine strength'. However, Bhattacharyya notes that Kripal never discusses this because it doesn't fit his agenda. Nonetheless, Ramakrishna is often seen

> engaging in persuasive conversation with well known intellectuals, scholars, and social leaders of his day, [...] asserting his will vis-à-vis his teachers, [...] preaching to varied audiences and closely guiding his disciples.

These would be classified as masculine roles in nineteenth-century India as well as in America. Bhattacharyya continues:

> In the *Kathamrita* and related texts we also find Ramakrishna playing multiple roles across genders and ages with élan. Women could evidently relate to him as one of their own group as much

as young boys and elderly men. This is especially significant at a time when social identities were largely compartmentalized.

Psychologically speaking, all humans have the potential for dual gender identification (social influences play a major role in defining our gender stereotypes), and Ramakrishna clearly had both these aspects well developed and harmonized.[69]

Unfortunately, to carry through his thesis of Ramakrishna's feminine identification, Kripal resorts to erroneous documentation. Thus a whole section is devoted to *bhagavatir tanu* or goddess body that Ramakrishna is supposed to have possessed. The actual *Kathamrita* term however is *bhaagavati tanu*, which simply means divine body, and has no engendered connotation. (The term is actually a Sanskrit term, and grammatical and physiological genders don't always go together in Sanskrit. E.g., the term *daara*, meaning wife, is masculine) *Bhagavatir* and *Bhaagavati* are two different words, and a person who reads the one for the other only reveals his lack of knowledge for that language.[70] Besides, Ramakrishna specifically identifies this *bhaagavati tanu* with the causal body, "by means of which one enjoys the bliss of God and holds communion with him", and notes its distinction from the gross physical body and the subtle body (or the mental complex). To assign a physical or even psychological sex to this category then is a reductive strategy, which robs the analyst of the possibility of deeper insight into human nature and its possibilities. Similarly, Ramakrishna's wearing silken clothes (*garader kapar*) during puja is taken to mean feminine dress simply because Kripal doesn't know that male priests in Bengal routinely wear silken clothes.

Bhattacharyya's footnote is telling of Kripal's cultural biases: "And why should [Kripal] not know? Don't the Roman Catholic clergy use silken apparel during mass"? He refutes Kripal's conclusions that tenderness between father and son is homoerotic, citing Bengali and Indian cultural nuances. He also shows numerous other records of Ramakrishna's interactions with his women disciples of all ages and classes. These records were all studiously ignored by Kripal. Those writings reveal that Ramakrishna's dealings with female disciples were as affectionate and close as were his dealings with his male disciples. Bhattacharyya warns the reader:

> It is all too easy to play around with the word *kamini* and say that Ramakrishna hated women (or for that matter women as lovers) and that when he spoke of sexual abstinence he only had heterosexuality in mind. As a matter of fact, in the *Kathamrita* we

find Ramakrishna repeatedly talking about *indriya sukha* (sense pleasures), *deha sukha* (bodily pleasures), *vishaya sukha* (object gratification), *kama* (lust in general), and *bhoga* (enjoyment) as impediments to spiritual growth.

Bhattacharyya summarizes: "All these terms stand for the pleasure principle and are indicative of the erotic, but organized in a 'much broader' . . . sense than just [Freudian] heterosexuality". He adds: "Of course, [there is no] specific comment from Ramakrishna about homosexuality simply because homosexuality as a construct was not current in Bengal of Ramakrishna's times".

Bhattacharyya devotes considerable time discussing the Goddess, since Ramakrishna's lifelong love and devotion was for the Goddess Kali. He shows that Ramakrishna's devotion to, and visions of Sita, Radha and other feminine deities clearly do not fit into Kripal's homoerotic thesis nor Ramakrishna's identification with Hanuman (the very symbol of Hindu masculinity), nor the mergence of numerous deities (both masculine and feminine). "To get past these hurdles Kripal simply falls back on caricature".[71] Bhattacharyya, as psychoanalyst, observes: "Somehow [Kripal] must include a castration story to get over this problem (That would make things appear more 'psychoanalytical' too!)."

Kripal attempts to justify the castration image by trying to prove that a banana offered during a goat sacrifice is actually the goat's penis. Bhattacharyya finds this ludicrous, and adds:

> [Kripal] has neither bothered to see a goat-sacrifice (the ritual has remained the same for centuries together), nor checked the manuals of procedure for these sacrifices. The sacrificial animal is decapitated at a single stroke, and any mutilation is sacrilegious.

From the perspective of an elder scholar, he cautions Kripal that he "*would also do well to remember that the female is not a castrated male.*"[Emphasis added]. As a trained professional, he finds Kripal's amateurish speculations laughable: "Equally comical are [Kripal's] attempts to weave in anal themes". He observes: "Unfortunately, [Kripal] claims to be a historian of religion . . . not a novelist. If he got angry responses he surely has invited them".

Bhattacharyya analyzes the manner in which Kripal selected the passages from the *Kathamrita* and concluded that Kripal's critical selectivity "**amply illustrates the basic problem in his handling of texts. Virtually any selected portion of his book is not just a matter of a few dozen, easily correctable translation errors neither is it simply a question** of textual relativism based on multivalent use of language." [Emphasis added]

Some Empirical Issues

Bhattacharyya offers many arguments that refute Kripal's thesis. The first study area that he investigates is the psychological impact of meditation and mystical experiences:

> In Kripal's own backyard, sociologist Andrew Greely of University of Chicago's National Opinions Research Council (NORC) tested people who had profoundly mystical experiences, such as being bathed in white light. When these persons were subjected to standard tests measuring psychological well-being, the mystics scored at the top. University of Chicago psychologist Norman Bradburn, who developed the test, said that no other factor had ever been found to correlate so highly with psychological balance, as did mystical experience.

Secondly he describes: "A landmark US national poll reported in the New York Times Magazine [in 1975] that found people with mystical experiences had happy and positive recollections of their childhood". The third example he cited was from an important study on the psychological effects of meditation, using subjects at various stages of Buddhist enlightenment. He reported:

> [The] enlightened subjects displayed evidence of normal conflicts around issues such as dependency, sexuality, and aggression. However, they showed remarkably little defensiveness and reactivity to these conflicts. In other words, they accepted and were unperturbed by their neuroses. Those few meditaters at the third stage of enlightenment gave reports that were unique ... they showed no evidence of drive conflicts and appeared free of psychological conflicts usually considered an inescapable part of human existence. This finding is consistent with classic claims that psychological suffering can be dramatically reduced in advanced stages of meditation.[72]

Bhattacharyya adds:

Ramakrishna's *samadhi* states were accompanied by very profound inward withdrawal of consciousness, and remarkable physiological changes, consistent with the highest stages of meditative absorption as documented in Hindu Tantra and Yoga as well as Buddhist literature. Thus the famous physician Mahendarlal Sarkar himself examined and found Ramakrishna without heartbeat and corneal reflexes during *samadhi*. These physiological changes (clinically taken as signs of death) . . . were not metaphorical changes [and] are not known to occur in a dissociative trance.

The fourth point made by Bhattacharyya traces its roots back to Freud, and a close contemporary, Medard Boss—an influential Swiss existential psychotherapist who had been trained by several prominent psychoanalysts and analyzed by Sigmund Freud. He had this to say about the holy men he met on his lecture-visit to India:

> [T]here were the exalted figures of the sages and holy men themselves, each one of them a living example of the possibility of human growth and maturity and of the attainment of an imperturbable inner peace, a joyous freedom from guilt, and a purified, selfless goodness and calmness.... No matter how carefully I observe the waking lives of the holy men, no matter how ready they were to tell me about their dreams, I could not detect in the best of them a trace of a selfish action or any kind of a repressed or consciously concealed shadow life. (Boss 187–88)

Finally, for his fifth point, Bhattacharyya discusses the dharmic perspectives of sex. He writes: "It is worth noting that although we commonly speak of a sex drive, sex does not fit the usual conception of drive, as a felt need that gets stronger and stronger, until it is satisfied". He explains, referring to Masters and Johnson: "Indeed, sexual abstinence probably decreases sexual motivation over the long run. There is no evidence, despite myths to the contrary, [that] abstinence from sexual activity is detrimental to a person's health".[73]

Hyper-Textual Sexualization

> [T]he book is not about... contemporary Hindu self-perceptions. It is about a nineteenth-century Indian mystic who was relatively immune from the last 150 years of Victorian and colonial sexual prudery that has, with other cultural forces, attempted to efface the ancient and very real phallic connotations of the lingam and the exquisite eroticism of much of Indic mythology, art and mystical practice.[74]
>
> Jeffrey J. Kripal

Bhattacharyya carefully investigates several instances where Kripal has homo-eroticized the heterosexual, hyper-sexualized the child, and 'masculated' the genderless. Through this methodology, she becomes he, and all signs point to penis envy or some equally loaded jargon. Indeed, the female is *not* a castrated male.

Bhattacharyya stresses, "Ramakrishna never [said the] practice [of celibacy] is applicable only to men." A story from the *Kathamrita* 'records in detail how Ramakrishna advises two young ladies in the worship of Siva'. The state of the child in Ramakrishna's language: "lacks engendered connotations . . . to illustrate abstract love for . . . a neuter entity'."

Kripal often feels that a passage is 'hyper-sexualized' and demands a sexual reading. Bhattacharyya suggests how Ramakrishna would probably have responded to such a simplistic reading: "Analogy is one sided . . . Suppose you say that a man is as terrible as a tiger. That doesn't mean that he has a fearful tail or a tiger's pot face." Bhattacharyya, tiring of the triumphalist theorizing, pegs Kripal as predictably smug in his absolutist assertion that the Self is the 'penetrating male'. Bhattacharyya adds: "Kripal's own approach [to the study of Ramakrishna] can correctly be termed 'sexualized'."

'Hypersexualization' is not a term that is found in the standard corpus of psychoanalytic literature [unlike] 'sexualization', which is defined as "endowing an object or function with a sexual significance that it did not previously have . . . in order to ward-off anxieties associated with prohibited impulses".[75] Bhattacharyya examines several of Kripal's writings and also looks at the articles written by Kripal's critics, such as Tyagananda. As a result, he writes lucidly across numerous theoretical subheadings. In one analysis, he exposes Kripal's view that looking upon all women as Mother needs to be translated as 'all vaginas are mother's vagina'. He then takes apart several Bengali sentences, looking at different forms of the word mother throughout—*matriyoni, matribhave, matristana*—comparing word usage with cultural meanings.

He stresses several times in his essay that Shakta worship of women as Mother aims at helping the aspirants transcend their sexual impulses. He adds: "Ramakrishna actually was of the opinion that such worship is possible only in the transcendent (God realized) state". For Bhattacharyya, "Reducing transcendence to sexuality or even eroticism, denies the very significance of this ritual." He points out that bringing the symbolism to the physical level of the breast or the womb immediately brings up associations of infantile states of symbiotic fusion, which 'is misinformed thinking'. Quoting Meissner, he writes:

It is clear that the sense of fusion with the object in mystical states is not the same as the regressive fusion to primary narcissistic union that might occur in states of psychotic regression. Rather, authentic mystical experience (as distinguished from pseudo-mystical or psychotic experience) not only does not undermine or destroy identity, but in fact has a powerful capacity to stabilize, sustain and enrich identit (151).

Bhattacharyya confirms:: "[This] can be clearly verified if one watches the two individuals (the mystic and the pseudo-mystic or psychotic) in a longitudinal study".

Kripal and Bhattacharyya are culturally miles apart regarding the manner in which each of them viewed Ramakrishna's use of the terms yoni and lingam. Bhattacharyya observed that Kripal is troubled by the use of yoni and lingam and, perhaps, because of shame or shock, he sexualizes, sensationalizes, eroticizes.[76] In contrast, Bhattacharyya sees worshipping a lingam or yoni as a cosmic symbol. Ramakrishna said they are symbols of fatherhood and motherhood so that one may not be born into the world again. Bhattacharyya advises: "If Kripal is bothered about the moral implications of such worship then he clearly needs to associate with the traditions that place a high moral value on this ritual". Kripal takes the easy road—first by discovering a new twist on the exotic Other, then asserting absolute authority to theoretically describe that entity.[77] Bhattacharyya is a bit dismayed:

Incidentally, when citing texts and arguments in support of his own claims, Kripal insists that things are 'crystal clear', while the other texts are all ambiguous ('simultaneously concealing and revealing'). Well! This is hermeneutics of convenience for sure!

Catachresis and the Hermeneutics of Convenience[78]

Kripal's textual mishandling is particularly grave because his primary claim is that he is a historian of religions. Professionally, Bhattacharyya cautioned: "Large scale distortions of source material in an ill attempted effort at establishing a thesis, is certainly not academically acceptable". He compared this tactic to what is known in scientific research as 'the sharp-shooter's fallacy'—analogous to the way a gunslinger might empty his six-shooter into the side of a barn and then draw the bull's-eye around the bullet holes.[79] He warned: "Citing fringe works and material of equally dubious value doesn't help in salvaging the case".

Throughout this debate, Kripal has tried to place his critics in the Hindu obscurantist camp, and he is keen on playing identity politics as well. Bhattacharyya reminds him:

[C]ritics of his methodology include noted academics like Huston Smith, Alan Roland and Gerald Larson among others; and they are neither Hindus nor Indians.[80]

Since Kripal states that his 'hermeneutical' strategy is inspired by Hans-Georg Gadamer's work *Truth and Method*, Bhattacharyya quotes from the noted Indologist Fritz Staal whose lengthy analysis of Gadamer's internally contradictory methodology, explained that, ultimately:

Either one disagrees with what Gadamer says, in which case one must agree with what he means; or one agrees with what he says by disagreeing with its meaning. One must in all cases agree and disagree, and Gadamer's originality lies in this combination. He has adopted from the positivist-empiricist tradition its most monumental error—the caricature of the scientific method—and failed to heed its most valuable contribution—the critique of meaninglessness.

Staal ended his discussion of Gadamer exclaiming, "And this philosophy aims at instructing us about interpretation!" Bhattacharyya quotes Staal: "not because he shows up Gadamer in rather poor light ... though the criticism is spot on [but because] it provides some insights into Kripal's own line of thinking". He points out, "the circularities of logic and internal contradictions strewn in the text of *Kali's Child*, as also [Kripal's] self-contradictory statements." Bhattacharyya concludes: "Evidently, [Kripal] is not supposed to mean what he says and not say what he means! He seems to construe Gadamer's 'horizon of meaning' as license to distort texts". but doubts Gadamer intended it that way.

Moving through two subsections of his essay, 'On Comparative Critical Studies, and Sex, Love, and the Erotic', Bhattacharyya discusses homoeroticism and sexual innuendos. Though Kripal claims to be using the standard methodology of advanced historio-critical studies as practised in the American Academy, Bhattacharyya has his doubts:

Do the Jesus Seminar scholars take Jesus' talk about his return to 'unite with his followers' or Paul's supreme desire to know Christ and be united with him (be 'in Christ') as mutual 'homosexual entry'? Is Jesus pathologized simply because people said 'He's gone

mad' and Jesus' parents were concerned; and the Pharisees affirmed
'He has Beelzebul in him' (Mark 3:21)? Does Jesus' foot function
as a sexual object—'the sinful foot of God'—when 'a woman with
a bad name in town' anoints it and covers it with kisses (Luke 7:38)?
And When Jesus sits down and dines with prostitutes and sinners
(Matt 9:10) is the 'intercourse' sexual? When Jesus proclaims that
it would be more tolerable for the land of Sodom and Gomorrha
in the day of judgement than for the city that will not receive his
disciples, is he taken to be projecting his own sexual perversions
and psychotic delusions of grandeur? Or, when Johann Tauler, the
14th century German mystic, writes 'one who would know much
about these (spiritual) matters would often have to keep to his bed,
for his bodily frame could not support this,' is this taken as evidence
of massive sexual trauma? Do Kripal's colleagues in the American
Academy take the Christian distinction between agape and eros
simply as 'so much theological talk'; and the early Christian 'love-
feasts' (that's where the concept of agape originated) as plain
'sexual orgies' of 'erotic communities'? This is precisely how Kripal
has argued throughout *Kali's Child*. It was with good reason then
that Huston Smith wrote that Kripal ought to have written about
homosexual eroticism in Christian mysticism before writing *Kali's
Child*.

In *Kali's Child,* Kripal defines the term erotic as "an experience
containing 'both sexual and sacred components, a dialectical term
refusing to separate the sexual and the mystical'". Bhattacharyya
pointed out that in *Evam*[81] Kripal "clarifies ... by 'homoerotic' that
he refers 'to the structure or direction of the saint's desire, always
towards males (deities or disciples)'". For Bhattacharyya this definition
is problematic. He explains that in conventional usage the term erotic
is associated with "sexuality in all its diverse aspects, but hardly
anything spiritual ... unless it is suitably qualified". Kripal, however,
"uses the term in very conventional ways ... despite his unconventional
definition". Bhattacharyya points out that Kripal also violates rules of
Bengali grammar, by confusing the gender structure of character, and
linguistic genders with sexual function. Agreeing with Tyagananda,
Bhattacharyya writes:

> The vocabulary of Kripal's desire is also very problematic [because]
> Kripal wishes to have his readers believe that anxious longing
> (*vyakulata*), charismatic attraction (*tana*), and associative reminder
> (*uddipana*) among other terms, and also of course Ramakrishna's
> love for his male disciples, all carry sexual meanings, the contextual

structure not withstanding. Now, besides the textual problems documented by Tyagananda, some very real psychological issues are also at stake here . . . Freud's conception of love as 'aim-inhibited sex' stands repudiated at present on empirical grounds. Love and sex are not synonymous. There can be love without sex and vice versa . . . Thus, when Kripal summarily characterizes all these different shades of love as erotic he commits what may be termed a 'category error'.

Bhattacharyya explains that Fromm also notes that tenderness is by no means a sublimation of the sexual instinct as Freud believes; it is the direct outcome of brotherly love and exists in physical as well as non-physical forms of love.

Bhattacharyya then addresses Kripal's conflation of the sacred and the sexual explaining that sacralization of the mundane is the very basis of religious ritual. He gives as an example the 'sanctity' of marriage. In that context, Bhattacharyya fails to see Kripal's point that he has discovered hidden sexual themes in scriptural texts. Bhattacharyya writes: "Of course, they are there, and quite openly [therefore] one need not imagine prudish cover-ups [or] dig out non-existent texts". However, he goes on: "The thesis in *Kali's Child* which tries to stand this sacralization on the head and sexualize the sacred is not as easy as Kripal imagines". Bhattacharyya mentions complex Hindu categories such as *dharma* and *moksha* and *kama*. And points out: "[Though] sexual motifs in the Hindu myths have strong transcendental underpinnings, [the] experience of the sacred [is quite] distinct from the sexual experience". He adds:

Most importantly, when a religious celibate like Ramakrishna makes this distinction he needs to be taken seriously, unless one has genuine (and not speculative) evidence to the contrary. Ramakrishna's own experience as recorded in the *Kathamrita* bears eloquent testimony to the validity of this distinction. As we have mentioned earlier, physiologically speaking, Ramakrishna's *samadhi* is of an order distinctly different from anything we know as sexual. Ramakrishna never denied his sexuality or its biological roots. Therefore, when he speaks about his great and successful struggle to overcome lust, or about passions like lust and anger being burnt up on God-realization, then we just can't afford to wish him away. This is exactly what the Tantra and Yoga psychologies speak of. And this is what the other mystic traditions affirm. Ramakrishna repeatedly asserts that his love for a select group of young men is because of their inherent spiritual talent and these men in turn go on to have exemplary spiritual careers; to caricature this relationship as erotic is a travesty of religious scholarship. It is also surprising that Kripal fails to notice the similarity between the Christian concept of seeing one's fellow humans as the present Christ and Ramakrishna's assertion about seeing and loving God in man. Is this brotherly Christian love also erotic?

Bhattacharyya examines a passage from *Kathamrita* in which Kripal idiosyncratically characterizes a story as erotic:

> One can hardly have any objection to someone affirming 'both the spiritual and the sexual' as entities. But when Kripal conflates them (and that is what he means by both), he walks in the face of massive phenomenological and psychological (especially the Eastern psychological) evidence to the contrary.

Bhattacharyya sees Kripal's manuscript as irreparably tainted by predetermined motivations: "His invariable need to distort texts is proof enough against his agenda".

'State of the Child' and the 'Psychology of Being'

While defending his controversial thesis, Kripal has shown a certain proprietorship—claiming that: "psychoanalytic paradigms are his cultural inheritance". Sudhir Kakar has said that, "Psychoanalysis occupies an ill-defined zone between the arts and the objective sciences." Bhattacharyya quotes Otto Fenichel from *The Psychoanalytic Theory of Neurosis:* "The subject matter, not the method of psychoanalysis, is irrational".

Bhattacharyya further explains, "Kripal claims his work to be in line with the writings of Sudhir Kakkar [whose own work on Ramakrishna] though avowedly Freudian and reductionist in nature, is much more sophisticated. Kakkar is careful to suggest that the feminine identification of mystics is best interpreted as circumvention of drives and instincts, or in other words as an 'experience of being'." Bhattacharyya points out: "Transpersonal and humanistic psychologists have worked upon this 'psychology of Being' taken in its own right in a non-reductive and ipso facto fashion". He compares this to the 'state of the child', "which is central to Ramakrishna's perception of himself as well as to the way he was perceived by his contemporaries". Ramakrishna spoke about this state as being unattached and beyond the *gunas* . . . possessing only an appearance of ego . . . only a semblance of anger and lust ... seeing 'no distinction between man and woman' ... 'beyond ideas of purity and impurity' or 'holy and unholy' ... possessing a pure heart and simple faith".

Bhattacharyya explains:

> Ramakrishna's characterization of this 'state of the child' remarkably anticipates the findings of the classic studies on 'peak experiences' (which included mystic experiences) of 'self actualizing' people by Abraham Maslow, nearly four decades ago. Maslow noted self-actualizing subjects, picked because they were very mature, were at the same time, also childish. [He] called it 'healthy childishness', a 'second naiveté'. He considered a god-like gaiety (humor, fun, foolishness, silliness, play, laughter) to be one of the highest ... values of the state of Being ... i.e. 'being one's real Self'.

Bhattacharyya notes that it is specifically Ramakrishna's 'state of the child' (*matribhava, santanabhava*), which is the very psychological state that Kripal studiously avoids or distorts into amorphous or polymorphous sexuality. Bhattacharyya finds this *especially ironical* because this book bears the title Kali's *Child*. He laments:

> If only Kripal had not ignored this central theme of Ramakrishna's personality—'the state of the child'—he could have made much better sense of Ramakrishna's *samadhi*, his uninhibited dealings with his devotees, his love and concern for his disciples and their reciprocation of the same ...

The practices of Tantras are informed by deep psychological insights into the workings of the human nature. Bhattacharyya notes:

> If these basic psychological principles underlying the tantric practices are *not* ignored it becomes much easier to make sense of Ramakrishna's own eminently successful tantric practices and experiences, his criticism of some of the tantric sects and their practices, as well as his open-hearted espousal of many tantric techniques ... without having to pigeon-hole the tantras into the 'sexy, seedy and strange', and paint a conflicted, ambivalent Ramakrishna through extended skewed and speculative glosses.

To Bhattacharyya, Kripal's iconography of Kali bears a striking resemblance to the New Age and feminist appropriations of Hindu goddesses in the USA.[82] This is in stark contrast to Ramakrishna's own perceptions of Kali. Bhattacharyya sees Kripal as an ingénue, who catches a phrase or two, then based on erroneous knowledge of India and Hinduism creates a static essentialized icon of goddess worship. Bhattacharyya concludes, "This says more about the fertile and wounded imagination of its Western authors than it does about deity veneration in India."

Chapter 16

Is There Prejudice in Hinduism Studies? A Look at *Encarta*[83]

BY SANKRANT SANU[84]

The scholarship of certain sections of the academic community studying Hinduism has been controversial in the Indian community. In this article we try to examine whether there is truth to this controversy, and whether such academics influence the mainstream portrayal of 'Hinduism' in standard sources. We use the Microsoft® Corporation's *Encarta*® Encyclopedia as the reference for this study.

Introduction

In this article we discuss the differences, in both approach and result, of *Encarta's* articles on Hinduism in comparison with the articles on some of the other major world religions in *Encarta*. *Encarta* Encyclopedia is published by the Microsoft Corporation, which claims that it is the "Best-selling encyclopedia brand". *Encarta* is widely used as a reference source in American schools. In particular, because of its widespread use among children, we would expect *Encarta's* coverage of religions to be even-handed, sensitive and unprejudiced. In a world of religious conflict, it becomes particularly important that children are given balanced viewpoints of the mainstream beliefs and practices of all religions.

In particular, we contrast *Encarta's* treatment of Hinduism, with the two other major religions—Islam and Christianity. On occasion, we also refer to the treatment of other religions like Judaism and Buddhism. The purpose of this article is not to make value judgments or a comparative study of the religions themselves. In studying such vast and complex phenomena as the major religions, one can always find conflicting or questionable issues, just as one can find highly elevating truths. What aspects of the religion get highlighted is a matter of editorial choice. Our interest is not in comparing the religions per se, but in understanding the differences in editorial choice—both in the selection of content as well as style in the scholarly treatment of these religions in *Encarta*.

Unless otherwise noted, all references below are to the main content article on each of the religions in *Encarta*. We have used *Encarta* Encyclopedia 2002 (US edition) for our reference, though a casual look at *Encarta* 2003 suggests that the articles on the major religions have remained the same as *Encarta* 2002. All actual quotes are in quotation marks preceded by the name of the article in *Encarta*.

The Contents Page

Our study begins with the main contents page for each of the religions. In some cases, the contents page contains, in quotes, a single highlighted statement about the religion. In the 2002 version of *Encarta*, these quotes are present for Hinduism, Buddhism and Judaism, and not for Christianity and Islam.

- Judaism: "The God of creation entered into a special relationship with the Jewish people at Sinai".
- Buddhism: "Karma consists of a person's acts and their ethical consequence".
- Hinduism: "Rama and Krishna are said to be avatars of Vishnu though they were originally human heroes".

We note that the one statement chosen to describe Hinduism repudiates Hindu belief, while the statements for the other two religions reflect a balanced, positive, or neutral stance. Notice also the use of 'said to be' in Hinduism while the statement on Judaism is presented in the editorial voice as a presentation of fact. To understand this representation, let us draw up a hypothetical quote on Christianity to parallel the quote on Hinduism.

- Christianity: Jesus Christ is said to be the 'Son of God' though he was just a human.

Irrespective of belief in the truth or falsity of this statement, or the parallel one in the case of Hinduism, when such a statement is the highlight of the commentary on a religion, it reflects a certain *attitude* about how the subject is approached. Let us see if this attitude continues to persist in the article on Hinduism in comparison to other religions.

Fundamental Principles

In the article on Hinduism, we find that the 'Fundamental Principles' are divided into four sections—'Texts', 'Philosophy', 'Gods' and 'Worship and Ritual'. We find the sequencing of ideas within this section fairly haphazard—generally moving to specifics without laying out the general—giving the impression of a somewhat incoherent system. Hinduism:

> The canon of Hinduism is basically defined by what people do rather than what they think. Consequently, far more uniformity of behavior than of belief is found among Hindus, although very few practices or beliefs are shared by all. A few usages are observed by almost all Hindus: reverence for Brahmans and cows; abstention from meat (especially beef); and marriage within the caste (*jati*), in the hope of producing male heirs.

By writing the above, the author takes the richness and diversity of Hindu thought and tries to approach it from the point of view of an orthodox church defining a single 'canon'. Failing to find the 'canon' or articulate the underlying worldview of a system that allows many paths to flourish within it, the author quickly gives in to start listing mainly social practices. Let us see how the same issue is treated in Christianity.
Christianity:

> Any phenomenon as complex and as vital as Christianity is easier to describe historically than to define logically, but such a description does yield some insights into its continuing elements and essential characteristics.

In the description of Christianity, *Encarta* approaches it from a point of view of humility—the problem being of the expository limitations of the author. No such humility is visible in the description of Hinduism, where the author quickly reduces any notion of complexity to an anthropological viewpoint. Further on, we explore various examples of how the anthropological viewpoint dominates the article on Hinduism.

Dealing with 'Contradictions'

Let us see how the articles deal with supposed contradictions.
Hinduism:

> Although Hindus believe and do many apparently contradictory things—contradictory not merely from one Hindu to the next, but also within the daily religious life of a single Hindu—each individual perceives an orderly pattern that gives form and meaning to his or her own life.

The article on Hinduism is very clear that there are contradictions, and highlights this aspect. The articles on Christianity and Islam are either unable to find any contradictions, or don't find them the most significant aspect of the religion to cover. In the few instances when they do, they use substantially different language to talk about these.

In Christianity, any contradictions of behavior are attributed to the limitations of individuals rather than limitations of the faith or of 'Christians' as a generalized entity.
Christianity:

> To a degree that those on the inside often fail to recognize, however, such a system of beliefs and values can also be described in a way that makes sense as well to an interested observer who does not, or even cannot, share their outlook.

The article on Islam does not mention any 'contradiction' at all, but a continued 'refinement'.
Islam:

> Recurring debates among Islamic scholars over the nature of God have continued to refine the Islamic concepts of God's otherness and Islamic monotheism.
> [...]
>
> Even when the article on Islam admits differences in contemporary practice, it puts the difficulty of these on the analytical or expository abilities of the author ('difficult to identify'), rather than on the religion.

Islam:

> Yet the radically different political, economic, and cultural conditions under which contemporary Muslims live make it difficult to identify what constitutes standard Islamic practice in the modern world.

The key to understanding both the diversity as well as the unity of Hinduism is neither in the search for a 'canon' (a strongly Christian worldview), nor in the anthropology of particular practices. It is in recognizing that the philosophical foundations of Hinduism have celebrated diversity of path and individuality (which itself is a distinctive feature), while at the same time encouraging theological debates to further understanding.

In the articles on Christianity and Islam the problem, if any, is usually depicted as that of the author's inability to adequately describe complexity rather than one of internal contradictions within the religions. The author of the section on Hinduism apparently faces very little difficulty—she carries on with an anthropological description of practices 'from above'—sure that any contradiction that is found is inherently in the religion itself, and not in any lack of understanding or expository ability.

Peaceful 'Jihad' and Violent 'Ahimsa'

A further study about the difference in approach and attitude in the articles on religion can be found in the description of subtle concepts. We take two—*jihad* and *ahimsa*, in particular, both of which may be somewhat familiar to the lay reader.

Islam:

> Many polemical descriptions of Islam have focused critically on the Islamic concept of jihad. Jihad, considered the sixth pillar of Islam by some Muslims, has been understood to mean holy war in these descriptions. However, the word in Arabic means 'to struggle' or 'to exhaust one's effort,' in order to please God. Within the faith of Islam, this effort can be individual or collective, and it can apply to leading a virtuous life; helping other Muslims through charity, education, or other means; preaching Islam; and fighting to defend Muslims. Western media of the 20th century continue to focus on the militant interpretations of the concept of jihad, whereas most Muslims do not.

Hinduism:

> The most important tenet of sanatana dharma for all Hindus is ahimsa, the absence of a desire to injure, which is *used to justify* vegetarianism (although it does not preclude physical violence toward animals or humans, or blood sacrifices in temples). [Emphasis added]

In both cases, the authors treat subtle subjects in the respective religions. In the article on Islam, the author presents a sympathetic view of Jihad, and attempts to favorably influence Western perceptions. In the article on Hinduism the author adds decidedly unfavorable editorial asides seeking to 'correct' possibly favorable perceptions by introducing 'contradictions'. The tone of the article again is of a higher entity looking down on lowly customs and illogical 'native' interpretations as in, 'ahimsa . . . is used to justify'. This is an illustration of the very different viewpoint (dare we say 'agenda') from which the article on Hinduism is written. While the articles on Islam and Christianity attempt to uplift the reader to a refined understanding of those religions, the article on Hinduism attempts to denigrate instead.

To understand what we mean by this, let us see how *Encarta* would present Christianity and Islam, if it were to use the same logic and attitude as used in the article on Hinduism.

Christianity:[85]

> The most important tenet of Christianity is love (although it does not preclude burning heretics and witches at the stake, the Crusades, Christian colonization and the Jewish Holocaust).

Islam:[86]

> Muslims claim that Islam is a religion of peace (although it does not preclude suicide bombing or other terrorist acts).

To be really clear, we are not suggesting that such descriptions of Christianity or Islam should have been in *Encarta*—they would be decidedly negative portrayals. Unfortunately, this tone of portrayal prevails in the article on Hinduism.

This is, surprisingly, not the only example of the technique of negative editorial asides in the article on Hinduism. Thus we see:

Hinduism:

> *Svadharma* comprises the beliefs that each person is born to perform a specific job, marry a specific person, eat certain food, and beget children to do likewise and that it is better to fulfill one's own dharma than that of anyone else (even if one's own is low or reprehensible, such as that of the Harijan caste, the Untouchables, whose mere presence was once considered polluting to other castes). . .

A positive portrayal of 'Svadharma' (literally 'Self-Dharma') would introduce it as a high statement to an individual to discover and understand their purpose and calling with the cosmos in order to actualize it. Yet in the hands of the *Encarta* author it becomes an excuse for an aside on the historical practice of untouchability that is derided in contemporary mainstream Hinduism. In neither of the other two articles of the major religions, Christianity or Islam, do we find the use of the technique of the denigrating editorial aside. Indeed, the purpose of the other two articles appears to be to elevate rather than to denigrate—and quite rightly so for a mainstream source dealing with religion.

Philosophy or Anthropology?

The article on Hinduism appears quite disjointed in its understanding of philosophy, anthropology, cosmology, and mythology. The 'Fundamental Principles' leads with anthropology. As we see below the section on 'Philosophy' is mostly 'mythology' depicting 'cosmology'—the very limited coverage of the well-developed schools of Hindu philosophy is relegated to a list in the section 'Rise of Devotional Movements', as a topic of History. Without setting out the philosophical principles, the underlying beliefs and practices of Hinduism, the coverage of 'Gods' and 'Rituals' appears particularly bizarre. Let us see how the section on 'Philosophy' begins.

Hinduism:

> Incorporated in this rich literature is a complex cosmology. Hindus believe that the universe is a great, enclosed sphere, a cosmic egg, within which are numerous concentric heavens, hells, oceans, and continents, with India at the center.

> They believe that time is both degenerative—going from the golden age, or Krita Yuga, through two intermediate periods of decreasing goodness, to the present age, or Kali Yuga—and cyclic: At the end of each Kali Yuga, the universe is destroyed by fire and flood, and a new golden age begins.

Firstly, this is not philosophy, but as the author points out, cosmology. Secondly, as a description of Hindu cosmology, it is fairly inadequate and reductive. It fails to point that there are multiple creation myths in Hindu texts. Also, as far as Hindu cosmology goes, people like the notable astronomer and author, Prof. Carl Sagan, have pointed that the calculations of the age of the universe based on this cosmology works out to be fairly close to our current scientific estimates—and "(Hinduism) is the only ancient religious tradition on the Earth which talks about the right time-scale".[87] Mentioning any of this, would, of course be quite contrary to the tone of the article. Rather than presenting the creation myth as a story and presenting the hidden elements of scientific truth, the article gives a reductive description, preceded by the phrase 'Hindus believe'.

To understand this better, let us compare it with the article in *Encarta* about the Biblical creation myth.

Adam and Eve:

> Adam and Eve, in the Bible, the first man and woman, progenitors of the human race. The biblical account of the creation of human beings occurs twice: in Genesis 1:26–27 and in Genesis 2:18–24. Marked differences in vocabulary, thought, and style between these accounts have led to the scholarly consensus that these creation stories reflect two distinct sources (see 'Bible: The Development of the Old Testament'). In the first account, the Hebrew common noun Adam is used as a generic term for all human beings, regardless of gender; Eve is not mentioned at all. In the second account, Adam is created from the dust of the earth, whereas Eve is created from Adam's rib and given to him by God to be his wife.

The first notable difference is that of the expository technique. The latter article presents different creation accounts in the reading of Biblical texts. Note how this shifts subtly if it were preceded by 'Christians believe . . . ' That there are differences in two different stories in the same book could then be extrapolated, as is done in the article on Hinduism to state: "Christians believe many contradictory things". Instead the article about Adam and Eve treats it as a scholarly study of text (where different 'accounts' are found), rather than conclusive statements about 'Christian belief'. Let us see how one would present a section on Christian 'Philosophy' with the same approach as in the case of Hinduism.

Christianity:

> Christians believe that all humans descend from one man and woman, called Adam and Eve and calculated the age of the world to be about 10,000 years. They believe also that the female Eve was created from male Adam's rib by God to be his wife (which is *used to justify* Christian attitudes towards women such as a historical denial of equal rights).

Christians believe many contradictory things—for example, that an all-loving, forgiving God puts human beings in everlasting Hell, if they sin without repenting in this life. [Emphasis added]

This would be a similarly reductive account presenting 'Christians' as irrational, and failing to grasp the multiple levels of subtleties involved in understanding a religion. As we see in the description of Hinduism, this is precisely the approach of the *Encarta* article.

An account similar to the one in *Encarta* on Adam and Eve would be a neutral objective treatment of similar material in Hindu mythology, rather than a treatment that 'boxes-in' the rich and diverse Hindu cosmology into 'Hindu belief'. Adding the relationships to modern scientific understanding would make it a 'sympathetic' treatment for current audiences. Instead, the *Encarta* article on Hinduism consistently chooses a subtle (and sometimes, not so subtle) negative portrayal.

Despite a very rich philosophical tradition, the anthropological view dominates the article on Hinduism. Both the articles on Christianity and Islam, lead instead with the philosophical ideas. Apparently the broadness of Hindu philosophical ideas like, *Vasudhaiva Kutumbakam* (the world is one family), and the ideas of religious pluralism ("many paths lead to God") that continue to guide most Hindus, find no place in the *Encarta* article.

'Gods'

Nowhere is the anthropological view more apparent than in the treatment of 'Gods'. Firstly, an inadequate attempt is made to put the idea of 'gods' in proper perspective for a Western reader. The word 'deva' in Sanskrit, is less akin to the 'God' of Christianity, but more so to 'angel' (a power higher than man but lesser than 'God'). Secondly, the concepts that 'God' is 'unknowable' and that different deities are thus representations of different aspects (*nama-rupa*) of 'God', is glossed over. The *Encarta* article also completely misses the concept of the Hindu trinity—that any Hindu child could recite—a key idea in the presentation of Brahma, Vishnu and Shiva as creator, preserver and dissolver, and their female counterparts as three aspects of the One God. That the male and the female energies coexist in Indian thought and the idea of God as both male and female (at the same time being beyond gender) is also missed. Having skipped all the structure, the topic of 'Gods' is presented as a confusing 'curio-shop' of unrelated deities and sects, complete with sensational descriptions of blood and gore.

Hinduism:

> Shiva embodies the apparently contradictory aspects of a god of
> ascetics and a god of the phallus. He is the deity of renouncers,
> particularly of the many Shaiva sects that imitate him: Kapalikas,
> who carry skulls to reenact the myth in which Shiva beheaded his
> father, the incestuous Brahma, and was condemned to carry the
> skull until he found release in Benares; Pashupatas, worshippers of
> Shiva Pashupati, 'Lord of Beasts'; and Aghoris, 'to whom nothing
> is horrible', yogis who eat ordure or flesh in order to demonstrate
> their complete indifference to pleasure or pain. Shiva is also the
> deity whose phallus (linga) is the central shrine of all Shaiva
> temples and the personal shrine of all Shaiva householders; his
> priapism is said to have resulted in his castration and the subsequent
> worship of his severed member.

While 'phallus' is just one interpretation of 'linga' there are many
others as well, notably 'symbol' for the divine ([as in] *Lingyate anena
iti lingam*). Apparently the author, whose interests appear to have a
limited focus, continues to find contradictions from that single point
of view—missing both other common interpretations as well as the
underlying symbolisms. A disproportionate interest in the dimension
of esoteric 'sects', 'phallus', 'skulls', 'flesh' and 'ordure' dominates the
article and we find that practices and aspects far more prevalent and
relevant to contemporary times—like Yoga or Chakras, meditation or
mantras, breath and Pranayama are practically absent in the article.

The article continues with these descriptions, clearly showing the
author's interest in particular ways of looking at Hinduism.

Hinduism:

> As Durga, the Unapproachable, she kills the buffalo demon Mahisha
> in a great battle; as Kali, the Black, she dances in a mad frenzy
> on the corpses of those she has slain and eaten, adorned with the
> still-dripping skulls and severed hands of her victims. The Goddess
> is also worshipped by the Shaktas, devotees of Shakti, the female
> power. This sect arose in the medieval period along with the
> Tantrists, whose esoteric ceremonies involved a black mass in
> which such forbidden substances as meat, fish, and wine were eaten
> and forbidden sexual acts were performed ritually.

In this well-embellished description of Kali, the intensity of the
language speaks for itself of the *Encarta's* author's interest in this
particular area.[88] Clearly blood and gore, erotica and exotica are of
much greater interest to this particular writer than Hindu philosophy,

or any of the symbolism of these ancient descriptions. Again, the article shows more interest in the portrayal of esoteric sects and ceremonies than exploring mainstream and commonplace Hindu rituals—like saying 'namaste', the sacred syllable 'Om', lighting *diyas* or wearing *bindis* (the 'dot' on the forehead)—practices that are vastly more familiar to a Westerner and a Hindu child alike, none of which find a place in the *Encarta* article.

The article instead describes various 'Gods' and 'Goddesses', particularly emphasizing the sensational, as we saw in the description of Kali previously, without presenting these within the unifying coherent theme that most Hindus view these manifestations—of different forms of One Supreme Reality, which cannot be boxed into a single set of attributes or descriptions.

As the section on 'Indian Philosophy' in *Encarta* states:

> 'Most of the poems of the Veda are religious and tend to be about the activities of various gods. Yet some Vedic hymns and poems address philosophic themes . . . such as the henotheism *that is key* to much Hindu theology. Henotheism is the idea that one God takes many different forms, and that although individuals may worship several different gods and goddesses, they really revere but one Supreme Being.' [Emphasis added]

Has the *Encarta* article on Hinduism lost all keys? While there is a passing mention of this concept in *Encarta*, it is, characteristically, watered down from the clearer statement above.
Hinduism:

> In this way Hindus *have been able to reconcile* their Vedantic monism (see Vedanta) with their Vedic polytheism: All the individual Hindu gods (who are said to be saguna, 'with attributes') are subsumed under the godhead (nirguna, 'without attributes'), from which they all emanate. [Emphasis added]

A common Hindu saying is—'As you are, so God's image appears to you'—since God is beyond images or attributes, we superimpose our own. Does *Encarta's* choice of subjects and descriptions in the article—scatological and incoherent, reflect the author's own state?

Finally, let us see how the article describes Rama and Krishna, considered as incarnations of God (as Vishnu).
Hinduism:

> Most popular by far are Rama (hero of the Ramayana) and Krishna (hero of the Mahabharata and the Bhagavata-Purana), both of

whom are *said to be* avatars of Vishnu, *although they were originally human heroes.* [Emphasis added]

The article appears to speak with the certainty of divine knowledge! Let us see how a similar issue, the divinity of Jesus is treated in the article on Christianity:

Christianity:

> The ultimate mystery of the universe, called by many different names in various religions, was called 'Father' in the sayings of Jesus, and Christians therefore call Jesus himself 'Son of God.' At the very least, there was in his language and life an intimacy with God and an immediacy of access to God, as well as the promise that, through all that Christ was and did, his followers might share in the life of the Father in heaven and might themselves become children of God.

We note both the subtlety of thought and the sensitivity of expression in description, versus the heavy-handed certainty by which the article on Hinduism speaks, of happenings and events further back in time than the historical Jesus. Is this certainty born out of knowledge of fact, or simply a disregard for the corresponding religious sentiment?

More 'Blood' and Animal 'sacrifice'

The presentation of 'Gods' is not the only place in the article that *Encarta* is interested in gory descriptions—of 'blood', 'skulls', 'ordure' and the like. Starting from the concept of ahimsa (which refers to 'blood sacrifices') to the celebration of the Hindu festival of Holi, this point of view permeates the article. In fact, the *Encarta* article on Hinduism has more references to 'blood' and 'animal sacrifices' than it does to Yoga. Yoga, arguably the most popular contribution of Hinduism to the West is mentioned in two places—both insignificant, as we see later on. Other than the quote above, let us see where else *Encarta* mentions themes related to 'blood' or 'animal sacrifice' in the article on Hinduism.

Hinduism:

> Holi, the spring carnival, when members of all castes mingle and let down their hair, sprinkling one another with cascades of red powder and liquid, symbolic of the blood that was probably used in past centuries.

Let us start with factual inaccuracies—Holi is celebrated with all the colors of spring—green, yellow, red, pink, not just 'red' as the article states. It celebrates the coming of spring with a riot of colors. Factual details aside, for *Encarta* the suggestion of 'cascades of red powder and liquid' works well to further the theme of blood and gore prevalent in the article. This goes on in the description of 'Worship and Rituals'.

Hinduism:

> In many temples, particularly those sacred to goddesses (such as the Kalighat temple to Kali, in Kolkata), goats are sacrificed on special occasions. The sacrifice is often carried out by a special low-caste priest outside the bounds of the temple itself.

Similarly, the majority of Hindus living today have probably never seen an animal sacrifice in their life. Why is this rare practice chosen when we don't find mention of commonplace practices like '*satsang*' (literally, company of truth, or good) meetings where people congregate to communally chant or read from scriptures in orders of magnitude more prevalent? The comment on 'low-caste' that rounds out that quote above is obligatory to keep the 'otherness' of Hinduism on centre stage—a technique we find employed elsewhere in the article.

It is also very worthwhile to compare this overall approach to highlighting 'blood and gore' with the treatment of 'animal sacrifice' in the *Encarta* article on Islam, a religion in which such sacrifices are obligatory that every Muslim is required to perform on Hajj (rather than a rare occurrence).

Islam:

> The final ritual is the slaughter of an animal (sheep, goat, cow, or camel). This is a symbolic reenactment of God's command to Ibrahim to sacrifice his son Ismail, which Ibrahim and Ismail duly accepted and were about to execute when God allowed Ibrahim to slaughter a ram in place of his son. (In the Hebrew and Christian Bibles, Abraham is called to sacrifice his son Isaac rather than Ishmael.) Most of the meat of the slaughtered animals is to be distributed to poor Muslims.

Notice how the stress is on symbolism and how the last line is used to soften the theme. We shall spare the reader a rewrite of the Islamic depiction with details of the animal's severed head and pouring blood and omitting any hint of symbolism. Would an anthropologist probing the Bible many millennia from now condemn Christians as cannibals when reading of Christ's disciples being asked to partake of Christ's 'blood and flesh'? If approached from the point of view of the *Encarta* article on Hinduism, devoid of either sensitivity or an understanding of symbolism, this would probably be the case. Surprisingly, the author chooses this approach to Hinduism, which is a living contemporary tradition rather than simply an anthropological reconstruction of relics and past rituals.

These are choices in both omission and commission that are worth noting. While including exotic details and rituals the author continually misses large and commonplace topics—like the forms of Indian dance as a component of the religion, the celebration of 'Ram Lila'— enactments of Ram's life common throughout the north, and major Hindu celebrations like Janamashtami (Krishna's birth), Raksha Bandhan or Onam.

Where is the real 'Philosophy' and 'Yoga'?

Now that we have read the description in *Encarta* of Aghoris, 'to whom nothing is horrible'—yogis who 'eat ordure or flesh in order to demonstrate their complete indifference to pleasure or pain', we look around for the yogis we have seen or known. Unfortunately, with the concern of the *Encarta* article on Hinduism in looking for scatology, it completely misses the highly refined theology and practices like Raja Yoga or Hatha Yoga or Patanjali or yogic meditation. In fact, the word 'yoga' has exactly two occurrences in the article (other than the one description of 'Aghoris' as yogis above):
Hinduism:

> Many elements of Hinduism that were not present in Vedic civilization (such as worship of the phallus and of goddesses, bathing in temple tanks, and the postures of yoga) may have been derived from the Indus civilization, however. *See* Indus Valley Civilization.

> [...]

> The philosophies of Shankara and Ramanuja were developed in the context of the six great classical philosophies (darshanas) of India: the Karma Mimamsa ('action investigation'); the Vedanta ('end of the Vedas'), in which tradition the work of Shankara and Ramanuja should be placed; the Sankhya system, which describes the opposition between an inert male spiritual principle (purusha) and an active female principle of matter or nature (prakriti), subdivided into the three qualities (gunas) of goodness (sattva), passion (rajas), and darkness (tamas); the Yoga system; and the highly metaphysical

systems of Vaisheshika (a kind of atomic realism) and Nyaya (logic, but of an extremely theistic nature).

The first reference serves to separate Yoga from Hinduism. In the second reference, it is buried in a list of themes, each of which is probably more significant to describe than long-winded descriptions of Kali. Note that this list of classical philosophies is the only significant description of these philosophies in the entire article on Hinduism – that too not in the explicit section for Philosophy, but embedded in the 'Rise of Devotional Movements' section of 'History'.

To be fair to *Encarta*, there does exist a separate article on Yoga that the article on Hinduism does not directly reference. That article states:

Yoga:

As a system of practice, Yoga has from the beginning been one of the most influential features of Hinduism.

Surely, as one of the most influential features of Hinduism, Yoga merits more than a single word (with no link or reference) mention in the article on Hinduism.

In the obsession with external aspects of myth and ritual, blood and gore, the article gives very little space to either the highly developed systems of Hindu theology and philosophy or its most commonplace practices in comparison to the other articles on religion, neither does it link directly to a separate article on Indian philosophy. In the next section we will see a surprising example of what it does choose to include as a link.

Contemporary growth of the religion

There are other differences in detail that consistently add an unsympathetic flavor to the reading on Hinduism. We will end with some examples relating to the contemporary spread of these religions.

Islam:

The Muslim community comprises about 1 billion followers on all five continents, and Islam is the fastest-growing religion in the world.

[...]

Today about 1 billion Muslims are spread over 40 predominantly Muslim countries and 5 continents, and their numbers are growing at a rate unmatched by that of any other religion in the world.

Both in the introduction and conclusion, the article on Islam repeats positively how Islam is growing, almost from the point of view of an evangelist.

Let use see how *Encarta* covers the spread of Hinduism.

Hinduism:

> In more recent times, numerous *self-proclaimed* Indian religious teachers have migrated to Europe and the United States, where they have inspired large followings. Some, such as the Hare Krishna sect founded by Bhaktivedanta, *claim to* base themselves on classical Hindu practices. [Emphasis added]

As is consistent with the tone of the article, notice the deprecating use of 'self-proclaimed' and 'claim to', words rarely used in similar ways in the other articles. The author also fails to mention the fast- growing 'Yoga' movement (which *Time* magazine reported as having over 15 million practitioners in the US) and the large influence of Hindu thought on the 'New Age' movement. The article completely misses movements like 'Transcendental Meditation' of Maharishi Mahesh Yogi and the Self-realization fellowship of Parmahansa Yogananda, or the influence on Americans of the beat generation or the 1960s culture (Swami Satchitananda was called the 'Woodstock guru'), people like George Harrison, Allen Ginsberg, Jack Kerouac, Mia Farrow, or Madonna. To do that would bring Hinduism in, leave it less 'other'. But, unfortunately, the quote above follows the general theme of the article—to obscure or denigrate anything positive, and find and highlight that which is likely to be misunderstood, failing to provide it in the proper context.

The article on Hinduism ends with a bang—something that can aptly demonstrate that deep-seated prejudice and even, perhaps, a political agenda. After failing to have links for 'yoga' or 'Indian philosophy' in the *Encarta* article, at the very end *Encarta* discovers the power of links.

Hinduism:

> For information on religious violence in India, See India.

Is this an appropriate ending for the article on Hinduism? We first surmised that this might be due to some current events (even then it would not be an appropriate ending for an academic article on Hinduism, other than motivated by considerable prejudice). But we find the same ending, for the same article, as far back as *Encarta* 1999! As a crosscheck, let us look at the other articles on religion.

Christianity:

For additional information, see articles on individual Christian denominations and biographies of those persons whose names are not followed by dates.

Islam:

No link suggested at the end

Given the thread of negativity that permeates the *Encarta* article on Hinduism, it comes as no surprise when, in the end, it suggests the topic of 'religious violence' as additional reading. If the articles of Christianity and Islam were written with the same intent, this is what last links could look like.

Christianity*:

For additional information about burning witches at the stake, see Witch Hunt.

Islam*:

For terrorist violence, see International Terrorism.

Again, we do not suggest these endings be used, nor does *Encarta* do so. They are provided for the purpose of illustrating the underlying attitude in choosing such endings—an attitude that pervades the article on Hinduism.

Analysis of Cause

We have established a significant difference in the treatment of Hinduism versus other religions, notably Christianity and Islam. In this section, we look at probable causes for the difference in treatment.

Selection of Authors

Encarta provides the following names and biographical information for the authors of the three *Encarta* articles in question:

- Christianity. Prof. Jaroslav Pelikan, B.D., Ph.D. Sterling Professor Emeritus of History, Yale University. Author of *The Christian Tradition: A History of the Development of Doctrine*, *Historical Theology*, and other books.

- Islam. Ahmad S Dallal, B.E., M.A., Ph.D. Associate Professor of Arabic and Islamic Studies, Yale University. Author of *An Islamic Response to Greek Astronomy: Kitab Ta'dil Hay'at al-Aflak of Sadr al-Shari'a.*
- Hinduism. Doniger, Wendy, M.A., Ph.D., D.Phil. Mircea Eliade Professor of History of Religions and Indian Studies, University of Chicago. Author of *The Origins of Evil in Hindu Mythology, Siva: the Erotic Ascetic,* and *Dreams, Illusion, and Other Realities.*

Emic or Etic?

The first observation we make is that scholars who profess those faiths have written the articles on Christianity and Islam; this is not the case with Hinduism. While the topic of emic (insider) and etic (outsider) study is often debated within academia, we would expect *Encarta* to choose uniformly either the emic or etic view of the major religions. In the *Encarta* article on Christianity, Prof. Jaroslav Pelikan strongly defends the emic viewpoint:

> Like any system of belief and values—be it Platonism, Marxism, Freudianism, or democracy—Christianity is in many ways comprehensible only 'from the inside', to those who share the beliefs and strive to live by the values; and a description that would ignore these 'inside' aspects of it would not be historically faithful. To a degree that those on the inside often fail to recognize, however, such a system of beliefs and values can also be described in a way that makes sense as well to an interested observer who does not, or even cannot, share their outlook.

The same logic, apparently, does not apply to Eastern religions. In general, though not always, we would expect the 'emic' view to be more sympathetic than the 'etic' view, particularly when the 'emic' author is a practising member of their faith.

Areas of interest of the authors

While the orientation of study of Prof. Pelikan and Dallal is towards the philosophical, scientific and theological aspects of the religions they write about, Prof. Doniger's orientation is more anthropological—studying rituals and myths rather than philosophy and theology. Even within that field, Prof. Doniger's dominant area of interest, going by the books she has authored, is in the exotic and erotic aspects of these rituals and myths. Thus the study of Prof. Pelikan and Dallal is a living, practising view of the religion, including theological, metaphysical and scientific issues that would positively engage contemporary audiences; Prof. Doniger's appears to be an archeological dig, turning over quaint specimens that strike her fancy for examination. While this is certainly a valid field for study, it is clear that it leads to very different viewpoints and results in the articles.

Acceptability of the authors in the represented community

The third aspect of authorship is the broad acceptability of the author in the religious community they purport to represent. In general, it is more likely for emic authors to be acceptable, though not universally so. Research on the web shows that while Profs. Pelikan and Dallal are not regarded as controversial, Prof. Doniger has come in for considerable criticism for her lopsided portrayal, and unsubtle understanding of Hinduism.[89] While Hindus, in general, are known for their tolerance of criticism (which is probably why the *Encarta* article has survived, without protest, for several years), we wonder why *Encarta*, as a mainstream encyclopedia, would deliberately choose to continue with authors that are highly controversial within the communities they write about. Note that, particularly in Hinduism, this could be very true for supposedly 'emic', but in reality, non-practising, authors as well.

Deliberate Prejudice or Error?

While there is some evidence of prejudice on the part of *Encarta's* author on Hinduism, it is not clear whether prejudice also exists in *Encarta* as well. Certainly, as the ultimate editorial authority, *Encarta* cannot evade responsibility for the situation, at the very least in the selection of authors and editorial oversight over prejudiced treatment in a sensitive topic like religion. However, *Encarta* may well have, knowingly or unknowingly participated in an environment of bias.

An Eastern graduate student of Hinduism at a US university suggests a broader prejudice:

"... in American academia it is politically incorrect to treat Hinduism in a positive light and it is taboo to deal negatively with Islam".[90]

Certainly, the comparison of the articles in *Encarta* would validate this thesis. However, more study of this topic is clearly required.

Effects

We have not studied the effects of such negative portrayals of Hinduism on Hindu children growing up in America. We can speculate that derogatory mainstream portrayals of Hinduism, quite different from what they have seen or experienced first hand, would at the very least be confusing, and ultimately damaging to the self-esteem of such children. In the author's personal experience, many Hindus are reluctant to identify themselves as such publicly, even when they are practising Hindus—we conjecture that this may result from unconsciously accepting the negative portrayals of their religion. We find that this subject has not been studied much—however, the one study[91] that we found supports this possibility. Such articles in 'Encarta' also get used by various religious fundamentalists and hate groups to label Hinduism a 'cult' —the *Encarta* article serves as a good 'objective' reference to make their point. The interested reader can do a web search on 'Hinduism cult *Encarta*' to find examples. Inaccurate, negative mainstream portrayals of a religion can ultimately only prove harmful to the community. Clearly much more work is needed to study the exact· effects and consequences of such portrayals.

Conclusion and Recommendations

In this article, we compare the treatment of different religions in *Encarta*. We find that there are significant differences in the treatment of Hinduism vs. the treatment of Islam or Christianity in both, the selection of content and the attitude displayed in the writing—resulting in a distinctly negative portrayal of Hinduism vs. the other religions. We conjecture that the reason for this difference is related largely to the differences in choice in the selection of authors—whether they are emic or etic, and their area of interest or specialization in the religion they study. We also find that Prof. Doniger, the author of the *Encarta* article on Hinduism is controversial within the Hindu community.

The authors of the article on 'Islam' and 'Christianity' have a mature and balanced viewpoint and they represent their religions in a way that the vast majority of adherents will find appropriate and positive. We commend *Encarta* for their choice of authors in portraying these religions in a sympathetic way. Unfortunately, the same balance and sympathy is not visible in the article on Hinduism. While we believe that Prof. Doniger is certainly free to pursue her specific areas of interest and scholarship in Hinduism, we do not believe that her article represents the mainstream of Hindu thought in both the selection of content and its interpretation, which would be appropriate for a widely read source such as *Encarta*.

Given that Prof. Doniger's specific interests and attitudes strongly influence the article, it would be insufficient to simply remove a few of the most glaring examples of negativism, while leaving the rest of the article unchanged. We recommend instead that an article written by someone 'emic' to the community, who can represent Hinduism in a positive, mainstream viewpoint, promptly replace the article on Hinduism in *Encarta*.

Epilogue

As a result of the reasoned arguments above, and community activism spurred on by the publication of this article, Microsoft Corporation decided to change the article on Hinduism in *Encarta*. This change is reflected in its 2004 edition. The larger problem of prejudice in Hinduism studies in academia remains unchanged.

Chapter 17

Paul Courtright's '*Ganesa, Lord of Obstacles, Lord of Beginnings*': An Independent Review[92]

By Vishal Agarwal[93] and Kalavai Venkat[94]

Editors' Note:

In this chapter, Vishal Agarwal and Kalavai Venkat provide a detailed review of Paul Courtright's book, *Ganesa, Lord of Obstacles, Lord of Beginnings*. Their analysis raises very troubling questions about the quality and integrity of Courtright's scholarship. Nevertheless, Courtright, Doniger, and her followers, continue to evade these questions about methodology by demonizing their critics.

Doniger has recently adopted an interesting new tactic to silence criticism while simultaneously appealing to American liberals. She has started comparing those who criticize her to fundamentalist Christians opposing the teaching of Evolution in schools. She casts herself in the role of Darwin, as a courageous 'scientist' being attacked by obscurantists who are unwilling to deal with empirical evidence. The allegation is that her critics are irrational. This charge is over and above her prior allegations that her critics—along with their deities and spiritual traditions—are violent and immoral. [95]

She deploys a tactic with deep emotional roots among American liberals going back at least a hundred years, from before the Scopes Monkey Trial. This seminal socio-political event, perceived as the triumph of obscurantism over science still resonates strongly. Many American liberals rightly carry a 'never again' attitude over this issue, with visceral feelings that tie into their personal identity. To enlist liberal sympathies against the Indian–American minority, Doniger disingenuously positions the debate as between scientific reason, represented by her school, and unreason, represented by the Hindu diaspora.

Ironically, most Indian-Americans who have criticized Doniger's scholarship are scientists or professionals with considerable technical training, while Doniger and her cohorts are typically trained in the humanities, and questionably, at that.[96] In addition, many critics within the Hindu diaspora have had lifelong instruction in many Indian languages and in Sanskrit. They have, importantly, knowledge of multiple versions of narratives based on regional differences, chronology, or schools of thought, besides a culturally rooted understanding of texts. Many in the diaspora see the Doniger school's methodologies as empirically flawed, arbitrary, irrational and ultimately harmful to American liberalism, as well as a prejudicial bulwark to the dignified inclusion of Indian-Americans into the American mainstream.

In an interview with a local American newspaper, posted on UChicago's public relations website, Doniger engages in undisguised us-versus-them branding and insinuation by misrepresenting her critics' positions. The newspaper reported that Doniger:

> sees some parallels with the debate in Kansas about how much teaching on creationism should be allowed in the classroom. 'This same fight is going on in my field,' Doniger says. 'Not literally, of course, about Darwin and the Hebrew Bible and Genesis, but whether the scholarly attitude of the events in the history of Hinduism or the faith attitude to the history of the events in the history of Hinduism is the one that should be taught in school. There's a very close parallel.'[97]

The primary problem with her analogy is that the particulars of the 'debate in Kansas' over creationism versus evolution are the inverse of the current situation. The 'fight going on in [Doniger's] field' is not a battle between modern scientific approaches, represented by RISA et al, versus a tradition-bound obscurantist Hindu diaspora. It is a debate between, on the one hand obscure, arbitrary approaches to Hindu Studies based on Eurocentric paradigms and poor evidence, which make unverifiable inferences about the meanings 'of the events in the history of Hinduism' versus an approach to Hindu Studies that insists on rigorous training, accuracy in translation, independent peer-review and cultural authenticity.

The reader should judge for herself whether Doniger is justified in calling her followers' approach to Hinduism 'scientific', i.e. comparable with Darwin or even 'historically accurate'. On the one hand, Courtright's book, carrying Doniger's endorsement, won a prestigious history prize.[98]

Courtright has also tacitly compared himself to noted historians and chroniclers like De Tocqueville and Myrdal, even though he is not trained as a professional historian.[99] Courtright's work was supposedly peer-reviewed by other Western academic scholars prior to publication to ensure scientific rigor in the use of evidence and theory. On the other hand, this chapter demonstrates the value of independent peer-review, when the academic peer-review system is broken. The reader can judge for herself whether Courtright's book is, in fact, scholarly and evidence-based; or relies upon fabricated data, shoddy research and arbitrary theorizing—dressed up with a scholarly gloss to disguise prejudice.

Introductory Remarks:

Background and Importance of Courtright's Book

In the years 2003–2004, a fierce controversy involving Hindu-Americans on one side and certain Indologists on the other, broke out over Paul Courtright's book on the Hindu deity Ganesha. The controversy gathered steam in November 2003 when a chapter of the Hindu Students Council (HSC), at the University of Louisiana, Lafayette, started an online petition criticizing the book. The petition reproduced several passages regarding Lord Ganesha from Courtright's book that were deemed pornographic in nature. Within a matter of days the petition successfully attracted almost 7000 signatures. Unfortunately some anonymous signatories took advantage of the privacy that the Internet offered them and posted death threats to Courtright on the petition. The HSC members who started the petition immediately took if off the website before the situation got out of control.[100] Meanwhile Motilal Banarsidass, which had published the Indian reprint of the book, withdrew it from circulation before the controversy reached Indian shores. The publisher also apologized to the protestors for hurting the religious sentiments of Hindus.

These two developments in turn raised a storm among a section of scholars of South Asian Studies in the American academic community. They went on to denounce the publishers and protestors as 'Hindu fundamentalists' bent on damaging freedom of speech in American Universities by intimidating the author of a 'scholarly', 'sensitive', 'thoughtful', 'peer-reviewed', and 'excellent' book.[101] This generalization is, in our opinion, quite crude and reductionist. We often hear these same academicians sermonize Hindus on how we should approach matters in a nuanced, sensitive, multivalent manner, and that we should consider many different perspectives of an issue. Why are the same people now trying to reduce the situation to an issue of freedom of speech? And why do we get the impression that these scholars are suppressing dissent in the academic discussion lists controlled by them?

Courtright's book cannot be ignored and it is in fact a prominent yet controversial Indological publication for several reasons outlined below. First, the text bears a Foreword by none other than Wendy Doniger, who currently acts as the reigning Czarina of Indological Studies in the United States. She is a cult figure for a very large number of her students, who have a profound influence on how India and Hinduism are depicted at American Universities. Even those who are not her students, nevertheless feel proud of their association with her, such as Courtright. Second, the book has received a national award for its presumed excellence. The award was given in 1985 by the Committee on the History of Religions of the American Council of Learned Societies. It may be noted that the History of Religions as a discipline emerged, for all practical purposes, from the University of Chicago, where Wendy Doniger is now in f. ct a Professor in the History of Religions!

Third, the dissension actually prompted Oxford University Press, one of the most reputed academic printers in the world, to publish a 2003 reprint of the book in the West.

Fourth, its reprint in India was brought out by Motilal Banarsidass, the largest publisher, exporter and distributor of Indological books in the country. As a result, the book was also noticed and commented upon in India. We will refer to some of these reviews in our own extensive comments here.

Fifth, it appears that perverse descriptions of Ganesha from the book have started to creep into mainstream society in the West. For instance, in a recent exhibit on the Hindu deity Ganesha arranged by a museum in Baltimore,[102] the book served as a seminal text that was quoted in citations accompanying the displays.

Sixth, since the publication of the book, Paul B. Courtright has been acknowledged as an authority on the subject of Ganesha. This is evident from the way in which numerous other writers of books on the deity not just acknowledge his help and guidance; they also often quote his text either approvingly or at least in a neutral manner.[103] Conversely, the list of people whom Courtright acknowledges in his book for their help reads like a veritable 'Who's Who' in the world of Hinduism studies in the United States.

Seventh, the book is derived, at least in part, from the author's Ph.D. thesis[104] and therefore should be considered a result of intensive research. The thesis was completed in 1974, eleven years before the publication of the book. It is reasonable to assume that the book therefore contains the fruits of his intensive research as a doctoral student, and perhaps a lot of other subsequent research in the eleven years thereafter. Moreover, the author has published several journal articles on themes related to the subject matter of his book.

Eighth, in the wake of this controversy, a number of professional scholars of Hinduism Studies and in related fields have actually gone on record with whole-hearted praise of the book. Such academic support not just defends Courtright's right to free speech; it actually praises his book for its content and analyses.

Ninth, Courtright has done better professionally than most scholars in Hinduism studies. He is currently a tenured professor and former co-chair of the Department of Religion at Emory University; a feat attributable to the accolades his book has drawn in the past.

Tenth, a cursory search on WorldCat and other electronic catalogs shows that approximately 300 college and school libraries in North America alone have a copy of his book on their shelves. This is a large number for any Indological publication and attests to the widespread acclaim and popularity that his text has attained in American academia, almost to the point of canonization.

Finally, a sourcebook[105] on Hinduism and Psychoanalysis cites long extracts from his book to explain the father-son relationship in the Hindu society! These citations actually constitute some of the most obscene and offensive sections of the book. Obviously according to the editors of this sourcebook, Courtright's psychoanalysis provides seminal understanding of family relationships amongst Hindus!

Being such an important book also means that the controversy raises many other issues besides the question of free speech and academic freedom. In our review, we restrict ourselves to the issue of Paul Courtright's misuse of primary data from Hindu texts for developing his theses. We argue that since the author has taken great liberties with Hindu texts and traditions, his interpretations depend on a flawed set of data and therefore cannot be valid. We shall examine his (mis)use of textual data under different classes of Hindu scriptures. We wish to emphasize that the examples given below are merely illustrative and form a small subset of distortions pervading the book. We will not examine the book from the perspective of a flawed application of psychoanalytical techniques themselves because a review by another author has done this task.[106]

Psychoanalysis and Indology in the United States: When the Cigar becomes a Phallus

Sigmund Freud had a lifelong relationship with cigars.[107] He was rarely photographed without one between his lips. It is said that he enjoyed as many as twenty of them every day. In the declining years of his life, he was beset with some ailments such as arrhythmia, which were blamed on his passion for cigars. On medical advice, he often tried to quit his obsession, but he would always experience withdrawal symptoms. During one such period of abstinence, he even exhibited hysterical behavior in a letter to his physician. When his friends suspected that he was addicted to cigars, he argued that they were a very private aspect of his life that should be insulated from psychoanalysis by others. This disagreement with peers supposedly gave rise to a statement at times attributed to Freud, "Sometimes a cigar is just a cigar." The implication being that people should not see something else in his cigar since it really was just a cigar.

Little did Freud know that several decades later, a 'gutsy' Indian novelist and high-profile socialite Shobha De would write a novel in which a woman sees a cigar lying on a table in front of her, only to discover that it is actually the phallus of her paramour standing nearby. While Freud's cigar was just a cigar, Shobha De's was certainly a phallus. But lest one credits steamy-fiction writers with too much originality, let us hasten to add that *some* Indologists and other academics on Hinduism in the United States foreshadowed Shobha De's innovative use of cigars by at least a decade, albeit in the guise of scholarship.

What we are referring to is the complete *Freudianization* of Indological parlance, or lingo, by a small band of academics. The phenomenon has advanced to such an extent[108] that words and phrases like 'castration', 'flaccid-penis', 'sexual-fantasy', 'erect penis' and such have become a sort of lingua-franca through which the intellectual intercourse of closely-related scholars achieves effect in their academic publications.[109] Wendy Doniger, the doyenne of academic studies on Hinduism[110] has summarized the *weltanschauung* of these scholars in the following words:

Aldous Huxley once said that an intellectual was someone who had found something more interesting than sex; in Indology, an intellectual need not make that choice at all.[111]

After all, did not Courtright's book on Ganesha precede Shobha De's novel by several years?

Who wrote the Mahabharata?

The Foreword to Courtright's book is written by Wendy Doniger O'Flaherty[112] who, in her typical colloquial and superlative style, praises his book without apparently adding anything substantial. Except she does reveal undisclosed lore about the writing of the Hindu epic the *Mahabharata*, " . . . in which Ganesa dictates the epic to Vyasa" (Courtright, viii.)![113] Hindu tradition, however, is unanimous in informing us that it was the Sage Vyasa who dictated the epic to Ganesha rather than the other way around as Doniger states. No, this is not a slip of the tongue on Doniger's part, unless it is some kind of a Freudian slip, because she actually constructs a pseudo-psychology out of her erroneous version of the tradition:

> . . . every book exists in toto in the mind of the elephant-headed god, and we scribes merely scramble to scribble down those bits of it that we can grasp, including the 'knots,' the obstacles to full comprehension, that the god of obstacles throws in on purpose to keep us on our toes and to keep us in awe of him.[114]

Courtright too returns the compliment of Wendy Doniger. He writes:

> A special word of gratitude goes to Wendy Doniger O'Flaherty, who not only shared her vast knowledge of the Puranic literature and Hindu mythology and made many valuable suggestions on several drafts of this book, but also graced this undertaking with her inexhaustible enthusiasm and confidence in its value.[115]

Doniger, for her part, reciprocates the lavish praise. She writes: "This is a book that I would have loved to have written". (Courtright, p.vii).

The mutual admiration club completes its protocol. In Courtright's defense, we must point out that he himself has correctly referred to the tradition about the authorship of the *Mahabharata* in his book (Courtright, pp.151–53). Doniger herself perhaps did not read the book thoroughly even though she wrote the ecstatic Foreword to it.

Lord Ganesha does not get to bask in the glory of his surprise, albeit ephemeral, promotion from a scribe to the narrator of the epic. Courtright brings Ganesha down from the heavenly realms to the earth and transforms him into something of a eunuch, an incestuous son, and a homosexual. Had Ganesha indulged in the ephemeral glory bestowed on him by Doniger then one must indeed pity his naivety, because Doniger had earlier forewarned:

> Ganesa has everything that is fascinating to anyone who is interested in religion or India or both: charm, mystery, popularity, *sexual problems, moral ambivalence,* political importance, the works.[116] [added emphasis].

Doniger had essentially made the same universal claims for Lord Shiva, when she herself wrote one of her first major books on Him in the year 1973.

> The mythology of Siva forms only a part of the material of the Puranas, but it is an ideal model which reveals a pattern which pertains to the material as a whole. Siva is not only an extremely important god; he is in many ways the most uniquely Indian god of them all, and the principles which emerge from an intensive study of his mythology lie at the very heart of Hinduism.[117]

But that was when there were no 'Wendy's Children'. Now she is *the* matriarch of Indology, who will shower her *anugraha* [blessings] on any of her children and *sakhis* [compatriots] who write anything on everything Hindu: the *Rig-Veda,* the *Kathasaritsaagara,* Ganesha, caste, etc. Euphoria and superlatives ooze from the numerous forewords she has written in the last twenty some odd years. Perhaps the author of these forewords is an ideal subject for Freudian studies in her own right.[118] We proceed to review the contents of Courtright's book.

Misuse of Textual Sources

Courtright attempts to base his study on the contents of Hindu texts and then interprets them to derive a particular thesis. The two major classes of texts he deals with are the Vedas and the Puranas. The Tantras and the Upanishads are largely left out, except for a stand-alone translation of the *Ganapati Atharvasirsa Upanishad* in the appendix. In this section, we examine the validity of Courtright's use of Hindu texts in his study.

Dubious Vedic Textual References

In Chapter I, titled 'The Making of a Deity,' he explores the evolution of Ganesha as a deity in the Hindu pantheon from a historical perspective. He begins with the antecedents of the deity in Vedic literature and proceeds to make dubious statements. For instance, while dismissing all Vedic references as evidence that the worship of Ganesha was known when the Vedic texts were the primary source of Hindu practice, he says:

> A similar invocation in another Brahmanic text addresses 'the one with the twisted trunk [*vakratunda*]' (Tā 10.1.5), also leaving it uncertain whether it is Ganesa or Siva who is being addressed.[119]

This is puzzling, because vakratunda is distinctly another name for Ganesha. Moreover, the last portion of the mantra (called the *Vighneshvaragayatri* in the Hindu tradition) reads—*tanno dantih pracodayaat* (*Taittiriya Aranyaka* 10.1.5), which is clearly a reference to the tusk of Ganesha.[120] Courtright also mistakenly classifies the text as 'Brahmanic' or from the Brahmanas, whereas in reality it is a mantra. Another obvious reason why this mantra containing the word vakratunda refers to Ganesha and not to his father Shiva is that the preceding mantra is in fact addressed to Mahadeva and Rudra (other names of Shiva), and the mantra after the *Vighneshvaragayatri* is addressed to Nandin, the mount or vehicle of Shiva. Moreover, the mantra that follows the *Nandigayatri* is addressed to the brother of Ganesha, Karttikeya. Thus from the words of the mantra and its context as well, we should infer that this mantra is clearly addressed to the deity Ganesha and not to Lord Shiva.[121] The parallel mantra in *Maitrayani Samhita* 2.9.1 reads *hastimukhaaya* (one with an elephant head) in lieu of *vakratundaaya* and this should again clinch the matter.[122]

Referring to Ganapati in *Aitareya Brahmana* 1.21, Courtright again claims that the reference is to Shiva (Courtright, p.9). The actual text reads "*ganaanaam tvaa ganapatim havaamah iti brahmanaspat-yambrahma vai . . .* ," showing that here Ganapati actually refers to Brahmanaspati (=Brihaspati) and not to Shiva. In fact, the Brahmanic text clearly refers here to *Rig-Veda* 2.23.1 that reads,

ganaanaam tvaa ganapatim havaamahe
kavim kaviinaam upamasravastamam
jyeshtaraajam braahmanaam brahmanaspata
aa nah srnvann uutibhih siida saadanam

The mantra is addressed to Brihaspati, who is indeed the *devataa* of this mantra according to *Saunakiya Brihaddevata*.[123]

Finally, Courtright claims that 'TB [Taittiriya Brahmana]10.15'[124] contains the word *dantin*. This reference by Courtright is problematic because *Taittiriya Brahmana* is divided into 3 books that are further divided into smaller sections. Therefore, the citation of TB 10.15 does not make much sense. The Vedic Word Concordance of *Vishvabandhu*[125] also does not indicate any occurrence of the word *dantin* in the entire *Taittiriya Brahmana*.[126] Courtright attributes the textual reference to a publication of Louis Renou.[127] After referencing Renou's article, however, we did not find any mention at all of the *Taittiriya Brahmana* in it. The reference in Renou's article is in fact to *Maitrayani Samhita* 2.9.1. The presence of so many erroneous and apparently invented textual citations in just one page of the book is simply unacceptable from an academic perspective.

Errors of Vedic citations are seen in other parts of the book as well. For instance in Chapter II of his book, Courtright claims: "The association of the thigh with the phallus in the Indian tradition dates from the *Rig Veda* (RV 8.4.1)."[128] The mantra in question reads:

yadindra praagapaagudam nyag vaa uuyase nrbhih
simaa puruu nrshuuto asyaanave.asi prashardha turvashe

Ralph Griffith's translation reads—

Though Indra, thou are called by men
eastward and westward, north and south,
Thou chiefly art with Anava and Turvasa,
brave Champion! urged by Men to come.[129]

There is no reference to the penis or thighs here.[130] We therefore question what Courtright was thinking.[131] A majority of references to Vedic texts by Courtright in Chapter I of his book and others in subsequent chapters are either interpreted incorrectly, or they are non-traceable.[132] Thus we question if Courtright even had a first hand, or even a reasonable second hand, knowledge of Vedic texts when he wrote his book.[133]

The examples we have cited here are for illustrative purposes only and do not constitute the entire list of errors in his Vedic citations. Despite the sloppiness of textual citations, Chapter I has two merits. First, it dismisses various prevalent theories about the origin of worship of Ganesha as variations on the Dravidian hypothesis, which are mere speculations not based on any concrete evidence.[134] This does not mean that he does not use the myth of the Aryan and Dravidian divide as a hermeneutic tool in his book. He uses it several times. But in the case of Ganesha, he elaborates later:

> The demon lineage from raaksasa, marut, and vinaayaka to Ganesa further supports the argument that Ganesa emerges from within the network of Aryan and Vedic symbolism in contrast to the view that he is an outsider from a Dravidian or non-Aryan folk tradition.[135]

The second merit of this chapter is that he proposes an alternative, novel hypothesis to explain how the worship of the deity came into prevalence. The explanation is pure speculation as well, but could nevertheless be treated as an alternative hypothesis by future researchers.

Mythology of Ganesa and Abuse of Puranic Texts

Chapter II of the book, titled 'Mythology of Ganesa,' deals with the different ways in which academics studying religion can approach the mythology of the deity. Courtright lists five such levels, of which Wendy Doniger is credited for explicating the first four while the fifth is Courtright's own contribution. This particular chapter seems to focus on the first or 'narrative' level, in which the story of the deity is stated in all its versions. This section of our review deals primarily with Chapter II of the book.

Varying divergent and convergent versions of the story of Ganesha are scattered throughout a diverse set of Hindu texts belonging to different centuries. Courtright treats these texts in a combined, holistic manner to explore the thematic, structural, and interpretative dimensions of these myths. He claims that his analyses are only peripherally affected by chronological considerations of these texts. Courtright says that he has treated all Puranic accounts as belonging to a single ongoing tradition in order to paint his picture of Ganesha.[136] We believe that this is *not* a sound approach, because each of the Puranas catered to the needs of a particular Hindu sect and some of them are known to display sectarian rhetoric against other sects and their deities. Some of these Puranic depictions tend to project the deities of a rival sect in a less than glorious light. Each sect had its own traditions that influenced the Puranas they wrote. Specific traditions were not necessarily influenced by the way a deity was portrayed by the Puranas belonging to a different sect.

Winternitz presents a very relevant example to demonstrate this sectarian bias, bordering on the absurd, as reflected in the Puranas regarding the deities of a rival sect. He draws readers' attention to the Uttarakhanda section of the *Padma Purana* that narrates a story of Shiva. Once, a quarrel arises among the sages as to which of the three gods, Brahma, Vishnu or Shiva is the greatest, and Bhrigu is made the adjudicator. He repairs to the mountain Kailasa where Shiva enjoys the love of his wife. Nandin, Shiva's mount and guard, prevents Bhrigu from entering.[137] Bhrigu takes this as an insult and curses Shiva to take on the shape of the Linga, to be worshipped not by Brahmins but only by heretics.[138]

Often, such narratives turn out to be later day interpolations, as is the case with the above example cited by Winternitz.[139] The question readers should ask is, what historical impact did this narrative of the *Padma Purana* have on the practitioners of Shaivism? The answer has been none. They simply ignored it and were quite content interpreting the meaning and significance of the Linga according to the Puranas of their own tradition.[140] This is true of any Hindu tradition, including those of worshipping Ganesha. To postulate only a single interpretation of a tradition using the divergent narratives found in the text of a rival tradition would be a problematic methodology and approach.

We get the feeling that the selection of such a questionable methodology is intentional and is done to force the data to fit preconceived notions. Through this 'methodology', Courtright uncritically uses every source, including those that are anecdotal and hence not verifiable, to taint Ganesha.

Elephant Mythology and Omission of Important Texts

Courtright initiates the discussion by first devoting a section to the symbolism of the elephant in Indian culture.[141] The treatment is rather uncertain and he surprisingly omits the mention of texts specifically referring to elephants—the *Gajasastra* or the *Hastyayurveda*.[142] The omission is unfortunate because Courtright primarily relies on, amongst other texts, the Puranas, when some of them (e.g., *Agni Purana*) actually refer to the authority of Palakapya Muni, the author of the *Hastyayurveda*. Courtright enumerates a number of metaphors for elephants in Indian culture but omits two very important attributes of the creature for which they are especially well respected, their profound memory, and their longevity. The elephant is also counted as one of the nine types of wealth or treasures (*navanidhi*) in the Hindu tradition. A discussion on all these would have enriched Courtright's study considerably, because these themes are very important in how Hindus perceive this noble creature.

Even more detrimental to the quality of his study is the scarce use (if not a total omission) of the two Puranas that specifically deal with Ganesha the Mudgala Purana and Ganesha Purana.[143] Courtright mentions editions of both of them in his bibliography, but practically ignores the former,[144] and uses the latter very rarely. Even when he does, most of the citations of the Ganesha Purana appear to be taken from secondary studies on the text, not from the original text itself. The scanty use of these important traditional texts detracts from the comprehensiveness and objectivity of his analysis. We shall give a few examples in this review, showing how data from these two Puranas invalidates some of the speculations of Courtright.

The elephant is also considered a noble animal, and a symbol of devotion (bhakti) via the story of Gajendramoska in Bhagavata Purana, skandha VIII, chapter 204 and other texts. Courtright ignores these aspects of elephant mythology here, dealing with it later[145] in relation to Ganesha where it really does not belong.[146] In his zeal to force-fit this story into the model of tension between asceticism and eroticism,[147] he interprets it in a very inconsistent and illogical manner. We will critique his interpretation of the Gajendramoksha episode a little later.

Instead of discussing these ways in which Hindus look at the creature, Courtright says:

> Elephant trunk and serpent share certain undeniable characteristics and carry associations of force and power, both political and sexual.[148]

We are not told why this association is 'undeniable'. This baseless assertion would serve as his launching pad for declaring elsewhere:

> The elephant trunk, which perpetually hangs limp, and the broken tusk are reminiscent of Siva's own phallic character, but as these phallic analogs are either excessive or in the wrong place, they pose no threat to Siva's power and his erotic claims on Parvati.[149]

Courtright says that an elephant, even if it were male, cannot be assigned any definitive sex because its movement is often compared to the graceful movement of a woman, and its temple, like a woman's breasts, give forth a different but no less desirable fluid. If this hypothesis sounds unreasonable, then it is outsmarted by the ensuing inference that since Ganesha is an elephant-headed god, his gender too must remain less than precisely articulated.[150] An illogical premise invariably leads to ridiculous conclusions, and Courtright doesn't fail to disappoint on this count. He concludes that Ganesha's head symbolizes phallic masculinity and feminine grace.[151]

Though Courtright uses several dubious, peripheral, and regional myths of doubtful veracity and non-verifiable antiquity to construct his thesis (we shall refer to some of these below), he practically leaves out the Tantric texts. This omission is again unfortunate, because these texts clearly distinguish between the deity's trunk and the phallus (whereas Courtright equates the deity's trunk to a limp phallus) and also describe clearly the functionality of these two organs. But then, incorporation of data from the Tantras would have dealt a deathblow to his 'celibate-eunuch-limp phallus' thesis on Ganesha. If one chooses data from Sanskrit texts in the piecemeal manner that Courtright does, any thesis can be 'proven' from them.

Misdating Puranic Texts

In the sole appendix to his book, the author claims[152] that the *Sri Ganapati Atharvasirsha Upanishad* probably belongs to the sixteenth or seventeenth century. He assigns no reason for this late date, something that other scholars have also noted and have found inconsistent with their own views.[153] Elsewhere, Courtright claims that the *Mudgala Purana* should be dated between the fourteenth and the seventeenth century, but again assigns no reasons.[154] However, on page 214 of the book, Courtright dates the Purana from fourteenth to sixteenth centuries. This would mean that the *Atharvasirsha Upanishad* is roughly contemporaneous or even later than the *Mudgala Purana*. However, the *Mudgala Purana* (2.31.12; 2.72.5, etc.)[155] clearly mentions the *Ganapati Atharvasiras* text, and therefore should be sufficiently later than the Upanishad, contrary to what Courtright implies.[156] Courtright certainly recognizes the difficulty of dating Puranic texts,[157] but he should have been more careful before assigning his own dates to them.[158]

Earlier we saw that Courtright's references to the Vedic texts in Chapter I were largely dubious. Chapters II and III of his book rely mainly on the Puranas. To ascertain whether Courtright has shown sufficient fidelity to the Puranic texts, we crosschecked his descriptions of the story of Ganesha with the original texts of the Puranas. To illustrate our findings, we chose only a few of these texts below, for the sake of brevity. We have also chosen a text from the *Buddhacharita* that is misinterpreted by Courtright.

A Beheading by the Compassionate One (Buddhacarita)

In Ashvaghosha's *Buddhacarita*, there occurs a story in which Devadatta sent a mad elephant to kill Bhagavan Buddha. However, when the elephant approached the Buddha, the latter's spiritual power tamed the creature. According to the text, as quoted by Courtright, the Buddha then stroked the head of the elephant.[159] A reader would normally interpret the Buddha 'stroking the head' of the tamed elephant as an act of blessing or benevolence, of compassion and love. Courtright, however, suggests, "... his hand strokes the head in what may be a faint echo of a gesture of decapitation".[160]

Readers familiar with Indian television would perhaps recall a scene in which an elephant raises his trunk to salute the Kanchi Acharya Jayendra Sarasvati. The Acharya in turn approaches the elephant after it lowers its trunk and then goes on to pat its head. Since Courtright sees a flaccid penis in the non-raised trunk of Ganesha, he would perhaps interpret the raised trunk in the televised scene an 'erect' penis and the patting of the creature's head as castration. He could then see the lowering of the trunk by the elephant before the Acharya pats it as the triumph of asceticism over eroticism! The point we are making here is that such Freudian interpretations are quite bunkum, and their juiciness depends merely on how fertile the imagination of the Freudian interpreter is.

Eroticization of Gajalakshmi in Vishnu Purana:

Courtright correctly identifies a passage from the *Vishnu Purana* 1.9.103 in which, when Devi Lakshmi emerges during the churning of the Ocean and the River Ganga, other sacred rivers appear at the site.[161] The celestial elephants then pour water from these sacred rivers on her with *golden* vessels. A few pages later he transforms this into a sexually titillating narrative:

> The male attributes of the elephant are so obvious as to need no comment. Not only the trunk but the tusk has phallic associations in some of the Ganesa stories. The myth of the elephant guardians anointing Lakshmi by spraying water over her seems the fullest expression of male fertility surrounding female fecundity. As O'Flaherty has shown, moreover, rain tends to be associated with male seed in the Indian tradition, whereas rivers appear as symbolic expressions of the feminine aspect of water ... [162]

Per conventions of Hindu tradition, Lakshmi and Ganesha stand in relation to each other as mother and son.[163] Courtright's erotic explanation in effect transforms the innocuous description of the Puranas into a tale of incest. In fact, it was and is fairly common in India for holy men, princes, and other great men to be honored by· flowers and with water poured on them by elephants. Would Courtright interpret all these as suggestive of homosexual encounters? Moreover, the text of the *Vishnu Purana* clearly states that the elephants take the waters of feminized rivers. So it is surprising that, according to Courtright and Doniger O'Flaherty, the waters from feminine rivers would be transformed suddenly into virile semen after the elephants pour them over Lakshmi. What we are trying to suggest is that the 'analysis' by Courtright is nothing but his own perverse imagination. We are in fact surprised why he failed to see the connection between '*hiranyam*' (=gold, light, brightness) and '*retas*' (=seed, semen) in the Hindu tradition[164] to further argue that the feminine river water changed its sex to masculine semen in the *gold*-pitchers used by the elephants to pour river waters over Lakshmi!

Conversely, Courtright misses some relevant passages in the *Ganesha Purana* (Upasana-khanda 15.1–7) in which Brahma has a vision of a banyan tree and sees the *baalaganesa* (baby-Ganesha) playing on a leaf of the tree. Brahma wonders how a human baby with an elephant head arrived there and how the tree itself could survive the waters of deluge. Suddenly the *baalaganesa* lifts his trunk and sprinkles water on Brahma's head. Brahma is filled with both joy as well as anxiety and bursts into laughter. According to the Courtright-Doniger's methodology, Brahma's dream should perhaps be interpreted as a homo-erotic fantasy because an 'erect' trunk sheds 'semen' on Brahmaji's 'head'. In any case, such passages clearly negate Courtright's 'limp-phallus' fantasy about Ganesha's trunk, which we will discuss in more detail later as well.

Inventing Mankind from the Divine Arse (The Linga Purana and The Bhagavata Purana)

Courtright claims:

Some Puranic sources maintain that demons and humans have come from the divine rectum (BhP 2.6.8; LP 1.70.199; cf. O'Flaherty 1976, p. 140)."[165]

This claim of Courtright and Wendy Doniger does not stand to scrutiny. Neither the *Linga Purana* nor the *Bhagavata Purana* derives mankind from the 'divine rectum'.

Let us consider relevant passages from the *Linga Purana* first. Prajapati desires to produce four kinds of creatures, so he merges with waters and meditates on creation. In the meantime, darkness sets in, and out of his anus are produced the asuras. The text also explains the etymological meaning of 'asura' (*Linga Purana* 1.70.197–99). Then he casts off that body, creates another one that was resplendent. From the mouth of that body are born the *devas* (*Linga Purana* 1.70.200–205). He casts off this divine body as well and assumes another one full of goodness. *Pitrs* are created from the sides of this body (*Linga Purana* 1.70.206–211). Finally, he casts off that body of goodness, and creates another one characterized by passion. From the **mind** of this body are born men (*Linga Purana* 1.70.212–25ab). The meaning of these verses will be very clear to anyone who has a little familiarity with the Hindu scriptural tradition. These verses involve a bit of word play and a bit of allegory. The *devas* are indeed the resplendent or the shining ones,[166] and Agni *devata* is considered the 'mouth' into which worshippers pour their oblations during Vedic rituals, or *yajnas*. Human beings ('*manushya*' in Sanskrit) are said to be descendants of Manu, a word which itself is associated with 'thinking', or 'reflection' which is an attribute of the mind ('*manas*'). Similarly, it is not difficult to understand the creation of asuras (= demons) from the divine rectum because they are embodiments of sin, evil, and filth in classical Hinduism. Creation of men and women from the two halves of Prajapati or Brahma[167] is a recurrent theme in Hindu narratives of creation. This explains the birth of *Pitrs* (elders) from two sides of Prajapati's body.

Coming to the *Bhagavata Purana*, the text deals with the mythical creation of various parts of the Universe from different parts of the body of the Creator God. The verse (*Bhagavata Purana* 2.6.8) cited by Courtright and Doniger actually reads:

apam viryasya sargasya parjanyasya prajapateh
pumsah sina upasthas tu prajaty-ananda-nirvrteh |

According to this verse, the genitals of God are the source of water, rains, and semen, i.e. the *procreative power* of humans and the pleasure associated with coitus. There is no mention of anus or of men. The next verse (*Bhagavata Purana* 2.6.9) then continues:

payur yamasya mitrasya parimoksasya narada
himsaya nirrter mrtyor nirayasya gudam smrtah |

Here, the anus and the rectal region of the Creator are related to death, violence, ill fortune, and hell.

Apparently, Doniger (and following her, Courtright) misread '*mitrasya*' in the above text as '*marttyasya*'.[168] The text of the Purana published by ISKCON has the reading we have reproduced above. We also crosschecked the reading of another edition of *Bhagavata Purana*.[169] In that edition the words, '*payur yamasya mitrasya parimoksasya narada*' form the second half of verse 2.6.8. But in this edition also, the text reads '*mitrasya*' and human beings are mentioned only much later and are not related to the 'divine rectum' at all. In short, the creation of mankind from 'The Arse' is not stated or implied in the texts cited by Doniger or Courtright. It is pure fiction invented by them.

Misinterpretations of the Kurma Purana:

The Dropping of Shiva's Phallus:[170]

Following a 1975 book by Wendy Doniger, Courtright interprets a tale in *Kurma Purana* 2.37 in the following words:

> The variant of the beheading tale introduces the act of self mutilation by which Ganesa tears out his own tusk and holds it like a yogin's staff, like his father holds the trident. The gesture is reminiscent of the time his father broke off his own phallus when he saw it was no longer of use except to create progeny (KP 2.37; O'Flaherty 1975, pp. 137–141). This act of self-mutilation makes Ganesa more like his father.[171]

The claim that, "[Siva] broke off his own phallus when he saw it was no longer of use except to create progeny" is a contrived interpretation of *Kurma Purana* 2.37. The context is actually this: Once upon a time, several thousands of sages, along with their wives and sons, practised intense austerities in a forest while also remaining engaged in worldly life. Lord Shiva wanted to demonstrate the great fault in mixing worldly life with penances, and therefore he and Lord Vishnu respectively assumed the form of a handsome man and a beautiful woman. They approached the settlement, with Lord Shiva naked, and Lord Vishnu (in the form of a woman) dressed beautifully. Upon seeing them, the wives of the sages were filled with passion for Lord Shiva, while the sages and their sons themselves were attracted towards the woman. Soon the sages realized what was going on and they approached Lord Shiva in great anger, asking him to put on his clothes and abandon his own wife (the female form of Lord Vishnu).

They also cast suspicion on the character of the lady (the female form of Lord Vishnu). Lord Shiva replied that he was an ascetic and rules of modesty did not apply to him. Moreover, he argued that his wife was pure and that the sages' accusations were unfair. Outsmarted, the hypocritical sages started assaulting Lord Siva physically and asked him to castrate himself. Lord Shiva replied that he would gladly do so if their enmity were with his linga (*Kurma Purana* 2.37.40). However, as soon as he did so, the world became dark, and the sages were unable to see Lord Shiva, Lord Vishnu and even the linga (*Kurma Purana* 2.37.41). As the story continues eventually Lord Brahma explained to the sages that all their sacrifices, Vedic learning and meditation are fruitless if they do not aspire to know Mahaadeva, and also described the glory of worship of the *shivalinga*. Therefore the statement of Courtright-Doniger that: "The gesture is reminiscent of the time his father broke off his own phallus when he saw it was no longer of use except to create progeny . . . " has no relationship to the context of the relevant passages of *Kurma Purana*.

The Beheading of Daksha:

In another case of misinterpretation of the same text, Courtright says:

> He [Siva] attacks Daksa's sacrifice, beheading him and turning his head into the sacrificial offering, thus completing the rite that he had originally set out to destroy (KP 1.14).[172]

The *Kurma Purana* actually says quite the opposite. Daksha conducts a Vedic sacrifice but does not offer anything to Lord Shiva. The Sage Dadhici urges him to include Lord Shiva also but Daksha refuses saying that all the other devatas are already present and he does not recognize Lord Shiva as a deity. All the deities and sages then leave, boycotting the sacrifice. Only Lord Vishnu stays back and Daksha seeks refuge in him. Nevertheless, Lord Shiva does arrive with his attendants. The latter go on a warpath, ruining the sacrifice and attacking the minor deities. At this juncture, Daksha realizing his mistake offers homage to Parvati (*Kurma Purana* 1.14.71), who intercedes on his behalf with Lord Shiva (*Kurma Purana* 1.14.71–73). Lord Shiva instructs Daksha to include all the deities and also himself in his sacrifices. This is followed by a sermon to Daksha by Lord Brahma who describes the greatness of Lord Shiva and then asks Daksha not to differentiate between Lord Shiva and Lord Vishnu because they are not separate, and therefore he should be devoted to both of them.[173]

To conclude, the *Kurma Purana* version of the narrative does not mention any beheading of Daksha by Lord Shiva, contrary to Courtright's assertion.

The Vamana Purana *on the Birth of Ganesa and 'Sexual Fluids'*

Describing a version of the story of the birth of the deity, Courtright states:

> The first type of story is represented by the accounts of Ganesa arising out of the sexual fluids of Siva and Parvati after their bath, but outside Parvati's body (Vamana Purana 28.64–66) ... [174]

Unfortunately, the bibliography section of Courtright's book shows that he used the non-critical edition of the Purana. We compared this edition with the critical edition of *Vamana Purana*.[175] The relevant text (*Vamana Purana* 28.65) clearly reads:

> *snaatastasya tatoadhastaat sthithah sa malapuurushah*
> *umasvedam bhavasvedam jalamrtisamanvitam*

The text explicitly says that the drops of sweat of Uma (=Parvati) and Bhava (=Shiva) fell on moist earth and from this combination sprang Ganesha (verse 66). There is no explicit mention of 'sexual fluids', which is characteristic of Courtright's Freudian analysis. Later in the chapter too, he terms their sweat as, 'fluids of their lovemaking' and as 'sexual fluids'.[176] Courtright may argue that various erotic Indian texts[177] do mention passionate lovemaking causing the lovers to sweat. This textual passage, however, directly stresses the asexual birth of the deity. Thus, it states that when the intercourse of Siva and Parvati was interrupted by the machinations of the gods, Shiva discharged his semen as an oblation to Agni (*Vamana Purana* 28.50), and after Ganesha is born, Shiva names him as Vinaayaka because Parvati gave birth to him without the help of a *naayaka* or husband (*Vamana Purana* 28.71–72ab). Hence, to see the birth of Ganesha from the 'sexual fluids' of Parvati and Shiva is a bit farfetched. The text certainly does not say so or hint at it. Rather, the text seems to glorify Shiva and Parvati by suggesting that even the sweat and dirt of their bodies is so potent that the mere combination of the two can result in the birth of a great deity such as Ganesha.[178] Courtright's interpretations merely seek to amplify (if not invent altogether) the sexual connotations of these sacred stories.[179]

Another recent review of Courtright's book clarifies our objection in the following words:[180]

The authors or Compilers of the Puranas are very frank and open. When they mean such sexual symbolism they state it openly. When they want to say that a person or even a deity is too much interested in sex they frankly say so and some times punish them also, as in the case of Indra and Brahma . . . It is advisable, therefore, not to read too much between the lines. As far as possible, such attempts of trying to find relevance of the ancient texts in connection with the modern phenomena, may it be science or the Freudian principles, should be avoided by scholars.

Earlier in his book, the author claims that a Marathi idiomatic expression *ganapatice kele* means 'to conceive a child' (p.6). The same reviewer as above, a Maharashtrian herself, disagrees, pointing out that at best: "This might be present in some particular region of community. It is not commonly known". One of the present reviewers has also lived in Maharashtra for more than 5 years and has not come across this idiomatic expression in Marathi.

Another example of excessive interpretation is Courtright's insistence[181] that the story of Ganesha growing to the size of the earth after Parvati threw him into the river recalls and mirrors the luminous Shivalinga growing to an infinite size so that both Lord Vishnu and Lord Brahma were unable to reach its ends in a version of the *Shiva Purana*. After all he must eventually link everything to a *linga*. The description of particular deities growing to an infinite size is in fact a generic theme in Hindu sacred lore. Thus, we also have the case of Yashoda seeing the entire Universe inside Krishna's mouth[182], of Krishna assuming an infinite form (the *Vishvarupa*) in the *Gita*, or of the Vamana Avatara of Lord Vishnu growing from a dwarf to a stupendous size to measure the three worlds in two strides.

Misrepresentation of the Gajendramoksha *Episode (*Bhagavata Purana, Skandha VIII*):*

The *Gajendramoksha* narrative, occurring in the eighth book (*skandha*) of the *Bhagavata Purana* (BhP), is a beautiful tale of devotion and divine grace that continues to inspire millions of Hindus even to this day.[183] The central theme of the narrative is that no measure of worldly power and happiness can save us in the time of dire calamity, only God can. Here is how Courtright looks at the story:

> Once, the king of the elephants, along with his wives and children came to a splendid garden at the foot of the mountain that was surrounded by an ocean like the ocean of milk. With musk fluid

oozing from his forehead, with bees swarming around it, the elephant plunged into the ocean to cool himself. He sprayed water over the females and the females and the young ones bathed and drank. Then a mighty alligator, which had become angry at this intrusion into the ocean, seized hold of the elephant's foot and held it fast in his jaws. When the wives of the elephant king saw that he was being dragged further and further into the ocean, they tried in vain to pull him back out. As the alligator and the elephant struggled with one another, the elephant became increasingly weaker while the alligator grew stronger. When he saw that he could not free himself from the trap of alligator's jaws, the elephant called out to Vishnu for refuge. When Vishnu saw the elephant's plight, he came there and pulled the elephant and the alligator out of the water. He transformed the alligator back into Huhu, the celestial gandharva who had been cursed by the sage Devala [Narada] because he had been sporting in the water with some women when Devala wanted to bathe. When Huhu pulled on Devala's leg he was cursed to take the form of an alligator, only to be rescued from it by seizing hold of the leg of an elephant. (BhP 8.204)[184]

Apparently the address 'BhP 8.204' is a typographical error in place of BhP 8.2–4. After summarizing a longish story, Courtright then interprets the tale in the following sexualized manner:

In this myth of conflict between the alligator and the elephant, we see some similarities to the myths of Airavata and Durvasas. At the conclusion of the myth, we learn that the alligator is really a disguise of an erotic *gandharva,* who had been cursed by the ascetic Devala for touching him while he was bathing, much as the flying elephants had been cursed by the sage Dirghatapas when they brushed against the tree under which he was sitting. By transforming the *gandharva* Huhu into an alligator, the ascetic reverses their roles, for now the alligator is the one whose watery territory is invaded by the elephant. His biting the leg of the elephant echoes the theme of beheading, which we have seen at work in other myths. The conflict between the alligator and the elephant surrounded by his entourage of cows—like the conflicts between the sage and the *gandharva,* between Siva and Gajasura, and between Durvasas and Indra—draws on the important theme in Hindu mythology of the tension between the powers of eroticism and asceticism. The tension between the alligator and the race elephant cannot be resolved, and so they both edge their way to destruction. At this desperate moment the myth turns to the solution of *bhakti . . .* [185]

In this manner, Courtright goes on and on with his racy language, bringing disparate, unrelated facts picked up selectively, and then forces them to fit together artificially and unconvincingly into models of 'beheading', 'tension between the powers of eroticism and asceticism' and so on. How does he do this exactly?

First, he enhances the sexual connotations of the passage in *Bhagavata Purana*. Though his summary is fairly *short*, considering that the text extends over 92 verses, Courtright does not refrain from amplifying the aspects that suit his theory. An example is the use of the words, 'with musk fluid oozing from his forehead'. The original text reads (*Bhagavata Purana* 8.2.23–24),

> *sa gharma-taptah karibhih karenubhir vrto madacyut-karabhair anudrutahgirim garimna-paritah prakampayan nisevyamano 'likulair madasanaih saro*
> *nilam pankaja-renu-rusitam jighran viduran mada-vihvaleksanah vrtah sva-yuthena trsarditena tat sarovarabhyasam athagamad drutam |*

In these verses, the word '*madacyut*'[186] could certainly mean that the elephant king was in rut, and this meaning is supported by the mention of the '*likulaih madasanaih*' (intoxicated black-bees)[187] following him. However, what needs to be kept in mind is that in accordance with the excellent poetical character of the *Bhagavata Purana*, the narrative in this chapter of the Purana merely conforms to the embellished *kaavya* style and a "somewhat pallid erotic tinge, derived from stereotypical landscape descriptions in the Sanskrit courtly kaavya ... emerges in one or two verses ... ".[188] In other words, the so-called 'eroticism' in these verses is 'formulaic', and only incidentally a part of the long narrative of this chapter, whose main intent is to describe the lordliness, the arrogance, the marital bliss and familial happiness of Gajendra, in conjunction with the beauty of his surroundings. Moreover, Gajendra is surrounded not only by his wives, but also his children. He is happy with his life, and even arrogant, crushing numerous creepers and thickets on his way to the ocean (verse 20), terrifying the large animals of the forest (verse 21), but yet showering his grace on the smaller creatures (verse 22). Yet, when the powerful lordly elephant, supported by his wives (and also his male elephant friends, according to verse 28—a detail that Courtright conveniently leaves out) fights the alligator without any success, he realizes (*Bhagavata Purana* 8.2.33–34).

*na mam ime jnataya aturam gajah kutah karinyah prabhavanti mocitum
grahena pasena vidhatur avrto'py aham ca tam yami param parayanam|
yah kascaneso balino 'ntakoragat pracanda-vegad abhidhavato
bhrsam bhitam prapannam paripati yad-bhayan mrtyuh pradhavaty
aranam tam imahi|*

(These other elephants, my relatives, are unable to save me in my misery—how much less so can my wives! Caught in destiny's snare embodied by this monster, I shall take refuge with the Supreme. There must be some god who protects a frightened person who turns to him from powerful Death, running after him like a vicious serpent—I seek refuge with that god, Whom Death himself flees in fear.[189])

The besieged creature then bursts forth in a splendid hymn of praise and entreaty to Lord Vishnu. Hearing the prayers of his devotee, the deity appears mounted on Garuda, his vehicle bird. Gajendra is freed of course, but so strong is the salvation-granting power of God that even the alligator is released from his ugly body and transformed into a *gandharva*. The narrative then reveals the tale of the previous life of Gajendra, when he was a pious king of the Pandya kingdom, and ends with verses describing the fruits of hearing this tale of devotion.[190]

So when Courtright emphasizes the incidental 'erotic' aspects of the inspiring tale of devotion, there is a 'sexual' purpose behind it. Why? Courtright compares the scene of Gajendra's struggle with the alligator with the episodes of the sage and the *gandharva*, Shiva and Gajasura, and Durvasas and Indra to force-fit the Gajendramoksha narrative into the schemes of beheading and the 'tension between the powers of asceticism and eroticism'.[191] In effect, Courtright has taken words from a one-half a verse out of ninety-two verses of the narrative to weave his thesis of tension between eroticism and asceticism!

We feel that the analogy between the beheading and the biting of the leg of Gajendra by the alligator is far-fetched. The *gandharva* was cursed because, while indulging in amorous sports with women in a lake, he had accidentally disturbed Sage Devala. What Courtright omits to mention is the past life of Gajendra, narrated in the *Bhagavata Purana* 8.3.70–13. The text says that in his previous life, Gajendra was the pious *vaishnava* King Indradyumna of the Pandyan dynasty in the Dravida country. He renounced his kingdom and went to meditate as an ascetic. He was so lost in meditation that he forgot to offer his

214 INVADING THE SACRED

respects to a Sage who happened to pass by. Therefore, the Sage cursed the ascetic Indradyumna and he became Gajendra. What we see here is a conflict between a king who had become an ascetic himself but is reborn as king-elephant, and an ugly alligator that was a *gandharva* who was cursed when he was sporting in water with women. Courtright tries to project Gajendra as the 'erotic' personality and the alligator as the 'ascetic' personality in his model of the 'tension between asceticism and eroticism'. In actuality the roles of Gajendra and the alligator can actually be reversed when the entire range of facts are taken into consideration. In other words, Gajendra represents the ascetic, while the alligator represents the erotic, and not the other way round as Courtright interprets the story. In any case, the 'erotic–ascetic' dichotomy does not exist between Gajendra and the alligator.

The episode of Indra and Durvasa[192] is also not analogous to the Gajendramoksha tale. Here, Indra indirectly insults Durvasa while engrossed in sexual acts with a heavenly nymph. Indra was having sex with an *apsaraa* when the Sage visits him. Indra hurriedly offers his respect whereupon the Sage gifts him a *paarijaata* flower with the ability to bestow power, glory, and wealth to the owner if it is worn with respect on the head. Indra, however, throws the flower on his elephant Airavata's head as soon as the Sage leaves so that he can promptly resume his amorous activities with the nymph. In doing so, Indra insulted the Sage Durvasa whereupon the latter cursed him. Gajendra was not insulting any ascetic when the alligator caught his leg. The alligator was not an ascetic either. So where are the parallels that Courtright claims?

Likewise, the third episode of Gajasura cited by Courtright is also not related to Gajendramoksha through the model of tension between asceticism and eroticism, despite Courtright's contrary claims. In Puranic narratives, Devi Durga had killed Gajasura's father Mahisha. To avenge his father's death, Gajasura practised asceticism and was granted a boon by Brahma so that no one overcome by lust would be able to defeat the asura. Invincible, he became arrogant and sinful and conquered the gods. A battle ensued between Shiva and Gajasura in which the latter was killed.[193] Here too, while Gajendra and Gajasura were both elephants and intoxicated with their power, the alligator was not exactly the same ascetic Lord Shiva. Thus, there is only a superficial and limited semblance between the tales of Gajendramoksha and Gajasura.

The entire book of Courtright is similarly filled with irrelevant parallels, loose or non-existent methodologies, and superficial comparisons drawn by considering selective data while ignoring or explaining away divergent facts. In 'scholarly' parlance, this 'methodology' is called Freudian free association.

Inventing an Incestuous Rape (Devibhagavata Purana 7.30)

Courtright narrates two tales in order to elaborate upon the erotic power of the *paarijaata* (Coral Tree) flower. He cites the first from supposedly related accounts in the *Brahmavaivarta Purana* 3.20.41–62 and the *Devibhagavata Purana* (DBP) 9.403–23.[194] In this tale, which we repeat here from the previous section for the sake of continuity, Sage Durvasa presents a beautiful *paarijaata* flower, with the ability to make its possessor powerful and wealthy, to Indra. The Sage says that the powers of the flower are manifest only when it is placed on his head by its possessor with reverence. When the Sage arrives, Indra is busy making love with a heavenly nymph named Rambha. When the Sage leaves, Indra continues his lovemaking and throws the flower on the head of Airavata, his elephant mount. According to Courtright, Airavata immediately transforms into 'a form of Vishnu', abandons Indra and runs into the forest, whereas Indra is completely deprived of his power and glory. When the Durvasa learns that Indra has insulted and has defiled his holy gift to him, the sage curses Indra and he loses all his powers.

Courtright then continues his analysis:

> This story also concerns the rivalry between Indra and Siva, who here takes the form of Durvasas. The powers of the sage make short work of Indra's wealth and sexual prowess. The parijata flower is an emblem of riches and erotic power, one of the flowers from the five coral trees that arose out of the churning of the ocean at the beginning of the cosmic cycle. In another story the goddess gave this flower to Durvasas who in turn gave it to Daksa, who became so aroused by the scent of the flower that he made love to his daughter Sati 'in the manner of a mere beast'. This shameful action drove her to burn her body, that is, commit sati, and provoked Siva to such a rage that he beheaded Daksa 7.30).[195]

The author thus links the two stories through the supposed common motif of the *paarijaata* flower. However, when the relevant passages of the *Devibhagavata Purana* are checked, there is no mention of the *paarijaata* flower at all. Verse 7.30.28 of the text reads,

*tatah prasannaa devesii nijakanthagataam srajam
bhramabhradamarasamsaktaam makarandamadaakulaam* |

The verse merely means that pleased with the Muni, the Devi gives him the fragrant garland that is on her neck, attracting clusters of bumblebees with its fragrant juice (*makaranda*). Now the word "*makaranda*" is typically used for the juice of the jasmine flower, which is also very fragrant and attracts the bees, wasps, insects, and bumblebees that can be seen in the gardens of India. No other verse in the chapter indicates that the *paarijaata* flowers were in her garland, and so the artificial linkage between the two stories by Courtright is brought about by an unjustifiable insertion of 'paarijaata' flowers into the text by him.

Before coming to Courtright's claim of an incestuous rape, let us recapitulate the story of Daksha's sacrifice for the readers. The story is very popular and is found in numerous Puranas, albeit in differing versions. Apparently the story was so well known in the milieu of the author of this Purana that the reader's knowledge of the same was presumed. This is clear from an extremely brisk narrative in the *Devibhagavata* and from the paucity of allusions to the incident, which serves as a background of sorts. In most versions of the story, Daksha organizes a grand Vedic *yajna* and calls all the deities except Shiva. Thrilled by the prospect of meeting her siblings and mother, Sati, who is the daughter of Daksha and an ideal and devoted wife of Shiva, nevertheless persuades her husband to participate in the *yajna* as well. In some versions Shiva agrees and they go together to the *yajna*. In other versions, she proceeds alone. At the yajna Daksha insults Shiva, and unable to bear the insults to her husband, Sati immolates herself by her yogic powers. The recurrent theme in these varying versions is that the cause of Sati's death is the insult heaped on her husband by her father. When Shiva sees the charred body of Sati, his rage knows no bounds. He and his followers destroy the sacrifice and he beheads Daksha, replacing his head with that of a goat.[196]

Now, the *Devibhagavata Purana* is a Shakta sectarian text extolling the Devi primarily, and secondarily Shiva, her consort. It narrates this entire episode in a distinctive manner. After Sage Durvasa receives the divine garland from the Devi, he reverentially places it on his head and proceeds to meet Daksha. In Daksha's home the Sage offers his homage and Daksha asks for the garland. Sage Durvasa, thinking that Daksha himself is a devotee of the Devi, gives the garland to him. The text then says (*Devibhagavata Purana* 7.30.34cd–35ab):

grhiitaa sirasaa maalaa munina nijamandire
sthaapitaa sayanam yatra dampatyoratisundaram

(Receiving the garland given by the Sage on his head, in his own chamber, Daksa then places it reverentially on the beautiful bed prepared for the couple.[197])

It is very important to pay attention to the word '*dampati*' in this verse because the word normally stands for husband and wife. It seems implausible that he would have placed the garland on a bed meant for Sati and her husband Shiva, whose presence is not even mentioned so far, although verse 23 does mention her betrothal with Shiva – an incident that is clearly not contemporaneous with the *yajna* of Daksha. It is more likely that it was the bed meant for Daksha and his wife, Sati's mother.[198] There is no evidence in the text that the bed was meant to be shared by Daksha and his married daughter!

What happens then is very evil (verse 35cd),
pasukarmarato raatrau maalaagandhena moditah |

(Aroused by the fragrance of the garland, Daksa was engrossed in animal-acts during the night.[199])

There is no hint what these bestial acts were, but it is reasonable to conclude that Daksha engaged in sex, and perhaps other activities such as imbibing liquor. The text certainly does not say that, "he made love to his daughter Sati in the manner of a mere animal" as Courtright claims (Courtright, p.37). The word *pashukarma* is used in several ways in Sanskrit texts, and in this context, the sexual connotation is clearly implied. The general sense of '*pashukarma*' in Sanskrit texts is non-regulated general activity that violates the norms of the scriptures— such as unwarranted sex, violence, destruction and so on. Rape and incest are more specific, limited meanings of the term, which are not necessarily warranted in this particular context, and are in fact totally negated by parallel versions in other Puranas.[200]

But why is indulgence in sex by Daksha considered a *pashukarma*? First, he has defiled the divine garland given by the Devi (and remember that the Purana is a *Shakta Purana*, dedicated to the Devi) by allowing it to act as an aphrodisiac. Second, he is in the midst of a *yajna*, during which the *yajmaana* (sacrificer) and his wife are to remain celibate. Sex during the period of a yajna defiles the rite. And the third reason is clarified by the following verse (*Devibhagavata Purana* 7.30.36):

abhavatsa mahipaalastena paapena sankare
sive dveshamatirhaato devyaam satyaam tatha nrpa |

(O Great King! Owing to (or under the influence of) that sin (of sexual intercourse), Daksa spoke evil of Shiva, and he was filled with an intense enmity for Shiva as well as for his daughter Devi Sati.)

So we come to the standard narrative wherein Daksha speaks ill of Shiva and is filled with hatred for him (and here also for Sati, who is but an incarnation of the Devi).

The beginning verses of chapter 7.30 narrate how Daksha was a pious king who had pleased Devi by intense austerities in the Himalayas. When the Devi appears before him, he requested her to take birth in his family. The Devi granted Daksha his wish, and she was born in his family as Sati. The Daksha, a completely transformed man, insulted the same Devi he had worshipped in the past. He became filled with enmity for Sati, who was not only his own daughter, but also the incarnation of the Devi. Therefore Sati can no longer stay in the body that is born of her sinful father Daksha.[201] The text continues (*Devibhagavata Purana* 7.30.37):

rajanastenaaparaadhena tajjanyo deha eva ca
satyaa yogaagninaa dagdhah satidharmadidrksayaa |

(O King! Because of Daksa's crime, Sati immolated her body, that was generated from him (Daksa),[202] with her yogic fire, so as to preserve the dignity of the eternal dharma of devotion to her husband.)

The crime of Daksha was that he had spoken ill of Shiva and that he was filled with enmity towards him and his own daughter under the influence of sin. The text then states that the *shakti* of Sati returned to the Himalayas (7.30.38ab), the abode of Devi where Daksha had meditated and had her *darsana* in the first place. The narrative continues in the standard manner—Shiva was infuriated with the death of Sati and he destroyed the *yajna* (7.43). Daksha was beheaded and his head was replaced with that of a goat.

So what we see here is a variant of the standard theme in which Sati commits suicide because she cannot bear the insult of her husband by her father.[203] And since the text is a Shakta text, it adds its own details that Daksha had defiled the gift of Devi, and was filled with enmity towards her own essence in his daughter Sati. The text certainly *does not* say: "This shameful action [of Daksha's incestuous rape of Sati—reviewers' addition] drove her to burn her body".[204] This 'scholarly' version is but Courtright's own invention. The manner in which Courtright gives sexual kink to Puranic passages reminds us of how his *gurubandhu* Jeffrey Kripal had interpreted the *Kathamrita* to make Ramakrishna Paramahamsa into a homosexual pedophile.[205]

It would not be an exaggeration to say that Courtright has left behind even his mentor Wendy Doniger in eroticization of Sanskrit texts. Consider this very example. Doniger has summarized these verses of *Devibhagavata* in the following words:[206]

> And so he [Durvasa] gave the garland to that man, Daksa, who received the garland upon his head and placed it upon the exquisite marital bed in his own palace. At night, the man was so delighted by the perfume of the garland that he made love in the manner of a mere beast; and because of this evil, the king conceived in his mind a hatred for Siva, Sankara, and even for the Goddess Sati. Because of this offence, Sati burnt that body, which the man had begotten, in the fire of her yoga, with a desire to demonstrate the dharma of '*suttee*' . . .

The parallels between Doniger's book and Courtright's book are clearly visible. While Doniger uses the words 'made love in the manner of a mere beast' (in her mis-translation of the word '*pasukarmarato*'), Courtright (p.37) goes a step ahead and translates the word as 'made love to his daughter Sati in the manner of a mere beast', adding his own commentary 'to his daughter'!

If the text did have any hint of rape (much less an incestuous rape), as Courtright claims, Doniger would not have failed to notice it and would have certainly discussed it.[207] The fact that she herself does not do so confirms our assertion that the description of an incestuous rape in *Devibhagavata Purana* 7.30 is nothing but Courtright's own fantasy. There is no cigar, yet Courtright sees a Phallus!

The Remover of Obstacles or the Creator of Obstacles?

Ganesha is also known as Vighneshvara that Courtright translates as, 'the Lord of obstacles'. The name is generally understood to mean 'remover of obstacles' by lay Hindus. Hindu tradition itself, however, associates some ambiguity with the name. In some Hindu texts, Ganesha is actually stated to be the creator of obstacles. Courtright cites a version[208] of the *Skanda Purana* (VII.1.38.1–34), according to which the heavens become crowded with people when even sinners start attaining salvation by visiting the temple of Somanatha. The gods then become alarmed and approach Shiva for a way out of this quagmire. He is unable to help them and therefore Parvati creates Ganesha out of the dirt of her body. She remarks that Ganesha will place obstacles before (sinful or undeserving) men so that they will get deluded, and will go to the hell instead of to Somanatha.

The notion that Ganesha creates obstacles without a just cause is merely meant to demonstrate his power, as well as the fact that he does not allow sinners to take short cuts to reach the heavens—this is what the above story from the *Skanda Purana* also demonstrates. The *Linga Purana* 105.12–16 says the same in a more elaborate fashion:[209]

> Hear Parvati, what this son of yours will become. He will be like me in might, heroism, and compassion. This son of yours will become one just like me because of these qualities. He will make obstacles that last until death for those evil and impious ones who hate the Veda and dharma. Those who fail to pay homage to me and Visnu, the supreme lord, will go to great darkness by the obstacles laid before them by the lord of obstacles. In their houses there shall be quarrels without end. Because of the obstacles your son makes everything perishes utterly. For those who do not worship, who are intent upon lies and anger, and are committed to fierce savagery, he will create obstacles. He will remove obstacles from those who revere the traditions, knowledge, and teachers. Without worshipping him, all actions and laws will become obstructed.[210]

Courtright too is aware of *Shiva Purana* 2.4.15–18 in which Parvati declares that Ganesha shall receive the worship of all and remove all obstacles.[211] Yet, how could a deity, whose morality Doniger has judged as ambivalent,[212] and whose father Shiva is labeled by Courtright as a notorious womanizer,[213] be depicted in such an exalted manner? Thus Ganesha is presented as the Lord of Obstacles, turning him into a malevolent deity. Courtright interprets the verses in the *Linga Purana* (105.4–22) and the *Skanda Purana* (6.214.47–66), in which Shiva tells Ganesha that he will help the gods and the Brahmins by creating obstacles in the rites of those who fail to pay the priest his *dakshina* for performing the sacrifice. This is quite out of context with the dubious label bestowed on Ganesha by the above-mentioned scholars. Apart from adorning the cover of Courtright's book, this label is later used as a tool to psychoanalyze Ganesha's supposed sexual ambivalence. Courtright would portray Ganesha as a jealous deity who inflicts severe punishments on those who dare ignore his immanent manifestations.[214] The joyous festival of Ganesha *caturthi* when women pamper Ganesha with sweetmeats just as they would pamper their own children is portrayed as an attempt by the devotees to propitiate

Ganesha, who as the readers are told, if not appeased would turn demoniac and lay obstacles in their path.[215]

In the course of this discussion, Courtright compares Ganesha to St. Peter, who is the keeper of the gate to the heaven as per Biblical texts. The author is quick to point out one difference though: Ganesha is comparable to the devious St. Peter of folklore, not to the sober and austere St. Peter of the New Testament and early Christian hagiography.[216] It becomes imperative for Courtright to differentiate between folklore and literature to present St. Peter in a positive light, but such scruples are dispensed with when it comes to using unreliable anecdotes to taint the Hindu deity Ganesha.

Referring to the story of the *Skanda Purana*, Courtright suggests that "the pattern of Ganesa's ambivalent behavior at the threshold links him with the actions of demons . . . "[217] This is a rather poor choice of words, and an unfair demonizing of the deity. Hindus interpret the deity predominantly as an embodiment of auspiciousness, benevolence and the like.[218] He is invoked at the beginning of all endeavors, religious or secular, because He is the remover of obstacles. If He places obstacles in front of the people or the gods, it is predominantly for the reasons stated in the passages from the *Linga Purana* and the *Skanda Purana* above. The essential character of Vighneshvara is that of *vighnahartta, sukhakartta, dukhahartta* and *mangalamurthi*. His obstacles are meant largely for people who want to take unethical short cuts in their lives and are a minor aspect of his character.[219]

But even in the 'Foreword' Wendy Doniger sees only his 'obstacle-creator' aspect, and says:

every book exists in toto in the mind of the elephant-headed god, and we scribes merely scramble to scribble down those bits of it that we can grasp, including the 'knots,' the obstacles to full comprehension, that the god of obstacles throws in on purpose to keep us on our toes and to keep us in awe of him.[220]

Perhaps, Doniger and her progeny always want to say something that is 'new', 'different', 'exciting' and 'sexy'. Or as a Sanskrit proverb goes: "The housefly ignores the entire clean body of its host and dwells only on the festering sore".

The Puranas and Conspiracy Theories

Courtright revisits the theme of the problem of the Vedic origins of Ganesha. It is true that there are not many unambiguous references to

Ganesha in the ancient Vedic texts, in contrast with the exalted manner in which he is referred to in the texts of classical Hinduism, the Puranas. To explain this discrepancy, Courtright comes up with a conspiracy theory. He argues that the Puranas attempt to cover-up his demon ancestry and are uncomfortably aware of the discrepancy between the malevolent, obstacle-creating powers of Vinayaka and the positive, obstacle-removing actions of Ganesha.[221] According to him, the Puranas seek to resolve this contradiction by various mechanisms such as "clever use of false etymologies for the name 'Vinayaka'". Courtright says:

> In one case, when Siva saw, much to his surprise, that Ganesa appeared out of the mixture of his and Parvati's sweat and bathwater, he exclaimed to her, 'A son has been born to you without [vinā] a husband [nāyakena]; therefore this son shall be named Vinayaka' (Vām P 28.71–72). This etymological sleight of hand obscures the association of Vināyaka with "those who lead astray" which is its etymologically prior meaning, and connects it with another meaning of nāyaka as leader or husband.[222]

The Purana has really not indulged in any subterfuge because in the second half of this very verse (28.72cd), Lord Shiva clearly says that Ganesha will create thousands of obstacles for devatas and others (esha vighnasahasraani suradiinaam karishyati). The meaning of the word vinaayaka given by the Purana is definitely possible grammatically, without any strain at all. The appropriate question pertaining to historiography is whether the meaning 'creator of obstacles' for 'vinaayaka' was in vogue or the norm at the time the Vamana Purana was compiled. If not, then we cannot accuse the author of the Purana with a proverbial sleight of hand.[223]

It may be noted that creation of such ad-hoc etymologies, mythologies, and cosmologies is seen very frequently in Hindu texts such as the Brahmanas, the Upanishads, and the Puranas, amongst other genres. These ad-hoc etymologies serve various purposes at hand, such as providing impromptu explanations or justification for a ritual act, or thematic completion of the narrative. One need not come up with conspiracy theories, as Courtright has done, to describe this phenomenon.

Maternal Aggression of Parvati against Ganesha—Dubious Passage of Varaha Purana

Courtright writes:

> The theme of maternal aggression in the myths of Ganesa is more veiled; but it is there—as we have seen in the myth where Parvati

curses Ganesa to be ugly and as we shall see in the myth where she places him at the doorway to be cut down to size by Siva . . . [224]

We are not aware of any Puranic text where Parvati curses Ganesha to be ugly. Courtright himself admits that this story is not found in any printed edition of the Varaha Purana. He, however, attributes the above text to a Christian missionary traveler to India, and to an ill-informed author writing from the first half of 1800s who may have relied himself on the missionary's work for this piece of information.[225] We shall discuss this issue more in detail later.[226] It is also questionable if Parvati's asking Ganesha to stand guard at the doorway should be taken as a 'veiled' instance of 'maternal aggression'. Courtright's fantasy of the 'maternal aggression' of Parvati evaporates when we consult the actual text of the Varaha Purana (20.11.18), according to which it is actually Shiva, not Parvati, who curses Ganesha to become ugly by having an elephant's head!

Who is older: Ganesha or Skanda?

Hindu tradition is not unanimous on who is the elder brother of the two. Courtright, however, states that Ganesha is the younger brother in a somewhat absolute manner.

> The iconography is clear enough; Ganesa is a child, a baby. So he remains, never growing into the full youthful stage of his elder brother Skanda or the maturity of his father.[227]

Later (p.123), he contradicts himself and states that in most areas, Skanda is considered the younger brother.[228] So we see that even incorrect and inconsistent facts do not prevent Courtright from inventing psychological analyses. The point is that if a matter is not settled within the Hindu tradition itself, then why does Courtright select one version alone to retrofit his preconceived thesis?

Imaginary Blackie in the Matsya Purana

A recent review[229] of his book makes the following additional remarks, which we reproduce below for the benefit of the reader.

> Further while dealing with the mythology he states, "Once in jest Siva called Parvati 'Blackie' [Kali] because her skin looked black like a serpent. She was offended . . . and so went away to practice asceticism to obtain a golden skin. Viraka begged her to take him with her . . . But she told him to stay at Siva's door . . . for Siva is a notorious womanizer. The references given to the passage quoted

are Skp. 1.2.27–29; cf. Matsya P. 154.542–78. See also Kramrisch
1981, pp. 364–65; O'Flaherty 1975, pp. 252–61.

The reviewer then criticizes Courtright in the following words:

The MatsyaP. does not contain the word *Kali* or any word similar
to womanizer. The *Skanda Purana* has the word *krsna* for black
complexioned one. Similarly what Parvati tells Viraka about Siva
is *gaurangilampato hyesah*...1(2).28.8 'enamoured of woman of
white complexion') (as is translated by Tagore), and not 'a notorious
womanizer' as the author says.

We have given just a few illustrations of various ways in which
Courtright has distorted data from the Puranas and the Vedas for his
questionable *and* strained psychoanalytical constructions. Many more
instances of distortion could be cited in relation to texts such as the
Skanda Purana and the *Shiva Purana*, but we will not include them
for the sake of brevity and move on to the next section.

The Cigar Now Becomes a Phallus[230]

The principal cause of the current controversy over Courtright's book
is his abuse of Freudian theories to impart perverse sexual meanings
to the otherwise innocuous aspects of the narratives on the deity found
in Hindu texts. Courtright's defense, however, is that his detractors have
taken his quotes out of context. We find this explanation disingenuous
because even outside Chapter III, where most of these sexual
interpretations are found, one can find other instances where he has
hinted at similar aspects. The previous sections of our review clearly
demonstrate how Courtright has exaggerated and even has invented
sexuality in several Puranic passages.

We have seen in our brief review of the textual analysis in the
book how Courtright manages to kink the narratives of the Puranas
by giving them numerous sexual twists. Completely unrelated
projectiles, missiles, electric poles, water pipes, tree trunks, elephant
trunks, stone pillars, walking sticks, obelisks, spider legs and lotus-
stems were reduced to 'cigars' (to put it facetiously). Now Courtright
asks us to see phalluses in all these 'cigars'. Indeed, such a wide variety
of choices that we are given makes his text very 'insightful',
'thoughtful', 'wonderful', 'scholarly', 'objective', 'nuanced', 'sensitive',
'sympathetic' etc., to use the buzz words of academic Hinduism
studies.

In a way, the narrative focus in Chapter II leads to Chapter III. Courtright himself explains the rationale for this earlier in his book:

> It is particularly difficult to know how to proceed from the point at which the various myths in their variant versions are assembled in the lush landscape of the Puranic texts (the narrative level) to an interpretation of these myths. We could start almost anywhere and work our way around, examining each theme and metaphor until all the myths are accounted for in a network or tapestry of meanings. My way out of this welter of possibilities is to seek the elements in the myths that are most common and recurrent or most striking in their uniqueness, to begin with these and thence be led to other myths that shed light on the first ones. The most striking, and obvious, recurrent element in the Ganesa cycle of myths is the elephant head. Hence our analysis begins with an inquiry into elephant symbolism and mythology and its relation to the Ganesa story. The elephant head in turn leads to the myths of Ganesa's birth, beheading, and the receiving of his elephant head, which in turn leads to myths of his beheading. Beheading connects his mythology to the larger metaphorical universe of sacrifice, dismemberment, initiation, and theogony. Because it is Ganesa's father who beheads him, the story is tied to the cycle of Siva myths and to the issue of father-son relations. This opens up the possibilities of psychoanalytic interpretations, centering on the Oedipal complex...[231]

Another reviewer[232] has shown that the version in which Shiva beheads Ganesha is *not representative* of the overall Puranic tradition because most Puranic narratives attribute different reasons responsible for Ganesha's elephant's head.

One wonders how Wendy's Children would interpret, using psychoanalysis as a façade, the episode of Parashurama beheading his mother Renuka at his father's behest. Would they argue that it reveals a possible homosexual relationship between Sage Jamadagni[233] and his son, and suggest that the beheading symbolizes the removal of the unwanted mother? Would he liken Renuka's head to the sexual organ and equate her beheading with genital mutilation?

One may argue that Courtright is imposing Western interpretations on an Indian deity and so there is bound to be some bias. Courtright argues, however, that his methodology is 'universal' or 'objective' in the following words.

> The myth of Ganesa parallels aspects of human experience beyond the restricted world of ritual initiation. It is a tale of family relations

and reflects the unconscious ambivalences of early forgotten childhood experience. One need not be an ideological Freudian to see the fruitfulness of raising psychoanalytical questions about a myth that involves such a violent and complex account of father/ son relations. The extent to which the myth of Ganesa explores these relations and the sensibilities that attend them, it reaches beyond its Indian context and takes on universal meaning and appeal.[234]

We invite the reader to read our extracts from Courtright's psychoanalysis and decide for him or herself whether there is anything worthwhile in this perverse verbal-jugglery. It appears that to give a 'universal meaning and appeal' to the persona of Ganesha, he started with his unflattering introduction of his protagonist Ganesha, of whom he says: "He appears tainted, trivial, perhaps even vulgar . . . In short Ganesa is too ordinary".[235] He wrote: "Repulsion at the form of the deity with an elephant head and suspicion that there may be more going on than meets the (Western) eye, is a good starting point for our inquiry . . . "[236] Ganesha's mythology is also declared as: "an elaborate rationalization for an invented deity".[237] Now that really sounds universally appealing and meaningful!

Courtright Invents a 'Limp Phallus'—Misrepresenting Vedanta and Tantra

Perhaps the most offensive statements made by Courtright relate to his description of Ganesha's trunk as a limp phallus. Let us reproduce them here, for the information of our readers.

> The elephant trunk, which perpetually hangs limp, and broken tusk are reminiscent of Siva's own phallic character, but as these phallic analogs are either excessive or in the wrong place, they pose no threat to Siva's power and his erotic claims on Parvati.[238]

That the tradition or the texts never attach any sexual connotation to this legend doesn't stop Courtright from thus trashing Ganesha. A sensible reader need not stop to think if any elephant's trunk is ever erect. While Courtright dwells incessantly and uncontrollably on the equation 'Ganesha's Trunk = limp phallus', he does not ascribe any Freudian significance (and thank God for that) to the fact that his trunk is also not really straight, but also slightly twisted or curved, which is why the deity is often termed as *Vakratunda*.

According to several versions of how Ganesha acquired his elephant-head, his beheading is caused by a battle that starts at the threshold

of Parvati's inner chambers. Courtright concurs with Robert
Goldman[239] and others in interpreting this location in sexual terms.

> From the psycho-analytic perspective, the symbolism as the location
> where the battle occurs is significant. It is the threshold to Parvati's
> bath and bedroom, symbol of her shrine, womb, and point of sexual
> entry. It is the place simultaneously of union and separation. Ganesa
> the child is coming out of the door at the moment Siva the husband
> is attempting to get in. The doorway is not big enough for both
> of them at the same time; one must prevail, and, of course, it is
> the father. The resolution, at least initially, must fall in his favor.
> The particular type of mutilation Siva inflicts on Ganesa is also
> significant. As Robert Goldman points out in commenting on
> Ganesa's beheading, 'This particular mode of displaced castration
> is a common feature of Hindu legends. Beheading is, moreover, a
> regular symbol for castration in dreams and fantasies' (pp. 371–
> 372,; cf. Freud, pp. 366–69). In traditional Indian yogic physiology
> the head is the receptacle of both thought and sexual potency or
> seed. In Tantric descriptions of the process of spiritual liberation
> [moksa] the seed is drawn up from the sexual organs through the
> various centers [cakra] along the spinal axis until it is released
> through an aperture at the top of the head [brahmarandhra cakra
> or sahasrara cakra] (cf. O'Flaherty 1980, pp. 17–61). In some
> versions of the myth where the Ganesa already has his elephantine
> form, the 'displaced castration' takes place on an even more obvious
> surrogate, the tusk. In separating Ganesa's head/tusk Siva, or one
> of his stand-ins, removes any potential threat of incest and thereby
> leaves Ganesa sexually ambiguous...[240]

We feel that the reference to a 'doorway' which two men cannot
enter at the same time could be interpreted by readers as a double-
entendre, and thereby could be seen as demeaning to Parvati, and
therefore even kinky and sexist in nature. Courtright and Goldman are
clearly alluding to the possibility that both Shiva and Ganesha are
trying to copulate with Parvati (their wife and mother respectively).
Courtright then injects more sexuality into Ganesha's beheading by
bringing in the concept of the Brahmarandhra Chakra. A yogi is
supposed to prevent his 'seed' (retas) from 'falling out' (skhalana) and
instead cause it to rise in his body till it reaches the 'head' (urdhvareta).

So far so good, but how is this relevant in this context especially
when Courtright himself is at pains to suggest that Ganesha's wisdom
is not the transcendental wisdom of the Vedanta and Upanishads and
he is 'not a deity of transcendental realization' and rather "rules the

concrete world of action and its fruits, success and failure, triumph and pain"?[241] It appears that in their zeal to make their interpretations more juicy and full, Goldman and Courtright would not have even a pretense of consistency, but would do whatever they find to affect a complete sexualization of all aspects of the deity's persona.

Relating the beheading of Ganesha to the *brahmarandhra cakra* in such a contrived manner is also contradicted by direct data from Tantric Hindu texts, which are ignored by Courtright. These texts actually relate the deity to the *muulaadhaara cakra* that is at the base of the spine, close to the anus.[242] The reason is quite transparent; Ganesha is the Lord of the threshold, and moreover Hindu prayer ceremonies commence with invocations to Ganesha. Likewise, in the initial stages of Yogic meditation, the focus is on *muulaadhaara chakra*. The practitioner of Yoga in his initial stages tries to awaken his *kundalini*, which is located in the *muulaadhaara chakra*. And things become easier once this has happened, just as our tasks become easier if we commence them with an invocation to Ganesha. The Rudrayaamala Tantra clearly states that Ganesha's elephant head with the curved trunk resembles the form of the *kundalini*, which resides in the *muulaadhaara chakra*.[243]

Courtright writes:

> An important element in the symbolism of the elephant head is displacement or, better, disguise. The myth wants to make it appear that the elephant head was not a deliberate choice but merely the nearest available head in an auspicious direction or the head of one of Siva's opponents to whom he had already granted salvation. But, from a psychoanalytical perspective, there is meaning in the selection of the elephant head. Its trunk is the displaced phallus, a caricature of Siva's *linga*. It poses no threat because it is too large, flaccid, and in the wrong place to be useful for sexual purposes. In the myth of the broken tusk, Siva does not restore it but leaves it for Ganesa to carry around and to use occasionally as a weapon or a writing instrument. The elephant head is also a mask, and, as it is a mask's purpose simultaneously to reveal and conceal, it both disguises and expresses aggression inherent in the story. So Ganesa takes on the attributes of his father but in an inverted form, with an exaggerated phallus—ascetic and benign—whereas Siva's is 'hard' [*urdhvalinga*], erotic, and destructive.[244]

While we do not see any mask on Ganesha's torso, we do get a hint of peek-a-boo pornography in Courtright's 'analyses'. We would let the readers decide if it is worth psychoanalyzing Courtright himself, based on his own statements in the book.

Courtright's 'Limp Phallus' not attested in texts of Ganapatya Sect

Anyway, his fiction of limp trunks and phalluses is not exactly supported by the Hindu texts. For instance, the *Ganesha Purana* (*Upasana Khanda* 12.38) states that the trunk of Ganesha is so strong that it is more powerful than that of Airavata and other elephants who are guardians of the eight quarters of the Universe.[245] Courtright thus misses a good opportunity to discuss 'Penis-Envy'. The Tantric texts, which Courtright ignores, distinguish clearly between the trunk and his phallus, and the latter does perform its intended functions according to these texts. In short, data from the texts ignored by Courtright completely negates his own fantasy about Ganesha's trunk.

Numerous depictions of the deity actually show him with a raised or an erect trunk. Courtright has ignored the diversity of the Hindu tradition with regard to the deity and has chosen only those aspects that fit his predetermined thesis.

Courtright should have considered the fact that in Indian culture, the lifted trunk of an elephant represents a salute by the animal. The deity is not really supposed to salute us, which is why He may have a lowered trunk in most of His iconic representations so as to symbolize His benevolence and omnipotence.

Ekadantin of Hindu Tradition—Courtright Castrates Ganesha Thrice

Now we have another curious fact regarding Lord Ganesha. One of the tusks of the deity is broken, or missing. How does Courtright unravel this mystery? As expected, under the subject 'The Tusk'[246] in his book, all kinds of disjointed, unrelated, disparate Puranic narratives are brought together in an artificial manner by Courtright to lay the ground for discussions on beheading, decapitation, amorous play and all such sexual, Freudian materials in Chapter III. Ignored of course are the mystical and spiritual interpretations of his single tusk in Hindu tradition (e.g., *Mudgala Purana* 2.52.13–14) wherein the tusk is related to *maayaa*.

It is definitely worth investigating what meaning Hindu tradition itself accords to the broken tusk of the deity. To determine the traditional meanings of the broken tusk, we explored a wide range of Hindu texts, from Kaavyas to the Puranas, and found the following explanations. In a major Purana text, Lord Vishnu explains the word *ekadanta* as follows: The word *eka* means 'supreme' or *pradhana*, and the word *danta* denotes strength. "To Him (Ganesha) who is supremely powerful/ strong, I (Lord Vishnu) offer homage".[247]

Far from being a castrated phallus, the broken tusk of Ganesha is a potent weapon. The *Ganesha Purana, Kridakhanda* (chapters 62–70) describes a battle waged between Devāntaka and Ganesha, the latter assisted by his spouses. Devāntaka uproots the tusk of Ganesha, but the deity uses this very broken tusk to penetrate the demon's chest and thus kills him. The *Mudgala Purana* discusses the eight avatars of Ganesha, in eight sections. The second section is the *ekadantakhanda*. *Mudgala Purana* 2.52.13–14 states that the word *eka* means *māyā* whereas *danta* represents the Atman that illuminates the *māyā* through superimposition or reflection. This is a Vedantic interpretation of the single tusk.

Sant Jnaneshvara (1275–1297 CE) begins his Jnaneshvari, a celebrated Maharashtri commentary on the *Gita*, with a devotional praise of Ganesha in twenty-one verses. Verse 16 states that the deity vanquished the heretical Buddhist doctrine with his broken tusk. In Sishupalavadha 1.60 of poet Maagha, it is stated that Ganesha has one tusk because Ravana uprooted his second tusk to make ivory earrings for the beautiful women of his kingdom. And of course, the tradition that Ganesha uprooted his tusk to serve as a pen for writing the *Mahabharata* at the dictation of the Sage Veda Vyasa is too well known to recount here. The tale is narrated by Courtright himself.

One could also refer to traditional *Shilpashastras*, which indicate that the icon of the deity can actually have more than two tusks. Many such icons and representations actually exist and can be seen in printed books quite often. In other words, tradition is not uniform on whether the deity has just one tusk. Therefore Courtright's kitsch-psychoanalysis is based on a crude reduction of the diversity seen in Hindu iconography.

In short, Courtright considers Ganesha's beheading as a castration, his trunk as a symbol of a limp phallus and now his broken tusk as another castration. It is therefore legitimate to ask if one person can be castrated and emasculated thrice! And from a psychoanalytical perspective, one may wonder who it is that has actually demonstrated a Penis Envy in this entire episode!

Indian Males in relation to Ganesha's Sexuality, Celibacy and Incest:

Courtright summarizes his Freudian interpretations on Ganesha in the following manner:

Iconographically Ganesa's body is that of a plump infant. Although at least one Puranic source has an account of his marriage, Ganesa is generally represented as celibate, a celibacy suggested visually and perhaps caricatured by his exaggerated but perpetually flaccid trunk. Finally, his insatiable appetite for sweetmeats [modaka]— a source of many amusing tales—raises the question (from a psychoanalytical perspective) of whether this tendency toward oral erotic gratification may not serve as compensation for his arrested development at not reaching the phallic stage as well as the severing of the maternal bond he underwent at the beheading hand of his father. Gananath Obeyesekere interprets Ganesa's celibacy, like his broken tusk, as the punishment he receives for incestuous fixation on his mother.[248]

This generalization of Ganesha is preceded by something even more sinister. Indians as a whole are force-fit into a stereotypical category by Courtright, and then this stereotype is subjected to a demeaning Freudian analysis. Courtright is not alone in treating the stereotyped Indian male as a subject of Psychoanalyses. In fact, he draws upon the works of Sudhir Kakar and the like repeatedly in this chapter. We will not reproduce his citations from their works here because similar citations are available already in an Internet review[249] of the book, *Vishnu on Freud's Desk*.

Coming back to Ganesha, Courtright says:

Ganesa's celibacy links him both to his father and his mother, but for opposite reasons. He remains celibate so as not to compete erotically with his father, a notorious womanizer, either incestuously for his mother or for any other woman for that matter.[250]

There is nothing in the tradition to defend this portrayal of Ganesha as an incestuous son. So, anecdotes that none can verify, are used to bolster the case.

Once Parvati asked Ganesa whom he would like to marry; he replied, 'Someone exactly like you, Mummy.' And Mummy got outraged by such an openly incestuous wish and cursed him with everlasting celibacy.[251]

Courtright quotes A.K. Ramanujan, who doesn't name his source. In any event, Ramanujan's version is very different from those that other South Indians are aware of. In that version, when Ganesha tells Parvati that he would want a bride just like her, she laughs at him, and jokingly tells him that he may never get married in that case, implying that there is none comparable to Shakti. It seems that Ramanujan has added his own spin to this tale in his amateurish attempt at psychoanalysis. The fact is that in a vast country such as India, with more than a billion people (or 700 million people in 1980s when Courtright wrote his book), there are literally thousands of tales and stories about different deities floating around orally amongst the Hindu masses. Should one bring together these stories with passages of older texts and then construct a psychoanalytical theory on them? Is this methodology sound?

Even though in this unverifiable tale, the child Ganesha alone is pronounced guilty of harboring incestuous thoughts, Courtright is quite eager to indict Parvati too on this count. He has no hesitation in invoking a tale that, by his own admission, does not find any mention in published editions of the *Varaha Purana*, but is only to be found in the writings of Abbe Dubois, the missionary that never concealed his hatred for Hinduism. In this invented and disparagingly presented tale, the beauty of the newborn Ganesha fascinates all women and this triggers a supposedly incestuous jealousy in Parvati, who curses his beauties to vanish.[252]

It is very common in India for sons when asked, what kind of girl they want to marry, to say that they would marry someone like their own mother. The Indian ethos emphasizes sacrifice, and the mother is often the embodiment of sacrifice. She sacrifices for the family, and when the time of reckoning comes, her children gratefully remember all that she has done. So, when a son says that he would like a spouse just like her, he is talking of a likeness in character and spirit. It is ironical that Wendy's Children must read such noble sentiments within a culture as incestuous thoughts.

Having unfairly declared Ganesha an incestuous son, Courtright proceeds to present even the most innocent events of Ganesha's life as sordid tales of incest. In a Sri Lankan legend, Ganesha competes with his brother Skanda for a mango. While the latter circumambulates the world, Ganesha simply circumambulates his parents and wins the mango. Courtright quoting Obeyesekere concludes that the mango is a symbol for the vagina, and hence this episode of Ganesha eating the fruit symbolizes his incestuous possession his mother.[253]

Now, mango is considered 'the king of fruits' in India and is included in hundreds of narratives in all parts of the country, in many different ways. Is it justifiable to pick one of these, and then impose a 'symbolic' meaning on the same in order to bolster a speculative psychoanalytical fantasy? It may be noted that many fruits have certain sexual connotations in various human cultures. For instance, several medieval Christian art traditions depict the apple as the sin that tempted Adam and Eve. Therefore, would it be justified to see a double-entendre in the English adage that "An apple a day, keeps the Doctor away"?

In the *Song of Songs* in the Old Testament, the breasts of a woman are likened to bunches of grapes. Should we, following Courtright-Obeyesekere 'methodology', see hidden meanings every time a Christian or a Jew offers wine? Bananas, oranges, papayas, and dozens of other fruits have some sexual connotation or the other. But fortunately, unlike Obeyesekere and Courtright, reasonable people do not invent cheap gossip every time we eat bananas, papayas, grapes, apples and mangoes. They are just fruits for us, nothing else.

There is a Maharashtrian folk tale that narrates the intrigues between a Mahar[254] soldier and a woman of the palace under Peshwa rule. The illicit liaison is exposed and the soldier, whose name is Ganapati, is punished by death. His spirit, according to the folklore, haunted the king. To propitiate it, he installed the effigy of the slain soldier at the gate of the palace in the form of the deity Ganapati and required everyone to pay obeisance to it. There is nothing in this story to compare with the legend of the deity Ganesha, except the name and the fact that the Mahar's effigy was installed in the form of the deity, but Courtright sees striking parallels in this tale with the supposed incest of Ganesha with his mother. Such meaningless parallels promote neither an understanding of the deity, nor do they promote knowledge.[255] Instead they offer an insight into Courtright's perverse mind.

Ganesha as a Eunuch

Several sacred stories pertaining to Ganesha describe him as a doorkeeper or guard outside his mother Parvati's inner chambers. Courtright sees in this a parallel to an old Indian practice of posting eunuchs as guards of the doors to harems. He then quotes an Indologist to the effect that these eunuchs had a reputation of being homosexuals, with a penchant for oral sex, and that they were frowned upon as the very dregs of society, implicitly ascribing the same qualities to the charming Ganesha and reducing his symbolism to 'an explicit denial of adult male sexuality'.[256]

Courtright extends this weak chain of parallels to imagine the deity himself as eunuch-like.

Like a eunuch, Ganesa has the power to bless and curse; that is, to place and remove obstacles. Although here there seem to be no myths or folktales in which Ganesa explicitly performs oral sex, his insatiable appetite for sweets may be interpreted as an effort to satisfy a hunger that seems inappropriate in an otherwise ascetic disposition, a hunger having clear erotic overtones. Ganesa's broken tusk, his guardian's staff, and displaced head can be interpreted as symbols of castration.[257]

Courtright then quotes Edmund Leach, an anthropologist,[258] in support of his own interpretations:

This combination of child-ascetic-eunuch in the symbolism of Ganesa—each an explicit denial of adult male sexuality—appears to embody a primal Indian male longing: to remain close to the mother and to do so in a way What will both protect her and yet be acceptable to the father. This means that the son must retain access to the mother but not attempt to possess her sexually. As a child, a renouncer, or a eunuch, he can legitimately maintain that precious but precarious intimacy with his mother because, although he is male, he is more like her then he is like his father. This may explain why Ganesa takes on these qualities through his own choice or why he willingly accepts them as mutilations from others—even from Parvati herself—so long as they will guarantee his continued proximity with her.[259]

The reader is also told that Ganesha represents, 'a primal Indian male longing: to remain close to the mother and to do so in a way what will protect her and yet be acceptable to the father. This means that the son must retain access to mother but not attempt to possess her sexually'.[260] From this and other instances, we feel that this entire psychoanalysis is not really restricted to a 'mythical deity' as Courtright may claim in his own defense. Rather, in our opinion, it demeans the category of the Indian male as such.

The Modaka as a (Sexual) 'Toy'

Hindus fondly depict Lord Ganesha as devouring a sweetmeat called *modaka*.[261] Courtright applies the 'oral' and 'anal' paradigms of Freudian ideology to interpret this in a sexualized manner:

The perpetual son desiring to remain close to his mother and having an insatiable appetite for sweets evokes associations of oral eroticism. Denied the possibility of reaching the stage of full genital masculine power by the omnipotent force of the father, the son seeks gratification in some acceptable way. As long as he remains stuffed full he is content and benign, like a satisfied infant at its mother's breast. If Ganesa should go hungry because of the devotee's failure to feed and worship him first before all other gods, then his primordial hostility is aroused, to the detriment of all. Feeding Ganesa copious quantities of modakas, satisfying his oral/erotic desires, also keeps him from becoming genitally erotic like his father . . . Ganesa's impatience for food suggests an anxiety, a hunger that is never completely fed no matter how many modakas he consumes. He is the child forever longing for the mother's breast—that fountain of life-giving elixir he once enjoyed without distress in infancy but is now denied because of the father's intrusion . . . Ganesa's story is, in part, the story of maternal attachment, loss, and indirect but incomplete compensation. As a celibate child, and resembling the ambiguous figure of the eunuch, Ganesa is one whose masculinity remains partial, trimmed, and contained. Unable to take full possession of his mother in the face of his father's beheading/castrating power, Ganesa lives a threshold existence—near but nor far enough— seeking his own fulfillment in dutiful service to his parents and taking pleasure in an endless flow of sweetmeats from adoring devotees. He is the mythical expression of the male wish for maternal intimacy denied in real life in the course of growing up, a fantasy in which the defeats of the son must suffer at the hands the father are compensated indirectly by an orally erotic celibate proximity to the mother.[262]

Earlier, the author refers to a story in which Ganesha trips and his belly rips open, with *modakas* spilling out.[263] The moon started laughing at Ganesha, whereupon the latter took out one of his tusks and hurled it at the moon. As a result, there was darkness all over the earth. The *devatas* implored Ganesha to restore the moon and retrieve his tusk. Ganesha did so but on the condition that henceforth the moon would wax and wane. Courtright interprets this incident in sexual terms and writes:

The myth opens with Ganesa already fused in his elephant-headed form and suffering from too much of a good thing: he had filled his belly to overflowing and has satiated his legendary appetite for oral gratification. This situation roughly parallels the pursuit of genital gratification between Siva and Parvati that forms the background for the story of Ganesa's birth. Ganesa's gluttonous excesses cause him to fall from his rat and split open his belly, as his parents' amorous play shook the universe.[264]

The reference to how the deity's "parents' amorous play shook the universe" apparently recalls a relevant verse in *Vamana Purana*, chapter 28.

As we extracted these and similar passages from Courtright's book for our review, we felt a lot of mental agony seeing that he could use words such as 'limp-phallus', 'castration', 'orally erotic', 'eunuch', 'amorous play' and so on in the context of a child, even if it be mythical for a Christian such as Courtright (but Divine for us). Our American readers could perhaps feel our pain by imagining a situation in which Courtright would use such language for the baby Jesus, or if you are not religious, an all-American anthropomorphic child-character such as Mickey Mouse.

Hindus invoke the presence of and blessings of Lord Ganesha at the start of all our prayers. Mickey Mouse is not worshipped of course, but he continues to delight millions of adults and children all over the world with his delightful antics. If someone were to obsessively and insistently see genitalia and other kinds of sexual stuff in the character or persona of the baby Jesus or Mickey Mouse, we would normally conclude that he is suffering from some pathological disorder requiring medical attention. While reading his book on Ganesha, the thought that kept repeating in our mind page after page was—how could he have written this? Why did he do this?

Sexualizing the Hindu Child: The Initiation Ceremony (Upanayana):

In her two-page Foreword, Wendy Doniger refers to the use of Freudian analysis in the following words:

> The episode of beheading by the father cries out for (and has been given by others) a party-line Freudian analysis; Courtright does, indeed, sail through this particular strait, but though he listens with unwaxed ears to the song of the psychoanalytical sirens, he is not seduced. He offsets the Freudian analysis with his own striking model of the parallels between the Ganesa story and the Hindu ritual of the initiation of a young boy . . . [265]

And what are these parallels that deserved a special acknowledgment by Wendy Doniger? While describing his sexualized version of Ganesha and the stories associated with Him, Courtright takes a step forward and transplants erotica onto the solemn Hindu ceremony of *upanayana* in which young Hindu males are initiated into their student life. In effect, after demeaning the Hindu male, Courtright targets the innocent

Hindu child. The *upanayana* ceremony involves a symbolic transformation of the would-be teacher of the student into his new father. This father-son relationship between teacher-student is maintained for a lifetime and does not sever the relationship of the student with his biological father. However, Courtright sees something sexual in this whole affair.

> This new father/son, guru/disciple. Acarya/brahmacarin relationship creates a new bond of affection in the context of absolute domination by the authority figure and utter dependence of the disciple. The sexual nuances of this relationship are well hidden, but it is significant that in the myth Siva gives Ganesa his weapons and in the ritual the acarya gives the brahmacarin the ascetic's staff [*yogadanda*]—symbols, like the broken tusk, of the detached phallus. Carstairs notes further 'There is also a powerfully repressed homosexual fixation on the father. This is shown . . . in indirect and sublimated form, in a man's feeling toward his Guru—in one context in which a warm affectionate relationship (although a passive and dependent one) is given free expression.'[266]

So, the scholarly pair of Carstairs and Courtright have debased even the 'teacher–student relationship' in Hindu society (perhaps privileging the Western version indirectly) by imparting perverse sexual connotations to it. We are indeed curious to know how Courtright would psychoanalyze his relationships with his own students.

Earlier in his book, Courtright assigns sexual connotations to several individual rituals constituting the *upanayana* rite. Thus, when the sacred thread has been placed on the boy-student, he takes it saying *"My staff which fell to the ground in the open air, that I take up again for the sake of long life, holy luster, and holiness"* (*Paraskara Grhyasutra* 2.2.14).[267] Courtright sees the *danda* (staff) as an 'alter-penis' and remarks:

> From a psychoanalytical perspective, this ritual move may be read as a symbolic castration, in that his ascetic/guardian staff protects him while he remains celibate.[268]

We would normally expect such interpretations from juveniles who have watched too many Hollywood or Bollywood movies. Not from an academic in an 'award winning' book.

In the Indian ascetic tradition, there is a long-standing controversy on whether the staff should be single or if it should be a triple-staff (*tridanda*). One wonders what would be Courtright's perspective on this controversy. Hindu tradition sees the *danda* as a symbol of chastisement[269] or discipline, whether inflicted or self-enforced. When a young student assumes a *danda*, he is in effect vowing that he will live according to the prescribed rigors of student life.

It may be pointed out here that Hindus have been performing the upanayana ceremony for their children, often aged five to eight years, for several thousand years now. If there is any reality to Courtright's imaginative interpretation that danda = penis, then the inescapable conclusion is that millions of Hindu children have been subjected unconsciously (or consciously) to sexual abuse by being handed a pseudo-penis in their hand by a male elder during the ceremony. While we find such sexualized interpretations of the *upanayana* defamatory and degrading, Wendy Doniger O'Flaherty finds *it so apt and insightful* that she made a special mention of it in her Foreword to Courtright. The consequences of such essentializing can indeed be grave for an American minority. One wonders how Doniger and Courtright (and the Prize committees that lionize these scholars) view Hindu-American parents who have celebrated their seven year-old's *upanayana*—as potential perverts who should be kept away from white children? Would similar academic-grade myth-making about Jewish parents celebrating an allegedly pedophillic *bar mitzvah* for their children be praised and valorized by the AAR? What would be next? Myth-making about the blood of little white children mixed with matzo balls?

Let us now turn to Hindu tradition itself to verify what significance and symbolism it attaches to the student's staff. The text cited by Courtright is *Paraskara Grhyasutra*, which has been blessed with a very strong commentatorial tradition.[270] The sutra 2.2.14[271] in question reads:

> *tam pratigrihnati yo me dandah paraapatadvaihaayaso*
> *adhibhuumyaam tamaham punaraadada aayushe brahmane*
> *brahmavarcasaayeti*

Courtright follows the translation of Hermann Oldenberg,[272] which is somewhat inaccurate, and he is gladly misled by it. A more accurate translation of the text would be:

> This staff of mine, which has fallen from the sky to the ground, that I take again (or take properly) for a long life, for Vedic study and for holy luster.

Oldenberg must be turning in his grave to learn that his words "*My staff which fell to the ground in the open air*" would be misused by

Courtright to create a phallus-centric interpretation in which the staff is seen as an exposed penis of which the young student has been deprived. When the text is translated more accurately as we have done above, the staff is seen to be a reminder and a symbol of Dharmic authority, or Dharmic discipline with which the teacher invests the student and motivates him to pursue his divinely ordained duty of studying the sacred texts before he gets married.

This interpretation is supported by explanations in numerous traditional commentaries.[273] The staff is widely used to symbolize authority and discipline in numerous cultures all over the world, and Hindu texts are no exception. Perhaps Courtright could explain to us what the staff of Moses, which parted the Red Sea, stands for in his Freudian world.

Courtright does not even make the pretense of acknowledging how the Hindu tradition itself interprets the staff of a celibate student, something that he could have found out by referring to even basic works on Hindu *samskaras* or sacraments.[274] He would have found that according to some authorities,[275] studentship was considered as a long sacrifice, and therefore, a student was expected to bear the staff just as a scholar would in a long sacrifice. *Paraskara Grihyasutra* 2.6.26 suggests that the purpose of the staff was to protect against human and non-human attackers. According to *Manava Grihyasutra* 1.22.11, the student is a traveler on the long road of knowledge. When this paradigm is considered, the staff assumed by the student then becomes reminiscent of the staff used by a traveler. According to the *Varaha Grihyasutra*, the staff was the symbol of the watchman. Apararka in the *Yajnavalkya Smriti* 1.29 states 'that bearing the staff makes the student self-confident and self-reliant when he goes out to the forest to collect fire-sticks for *yajnas*, for tending the cattle of his teacher, or when he travels in darkness.

In other words, while the Indian tradition takes the staff as a symbol of authority, discipline, protection and so on, Courtright sees just a Penis. Another scholar[276] looks at parallel Vedic texts in a very comprehensive manner and arrives at a similar translation and explanation as we give above.

In his Ph.D. thesis too, Courtright refers to the staff which Parvati gave to her son Ganesha for guarding her chamber and says:

> Parvati arms Ganesa with a stick, an implement which might be interpreted to represent a detachable phallus, the emblem of male physical prowess.[277]

How would Courtright interpret the instances in his childhood wherein he was handed a pen, or a broom, a baseball bat, or a stick or even a candy bar by his parent(s)? We leave it to the reader to decide if Courtright's interpretations are genuine or reasonable scholarship, or if they are just pornographic fiction.

Marriage of Ganesha

Hindu tradition is not uniform on the marital status of the deity.[278] While the dominant view depicts him as a son devoted to his mother and as a bachelor, other traditions state that he has two wives. Courtright expends a lot of energy in depicting the 'eunuch' and 'oral' nature of Ganesha, in keeping with his Freudian paradigms. So when conflicting textual evidence relating to his marital status emerges, it has to be explained away in some way. Courtright does this with the following words:

> Iconographically he is sometimes represented sitting between Siddhi and Buddhi, but there is little in the way of mythology about his marriage in the textual tradition. These women appear more like feminine emanations of his androgynous nature, saktis rather than spouses having their own characters and stories.[279]

Courtright's claim that there is little in the textual tradition about Ganesha's marriage to Siddhi and Buddhi stems from the author's presumed ignorance of the *Ganapatya Puranas*. Thus, *Ganesha Purana* (upasana-khanda 49.23 etc) speaks of Buddhi and Siddhi as his two consorts, and *Mudgala Purana* (7.11.35 etc.)[280] calls him the husband of these two. And these references are in addition to the one from *Shiva Purana* that Courtright cites. There are similar other references (e.g., *Parashurama Kalpasutra* 2.4[281], *Narada Mahapurana*, purvabhaga 3.66 etc.). How many more references would one want to say that the textual references are not 'little'? Perhaps the references would be sufficient for Courtright only when he can find anecdotes of beheading, castration, decapitation, sexual fluids, phalluses and the like, which can be given a titillating tilt by his 'analysis'. In fact, had Courtright consulted Tantric texts, he would have indeed found a lot of such texts about his 'marriage' of immense use to his 'analyses'.

Courtright continues:

> The celibate character of his marriage is evoked by the seventh-century poet, Bana, who wrote of Ganesa and his bride as the fused-androgyne, lacking sufficient separateness from one another to

engage in the erotic possibilities of marriage. 'May the single-tusked Ganesa guard the universe, who imitates his parent's custom in that his bride, it seems, has been allowed to take that half of him wherein his face is tuskless.'[282]

Banabhatta is in fact referring to the concept of *ardhnaariishvara*[283] that depicts Siva and Parvati (who definitely are not a celibate couple) as two halves of one deity, and suggests that the wife of Ganesha, being tusk-less, represents a similar conception with her constituting that side of his which does not have the tusk (since one of his tusks is broken).

The reckless free-association, inconsistency and ad-hoc nature that characterizes Courtright's work in general gets exhibited here again when he uses his preconceived notions of a celibate Ganesha to explain away references to his children in the Puranas:

He lives a celibate marriage; yet, according to the above myth at least, he has children; this is another way in which he is the inversion of his father, who has sex but no children—at least none engendered naturally. Reference to Ganesa's children are indeed rare, this one in the Siva Purana being the only one known to me among the Puranic sources.

I hope that since 1985, Courtright has had the opportunity to read the Tantras to realize that Ganesha's marriage was not really celibate.[284]

Ganesha as.a Trickster

Courtright cites the British anthropologist Edmund Leach approvingly:

Leach sees this characteristic as Ganesa's closes link to the trickster: Ganesa's broken tusk and severed head with the long flaccid trunk are the clearest signals of his sexual ambiguity.[285]

Concluding his own estimation of Ganesha as a 'trickster', Courtright then likens the deity to a eunuch:

His sexuality remains ambiguous, as his relationship with his mother and father, his detachable tusk/phallus and his similarities to eunuchs all suggest.[286]

All the above passages of Courtright are not only dubious from an academic perspective, they are also plainly offensive, and perverse. Perhaps, Courtright *et al* always see life through a different aperture than most of us.[287] Perhaps, they always see everything as a cigar, and the cigar as only a *Lingam*.

The Worship of Ganesha

Chapter IV deals with the worship of Ganesha in homes, in temples, and during public festivals in Maharashtra. Overall, the description is balanced, readable and nothing out of the ordinary. It is clearly written from the perspective of an observant outsider. A few references to Indian literature on the subject are thrown in, besides some from the works of the Indologists as well, perhaps to give the entire narrative a quasi-academic flavor. For the Hindus, the chapter perhaps does not offer much that is not already known to them in general terms. For the Westerners or even Westernized Indians, the narrative could serve as a useful and informative background on how the tradition of worship of Ganesha is actually practised in our times. The public celebration of the Ganapati festival in Pune and Mumbai is well known. In a welcome departure, and for the sake of simplicity, the author studies the public festival in the city of Ahmednagar instead. This chapter, as well as the next conforms to the fifth level of studying the deity that is proposed by Courtright in chapter II (pp. 18–19). This is the etiological level, wherein the "narrative, metaphorical and sociopsychological levels are joined in the immediacy of the image and the ritual actions to be performed in response to it", to quote the words of the author himself (p.19). It is not exactly clear in this chapter, however, how the author has related the first three levels to the ritual performances to Ganesha's *murtis*. At best, the attempt is very sketchy and incomplete.

Chapter V titled, 'Ganesa in a Regional Setting: Maharashtra' deals with the well-known fact of deep devotion of Maharashtrians to Ganapati. It opens with a strange comment, based on an old work, that in South East and in East Asia he is more often portrayed as demon.[288] Perhaps this has changed in the last six decades since the book referenced by Courtright was written. One of us, who has worked in and has traveled to that part of the world (Thailand, Bali and Java, Singapore) would clearly question this characterization today. At least in our own times, he is a beloved deity for the Hindus of Bali (and even more so in eastern Java), as well as for the Buddhists in urban Thailand.[289]

The author makes a minor error on page 204, in stating that Muslims account for only 5% of Maharashtra's population.[290] The author sketches the general religious background of the Indian state, and credits the Varkaris (with their pilgrimages and other devotional practices) for giving the state its vital and genuinely religious character.

He goes on to enumerate the major religious shrines of the state, and numerous omissions are seen in his brief list—for instance those of Alandi and Dehu, which are very important areas for the Varkaris.

Courtright then proceeds to narrate the sacred stories associated with some important shrines of Ganapati in Maharashtra, relying on the famous *Ganesa-kosha* of Gadgil.[291] However, some of Courtright's paraphrases and translations from this Marathi text are inaccurate. For instance, Courtright narrates the legend related to the Ashtavinayaka Temple at Siddhateka in the following words:

> When Brahma began creating the universe, two demons, Madhu and Kaitabha, appeared out of Vishnu's ear and began to disturb Brahma. Vishnu tried to kill the demons, but they proved too powerful. Then he went to Siva, pleasing him with devotional songs, and asked for his help. Siva scolded him, saying that if he had worshipped Ganesa in the first place he would not be in this predicament . . . (Gadgil, 2.43–4).[292]

One wonders where Gadgil has stated that the demons emerged from the ear of Vishnu. The exact words of the text, in Marathi, are:

> *madhu aani kaitabha yaa dona atishaya paraakramii daityaani brahmadevaalaa tyaacyaa srshtiracanecyaa karyaata uddanda vighnen aanuun traasa dyaavayaasa suruvaat kelii*[293]

There is no mention that the demons emerged from Vishnu's ears in Gadgil's version.[294]

Further, the claim that Shiva 'scolded' Vishnu is also Coutrtight's own commentary, and is neither stated nor implied by Gadgil. He merely says that Shiva told (*mhanuna*) Vishnu to worship Ganesha with the *Shadaaksari Mantra*. In tracing the origin of the *Gaanapatya Sampradaaya*, Courtright speculates that their tradition of considering their deity as the Supreme Deity probably arose in the tenth century CE or perhaps even earlier. As a supporting piece of evidence, he offers

> A hagiographical text from about this time, the Sankaravijaya of Anandagiri, gives us a picture of some aspects of Ganapatya thought and practice.[295]

There is no evidence that the *Sankaravijaya* of Anandagiri is such an old text, it is typically assigned a much later date.[296] The Advaita tradition knows of many Anandagiris and the authorship of this particular *Sankaravijaya* is very uncertain. Therefore, this text cannot be used reliably for dating the origin of the *Ganapatya Sampradaaya*.

One does wish though, that Courtright had included a more rigorous treatment of the core texts of this *sampradaaya*, namely the *Ganesha Purana, Mudgala Purana* and so on.[297]

The rest of the chapter deals with some important shrines such as the Moragaon Ganapati, the temple at Chinchavad, Theur and so on.[298] Then there is a long discussion on the genesis and growth of the Ganesha festival, with the narrative stopping roughly at the time Lokamanya Tilak died. All these are subjects of common knowledge and the summary and overview provided by Courtright, in this context, are very readable and over-all, balanced. The chapter erroneously says that India won its freedom in 1948, which is probably a typing error for the correct year, 1947.[299]

The last chapter named 'Ganesa: The Protean God' is lyrical and poetical and acknowledges the continued relevance and importance of the deity to Hindus in general, and to Maharashtrians in particular.

Taking Liberties with Liberal Arts (Courtright's Ph.D. Thesis)

We had an opportunity to obtain a copy of Courtright's Ph.D. thesis[300] of which the book under review is an expansion. Interestingly, in the Preface of his thesis, the author states:

> Nearly ten years ago, while I was teaching conversational English at Ahmadnagar College in central Maharasthra, several of my students invited me to join them and their families for the annual celebrations to the Hindu god Ganesa. At that time all I knew about Ganesa was that he was the elephant-faced deity who Hindus regarded as the god of good fortune. I had seen his picture in numerous shops in the city and had gathered the impression that the good fortune he was believed to bring had largely to do with the financial success and material well-being. Hindus seemed to view him with a compelling light-heartedness which I found quite different from the more somber attitudes my Protestant upbringing had taught me were appropriately religious.[301]

He states that during the Ganesha Festival at Ahmadnagar the Maharashtrian dancers made him dance with them and as a result, "I had become united with them. It seemed that I had finally experienced India 'from the inside'." He expresses his acknowledgements to his informants in the following words:

> Although the title page lists me as the author of this dissertation, many others have been involved in its completion. The people of

Maharashtra, displaying attitudes of hospitality for which India is famous, welcomed my frequent inquiries about their festival and its traditions, patiently submitted to my interviews, and made my research pleasurable. No scholar could hope to have greater cooperation than I received from them.[302]

Through our analysis of the resulting book, we have seen the manner in which Courtright expressed his gratitude for the cooperation offered by Maharashtrian Hindus: calling the cherished deity of his 'native informants' as something of a eunuch, something like a homosexual, and a pervert harboring sexual fantasies for his mother!

Perhaps, it is not out of place to mention that even Courtright's PhD thesis is so full of errors, that it does not even spell the names of Hindu texts and common Hindu terms correctly. For instance,

On Page 5, Atharva Veda is mis-spelt as 'Athārva Veda'
On Page 14 and 17 etc., the Mahābhārata is mis-spelt as 'Māhabhārata'
On Page 14 and 15, the Mānavagṛhyasūtra' is mis-spelt as 'Mānavagṛhasūtra'
On Page 16, the Yājñavalkyasmṛti is mis-spelt as 'Yajṇavālkyasmṛti'
On Page 18, Mahābhāṣya is mis-spelt as 'Māhabhāṣa'
On Page 18, Rāmāyaṇa is mis-spelt as 'Rāmayāna'
On Page 19, Mahāpurāṇa is mis-spelt as 'Māhapurāṇa', Matsyapurāṇa as 'Matsyapûraṇa', Vāyupurāṇa as 'Vayupurāṇa'.
On Page 20, Jaya is mis-spelt as 'Jāyā', Vijaya as 'Vijāyā'
On Page 22, Śakti is mis-spelt as 'Śaktī'.
On Page 24, Prahara is mis-spelt as 'Prahāra'
There is no consistency of transliteration. Sometimes, Vinaayaka should have been spelt as vināyaka but instead we see vinayaka (e.g., p. 14, 18). Apparently, the transliteration marks serve more an artistic than a phonetic purpose. A new meaning to the phrase 'Liberal Arts', should we say?

To give an example of errors in his thesis, on p.19 he claims,

Ganesa is conspicuously absent in the two oldest Purāṇas, the Matsyapūraṇa (sic) and the Vayupurāṇa (sic), and in the explicitly sectarian Vaiṣṇavite Bhāgavatapurāṇa. Although he does appear in the remaining fifteen of the eighteen Māhapurāṇas (sic), he does not figure prominently in any of them. His character in all of his Puranic appearances is markedly similar.

This claim is wrong. For instance, we may point out that the story of Ganesha is narrated in brief in *Matsya Purana* 154.495–505, and the deity is also mentioned in chapter 260 of the same Purana as the husband of Riddhi and Siddhi. Ganesa does figure prominently in the *Brahmavaivarta Purana*, a Maha Purana, which has an entire portion titled 'Ganapatikhanda' containing forty-six chapters.

Conclusion: Academic Scholarship, or 'Peer-Reviewed Pornography'?

The above examples are but a small specimen of erroneous translations, selective use of Hindu textual evidence, insufficient knowledge of Tantric and Yogic traditions, and the over-sexualization of passages in Hindu texts that characterize Courtright's book, page after page, and chapter after chapter. It is fair to say that being based on incorrect data, his interpretations and his reconstruction of the Hindu deity Ganesha are by and large invalid.

To conclude then, Courtright's book may be considered as an example of excellent pornographic fiction, and also as an example of careless academic scholarship. It is therefore surprising that scholars in South Asian and Indology programs in the United States have praised the book and awarded it prizes. It makes one wonder if this is due to the fact that the level of scholarship in Indian and Hinduism studies is really substandard in American Universities.

In an apparent effort to defuse the crisis, Courtright wrote an email to an internet list of scholars in South Asian Studies:[303]

> I wrote it over twenty years ago, in a different discursive environment than we have now ... were I writing that book today I would, hopefully, be more aware of how it might be read by some Hindu readers in both India and its diasporas.[304]

This confession must be quite puzzling to any honest academic. This approach raises questions regarding ethics and honesty in scholarship. Is an academic expected to play to the gallery, as Courtright has confessed he did and perhaps intends to do in the future as well? If so, is it not a violation of objectivity, ethics and honesty? One may understand that interpretations of literature, history, or any other observable phenomenon changes as new proven theories and data emerge. But why should the interpretation change according to the readers? What kind of academic objectivity is that? Is it not a corroboration of the accusation that there is a deeply entrenched anti-Hindu bias among Wendy's Children?

Courtright apparently felt that so long as his audience was not Hindu and annoyingly knowledgeable, he could depict Hinduism in an obscene manner—perhaps as an 'inside' ethnic joke shared with his white colleagues. One cannot help but recall Doniger's thigh-slapping, triumphant amusement upon 'learning' from Kripal that the Sri Ramakrishna that many 'moronic' Hindus worship as the epitome of their religion could be academically *tried and convicted* as a conflicted, maladjusted homosexual, and a pervert to boot.[305] Those were cozy times indeed to laugh about the heathen and his blindness, with one's buddies. Today, with more Hindus constituting the audience, Courtright feels that he has to calibrate his interpretations differently. Strangely, the academic reaction to this bizarre phenomenon ranges from a deafening silence to showering praises on him.

Books such as those of Courtright and Doniger merely conform to the latest fad in eroticizing 'exotic' cultures, just as a few decades earlier it was very fashionable for some Western anthropologists to go 'bravely' to some remote island in the Samoa archipelago to study the sexual practices of Samoans. Such studies not just demean the culture that forms their subject. They are like the gaze of a pervert that mentally disrobes a lady standing in front of him. Indeed, the book reviewed by us does not necessarily illuminate its purported subject matter. Rather, it allows us to act as voyeurs of the mind of the author. Hindus and Indians do not need such 'dedicated', 'thoughtful', 'respectful' and 'loving' scholars to promote an understanding of our heritage in the West, just as an abandoned orphan would do well without the love of a pedophile.[306]

III

WHISTLEBLOWERS, WITCH HUNTERS AND VICTIMS

✦

By Aditi Banerjee

Turning and turning in the widening gyre
The falcon cannot hear the falconer;
Things fall apart;
The centre cannot hold.
                    —*The Second Coming*, William Butler Yeats

This comic is intended to be satirical, and any resemblance herein to actual events or persons living or dead is purely coincidental.

This comic is intended to be satirical, and any resemblance herein to actual events or persons living or dead is purely coincidental.

Chapter 18

Myth of the Savage Frontier[*]

The previous section documented the beginnings of a dialogue revealing serious and troubling issues regarding American scholarship on Hinduism. The remaining two sections of this book examine how the RISA establishment and the mainstream media sought to hijack and recast the substantive challenges made by public intellectuals as an 'attack' on scholars and as a 'threat' to academic freedom. In this retelling, the RISA scholars whose works were critiqued were portrayed as 'victims' of a conspiracy from dangerous and violent 'others'.

Due to the power imbalance between the RISA cartel and the diasporic public intellectuals, and the cultural complicity of the mainstream media with the academy, this strategy succeeded in distorting the issues and thwarting sincere efforts to re-evaluate the academic objectivity and credibility of RISA scholarship. Sections III and IV examine how this red herring—the claim of savage attacks against American scholars—played out both in scholarly discussion groups as well as in mainstream media reports.

A Brief History of the 'Savage' Trope

In order to understand why this *Victim versus the Dangerous Other* trope resonates so strongly with the American academic establishment and mainstream media today, we must understand its deep roots in

---

[*] This chapter is based on discussions with Rajiv Malhotra, and it summarizes a core thesis he has researched about American national character. His full thesis based on an analysis of 400 years of American history will be the subject of his forthcoming book. This chapter paraphrases portions of his unpublished manuscript with his permission.

American mythology and history. The RISA scholars who have cast themselves as victims are actually tapping into an internalized mythology of the 'savage versus the civilized', also known as the Frontier Myth. This has long formed the collective subconscious of white Americans and has given them meaning and direction since they first established colonies at Plymouth Rock and gazed covetously across the vast North American continent. Richard Slotkin, the preeminent historian of the American Frontier, explains:

> The Myth of the Frontier is our oldest and most characteristic myth, expressed in a body of literature, folklore, ritual, historiography, and polemics produced over a period of three centuries. According to this mythic-historiography, the conquest of the wilderness and the subjugation or displacement of the Native Americans who originally inhabited it have been the means to our achievement of a national identity, a democratic polity, an ever-expanding economy, and a phenomenally dynamic and 'progressive' civilization.[1]

The development of the Frontier Myth has been documented by various notable historians such as Turner, Smith, Slotkin, Horsman, Drinnon and others.[2] This Myth is played out in the Eden-Frontier dichotomy. Eden is 'our' space and the Frontier is the 'satanic' wilderness inhabited by uncivilized, unknown 'others'. The mission entrusted to Americans—purportedly by Providence—is to constantly expand Eden, or Civilization (its secular equivalent), by conquering and colonizing the wild Frontier. The Frontier Myth helped to generate cohesiveness among the settlers by evoking varying degrees of 'otherness' towards the Native Americans (and later the Blacks and the Mexicans)—ranging from exoticization to suspicion, tension, and outright hostility. The Natives were otherwise invisible—seen as part and parcel of an *uninhabited* wilderness—thus providing untrammeled rights to the Whites to reshape the wilderness as they saw fit.[3] A similar situation can be seen as prevailing in academic studies of Hinduism—the intellectual space is seen as an uninhabited wilderness, thus granting full rights to scholars to recast Hindu religious thought as they see fit. Perhaps the shock of having the invisible other rise up and ask for a place at the table is what leads to heated rhetoric about the field being 'hijacked' from the 'outside'.

The landscape of the Frontier Myth is partitioned by a moral demarcation separating civilization from the wilderness. The civilization-wilderness dichotomy is a device to distinguish civilized Whites from uncivilized non-Whites. The Frontier has been both a geographical place and a mythic space populated by various imagined casts/castes: Native American Indians as savages, Blacks as inferior, Whites as heroes, white women as needing rescue from savages, and so on. The underlying motivation for such imaginations of the other was, of course, lust for land and the need for hegemony, but such materialistic aspirations had to be *justified* in order to quiet the rumblings of the collective white conscience. Reginald Horsman, a noted historian who has traced the role of the American myth in defining and controlling the non-White 'other' writes:

> Although the white Americans . . . wanted personal success and wealth, they also wanted a clear conscience. If the United States was to remain in the minds of its people a nation divinely ordained for great deeds, then the fault for the suffering inflicted in the rise to power and prosperity had to lie elsewhere. White Americans could rest easier and the sufferings of other races could be blamed on the racial weakness rather than on whites' relentless search for wealth and power.[4]

The quest to blame the Natives for their own suffering gave rise to an abundant flowering of popular narratives and media images of the 'primitive savagery' of the Natives that warranted their subjugation—not dissimilar to some of today's ethnographies and reports about various kinds of Third World peoples. This bestselling 'Indian atrocity literature' chronicled the kidnapping, capture and torture of Whites, especially women and children, at the hands of Native Americans on the Frontier. In today's language, one might say that the Natives were portrayed as egregious violators of human rights, their religion and culture blamed as the cause of their inhumanity. These sensationalized stories included one-sided exaggerations of some actual incidents and outright lies about others. Their main application, however, was not to provide insight or accurate accounts, but to offer an excuse for the usurping of Indian lands.[5] The whites achieved this by devastating the image of Native American culture and questioning whether natives who clung to such 'evil' culture deserved the same human rights as the civilized (white) people.

This literature glorified the white 'frontiersman' who ventured fearlessly into the wilderness and dealt with the 'savages' on their own savage terms, while bringing back valuable experiences and insights that helped further the project of advancing 'civilization.' The atrocity stories served as 'anecdotal data' to reinforce theories about Native 'savagery'. Repetition of these stories in the popular media, as well as by scholarly writers, was sufficient to kill off debate on substantive issues regarding Native Americans' *own* rights.

Even those who did not indulge directly in this sort of atrocity literature were heavily influenced by the attitudes projected in it. Most Americans simply assumed that the *uncivilized* Native American was doomed for extinction in the face of *civilization*—similar to the idea that traditions such as Hinduism are doomed to succumb eventually to what is called 'progress'. This idea had permeated literature about the Natives for over two hundred years.[6] The theoretical framework created by Christian theology and Enlightenment notions of progress and history became the received wisdom about the Natives' inevitable fate. It is within the context of this 'high' theoretical framework formulated by the leading intellectuals of the day that the 'lower-level' atrocity literature (i.e. the 'field data' gathered by other Whites) produced its true impact and power. The white control of theoretical frameworks, institutions, and publication outlets also defined what kind of data was collected, documented, and highlighted, and, more importantly, what was not.

An 'Open Society' Debates the Rights and Wrongs of Indian 'Removal'

The early development of an independent America was fueled by a seeming paradox: on the one hand, a systemic genocide of the Natives was being carried out across America, while, on the other hand, the nation was celebrating the beginning of a liberal democracy with participatory voices from many sides. The dissonance between a liberal society and a wholesale decimation of a people gave rise to an 'Enlightenment' view that sought to romanticize the Natives while justifying their destruction. This Enlightenment view of the Natives sought to revise the fundamentalist Christian view of them as subhuman 'beasts' by positing the Natives as innately equal humans beings who, given proper training, could become civilized. This romantic image of the Native American as a 'Noble Savage' influenced important American writers such as Nathaniel Hawthorne, Henry David Thoreau, Herman Melville, and James Fenimore Cooper, who continued to portray the Native as a noble albeit tragic figure. These writings had a sense of tragedy built on fatalistic inevitability—that nature had predestined the Indian for destruction in the face of progress.[7] They presented a more humane portrayal than the 'beastly savage' image. However, this did not prevent the Natives' extermination. The intellectuals of the time also failed to identify Christian intolerance or Enlightenment-based European supremacy as problematic ingredients in the process of genocide.

In fact, the Enlightenment model of the Natives served less as a challenge to the prevailing 'beastly savage' model than it served as a reinforcement of both models' underlying perception of the Natives as an 'uncivilized' and inferior people. The main difference between the two models was that the Enlightenment view sought to civilize the Natives while the fundamentalist view sought to conquer them. Both aimed at denigrating and exterminating native cultures and religions.

For example, Jeffersonian Democracy, though a product of the Enlightenment, had an ambivalent position on the Indians and a worse one on the Blacks. Jefferson admired Native Americans and saw their extinction as tragic; yet during both terms of his presidency, tens of thousands of Indians were forcibly relocated from their native habitats to reservations west of the Mississippi River. The sleight of hand that allowed Jefferson and others to purport to admire the 'Noble Savages' while actively supporting and enabling their destruction was a belief in the predestined destruction of the Natives in the face of the inevitable triumph of 'Enlightenment' and 'progress'.

Playing 'Victim' to the Savages

The liberal impulse, fostered by the democratic leanings of the American people, contributed in a curious way to the development of the Frontier Myth, as the introduction of a liberal voice (the 'good cop') played counterpoint to the frontiersman (the 'bad cop') and yet came to the inevitable conclusion that the Natives were an unchanging threat to white 'victims' that had to be removed.

The historian, Richard Drinnon, graphically illustrates how the literature produced during the process of the white takeover of North America provided justification for ignoring the rights of the Natives who lived there.[8] The literature often acknowledged as a starting point that the Natives had a favorable case for the ownership of the land and the practice of their culture. The American Frontier and its perpetual expansion were justified through a kind of 'soft' debate that was managed through these stories. Drinnon shows that the debate was never allowed to get serious, but was simply used to assuage the American conscience. Indeed, the health of the American Myth has depended to a great extent, as Slotkin and others have shown, on blocking out genuine debate while claiming to champion intellectual freedom.

In many of the atrocity stories, a token white person would try to make a sympathetic case for the Indians. This is a historical version of the modern urban, liberal white 'good cop' who feels pity and objects to the unfair demonology and the killings of Natives by a courageous but unsophisticated frontiersman—the 'bad cop'. The good cop can be seen as the spokesman for the Enlightenment who expresses shock at the cold-blooded hunting down of Native Americans. He pleads that humane values and fairness in battle be respected and not forgotten—even when dealing with savages. He may also raise uncomfortable questions about the Natives' inherent right to control their own land and the frontiersman's desire to take it away from them.

There is a classic device in these stories that comes to the forefront and serves to end the debate started by the liberal 'good cop'. The frontiersman (often the hero of the tale) does not waste his time arguing over grievances that the Natives may have about his methods and ambitions. Instead, he shows the liberal visitor (and thus the reader) extensive evidence of the personal threats directed at him and the dangerous everyday life he leads in an *age of terror*. He shows the graves of slain family members and tells tales of Native atrocities against Whites, especially women and children, and also against other Natives. The frontiersman, in effect, ends the argument by playing the victim and appealing to the sympathy of the 'good cop' and, by extension, of the reader. (**A remarkably similar ploy is used by Paul Courtright,** as we shall see in Chapter 24.)

At this point, the good cop in the Frontier Myth backs off, reluctantly conceding that he, like other educated white consumers of these stories, should not be so quick to judge the frontiersmen who, after all, seem to have ample justification for their contempt and hatred for the Natives. These frontiersmen *know* the problems with the Native culture as experts *in the field*. This qualifies them to speak with authority. Moreover, they clearly have been victims of the savages' threats and actions.[9] Similar assumptions about *expertise* and special knowledge about native cultures are carried over to today's Area Studies experts in the American academy.

The same story was writ large in contemporaneous historical developments. By the time of Jackson's Presidency, the debate between the Enlightenment and fundamentalist Christian views of the Native was dying down: even those who considered Natives to be innately equal humans had largely internalized the atrocity literature (which in addition to portraying the Natives in debasing and cruel ways showed Christianity and Civilization as the solution). Jacksonian Democracy fully embraced the doctrine of Manifest Destiny that vowed to remove and relocate Native peoples so that white Americans could occupy the land. Andrew Jackson is infamous for causing the Trail of Tears—the forced removal of the Cherokee people from their sacred homelands in the southeast to Oklahoma—a tragic ethnic cleansing of an enormous number of people.

Andrew Jackson provided ready justifications by graphically depicting the depravity and cruelty of the Natives. Images of women and other helpless victims were especially useful. For example, Jackson would call for action using words like, "The Seminole Indians . . . have for more than two years past, visited our border settlements with all the horrors of savage massacre—helpless women have been butchered and the cradle stained with the blood of innocence."[10] Such rhetoric about the devilish Natives and their treatment of women was also a staple of church sermons and dictated how Whites perceived the Natives.[11]

Some apologists argue that greedy white settlers and militias acted on their own, while the U.S. federal policy towards the Natives was more benevolent. However, evidence presented by Drinnon and other historians reveals an interesting partnership based on Manifest Destiny between the government and the frontiersmen.[12] This again can best be described as a good-cop, bad-cop relationship. Andrew Jackson's excesses as the bad cop were met with public criticism by the presidential cabinet playing the good cop. But, ultimately, as Drinnon points out, such violence was protected and justified by powerful cabinet members such as John Quincy Adams (who later became President). When Adams was asked to investigate Jackson's actions, he produced a White Paper that adroitly avoided dealing with substantive issues such as the unprovoked atrocities of white militias, the white lust for Native lands, and the *internal causes* of such brutality within the white communities. Instead, in the report:

> he laid the groundwork in international law for genocidal acts against a ferocious nation that observes no rules . . . if a commander has to contend with an inhuman enemy . . . he may take the lives of some of his prisoners, and treat them as his own people have been treated. The justification of these principles is found in the salutary efficacy for terror and example.[13]

Once again, the focus of the debate was easily shifted by raising the bogey that *civilization is in danger* from savage attacks by Natives. This sensationalized approach eliminated any need for serious analysis and soul-searching. Adams was not acting in isolation but relying on the Frontier Myth.

This 'switch the debate' tactic has always enjoyed tremendous support from the American establishment, sometimes quite openly. All the living American ex-presidents at that time explicitly endorsed this creative re-imagining of the problem of white militia brutality against Native Americans. Thomas Jefferson, for one, felt that Adam's White Paper linking the US usurpation of Native lands to the Natives' inherent savagery was a triumph of logic. Further, Jefferson noted that this would help "maintain in Europe a correct opinion of our political morality".[14] Once the Europeans accepted the status of Whites as *victims* and the status of the Native Americans as *savages*, they were less likely to doubt the success of the American experiment in democracy and its claims to Manifest Destiny.

These atrocity stories reinforced theories about Indian savagery. Both in the theorizing and in the anecdotal data-gathering, **no effort was made to interrogate and investigate issues from the opposing point of view.** Enlightenment and biblical frameworks were never challenged to the extent to which Native culture and religion were critiqued and demonized. This is analogous to the privileged position given today to Western social theories in the academy, along with the lack of agency given to the voices and viewpoints of others. Furthermore, the brutalities of settlers and missionaries were never highlighted on par with Indians' actions, even in cases when these actions were in direct retaliation against white brutalities. There was no reverse gazing by Native scholars looking at white culture to counterbalance the discourse.[15]

Once the savagery of the Native is expertly 'proven', the story and discussion ends. The Natives' inherent human right to defend their sacred sites and families in the face of white greed and aggression, and the huge discrepancy between White and Native atrocities, are never discussed. Drinnon writes: "Yes, the reader was asked to reflect, 'Is it not too easy to be virtuous at a distance?' A little cheap to forgive merciless savages when we ourselves have not suffered . . . at their hands?"[16] **The same appeal is made by Wendy's Children to fair-minded Americans who may otherwise be swayed by the evidence presented by the diaspora. The 'others' may have a point, they reluctantly acknowledge, but how can you judge us when we are being** threatened—especially when you have not suffered at the hands of Hindu savages like we have? Thus, the model of the Savage Heathen versus the Civilized, so deeply embedded in America's self-mythologizing, comes to life in the contemporary context.

The remainder of this section narrates the range of responses from RISA scholars, beginning with a small minority who expressed genuine concern over the quality of scholarship when confronted with the evidence, and moving to the vast majority who decided to circle their wagons against this new 'threat' from the natives. Section IV will examine how journalists in the mainstream American media have in the same way allowed certain American academicians to manipulate the debate. Reporters—either consciously or unconsciously—often used the 'savage versus victim' trope, Section IV will examine the role played in this regard by *Washington Post*, the *University of Chicago Magazine*, *New York Times*, and *India Abroad*, as well as by writings on the interfaith Internet portal, *Beliefnet.com*.

In order to properly understand, however, the extreme hostility and paranoia with which these challenges to academic orthodoxy were received by the academy and mainstream media, the particular debate regarding Hindu scholarship must be located in the larger historical paradigm of the American Frontier Myth described above.

Hindus are the latest in a long list of 'savage' minorities to be pitted against the 'civilizing' force of the America's Manifest Destiny. Unlike the frontier struggles of the past, this is not a physical battle with literal bloodshed, but a battle of ideas, where indigenous traditions and ways of knowledge are sought to be decimated by Western tropes and ontologies (brought forth by academic 'pilgrims' venturing into foreign and exotic intellectual and cultural territory), where the 'dead Indian' is not a physical body, but a deity (Ganesha, Shiva, the Goddess—victimized by the psychoanalytical weapons of the academic battalion) or a saint (Sri Ramakrishna, defamed as a pedophile) or spiritual practices (Tantra, denuded of spiritual value by being recast as an appropriation by sexually repressed upper castes of lower-caste sexual practices). It is only when we view the ongoing controversy in this paradigm that we can make sense of the war cry put up by the RISA cartel against the indigenous Hindus re-staking their claim over their own intellectual and philosophical territory.

Chapter 19

An American Community Gets Awakened

The *RISA-Lila* articles became what Arvind Sharma has called the "tipping point in the relationship between the academic and faith communities", because the articles "transformed the Hindu perception of the Western academic community from one of adulation, or at least acquiescence, to one of suspicion and even hostility".[17] Following these articles (in 2002 and 2003), many student groups, community organizations and other members of the Hindu diaspora joined in the protest about what they perceived to be academy-endorsed defamation of their religious traditions. Objections and concerns were expressed through articles of varying levels of intellectual depth, community meetings, online petitions, letters to editors, and contacts with universities, news bureaus and other institutions.

Indian-Americans have successfully made the United States their home, contributing immensely to its economic, social, and educational systems. Many of them have observed that their Indian heritage is often misportrayed in popular culture, and that their religious beliefs and traditions are routinely mocked in what is meant to be a multicultural educational system. These include everything from mocking the Hindu vegetarian diet, to demonizing the Goddess in school textbooks, to implying that Hindu beliefs are laughable superstitions[†]. Up until

---

[†] This on-going insensitivity is exemplified by a Social Studies textbook for sixth grade American students, published by Oxford University Press in 2006. The chapter on ancient India discusses Hindu dietary practices on page 144, where a sarcastic caption belittles the Hindu emphasis on vegetarianism and mindlessly, in bold font, taunts Hindu and other vegetarian students with the words from an outdated television commercial, "Where's the Beef?" In that same textbook, Kali and Durga are referred to as 'terrible and blood-thirsty' goddesses that the students are warned to watch out

recently, there has been a lack of organized, coordinated action to address these issues. Consequently, Eurocentric and idiosyncratic narratives about Indic traditions have persisted.

The continuing existence of strange distortions and exoticized stereotypes through which Indian culture is represented in the mainstream American educational system may be partially due to the relatively recent arrival of immigrants from India and their inexperience in American activism. Other American minorities have faced similar obstacles in the past, given the historical tendency of the white Christian establishment to resist the admission of each new ethnic group. Time and again, there has been a struggle against the status quo of institutional power, and each time the paradigm has shifted to allow greater membership to a new group of American citizens. Peoples from other ethnicities and religions such as the much older Jewish-American community have proactively formed groups to fight social pathologies such as anti-Semitism. For instance, the Anti-Defamation League was formed in 1913, and had a long upward struggle.[18] In the past few decades, Muslim-Americans have followed suit and formed several organizations to work with curriculum committees and textbook publishers.[19] Prior to the events described in this book, Indian-Americans acting on their own, or in small ad hoc groups, would sometimes approach their children's school districts to express concerns about misinformation. But it is only in the past few years that there has been any coordinated effort to contest the defamation of Hinduism.

In this manner, Indian-Americans, the so-called 'model minority,' became the latest American minority group to take direct interest in, and make proactive actions in favor of, their cultural representation, following a long line of other similarly hyphenated American groups, including African-Americans, Arab-Americans, Chinese-Americans, Hispanic-Americans, Japanese-Americans, Jewish-Americans, and Muslim-Americans.

---

for. On page 87, in the few sentences that discuss the Indian epics, the textbook explains that, "Hanuman loved Rama so much that it is said that he is present every time the Ramayana is told." Then the sixth grade textbook again mocks this beautiful Hindu tradition, asking the children to "look around—see any monkeys?" Eleven year-old students in American classrooms are encouraged by this unnecessary taunt in their textbook to tease or ridicule their mostly brown-skinned Hindu classmates: "See any monkeys?" These are just three examples from one chapter of only one of the sixth grade textbook in common use in American classrooms. The content about India as narrated in the OUP textbook is actually less egregious than descriptions about India found in other mainstream Social Studies textbooks by different publishers.

This engagement requires that Hindu-Americans be recognized as equal participants at discussion tables where Indic traditions are considered—including curriculum committees, educational institutions, museums, media outlets, political think tanks, and corporate policy committees. Obtaining such a seat at the table is a slow and difficult process.[20]

American Business Schools Respect India while RISA Denigrates it

The strikingly derogatory portrayals of Indian traditions produced in RISA-related academic forums are in contrast to other areas of the American educational system. Contrary to the often grim positioning of Hindu culture and India in South Asian Studies, there is a burgeoning appreciation for India and Indians in American business schools that reflects India's new position in the world economy. Indian entrepreneurs, businesspersons, management consultants, and industrialists are invited as guest speakers in business school courses, and as equal participants in debates and seminars. That is to say, *practitioners* of business in India are treated as experts whose opinions and experiences are listened to with respect—setting the precedent that the *practitioners* of Hinduism should be given similar positioning in Religious Studies (practitioners of Christianity, Judaism, Islam and Buddhism already enjoy this status in Religious Studies). American business schools have a pragmatic and merit-based intellectual tradition that has enabled Indians to advance rapidly.

Unfortunately, the representation of India is very different in the Social Sciences and Humanities. Indian-Americans have long witnessed that practitioners of Hinduism, Jainism, and Sikhism, along with their respective teachers or gurus, are positioned as *targets* of study (i.e. as 'native informants') rather than as *subjects* entitled to respect and as scholars and experts with an equal share in shaping the understanding of Indian civilization.

This section shows that, even with their high levels of education and professional/business success, the Indian diaspora faces obstacles in entering into a dialogic process about their culture with an American academy deeply entrenched in its own cultural pathologies. We will examine a few examples of the self-perpetuating supremacy and defensiveness exhibited by the Ivory Tower. Many academics react against interventions by members of the diaspora with hostility, and many brand their critics as extremists, even stretching the facts to try to link them to political events in India. This is unfortunate:

> Such a phobic attitude in the academy sadly fails to acknowledge that the adherents of these traditions are not primitive foreigners, but they are increasingly one's Indian-American neighbors, doctors, classmates and friends. Furthermore, it fails to recognize that these traditions are finding adherents among a significant number of white Americans and other Westerners who find them compelling and important. This increasing presence and participation of Indians and Indian culture in American society not only provides new and valuable resources for scholarly research understanding, but it also demands that scholars become more aware of and sensitive to the traditions and their followers.[21]

Internal Challenges for the Indian-American Community

By no means can all of these problems be blamed on the academy. Through the years, many well-placed members of the Indian diaspora have opted to downplay their Hindu heritage, even though most other Americans very publicly celebrate their religion and welcome others to do the same. Many modern Indians, raised in urban India's English-medium schools, have not developed an authentic indigenous viewpoint. They implicitly equate received Eurocentric viewpoints with 'universal' values.[22]

Indian spiritual leaders also tend to not engage the mainstream *academic* establishment. While they provide competent leadership and guidance on spiritual philosophy and rituals, they remain introverted within their cocooned organizations and are largely ignorant of the massive Western academic establishment that represents Hinduism by default. These traditional experts are disadvantaged by their lack of American-style strategic thinking skills and their lack of understanding of how 'the system' works. The clergy, or scholar-practitioners of Judeo-Christian traditions, have developed the required communication skills and the organizational mechanisms to gain equal standing with secular academics studying their religions. A similar movement has not yet developed among the traditional gurus, pandits and scholar-practitioners of Indic traditions. This may also be due in part to the fact that a comparable academic field of Religious Studies does not exist in universities in India; therefore, the very idea of such an engagement is a non sequitur.

In today's RISA-dominated world of Hinduism Studies, there are very few knowledgeable individuals who are willing to stand their ground in the middle of a hostile academic environment in order to defend their living culture against false representations. This vacuum is sometimes filled by voices that are informed and articulate, but often by those who lack the political savvy or intellectual depth to engage the academy. In the absence of a coordinated and coherent representation, the enormous diversity of Indians confuses most Americans who prefer a simple way of understanding 'others'. Some recent initiatives by Indians to address this are examined below.

Hindu-American Student Activism

Many second-generation Indian-Americans have recently become involved in counteracting the educational bias. Having gone through the American educational system, they are keenly aware of the often humiliating nature of the textbook narratives about India and are motivated to solve the problems before their children have to deal with the same issues.[23]

One example of this activism took place in October 2003, when an email was mass-distributed by the Hindu Students Council (HSC) at the University of Louisiana, asking people to sign an online petition.[24] The petition was addressed to, among others, President Wagner of Emory University (where Paul Courtright teaches). It listed over ten separate quotes from Courtright's book on Ganesha that the petitioners considered 'clear-cut examples of hate-crimes inflicted on innocent Hindus' and their forms of worship.[25] They asked that the author and publisher apologize, and that Courtright withdraw the book, pending corrections and clarifications to the offensive passages. Because this petition triggered a very serious controversy, it is reproduced in full in Appendix-4.

Unlike the various intellectual essays reproduced in the previous sections of this book, the petition focuses on the *emotional* impact of Courtright's work. While some have criticized the emotional nature of the petition on the grounds that it did not challenge the intellectual failings of Courtright's scholarship, this kind of activism has precedents in and is consistent with both the Indian and American traditions of protest using petitions and peaceful mobilization. However, as we shall see, the academic defendants manipulated the facts to block open debate.

Debating Student Activism

Paul Courtright falsely accused Malhotra of instigating the petition, when, in fact, Malhotra had learnt of the petition only after it was posted and had played no role in drafting it. In fact, he refused to sign the petition when it came out, and explained at length that he disagreed with its approach[26]—he was critical of the Louisiana students' petition because he felt it had done more harm than good. He critiqued both sides, hoping to 'raise the level of abstraction in the discourse' and emailed his analysis to many persons in the diaspora and in Hinduism Studies, calling the petition 'facile in its lack of critical analysis' because it failed to deal with the lack of authenticity of scholarship and relied too much on sentiments being hurt.[27] Despite such attempts to initiate a meta-level discussion of theories, including Wendy Doniger's theories of myths as agents that deny Indians' individual agency, the reply from most RISA scholars was a deafening silence.

Courtright insisted, without citing any evidence, that the year-old *Risa Lila-1* essay had inspired the 'attack', and that the quotes excerpted from his book had 'taken on a life of their own'. Courtright appeared eager to shift the blame for the words that offended and hurt readers, though they were his own writing. Moreover, others had pointed out the quotes independently of *Risa Lila-1*.[28] Yet, Courtright refused to debate the issues raised about his scholarship.[29]

The Petition is Hijacked

The HSC petition gained momentum and gathered over 7,000 signatures in just a few days. However, this well-intentioned activism turned out to be poorly executed, because it permitted signatories to add their own closing comments without prior screening. This loophole was exploited by about 20 or so signatories who added threatening comments about Courtright; someone even posted Courtright's home address online. The threatening language was abhorred by the authors of the petition, who did not want the substance of the message to be derailed by a few extreme remarks. Unfortunately, that's exactly what happened. The few tacked-on threats quickly became the focus of the academy's attention, rather than the activists' concerns about the contents of the book. Such comments served as a decoy and triggered a new series of unfortunate events in which Courtright's academic supporters responded by repositioning themselves as 'victims'.[30]

Mediation to Stop the Petition

Several scholars in Hinduism Studies decried the threats some hooligans had made and privately requested that Malhotra help reduce the tension. Agreeing that threats had no place in an intellectual debate, he took immediate steps to de-escalate the situation, offering to facilitate a dialogue, and was thanked and complimented in return for his role in ending the 'cyber attack'.[31] He advised someone associated with the petitioners to delete and prevent all abusive comments or else to remove the entire petition.[32] The student activists and their faculty advisors, who were all deeply distressed by the threats that diverted attention away from their substantive concerns, found it technically impossible to remove only the threats and so, within a few days, the entire petition was removed from the Internet.

Diaspora Support for the Petition

Interestingly, Malhotra's criticism of the petition was *challenged* by many in the diaspora.[33] Given the diversity of people who were appalled by the misrepresentations of Hinduism, this is hardly surprising. For instance, Alex Alexander[34] wrote:

> I agree with [Malhotra] that this petition lacks much of the sophistication that is needed in pursuing an item of this kind. However, I do believe that the concerns that are being voiced by people on issues like these ought to be heard by leaders who have the responsibility to both oversee academic standards and also preserve civility among communities that practice different faiths.

Another Indian-American, Chitra Raman, also posted her thoughtful rejoinder:[35]

> The drafters of this petition are equally entitled to express their deep outrage over the book. Though the issue is not about 'feelings' being hurt; but to them, at the level they operate, it is . . . I hope [those who object to the petition] realize that this petition should be read purely as a barometer of collective sentiment, not as an incitement to inflict harm.
>
> There appears to be a perception that 'progressive and secular' Hindus ought to be able to roll over and take anything that is written about their religious traditions. They should be 'objective' about people who turn some of their most sacred iconography into an object of obscene,

practically derisive interpretation. Those who stand up and protest are either ignored as either excessively 'emotional' or, if their language turns extreme, are eyed warily as recidivist fanatics.

[...] **Do representatives of all religious traditions in the West have to try so hard to maintain the right tone, to calibrate their approach to such an extent, in order get a proper hearing?** Do they take a tuning fork to their arguments to ensure that it resonates with the right 'objective' frequency if they believe they have experienced an opprobrious assault either to their belief systems, their community, or their culture? [...] I never cease to be amazed at the double standards that permeate the Western perspective . . .

Professor Courtright . . . writes as an academician with the expectation of influencing young minds in his classroom and beyond. He writes about the most widely beloved and central deity in the Hindu religious tradition. I do think it is uncivilized and deplorable to level threats of physical harm to anyone on the basis of any level of disagreement. However, it is necessary that Prof. Courtright and other luminaries at Emory University understand what they are taking on, and be prepared and open at the very least to face fierce opposition and spirited debate over his book.

In summary, I believe that double standards in the treatment of faiths exist for a number of reasons and that fear of repRISAL (sic) is only one of them . . . It is truly energizing to know that people such as Rajiv continue to push for the move from double standards to higher standards of academic accountability. But this effort is in no way diluted by diverse voices. Let them be heard. [Emphasis added]

The Hindu American Foundation (HAF), a US-based international human rights organization, deplored the threats but also noted that the petition had a role to play:

It was that petition, however, that seemed to awaken a slumbering Hindu consciousness in the United States. The spectacular momentum [was] generated by a petition that garnered nearly 5000 signatures before it was closed within a few weeks (sullied unfortunately by few indiscriminate fulminations about Dr. Courtright).[36]

HAF has also shown that works such as Courtright's help fuel Hinduphobia and hatred towards Hinduism in America, even as recently as 2007. This is particularly true among evangelical and fundamentalist Christians. Thus in a recent human rights report, it shows that several websites exist that demonize and denigrate Hinduism, and one Christian website in particular puts Courtright's fictions to good use. To quote the HAF report:

> This website contains some of the more malicious attacks against Hinduism. The website's Hinduism section is called, 'Hinduism: The Pig Pen from the East.' It refers to the religion as, 'one of the world's most dirty and dignity destroying religions' and also speaks of it as being 'filthy' and 'sexually perverted'. It uses sexually explicit imagery to assert false notions, such as when it states, "The penis, (particularly if flaccid), may be adored as Ganesha's trunk.[37] [Emphasis added]

Community Groups Engage the Academy

While a handful of hijackers succeeded in derailing the HSC petition, the Hindu-minority community had become energized about what it saw as 'hate-speech' emanating from the academy. This jumpstarted many diaspora efforts to pursue the issue with the academic community.[38]

For instance, independent of the HSC petition, the President of the Vedic Center in Greenville South Carolina presented another petition with numerous signatures to the President of Emory University, expressing deep concern about the prevailing Hinduphobia. Several national and local organizations such as the Hindu American Foundation, Hindu International Council Against Defamation, Atlanta Hindu Society, Shakti Mandir, Hindu Students Council-National, the World Association of Vedic Studies, among others, also protested the distortions in Courtright's book.[39]

Even *prior* to the HSC petition, a group of Hindus in Atlanta, organized under the name Concerned Community, had written to President Wagner of Emory University in September 2003. It conveyed outrage its the book and requested a constructive dialogue with the administrators at Emory. Its concerns included the book's impact on mainstream American culture and the attitudes it could foster. It wrote:

> Negative attitudes and stereotypes about Hinduism and India as taught in the American classrooms have a devastating impact on Hindu students who are already struggling to find their identity in a multicultural but predominantly Anglo-Christian society like America.[40] This also conveys a negative picture about Hinduism and Hindus to the mainstream North Americans resulting in hate crimes and violence against the minority community. Even a

museum like The Walter Art Gallery, Baltimore has depicted [a] Shri Ganesha statue with the sexually perverted writings: 'Ganesa's potbelly and his childlike love for sweets mock Siva's practice for austerities, and his limp trunk will forever be a poor match for Siva's erect phallus'. [The museum] cited 'academic scholarship' as authority in its defense.[41]

Sadly, the response from Emory was defensive and appeared to endorse Courtright's egregious remarks against the traditions of Hindus. The Concerned Community found these replies arrogant and a trifle disingenuous:

[The Community] got a sanctimonious and patronizing letter from the Dean of the College of Arts and Sciences, Robert Paul, who said that like 'any great research university', Emory 'never condemns any point of view simply on the grounds that it may be controversial or even offensive to some people'. Would he dare say that about Islamic scholarship, or about Judaism studies, or about inquiry into African-American life at Emory University? The Dean claims that the only exceptions that Emory University makes 'are for claims made on the basis of willful untruths or which otherwise violate the rules of academic integrity, or for statements made solely for the purpose of willfully demeaning or insulting some person or group.'[42]

The Dean ignored the very troubling *prima facie* evidence of Courtright's shoddy scholarship, which may well have 'violate[d] the rules of academic integrity', marshaled by Agarwal and Venkat, [43] even after the document was handed to him in person.[44]

The Diaspora Tries to Dialog with Emory

After much back and forth, a meeting finally took place in February 2004, almost *six months* after the Community first requested a dialog. Both sides were present at the meeting—including diaspora activists, academic scholars from both sides, and the Dean of Emory University.[45] The Briefing Book created by the Concerned Community, and later, the minutes of this meeting were given to Emory University. The community's official statement to the university is quoted at length below and reveals a sincere effort to approach the academicians through dialogue, asserting that "Emory University has a moral obligation to respect members of all religious faiths including Hindus." The Community's objective was "to work towards a mutually rewarding relationship between Emory University and the Indian/Hindu communities that it serves".

Each member of the Community had carefully read Courtright's book and become convinced that it was highly problematic.[46] While expressing appreciation for the academic and cultural contributions made by Emory University over the years, the Community complained: "Professor Courtright's work and his irresponsible scholarship and misleading representation concerning Hinduism has become a matter of much concern and distress to Indian-American communities across the nation".

The following document, included in the Briefing Book, was delivered to officials at Emory University on February 18, 2004:

Action Items for the Department of Religion/South Asian Studies

1. Curriculum on Hinduism/India:
The Department should take a serious look at the political biases and prejudices that guide the selection of textual and audio-visual material, sensational films, recommended for reading and viewing in Hinduism studies. Balance, fairness, and accuracy demand that when controversial material is introduced in classrooms that instructors go the extra length to provide their students the oppositional view. For this to happen, we recommend that the department start a dialogue with the Hindu community on the political and prejudicial nature of some of this material.

2. Faculty teaching Hinduism:
Emory University must make a good faith effort to find practicing Hindus and scholars in Hinduism and/or Sanskrit to teach Hinduism.

3. Programs/Activities and use of Emory facility:
(a) Programs, activities, film festivals, and lectures (including visiting Fellows) related to Hinduism/India at Emory University should be unbiased, reflecting the diversity and progress of India, and not be captive to political, social, religious and ideological affiliations.
(b) Religion/S. Asia department should refrain from discriminatory and unfair practices in dealing, joint-venturing and aligning with the Indian Atlanta community. Maneuvering and favoritism by Emory faculty towards a select few friends or partisan groups should be avoided, especially when co-sponsoring programs/activities with the community. Temporary allocation/leasing by Emory of its facilities/space for activity/program use by the Indian Atlanta community should be fair and not selectively restrictive.

4. Emory/Courtright should prevent further spread of biased and misrepresentative depictions of Hinduism:
Emory University must halt the further dissemination of Dr. Courtright's work in question. Emory must also remedy damage already caused by this work, such as use of excerpts of the book by the Walter Museum in Baltimore, MD in a recent museum display on Shri Ganesha.

5. Press releases and Media Interviews:
Non-practicing Emory faculty should refrain from calling themselves as 'experts on Hinduism' and thus be speaking on behalf of a billion Hindus while issuing press releases or interviewing with media on Hinduism related interpretations. The faculty, may, however, deem it as their personal opinion instead of being called experts, as unfortunately claimed by the recent Atlanta Journal Constitution report.

6. Sensitivity and Intercultural Communication Training:
Emory University must provide opportunities to faculty and administrators and require them to attend intercultural communication training to sensitize them to issues of bias, objectification, and misrepresentation.

Issues Raised by the Community

In order for these demands to be taken seriously, the Community needed to show that Courtright's scholarship concerning the psychoanalytical interpretation of Ganesha was not just offensive but was the product of sloppy scholarship. Its research on this topic identified where his work was undocumented, fabricated or arbitrary. It compiled an extensive set of research papers questioning Courtright's methods of scholarship and raised many issues during their meeting. The papers that were delivered included two kinds of criticisms: analyses of Courtright's translations and interpretations, and general criticisms of the applicability of Freudian analyses.[47]

One of the papers included in the packet was by John F. Kihlstrom, a leading academic psychologist from the University of California, Berkeley. It exposed the unscientific and questionable nature of much of Freud's theories:

> Freud's cultural influence [on the West] is based, at least implicitly, on the premise that his theory is scientifically valid. But from a scientific point of view, classical Freudian psychoanalysis is dead as both a theory of the mind and a mode of therapy (Crews, 1998; Macmillan, 1996). No empirical evidence supports any specific proposition of psychoanalytic theory, such as the idea that

development proceeds through oral, anal, phallic, and genital stages, or that little boys lust after their mothers and hate and fear their fathers. [...] It is one thing to say that unconscious motives play a role in behavior. It is something quite different to say that our every thought and deed is driven by repressed sexual and aggressive urges; that children harbor erotic feelings toward the parent of the opposite sex; and that young boys are hostile toward their fathers, who they regard as rivals for their mothers' affections. This is what *Freud* believed, and so far as we can tell **Freud was wrong in every respect.** For example, the unconscious mind revealed in laboratory studies of automaticity and implicit memory bears no resemblance to the unconscious mind of psychoanalytic theory (Kihlstrom, 1999) [Emphasis added.].[48]

Kihlstrom also explained that Freud is a Western cultural icon who has enormously influenced the way a large number of Westerners see themselves and others. This has made Freud an object of deference and an integral part of Western culture, giving him a legitimate place in studies of Western culture and literature. However, he was *not a scientist* and his theories are not based on empirical data that can be generalized to all cultures. Kihlstrom wrote:

> Freud also changed the vocabulary with which we understand ourselves and others. [...] While Freud had an enormous impact on 20th century culture, he has been a dead weight on 20th century psychology ... At best, Freud is a figure of only historical interest for psychologists. He is better studied as a writer, in departments of [Western] language and literature, than as a scientist, in departments of psychology. Psychologists can get along without him [...]

> Of course, Freud lived at a particular period of time, and it might be argued that his theories were valid when applied to European culture at the turn of the last century, even if they are no longer apropos today. However, recent historical analyses show that Freud's construal of his case material was systematically distorted and biased by his theories of unconscious conflict and infantile sexuality, and that he misinterpreted and misrepresented the scientific evidence available to him. **Freud's theories were not just a product of his time: they were misleading and incorrect even when he published them.**[49] [Emphasis added]

The Concerned Community's presentation included the positions of competent academicians on the problem of using psychoanalysis to dissect Hindu traditions. They stressed that scholars who are untrained in psychoanalysis should refrain from using Freudian theories because this can easily deteriorate into indulgence in Eurocentric fantasies about the other. As we shall see, Emory University did not respond to these important issues about training, methodology and cultural hegemony in any detail.

Substantive Issues About Courtright's Scholarship

The Briefing Book cited numerous comments from senior academic scholars, presenting *prima facie* reasons to question Courtright's approach to his work on Ganesha. The document raised questions from a theoretical perspective, as well as pointing out textual discrepancies. The Briefing Book quoted Prof. Antonio de Nicolas, who wrote regarding Courtright:

> His degree is a privilege of knowledge, not ignorance. Freedom stops here. Opinions are not the food of the classroom at the hands of Professors. They guarantee knowledge.

The Concerned Community added that they "believe, Emory as an institute of learning, is obligated to call into question the scholarship of Dr. Paul Courtright and provide a correction of some kind to a billion strong Hindus worldwide".[50]

The Briefing Book also included a presentation by Shree Vinekar, an award-winning psychiatrist and professor of Psychiatry and Behavioral Sciences. He noted that while Courtright claims to use psychoanalysis to derive knowledge about Ganesha, "Courtright has little or no understanding of psychoanalysis . . . [Courtright] used psychoanalysis to interpret the image of Ganesha like a Rorschach card upon which he had projected concepts and practices from his own culture as represented in his own unconscious . . ." Thus, in Prof. Vinekar's opinion as an *expert peer-reviewer*, "Courtright's book was a disgrace [to] . . . Applied Psychoanalysis." He pointed out that Courtright ignores or downplays the understanding of Ganesha's form explained in works like the Atharvashirsha, Jnaneshwari and other treatises. Instead he had tried to 'deliberately stretch and manipulate meanings'. These descriptions in both the traditional references (which Courtright claims to know and cites as references) insist that Ganesha was an anthropomorphic representation of 'AUM'.

Jnaneshwari graphically illustrates how the image of Ganesha was formed or derived from AUM. Vinekar opined that by ignoring these traditional views, Courtright "avoided giving prominence to these facts and has chosen to delve into the mythology and concrete interpretation of the form to suit his preconceived Freudian fantasies. He delights in reading the Puranas to give the stories a psychoanalytic twist while the image was formed to illustrate . . . lofty philosophical principles".

In his presentation, Ramesh Rao, a professor of Journalism,[51] explored the limits of academic freedom when it is used to manipulate facts and make misrepresentations. Other members of the Community highlighted the negative impact of such works on Hindu children and others who relate to Divinity through the form of Ganesha.

Emory's Dismissive Response

The Community felt that Emory's response showed a remarkable lack of interest in whether Courtright had breached academic integrity. Emory had assembled a team of scholars, including many of Hindu origin, who provided character references for Courtright or made generic statements about the problem without discussing any concrete steps to address the issues.[52] Some of the comments from Emory's team include the following:

- P.V. Rao claimed that he had learnt a lot about reading Hindu texts from Courtright, and expressed a desire 'to have Dr. Courtright as his friend in his next life'.
- Rakesh Ranjan, a Hindi language teacher at Emory, recalled that when he first arrived in Atlanta, Courtright had taken him to Hindu temples and introduced him to many Hindus.
- Deepika Petraglia-Bahri of the English Department, who specializes in Postcolonial Studies and Critical Theory, felt that "what we were dealing with here was 'pain' caused by colonialism and that we can mitigate the 'pain' through communication".[53]
- Joyce Flueckiger commented on how much she treasured her growing interaction with the Indian-American community, and said that Emory was keen on hiring Hindu practitioners in the Religion faculty, but bemoaned that Indian universities did not offer a PhD in religion.[54]

Soon after the meeting, both Dean Robert Paul and Prof. Flueckiger wrote letters to the Concerned Community in which they did not refer to any of the issues regarding Courtright's scholarship that had been raised at the meeting and in the papers compiled in the Briefing Book. While acknowledging that the local Hindu community had initiated 'a constructive dialogue', Dean Paul focused instead on the *feelings* of Hindus:

> Emory University acknowledges your position on Professor Paul Courtright's book on Ganesa, and regrets that any unhappiness or insult has been experienced by anyone in connection with the work of a member of our faculty . . . I feel quite certain that many members of our faculty have heard your concerns and are taking account of them in thinking about their own future research and teaching. [...]Let me also state clearly that I now better understand the hurt some Hindus feel, and that I deeply regret, on behalf of Emory University, that you and others have felt insulted and experienced distress.

He also acknowledged the Community's right to speak out as it had done:

> We respect absolutely your right to critique the book in question, to express feelings of anger, insult, or outrage about it in print or other media, and to offer arguments against the interpretations put forward in the book, as you have indeed done forcefully at our meeting and in the documents you have assembled. These activities are all in the spirit of scholarly debate that Emory University espouses and defends.

Even though the documents presented included Venkat's and Agarwal's detailed and troubling critique of Courtright's scholarship, the Dean was not open to any examination of these charges. Indeed, his letter took an admonishing and patronizing tone, characterizing the Community's demands as an 'assault' on academic freedom. After having commended the Community for speaking up, Dean Paul wrote in his letter:

> That being said, however, insofar as your proposals concerning what you expect from Emory ask us to violate the principle of academic freedom, the possibility for further constructive dialogue between us is limited. You are of course free to express your views on Professor Courtright's book, but further dialogue with the Administration of Emory University will not be productive if you continue to propose actions by Emory limiting or in any way infringing on Professor Courtright's academic freedom, or to any degree censoring or stifling the free expression of his ideas, however much you may not like them.

After boasting that Emory espouses constructive dialogue and scholarly debate, the Dean rebuked them for that very act! Joyce Flueckiger, Emory's Director of South Asia Studies at that time, also wrote back expressing regret for any hurt that was caused and gratuitously reminded the Community of the Dean's position on academic freedom. The bulk of her letter related to the action items in the Community's complaint to the University. For each point raised by the Community, Flueckiger's answer, in effect, was, "Emory is already doing it, thank you." The Community expressed its concern as follows: "Neither Emory nor Flueckiger offered to set up a formal process to invite the participation of a joint committee of faculty and the Community in order to ensure that diverse views were represented. Nor did Flueckiger promise to investigate the disturbing findings about Courtright's works".[55]

Interestingly, neither Flueckiger nor Courtright was willing to take any responsibility for the prejudiced and defamatory scholarship entering mainstream America through exhibits like the one at the Walters Museum in Baltimore. Unlike their stand on the few threats posted by unauthorized and unknown persons—which they tried to pin on *every* critic of Courtright—they completely washed their hands of the Hinduphobia that an employee of the University had generated. Flueckiger wrote:

> As far as other institutions, such as museums, using the publications and scholarship of our faculty, **those institutions are responsible for fair usage, not the authors of the scholarship.** I am sure you have already contacted the Walter Museum directly with your legitimate concerns. [Emphasis added.]

While both the Dean and Flueckiger claimed to respect Hindus, neither was willing to help correct the situation by writing to the Walter Museum to caution that Courtright's speculative and poorly evidenced psychoanalyses of Ganesha were not 'facts' and should not be presented as the authoritative interpretation of Ganesha.

Conclusion

Ramesh Rao noted that Emory had assumed quite a patronizing attitude towards the Community, with the Dean 'admonishing' the Hindu community, lecturing that the next time they wanted to complain about a scholar's slander it would be better not to "seek its suppression or condemnation", but to "put forward their own views in the free market-place of ideas that we at the university guard as our most basic principle." However, Rao observed that this facile advice from Emory, a leading Methodist Christian institution:

> presumes that the playing field in these matters is level. At present there are no Hindu equivalents for academic journals in the US, there are no Hindu presses and radio and television stations, no central body to represent Hindu interests and only one 'infant' Hindu university that can take on the might of well-endowed universities and their well-paid scholars.[56]

In the aftermath, the Concerned Community felt cheated that its sincere efforts seemed to come to naught. It concluded:

> There was no credible or even apparent concern expressed by Emory about its Professor's perverted depiction of Hindu religion, which is a major cause of concern of the community. **In fact, Emory panel members, citing close friendship with Courtright, focused on character references or programmatic friendship of Courtright rather than on the specific concerns and evidence pointed out by the community.** The Emory panel side-stepped the insulting contents of the book despite vigorous protest letters from the CC to the President and to the Department of Religion, despite numerous nationwide Petitions and hundreds of letters to the President, and in spite of the CC convincingly refuting the [misplaced] claims of 'academic freedom,' 'scholarship' and 'psychoanalysis' at this meeting at Emory.[57]

It was obvious to the members of the Concerned Community in Atlanta that Emory University had assembled a politically correct team to placate 'hurt feelings' and provide a pretence of due process, but that it never had any genuine intentions of investigating the substantive issues.

Chapter 20

Attempts to Refocus on the Issues

In the wake of the Hindu-American protests against denigration and inauthentic representations of their cultures by the academy, one particular concern was the asymmetry of power that prevented a level playing field on which a dialog among cultures could emerge.[58] In those disciplines where the personal and cultural conditionings of scholars can radically influence how questions are framed and which methodologies and contexts are used, it becomes even more critical to reduce the asymmetries of power between the Ivory Tower and the people they study. This involves setting up mechanisms so that criticisms from outside the academy, especially from the emic practitioners being analyzed, are welcomed and treated with respect. Unfortunately, during this ongoing RISA-Lila saga, a reactionary resistance and hostility emerged as RISA demonized its diaspora critics.[59]

As this lila was unfolding, numerous supportive scholars, such as Stuart Sovatsky,[60] contributed to the conversation:

> Foucault [seems] to be a primary ally in critiquing the 'Power-Knowledge' game of academia. In reference to tantra and its distortion by psychoanalysis, his concept of erotica is the only Western lens (I know of) that is capable of understanding the former while critiquing the latter. Thus, he is one example, I think, of what you are looking for, from Western academia.

Antonio de Nicolas also sent Malhotra a supportive email:

> Your exchange on the issue of the book is exemplary and leaving the lesser issue (feelings) you have managed to force the focus on the real (RISA) issue: incompetence and dissemination of trivialities and dis-information about Indic studies.

Father Francis Clooney[61] wrote that he found *RISA Lila-2* to be 'stimulating as usual'. Clooney explained that scholars were "rather individualistic in their work, and rarely argued, preferring to stay out of each other's way". This was a tacit admission by a leading academic Christian theologian of Hinduism that the vigorous debate and bruising disagreement, and careful examination of each other's claims, the separation of fact from opinion—all of which is supposed to help the advancement of knowledge in such fields—was not taking place sufficiently.[62]

A Systemic Hegemony is Exposed

This ongoing investigation of the field continued to bring forth more voices that acknowledged the serious asymmetries of power inherent in the Western study of other cultures. The problems are not limited to stereotypes about Hinduism, but attacks upon the broader Indic culture and India's secular civilization as well. Susantha Goonatilake,[63] who has explored these issues in his own works, sent a lengthy email:

> I broadly agree with what Rajiv [Malhotra] is saying. The study fields that he mentions started about 25 years ago as a response to western hegemonic thought. But they were picked up as mechanical tools by others to do its opposite on S Asia. **Post colonial studies became pro colonial studies.** Feminism, whose aim was to understand what white males left out, became about repeating what white females said. So [even] without a [Samuel] Huntington you have civilizational ideologues for the west. What you are saying about Indic Hindu studies is worse in Buddhist studies. Buddhist studies in the 19th & 20th c. were an attempt to grasp what Buddhism was. It was a good effort. During the last 25 years there has been an anthropological turn in Buddhist studies and instead of careful scholarship one has gross inventions and partial truths that do not meet basic criteria of scholarship or tests.

Goonatilake was skeptical about scholars' claims to act without fear or favor. He was aware that scholars ultimately respond quite positively to those cultures and groups that gaze back at the scholars and are powerful enough to challenge them. Thus, he noted, "Nobody messes up like this with China," adding that he has personally "seen Western scholars kowtowing there [or in] Japan or even S. E. Asia." Regarding the Western approach to Indic traditions, he anticipated a paradigm shift driven by economic growth rather than the academic establishment's open-mindedness:

> But we have to see this in broad geo political terms. In 25 years' time India—in spite of numerous problems—will probably be the number 3 or 4 economic power in the world. With this clout it can dictate the terms of scholarship and [remedy] its anti Indic biases. I think one should let the Indic Studies community know this inevitability.

Others also noted the system-wide nature of the problem. Expanding the analysis to relations between academic scholars and the religious laity in America, but appreciating the validity of the particular problems faced by the Hindu minority, Dr. Cleo Kearns[64] wrote:

> The outrage some Hindus feel about this book [by Courtright] is similar to (though not identical with, due to the unequal political context) the outrage felt by many Christians in this country about the treatment of Christianity in the academy (and in the arts as well). In saying this I am not trying to equate the two situations, **because the power relations are very different,** but merely to draw what I hope will be a warning parallel. The result here has been a deep split between the popular consciousness and the intelligentsia—the so-called 'culture wars.' This rift in our society has been and is very dangerous. [Emphasis added]

Kearns further urged perseverance in trying to widen participation in the discourse by including both academics and non academics:

> The only way to resolve this is by open, educated and critical debate of the kind you have been trying to foster. This debate, while always civil and respectful of good form, should involve both academics and non-academics, those who speak from within and those who speak from without the traditions involved, and informed minds should not in my opinion hesitate to exert leadership here as [Malhotra has] done.

David Freedholm, who teaches comparative religion and philosophy in a prestigious American school system, raised a third issue in discussions of systematic bias in the academia. He noted that the 'culture wars' were not uniform in their impact. He did not support a ban on Courtright's book but remarked that the debate should have caused RISA scholars to introspect about what they were doing to help reduce prejudices against Hinduism. He hoped that relations between academia and the religious communities they study would not remain so antagonistic. He pointed out the tremendous difference between the missions of RISA and those of Islamic Studies faculty in America:[65]

Contrast this [RISA attitude of antagonism to the Hindu community] to the Study of Islam section of AAR. In its mission statement, the Study of Islam section recognizes the key role it has in shaping the understanding of Islam in public schools, universities, and in the public consciousness. They explicitly state that they need to contribute to the 'public understanding of religion' in general and of Islam in particular. This concern that Islam be understood in ways that are balanced and fair from both the emic and the etic perspective is seen in the various projects they take on. They created a website[66] in order to deflect criticism of Islam after the terrorist attack on the WTC. Many scholars of Islam Studies have dedicated themselves to making Islam better understood in the West. Prof. Alan Godlas has created an award-winning website[67] that is "intended to be of use for non-Muslim and Muslim students and teachers at all levels as well for members of the general public who wish to get a non-polemical view of Islam." On his site, Godlas provides links to a number of other efforts by Study of Islam members to make Islam better understood and to present a positive spin on Islam.

He observed, regarding Islam: "It is clear that these efforts emerge because scholars of Islam in AAR, whether Muslim or non-Muslim, feel a responsibility to the community they study." He asked, incredulously,

Why are there no similar efforts by RISA? Where are the websites, public talks and statements, and books that try to provide a fair and balanced presentation of Hinduism and to correct misunderstandings of Hinduism in the public sphere (in the media, in schools, etc.)?

On the contrary, he observed, "RISA scholars appear more interested in the exotic and erotic aspects that they identify in Hinduism. They appear more concerned with trying to highlight social problems in India which they blithely blame on Hinduism." He concluded, "It is no wonder there is such disconnect between the Hindu community and RISA scholars."

As a second-generation Indian-American law student, I wrote that such disparaging and antagonistic scholarship was not limited to Religious Studies but was also used to blame Indian culture, its people and the Indian nation-state as oppressors. This had a psychological impact on young Indian-Americans like myself. *RISA Lila-2* had eloquently articulated the need for Indian/Hindu scholarship that remains authentic to the traditions of the people while retaining the rigor and objectivity required of academic work. As a student I went through the torment of taking college classes pertaining to South Asia and had been so disappointed in and frustrated by the quality of the teaching. I'd gone to innumerable talks purporting to explain the phenomenon of rioting in India when in reality, they were more like tabloid-style talk shows using sensationalist stories of brutality to demonize a populace and wax nostalgic for the Dalit and Naxalite[68] movements. This kind of lazy scholarship sapped me of any desire I once had to enter academia. I wrote how refreshing it was to read such a piece in the midst of all the recycled, exoticized, too rightist or too leftist, and apologist literature about Hinduism that exists today.

There was a growing understanding and relief among many in the diaspora that they were not standing alone. Indian-Americans welcomed the spotlight that was finally shining upon long-ignored issues, which, if left untreated and unscrutinized, threaten to completely corrode the quality of research coming out of the academy on Hinduism.

They were also concerned about the social and psychological consequences for the children of this new American minority if the puerile, psychopathological, and trivializing approaches to their religion and society remained unquestioned. Indian-Americans of all ages and from all regions of the country were tuning in and contributing to this debate. However, as will be seen in the next chapter, even while these lively and deliberate discussions were earnestly taking place, less than noble diversions intervened. Ironically, it started with a hopeful sign: a well-respected member of the academy breaking ranks and calling for honest self-examination from his fellow professionals.

Chapter 21

Circling the Wagons: Dissent and Censorship

The previous chapter described efforts to elevate the debate beyond the issues of emotional pain and defamation caused to the minority Hindu-American community to a serious consideration and criticism of the methods used by scholars. Nonetheless, RISA did not get fully involved until one of their own posted a stinging critique of Courtright. His courageous act of whistle-blowing unleashed a passionate and bruising argument that was sadly prevented from becoming a substantive debate.

On one side of this fight were a few scholars concerned about the hegemonic nature of some of their colleagues and on the other side were the establishment voices that wanted to preserve the status quo by quashing dissent and by trying to paint *all* of Courtright's critics as radicals from the 'Hindu Right'. The unscholarly mayhem included many distinguished professors with considerable institutional authority to shape the academic field. Junior scholars hoping to prove their loyalty to the RISA establishment were also drawn in by the political opportunity.

On November 1, 2003, Prof. Antonio de Nicolas posted the following critique of Courtright's book on the RISA-list.[69] He focused on the quality of Courtright's work and appealed to the scholarly community's sense of professionalism. He reminded them of their obligation to conduct rigorous peer-review of all such works and to take corrective action whenever questionable work slips through the cracks. Courageously, he raised the core issue that was being evaded by Emory: whether Courtright's work could be considered scholarly and methodologically sound, or whether it should be investigated for academic malfeasance. Had Courtright dealt with the evidence honestly, or had he manipulated it? Was he dealing in facts or merely presenting his *speculations* as fact? De Nicolas reminded the RISA community that, in the classroom and in research, Courtright was obligated to, "impart knowledge, not falsehood or opinions". His post to the official RISA online discussion list is quoted in full:[70]

Dear friends,

It is now obvious that we have a revolution of sensitivities on our hands, and the correction of such a distempered situation is now in the court of Indic Studies scholars and the Universities we serve. Are we, as scholars commanded by the freedoms and privileges of our professional degrees, entitled to stand the ground of silence in the case of Dr. Paul Courtright and his thesis on Ganesha, or is it our obligation as such scholars to call into question the scholarship of Dr. Paul Courtright and demand a corrective of some kind?

In more veridical terms, did Dr. Courtright act, in writing his book on Ganesha, with the discipline and scholarship demanded of him by his degree or did he act irresponsibly and unscholarly in such a manner that his freedom of speech and his freedom to teach are both in jeopardy?

Point number one: The first responsibility of a scholar in describing, writing, speaking, teaching other cultures is to present those cultures or the elements of those cultures in the same manner those cultures are viewed by themselves and by the people of those cultures. If not, then the scholar is using those cultures in name only and his goal is their destruction, if not in intention at least in fact. 'The flaccid phallus of Ganesha' is an invention of the author when this is not the only depiction of Ganesha, since He appears in other statues with a large erection.

A scholar who does not know how to present other cultures by their own criteria should not be allowed to teach those cultures. His freedom of speech is not guaranteed by his ignorance. His degree is a privilege of knowledge, not ignorance. Freedom stops here. Opinions are not the food of the classroom at the hands of Professors. They guarantee knowledge.

In the case of Lord Ganesha and Hindus, the case is even more dramatic and irresponsible, or demands even more responsibility than in other cases. Lord Ganesha is considered a God [by] millions of Hindus. We Westerners may think whatever we want about Indic gods, but it is the case that in the Indic classical texts gods are 'intelligence centers', pilot brains to give light to our lives and decisions. Who is the Western scholar that can use his freedom of speech (but not his responsibility to know better) in order to destroy, dethrone, or laugh at a God made naked for that purpose or consequence? And which is the institution of learning that will condone such behavior from one that has promised, by accepting his degree, to strive to continue to impart knowledge, not falsehood, or opinions?

Would Dr. Courtright like to open a door to the enemies, or outsiders, of Christianity to do the same with the Bible, for example? Would he or others find it offensive if a Hindu scholar with full credentials and knowledge described the Creation myth of the Bible as an absurd and gross sexual representation? For one thing Freud would not be needed. The Bible is very explicit. The creation myth (history) says very clearly that the Creator created the world by ejecting his semen (ruh= pron.ruah) and mingling it with the waters. In other words, the creator created through masturbation. And if you stretch the story all the way to Jesus and follow the patrilineal lines given to him, turns out that Yahweh is his father. Can you be more gross? And would any Ph.D. in Religion be able to answer this attack?

You see, a Pandora's Box is let open to inflict enormous pain on believers. Why not see the same pain on Hindus when their gods are attacked? We are talking about interpretations not realities!!! All stories about gods are bad stories.

I think I am making my points clearly. Emory University and the AAR should investigate this and similar cases and keep an investigating body available to make sure this does not happen again. And also make sure that the present crisis is immediately stopped from spreading, with a large apology for such irresponsible behavior. [Emphasis added].

One of the first responses posted on RISA-l came from Prof. Narasingha Sil, who referred to the asymmetry of power inherent in the academy. He used the technique of reverse psychoanalysis to satirize the Eurocentric academics:[71]

Professor Courtright's depiction of Ganesha reflects his idealization of a particular state of the male organ and we need not exercise ourselves unnecessarily on Ganesha's proboscis seen as a limp phallus. I have seen (so have many others) limp phallus of most of the male nude statuary sculpted by the Greeks and even by the Renaissance Italians. Nobody has interpreted the statue of a young David or a muscular Adam (the perpetrator of the 'Adamic' sin!) with a small and limp phallus in Florence or in the Sistine Chapel as something to be excited or exercised about. Let Ganesha have his phallus limp when he is not shown as gawking at a divine female. If Courtright intends to insinuate impotence of Ganesha (which I sincerely doubt he does), then that may be an instance of his personal anxiety about a male organ to be ever up and ready for action.

The interesting and intriguing point to underscore here is that Ganesha being a 'pagan' god with juicy legends about his origin is an object of curiosity to those who really have no stake in stuff Hindu. [Emphasis added]

Attacking the Whistleblower

Essentially, de Nicolas was breaking the silence and joining those who had called the emperor naked. This could have been an outstanding opportunity for RISA scholars to take up a point-by-point examination of Courtright's work and to see if it held up to their standards of rigor. Agarwal and Venkat's work had raised several questions and would have made a good starting point. Unfortunately, the responses from the RISA establishment were knee-jerk and defensive. Rather than presenting a systematic and scholarly defense of Courtright's work, they began an *ad hominem* attack on de Nicolas and racist attacks by calling Indians pejorative names such as 'dim' and 'different'.

William Hartman[72] fired the opening salvo to attack de Nicolas:[73]

De Nicolas has assumed that he and he alone knows the Truth about Ganesha and about how the culture that reveres Ganesha thinks. In fact, I know many Indians who much appreciated Courtright's meticulous scholarship, and who felt that it represented an affectionate, provocative, and exploratory study into the nature of this wonderfully protean Hindu deity.

Hartman's response was not based on citing evidence of Courtright's scholarship but on providing anecdotes claiming his popularity among some Indians—hardly an *academic* argument. De Nicolas's serious charges were simply disregarded and his appeal to professional responsibility was repositioned as one man's arrogant *opinion* about Ganesha.

John Oliver Perry,[74] a retired literature professor who has studied contemporary Indian poetry but has no Religious Studies background, chimed in against Indian scholars in a startlingly dismissive and racist fashion. Without revealing a shred of the post-Orientalism championed by his field of Critical Theory, he wrote: "Freudian thinking has, after all, penetrated even the apparently 'dim' and 'different' [Other? unable to be scholarly, only sensitive to slight][75] minds of scholars in India".[76] In his effort to sound clever, Perry made a blatantly racist statement that scholars from India are too dim to understand advanced and sophisticated Western techniques such as Freudian analysis and other 'scholarly' methods. Perry stated that the minds of scholars in India can be judged not only as 'different', but also as inferior: 'dim', emotional rather than rational, 'unable to be scholarly, only sensitive to slight'. It is a measure of how pervasive and 'normal' contempt for Indians and their culture is in RISA that Perry's peers *did not raise any objections whatsoever.*

It is astonishing that in America's pluralistic, multicultural environment, when Indian scholars were dismissed and belittled on an academic forum that specializes in the study of Indian culture, their peers remained silent and allowed white supremacist stereotypes of non-whites to go unchallenged. A steady diet of Eurocentric scholarship appears to have convinced RISA's predominantly Western membership that Indian scholarship *is* inferior. After all, the reasoning seems to be, most of these Hindus are phallus worshippers who are too dim-witted even to realize it and require a white person to point out to them that they are worshipping a phallus. Regrettably, this was not the only nor the most insidious example of such ideas in RISA.

Ramdas Lamb,[77] from the Department of Religion at the University of Hawaii, also broke ranks with his cohorts and described the situation from the perspective of a practising white Hindu-American. He was critical of Courtright's work:[78]

> I cannot help but believe that the vast majority of Hindus would be appalled at such an approach, which seems to say far more about the writer and his focus than about the way Ganesha has been historically understood by Hindus. If the text was simply meant to take a Freudian approach to Ganesha, with the inevitable outcome of such tact, then, maybe, it was successful. However, if it was meant to provide good historical scholarship on Ganesha, then I do not see where such depictions accomplish that, unless they have been integral in the development and understanding of Ganesha within the Hindu tradition. **Is it wrong to suggest scholarly understanding should take historical reality into consideration?** While I am sure that there are currently, and may have long been, some Indians who may view Ganesha in that way, but when have such views been characteristic of Hindu thinking with respect to Ganesha? **Just because we are scholars, does that mean we can**

say and write whatever we wish, irrespective of its accuracy or impact? [Emphasis added]

Lance Nelson,[79] the long-time moderator of the RISA online discussion list, sought to legitimize the naked Ganesha cover picture on Courtright's book by asking how it differed from naked pictures of baby Krishna that were part of the tradition. Swami Tyagananda's post seemed to slip past RISA without comment: "A naked Ganesha is certainly *not* a 'tradition' the way a naked baby Krishna is part of the popular culture expressed through songs, pictures and images."[80] Moreover, the issues are not reducible to one isolated item of 'offense' but are about whether Courtright's scholarship holds up to scrutiny in the face of the numerous problems identified.

Joanna Kirkpatrick mentioned that de Nicolas's complaint was trumped by the fact that Carstairs's famous work on Rajputs and Doniger's work in general was based on Freudianizing.[81] This is Eurocentric circular reasoning, because it assumes that the mere adoption of a theory by Western scholars proves its legitimacy. Kirkpatrick did not bother to offer any arguments other than citing that Doniger had used the same approach. The mere popularity of particular writings does not legitimately entitle them to a self-perpetuating legacy.

Deepak Sarma, who received his PhD under Doniger and is the co-moderator of the RISA discussion group, chastised de Nicolas for supporting the Hindu students' petition and warned him to stop further posts that criticized RISA members.[82] While protecting the powerful may have helped his career, Sarma's officious and heavy-handed censorship muffled healthy debate and aggrandized privileged, syndicated perspectives. De Nicolas informed his colleagues about the mafia-like clampdown to muzzle him, complaining, "I was told to shut up and/or be approved by the RISA administration."[83] It is important to note that in spite of making this public, no outpouring of support from the champions of academic freedom was forthcoming in de Nicolas's case.

Gene Thursby did offer de Nicolas support offline, defending his right of free speech.[84] Thursby confided that de Nicolas's interesting posts were far more important than many of the other topics that are routinely discussed on RISA and that such posts added substance to RISA's list. However, Thursby deflected the question of whether Courtright's work should be investigated by scholars by bringing in an unrelated controversy involving Sikhs in order to suggest that scholars were victims regardless. Thus, he seemed to suggest that intelligent public debate about the specifics of Courtright's scholarship was useless, since scholars were damned if they did and damned if they didn't in dealing with Indians:[85]

> The current flap itself mirrors earlier ones. For instance the complaint a decade ago that Harjot Oberoi ought not occupy a "community" chair of Sikh Studies because his book *The Construction of Religious Boundaries* represented Sikh history inaccurately and inappropriately. Ironic in the context of the current flap since in a way Oberoi had done too much historical study and it is claimed that Courtright has done too little.

Thursby would have been right on the money if he had called for an actual examination of *whether* Courtright had indeed done 'too little' history. After all, this was the crux of the matter—whether the book was based on speculation, fabrication and fantasy versus rigorous evidence. Other professors who joined the debate in various forums also avoided dealing with the troubling questions that de Nicolas had raised.

A group of academics began a campaign in which critics of Courtright's scholarship were linked to unrelated events in India and London—the problematic but isolated issue of threats made by a few of the petition signatories, coupled with a completely unrelated attack by ethnic chauvinists and anti-Brahmin groups on the Bhandarkar Institute in India, were brought in to muddy the waters and deflect from the issues surrounding Courtright's work. These events were quickly seized upon to depict the Indian 'others' as dangerous culprits. The RISA establishment mobilized established professors, young career-climbing faculty members and graduate students to torpedo de Nicolas's initiative. In doing so, the academy lost a golden opportunity for critical self-examination.

Admirably, Kathleen M. Erndl[86] suggested some guidelines to follow in order to improve communication among RISA scholars:[87] "Whatever the merits or demerits of certain types of analysis and interpretation may be, they ought to be debated in an informed, scholarly (and dare I suggest) civil manner". Nonetheless, several of Erndl's RISA colleagues failed to apply these principles. Unfortunately, Prof. Erndl did not object when the 'civil' conduct was suspended to facilitate attacks on the diaspora and on those scholars who criticized RISA.

Colonialism Updated: Attacking an Indian Publisher

While these disputes were occupying considerable Internet bandwidth in the U.S., Courtright's publisher in India, Motilal Banarsidass, announced in large newspaper advertisements across India that it was withdrawing Courtright's controversial book. The issue received broad, but rather shallow, coverage in the press. The press reports did not refer to the scholarly issues with the book, but singled out the 'offending picture' of Ganesha on the book cover as the sole cause for the apology. The following press release was issued:

Publishers apologize for 'offending' Ganesha picture
[Monday, November 3 2003 23:11 Hrs (IST)]

New Delhi: Motilal Banarsidass Indological Publishers and Distributors, who had published a book containing an 'offending' picture of Lord Ganesha, today (November 3) offered their apologies and announced withdrawal of all the copies from the market.

Motilal Banarsidass Indological Publishers and Distributors said they were 'deeply hurt' to note that the book *Ganesh: Lord of Obstacles, Lord of Beginnings* which was originally published by Oxford University Press in 1985 has 'appeared to be offensive to a section of beloved readers'.

A press release stated: 'Respecting the sentiments of the culturally conscious scholars, the publisher and distributor have withdrawn the circulation of the book from the market.' The publisher and the distributor also offered apologies to the readers.

The press release concluded: 'The reason that we undertook the publication and distribution of the book is because we thought that the book, originally published by Oxford University Press with no adverse response and reviews, deserved a wider circulation in a relatively lower price for the benefit of the academic world.'

Immediately, a roiling controversy erupted on the RISA online forum; a political movement formed to boycott Motilal Banarsidass publishers. Amidst tumultuous exchanges in academic forums, an open letter to Motilal Banarsidass was posted by Patrick Olivelle, a well-placed and senior Sanskrit scholar in America.[88] He wrote to Motilal:[89]

> This is a book that won the 1985 prize of the Committee on the History of Religions of the American Council of Learned Societies, the most prestigious scholarly organization of America, an

organization to which almost all scholarly associations of America belong . . . I think your reputation as a serious publisher of scholarly books is being undermined by withdrawing a good scholarly book from circulation for non-academic reasons. I will find it difficult to recommend you to my colleagues as a venue where they may publish their works.

Olivelle blithely pretended that there were no serious issues about the authenticity and scholarly rigor of Courtright's book. He did not try to examine whether the Committee on the History of Religions of the American Council of Learned Societies—the most prestigious scholarly organization of America—had performed a rigorous peer-review and, if so, how the numerous errors and problems were missed by the prize committee. Perhaps someone should have pointed out Gene Thursby's ironic comment to him that Courtright was being blamed for knowing too little history and that a *History of Religions prize was given for a work that largely ignores history—a truly bizarre phenomenon.* Instead, his argument seems to scream: "How dare you Indians differ with 'the most prestigious scholarly organization of America!'" No wonder that a dissenting RISA scholar, who requested anonymity, wrote privately: "Doesn't the insinuating, blackmailing tone of this just set your teeth on edge?"

Contradicting her earlier clarion call for objectivity, Kathleen Erndl gave her boycotting colleagues an encouraging 'shabash:'[90] "I'm happy to see RISA members rallying to support our colleague, *whether we agree with every word or not.*[91]" [Emphasis added] Though they may not agree with the methods, suppositions or conclusions of the book in question, *and may not have even read it,* closing of ranks is typical of many RISA members, contradicting their claims of objectivity and individuality. Cynthia Humes openly rallied the RISA troops to charge against Motilal as her following comment indicates:

> I suggest that scholars should either lobby Motilal Banarsidass to reverse this decision [to withdraw the book], or to begin boycotting Motilal Banarsidass, or both. Paul Courtright's book was peer-reviewed. If we allow ourselves to be censored, then there is no point to the academic enterprise. Friends, this is something to take a stand about.

Like Olivelle, Humes understands 'peer-review' as infallible and as a way to kill uncomfortable questions.[92] Later that day, Humes again came out against Motilal Banarsidass in no uncertain terms, advocating legal action in American courts. Moreover, she suggested that Western scholars circle their wagons and start assigning the book to their students just to send a message to Indians:

> If I were he [Courtright], I would get some of those famous Emory lawyers on the case and sue both the company as well as Jain individually. I would take that book, and with all of its newfound interest, find a reputable publisher and come out with a new foreword detailing the story, excoriating the press linking them to the petitioners, and publicizing it on the back cover with retorts to choice absurd quotes from the websites. People will come out of the woodwork to buy it, because of the frenzy. **It will be adopted in courses, not just for the subject matter, but also to reveal the importance of academic freedom.** I would then create a website on the controversy, with direct sales of the book offered at the click of a button. [Emphasis added]

Others quickly caught on to their financially privileged position over Indians. Jack Hawley, professor of Hinduism at Barnard College and Columbia University, further intimidated Motilal Banarsidass, using the power vested in him as a member of the dominant culture. In his letter to Motilal Banarsidass, Hawley's threat was loud and clear:

> May I ask for the current status of copyright information on any titles of mine that MLBD has published? Are AT PLAY WITH KRISHNA and DEVI: GODDESSES OF INDIA still in print? In both cases, other authors/editors are also involved, as are other presses, but once I have consulted with them, I would like to initiate a process that would allow me to withdraw those books from your care, if possible.

Kathleen M. Erndl again wrote in support of the boycott:

> As far as a boycott of MLBD is concerned, my thinking is this: I have spent thousands of dollars on MLBD books over the years. I have a limited amount of money to spend on books, and I am loathe to give my hard-earned money to a publisher who engages in censorship and denial of academic freedom and who has participated in a smear campaign to defame a respected friend, scholar, and colleague. If the decision is reversed, I'll be happy to return as a customer of MLBD.[93]

Meanwhile, Humes made sure that the frenzy would not die out with her cheerleading exhortations:[94]

If nothing else, a no-holds-barred academic boycott against Motilal Banarsidass will provide Indian presses with an answer to extremists on why they should not censor peer-reviewed works in the future [...] RISA, take a stance against efforts to deny academic freedom. **Boycott Motilal Banarsidass. Spread the word. Act.** [Emphasis added]

Erndl's and Humes's position is that of a relatively well-off American (in contrast to most Indian scholars) with the funding power giving her the ability to influence and control the distribution channels of knowledge. Malhotra's analysis located these events in the larger historical context of India's colonial past: The British East India Company first focused on controlling the distribution channels of trade, and this enabled them to control India's production as well. The rest, as they say, is history. Likewise, in the field of knowledge dissemination, the academic scholars know the strategic implications of keeping Motilal Banarsidass on a leash controlled by Western interests. Motilal Banarsidass is the *only* major Indology publisher with global reach and reputation that is controlled by Indians. Therefore, it is incumbent upon RISA to remind it of who the *boss* is, and thus also teach other Indians a lesson on the limits to their independence.

Publishers, even academic publishers, usually make decisions about whether or not books will see the light of day based on market conditions. It is also not unheard of to cease publication and withdraw copies of books with serious problems. The fact that an Indian publisher was being targeted while similar decisions by Western presses went unchallenged was certainly worth noting. The noted Abhinavagupta scholar, Sunthar Visuvalingam, exposed this double standard by revealing that SUNY Press had recently rejected one of his scholarly works on the excuse that it was 'too inflammatory'. He felt that SUNY's take-it-or-leave-it pressure was without any academic due process—no specific errors in the work were raised or debated with the author. Given the numerous problems with Courtright's book, Motilal had every right to be wary of such a work. (One does wish it had been more courageous and actually said so, rather than just talking about the *feelings* of their 'beloved readers'.) So there *is* a double standard. Western presses can and do reject Indian authors' books if they might offend white readers' sensibilities (as illustrated by Visuvalingam's personal experience); but when an Indian press dares to be sensitive to Indian sensibilities, the power hierarchy gets threatened and unleashes an attack!

An academic scholar, who had been the target of attacks by RISA, anonymously wrote exposing the selective nature of American academic outrage:

It is amusing that folks at RISA are calling for a boycott of MLBD. I haven't heard a word anywhere about boycott of CBS that pulled the movie on Reagan (peer-reviewed etc) only yesterday. Neither is the Republican Party that carried out this campaign against the movie, being called fascist.[95]

Laughing at RISA's Lilas

A sorrier spectacle is hard to imagine. Scholars refusing to exercise their professional obligation to investigate a case where serious and troubling questions had been raised were instead mobilizing an economic and political attack on a publisher in distant India. Perhaps only satire could make sense of the absurdities. As the anti-Motilal boycott picked up momentum, Prof. John Grimes, cut from a different cloth than the usual weave of RISA members, was the first to poke fun at the threatened boycott and the ridiculous specter of the scholars' self-righteous outrage.[96] He suggested ironically that scholars should burn all of the Motilal books in their libraries.[97]

Lampooning the situation, a spoof was written using a pseudonym and forwarded to various diaspora online discussion groups. This spoof by an anonymous author brings welcome humor to the controversy, and highlights both the tone of cultural superiority and the often amateurish efforts of RISA scholars to use pop psychology.

Mr. Ramesh Jain
Motel Benares Bookstore, Delhi

Dear Mr. Jain,

I deeply regret your recent decision to discontinue publication of Paul Courtright's book on the pagan God Ganesha. Employing psychoanalytical methods is an old tradition in the English speaking academia: but how can an unwashed coolie like you know about such things? These methods reveal a great deal about the person doing the analysis, much like a Roshak test [sic: Rorschach test]. That is another little psycho-babble concept that you don't know about.

So let me explain it to you. I will speak very slowly for your benefit. Paul Courtright's limp phallus imagery is clearly derived from his own lack of fertility as a scholar. He tends to see limp phalluses everywhere.

In fact, the limp *phallus* is a good symbol for the state of Indology in general. That is why we are all obsessed with phalluses, limp or otherwise. Where would we be as a field without our little limp phalluses? You have seriously tarnished your good name (in my opinion) by missing such an obvious point. It is our right as scholars to publish anything we like. It is your duty to publish everything we ask you that has been peer reviewed. No real (i.e., European) publisher ever considers the marketability of a book. Am I speaking slowly enough for you?

May I ask for the current status of the books I sent to you to publish because I could not find a real (i.e., European) publisher for them? Are AT PLAY WITH PAUL and WENDY: GODDESS OF INDIA still in print? I know I am striking terror into your heart, by threatening in my devilishly clever and subtle way, to withdraw these books from your care. Take that and add that to your curry!

Yours sincerely
John Yes, Holy
The One and Only

A commentator on Sulekha responded to *RISA Lila-2* with this ironic take on Western influence over Indian intellectuals. The boycott, he observed only half-jokingly, would actually *promote* intellectual freedom:

The boycott of Motilal Banarsidass, and withdrawal of the current scholars' copyrights, if it happens, would be one of the best things possible for Indian scholarship. For, the problem is American scholarship or European scholarship on India masquerading as *the definitive and scientific and objective* knowledge about India. That this happens unchallenged is only because there is a vacuum in India; but, as you point out, it is inevitable that this vacuum will be filled in the next few decades. If Jack Hawleys' and Cynthia Humes' books were not available inexpensively in Indian editions, then it will help ensure that Indian scholarship is not merely a slavish imitation of the West.[98]

An Academic Witch Hunt

One may find a parallel between the plight of medieval witches and the contemporary methodology of academic Hinduphobia:

During the three centuries of witch-hunting across Europe, it was sufficient to accuse someone of being a witch, and then the accused person had the burden to prove his or her innocence. If one were even remotely linked, howsoever indirectly, to any person or organization that had been demonized by the Church, or if one were charged with wearing a symbol or using certain terminology that had been condemned, it was enough to be declared guilty-by-association and burnt at the stake.[99]

As the Courtright vs. whistleblowers controversy unfolded, RISA scholars publicly engaged in a series of witch hunts, using theories and methods against fellow-scholars and the Hindu diaspora that bear a striking resemblance to the Church's demonology of pagans and witches in the Dark Ages, and in American history. RISA's rules for scholarship and civil behavior seemed to have been conveniently suspended to allow this witch-hunting to proceed with impunity. Sarma's attempt to muzzle de Nicolas, silently approved by a shameful majority of RISA's members, was only the beginning.

Prof. S.N. Balagangadhara (popularly referred to as Balu) and Prof. Jakob De Roover, another scholar from Belgium, became targets of libelous attacks that clearly violated RISA's rules. On RISA's list, Prof. Zydenbos pronounced Balu guilty-by-association on the sole grounds that Balu was listed on an Indian diaspora yahoo egroup as 'an author' alongside 'well-known names', including a "fellow who campaigns against this RISA list as a whole (as well as against academic freedom and freedom of the press, as the present Courtright case has shown)".

Zydenbos did not supply any evidence behind these insinuations in this petty and sensationalist attack. Another 'crime' that Zydenbos accused Balu of was that he was referred to as 'Balu' on that demonized egroup—a sign of being uncomfortably familiar with and 'close to the Devil'—even though Balu pointed out that many people routinely called him 'Balu'. Zydenbos expressed anger that Balu had been elected to lead the Hinduism Unit at AAR, and went on the record wishing his peers 'sagaciousness' as he publicly warned them against Balu's election.

The frenzied witch-hunting continued as Zydenbos took aim at Jakob De Roover.[100] Zydenbos accused De Roover of committing a scholarly sin simply by raising questions about the manner in which secularism is practised in India. (De Roover had written several articles explaining that secularism is not interpreted the same way in India as it is elsewhere.[101]) Zydenbos neither respected the academic freedom of a peer nor dealt maturely with a position on secularism that differed from the established dogma. As De Roover noted:

It was disquieting to read Prof. Zydenbos' recent post concerning the discussion on Indian secularism. The main purpose of his remarks seems to be to associate Prof. Balagangadhara and me with the anti-Muslim agenda of certain political organizations in Flanders and in India. He does not in any way address my arguments on secularism, but merely tries to discredit me by making insinuations about my political affiliations. This is unworthy of any intellectual.[102]

De Roover defended his right to propose alternative conceptual approaches to Indian cultural studies. He challenged RISA scholars to respond to his thesis using legitimate methods of criticism, rather than the unproductive and unprofessional character assassination pursued by Zydenbos.[103]

Like many other critics, De Roover was forced to clear his name of a false but loudly proclaimed accusation of fascism. He is in the company of scholars such as Ashis Nandy and T.N. Madan, who were also labeled 'saffron', simply because they dared to suggest that the people and/or the lawmakers in India should discuss, or re-evaluate how secularism is defined in the Indian context.[104] De Roover was forced to declare in his own defense:

Let it be clear that I do not have any connection to the fascist political party that is popular in *Flanders* or to the Sangh Parivar in India. Neither have I ever had contact with any 'notorious Indologist' who is associated with these political movements. My argument about secularism in India should be taken at face value.

Guilt-by-association extended beyond Balu and De Roover. Zydenbos laid blame on the entire University of Ghent. Balagangadhara protested this attack on academic freedom and wrote to the RISA list:[105]

Zydenbos launches personal attacks on me, on Jakob De Roover, and on those coming from the University of Ghent. He tries to make my credentials appear suspect because, heaven forbid, *www.bharatvani.org* provides a link to an article I wrote and published elsewhere! Koenraad Elst hails from Belgium, I teach at a Belgian University, my article is referenced to by a 'Hindutva filth factory' and, voila, he suggests, 'perhaps a glance at Bharatvani helps us hermeneutically to gain an insight into the intentions behind the writings coming out of Ghent.'

Balagangadhara criticized Zydenbos for engaging in character assassination, yet was compelled to formally declare that he was not associated in any way (directly or indirectly) with any political, religious, or social movement in India and that he was not nor had ever been a member of any of the Sangh Parivar.[106] Balu also sent a notice to Sarma, the co-moderator of the RISA list:

> Because this is a moderated list, the listserv is liable if someone takes it into his/her head to prosecute for libel. [...] In any case, it is just about conceivable that my next response to libel and innuendos will not be a friendly warning. I hope earnestly that people like Stephen Brown and Zydenbos also realize that they cannot simply go around assassinating the characters and reputations of people with impunity.

Whereas Sarma had earlier silenced de Nicolas for raising questions about Courtright's scholarship, Zydenbos was not similarly scolded for a blatant violation of professional decorum, even though he had relied on false hearsay to indulge in gross *ad hominem* attacks. Without any evidence to prove his assertions, Zydenbos was able to use smear tactics that did not analyze scholarship and simply pronounced the scholars guilty by imagined associations that they did not actually have. Contrary to basic norms of fair play, not only was Zydenbos not cited for his attempt to smear Balagangadhara and De Roover, but also these two scholars were warned by Sarma in his capacity as a representative of the RISA hierarchy: "If those two Belgians persisted in carrying on with the discussion, their posts would be put on 'moderation'".[107]

Commenting on this orgy of guilt-by-association and *ad hominem* attacks by the academics, Sankrant Sanu noted in a comment to *RISA Lila 2*:

> As I was reading the RISA posts, as well as the article, one of the things that struck me was the relative lack of *introspection* that was occurring in this academic citadel that was choosing instead to quickly find the 'other' to blame. Perhaps this lack of introspection may also be regarded as a cultural difference arising from the constraints of the Christianized framework ... Another very interesting dimension of this that you point out is the fairly liberal use of demonization by association in this academic community. This is done both by using the 'Hindutva' label as a demonizing technique, not only for all those who do count themselves as supporters for Hindutva, but also for anyone who speaks up for Hinduism (or even makes known they find certain scholarship offensive), somehow assuming that anyone who belongs in all these categories is automatically labeled as 'Hitler-worshipper', 'Muslim-killer', 'Gujarat-riot-supporter' etc.[108]

Conclusion

The Courtright controversy highlights the unwillingness on the part of the most prominent academic scholars to investigate with honesty cases of apparent scholarly malfeasance, or even cases where simple malarkey is heavily codified and footnoted. The detailed list of Courtright's errors, inventions and omissions—diligently compiled by Agarwal and Venkat—were ignored, as was the forthright challenge from de Nicolas regarding the academy's professional quality control. Indeed, for de Nicolas it must have been shocking to realize that none of his colleagues would publicly come to his support and defend his freedom to raise uncomfortable questions.

The officially moderated RISA-l responses were full of excited calls to arms and scurrilous invectives and wild guesswork regarding the hypothetically 'fascistic' motives behind the diaspora criticisms. This lack of scholarly decorum established an unprecedented level of tolerance of *ad hominem* attacks and unsubstantiated assumptions. Among those knee-jerk replies from RISA scholars were flagrant examples of intentional omissions and irrelevant distractions. This unbridled strategy of derogatory sneering calls into question the intellectual and moral qualities of the moderators of the RISA list.

A double standard becomes evident—freedom of speech is to be defended for certain academicians but not for the 'intruders.' The contradiction that escaped the attention of many RISA scholars was that, "They champion the freedom of those who are presumed to be among the 'Good'—and the chosen 'us'—while lobbying in the fiercest manner against the freedom of 'others' who are declared as 'Evil'."[109] This delineation based on Good/Evil people is an important archetype of the American Frontier Myth that was explained earlier in this section.

This is particularly worrisome, because RISA is the official body of scholars who study Hinduism in the American Academy. In the popular American mind, India is *inseparable* from these received images of Hinduism.

The prejudice in RISA-l against critics of Doniger and Courtright is not fuelled by a naïve ignorance about Hinduism but by something far more insidious, as noted by Madhu Kishwar, the well-known Indian author, editor and feminist. She opined that the academy's handling of the Courtright controversy was an example of Eurocentric chauvinism rather than simply an individual's ignorance about Hinduism. She wrote:

This is a classic example of conflicts arising *not* out of ignorance but surfeit of knowledge combined with the unconsciously imbibed arrogance of Western academia which assumes that its tools of analysis and value systems enable them to understand and pass judgment on the experiences and heritage of all human beings including those who operate with very different world views. Instead of dealing with the criticism leveled at their intellectual tools, many Western Indologists treated the conflict as a case of 'academic freedom' versus the intolerance of Hindu community leaders, thus leading to a bitter stalemate.[110]

Chapter 22

Character Assassination

Although a variety of intellectuals had offered diverse critiques of RISA, Malhotra, as a prominent public intellectual, and an 'outsider' to the academia, became the main target of a vicious defamation campaign by the RISA cartel. These defenders of the academy ignored hard facts and falsely assumed that he was the source of each and every one of the criticisms. Despite the fact that Malhotra had not started the petition to Emory and had criticized it, several RISA scholars persisted in making him the scapegoat—often as a way of evading the substantive issues raised by so many voices. As with de Nicolas, Balagangadhara and De Roover in the previous chapter, he also became the latest target in the campaign of demonization.

Talking Down at 'Jackals'

From the earliest moment when diaspora intellectuals like Malhotra approached Doniger to debate her ideas, she dismissed them as unfit to debate, indeed, called them inferior. Later, she would claim that she was not given a fair chance to address their criticisms.[111] However, prior to publishing *Wendy's Child Syndrome* on Sulekha.com, he had contacted Doniger by email and sent her an advance copy of her namesake article. In August 2002, he sent the unpublished draft to numerous scholars asking for feedback, in order to make changes prior to the column being posted on the website.[112] He also sent it specifically to those scholars featured prominently in his analysis—Doniger, Kripal, Courtright, and Caldwell—inviting them to debate prior to its publication.[113]

Malhotra described his role in writing the essay as trying to 'synthesize, summarize, and simplify' RISA's scholarly perspectives and that his writings had given the Hindu diaspora a voice. He explained that over 70 per cent of his *Wendy's Child* essay merely summarizes prior critiques by others, and asked: "What's wrong with an Indian journalist who covers Indologists for the benefit of his community? This is merely reverse anthropology". He hoped to break new ground in educating the Indian-American community regarding the academic portrayal concerning them.

In reply, Jeffrey Kripal agreed to respond on the Sulekha website. His article, *The Tantric Truth of the Matter*[114] was published two weeks later. In the introduction, Kripal wrote: "I take Mr. Malhotra's main point to be that a greater dialogue or 'hermeneutical fusion' of civilizations is necessary to ensure a more hopeful future for us all". Kripal's rejoinder drew considerable interest from readers at Sulekha, as well as critical responses from other scholars.

Caldwell and Malhotra engaged in a dialogue, working offline to write up their debate into a single article using both voices. This resulted in the publication of an online essay, *The Insider/Outsider Academic Game*.[115] Caldwell had felt negatively portrayed in the original *RISA Lila-1* and this new piece was their mutually agreed enterprise to bring out both sides of the story.

Courtright also replied to the request for feedback, and "pointed out several specific statements in the draft that he considered erroneous or misrepresentations"; Malhotra indicated that he made the suggested corrections.

Doniger's response to Malhotra's overture was very different and dismissive. She wrote: "It is true that I have, and am glad that I have, a *parampara*. But everything else that you imply about me—and it's all vague innuendo, never a reasoned argument—is untrue". Malhotra suggested that psychoanalysis requires that 'both parties be in direct dialogue' and urged her to interact, but Doniger concluded with a tone of exasperation: "We are talking past one another".

Satya Prabhakar, CEO of Sulekha.com, wrote an email to the scholars explaining that "the issues being discussed are controversial" and invited them to respond to the criticism.

Malhotra, who had been copied on Prabhakar's email, replied that he had been critical of "Western scholars for excluding the voice from within the tradition, except as reduced to 'native informant'". He therefore did not want to be 'guilty of the same in reverse'. He invited Doniger's participation, because, "In the long run, we could be breaking new ground for this discipline. It might be an important contribution towards the secure and respectful integration of Hindus into American culture without losing their distinctiveness or self-esteem."[116]

Unlike the other scholars, Doniger refused the offer of debate. She wrote back sarcastically, trying to put Malhotra in his *proper place* as a native informant: "Thank you for inviting me to participate in a conversation with you in which you propose to assume the role of native informant." Her email was inflammatory, since such an asymmetric relationship is clearly what the diaspora was fighting. Doniger continued in the same vein, dismissing the very prospect of communing with the disapora untouchables:

> Harvard-trained as I am (in what I often mock, but actually do respect, as the 'Take a Buddhist to Dinner' school of comparative religion), I profit greatly from such conversations and seek them whenever I can.

She continued provoking: "I would indeed be happy to speak with you as scholar to native informant." Moving to a taunting personal tone, she wrote: "I would be very curious to know what prayers you recite, what rituals your two grandmothers performed, what stories your aunts told you when you were a little boy". She conceded sarcastically that: "As a Hindu you do indeed have some authority with me on the subject of Hinduism". She then slipped from her playful mode and came out with both barrels blazing, dropping the condescension, and moving into open insults. Knowing well that he didn't want to be seen as another native informant, she wrote: "But this is not what you intend". She tripped over her own stream of insults, and considered him to be 'grotesquely ignorant'. She characterized his attempts to participate in academic gatherings as hanging out in "places where real scholars gather as jackals hang about the congregations of lions", and named Harvard as a place "where they will do anything for money". Dropping the mask of her Ivy League decorum, she wrote more like a street-fighter:

> In the world of scholarship, you are what my sainted mother, who was Viennese, would have called an 'aufgestellte Mausdrek', a mouse-turd standing up on end. You do not even know enough to know how much you do not know; you have no training, nor even the rudiments of a self-education in the most basic principles of academic discourse. I would no sooner take your advice on how I should write about Hinduism (let alone how Jeff Kripal should write on Hinduism) than I would expect you to take my advice on how to run your business, whatever it is. I'm sorry I wasted all

this time even drafting this reply to you, but I confess I finally lost my temper. Please don't bother me any more.

Doniger has used similar demeaning and egregious language as an intimidating tactic before, against others with whom she disagreed. For instance, Doniger used *ad hominem* attacks, rather than reasoned analysis, in reviewing a work about the late scholar Joseph Campbell. Because Campbell's largely Jungian interpretations are at variance with her Freudian approach to Hindu symbols and myths; Doniger claimed that Campbell "never got below the surface of anything".

Ironically, Doniger, an amateur psychoanalyst, characterized Campbell's decades of scholarship as pop psychology in which, according to her, he "cooked up the TV dinner of mythology" so that "people in California could feel better about themselves". While accusing him of anti-Semitism, Doniger claimed that Campbell was 'neither a scholar nor a gentleman'.[117] Doniger's rhetoric about Campbell's life's work was dismissive rather than reasoned. She characterized his *magnum opus*—the editing of the Indologist Heinrich Zimmer's work—as having 'Campbell's dirty pawprint' which she claimed "soils the work of Zimmer everywhere".[118] Campbell's official biographers, the Larsens, noted that Doniger's cheap rhetoric was 'outrageous' and "cast aspersions on his scholarship and character" rather than engaging in scholarly debate. They asked:

> What should we expect from scholars? Certainly a firm command of the facts, but also subtleties of dialogue and intellectual confrontation, not the histrionic broadsides and wholesale denunciations that characterize Ms. Doniger's approach to Campbell and are also found in her review.[119]

Many experts on the works of Joseph Campbell feel Doniger is motivated by jealously and dislike of those who differ from her; they accuse her of not approaching debate honestly.[120] Campbell's biographers contend that because of scholars like Doniger, "Serious debate is sacrificed to scandalmongers and jealous contenders."[121] Apparently, her tactics of personal attacks are rarely censured by the scholarly community because of her ferocious clout and influence. Campbell, as a part of the elite academic establishment, was accorded a strong defense by his colleagues. However, the path is more arduous for other less prominent commentators such as Malhotra, who has been critical of Western scholars for excluding the voice from within the tradition, except as reduced to 'native informants'.

Doniger's Claim as a Champion of Hinduism

A few hours after she tossed her Viennese mouse turds at the Indian jackals, Doniger replied to Prabhakar in a more civil tone. Claiming close connections with Indians, and dropping many names, she emphatically stated that she does "not object in any way to discussing my ideas about Hinduism with Hindus—the 'community being studied'". She laid claim to having understood Hinduism authentically from practising Hindus.[122] But then, with her pen dipped in venom, she wrote:

> I refuse to have a conversation with YOU, RAJIV MALHOTRA, [Original emphasis] because of the ill-informed, inaccurate, and malicious things you have written about me and about Jeffrey Kripal, statements that disqualify you as a valid spokesperson for anything at all, let alone the Hindu community as a whole.

To avoid engaging the issues raised, Doniger disqualifies Malhotra's validity as a representative of the Indian-American of Hindu community. It is important to note that this is not just Doniger's personal bias: She is swept away by the deeply embedded civilizational mindset inherent in White culture when dealing with non-Euro-American cultures. Interesting parallels to this attitude can be found in various colonial contexts. In the American Frontier this game of 'who speaks for the natives' was frequently played out.[123] Only those natives who were deemed safe and pliable were dealt with as authentic negotiators. Those who mounted a concerted defense, like Tecumseh, were to be eliminated by any means possible. Especially those who were sophisticated enough to understand and employ Western-style negotiations and legalistic methods were ignored or sidelined as being 'inauthentic'. President Andrew Jackson's biographer pointed out that in the frontier era, the US government often used this tactic in negotiating land rights and treaties with various native tribes.

When Andrew Jackson was determining a boundary line that was disputed between Cherokees, Creeks, and Whites, he told his underlings not to be too preoccupied with listening to the claims of the Indian representatives, *especially if they were relatively sophisticated about the law.* He didn't see them as legitimate voices even if they were raising legitimate issues about the demarcation of boundaries. Jackson asserted:

> In this matter the Indians—I mean the real Indians, the natives of the forest—are little concerned. It is a stratagem only acted upon

by the designing half-breeds and renegade white men who have taken refuge in their country.

He claimed that negotiating with savvy, assertive Indian spokesmen would disadvantage not only hard-working white settlers, but also other Indian tribes! Jackson used this self-serving but noble-sounding reasoning to bypass the educated negotiators and turn to less sophisticated and more naïve Indian chiefs, pressuring them to endorse the boundary settlement as Whites wanted.[124]

The Indian-Americans involved with this contemporary debate with Doniger are educated in Western ways and dare ask inconvenient and impertinent questions. Yet, in the mythical mechanisms employed to imagine them, they are classified by Doniger as 'not real Indians' and thus illegitimate as participants in the discussions.

Doniger's assertion of her proximity to certain Hindus is also reminiscent of the rhetoric of the Frontier Myth. Andrew Jackson, who was responsible for untold misery and genocide through his policy of Indian removal, also *claimed to love* Native Americans, and to be acting in *their* best interests. Indeed, as Brands points out, Jackson and his wife even adopted Indian children to show their "sincere good intentions", but this did not stop him from pursuing a policy that devastated native cultures.[125]

Doniger's dehumanizing classification of Malhotra as a 'jackal' also recalls frontier white attitudes towards 'dangerous' Native Americans. In the frontier narratives, Native Americans were dehumanized repeatedly as vultures, jackals, wolves and snakes. Later, perhaps as a form of damage-control, Doniger excused this name-calling as 'a joke'. However, this is not quite convincing as Doniger repeatedly plays the race card claiming she is a victim of reverse discrimination.

Prabhakar made one last effort to foster debate, asking her to reconsider her decision against writing an article on Sulekha: "I think it would be of enormous benefit for the audience to understand your point-of-view and your take on the issues being discussed". He stressed that the "issues, inferences and implications" of her "research related to Hinduism" has touched a "very sensitive nerve among the vast majority of Indians who are uninitiated in these discussions that are largely restricted to academic fora": He counseled her that

> The downside of not responding is an increasingly intensified opinion (that we as managers of the site have observed) that all of this is part of a concerted and prejudiced attempt, led by a mutually-reinforcing group of Western religious scholars, to

denigrate Hinduism as a religion and vilify its intellectual and spiritual output.

He stressed that Sulekha 'is agnostic and encourages expression and discussion'. An hour later, Doniger sent Prabhakar a reply, copied to Malhotra, Kripal et al, in which she positioned herself as a champion of Hinduism—a patronizing attitude that other white scholars such as Martin Marty would later endorse. Doniger cited a list of her books to prove that she had dedicated her life 'praising and glorifying' Hindu mythology, and arguing for its 'wisdom'. She therefore found it preposterous

> that anyone should accuse me of a 'prejudiced attempt . . . to denigrate Hinduism as a religion and vilify its intellectual and spiritual output' that I am simply flabbergasted. HAVE YOU EVER READ ANY OF THESE BOOKS OF MINE? [Original emphasis]. I refuse to defend myself against people who know nothing of my work and simply repeat what they hear other people say about me. This is why I feel that this discussion is totally useless and has nothing at all to do with me or my work. There is nothing about any of my work in any of what Rajiv Malhotra says about me.[126]

An hour later, Doniger sent Prabhakar another email, again copied to the others. She lists a variety of her 'lovingly and carefully translated' works which she felt helped readers 'to appreciate Hinduism'. She then plays the race card: "Does none of this mean anything to you? Is there ANYTHING in any of these attacks other than pure and naked racism, and objection to the color of my skin?"[127] Doniger has repeatedly claimed that her *Encarta* essay and other works were criticized because "my name is not Sharma." She disingenuously accused her critics—and, by implication, Microsoft *Encarta*—of racism and refuses to debate them. Anyone can see that her skin color and last name have nothing to do with Sanu's critiques of her *Encarta* essay or other work.

After several more angry emails passed between Doniger and Malhotra, they agreed to disagree and not to schedule any kind of *samvad*.[128] Her charge that he had attacked her was reminiscent of early Christianity when the Church in Rome encouraged its followers to 'get attacked' so they could be declared martyrs and give the authorities an excuse to kill the 'evil heathens'. Dharma traditions never glorified martyrdom; hence the mindset to claim victim status is simply not there. White Christians have established the right for the past 400 years to examine other peoples in the minutest and most intimate details, but they deny the same right to be examined by others in reverse. When scholars write denigrating accounts of Sri Ramakrishna, Ganesha, the Goddess, and Gurus, they are classified as 'analyses' and 'interpretations' and defended as the outcome of intellectual freedom. But when this process is reversed and the gaze is inverted, why is it seen as an attack? Malhotra sees the claims of victimhood like "a fig leaf used to hide the real issues of incompetence, cronyism and cartel behavior".

Keeping the Savages at Bay

While Doniger viewed Malhotra as the 'savage other' before the publication of his essay, other RISA scholars entered the fray once numerous critical essays and petitions began to appear. RISA officialdom's attempt to defend its hegemony provided an opportunity to otherwise unnoticed junior scholars for some serious career climbing. Many RISA scholars and graduate students, even those who rarely contributed to the online discussions, took advantage of this to prove their establishment-friendly credentials.

For example, one graduate student named Stephen Brown alleged Malhotra to be behind all sorts of attacks and conspiracies against scholars. He was challenged on the RISA online list by others such as Balagangadhara, leaving Brown and other RISA henchmen embarrassed.[129]

Attempts at demonizing continued with John Pincince, who was then a graduate student in history at the University of Hawaii, wildly fabricating secondary and tertiary links between Infinity Foundation and the 'usual suspects'.[130] Cynthia Humes eventually reminded the group that Malhotra was not in favor of the petition in question and that his financial support for dialog efforts between Hindus and Western scholars was 'a matter of public record'.

Prior to the events described in this section, messages sent to RISA's online list had been open to the general public even though only its members were allowed to post messages. But once its scholars were being criticized, RISA's conversations were quickly closed to outsiders, its online list made secret and underground.

A few weeks later, as the controversy spread to other scholarly forums, Prof. Miriam Sharma of the Asian Studies Program at the University of Hawaii, took a superficial glance at the Infinity Foundation website and reported her findings to yet another academic online discussion group, H-ASIA. Sharma warned her colleagues that the 'particular affiliations and views' of Malhotra would leave one 'exceedingly alarmed'. Such 'alarm' seems misplaced. The foundation's website is very multifaceted and pluralistic, hosts essays by numerous diverse scholars, and that provides considerable room for dissent.

Though Miriam Sharma and John Pincince are both at the University of Hawaii, they nevertheless failed in their examination of Infinity Foundation to mention the programs that it sponsored at the University of Hawaii since the mid-1990s. The single largest set of grants cumulatively given by Infinity Foundation to anyone in its entire history went to the University of Hawaii, including conferences, talks by eminent and controversial scholars—including Wendy Doniger— stipends for graduate research, and grants for faculty research.[131] Some observers have suggested that the quality and quantity of work on the website of this small foundation is frightening to those scholars who do not expect such sustained involvement from their erstwhile 'native-informants'.[132]

In her letter to H-ASIA, Miriam Sharma compared Malhotra to those who attack 'leftist-dominated' academia and lumped him with those who accuse all others 'of aiding and abetting the enemy'. However, the critics featured in the present book are the opposite of neo-conservative ideologues and are squarely in the multicultural camp. The shallowness of this attack became apparent when she used the standard cliché against conservative foes: mocking them for criticizing 'Edward Said and Cultural Studies, among others', when in fact Malhotra has gratefully utilized Said's works in his own arguments and is critical of the approach of those South Asianists who only give lip service to Said. If Sharma is claiming the leftist 'higher ground' for herself then she must deal with the evidence presented here that shows RISA to be elitist, anti-Hindu-American minority, anti-change, anti-dissent—in every way contrary to a progressive, humanistic approach.

Sharma attempted fear-mongering, reminding her colleagues of 'the recent [U.S.] Congressional attacks on Area Studies'. Having failed to conclusively link Infinity Foundation to the Hindu right or 'deviate' types, Sharma ended up comparing Infinity Foundation to the US Congress' debates on post 9/11 governmental controls of Cultural or Area Studies through Title IV funds. Sharma once again got things backwards. She got the totally different dynamics between Islamic

Studies and Hinduism Studies mixed up. Neo-conservatives protest the *lack of criticism* of Islam in the academy. For the past few decades, professors of Islamic and Middle Eastern Studies have worked to make Islam more acceptable to American sensibilities and in particular to smooth out the textbooks and curricula. The respectful interface with practitioners, the preponderance of Islamic 'insiders' on the faculties, and coziness with Saudi funding sources has significantly impacted the presentation of Islam in US schools and universities. The same has *not* happened with Hinduism, as noted by David Freedholm and others, where the situation is the exact opposite: Hinduism has been subjected to fetishizing and psychoanalysis.

Sharma ended with a flourish, warning her colleagues with "a strong reminder that the views of Rajiv Malhotra must be attended to seriously and counteracted with all the critical faculties that scholarly endeavors possess". This invitation to use critical faculties and debate is exactly what Hindu-Americans have been asking for all along, insisting that it would be healthy for the discipline. But Sharma was advancing not a good-faith exhortation to debate but rather a coded call to arms in order to preemptively squash a threat to the status quo by any means available. Notably, each negative category in which she tried to paint the 'other' crumbles upon close scrutiny. The only tool that was left for her to deploy was guilt-by-association, a device that enables insecure scholars to ignore or misquote the diaspora, and thereby position it as a threat.[133]

Some of the RISA scholars also tried to derail an Indian academic conference sponsored by Infinity Foundation, using guilt-by-association in order to discourage others from participating. Prof. Jack Hawley tried very hard to negatively brand Malhotra in the mind of one of the main conveners.[134] But he was unsuccessful because she chose to think for herself and not rely upon second-hand information or jealous allegations. Hawley had earlier been keen to organize a panel at the conference but backed out once he realized that IF (Infinity Foundation) was the sponsor. He wrote to the convener, explaining that 'the IF connection' with the conference was a reason to be 'more than ordinarily wary'.[135] The convener's reply to Hawley made her stand unambiguously clear and is worth quoting at length:[136]

Dear Jack,

If the IF connection makes you wary, then please feel free to keep your panel papers to yourself. I do not wish to have the papers of anyone who has misgivings about our integrity and intentions. For 25 years I ran [my organization] without any funds or grants precisely because I wish to preserve my intellectual and political freedom and sense of priorities free from the influence of donor agencies. Having experienced such a rare quality and quantity of freedom for such long years, at great personal cost because I had to work with very small amounts of money, I am not likely to surrender my freedom for this or that grant. Even those who may differ with me or hate me have so far not cast aspersions on my integrity. That is why many of those who may be uneasy about Rajiv's critiques have not hesitated to be associated with our Conference. My experience with IF has been very uplifting. Unlike all the other funders who gave us small amounts of money for the Conference after a great deal of power play, IF has been more than gracious in allowing me total freedom with no questions asked, no demands made and no hidden agendas pushed down my throat. That is why I see myself working with IF to make this Conference an annual event . . . I know some of you are upset at Rajiv's criticism of Wendy's and Paul's work. But why not respect their right to challenge your scholarship as long as we respect your right to defend and uphold it? . . . [Emphasis added]

Hawley replied, charging that he had been 'attacked by Rajiv as being anti-Hindu'.[137] But he failed to furnish details on what constituted the alleged 'attack'. It turns out that Hawley had written in a prestigious and influential American journal that Hinduism is an illegitimate religion, and Malhotra had exposed this as part of taking the debate to the public. Here is what Hawley wrote in an academic journal and felt embarrassed about when it was brought to the attention of the diaspora:

> Hinduism—the word and perhaps the reality too—was born in the 19th century, a notorious illegitimate child. The father was middle-class British, and the mother, of course, was India. The circumstances of conception are not altogether clear.
> [Jack Hawley, "Naming Hinduism," in The Wilson Quarterly, summer 1991. p. 21.]

Hawley has not explained why he should be exempt from criticisms, or why his words should not be discussed by the community. He continued to warn the conference convener that Malhotra has 'a very dark side, in my opinion'. Invoking mysterious dangers posed by 'dark savages', Hawley expressed how his "hopes and wishes" did not 'align with those of IF' and that he "had to learn to be very cautious, and in this I know I am far from being alone". He gave up further attempts to poison the conference after his final words about Malhotra: "He's a man with many sides—well, at least two".[138]

Attempts to Subvert Intellectual Freedom

Similar attempts have been made to scapegoat critics of the Western academy and to blacklist the events where they participate. But many self-assured scholars in India choose to remain uninfluenced by such attempts. Madhu Kishwar is a good example of those who went public to expose that some scholars were blocking a free exchange of ideas. She wrote:

> When I organized the First International Conference on Indic Religions through the Centre for the Study of Developing Societies in December 2003, many activists and academics let loose a defamation campaign arguing that this was a Hindutva inspired initiative and therefore, ought to be shunned. Fortunately, very few people believed this slander, given the track record of CSDS and Manushi on the issue of minority rights. But it did frighten several scholars who stayed away from the First Conference lest they be forever tainted. Such blind targeting and hate campaigns have meant that only politicians from the extreme right articulate religious concerns, while serious scholars who do not trash the religious and cultural traditions of India or do not join partisan campaigns on behalf of left-leaning political parties run the risk of being dumped in the RSS-VHP camp and are assumed to be responsible for everything from the Gujarat riots to the demolition of the Babri Masjid.[139]

Kishwar noted that such campaigns of guilt-by-association choke off participation by those who have an Indic viewpoint or wish to challenge a Eurocentric construction that demeans or trivializes Indian culture. By trying to malign alternative models in which Indic paradigms are valued and discussed, Eurocentric scholars kill real diversity in the debate, and the result is further cultural hegemony. Kishwar continued:

> Thus, most of the serious scholarship ends up being processed in Western universities with the inevitable inbuilt biases. This is not to deny that works of great scholarship have also been produced

in these universities which have made knowledge of distant cultures accessible to people educated through the English language. But such insightful studies are small in number and remain confined to a very tiny intellectual elite.[140]

By branding those who challenge Eurocentric notions and seek a more Indic framework as 'untrained,' 'unsophisticated,' or 'dangerous,' the scholars are helping further the exoticization and demonization of Indic culture. These currents filter down into the mass media, as we saw with Doniger's smug 'expert' comments on the Bhagavad Gita and the Goddess, producing more prejudice. Kishwar explained how such narrow control of the flow of information about religions caused social harm:

> Today, most people know the faiths of others through brief exposure to superficial descriptions on TV, in newspapers, films and other mass media. The dominant forms of international mass media have deeply imbided a distorted Eurocentric worldview, with its tendency to see the cultures and faiths of non-European peoples as intrinsically inferior and backward, as mainly of anthropological interest, existing as a curious hangover of a lower stage in the evolution of human kind. Therefore, instead of leading to greater understanding, fleeting mass media images of alien practices, when viewed in very different cultures, have so far tended to increase divisions, strengthen prejudices and negative stereotypes.[141]

Visualizing a Level Playing Field

Very few Indian-Americans who are interested in these issues directly witnessed this unfolding of events in the RISA online group. However, those who followed the discussions were astounded to see such blatant instances of bias unfold publicly right before their eyes. The most disheartening realization was that this mean-spirited orientation was produced and disseminated by RISA, which is a part of the AAR, the mother ship of Religious Studies in the USA. Most AAR scholars remained silent and many of them encouraged the bias.

This raises especially troubling questions about the validity of the fieldwork of such scholars. One shudders to think how much false academic reporting there could be in some scholars' work with Indian villagers and pandits. After all, the Indian native informants do not get to read what is published after the scholar returns to the West, and, even if they were to find out, they lack the power, the self-confidence and the means to protest in any manner at all. Moreover, there are seldom any credible or neutral witnesses to attest to the authenticity of the data. This issue of patronizing the powerless native informants while refusing to acknowledge the courageous and articulate Indian 'other' has been addressed in detail by McCutcheon, as we will see in chapter 24.

It is important that RISA should establish clear policies of engagement. Malhotra proposed that the following three issues regarding methodology should be of concern to scholars who consider themselves post-Orientalist—i.e. devoted to giving voice and agency to the subjective self:[142]

1. *What is the RISA policy on using guilt-by-association?* If a RISA member belongs to institution X (which could be their University or Church, for instance), to what extent is the person guilty by association with every other member of X? Furthermore, if an article posted at a website of institution X has a bibliography listing of another person Y then is every member of X guilty by third or fourth level of indirect association with Y? In addressing these questions, RISA must bear in mind that if Pincince's methodology was applied to RISA members, every student and faculty at a Catholic school or college and every Catholic in RISA would have to be accused of [links to] the child molesting cases in the Catholic Church. One can see how this policy could implicate just about everyone in RISA by association with their universities, social and political associations, synagogues, churches and temples.

2. *What is the hermeneutical role of guilt-by-association?* Once guilt-by-association has been established pursuant to Policy #1 above, what is its relevance in the examination of a **proposition** [or thesis] whose author is deemed guilty-by-association? In other words, are propositions to be examined independently of their authors or not? Again, this must be consistently applied to RISA members with the same standard as to outsiders.

3. *Can and should the scholars be psychoanalyzed?* Can psychoanalytical techniques be used to inquire whether the scholar could be projecting his or her own fantasies on to the Indian cultural psyche? Tying together the loose threads of their traumas that may have impacted their work, one might identify the Freudian obsessions that drove a scholar to interpret, for instance, Ganesha

as craving oral sex. The use of reverse psychoanalysis might reveal that the subject, in this case the Indologist, has a limp phallus complex, which is, of course, pathological depending on the context. It might be determined that sexual abuse as a child compels certain interpretive strategies: Could he have been abused as a child by someone with a potbelly who ate sweets and who performed oral sex, leading him to subconsciously superimpose this on to Ganesha's imagery? Is it conceivable that, as a child, the scholar might have had some sexual encounters with his mother, in competition with his father's harder penis, and that this latent unfulfilled fantasy now gets superimposed as the interpretation of Ganesha competing with his father, Shiva?

Unfortunately, RISA has done nothing to evaluate, much less enact, any such policies as steps towards transparency and a level playing field.

How do the Two Sides Compare and Contrast?

Many people have pointed out similarities between the methods of Doniger's camp and the methods of the diaspora critics. We decided to analyze how both sides overlap and diverge.

It is important to bear in mind that there is no unified Hindu diaspora approach. A wide variety of Hindus have taken positions across the spectrum. There *are*, indeed, those who should be classified as chauvinists for claiming the Puranas to be millions of years old along with similar positions, in the same camp as Christian-Americans who support creationism. There *are* also Hindu voices that advocate hegemony over other Indian groups, and these deserve to be considered right-wing nationalists, on par with those who see America solely as a Judeo-Christian or Anglo-Saxon nation.

But the Hindu voices featured in this book cannot be lumped with such orthodoxy or extremism. The *Postcolonial Hinduism School* referenced below is shorthand for the critics of RISA featured in this book and consists of those who have investigated the research and writings of various historical and contemporary academic scholars of Hinduism. The Postcolonial Hinduism School includes informed insiders as well as non-Hindus (such as Alan Roland, for instance) who challenge RISA's colonialist ways. These are RISA's feared 'savage others'.

SIMILARITIES

RISA Hinduphobia School	Postcolonial Hinduism School
Claim to uncover/decode the 'real' Hinduism, which Hindus allegedly wish to hide for sociopolitical reasons. Investigate the hidden motives behind symbols, rituals, gurus, texts, and contemporary Hindu society.	Reverse the gaze and claim to uncover/decode the 'real' motives of certain RISA scholars. Investigate the personal psychological conditionings, the institutional agendas of funding agencies, academic politics and games played to project the appearance of objectivity.
Claim that the realities about the targets of inquiry are more complex than what is publicly known. Hinduism has its 'dark side'.	Claim that the realities of the lives, politics and peer-pressure of the RISA scholars are more complex and influence their work more dramatically than what is publicly known. RISA scholars have their 'dark side'.
Many Hindus and Indian-Americans are troubled by this speculative scholarship.	Many RISA scholars are troubled by the investigative scholarship from 'outsiders' who they have known as 'native informants'.
These reactions from Hindus are seen as natural and expected; the academic work must continue as a part of intellectual freedom.	RISA scholars' reactions to this research are seen as knee-jerk reactions to be expected; the work to expose Hinduphobia must continue and enjoy intellectual freedom.
Scholars in this camp take their intellectual positions seriously and write provocatively to get their points across. (This expands the possibility of future funding). They use/create Eurocentric theories through which to explain Hinduism.	Scholars on this side are also very serious about their analyses and write provocatively to get their points across. (This expands their readership base). Malhotra, for instance, has developed some postcolonial theories (some of which are summarized in section I) through which he interprets RISA's scholarship.

DIFFERENCES

RISA Hinduphobia School	Postcolonial Hinduism School
Scholars work full-time in this pursuit usually for their entire careers. They are interconnected with various academic, governmental, grant-making and/or church-related organizations. Thus a given scholar may simultaneously be an ordained minister in an organized church, on the board of a foundation, a powerful advisor to the US State Department and an 'objective' professor training students on Hinduism—all at once. Institutional settings foster 'networking' for collaborations and dissemination into education and media.	Scholars are volunteers in this work, and their main professions and businesses are entirely unrelated. They are not dependent upon each other for their careers and their interconnections with each other are limited to Internet discussions and infrequent meetings. Their influence in established educational settings is limited as they have no backing in institutions that control knowledge flow. Their access to mainstream media is limited.
Indic claims to spirituality are treated superficially—reduced to myths, metaphors, and symbol libraries that are to be dissected into parts—and often positioned as a sociopolitical charade. Theories syndicated by the academicians are applied on an *ad hoc* basis, and Indic traditions (once so dissected) may be selectively used as 'data' at the personal discretion of the scholar, including for the purposes of voyeurism, catharsis and/or politics.	Spirituality is respected as having claims worthy of serious discussion. Legends, metaphors, and symbols are imbued with possibilities of experiential spiritual meanings. Indic traditions provide methodologies for personal growth and societal improvement. Certain interpretations by RISA-type scholars are seen as triumphantly parochial and disconnected from the traditions.
Exercise significant formal and informal control over the work of other, especially junior, scholars. Have the power to reward, promote, marginalize or punish those who dissent.	Little or no control or co-ordination over the actions of intellectuals, activists and scholars inside or outside their camp.

Differences (contd.)

RISA Hinduphobia School	Postcolonial Hinduism School
Scholars have failed to make positive initiatives to reach out to practising Hindus or to correct American mainstream prejudices against Hinduism (unlike professors of Islamic Studies who have developed synergistic connections with practising Muslims.) Many have boycotted the initiatives of the Hindu diaspora and denigrated their efforts, rather than engaging them. Diaspora attempts at engagement are perceived as interference, as the Emory interactions illustrate.	The diaspora has tried repeatedly to engage the academy. Several diaspora organizations, such as Infinity Foundation, have sponsored conferences in which scholars from various backgrounds came together. Infinity initiatives include encouraging academic Religious Studies within India, researching Indic theories of mind and psychology, reviewing American textbooks, and surveying the American public for Hinduphobia.

The *RISA Hinduphobia School* is shorthand for scholars who use psychoanalysis and other Eurocentric categories and theories to interpret dharmic traditions such as Hinduism. They study Hinduism from a reductionist 'outsiders' point-of-view. The RISA Hinduphobia School is deeply implicated by generations of Indological research and the politics of Western dominated institutions of research, teaching and funding.

The following charts indicate where the two 'schools' overlap and share methodologies, and where they diverge. These tables present the debates from multiple perspectives, allowing for a holistic, interactive understanding. This understanding of one another is known as the *purva-paksha* in traditional Indic discourse.

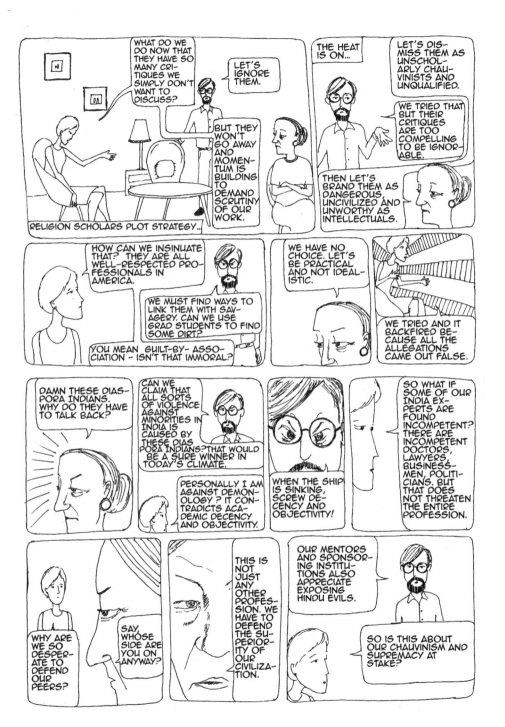

This comic is intended to be satirical, and any resemblance herein to actual events or persons living or dead is purely coincidental.

This comic is intended to be satirical, and any resemblance herein to actual events or persons living or dead is purely coincidental.

This comic is intended to be satirical, and any resemblance herein to actual events or persons living or dead is purely coincidental.

Chapter 23

Restoring the Debate:
Silenced Voices Speak Out

Against the backdrop of demonization attempts in which graduate students and RISA scholars closed ranks, there were a few courageous interventions on RISA list by those who sought to restore the debate to a scholarly plane. This involved discussing the serious issues of asymmetries of power between Hindus and the academy. Prof. Ram-Prasad Chakravarthi[143] wrote a very extensive and thoughtful piece on the RISA online list[144] concerning the strange silence of Hindu scholars who are also RISA members:

> It has struck me how few [RISA discussants are] scholars of Hindu origin. Are there so few people of Hindu cultural background on the list? If so, it does speak, one way or another, of some fundamental problems of scholarship and representation . . . If not, I am intrigued by the silence, for it must say something about the complexity of their personal positions?

Perhaps it is because he is at a university outside the US that Chakravarthi felt less intimidated by the power of the RISA establishment. Whatever the reasons, he was one of the few practising Hindus in Hinduism Studies who felt free to express his sensitivities as a subaltern and a minority.[145] Chakravarthi tried to restore perspective to the withdrawal of Courtright's book by the publisher. Like the overwhelming majority of Hindus involved in these debates, he rejected any form of book-banning. But he saw Motilal's decision in a bigger context that also put the spotlight on Western publishers and media— he pointed out the pragmatic concerns that often lead to banning, withdrawals and censorship, even by western-owned media, such as, for example, the *Satanic Verses* and *Last Temptation of Christ.*

Chakravarthi wondered if Patrick Olivelle had missed the point when he facilely invited those who disagreed with Courtright's reading of Ganesha to write their own version. The legitimacy bestowed upon Courtright's interpretation by powerful institutions would be simply unavailable to diaspora accounts written outside the American educational setting. Chakravarthi analyzed his RISA peers' responses to the scholarly interventions of modern Hindus, pointing out that demanding lay Hindu interventions to conform to RISA's norms revealed a bit of 'snobbery'. Chakravarthi pointed out that the academy would reject a similar demand by Christian theologians as 'intellectual snobbery'. He noted that Christians had refused to be reduced to the status of passive consumers—they demanded a direct voice.

According to Chakravarthi, Indian-Americans have not been in the US long enough to develop a self-sustaining power-base with pro-. Hindu journals, presses, radio and television stations and universities to support their identities. Part of the problem is the relative powerlessness of Hindu groups to self-define and self-represent. Over the past few decades, Christian, Jewish and Islamic groups have structured a rapport with academia through their funding, publishing and activism. They have political-educational power-bases in order to inveigh against and counter the perceived academic excesses of the same kind that Hindus are now dismantling.[146]

Chakravarthi did not entirely spare the diaspora, blaming them for neglecting serious scholarship about their own tradition:

> Western Indians have pushed themselves into a strange place in which high standards of professional education have combined with ignorance of and engagement with their ancestral traditions (only very recently and rarely do I get British Hindus taking Religious Studies at Lancaster, because they are all off to become doctors and engineers and management consultants). So they [Indians] do not find themselves usually able to intervene in the way that western scholars demand.

Leftists and Rightists: Perversions and Inversions of Labeling

Chakravarthi criticized the characteristic methodology of demonization by imposing labels. His words should provoke us to question the transferability of terms such as 'Left' and 'Right' as understood in America to the Indian context. In which camp would one classify

Indian scholars who use Marxist discourse but thrive in the Western academy, funded by Western foundations that are formed by capitalists to perpetuate their ideological hegemonies? What about Gloria Steinem who helped to liberate white women but was simultaneously working for the CIA? Unfortunately, 'saffron' and 'Hindu Nationalist' are convenient labels that mask complexity and nuance and are all too readily applied by Western scholars to demonize all those whom they see as enemies.

This is why Chakravarthi urged his colleagues in the academy to treat "Hindu conservatism on par with religious conservatism in the West", and to also bear in mind a critical difference, namely, that there is much less self-representation or socio-political empowerment in the case of Hindu-Americans.[147]

As a Hindu intellectual living in the West, Chakravarthi took exception to the privileged position occupied by Westerners in the study of Hinduism and asked whether Western scholars alone can be entrusted with writing in the *New York Times* or the *London Times Literary Supplement*. He stressed that Hindus must ask themselves again and again: "Are none of us really good enough to be asked to write about our culture and our philosophies? Or is it something else?" He was also 'disquieted' by Courtright's psychoanalytic passages about Ganesha, even though he came 'from a Sri Vaisnava family' (i.e. a family primarily devoted to Vishnu). He explained that Freudian methodology is not scientific but a matter of speculation; not something falsifiable through evidence or counter-argument. Nevertheless, the Freudian interpretation has become privileged, while Indic interpretations are sidelined:

> There are conflicts between the academic process of review . . . on the one hand, and **the vast asymmetries of access, exposure and privilege that still mark non-Western efforts to have a voice in the West.** [Emphasis added]

Chakravarthi suggested that in order to understand where the diaspora is coming from, the vigor of his colleagues' scholarly and cultural convictions could be leavened by 'an understanding of those who perhaps perceive their stake in the matter differently'. On a separate forum, but around the same time, David Freedholm was also writing about the vast asymmetries of access, exposure and privilege:

Unlike with Christianity, Judaism and even Buddhism in North America, there is no more mainstream counterbalance to the more radical approaches taken by scholars to Hinduism. Christians of a more traditional or mainstream inclination have many seminaries and publishing houses to train scholars and publish books. For every scholarly work on Jesus that takes a more radical approach (and such books and articles do exist) there are several others that critique them and offer more traditional views. At AAR/SBL one can find evangelical Christian and traditional Catholic scholars rubbing elbows with more secular and radical scholars of Christianity.

This is not the case with Hinduism. There is very little representation of more mainstream or traditional Hindu views in Western academia. When such views do appear they are scorned as 'fundamentalist' or worse. And, even worse, these scholarly views are seen to become the authoritative interpretations of Hinduism in the West. For example, Courtright's book on Ganesha is one of a relatively few books on the subject in English available to a wide audience. Because it has received approving accolades from the RISA community, it will be taken as an authoritative perspective on Ganesha, despite the fact that its interpretation is wildly at odds with that of most Hindus. It will be cited by authors of textbooks and its views disseminated into material designed for non-scholarly audiences. This would almost certainly never happen with a Freudian analysis of Jesus because it would be just one of many scholarly and popular interpretations of Jesus available. There is no such balance in Hinduism studies.[148]

Another balanced voice in the discussion was that of Ramdas Lamb who pointed out the intimidation directed at Hindus for representing a Hindu point of view:[149]

Can we question nothing any other scholar writes? Clearly, if we wrote nothing that offended anyone, there would soon be no books at all, but at the same time, should we not consider the implications and value of what we write? **What happened to the emphasis in academia on cultural awareness and sensitivity?** I thought that is one of the concepts we are supposed to teach at liberal academic institutions. **Is it that we just teach it, but not actually practice it? I guess we should not let the views of Hindus get in our way** ... Another [RISA scholar] labeled me an 'anti-free speech Hindu fundamentalist' for my comments ... For a long time, people have looked at academics as residents of an ivory tower, out of touch with 'the real world.' If our research does not reflect reality, then we are out of touch. If our writings are not relevant to the people and traditions about whom we write, then we also make ourselves irrelevant. [Emphasis added]

Ramdas Lamb's position led Prof. Rambachan[150] to make an appeal to RISA scholars to stop the demonization, and to affirm that Hindus must remain mindful of their traditional commitment to free inquiry:[151]

As a Hindu scholar . . . if we delight in representing our tradition as one that encourages the freedom of inquiry and discussion, we must not condone measures, directly or indirectly, that limit such freedom, even when the fruits are not to our liking. If we affirm the universal relevance of the Hindu tradition, our notions of 'ownership' must be examined critically. **At the same time, a faith-community has a right to express its thoughts and feelings about our scholarship, without everyone being branded as fanatical extremists, as a reminder to us that the subject of our study is a living sacred tradition in which deep emotions and meanings are invested.** Scholarly discernment is required also to know the pain of those whose traditions we make the object of our study.

Hopefully . . . we [scholars] will embrace the opportunity to thoughtfully consider the broader issues involved. How can our exercise of academic freedom be balanced with sensitive responsiveness to concerns of the faith community and its self-understanding? How are such concerns relevant or irrelevant to our scholarly pursuits? How can dialogue between these two communities be facilitated in order that the nature of the academic study of religion be properly represented and mutual stereotyping, suspicion and mistrust, so evident in these exchanges, be overcome? [Emphasis added]

Laurie Patton echoed this new attitude in RISA: "We might think about how we might write differently, too." She asked, "Who is our audience and readership and how do we focus on the balance between freedom and offence?" In the context of the recent email exchanges, she wondered, "How does the Internet contribute to the problem, and how does it help?" Ultimately, for Patton, the practical question was, "How can the issue of offence be dealt with in a constructive and positive way, through mechanisms which do their best to avoid unnecessary suffering?" She concluded with hope that lessons would be learned from "this episode, which is far from over", and that though "sad and hurtful to everyone on all sides, can be turned around for new and hopeful conversations".

Once Chakravarthi's intercession had let the genie out of the bottle, Courtright acknowledged his own change of perspective: "One of the things that has been painful for me in the controversy around my book is that I wrote it over twenty years ago, in a different discursive environment than we have now." Courtright thus acknowledged that when he wrote the book back in 1985, he had, as others had pointed out, 'started a dialogue with the Hindus' even though there were fewer in the diaspora with whom to dialogue at that time. However, in today's America, as was pointed out to him, sustaining an asymmetry of power/privilege is no longer as easy as it once was.

Courtright stated, "Were I writing that book today I would, hopefully, **be more aware of how it might be read by some Hindu readers** in both India and its diasporas." [Emphasis added]. Many people following this issue were surprised and gratified by his admission.[152] For years, many RISA-type scholars had hurled insults at the Hindu diaspora. It seemed that some RISA scholars finally heeded the call to stop treating Hindus as native informants and to start interacting with them as equals. This signified a new position from Courtright, who contemplated the changing milieu:

> In the early 1980s, when I wrote my book, the audiences for our work were much less interactive than they are now. I think there would be value in featuring a RISA or Hinduism Group panel on the issue of changes in audiences and how to think better in advance about how we present our scholarly work today. I hope we will think carefully about the methodological applications of the sorts of concerns Professor Rambachan articulates and develop more nuanced hermeneutical approaches to our research and writing.

Once Courtright appeared to acquiesce and to back away from the blame game, other voices of reason within the academy spoke up in a constructive manner. On November 6, 2003, Constantina Rhodes Bailly, Professor of Religious Studies at Eckerd College, noted that systemic meta-level issues about the study of others' religions by Western scholars needed to be taken seriously, and wrote:

> As Paul has graciously pointed out, if he had written the book today, some of the issues would be framed differently than they had twenty years ago. One of the interesting and disturbing points here is that what is happening with Paul's book and with 'Hindu Studies' is happening in other areas of religious studies as well. Similar and perhaps even more heated debates are going on, for example, in Native American studies. In our RISA discussions, there has been

mention of the possible origins of such sentiments against the way we Western scholars approach the study of 'other' religions, but much of it seems to be heated and volatile reactions against particular works, and the objections are mostly coming from non-academics.

Bailly commented that she was not familiar with various writers from the Indian diaspora and their approach to the issue of subaltern and post-colonial studies. She expressed interest "to read [those] works to acquire a more systematic understanding of what native Hindu scholars are saying about how non-Hindus do scholarship". She asked, within the Hindu diaspora, "Who are the 'respected' writers on post-colonialism?"

The literature from the Hindu diaspora is not yet a genre of study that has developed sufficiently so that multiple schools of thought can flourish within it. Bailly asked again, "Can anyone recommend any such writers and/or their works?" She concluded, suggesting that the members of RISA might "want to invite them to join any such panel that seems to be in the process of formulation". This group that she proposed to invite has been banging on RISA's door for several years with little response.

Prof. Fred Smith from the University of Iowa continued to push the door open wider, as RISA's old guard began to realize that there was a new reality to deal with, in which its days of chauvinism and Hindu-bashing seemed to be drawing to a close. Smith made a balanced suggestion:

> [T]his proprietary stance towards the study of religion is not something indigenous to recent South Asia. [...] To set our own situation in a broader academic context, I would like to suggest a series of interrelated panels at next year's AAR, dealing with these issues in different regional and conceptual areas of religious discourse (e.g., South Asian religion, Japanese or African religions, gay and lesbian issues, etc.).

Prof. Pratap Kumar joined this RISA soul-searching, capping the conversation with the moral of the story, that there should be more interaction:[153]

> Paul [Courtright] is right in identifying the 'changes in audiences' in today's classrooms and also in society, who read the academic books. In my humble view, it is not so much that the earlier audience was 'less interactive' as Paul suggests, but **rather there**

is a new audience who are not merely scholars but practitioners. Secondly, there is growing concern in our contemporary world about the way [the] 'west' in general depicts the non-western world . . . One thing that must happen . . . to progress in our scholarly endeavors, is that there should be more interaction and contact between scholars from outside and from within. [Emphasis added]

This welcome soul-searching that started within RISA in November 2003 may lead to the recognition that Hinduism is a minority religion in the US and deserves the same treatment by the academy that is already being given to other American minority religions—such as Native American, Buddhist, and Islamic.[154] Or, it may not. As this book shows all too well, Hinduphobia is deeply entrenched. The little shake-up here may be only the first of a series that will be required to lift the haze of Hinduphobia.

Up until this time, there have been precious few members of the Hinduism Studies academy who have recognized the tremendous value that debating the issues openly and provocatively brings to our understanding of the field. The fact that the scholars in the Hindu diaspora have largely produced their writings on the Internet means that a documented record exists. Thus, Jayant Kalawar wrote in appreciation of the documentation of events being provided by *Risa Lila-2*:

[These writings] are sure to be studied in the future as evidence on how Indic Traditions negotiated their place with the dominant culture as represented by its Brahmins, the Western academics. Their polemical responses to fact based analyses need to be analyzed and presented independently, as well.[155]

Indeed, some courageous Religious Studies faculty announced that they would be using the documented record on Sulekha, including the two *RISA Lila* essays, as assigned materials for class reading along with presenting the other side's arguments. Ashok Aklujkar,[156] a prominent Sanskritist, wrote to appreciate 'the well-reasoned and reasonable, clear stance' of the *RISA Lila-2* essay.[157] Sushil Mittal[158] wrote to Malhotra, enthusiastically telling him that this was "another article of yours that I will be assigning in my classes, especially Hindu Traditions".[159] Columbia University's Jack Hawley also assigned these essays for reading on his course, 'Hinduism Here', and encouraged his students to study Infinity Foundation as a new intellectual competitor playing on RISA's turf.[160]

Surely Some Revelation is at Hand[161]

This lila within RISA generated a lot of attention. The petition had occurred only a few weeks before the AAR Annual Conference was held in Atlanta, which ironically, is also home to Emory University where Courtright is a professor. In the tumultuous wake of the Ganesha petition, several commentaries were written by members of the Indian-American community, some of which were featured in section II.

As discussed, the Ganesha petition from the Hindu students' group was a legitimate attempt at protest, but a few random threats reduced its legitimacy and so it was quickly and easily hijacked and removed. However, even though some persons tried hard to refocus on the substantive issues, many in RISA preferred to play the victim card. The diaspora became alerted to a spiritually troubling and culturally threatening situation that they would need to engage with as an American minority. The thunderously defensive responses from RISA scholars were at first filled with self-righteous condemnation of others. Religious Studies scholars claimed the exclusive power to interpret Hinduism however they pleased and the power to demonize their opponents with impunity. *Ad hominem* attacks against both dissenting RISA scholars and Hindu-American public intellectuals became the norm, including using deplorable tactics such as guilt-by-association.

The frenzied outrage culminated in an organized political campaign of economic intimidation against a prestigious Indian publishing house. Only after the Kafkaesque absurdity of this approach became apparent to many witnesses did the atmosphere change somewhat. This white American instinct of circling the wagons against the 'savages' was followed by a quasi-contrite recognition that scholars of Hinduism needed a working rapport with modern Hindus.

Nonetheless, as Kishwar reported, attempts to undermine academic conferences and diaspora institutions by demonizing them with the label of Hindutva, simply because they are seen as *too* independent, continued. The Concerned Community's meeting with Emory in February of 2004 failed to yield tangible results beyond a patronizing recognition that Courtright's book caused 'deep hurt and pain'. The solutions that were proffered—such as the one by Prof. Smith of interrelating panels at AAR to bring together academics and practitioners—have yet to be implemented, four years later. As for the academy taking the responsibility of self-monitoring, we should note that while Courtright conceded some of the issues raised by his critics, he has still never engaged in a debate over the specifics of his scholarship on Ganesha—the serious questions raised by Agarwal and Venkat have never been answered by him. Even after de Nicolas's courageous whistle blowing, the academy has never demanded an investigation into these troubling questions.

After all, lest we grow complacent over these signs of apparent reform, we must remember that the academy's overtures are a tactical move, premised on its pragmatic calculation of the shifting power balance between the academy and members of the Postcolonial Hinduism School rather than a sincere re-evaluation of its serious and systemic breaches of academic duty and responsibility. As Courtright himself noted, the power asymmetries and privileges of the past are no longer as available to the academy vis-à-vis Hindu practitioner-scholars as it was in the heyday of Hinduphobic scholarship. This monopoly was able to exploit the public so long as it was the only player in town, but is now under threat by the opening of the 'economy of ideas' to new competition. The pressure has to be sustained and rival interpretations and scholarship encouraged and promoted to create an open marketplace of ideas. Just as free market economies lead to the best products, so too, de-monopolizing RISA's stranglehold over scholarship will bring higher standards of quality and rigor.

Chapter 24

Calling Courtright's Bluff

In the wake of the *Risa Lila* essays, many academic scholars have become self-conscious about the biases and asymmetries in the discipline and have made the required adjustments to their work. There has certainly been a dampening effect on fresh Freudian psychoanalyses claiming to uncover the 'real nature' of Hinduism. But other than de Nicolas, few have courageously called for an investigation into the existing work of scholars like Courtright. As the chapters in this section show, in order to bulldoze their critics into silence, the scholars have tried to squelch debate about their scholarship by portraying themselves as victims.

Yet the debate refuses to die. In a recent article in the *Journal of the American Academy of Religion* (JAAR), Russell McCutcheon[162] criticized Courtright for having a double standard.[163] One standard applies to dealing with the silent and powerless native informants, who McCutcheon describes as "others whose differences can easily be tolerated or overlooked with little or no cost". This refers to the villagers and poor Indians who will not talk back, who have no means to respond to the powerful Western scholar's depictions regardless of how ludicrous these depictions might be. These native informers, in almost all cases, never find out what was written about them after the scholar returns home to publish the story.

However, as McCutcheon points out, a *different* standard applies to those 'others' such as the members of the relatively well-to-do Indian diaspora who have the communication skills, the means, the courage and the tenacity to challenge the scholars' depictions of them. McCutcheon calls these the "others for whom they [i.e. scholars] feel little affinity and whose interests conflicts with their own". In this latter category are those like Malhotra, Agarwal, Venkat and numerous others, who have written scathing but thoughtful indictments against the work of what could be called the Hinduphobic academic cartel. McCutcheon thus tacitly acknowledges that the clash is not about academic freedom, but about the once-privileged India Studies scholars' discomfort in dealing with those who demand equality and dignity.

To clarify further, McCutcheon cites Robert Orsi's essay on the ethics of studying others. Orsi criticizes the scholar of religion for

> [Ignoring the] moral requirement of obtaining the *consent of those upon whom* this theoretical action is to be performed . . . Rather the assumption appears to be that the scholar of religion by virtue of his or her normative epistemology, theoretical acuity, and political knowingness, has the authority and the right to make the lives of others the objects of his of her scrutiny. He or she theorizes them.[164]

He also refers to Wilfred Cantwell Smith's well-known methodological rule of thumb according to which *both scholar and religious participant are involved in a consensual conversation*. Smith had famously and unequivocally stated that: "No statement about a religion is valid unless it can be acknowledged by that religion's believers".[165] McCutcheon goes to on explain this perspective that, "scholarship is a type of Habermasian conversation, comprised of [sic] a series of good-will negotiations between partners in which the goal is to arrive at some sort of mutual understanding that at least addresses, if not resolves, the differences between potentially competing systems of representation." Cabezon has also recently recommended dialogues intended to reach 'theory parity' between the cultures, warning that otherwise there will be denigration and manipulation and a mutual rejection.[166]

McCutcheon was reacting in part to Courtright's paper in which Courtright defended himself by lobbing blame at his critics. His paper's title itself shows how he tries to deflect attention away from the issues of his scholarship into a problem of 'dangerous wild savages' attacking a serious white scholar who is going about his job of enlightening the world with his research. Courtright's paper is titled, '*Studying Religion in an Age of Terror*'.[167] McCutcheon writes that Courtright's paper, 'makes use of the now well-known rhetoric of terror' to claim the innocence of his book juxtaposed against the unexpected and therefore 'frightening' criticism from diaspora.

Courtright's article describes his critics as 'well-financed and organized groups on the political and religious right' and accuses them of wanting, 'to control the memory of India's past . . .' Doniger has also made this charge. Martin Marty, a loyal friend and colleague of Wendy Doniger at the University of Chicago, branded all the critics of Courtright as Hindu 'militants'.[168] William Dalrymple joined in support by calling it a 'war' over India's history with profound political implications—with the non-Hindus naturally being the good guys.

Courtright conveniently fails to document how well-funded, well-organized and well-networked the American academy is, as compared to his critics in the Indian diaspora. The politics and agendas of the agencies funding RISA scholars were not investigated by Courtright, nor were issues surrounding their privileged access to the mainstream media for propagating fanciful opinions and culturally parochial views as 'authoritative'. Not asking or answering these inconvenient questions is vital to keeping afloat this evasive thesis of victimhood. Playing the helpless victim hides the reality of being a Eurocentric scholar who enjoys an enormous advantage of epistemic power and money.

Courtright's Approach to Demonizing his Critics

Trope	Scholar(s) Claim	Issues
Militants	Courtright claims that his critics are threatening him with violence.	The attack on a library in Pune, India is linked with Courtright's critics in the US. However, that attack was by a totally unrelated political group that was not even Hindu-centric. (It was by a local pro-Maratha and anti-Brahminical party that was offended that a popular historical Maratha king had been denigrated by a book, whose author is unrelated to Courtright.) Courtright falsely claims a conspiracy of dangerous third world 'savages' against 'objective' Western scholars.
Right-Wingers	Courtright claims his critics are right-wingers.	There is no evidence for this politicized claim. Yet other scholars in the academy have parroted Courtright's charges

Trope	Scholar(s) Claim	Issues
		without due process of inquiry, much less giving the other side a chance to speak for itself. In contrast to this, Courtright and colleagues do not attempt to investigate the politics of the academy: How many Religion scholars are right-wing Christians? How many of them are 'liberals' using Eurocentric Enlightenment theories in their work? How many of them are committed 'insiders' to other (competing) traditions, ideologies, churches and other organizations that may intimately color their representations of Hinduism? Alleging a certain politics on one side and refusing to investigate the politics on the other is clearly unfair.
Political Assault on History	Dalrymple and others rightfully criticize attempts to politicize history—which is sadly the reality not only in India but in the US, UK, China, Japan, France, the Arab world, Iran, and almost everywhere in the world.	The criticism of Courtright's book is *not* about history—Ganesha is not a historical figure. The criticism is about mistranslations, inventions of evidence, *ad hoc* and amateurish uses of Freudian psychoanalysis, refusals to discuss detailed and troubling questions about poor scholarship such as those discussed in this book.

It is ironic that even McCutcheon cannot help referring to Courtright's critics as 'nationalists', as though all those who have opposed Courtright can be so flippantly essentialized in one sweeping brush. No one would call all white middle-class Americans who criticize an off-the-wall, sexualized, fringe interpretation of Jesus or the Madonna, as 'right-wing nationalist militants'. This is a lingering deep prejudice against Hindus who speak out, one that even McCutcheon could not avoid.

McCutcheon notes that 'there is a fascinating triumphalism' among scholars who see their work's goal as overcoming parochialism. But he suggests that the opposite is true in practice: "All human systems of knowing and acting are best understood as parochial." This implies that scholars' interests do not coincide with the interests of those being studied by them. McCutcheon adds, "To presume otherwise—to presume that one's interests set the parameters of the so-called level-playing field, thereby providing the terms in which all representations can be assessed—strikes me as the height of imperialism."

McCutcheon examines the treatment of *Others* who are seen as fellow humans by scholars, such as Mexican immigrants, suburban Pentecostal women, a distraught widower, an Orthodox family, etc. He writes: "Who would not first seek these people's consent before sharing with others the stories they may have told us over a cup of coffee in their homes?" He contrasts this with the attitude of the very same scholars towards "so-called agitators, revolutionaries, militants, or vigilantes . . . "—i.e. people opposing the scholar's paradigms or violating her sensibilities. The former get sympathy because they are seen as 'crying, in pain, and engaged in . . . ritual behaviors' (as opposed to political behaviors). McCutcheon calls these people the 'no cost Other' and explains the contradictions in approach:

> [T]he liberal humanist scholar [must] make the tough calls and distinguish between the toothless pious and the radical fanatics, authorizing the former whereas paving the way toward dispensing with the latter by defining them out of 'the faithful'—which is nothing other than excommunication by other means.

He questions the motives of scholars like Courtright and Kripal for applying a different approach when dealing with diaspora critics: "We should ask why *they* are so ripe for the kind of theorizing from which we must refrain when studying the politically harmless". When examining the grieving widower (as an example of the politically harmless 'other'), these scholars suspend speculation of ulterior motives, sincerity, or subconscious desires, and importantly, what these 'others' have to say is taken seriously. Why not—McCutcheon seems to suggest by implication—give the Hindu critics the same treatment? He writes:

They likely see themselves as being not ideological but simply correct, righteous, and expressing self-evidence about India, Hinduism, world affairs, or even reality as such . . . What warrants do we, as scholars, have for instituting a different set of rules for their study? Why do we so easily suspend this particular group's rights to describe themselves, thereby failing to entertain that their views are but one more 'indigenous theory' that shed light on our own sad parochialism?

He concludes that the excuses for not including those declared 'indecent' are arbitrary and as a result not genuine:

> It therefore appears to me that those who speak back indecently (*i.e., those who are unwilling to put up with our presumed ability to speak and act as we wish*) are no longer counted among the sincere and are therefore fair game for theorizing—and just what are the limits of decency, how are they judged, established, and authorized; these are the questions that ought to attract our attention as social scientists. [Emphasis added]

In his response to McCutcheon in the same issue of JAAR, Courtright once again avoids the challenges to his scholarship. He focuses *only* on why he has refused to engage any of his critics. He writes, in language reminiscent of self-esteem affirmations: "I do have the power to decide whether to engage their critiques". He then explains or rather excuses himself—predictably—by claiming, "When the Other is threatening your life, I am a scholar, not a saint." End of story for Courtright. He is off the hook, he insists. It's a matter of repeating as often as he can, in as many fora as he can, that he is a 'victim' of 'threats' no matter how far-fetched and questionable his evidence is.

The critics who have raised the most troubling questions about Courtright's *scholarship*—such as Malhotra, Agarwal, Venkat, and de Nicolas—have never threatened him personally. Neither has he been threatened by the Concerned Community of Hindus in Atlanta who petitioned Emory University for redress. But by framing his story using random episodes of reported violence from remote corners of the world he can constantly keep his victim status alive.

The question that remains is why have other scholars not asked him to respond to *them* concerning his scholarship? They could demand, "Never mind what you think of *those* evil Hindu critics thus far; let *us* hear a defense of your work." Imagine if a person accused of corporate corruption is able to slip away simply by accusing *all* his accusers of being 'bad' people. And imagine that nobody else bothers to conduct an inquiry into the corruption charge because he shifts attention towards the 'bad' guys' who blew the whistle on him! This is exactly what has happened in the cases of Doniger, Kripal and Courtright, in spite of the detailed evidence questioning their scholarship. How was this amazing feat managed?

A part of the answer, at least, may lie in the deeply held American national and racial myths about 'us' versus the 'other,' as described at the beginning of this section.

IV

✦

MEDIA IMAGES: DIASPORIC 'SAVAGES' VERSUS ACADEMIC 'VICTIMS'

This comic is intended to be satirical, and any resemblance herein to actual events or persons living or dead is purely coincidental.

Chapter 25

Hyping Hindu 'Wrath': Mythmaking and the *Washington Post*

By Krishnan Ramaswamy

This section documents how the RISA establishment deployed the media to frame the central issue as being about 'savages' trying to censor, intimidate and control the work of scholars. With a few exceptions, the media reproduced the sensational stories fed by the academic establishment, while failing to ask tough questions about the quality of scholarship. The resulting images thus tapped into the 'Dangerous Savage' trope (discussed in Chapter 18) in the public imagination.

In April 2004, the *Washington Post* published an article entitled: 'Wrath over a Hindu God: U.S. Scholars' Writings Draw Threats From Faithful'. Appearing almost three years after the *RISA Lila* essays in Sulekha, this was the first mainstream media article that covered the debate at the heart of this book.[1]

A few weeks before the article was published, Shanker Vedantam, a staff journalist at the *Post*, contacted certain diaspora intellectuals about the controversy. Glad to finally have the opportunity to inform a wider American public about these issues, Malhotra wrote to Vedantam to explain his position:

> I have championed the case for de-monopolizing religious studies by adding practitioner-scholars . . . We seek the same kind of seat at the table of discourse about our traditions as Blacks have in Black Studies, Jews, Christians, Muslims, etc. each have in their respective portrayals. But [in India Studies] when the native informant starts to answer back, it is seen as an 'attack,' because they are just not

used to treating us as equals. However, over the past 32 years since I have been in the US, Indians in many other professions have upgraded their standing and are not second class anymore—so why not in the academic field of Religious Studies? Why is that a bastion of prejudices still? It is only a matter of time before they will realize that the field will get enriched and expanded with more voices. My sense is that this resistance comes from the old guard who has lots to lose.[2]

Attempting to ensure that the substantive issues would not be buried under the spin of victimhood and branding, Malhotra compared the contemporary academic treatment of India with the construction of Indian culture by Indologists of the British Empire. He offered several other analogies that framed the movement against powerfully entrenched systems, such as Gandhi's satyagraha or Ralph Nader's Consumer Rights. If the story became framed as 'dangerous Hindu hooligans attacking scholarly Western academicians', he warned that it would be a grossly unfair mischaracterization.

Unfortunately, the *Post* completely evaded the range of issues explained to Vedantam, such as the inadequate training of scholars, the politicized peer-reviews, the parochial portrayals, and the asymmetries of power in the academy. Focusing instead on juicier offerings, the *Post* framed the story in the mythic trope of savages (i.e. the Hindus) victimizing the civilized Whites (i.e. the scholars). Thus, what began within RISA as a crude tactic to derail debate took on a new life in the national press. This reframing of the controversy supplied key talking points for other media outlets as well.

Academics as Victims, Critics as Savages

Sensationalism runs deep in the *Post's* article. The title itself ('Wrath over a Hindu God: US Scholars' Writings Draw Threats From Faithful') instantly signals to the reader that wrathful Hindus are threatening American scholars. The entire collection of evidence-based essays published between 2001 and 2004 (see section II for a sample), is reduced to a mere 'scathing posting' rather than thoughtful critiques of the academy that generated vibrant debate:

[A]fter a scathing posting on a popular Indian Web site, [Courtright] has received threats from Hindu militants who want him dead ... Gopal from Singapore said, 'The professor bastard should be hanged,' said Courtright, incredulous. 'A guy from Germany said, 'Wish this person was next to me, I would have shot him in the head.' [...] Other academics writing about Hinduism have encountered similar hostility, from tossed eggs to assaults to threats of extradition and prosecution in India.[3]

By highlighting *only* the very few aggressive comments on the Internet petition, the merits of the petition were ignored and the numerous independent articles on Sulekha simply painted with the same brush. Faraway places like Singapore and Germany and egg-tossing in London had little bearing on the issues and merely served to create alarm and engender sympathy for the beleaguered academics.

The article failed to mention that Courtright's questionable and speculative scholarship was now being presented as standard fact at American museums and other venues. The implications to an American minority were ignored, even though the journalist is from that same minority. It appeared that he *intentionally* refused to look at the situation from the perspective of the Hindus he interviewed. Sadly, he saw the tale only through the eyes of the dominant culture. Chitra Raman, a member of the diaspora from Detroit, dissented in a letter to the *Post*:

> It is rather cavalier to dismiss the painstakingly analytical responses to the book as Internet demagoguery. Besides, Mr. Vedantam completely ignores the circumstances that fuelled those writings, including the discovery of phraseology from the book at a museum's Ganesha exhibit. One does not have to be a Hindu zealot to see Dr. Courtright's analysis as lewd conjecture, crudely disrespectful of a central Hindu symbol. The prospect of it being displayed at a site visited by thousands of schoolchildren was appalling. The articles by Rajiv Malhotra and others on the Internet were a wake-up call to Indian parents in America already struggling to help their children deal with ignorant and shallow stereotypes of Hinduism at school.[4]

Deploring the sensationalism of the *Washington Post's* presentation and the undue emphasis on unsubstantiated threats, Malhotra posted a rejoinder to the article, suggesting that the journalist should have put things in perspective:

> The only legitimate statement about these so-called 'threats' that a responsible newspaper should have printed, would have been something along the following lines: A small handful of 'threats' were posted by anonymous person(s) who adopted Hindu identities and who claimed to be located in various parts of the world. But there is no way to authenticate any of these.[5]

He suggested that the reporter might have qualified the ambiguous origins of the threats by writing: "It was also alleged that these threats could have been posted to derail the petition and to portray Courtright as a victim". Vedantam reported exclusively from the angle of the white Ivory Tower, dismissively deriding the Hindu plebeians on the swarthy plains.

To further reinforce the imagery of the victim/savage trope of the American Frontier, he brings in an *unrelated* controversy concerning a *different* book, involving an entirely *different* set of issues and actors. That book, *Shivaji: Hindu King in Muslim India*, was written by an American theologian named James Laine. According to angry groups in the state of Maharashtra, it defamed a beloved seventeenth century King.[6] Ironically, the violence that this book instigated in Pune was directed *against* orthodox Hindus and their institutions for being too Brahminical and was committed by a group of ethnic and regional chauvinists, whose orientation has little to do with religion per se. The *Post* surreptitiously mixes this vignette of ethnic violence in India to tar the face of Hindu-Americans and to show Courtright as a victim of pervasive Hindu aggression. In a story that claims to be about a controversy over a 'Hindu God', there is a remarkable amount of space devoted to Laine's unrelated problems in order to raise the alarm level.

The chronology given in the column is incorrect in claiming that Malhotra's original article produced 'a swift and angry response' from the Atlanta Concerned Community. The gradual intellectual mobilization described in earlier sections is reduced to, in Vedantam's words,

> a swift and angry response from thousands of Hindus. An Atlanta group wrote to the president of Emory University asking that Courtright be fired. 'The implication,' said Courtright, 'was this was a filthy book and I had no business teaching anything.' He said the quotes had been taken out of context and ignored the uplifting lessons he had drawn from Ganesha's story.[7]

The article *falsely* accused the Concerned Community of demanding that Courtright be fired for writing a 'filthy' book. The well-documented proceedings of the exchanges at Emory show that the Concerned Community never made this demand.[8] Moreover, the members of the delegation that met with the Dean of Emory made it clear that each of them had read the entire book and were not talking about a *few* quotes. By not interviewing the Concerned Community, the *Washington Post* privileged Courtright's version of the events. A member of the

Concerned Community wrote to the *Washington Post*, protesting this one-sided presentation:

> My father was involved with the group in Atlanta that you stated asked Courtright to be fired. I have a few questions: Why did you not contact that group? Did you see their original letter (it did *not* ask that he be fired, though it was strongly worded)? Did you know that they in fact had a meeting with Emory officials in February well before your article was published that was conducted in a civilized and rational way? [...] Your article gives the impression that there were no Hindus who had any kind of productive debate with Emory.[9]

Moreover, Courtright's disingenuous claim that his book was being 'attacked' as 'filthy' feeds into the myth about the Hindu 'other' as ignorant, intolerant and sexually prudish. Indian religions and culture are not particularly prudish about sex, although, just as with other religious groups, there are some Indians who are. Malhotra, Balagangadhara, Kishwar, Venkat, Sanu, Agarwal and many others have discussed sexual matters quite openly and comfortably in their writings.

Vedantam leaves out any serious discussion of Hinduphobia in the academy. He ignores that Eurocentric Freudian psychoanalysis and mistranslations are employed by amateurs to describe Hinduism, perpetuating a legacy of colonial era distortions. Many scholars interviewed by Vedantam subsequently complained that he had ignored all the specific instances they had supplied about Hinduphobia at American universities. This selective use of data was pointed out:

> By ignoring them, especially those scholars who told him point-blank of specific instances of anti-Hindu bias in his telephone interviews, Mr. Vedantam conveys the impression that the complaints came only from 'Hindu activists' and not from academic scholars, and from Indians and not from white persons. Both implications are untrue.[10]

Vedantam's defense to this striking omission was to claim a lack of column space. This does not address why he chose to exclude *all* the scholarly voices that cited examples of academic Hinduphobia.[11]

Doniger as the Authority on Hindu-Americans' Motives

The article presents Doniger as an objective bystander and fails to disclose the close working relationship between her and Courtright, merely noting that she wrote the Foreword to the book. Her perspective is positioned as authoritative and sympathetic:

> Doniger, a 63-year-old scholar at the center of many controversies, is distressed to see her field come under the sway of what she regards as zealots. 'The argument,' she said, 'is being fueled by a fanatical nationalism and Hindutva, which says no one has the right to make a mistake, and no one who is not a Hindu has the right to speak about Hinduism at all.'[12]

But the critics whose articles appear in section II did *not* base their complaints on nationalism or the fact that the scholars were non-Hindu. She politicizes all of her critics' motives and does not deal with their diversity. In effect, her approach mimics the very methodology she claims to oppose: (1) not reading the relevant materials, (2) a lack of nuance that hangs one undifferentiated mask on a diversity of faces.

Only later in the article do we learn that Malhotra not only does not object to non-Hindus studying India, but in fact has encouraged many such scholars to do so through his sponsorship of a variety of mechanisms. The article also fails to note that control of the field is almost completely in the hands of white non-Hindus who deny the rights of Hindus to critique the discipline.

Doniger's characterization of the diaspora who read Malhotra's article—over 20,000 readers at the time the *Post* article was written—is deeply racist and contemptuous. However, it is presented without critical comment:

> Doniger blames the Internet campaigns, 'Malhotra's ignorant writings have stirred up more passionate emotions in Internet subscribers who know even less than Malhotra does, who do not read books at all.' Doniger wrote in an e-mail. 'These people have reacted with violence [and] I therefore hold [Malhotra] indirectly responsible.'

How could Doniger know whether the 'Internet subscribers' in question read books or not? Unless she has done a systematic survey of Sulekha readers, this conclusion can be the result *only* of ingrained contempt and prejudice for the largely ethnic Indian readership of the website. The tiny fraction of signers of the Internet petition who reacted with threats are called 'these people'—implying 'savage' Indians—all of whom are said to be 'violent'.

Basically, Doniger is claiming that a public debate about potential biases and shortcomings in her scholarship is useless because the diaspora is uneducated and dangerous. Historically, this is precisely how the 'native informant' was constructed and how the various non-white Others were denied a seat at the table when the fates of their cultures, and ultimately their very survival, were being bandied about. Malhotra is, in effect, being blamed for meddling with this power structure and trying to bring previously silenced voices into the debate.

Vedantam is silent about Doniger's articulated contempt for Indians. Nor does he independently evaluate why Malhotra's writings are supposedly 'ignorant'. Instead of challenging Doniger for making such sweeping attacks, he immediately provides a character reference from a little-known 'Hindu psychoanalyst' in Ann Arbor, Michigan, who opines that Doniger had written 'moving interpretations' of Hindu texts and is a pioneer who has 'made [Hindu texts] accessible for the first time in North America'. This gentleman, who also claims that Doniger has no disrespect but 'love' for Indians, is merely trotted out as an ethnic spokesman.[13] The article does not quote psychoanalysts like Alan Roland and Somnath Bhattacharyya, who have thoughtfully questioned these methods of interpretation.

Serious matters of methodology and authenticity are replaced by patronizing *opinions* about 'disrespect' for Indians or 'love' for India. Malhotra noted in his rebuttal, "It is telling that Wendy Doniger is defended not on the basis of her positions but through attacking those who raise objections to her scholarship."[14]

Doniger is accorded the final say in the article, and she mischaracterizes her debacle with the online encyclopedia *Encarta* as racism. Sankrant Sanu was interviewed by the *Post*, but his evidence-based critique of Doniger's *Encarta* entry is barely examined. His evidence convinced Microsoft to remove Doniger's essay from *Encarta*, and yet the *Post* failed to cite *any* item from his critique or Microsoft's reasons for withdrawing the essay. Instead, the article concludes with a racist comment by Doniger: "The only important thing about it is that I wrote it and someone named Sharma did not". Doniger is implying that she was a victim of racial bias, because a white scholar's work was superseded by a non-white scholar's essay.

Many readers of the *Washington Post* were appalled. An Indian-American academic scholar, Beloo Mehra, pointed out how the story had been 'spun.' It was,

> an interesting example of how truths can be so easily constructed and perceptions so easily altered depending on how an issue is

introduced, how an argument is developed, what facts are highlighted, what details are selected and what are ignored. Basically, it's all in the 'telling' of the story.[15]

A Hinduism scholar and a RISA member, Jeffrey Long, also thought that the *Washington Post* article was skewed. He found it to be "disappointing [...] Hindus were made to look like fanatics".[16] Another scholar, named Lucinda Hopkins, criticized the article:

> [It] seemed intent on pitting people against one another on the basis of a superficial difference—their heritage . . . It saddens me to see this debate portrayed as a battle of bullies out to protect their own turf. Particularly distressing is Doniger's statement: 'The argument is being fueled by a fanatical nationalism and Hindutva . . . and no one who is not a Hindu has the right to speak about Hinduism at all.'

She continued:

> My experience is exactly the opposite. I am not Indian . . . I could not and would not make any exclusive claim to being Hindu. Yet, I have spoken about Hinduism, and I know not of what Doniger speaks when she claims that because she is not a Hindu her remarks are rejected. People I have met who are steeped in the Hindu tradition have respectfully considered my thoughts, observations, and questions, even when, perhaps my comments easily could have been found to be disrespectful or ignorant. So, from personal experience, Doniger is wrong.

Hopkins then provided her succinct and insightful analysis of Doniger's shortcomings:

> To be blessed with understanding a tradition one must have the patience and humility to learn the tradition from those who know it. This is Doniger's greatest mistake. It is why she makes such an appalling statement as holding [Malhotra] indirectly responsible for stirring up passionate emotions. She is 'stirring up emotions' by not learning, not understanding. Rather than listening to the disturbed outcries she has unleashed, she retreats to the cover of claiming that she is being discriminated against because she is not from India. But the discrimination is her fault: both for portraying the criticism against her as nationalistic and for lacking true discrimination to take what is being said and gain from it.[17]

Responding to the *Post*

The *Washington Post* article caused a public outcry in the Indian-American community. Numerous people wrote about their dismay at the distortion of what they saw as a groundbreaking debate. Malhotra posted two online responses and the *Post* reporter was accorded space on Sulekha to respond. The *Washington Post* did *not* offer a similar chance for Malhotra or any other diaspora critic named in its article to respond. Strangely, Vedantam was highly critical of Sulekha for allowing Malhotra to post his response before giving him a chance to review and respond to it ahead of time![18]

In his article, 'Ten Challenges', Malhotra asked the *Post* to stop spreading Hinduphobia by combining unrelated data and sensationalizing unsubstantiated claims, such as the issue of Laine's book discussed earlier in this chapter, and the anonymous threats posted on the student petition. Other important points from his rejoinder are summarized below.

Double Standards

While the religious affiliations of white American scholars such as Courtright, Doniger, or Laine are never mentioned in the article, the religious affiliations of Indian-American scholars such as Arvind Sharma and T.R.N. Rao are repeatedly highlighted. This gives the false illusion that the Doniger camp is speaking from a supposedly unbiased and universal perspective. As McKim Marriott has noted, the *etics* (i.e. those who study a religion from the outside/objective posture) are insiders to their own cultures and religions, and this biases their worldview. Noting the religious and ideological affiliations of the Doniger camp would actually have been illuminating.[19]

Vedantam's response did not address this issue of unbalance in portrayal. Malhotra notes that the *Washington Post* seems to grant higher credibility to white academic scholars like Doniger and Courtright than to the Hindu community:

> How are the *Post's* readers expected to evaluate the 'reaction' of the Hindus when they are not told what exactly Doniger said to provoke them? He refuses to even mention Wendy Doniger's telling statement, as quoted in the *Philadelphia Inquirer* that 'the Gita is a dishonest book.' Mr. Vedantam camouflages Doniger's denigration of the *Gita* and many other hate-ridden statements by dignifying her work as an 'academic' and 'scholarly' use of 'Freudian psychoanalysis' of Hindu texts and symbols. The reader is left to

imagine that a bunch of irrational, uninformed, and emotionally charged Hindus are ganging up on a scholar.[20]

Vedantam responded that Doniger claimed the *Philadelphia Inquirer* had misquoted her. He chided, "No responsible person would repeat such an unsubstantiated statement."[21] This was precisely the issue Malhotra found troubling—the journalist's blind belief in one side and automatic suspicion of the other. He wrote:

> In deciding which claims are credible, Mr. Vedantam fails to apply consistent standards . . . Even if Doniger denies saying these words, the *Philadelphia Inquirer*, a credible newspaper, has not agreed to retract its story . . . Doniger's mere denial compels Mr. Vedantam to override the *Philadelphia Inquirer's* report without even calling the *Inquirer's* reporter to get his account. On the other hand, despite the Hindu community contesting the authenticity of anonymous Internet 'threats,' Mr. Vedantam blindly believes what Courtright told him.[22] He always gives the Courtright/Doniger camp the overall benefit of doubt.

Vedantam posted no response to this charge.

Misinterpreting Hindu Symbolism

Vedantam explains Ganesha by using one of the more obscure stories about him as though it were literal history and ignores how Hindus interpret symbolism. Resorting to literalism is a misuse of the Abrahamic approach to interpreting Hindu narratives:[23] because Abrahamic faiths are 'religions of the book,' such stories must be reconciled with each other literally, but no such pressure to reconcile the literal meaning of various stories exists within Hinduism. Meanings are derived just as much from traditional practices as they are from texts. Vedantam disregards this key distinction between the Abrahamic and Hindu approaches to literature. As a result, Courtright's scholarship on Ganesha is shown as perfectly legitimate and the Hindu critics caricaturized as emotional and irrational.

Trivializing Intellectual Debates as 'Public Relations'

The article was not adequately contextualized for a mainstream American audience. It completely ignored the fact that minorities in America have always organized movements to take charge of and participate in their cultural representation, for example, through massive and well-funded organizations such as the Japan Foundation, the Chinese government's

Confucius Institutes, the Qaid-e-Azam academic chairs sponsored by the Government of Pakistan in US universities, and the Pew Charitable Trust's role in championing Christianity on prestigious American university campuses. Vedantam avoided these thought-provoking comparisons.

Ignoring Hinduphobia

As already noted, Vedantam chose to ignore the various examples of Hinduphobia cited by the sources he interviewed. The *Post* has not educated its readers about Hinduphobia, despite some disturbing trends in America. It needs to review the research data available on stigmas against Hinduism in America and should conduct further surveys amongst its own readers (and its journalists and editors) to gain a better insight into the level of misinformation that exists even amongst well-educated Americans. This would enable it to better position its own coverage and to avoid inadvertently fueling more hate crimes similar to the *Dotbusters* and attacks such as temple vandalism.

Notably, by contrast, Western media and universities are rich with research regarding Islamophobia. By directly facing this unfortunate social malaise, mainstream journalists and academicians hope that Islamophobia will eventually be uprooted and eradicated.[24] Ironically, those same professionals roll their eyes when they hear the term Hinduphobia. Even when Hindu temples are vandalized in Middle America, or temples are denied zoning permits, and when those whose dress and appearance is overtly Hindu are mocked (the followers of ISKCON, or 'Hare Krishnas' are routinely mocked in movies and on TV), the term Hinduphobia is never used. The violent 'Dotbusters' who killed Hindus and Parsees and attacked their properties in New Jersey have not been seriously studied by the academy or mainstream media.

Chapter 26

Muddying the Waters: Doniger Rolls Out the Big Guns

By Krishnan Ramaswamy

Soon after the article by Vedantam appeared in the *Washington Post*, another article appeared on a popular interfaith website called 'Beliefnet'. The essay, 'Scholars of Hinduism Under Attack', further reinforced the 'non-white savages attacking white scholars' framework. The piece on Beliefnet was written by a true heavyweight in the field of Religious Studies: Prof. Martin E. Marty, an ordained Evangelical Lutheran pastor who is considered a doyen of Religion at the University of Chicago. Just as Billy Graham is the acceptable face of Christian Fundamentalism in the American mainstream, Marty is on the same plateau of respectability and acceptance in the mainstream of Religious Studies.[25] Indeed, *Time* magazine called him the most influential Christian religious interpreter in America.[26]

A noted scholar like Marty does not often write on a site like Beliefnet, and so this article was obviously contributed under special circumstances. Given that the controversy around Courtright and Doniger involved allegations of shoddy scholarship, one would expect him to present a deeply reasoned analysis taking into account the evidence presented on both sides. Instead, readers were treated to the following journalistic hyperbole:

> Some **militants** were stirred to be critical of it, rejecting the psychoanalytic elements in Courtright's analysis of a Hindu god with the head of an elephant. While a few are themselves scholars, **most of the roused attackers lack context and understanding.** Courtright and other experts have had death threats, while others

know that persecution or exclusion from India could await them. [Emphasis added] [27]

It is unclear how Marty was able to determine the lack of context and understanding of the tens of thousands of Sulekha readers. An undergraduate student writing such a paper would have been instructed to examine the evidence presented by Roland, Bhattacharyya, Witzel, Swami Tyagananda, Venkat, Agarwal, among others, in which they challenge the quality and rigor of RISA scholarship.

Marty then went on to paint his friend and colleague ('Wendy down the hall' as he affectionately thinks of her) as a victim, presenting yet again the egg-throwing incident. Vedantam and Braverman (Braverman's article in the *UChicago Magazine* is discussed later in this section) had made sensational use of this 'incident' but not as repeatedly and centrally as Marty. "Doniger has not escaped completely. She had to duck an egg thrown by a militant Hindu as she lectured in London."[28] It is unclear how Marty was able to determine the religion or the politics of the anonymous egg thrower. Egg-throwing is certainly not a Hindu tradition. In fact, most Hindus we've spoken to find it to be a bizarre and aggressive form of behavior; whereas, it is actually a very common British (White Anglo-Saxon Protestant) mode of protest. Marty avoids mentioning that throwing eggs at speakers and politicians has a long and noble English history[29] that has been around since before 1914.[30] In British culture, egg-tossing is widely considered a comic act of protest, not a threatening one—its purpose being to take a pompous speaker down a notch or two.[31] Indeed, famous British politicians and political commentators have claimed "that throwing eggs at politicians, possibly tomatoes as well, was the constitutional right of every true-born Englishman".[32] Students at Oxford and other British universities routinely throw eggs at each other as a prank or as a celebration, although it is now being frowned upon by the authorities.[33] Surely, Marty, who has been to England many times in the course of his long career, is aware of this non-Hindu but authentically eccentric British tradition. Why do Marty and others continue to milk this egg incident and pin it on 'militant Hindu savages'?

Lending an Ugly Racial Tinge to Criticism of Academics

Marty provides a clue in the next point he makes: Hindus, he hints, are not as mature as Jews or Christians. He makes a direct, odious, *and* historically false comparison:

As for the psychoanalytic aspects in Ganesa, Freudians and post-Freudians have had their rounds with Moses, Paul, Christians, and Jews through the ages, without having to duck eggs, harassment, or death threats.[34]

To say that Freudians have never had to contend with harassment or threats from Christians 'through the ages' is patently false. Marty also refuses to acknowledge the asymmetry of power between well-established Judeo-Christian groups in America and a politically nascent minority. For every Freudian scholar who is sexualizing or pathologizing Judeo-Christianity's gods or religious figures, there are ten scholars challenging her, providing nuanced and alternative interpretations from within the tradition.

In the case of Hinduism, Freudian analyses—no matter how far-fetched—are not received as fringe views. Rather, they become a central way in which America and the West perceives Hindu Gods and religious figures. Marty avoids looking at the impact of these poorly evidenced and subjectively driven analyses, which nevertheless become the *authoritative* portrayals used to form mainstream America's perceptions of Hinduism. A Beliefnet reader criticized Marty on this facile omission: "I am an Indian Christian by birth and now a naturalized American who is a witness to the negative influence of the writings of Courtright, Doniger, Kripal and others on the minds of young Americans who want to learn about Hinduism through formal college courses or visiting our museums".[35]

Instead, Marty provides a superficial and misleading analysis of the motives of Doniger's critics, giving the whole debate a strongly racial tinge. The discussion about balancing insider and outsider perspectives, i.e. emic and etic discourses on Hinduism, slips away. He simply parrots Wendy Doniger's accusations in the *Post* that shadowy forces [i.e. savages] were trying to 'control' the discourse on Hinduism and exclude white non-Hindu scholars. Marty faithfully quotes Doniger claim that: "it is all fueled by a fanatical nationalism and Hindutva".

He accuses Doniger's critics of being 'hyper multiculturalists' who want to silence non-Hindus from talking about Hinduism and deplores this as a narrow, racist interpretation of multiculturalism that has victimized white scholars in the past through 'blighted tenure decisions, negative reviews, and probably harm[ing] some careers'. He suggests that America is now 'moderating' these past multiculturalist excesses, and he fears that Doniger's critics want a return to this period of 'bad' multiculturalism. His article is thus a coded warning to white scholars to circle their wagons around Doniger or risk having their power, influence, and careers undercut by 'Hindu multiculturalists'.

In Marty's view, the whole affair is merely a sensational episode in which his friends are being victimized for innocently sharing with other Americans their 'love' of the fascinating field of Hinduism and the 'good stories' they have picked up in their studies. Marty, who has looked deeply into the many faces of religious fundamentalism within Christianity and published broadly on this topic, can, nonetheless, see only a monochromic silhouette of threatening militants when it comes to Hinduism. In so painting Doniger's critics, he has precluded all possibility of nuanced discourse by using an all-or-nothing fundamentalist approach. He glorifies the work of Doniger's team:

> All great literature, canonical or not, is born of particular experiences, and if it is great, it gets shared. That was happening with Hindu mythology, but for the moment the eggs and threats fly and the barriers are up.[36]

Had he bothered to read any of the dozen or more critiques of the field written from a diversity of perspectives prior to writing his article, it would have been difficult for him to see them as 'barriers' to growth. Having failed to familiarize himself with the issues, Marty resorts to mere character reference: "Wendy . . . had and has a love affair with India and Hinduism".[37]

His next comment is a gratuitous warning that if Hindus continued to insist on contributing to the discourse about Hinduism Studies, the resulting scholarship about their religion would 'suffer for decades to come'. He stresses that Doniger, Courtright, Kripal, and others like them are not just indispensable to Hinduism Studies but are really the best *public relations* agents for Hinduism. He accuses Hindus of objecting to the bloodlines and geographical origins of Wendy and her children rather than admiring their public relations work to enhance Hinduism's image. He says, in effect, that Hindu-Americans are shooting themselves in the foot by being intolerant and ignorant racists. All the voices of the diaspora are derided as 'militant' and the expressed hope is that the establishment view will prevail:

> [Doniger], Courtright, and others should outlast the militants. Otherwise Hindu scholarship will suffer for decades to come. If this happens, some of the best public relations agents for the religions of India will be under a cloud and it will be a bit darker for all of us—including those who attack scholars who do not have the right blood line or geographical context.[38]

Marty seems to be suggesting that it is best for Hindus to outsource both scholarly discourse and public relations to Doniger and family because, quite simply, they do the job better. The one-sidedness and patronizing tone of the article provoked many troubled responses by readers who expected the distinguished scholar to take the high road and examine the issues. For instance, Dr. Alex Alexander wrote:

> I was troubled by Martin Marty's article on 'Scholars of Hinduism Under Attack'. It reminded me of the criticism unleashed against the late Columbia University Professor Edward Said when he first began to challenge the prejudiced writings of American 'orientalists'. To call the Indian critics of Doniger's and Courtright's writings as 'Hindu militants' as Marty does is like spitting against a breeze of fresh air. Rajiv Malhotra, Sankrant Sanu and others who have critiqued Doniger and Courtright are not Hindu militants but serious scholars of Hinduism. They are not the protégés of Doniger or Courtright. That may be the real issue here.[39] [Emphasis added]

Attempts to Restore the Debate

Marty's unfortunate and partisan polemic ignored and devalued the efforts of scholars like Arvind Sharma who have presented a balanced view of the debate and also of the attempts to derail it. In the spring of 2004, prior to Marty's Beliefnet article, Arvind Sharma wrote an opinion piece for *Religion Newsletter* called 'Scholars and Hindus'.[40] Like other Hindu critics, he deplored the threats and other emotional gestures as distractions from a substantive debate and courageously noted that the academicians of the Doniger School have also undermined the debate. He pointed out that they have repeatedly refused to address any substantive issues that are being raised by their learned and earnest critics. For example, Sharma noted that Kripal has never responded in any detail to the point-by-point refutation made by Swami Tyagananda of his mistranslations and extrapolations.

The academic community was acting inappropriately and harming the cause of intellectual discourse by not recognizing and welcoming their well-informed Hindu neighbors into the debate. Sharma wrote:

> For their part, Western academics should understand that depicting Hinduism in a manner perceived as provocatively demeaning by the Hindus themselves does nobody any good. Nor is the cause of civilized intellectual discourse advanced if they decline to respond to informed critiques simply because the critics do not happen to

be academics. It tempts the critics to conclude that the emperors have no clothes. [Emphasis added]

[...]

Previously, North American academics could write without having to take into account the reaction of the Hindu faith community, which lay halfway around the world. But immigration was now bringing Hindus to the door of the American ivory tower.

Others responded to Marty's polemics by attempting to restore the focus of the debate to the substantive issues. One example is Sankrant Sanu's thoughtful response that was posted on Beliefnet, reproduced in full below:

U.S. Hinduism Studies: A Question of Shoddy Scholarship[41]

By Sankrant Sanu

In a recent column on Beliefnet.com, prominent religion professor Martin E. Marty says that scholars of Moses or Jesus haven't had to 'duck eggs or death threats' lately[42] and asks why Hindu groups are attacking U.S. professors of Hinduism. This unfortunately shows that people in the academy are still talking past those in the Hindu community rather than attempting to have a conversation.

Many Hindus have expressed concern about the quality and nature of Hinduism scholarship emanating from the U.S. academy. What kind of work has drawn criticism from the Hindu community? Here are just a few examples:

- In his book on Ganesha, the beloved elephant-headed deity of Hindus, Emory University professor Paul Courtright made claims that Ganesha's trunk represents a limp phallus and the fondness for sweets of this child deity carries 'overtones' of a desire for oral sex.

- University of Chicago professor Wendy Doniger has been quoted in the Philadelphia Inquirer calling the *Bhagavad Gita*, a sacred Hindu text, 'a dishonest book' that 'justifies war'.

- In her article on Hinduism for *Encarta*, the online encyclopedia that serves as a mainstream introduction for general audiences, Doniger highlights what she calls 'contradictions' in the Hindu tradition—often using deprecating parenthetical asides, unusual for such an encyclopedia entry.

- In *Kali's Child,* Rice University professor Jeffrey Kripal portrays Sri Ramakrishna, a much-revered Hindu spiritual teacher, as a sexually abused homosexual child-molester.

Kali's Child has become a standard reference on Ramakrishna in U.S. academia. The works of Courtright, Kripal and Doniger are similarly served up as mainstream interpretations of the Hindu tradition, finding their way into museum exhibits and primary references for encyclopedias.

Many learned people in the Hindu community, most of them non-academicians, have taken a critical look at the work of these scholars. Rajiv Malhotra's 'RISA Lila I: Wendy's Child Syndrome' examines the work and assertions of Doniger, Courtright, Kripal and Sarah Caldwell. "When the Cigar Becomes A Phallus" by Vishal Agarwal and Kalavai Venkat is a detailed examination of Paul Courtright's book on Ganesha. And my article, "Are Hinduism Studies Prejudiced?" compares Microsoft *Encarta's* article on Hinduism, written by Doniger, with articles about other major world religions. The list goes on.

So are we critics just ticked-off Hindus trying to censor legitimate scholarship? Is this just a 'fundamentalist' response by 'militants', as Marty and others imply? The central question, at least for me, has been, "What constitutes knowledge". As I write in my article: "The Courtright Twist", I am bothered less by the issues of 'blasphemy' (which is less meaningful in the Hindu context), but by the question of whether this purported scholarship manufactures a distorted understanding of the Hindu tradition. If the academy is engaged in the production of knowledge, its freedom of speech is meaningful only within that boundary. Otherwise, there is no way to prevent anyone's personal fantasies or works of fiction from being passed off as non-fiction academic writing.

Critical articles, including my own, raise the issue of the quality of scholarship of some of these prominent members of the academy. These articles have pointed out errors, inconsistencies, mistranslations, missing references, suspect theories and interpretative techniques and, in some cases, troubling evidence of outright prejudice displayed by the academicians.

These arguments may be refutable. But, given the widespread support they have received from the Hindu community, it would behoove the scholars to engage with their critics and enter into a dialogue about the issues. The website Sulekha.com invited Wendy Doniger to offer a response to one of the early articles that Rajiv Malhotra had written. She refused.

Let's look at what happened when the Hindu community tried to address Courtright's work. Serious questions have been raised about the book, such as the non-existence of the references that Courtright cites in several cases as well as his clear misconstruing of others.

A community group started a petition to express its concern about Courtright's book. The petition contained quotes from the book that were considered offensive and hurtful; it asked for an apology from the author and a republication of the book with clarifications and corrections. While this petition was not initiated or signed by many of the people who had written critical articles, including by Rajiv Malhotra or myself, the large number of signers reflected the Hindu community's widespread concern about the book. This concern was being expressed in a democratic way.

When this petition was online, a few posts among thousands contained some angry language against the scholars. The anonymity of the internet easily allows many forms of verbal diarrhea visible in practically any large internet message board, especially on a contentious issue. Because of the posted threats, the organizers of the petition closed it down. Even though the petition had tremendous momentum, the organizers clearly did not want to provide a platform for personal threats of any kind.

Yet Marty reduces the entire debate about the Courtright book to stating that "some militants were stirred to be critical of it". He expresses the hope that "saner voices will prevail".

In reality, it's the academicians themselves who have marginalized "saner" voices by framing the issue as one of "death threats" and "militants"—using a few random posts on an un-moderated group to sideline the hundreds of pages of reasoned criticism that has been put out by the community. Doniger wants to make it an issue of "fanatical Hindutva" and Courtright chooses to play the victim by writing about it as "Scholarship in the Age of Terror".

Unless these high priests of academia can substantiate how these articles, which criticize their work, even remotely espouse militancy, the scholars' reaction can only be considered as a deliberate and dishonest distortion to avoid the substantive issues of scholarship that have been raised. Nonetheless, power has the ability to frame discourse. A *Washington Post* article on this issue follows the line put out by these academicians; it describes the issue primarily in terms of "death threats" and "violence" rather than the quality of scholarship.

Criticism of crude academic writing on Hinduism is coming from the community because it is not present in the academy. The Christian or Jewish community need not overly concern itself with psychoanalytical fantasies about Moses or Jesus because there is a vast body of scholars *within the academy* who would take this on. A Courtright-like narrative with far-fetched psychoanalytical interpretations would be marginalized in the study of Jesus or Moses. Not so with Hinduism, where such interpretations form part of the mainstream narratives by "authorities" like Doniger. Those who *object* are likely to be marginalized instead.

The balance of power within the academy for the Judeo-Christian traditions is vastly different from the case of Hinduism. Apparently, no one in the academy has even bothered to check the references of Courtright's "well-received" book on Ganesha in the 20 years that it has been out, let alone write a critique. This would be unimaginable in the case of a similar work about Jesus or Moses or even the Prophet Mohammad. And this is why the ideas of Courtright, Kripal, and Doniger can be put forward as *mainstream interpretations* of Hindu thought, unlike the alleged homoeroticism of Jesus.

While Doniger et al make exaggerated claims of violence based on ducking a stray egg, the real issue they have been ducking is that of shoddy scholarship. They charge that their critics do not read books; yet it is these academicians who haven't bothered to read their critics. Perhaps they don't need to. It is easier to remain ensconced in an Ivory Tower and make sure that the airwaves carry only the story of the scholars being "attacked." The alternative would be to engage in dialogue with the community who find their traditions unrecognizably mauled at their hands rather than talking past them, as Marty does, by caricaturing all criticism as "fundamentalist" and "militant." This engagement can only help all those that genuinely care to see the academy as a place for the dissemination of knowledge, rather than of one-sided propaganda.

Chapter 27

The Power of 'Connections': Using the *New York Times* for PR

By Krishnan Ramaswamy

On January 31, 2005, the *New York Times* published a strange article in the Arts Section entitled: 'Connections: the Scholar who Irked Hindu Puritans'. Written by Edward Rothstein, an art critic, it provided a now familiar spin on the Wendy's Child Syndrome controversy. As with the *Washington Post* and the *UChicago Magazine* (discussed later in this section) versions, this retelling had some strikingly confrontational and misleading features. Interestingly, it almost completely paraphrased the key points made by Martin Marty in his Beliefnet.com article a few weeks earlier. Some of the similarities between these articles included:

i) Characterizing Doniger and her students as 'victims of threats and attacks';
ii) Stereotyping her opponents as 'irrational fundamentalists and Hindu puritans';
iii) Slanderously conflating the critics' work with unrelated political violence in India and protests in the UK; and
iv) Obscuring the serious and substantive issues that have been raised about the quality of academic work.

The article focused on personalities rather than issues and attempted to enlist readers' sympathies for Doniger through various disingenuous means. In contrast, Doniger's critics were grossly caricatured, labeled as Hindu Puritans and Hindu Fundamentalists—a questionable approach when the ostensible purpose of the article was to discuss a controversy centered on the work of Doniger and other University of Chicago scholars. Most importantly, in violation of established journalistic practice and ethics, Rothstein did not attempt to interview the other side even though he named key players like Malhotra and Sanu. Doniger was the sole source and quoted multiple times.

The article seemed to be the product of a rather cozy and privileged relationship enjoyed by Rothstein, a University of Chicago alumnus, with key figures at the University of Chicago who are parties to this controversy. Many of these issues appeared to be violations of the *New York Times'* own *Code of Ethics* which are a set of covenants that the *Times* publicly made with its readers. Therefore, I wrote at length to the *Times* Ombudsman (or Public Editor), Mr. Okrent, and to its publisher, Mr. Sulzberger. My letter and their responses are discussed below.

Frontier Myth and White Victims

Featured prominently in the article was a decades-old picture of Wendy Doniger when she was a young woman. This use of her youthful appearance was deliberate. The article refers to it as "the image of an ingénue, perhaps barely out of her teens, gazing into the distance with earnest, sensuous grace". Such a picture has no relevance to Doniger's recent writings, or to the controversy discussed by the article. Rothstein explicitly intends the reader to link this tender, beautiful image with the trope of a white woman under threat from dangerous savages. He invites the reader to look at this photo and "get some idea of why in recent years this woman has had an egg thrown at her at a lecture and received threatening e-mail, and why just last week she was worrying about a student who was being ominously followed".

Thus, the article establishes from the outset that this earnest, beautiful and vulnerable white woman is a *victim*, a target of dark and malevolent forces linked to the 'Hindu puritans'. A photograph of Doniger taken in 2005 would not have had the same impact—it would show a formidable-looking woman in her sixties with a reputation for toughness and coarseness. Indeed, the picture on the University of Chicago's professionally managed public relations site shows an upper-crust woman petting an expensive horse. She looks simultaneously rich, successful, street-smart and tough.

In writing to the *New York Times* Ombudsman, I pointed out how manipulative this ingénue image was:

It is really in questionable taste that [Mr. Rothstein] tries to milk readers' sympathy by publishing an outdated but glamorous photograph from 1959 of a young, fragile white woman. The connection of the photograph to the article seems tortuous and artificial, since the subject matter of the article has little to do with the book in which the photograph appeared. Mr. Rothstein seems to be juxtaposing her youthful innocence—('an ingénue') with the assertion that 'violent' 'Hindu Fundamentalists' are after this woman, who needs to be protected. The bottom line is that such manipulation chokes off all debate, by calling on the readership to react emotionally rather than thoughtfully. To my mind this strange choice of Ms. Doniger's image recalls—in reverse—Time Magazine's infamous 'enhanced' cover in 1994 featuring Mr. O. J. Simpson, which showed him with darker skin, exuding menace at least for those who are menaced by dark skin [...]. Rule # 39 of the [New York Times ethics] manual considers public relations work, paid or unpaid, an inherent conflict of interest for its journalists. One may be forgiven for wondering if Mr. Rothstein is aware of this rule. Indeed Mr. Rothstein does seem to go all out in a PR effort for Ms. Doniger.

While the New York Times Ombudsman responded to some issues I raised, he completely avoided this important one. As a media specialist, he undoubtedly understands that such images are deeply rooted in American history and mythology and that through such images Rothstein was tapping into an integral aspect of the Frontier Myth. Thus, while the infamous Time magazine cover featuring O.J. Simpson was rightly condemned by many Americans for playing on White fears of Blacks, the Ombudsman for the New York Times let a similar abuse of racial and cultural stereotypes pass through.

Popular stories, art, and theater in the seventeenth, eighteenth and nineteenth centuries commonly showed 'pure white maidens and peaceful white men' being captured by fierce and atrocious Native American raiders, only to be rescued by heroic white men who fended off the beastly savages. Prof. Richard Slotkin explains, "The great and continued popularity of these narratives, the uses to which they were put, and the nature of the symbolism employed in them, are evidence that the captivity narratives constitute the first coherent myth-literature developed in America for American audiences."[43]

This 'captivity narrative' was among the most popular form of American adventure story in seventeenth and eighteenth century America. It became an important part of white Christian mythology and was often woven into church sermons.[44] The mythic uses of this narrative bear a striking resemblance to the work and attitudes of several Western scholars studying Indian Religions. As Slotkin notes, in the myth, "civilized men and women leave contemporary society and enter—willingly or as captives—a primitive, primal world. If they can maintain their racial/cultural integrity in that world, they can seize the natural, original power immanent in that world." Moreover, "if they can defeat the forces that seek to prevent their return to civilization, then . . . they will be capable of renewing the moral and physical capabilities of the [western] society they originally left."[45] Thus, the anxiety shown by Doniger and Children to impose Eurocentric lenses on Indic religions while simultaneously erasing or devaluing Indic interpretations goes back to this primal anxiety of keeping one's cultural and racial purity intact. Slotkin notes that by going to the Indian, i.e. by becoming *too much* of a native, "the hero risks the integrity of his or her white soul; he or she may be tempted to . . . become a racial renegade". For scholars like Doniger, privileging or even *respecting* indigenous interpretations of events and symbols, and *not* imposing a speculative, Eurocentric gloss on them is too frightening—**perhaps it feels too much like being intellectually captured by the 'primitive' Indic religious philosophies.** Interpreting criticism from Indians as attacks and threats is a small step under these circumstances.

In the classic version of this tale, the victim of the captivity narrative is typically a white woman or a Christian minister who is captured by Natives. The captive symbolizes the values of white civilization that are imperiled in the wilderness by the heathen savage. This is the "Myth of the Frontier in which the triumph of civilization over savagery is symbolized by the hunter/warrior's rescue of the White woman held captives by savages".[46]

The art and imagery of the period was filled with portrayals of the Natives as merciless savages. An endless series of such images established this as fact in American minds. Prof. Drinnon explains: "Always **the contrast was between dusky evil and fair innocence,** between maddened red cruelty and helpless white virtue".[47] [Emphasis added]. Drinnon explains how a popular painting called 'the Death of Jane Mcrea' was a prototype of this 'dusky evil' versus 'helpless white virtue/fair innocence' trope that galvanized emotions against the 'savagery' of the Indians. This kind of art was officially endorsed: massive sculptures were installed in the US Congress and other public spaces depicting white frontiersmen arriving in the nick of time to save white women and children from the maddened assault of dark-skinned Indians. It provided Americans a safety valve for their conscience while they carried out the task of displacing the natives and claiming Indian property as their own.

Rothstein—an art and music critic with a degree from University of Chicago, as well as the Editor of the *New York Times* Arts Section—should have been well aware of this history. Why then did he choose to run with these deeply prejudicial and emotive images unless the intention was to kill debate? Perhaps Rothstein felt a need to position himself as the hero rescuing Doniger from Hindu 'attackers'. The deployment of America's oldest and most robust myth against a non-white minority seen as 'savages' could not have been more vivid.

Savage 'Attacks' and Threats:

Rothstein characterized Malhotra's thoughtful but necessarily provocative essay as an 'attack', accusing him of wanting to preserve Hindu 'purity' and 'power':

> Though sexual imagery is found throughout Hinduism's baroque mythology, many groups would like to minimize its importance. They have different concerns: some with purity, some with Hindu power, some with minimizing the influence of 'Eurocentric' commentators. In 2002, for example, Ms. Doniger and some former students **were attacked** in a 24,000-word essay on Sulekha.com, an 'online community' for Indians. The essay, by Rajiv Malhotra, an entrepreneur whose foundation is devoted to improving the understanding of India in the United States, accused Ms. Doniger and her colleagues of Hindu bashing with their obsessive preoccupation with sexuality. [Emphasis added]

None of the substantive and troubling issues raised in Malhotra's essay about the quality of Doniger's scholarship were even mentioned in the *Times'* analysis. Rothstein apparently did not read the essay, even though he counted the words in it. Malhotra is linked to shadowy groups that would like to minimize the importance of sexuality without any attempt to substantiate such claims.

Here is Rothstein's version of the 'helpless white virtue in danger from dark, threatening, mysterious forces':

> That essay seems to have galvanized the opposition. A Sulekha.com article posted in 2002 accused Ms. Doniger of denigrating Hinduism

in her article written for the Encarta encyclopedia. Microsoft, the encyclopedia's publisher, ended up replacing Ms. Doniger's contribution. Meanwhile threatening e-mail messages were sent to Ms. Doniger and her colleagues. And in November 2003, an egg was lobbed at her at the University of London, after she lectured about monkey imagery in 'The Ramayana.'

No analysis is provided of the nuanced points in Sanu's article or Microsoft's reasons for replacing Doniger's sensationalist and skewed essay. Instead, the *New York Times* article focused on bringing in unrelated images of violence directed at scholarly victims in foreign countries.

Distracting and Slanderous Conflations with Indian Politics

Following Marty's lead, Rothstein obscures the issues by using images of unrelated violence and unrest from India. This is reminiscent of the American Frontier images that were constantly fed to white Americans in order to remove any white guilt from the brutal oppression of the non-white peoples. Unrelated attacks on scholars and rumors circulated by Doniger are repeated as *fact* in the article. Doniger could have written the journalist's script:

> In India things have become even more serious. Hindutva, a form of Hindu orthodoxy, was enshrined during the Bharatiya Janata Party's reign (from 1998 until this May). But even with that party's fall from power, violence from Hindu groups has grown along with violence from radical Muslims. Scholarship about Hinduism has also come under scrutiny. Books that explore lurid or embarrassing details about deities or saints have been banned. One Western scholar's Indian researcher was smeared with tar, and the institute in Pune where the scholar had done his research was destroyed. Ms. Doniger said one of her American pupils who was studying Christianity in India had her work disrupted and was being relentlessly followed.

Independent Indian scholars who collaborated with Laine are listed patronizingly as 'One western scholar's Indian researcher'—a slip that exposes the implicit White supremacy permeating the article: Indian scholars can rarely be equals as co-authors, and their proper place is that of junior researcher toiling like Robinson Crusoe's Man Friday.[48]

The phrasing of Rothstein's article gives a sense of dealing with *established facts* about Hinduism rather than highly debatable claims:

"Books that explore lurid or embarrassing details about deities or saints have been banned". The implication being that these 'lurid details' are settled issues, objectively arrived at, rather than the result of subjective Eurocentric bias, shoddy scholarship and even shoddier peer-review. Thus he undercuts the very basis of the debate with arrogance, reminiscent of Kripal's when he pompously claimed that the case about Ramakrishna's conflicted homosexuality was 'closed'.

Rothstein's mindset illustrates how an average American might view Doniger's sexualized analyses of Hinduism. Doniger has often claimed that the *centrality* of sex to understanding Hinduism is liberating and appreciated by Americans as a result of her efforts. This is her claim of championing Hinduism. But Rothstein does not find Doniger's Hinduism liberating or empowering, and, rather, finds it titillating, 'lurid and embarrassing'. No wonder his tone is disrespectful of Hinduism and is in tune with an imagined religion of chaos, violence and decadence.

Rothstein then enlists the authority of Doniger to *confirm* that such fanaticism and fundamentalism are an inherent part of Hinduism. At the same time, he also takes the opportunity to hint that Tantra's origins were in a South Asian sexual cult that required the consumption of all manner of bodily emissions.[49] Those who disagree are part of "a revisionist Hindu tradition that had led to intemperate attacks on European and American scholars". He cites Doniger's *London Times* article that links this with the growth of 'right-wing Hindus' in the diaspora in America. Rothstein—a novice to India Studies and Hinduism—has no basis for the sweeping conclusions he makes, other than uncritical acceptance of Doniger's version. The reader is left with the implication that a serious study of a chaotic and messy civilization like Hinduism is best left to Doniger and her school of experts, who can get all the dirt on 'them'. Deviousness is implied for one side and scrupulous honesty for the other.

What Happened to the Evidence of Shoddy Scholarship?

Rothstein mentions in passing that at least a part of the struggle is about the authentic self-representation of Hinduism, acknowledging that "it echoes the complaints of many Western groups that have not developed traditions of critical scholarship, but find themselves subject to what they consider outsider examination. In this, the Hindu right is echoing the Western left." This is flawed because Hinduism *does* have

a well-developed 'tradition of critical scholarship' that simply wishes
to have a seat at the debating table at par with other voices. Rothstein
never contacted anyone on the other side of the debate, but continued
as a mouthpiece for Doniger, alleging that Hindus were unleashing
'terror':

> Unfortunately, the alternative offered is usually not scholarship but
> self-promotion. In this case, Ms. Doniger wrote in her review, the
> 'righteous revolution' also threatens to become a 'reign of terror.'
> Moreover, the insistence on stripping away masks created by others
> may be an attempt to create a single rigid mask that presents a
> supposedly appropriate visage, an idea that flies in the face of the
> multifaceted Hindu traditions that Ms. Doniger explores.

Thus, attempts to challenge Eurocentric masks are framed as sinister
attempts to foster 'a rigid mask'. I pointed this out in my letter to the
New York Times Ombudsman:

> Both Marty and Rothstein have shown a remarkable single-
> mindedness in ignoring the fact that many renowned scholars have
> raised substantive and troubling issues regarding Ms Doniger's
> work, in addition to public intellectuals like Mr. Malhotra. Perhaps
> they are too inconvenient—too difficult to label & dismiss as
> 'fundamentalists'? These include persons like Prof. Witzel of
> Harvard (who has aggressively and publicly questioned Doniger's
> grasp of Sanskrit and the reliability of some of her translations),
> Swami Tyagananda of the Ramakrishna Mission (who has provided
> a detailed analysis of defamatory mistranslations from Bengali that
> Doniger supervised), Prof. De Nicolas of SUNY (who has criticized
> a certain mindset among Indologists at UChicago—including
> Doniger—that he believes leads to trivializations and
> mischaracterizations of Hinduism); Prof. Balagangadhara of the
> University of Ghent (who has weighed in on the impact on Hindu
> society of such mischaracterizations).

The *Times* Ombudsman's flippant response was to claim that, even
without interviewing anyone on the other side, Rothstein had taken
pains to represent all sides!

'Connections'

Rothstein is an alumnus of the University of Chicago. Access to the
New York Times in order to air their views is not easily available to
diaspora intellectuals. But it is easy for the likes of Doniger, especially

when the reporters and columnists are friends and alumni of the same university where she is a powerful faculty member. This is perhaps the classic definition of the 'old boys' (and old girls) network, where all the key players from similar cultural backgrounds are tied to the same alma mater. In formulating its Code of Ethics, the *New York Times* recognized many of these conflicts of interest. My letter was a test to see how seriously the *New York Times* took its own rules in correcting violations and lapses when they occurred. My letter is quoted at length:

> This article in the *Times* sadly gives the impression that the reporter set out deliberately to do a one-sided story that would deny members of the Hindu-American community a chance to voice their substantive issues with the work of Doniger et al. There are reasons to suspect that Mr. Rothstein did this laudatory article as a 'favor' to his friends and business partners at the University of Chicago (UC).
>
> Many *Times* readers I have spoken to believe that several clauses from the *New York Times Manual on Ethical Journalism* have been compromised by Mr. Rothstein in writing this article about Ms Doniger.
>
> Clauses #140 and #141 of the *Times* Ethical Journalism Manual recognize that a writer's arrangement with a publisher (in effect a co-author) 'can be a breeding ground for favoritism, actual or perceived'. It advises staff members who have a publisher, or a movie contract, to 'be exceedingly sensitive to any appearance of bias in covering other publishers or studios' i.e. competing or opposed parties. Mr. Rothstein co-authored his most prominent book with Prof. Martin Marty, who besides being a close friend of Prof. Doniger at UC, is a partisan of hers in this controversy and has attacked Ms Doniger's critics publicly. (See: *http://www.beliefnet.com/story/128/story_12899_1.html*.)
>
> Mr. Rothstein's article adopts exactly the same approach (but a more fawning tone) that Mr. Marty used: i) Choosing to ignore that serious and substantive issues about Ms. Doniger's work have been raised, ii) characterizing her as a 'victim', iii) stereotyping her opponents as irrational 'fundamentalists', and iv) obscuring the issue by slanderously conflating the critics with unrelated political violence in India and protests in the UK.
>
> Ms. Doniger has been picked to be the successor to Mr. Marty—as head of the Martin Marty Center at the Divinity School at UC. Controversies regarding the quality of Ms Doniger's scholarship, if given credence and investigated are liable to detract from the prestige of the Center and

potentially could even tarnish Mr. Marty's legacy. But if the controversy can be reduced to Ms. Doniger playing the innocent victim of religious fanatics then this risk is substantially alleviated.

Did Mr. Rothstein allow his personal and commercial relationship with Mr. Marty to cloud his judgment, and did he consciously or unconsciously set out to disseminate Mr. Marty's 'circle the wagons' stance on this issue as a favor?

Rule 140 and 141 require that Times staff members who have any arrangement such as the above conflict of interest to disclose it to their supervisors, who may then require them to withdraw from the coverage of the parties involved.

The question for the Ombudsman is twofold: 1) Did Mr. Rothstein in addition to disclosing his relationship with Mr. Marty, *divulge Mr. Marty's active role as an interested party in the controversy to his editors* and 2) *the fact that he (Rothstein) planned essentially to echo many of Mr. Marty's stances in the pages of the Times?* If so, did the editor act in accord with the Times ethics rules in allowing him to proceed? Surely, as Ombudsman, you will grant that there is here at least the appearance of something improper that merits investigation.

Next, I raised the question of whether Rothstein followed rules regarding the ethical reporting of controversies. These rules require him to maintain a working relationship with *both sides* of any controversy. There are also strict rules about how socially engaged the journalist can be with the persons one reports on.

Mr. Rothstein has (at least overtly) chosen to rely on Ms. Doniger as his primary and only source for this article. He quotes from an interview with her, but has not chosen to interview Mr. Malhotra (whom he mentions by name), or Mr. Sankrant Sanu, whose analysis of biases in Ms. Doniger's articles on Hinduism led to its withdrawal by Microsoft Encarta, or any of the other prominent scholars involved.

Rules #22, #23, #24 and #28 of the Times Ethics Manual caution the staff that personal relationships with sources can erode into favoritism, in fact or appearance; even a weekly round of golf with a person being covered, or spending weekends or eating dinner with a person and not paying for it—i.e. being a part of certain social circles—could lead to errors of judgment in writing about its members. To quote Rule 22, **'Scrupulous practice requires that we step back and take a hard look at whether we have drifted too close** to sources we deal with regularly. *The acid test of freedom from favoritism is the ability to maintain good working relationships with all parties to a dispute.'*

[...]Many Times readers I have spoken to have the impression of coziness, given the tone of the story, and their mutual connection to Mr. Marty and UC pedigree. Furthermore, *neither Mr. Malhotra nor anyone else on the other side of the dispute were given even a chance of developing any working relationship with Mr. Rothstein.*

Rothstein flunks the *Times' acid test of freedom from favoritism* laid out in its Ethics Manual: he *does* have a good relationship with one side and *none* with the other.

Asymmetry of Power to Reward or Punish

I also raised another very significant issue for any minority dealing with powerful established institutions like the *New York Times* and University of Chicago: Was it fair to allow Rothstein to write this article given how much influence University of Chicago has on his career versus how little the Hindu minority can influence his future? The real test is whether Rothstein could have afforded to write *against* persons closely linked with University of Chicago.

One cannot but wonder if Rothstein would face adverse consequences if he had not mimicked the stance of other powerful Chicago old boys/girls like Marty, or had dared to question the quality of Doniger's work. On the other hand, since Hindu-Americans and the scholars who challenge Doniger are not part of his professional and social circle, he faces no career pressure from them. Recently the *UChicago Magazine* selected Rothstein out of the 133,155 living alumni of University of Chicago for a career-boosting endorsement in its pages, highlighting his talents and achievements. Would such endorsements be forthcoming for a reporter who seriously questioned the quality of scholarship coming out of that university? By contrast, there is little that the Hindu-American community can do to reward a writer from the *Times*. Perhaps this is why ethics clause 138 prohibits *Times* staff from accepting awards from those they cover. Therefore, I asked whether the *Times* could reasonably ensure that Rothstein was fair and objective given these circumstances.

My letter pointed out that in framing its ethics rules, the *Times* seems exquisitely sensitive to its staff misusing its pages to further personal agendas. But these rules lose their effectiveness if exceptions are made allowing certain reporters to cover up skeletons in the closet of their alma mater in exchange for the university giving them special recognition to boost their careers. This could partly be mitigated with public disclosure of all ties and by making sure that the opposing party in the controversy gets an equal say. But this was clearly not done in this case.

The *New York Times* Responds

After I failed to receive any response from the *Times* to my detailed letter,[50] I wrote an email to Mr. Okrent's office. I received a reply claiming that they had never received my letter. I then sent them proof from the US postal service's website that the letters had indeed been delivered to the *Times* offices and signed for by an employee. I asked them to investigate how such mail to important persons could be misplaced so easily. In addition, I re-sent my letter to them electronically, which the Public Editor's assistant promised would get read the same day by Mr. Okrent. Having jumped through these bureaucratic hoops, I was hopeful that the *Times* would look seriously into the many ethical issues I had raised. Here is the reply I got:

Dear Dr. Ramaswamy,

Thank you for your patience. I have now had the opportunity to look into the issues raised in your letter, and although I find one aspect of this article's presentation somewhat distressing, I see no violation of *Times* policy or of generally accepted journalistic ethics.

Mr. Rothstein has met Prof. Doniger, but their acquaintance is slight, and it is strictly professional. He does not have any kind of financial relationship with Martin Marty. They are not in any conventional sense 'co-authors'; the book that bears their names (and Herbert Muschamp's) is a collection of three speeches delivered at the New York Public Library and subsequently collected in one volume by the Oxford University Press.

What troubles me is *the Times* ongoing failure to make clear the distinctions between news stories and columns that bear the writer's opinion. I know the piece was assigned as a column, and in that context I find nothing objectionable about it. Additionally, although he is clearly sympathetic to one side in the dispute, Mr. Rothstein takes pains to present the position of the other side as well. But the heading on the piece ('Connections') is so vague as to be meaningless; the piece is typographically indistinct from news stories; and that most obvious signifier of opinion pieces—the first person singular—isn't there to help the reader along.

I continue to nag *the Times's* editors about this lack of clarity, and expect to be writing about it at some point in the next several weeks.

Yours sincerely,
Daniel Okrent
Public Editor

N.B. Any opinions expressed here, unless otherwise attributed, are strictly my own.

Thus, while addressing issues of whether Doniger and Rothstein know each other beyond the professional level, and whether Rothstein has a *direct* financial link to Martin Marty, the reply refuses to look into other, subtler forms of influence that I had highlighted—the University of Chicago's Old Boys' influence. It does not address whether Rothstein disclosed these links to his editor *before* filing the piece, or the fact that he essentially planned to echo Marty's reading of the situation. The *Times* Code of Ethics is well aware of the covert forms of influence on which America's Old Boys/Girls Network operates. But Mr. Okrent was not keen to investigate this angle. Apparently, the *Times'* Code of Ethics is rhetorical and superseded by other considerations. The reply also states preposterously that "Mr. Rothstein takes pains to present the position of the other side as well"—ignoring the fact that the other side never got to tell its story at all. The rest of the reply is about form rather than substance—the confusion between objective reporting and subjective commentary—while the issue of one-sided reporting about a related party is ignored. Also the manipulative use of the 30-year old photograph and the playing up of Doniger and her students as victims is completely ignored.

I had appealed that they needed to present the other side's story as well: "As Ombudsman, you have a responsibility to your readers to inquire into the above issues and publicly write about the results of your inquiries. And to take measures to rectify the harm that Mr. Rothstein's one-sided article has done to readers' understanding of an important issue to do with academic rigor, standards and quality at U Chicago." In effect, their reply was telling me to go find another forum for a discussion on real issues.

Other critics of Hinduphobia, even those within the academy, were also unable to find a forum in the mainstream press to discuss the issue. They were confined to doing this only within the minority press. What is remarkable is that while the mainstream media quickly transformed the issue into a racist and emotive one of 'scholars under savage attack', the minority press continued to print both sides in a more balanced way.

Chapter 28

University of Chicago Magazine: Obscuring the Issues

BY YVETTE C. ROSSER

In December 2004, the *University of Chicago Magazine* ran an article titled, 'The Interpretation of gods' that relied primarily on an interview with Wendy Doniger. The article featured several sordid tales alleging that numerous Hindus had, through the years, responded with open hostility to Doniger's analyses about their religious traditions. This magazine article investigated only one side of the story and emphasized only the sensational aspects.

The article briefly summarized the field, mentioning essays that have emerged in the past few years critiquing and deconstructing the perceived Hinduphobia in American academia. The journalist, Amy Braverman, begins: "Do leading religious scholars err in their analysis of Hindu texts?" She grabs the reader's attention with a journalistic hook that sets the tone for the rest of the story: "Wendy Doniger didn't see the egg fly past her head, but she heard it splatter against the wall behind her".[51]

This ovoid tale of Hindu horror has now become a standard cliché in the academic narrative of oft-repeated one-liners among Indologists and South Asianists. After describing 'the trickle of raw goop' running down the wall near the podium, and the quick exit of the 'man who'd thrown the ovoid missile', Braverman begins the story, as narrated by Doniger, that "During the post-talk discussion an Indian woman took the microphone and quietly read a series of questions that went, as Doniger recalls: 'From what psychoanalytic institution do you have your degree?'" When Doniger replied that she had "None", the lady from India asked, "Have you ever been psychoanalyzed?" When Doniger replied in the negative, another question came: "Then why do you think you have the right to psychoanalyze Hindu texts?"

Braverman presented Doniger's view without critical examination, though the University of Chicago prides itself in teaching students to think critically. If Braverman had been a trifle more independent, she may have had the temerity to ask Doniger if indeed she had ever been trained as a psychologist and undergone the hours of therapy required of a professional. But when the reply came back in the negative, Braverman's readers would realize that a Freudian approach to Indian Studies is no better than pop-psychology. Braverman doesn't ask these questions because the answers don't fit in with the assumptions laid out in her tale about professors of Hinduism Studies who are being attacked by fanatical Hindus.

Doniger has had seemingly little professional training in the use of psychoanalysis. Yet, as an amateur, she nonetheless not only applies such analytical techniques to her cultural subjects, but she also supervises graduate students – who are equally untrained—in applying these same tangential techniques. Moreover, the journalist does not ask the professor to offer any proof that the techniques she is using are verifiable and reliable, especially when applied to a culture that is not European. Instead, Braverman channels Doniger's annoyance when she parrots the observation that the questions from the Hindus in the audience, 'were questions that Doniger had heard before'—indicating that Doniger found the objections tiresome and repetitive, and therefore unworthy of serious attention.

The article positions Doniger's critics so that whatever they say is tainted beforehand. Braverman biases her liberal academic audience by referring to all of Doniger's critics as arch-conservatives. The generic terms 'liberal' and 'conservative' have very different meanings in the Indian context than their respective applications in America. In this particular case, the liberal/progressive and conservative/regressive labels are being thrown around without context, when in reality Doniger's critics consist of many diverse voices. She refers to them all as 'some conservative Hindus in India, the United States, and elsewhere'—a phrasing reminiscent of the former U.S. Secretary of Defense Donald Rumsfeld's airy certainty when he said Iraq's weapons of mass destruction were, 'east, west, south and north somewhat'.

This labeling prohibits understanding and prevents communication. These misapplied terms paint all Hindus as obscurantist, stuck in traditional modes and hypersensitive regarding their ancestral traditions. In actuality, the critics in the diaspora[52] work in some of America's finest scientific, technological, industrial, media, and medical institutions, and entrepreneurial establishments. They are successful intellectuals, technocrats, scientists, and business executives. The last thing one could say about them is that they are irrational, pre-modern or somehow frozen in their ideas. The Hinduism they practise is itself very eclectic, syncretistic, and dynamic, a living tradition, changing over time, and varied from one region of India to another. Hinduism is also adapting to America in a variety of ways—from adaptations by many millions of non-Indian Hindu Americans to various Indian-American acculturations. In fact, most Hindu-Americans who are actively contesting Doniger's representations consider themselves to be liberal-minded citizens. Doniger, through Braverman's pen, obscures the multi-facetedness of her Hindu-American critics. Writing for a liberal academic audience, Braverman easily colors the anticipated response by simplistically referring to Doniger's critics as a vast conspiracy of Hindu neo-cons.

Until very recently, most students of Hinduism in American classrooms were non-Hindus without the lived experience or a personal stake in the discourse. Today there are Hindu students in American classes who have access to competent knowledge from a wide variety of sources, not only family traditions. During the past four decades, the material and professional success of the Indian-American community has gradually brought a level of self-confidence that is now in a position to challenge inaccurate descriptions and exoticized depictions of Hindu traditions. Many faculty members find themselves unprepared to deal with this new reality. The *UChicago* article alludes to but ultimately fails to appreciate this dynamic evolution in the manner in which Hindus have protested, become organized, and raised questions—on their way to becoming involved American citizens.

In spite of her circuitous approach to the topic, Braverman pegs the argument when she states that Hindu-Americans have objected to the hegemonic use of Western constructs and categories to describe Indian culture. These concerned citizens feel that their valid perspectives are intentionally excluded from the narrative. Braverman quotes Hindu-Americans, who stress that there are multiple ways to teach religion. She refers to Malhotra's 2002 *RISA Lila-1* essay that 'in two years ...received more than 22,000 hits'. Noting the '445 online comments' she writes, "Most readers agreed with his conclusions," that:

Rights of individual scholars must be balanced against rights of cultures and communities they portray, especially minorities that often face intimidation. Scholars should criticize but not define another's religion.

Braverman falls short of acknowledging the concerns of Indian-Americans who see that their traditions are being misconstrued in untenable, manipulated interpretations. She does not examine the many detailed and well-reasoned arguments by scholars and intellectuals about these issues. Unfortunately, she turns a serious scholarly debate into something sensational and quite juicy, explaining that, "Other readers took their anger farther, calling for the scholars' resignations, sending hate mail, tossing eggs, or issuing death threats." At the lecture in London, when the egg splattered on the wall behind Doniger, the host William Dalrymple politicized the debate when, according to an observer, he publicly blamed 'an Indian political party for the egg toss'!

The same London source related that when Doniger resumed speaking, she also made a "humorous remark ... hinting that the cadres of that [Indian right-wing] movement were present".[53] Braverman picks up this thread, unquestioningly linking the concerns of Hindu-Americans in the USA to politics in India. Doniger's imagined conspiracy theory is given prominence. She describes the "adamant ... violent responses [that] parallel a political movement in India, where conservative Hindu nationalists have gained power". In the very next sentence, the article mentions Malhotra by name, journalistically linking him to those 'conservative Hindu nationalists'. Imagined politics displaces substantive arguments.

Braverman unknowingly exposes the overriding paradox that flavors the field when she explains that even though the 'academic targets' agree that many 'valid discussion points' have been raised and the message is accurate, these very same scholars won't listen because they argue that the "rhetoric taps into the rightward trend and attempts to silence unorthodox, especially Western, views". However, based on an analysis of the objections of Indians in the U.S., this narrow perspective is the opposite of their expressed positions. Hindu-Americans continue to focus on their efforts to include a Hindu approach to the study of Hinduism, *along* with the existing 'unorthodox ... Western views'. Ironically, most Western approaches, far from being 'unorthodox' as claimed by Doniger, actually tap into Eurocentric orthodoxy, rejecting and marginalizing indigenous approaches. Indian-Americans contend that an Indic approach to Indian Studies is at least

382 INVADING THE SACRED

equally valid and certainly more authentic and less prone to quirkiness than experimental, post-modern, or psychoanalytical methodologies.

As an example of this alleged attempt to 'silence unorthodox' views, Braverman cites the essay, 'Wendy's Child Syndrome', summarizing correctly that it critiques 'the eroticization of Hinduism'. In the objective academic world, that is, in the halls outside RISA's lila, finding faults with scholars in the mainstream establishment by questioning their work does not amount to 'silencing' them. Indeed, establishment stories dominate, and it is the dissenting critics who are rarely given a voice.

Doniger misdirects the readers, alluding to the imagined Hindu puritan, she states that her critics 'think sexuality is a shameful thing [and therefore] it's embarrassing for them to have the texts . . . discussed.' Courtright also used this decoy in the *Washington Post* in order to distract attention from the troubling questions about the quality of his scholarship. Indeed, multiple commentators have written innumerable times that Hinduism's open-mindedness on sexuality is liberal when compared with Medieval, Victorian, or even 1950s' mores. Hindu images and icons were millennia ahead of their time, in contrast with the prudishness and patriarchal male dominance in Abrahamic religions.[54]

Braverman basically restates Doniger's defense for choosing the sexual meanings. Naturally, this laudatory article does not discuss criticisms of inaccuracy in Doniger's Sanskrit translations (noted in section I of this volume). Doniger explains the obvious:

> A Sanskrit word can have ten different meanings. A translator must choose, based on her knowledge of the context. Choosing the sexual meaning [...] is not incorrect if that is one of the attested meanings. It's a matter of, 'Did the author mean that?' You can make a judgment, and another person can argue and say you chose the wrong meaning.

However, the right to make judgments is seemingly only vested in and vetted by those certified by Western academia. A few influential Western scholars are able to select their favorite meanings among the wide range available, and if the quality of peer-review is not rigorous, and the field is not open to criticism from outside, then virtually everything is a consensus of opinions within a closed network of scholars. In this scholarly environment, new and bizarre meanings, often at great variation with the source traditions, become the standard. Sanskrit concepts and phrases are subjected to reductionist dilution—

exactly the opposite of the principle that post-colonialism and critical theories espouse.

For example, Hindu practitioners and scholars have complained that *jati* and *varna* are words that are being collapsed into 'caste', a European category that fails to convey the fluidity and flexibility in *jati* and *varna*. Hindu intellectuals—or 'elites' as they are often derisively called—get condemned for trying to deepen the discussions by pointing out more complex, nuanced meanings, whereas, through this dynamic process, they are actually engaging in constructive theology, and being part of a living tradition.

Many Hindu-Americans have come to realize that sometimes Hindu traditions are (intentionally or unintentionally) misconstrued by certain Western scholars. There is an overriding concern that this bias could in fact damage the self-image of American children of Hindu descent. There have been several studies and much written about the negative influence on the identity formation of Hindu-American teenagers who study sensationalized representations about their heritage in Social Studies classes in American high schools. See for example, an article written by Trisha Pasricha, a 15 year-old girl from Houston, 'The Abuse Hinduism Receives In US Schools Is Intolerable'.[55] There have been several studies that confirm the assessment that Hinduism Studies, as presented in mainstream academia, is exoticized and essentialized such as 'Stereotypes in Schooling: Negative Pressures in the American Educational System on Hindu Identity Formation'.[56] There is serious concern that Hindu-American youths are negatively impacted by misrepresentations about their religious traditions.[57]

Now that Hindu-Americans have come of age, many have vowed that, on their watch, the remnants of the academic biases they have lived with for a generation, will be washed away. These citizens refuse to sit by as their religious beliefs are ravaged through the decades, using alien categories with predetermined trajectories. As this book indicates, change is on the horizon. Unfortunately, many mainstream scholars studiously refuse to reflect on the impact of their work or acknowledge the legitimate concerns of Hindu-Americans such as Trisha Pasricha in Houston or Nina Appareddy in Chattanooga.

Threatening Innocent White Victims

Without verification, Braverman passes on the rumor that all the critiques come from persons linked to violence associated with a particular Hindu nationalist political movement in India. True to form, she sensationalizes not only stories about the Gods of Hinduism, but also the dangers faced by professors of Hinduism, reminding her audience that Paul Courtright has 'faced harsher threats' from supposedly dangerous and sinister groups such as the Hindu Students Council and their Hindu-American parents. She seems disconnected from the fact that in their individual capacities these Hindu-Americans are extolled as the 'model minority'. Yet their culture and identity is demonized by academic authorities based on their supposed nefarious social or political associations. A similar denigration and demonology of Jews would be called anti-Semitism and if aimed at Muslims would be described as Islamophobia.

Braverman mentions an important aspect which Courtright has stressed repeatedly, that his book on Ganesha 'received little attention outside academia when it was first published in 1985'. Courtright and others have offered this as evidence of a coordinated 'attack', that for almost twenty years no one from the Hindu-American community objected to the book's contents. However, they fail to mention that the book's 2001 edition had recently come out in India, sparking new interest. It was far from being a dormant tome. Nor does she mention the slow percolation of the book's fanciful conclusions based on amateur psychoanalysis into mainstream America through museums and other venues. Importantly, during previous decades, there were fewer Hindus in US classrooms and certainly a paucity of Hindu organizations, and therefore nobody willing to talk back.

Braverman defends Courtright's use of psychoanalysis, without mentioning his lack of qualifications in the field, or the basic Eurocentric orientation of Freud's ideas. Instead, she reverts to references to the BJP, a political party in India, discussing how "Courtright received hate mail, including some threats." She tries to pinpoint Malhotra as the ultimate source of all such so-called attacks. For instance, Courtright tells Braverman that 'recently on Malhotra's radar screen' is a book by another graduate of the University of Chicago.[58] (See chapter 8 for a discussion on that book.)

Comparisons to Academic Scholarship on Christianity

Braverman tries to downplay the extensive harm *Kali's Child* causes in the Hindu community, by mentioning that scholars also use similar devices to uncover homoerotic inferences in the Bible. In the context of reinterpreting classic texts to tease out hidden homoerotic meanings, she mentions a book by another University of Chicago professor, Theodore W. Jennings,[59] *The Man Jesus Loved: Homoerotic Narratives from the New Testament*. Jennings' book was published in May 2003 and by June of that same year the president of the Chicago Theological Seminary issued an official notice defending the professor's right to write such a controversial book.[60] Since Ramakrishna is often compared to Jesus as a spiritual figure, at least the comparison is appropriate when contrasting the respective responses from Hindus and Christians.

Some of the criticism of Jennings' book is similar to that offered to Kripal, concerning the extrapolation of arbitrarily selected erotic elements and the use of radical hermeneutics. In July 2004, R. Albert Mohler, Jr. wrote a critique on a Baptist website, asserting that what

> Jennings proposes is a radical re-reading of the New Testament material in order to claim Jesus, not only as a proponent of the homosexual movement, but as a man involved in homoerotic relationships. He intends to appropriate the Bible for a 'gay-positive perspective.'[61]

Mohler continues:

> Those unfamiliar with the bizarre science of liberal theology and modern biblical studies may be unfamiliar with the way [...] they look for hidden 'strategies' by which the text can be read to mean the opposite of what it clearly states.

He then quotes Jennings' description of this alternative methodology:

> The task of a gay reading thus entails a multiple strategy of interconnected readings of texts [that attends] to the distinction between and relations among these strategies, we become better acquainted with the biblical text itself as well as with the varied aspects of liberationists readings generally.

Mohler jests, "If that sentence makes clear sense to you, you probably need counseling." He calls it the "pattern of convoluted argument and excessive verbosity [that] is characteristic of postmodern biblical interpretation." He concludes, "Those who apply these methodologies are not seeking to understand the text itself, but are determined to read their own interpretations into the texts in order to use the text for their own purposes."

The criticisms of Jennings' homoerotic interpretations of Jesus parallel similar critiques of Kripal's homoerotic interpretations of

Ramakrishna. But Braverman fails to point out the big difference between the impact of the works of Jennings and Kripal. Jennings' readers are intimately familiar with the stories in the New Testament beforehand, so his theories float around like funny fireflies that don't fundamentally challenge what is already well known. His novel ideas concerning Jesus' homosexuality just add alluring color—they are certainly not taken as irreducible *fact*.

On the other hand, Kripal's American readers come to the story of Ramakrishna's life without any background, either historical or cultural. Therefore, *Kali's Child* becomes the normative view of Ramakrishna as a conflicted and neurotic gay man, whereas Jesus is seen as queer only by a few overzealous homosexuals. Jennings' thesis is a constructive strategy for gays to validate themselves in a homophobic society rather than a challenge to the authenticity of Jesus' religious visions or of Christianity itself. Jesus' visions of divinity and his claim to speak for God are not psycho-pathologized as being the outcome of conflicted homosexuality. For Kripal, however, his precise claim is that without Ramakrishna's psychopathologies, there would have been no Paramahansa and no Ramakrishna-led revival of Hinduism.

Another key difference is that Mohler is backed by a formidable battalion of Biblical theologians who are ready, willing, and able to counteract one-sided and fanciful depictions the very moment such depictions come out. They comprise the Christian 'home team' of insiders in the establishment, with their own academic journals, PhD granting institutions, scholarly conferences, funding mechanisms, media connections, and even deep links to the US government. On the other hand, Hinduism simply lacks comparable institutional mechanisms and champions in the intellectual establishment.

This is why Jennings' eccentric Biblical interpretation was not referenced in Encyclopedia Britannica as the top choice for learning about Jesus, while Kripal's book got listed as a top reference choice on Ramakrishna! *The Man Jesus Loved: Homoerotic Narratives from the New Testament* is not seen as authoritative, and is certainly never used to teach Christianity, at universities in India, China, or other places where Christianity is a minority religion. On the other hand, because most Americans know very little about the nineteenth century saint or about Bengali culture, or even about Hinduism, Kripal's book and his fantasized eroticization of Ramakrishna's life become the accepted authority.

Additionally, Jennings is a Methodist, so even though he used far-out hermeneutics to tease out his pet thesis, he writes from the perspective and sympathy of an insider. He does not blame American brutalities on Jesus, for instance, in the same manner as Wendy's Children expand their psychoanalysis of Hindu texts to demonize Hindu culture at large. Braverman acknowledges that most academic scholars of Hinduism come from outside the faith but does not contrast this to the insider's approach to Christianity.

Braverman's article continues:

> [Malhotra has] begun to research 'Whiteness Studies,' which analyzes the 'anthropology of white culture and uncovers their myths . . . [He wrote] 'I am researching issues such as white culture's Biblical based homophobia, deeply ingrained guilt of sex (Garden of Eden episode) and condemnation of the body . . . I posit that many white scholars are driven into Hinduism studies by their own private voyeurism or fantasies, or an attempted escape from white culture's restrictions. This is what I earlier called *Wendy's Child Syndrome* because my sample was a few of Doniger's students. But now the sample is much larger . . . '

Eventually, the article returns to Doniger. Braverman writes that in September 2002,

> Sankrant Sanu, a former Microsoft manager and freelance writer, argued in a Sulekha.com essay that Microsoft's online Encarta encyclopedia article on Hinduism – written by Doniger—put forth 'a distinctively negative portrayal of Hinduism,' especially when compared to the entries on Christianity, Judaism, and Islam. Sanu recommended that someone 'emic' to the community rewrite the Hinduism entry, as had been the case for the other religions.

Based on Sanu's critical analysis (which is reproduced in chapter 16), "Microsoft obliged, exchanging Doniger's essay with one by Arvind Sharma, a McGill University professor of comparative religion". Mercifully, Braverman does not give credence to Doniger's opportunistic charge of being ousted because of racism. On the emic v/s etic debate, Braverman quotes Arvind Sharma:

> [T]he debate has shades of gray. Both the insider and the outsider see the truth [...] but genuine understanding may be said to arise at the point of their intersection. At this intersection one realizes that the Shivalinga (the icon of the god Shiva) is considered a phallic symbol by outsiders but rarely by Hindus themselves, or that the Eucharist looks like a cannibalistic ritual to outsiders but not to Christians. [...] If insiders and outsiders remain insulated they

develop illusions of intellectual sovereignty. Each is required to call the other's bluff.

However, moving immediately from Arvind Sharma's careful explanation, she writes: "Some scholars say [...] there's a fine line, between legitimate Hindu concerns and the right-wing political wave". This simplistic statement captures the very heart of the strategic framing to turn Doniger's critics into demons. Legitimate Hindu concerns, such as those articulated by Sharma, are erroneously conflated with right-wing fundamentalists who must be ignored and/or controlled, and with heinous crimes against humanity.

Ironically, a Freudian analysis would reveal that Braverman's choice of verbs shows her biases. Her perception that academic challenges from the Hindu-American community are a form of aggression rather than debate shows through when she writes that scholars have *scuffled* with Hindu-American critics. This is a manifestation of precisely the kind of reductionism that the University of Chicago proudly claims to have taught its students to avoid! It is a Chicago style of George Bushism that forces everyone into two camps where the other side is always wrong.

Why can't the scholars accept the fact that there *are* critics who are not right-wingers or fundamentalists? There are articulate Hindu intellectuals who have legitimate grounds on which to complain. Why do so many RISA-related scholars describe these critics as terrorists? After all, many Muslims complain about Islamophobia and are not attacked as Islamic fundamentalists by the scholars in Departments of Middle Eastern Studies. Why are mainstream scholars forcing every Hindu to remain silent in the face of Hinduphobia or else get attacked as a right-winger? The academicians cannot see the criticisms by practising Hindus as free from contemporary politics of India. They have not considered that most of the Hindus involved with the effort to engage scholars and correct textbooks are American-born with American citizenship; hence their political stakes are in the USA and not in India.

Braverman closes the article with an interview with Vijay Prashad, who seems eager to lend his 'Brown folk' legitimacy to defend Doniger. Since a *Washington Post* article was criticized for not revealing Prashad's radical political affiliations, much less his lack of expertise in Hindu matters, Braverman covers this base. She informs her readers that Prashad is 'a self-described Marxist who studied history and anthropology, not religious studies, at Chicago'. However, beyond this,

Braverman fails to question Prashad's unsubstantiated claim that because of academic insularity, "The oxygen in public opinion is being sucked (*sic*) by people like Rajiv. He's the only one pressing so hard. He uses that silence to say that people are arrogant and they don't have any answers." This statement that Malhotra is 'the *only* one pressing' is more aptly a comment on Prashad's own insularity—as the articles in this book demonstrate, the voices of protest are many and diverse. Moreover, as section III shows, the academy has responded to criticism *not* with silence but with powerfully mobilized attempts to demonize its opponents.

Prashad also disingenuously accuses Malhotra of promoting 'the idea that there is one Indic thought'. Prashad and Malhotra had a prior lively online debate in which these and many similar topics were extensively covered by both sides. Prashad not only deflects away from the archive of that debate which is available online[62] but he deliberately misrepresents its substance. Hinduism's great strength is its *internal* diversity. Malhotra sees this as the result of 'not being held in bondage by any One Prophet or One Canon or One Historically Unique Event'. Prashad seems to make up a straw man as an opponent to suit himself. This accusation of imagined homogeneity/conformity is constantly lobbed at Malhotra and many other Hindu-Americans, in order to neutralize their effectiveness by assigning nasty right-wing epithets.

When questioned, Malhotra explained that he "celebrates the multifaceted qualities of Hinduism, and does not promote any one section of Hindu scriptures over another". He pointed out that the Infinity Foundation has "facilitated serious works on a wide diversity of research themes and on various interpretations of Hinduism", including ideologies of 'Hindu Left,' 'Hindu Feminist' and so forth. His own position has often been described as that of a 'non-Hindutva Hindu'. Prashad knows this well because it was discussed in their online debate. Sadly, Braverman fails to research this debate or Malhotra's stances, nor is she adequately skeptical of Prashad's sweeping claims.

Prashad also posits that, 'the current protests derive from ... a Victorian sense of decorum' and the Hindu right's 'protofascist views'. Prashad's wild and woolly views of Hinduism must be taken with a grain of salt. For example, in his pamphlet *'Suburban Whites And Pogroms In India,'*[63] **Prashad attacks Deepak Chopra and the Dalai Lama for promoting Indic forms of spirituality and accuses suburban American Whites who have embraced Hindu practices like yoga of contributing to genocide in India!** A similar cultural shortsightedness and one-pointed agenda can be seen in his article, 'How the Hindus Became Jews: American Racism after 9/11'. But none of this is relevant to the issues at hand and it is brought in merely to sensationalize a 'dangerous frontier' filled with 'savages'.

Having painted her opponents as 'homogenizers', Braverman contrasts this with Doniger for whom, 'it's a matter of considering multiple explanations'. However, Hindus also experience Hinduism as multihued, honoring many kinds of practitioners with many histories, many teachings, many rituals, many esoteric practices, and beyond.

Devaluing the Hindus in the Debate

The *UChicago Magazine* article draws to an end with yet another warning about dangerous Hindu activists. Hindu-Americans are agitating against Western scholars, claims Doniger, because they think that the scholars 'have pushed out Indian views the same way Coca-Cola has pushed out Indian products'. Her use of this analogy is either heartless or simply uninformed. There is a broad-based movement in India from the left and the right that is very concerned about the severe damage that Coca-Cola factories are doing to the environment and the water table.[64] By using this metaphor, Doniger has unknowingly evoked a telling comparison between the devastation of Hinduism by the use of Freudian theories by powerful multinational social sciences and the devastation of India's environment by powerful multinationals like Coca-Cola. She then tries to invalidate her critics, arguing that it is 'a false model to juxtapose intellectual goods with economic ones', even though she herself created the analogy.

Braverman again ominously refers to communal tensions in India: "Though such violence hasn't occurred in the United States, Western scholars have felt the effects of India's new politics". Once again, this article cleverly uses images to muzzle critics by branding middle-class, middle-of-the-road American citizens of Indian descent as dangerous.

The article finishes with an ironic twist, invoking the colonial legacy's acquisition of antiquities by describing Doniger's private Indian art collection with its 'colorful tapestries, bronze sculptures including dozens of Ganeshas, and paintings [that] adorn every surface'. Doniger is shown in a photograph surrounded by Indian artifacts, proud of her appropriations like a socialite at a party of antiquities, saying, "A lot of these things you couldn't buy in India now." Since she obtained them in the 1960s, they are today 'protected from exportation'. This Freudian slip points to the abuse of power by some Westerners. Doniger brags about owning rare Indian art whose looting and smuggling out of India is now illegal. Native American artifacts decorate America's museums after the people were virtually exterminated. Colonialists often glorified native people's exotic antiquities while facilitating their cultural genocide—proud to 'own' a piece of that primitive tradition to ornamentalize their homes.

'... but in all the shouting, no one's listening' [65]

The February 2005 issue of the *University of Chicago Magazine* printed seven letters to the editor in response to Braverman's article about Doniger. The magazine received 'scores of letters' and printed a 'representative sampling'. The first letter printed is from Rajiv Malhotra and begins by pointing out that the "blind spot in [the article] and in Wendy Doniger's camp is that they give no consideration to education's ethical consequences". Malhotra wrote:

> The propagation of caste, cows, and curry stereotypes of India is a disservice to Chicago's students, many of whom will hold globalized careers. The times demand a radical departure from the prejudiced constructions and dubious scholarship peddled by segments of the old guard of the American intellectual establishment and transmitted through a Eurocentric core curriculum.

> Arriving at more accurate, balanced representations of Indian culture requires the participation of non-career intellectuals, not bound by academic cronyism or prepackaged 'theories' by which Chicago's PhD factory churns out India 'experts'. Academicians should dialogue with public intellectuals like me, rather than caricaturing us as political 'activists' and psychoanalyzing us as native informants under the white gaze.

> Reversing the gaze—allowing the Indian gazer to anthropologize and psychoanalyze the dominant white culture—is a prerequisite to the honest intellectual debate evaded by Doniger and her ilk. Unfortunately, the article re-reverses the gaze upon the dissenters personally. The whole affair is choreographed as a violent conspiracy in which Doniger plays the innocent victim. Are Doniger and Braverman subconsciously applying the doctrine of *Manifest Destiny* in which white supremacy was legitimized by framing others as violent, irrational, and unfit to self-govern?

The article's credibility is also compromised by lumping together unrelated Indian political antics with legitimate intellectual challenges from the Hindu American minority. Political correctness has superseded journalistic rigor.

I introduced Braverman to 30 knowledgeable scholars, many of whom e-mailed their views to her and expressed willingness to be interviewed. She ignored almost all of them. Instead, Vijay Prashad, who does not claim to be a Religious Studies scholar or a spokesman for practicing Hindus, is used as a loyal proxy for the establishment. Prashad scored political brownie points by demonizing me, although my dissent is against the very imperialistic system he frequently attacks to prop up his own brand value as a Marxist.

Will the incumbents in control of institutionalized discourse on India respect the challengers' intellectual freedom, including the right to a Gandhian satyagraha (campaign for truth)? Or will their teachings produce more Abu Ghraibs?

The second letter was from Prof. Volney P. Gay,[66] who received an MA and PhD from University of Chicago. As the Director of the Center for the Study of Religion and Culture at Vanderbilt University, he wrote authoritatively. He agreed in part with the objections of the Hindu-American community, but he was also protective of the privileges of academic Religious Studies. He wrote:

At the end of Rajiv Malhotra's lengthy criticism of Wendy Doniger's studies of Hindu texts, he writes: 'Rights of individual scholars must be balanced against rights of cultures and communities they portray, especially minorities that often face intimidation. Scholars should criticize but not define another's religion.' If this means that slander is wrong and colonialism is pernicious, who could disagree?

Prof. Gay adds, misinterpreting Malhotra's position, "Yet, if this means, as I read him, that scholars should contort their readings of sacred texts to honor the opinions of traditionalists, I must dissent." Gay explains that the "university's role . . . is to refuse rights of censorship to any group, native or nonnative, elite or nonelite." However, he adds, "This does not shield Doniger or any of us from criticism; many of Malhotra's complaints about biases and errors in Western scholarship are worthy of sustained dialogue." But he insists, "scholars should challenge the 'rights' of the group, which always means the power elites, to control what counts as valid."

Gay writes: "Humanities professors should respect the lives, meanings, and values of those whom we study and whose sacred texts we read". But he warns that "respecting a tradition does not mean we should grant to its leaders additional rights." Gay makes the point that "Traditions are always in danger of redefinition from within and without." But why is this seen as a *danger*? This is odd coming from a professor of Religious Studies, where historically there has been a significant focus on applied, interactive and progressive theology. Hindus feel they have the right to define/redefine their religion, whereas many of the scholars denounce them for attempting what other faiths have been doing all along. Christians have been redefining their religion for 2,000 years, using constructive theology. For thousands of years, Hindus have also experienced the same evolution of their faith, until it was frozen into Western tomes.

Gay writes: "Doniger may be wrong some of the time, all of the time, or never (which seems unlikely) . . . [but] the place to assess her work is in the academy, not polemical billboards or web pages". This sleight of hand automatically denies a voice to those who the academic establishment chooses to exclude.

The third letter to the editor was from a man in Los Angeles who received his undergraduate degree from Chicago in 1973. He compares the "narrow and pretentious outpourings of Doniger, Kripal, et al [as] not a little strained and frivolous to anyone with a mite of spiritual sensibility". Admonishing his alma mater, he writes: "Please, Chicago, recruit scholars of grander vision than these!"

The author of this letter, Karl Gores Whitmarsh, adds a caveat that "Doniger's bullying detractors show a similar smallness of mind." He sees that there is now a "shouting match [where] each side digs in its heels, mired in its own self-righteousness—*but in all the shouting, no one's listening.*" He warns the scholars not to "dismiss Malhotra and his ilk too quickly. Their tactics may be mean-spirited, but their outrage is genuine." In concluding, he writes: "Let the University do its part to bring clarity to this academic fog". Then pinpointing the main issue of closed-mindedness he concludes: "It's high time the University recruited scholars to its fold who really do see both sides of this issue."

The fourth letter to the editor, written by Prof. Antonio de Nicolas, was titled, 'Academic Arrogance?' He wrote in support of Malhotra that:

> The real fight is that the [study of religion at Chicago] is deeply immersed in social-science methodologies which do not provide

legitimate interpretations of classical Indic texts dealing with religious experience.

He continued:

While Christian traditions argue theology based mostly on the 'rational' faculty, this is not the faculty Indic texts use, or even acknowledge as a faculty, but accept only as one of the senses, an instrument of translation of experience, of re-gathering of habits. Indic texts (Sruti) are from 'experience', not theory. Where do we find in the works of your Chicago heroes the categories that lead to the type of experience Indic texts lead to, point to, or come from?

Antonio de Nicolas has vast experience in philosophy, religion and mysticism. With these credentials, he expressed his criticism of the methodology:

The story of the decapitation of Ganesha is not the Oedipal theme but an invented story carelessly linked to Oedipus and Ganesha, *because the methodology used allows for this kind of arbitrariness* [Added Emphasis]. The Chicago school of interpretation that is trying to decapitate Ganesha and the memories of a culture is the same one that had already done so with Plato, and with this decapitation our access to memory in our own Western culture.

He criticized the demonization of the Hindu diaspora and finds 'conspiracy suggestions about Rajiv Malhotra' in the article 'distasteful'. Then, de Nicolas asks, "Does he not try to correct an injustice done to his people and religion the way you would protect your own people?" He concludes his letter with the same ironic twist described above:

It is an ironic ending of the article that while Doniger utilized her visits to India to accumulate wealth through antiques expropriated from there, Malhotra uses his own wealth to correct her page.

The fifth letter to the editor was from Prof. Ramdas Lamb, who teaches Religious Studies at the University of Hawaii at Manoa. Prof. Lamb writes that the article "seems to suggest a simplistically bifurcated way of viewing Hinduism: that of the objective scholar and that of the narrow-minded, conservative Hindu". He asks: "Is it really so clearly defined? What happened to the critical thinking one would expect in a University of Chicago publication?" He acknowledges, "Wendy Doniger is a respected, astute, and well-known scholar, and she has a right to her views. The other academics mentioned do as well". But he states, however: "At the same time, no academic's work should be off-limits to critique". Lamb argues that this is especially true

> When one assumes that clearly questionable and often discredited methodological tools such as those of Freud can be used unequivocally to deconstruct and analyze the cultural beliefs and practices of others, while rejecting indigenous understanding and interpretation, is this not a form of intellectual colonialism?

He wonders if 'Braverman has read Michel Foucault,' and states:

> Even Louis Dumont acknowledged that as scholars, we 'must learn from the people themselves which modes of thinking we have the right to apply [to them] and which we should reject'.

He ends his letter profoundly critical of the article:

> Scholars and practitioners are not inherently distinct groupings, and there are many of us who coexist in both realms. There is much in the approach and understanding of each that can further and enhance the other. Unfortunately, Braverman's article will do more to hamper than promote that process.

The next two letters both appear under the title, 'Forget Freud, Deep-six Marx'. The first letter from Rex J. Styzens thanked the magazine for the article about "objections to non-Hindu psychoanalytic interpretations of Hindu scripture". Though Styzens objects "to most psychoanalytic interpretation of literature ... as reduction by an immature hermeneutic," he admits that "The issues in the present case are complex ... In any case ... psychobabble ... exploits the vocabulary of diagnosis". He stresses that the vocabulary of psychoanalysis is only justified "preliminary to a program of therapy. In the absence of therapy, it is jargon".

Thomas Murray, a 1987 University of Chicago graduate, wondered "why so many of the professors of the great universities of our country are still so enamored by the bankrupt ideologies of Freud and Marx". He continues:

> Using these to interpret and explain complex religions like Hinduism is really not very useful. I would suggest that using the knowledge from comparative mythology that scholars like Joseph Campbell and Carl Jung have given us would be much more helpful in understanding the metaphor of the world's mythology and religions. From this understanding, we might realize the essential unity of the human condition and that all paths lead to the same mountaintop.

The final letter to the editor was sent from Tista Bagchi, a resident of New Delhi who received her PhD from the University of Chicago in 1993. She wrote:

> I am . . . extremely disturbed by the hegemonic attitude to Hinduism studies on the part of University of Chicago scholars I myself have publicly gone on record in India against the excesses of the Hindu right (in my country and abroad), and during my years as a graduate student at Chicago I took particular pleasure in tearing up and throwing away the optional religious affiliation form, given my mixed atheist, Hindu, Brahmo, and Unitarian upbringing and refusal to be pigeonholed as a 'Hindu'. During my student years at Chicago and much more recently during a visit to the University in June 2004, however, I experienced both humiliation and substantive discrimination directed quite obviously at my ethnicity and gender, mitigated only by the unexpectedly warm support of individual faculty members who have themselves been marginalized within the University in significant ways. Not all of the reactive animosity toward these scholars of Hinduism can, therefore, be ascribed to the excesses of Hindu fundamentalism.

As can be seen from the writings in this volume, and confirmed by Tista Bagchi's experiences, Hinduphobia is not an illusion. This discussion of the *UChicago Magazine* article and the subsequent chapters in this section investigate the manner in which the mainstream media simplistically and erroneously characterizes this vitally important ongoing cultural interaction as a clash between urbane, objective scholars and savage fundamentalists. It is hoped that analyses such as these will change that prevalent paradigm.

Chapter 29

The Diaspora Press: *India Abroad* Encourages Debate

By Krishnan Ramaswamy

Unlike the mainstream American press, the Indian diaspora press covered the controversy with restraint and balance, by and large avoiding sensationalism. On November 28, 2003, Prof. Ramesh Rao[67] published 'Hindu God, Must Indeed Be Heathen' in the Indian-American newspaper, *India Abroad*. Rao addressed the very important issue of the asymmetries of power between the behemoth of Western academia and the minority Hindu-American community. Rao focused on the Courtright controversy as an example of how a culturally in arrogant and elitist academic establishment not only facilitates insensitive and inaccurate work on Hinduism but also throws up road-blocks by bringing in tangential and sensationalized matters.[68]

In contrast to the way the *Post*, the *Times* and *UChicago Magazine* handled the issue, *India Abroad* also published, **on the same day as Rao's article**, an even longer (1700 words as opposed to Rao's 1400 words) interview with Paul Courtright to give his side of the story. Courtright uses the interview to claim that he never meant to cause hurt. The substantive issues raised by Rao are not addressed, nor does Courtright provide a point-by-point justification of the many errors and misrepresentations in his book. Nevertheless, he is offered a forum to air his views and to let the readers decide for themselves[69]—an opportunity denied by the American mainstream press to critics of the academy.

The framing of the issues and the players is also very different in *India Abroad* when compared to the *Times* or the *Post*. While those papers portrayed Malhotra, Sanu and others as 'conservative' or 'radical' or 'right-wing' Hindus, *India Abroad* avoids a similar pejorative characterization of anyone on either side. While the mainstream press insinuated guilt-by-association by linking diaspora intellectuals with forces of religious intolerance, *India Abroad* avoided linking Courtright to the activities of the Christian right or of missionary organizations that routinely denigrate Hinduism. Unlike the mainstream press, the article is not entitled 'Scholar attacks Hinduism', but rather with a quote from Courtright expressing his pain at being 'misunderstood': "I am distressed that anyone found my discussion of Ganesha offensive".

The reporter for *India Abroad*, Tanmaya Kumar Nanda, goes out of his way to portray Courtright in a sympathetic light as opposed to sensationalizing his motives and the deleterious impact of his work (which was how critics of the academy were treated by the mainstream press). This is how Courtright is characterized in the opening lines of Nanda's interview:

> Professor Paul B. Courtright, interim chairperson (2003–2004) of the Department of Religion at Emory University in Atlanta, Georgia, is an Indophile, who loves India. He calls it the 'most hospitable place in the world.' [...] The controversy has not fazed Courtright, who maintains he has the highest regard for Indian and Hindu culture.

In spite of the sympathetic treatment accorded to Courtright, the key issues do come through in the pages of *India Abroad*. Rao's and Courtright's articles are a study in contrast. Rao focused on real issues, such as the primacy and the limits of free speech in the academic setting, the need for cultural sensitivity, paucities in academic training and standards, and the percolation of religious prejudice and cultural hatred from the academic to mainstream settings. Courtright, by contrast, gave an emotionally charged interview in which he repeatedly presented himself as a bewildered victim, professed his love for India, and accused his opponents of never having read his book. He even claimed that he could not understand what in his book could possibly have caused offense! While he indirectly expressed regret for the hurt it caused, he took no responsibility for the glaring errors in the book, or for his lack of training in psychoanalysis, or for the use of his book by other institutions to perpetuate Hinduphobia.

Rao, as a professor of Media Studies, wrote that "Academic freedom and free speech rights are vigorously . . . vociferously defended in the

US", but at the same time he also pointed out the responsibility implied in that privilege:

> Courtright seems to have ignored what his peers in the American Association of University Professors [AAUP] recommend about the pursuit of free inquiry: 'College and university teachers are citizens, members of a learned profession, and officers of an educational institution. When they speak or write as citizens, they should be free from institutional censorship or discipline, but their special position in the community imposes special obligations. As scholars and educational officers, they should remember that the public may judge their profession and their institution by their utterances. Hence they should at all times be accurate, should exercise appropriate restraint, should show respect for the opinions of others, and should make every effort to indicate that they are not speaking for the institution.[70]

Rao noted that these injunctions of accuracy and restraint "become even more important when scholars write about other people's beliefs and life experiences". He wondered whether Courtright 'had accurately analyzed the various Ganesha myths and stories' and if he had found any traditional text that contained anything close to his interpretation. Nanda asked a similar question of Courtright, to which Courtright could not or would not provide a direct answer other than to claim that he was justified in making up Freudian interpretations willy-nilly simply because Hindu tradition in general "has drawn upon the human body, including its sexual dimensions, as contexts for religious reflection and understanding". While conceding that these traditional Hindu insights had deep value—"These understandings are profound and instructive for us all"—Courtright does not directly illuminate why he undervalues and obscures these traditional insights in preference to Eurocentric methods like applied psychoanalysis.[71]

Perhaps the answer is contained in his response to Nanda's question about what started him on the path of Freudian analysis. **Courtright claimed that he was *culturally constrained* to use Freudian Psychoanalysis, because it was expected of him by the Western academic establishment.** This peer-pressure to conform to the dictations and cultural expectations of a Eurocentric establishment is a revealing if inadvertent admission, but unfortunately neither Courtright nor the interviewer explored the implications further. Moreover, Courtright also claimed that Ganesha's stories are themselves suggestive of Freudian themes—and that his untrained and culturally constrained speculations should nevertheless be treated as deep 'insights':

My use of psychoanalytic insights emerged from the Ganesha stories. [...] No responsible scholar, writing in the West for an audience well-acquainted with psychoanalytic methods and insights, could [afford to] not engage the issues of Ganesha's story as offering an opportunity to reflect on the deeper, and often hidden, dimensions of human relations.[72]

Rao had a more forthright assessment, observing that Courtright had "transgressed the boundary of 'ethical' and 'responsible' inquiry". He pointed out that Courtright is not a trained psychologist and that he "does not provide a single piece of evidence to show that his analysis has either a traditional/historical/factual basis or whether it can be corroborated by any social scientific methods".

Courtright tried to downplay the percolation of such distorted understandings of Hindu deities into the American mainstream, stating emphatically that his book is not part of the undergraduate curriculum, although "Graduate students read it, and occasionally an undergraduate who wants to do a research project on Ganesha might read it along with other books I would recommend, including books written by Hindu practitioners." No further discussion of the social impact of the book takes place in the interview. However, Rao notes with grave concern that Courtright's 'pronouncements have now been sanctified by academe and reified by public institutions'. He gave the example of a large eleventh century Ganesha carving displayed at the famous Walters Art Gallery in Baltimore where the description of Ganesha was exactly as speculatively interpreted in Courtright's book. The display at the art gallery stated that

Ganesa, is a son of the great god Siva, and many of his abilities are comic or absurd extensions of the lofty dichotomies of his father... Ganesa's potbelly and his childlike love for sweets mock Siva's practice of austerities, and his limp trunk will forever be a poor match for Siva's erect phallus. [73]

Rao pointed out, "The only way the curators of the museum could have got the idea that Ganesha's elephant trunk symbolizes a limp penis would be from Courtright's tome." No other book about Hindu symbolism would even remotely imply that Ganesha's trunk is a phallic symbol, because it is not part of any of the multitude of traditions surrounding Ganesha's worship and stories.

Interestingly, Courtright refuses to take any responsibility for this, and also does not offer to write to the museum to explain the difference between fact and speculation. But several times in the interview he implies that writings by the Hindu-American public intellectuals are somehow responsible for the unrelated threats made about him in the comments to the Internet petition. Courtright had explicitly asked Malhotra "what are you going to do now?.".[74] but did not ask the same of himself when it came to light that his speculations have taken on a life of their own and have poisoned American understandings of Hinduism. Indeed Prof. Fleuckiger, Courtright's supervisor at the university, explicitly told the Atlanta Concerned Community that neither Emory nor Courtright felt responsible for what the Walters Museum or other institutions did with Courtright's work.[75]

Courtright has claimed elsewhere that "it is more important to trace the thematic and metaphoric connections between the myths and rituals" than to trace the historical development of ritual practices with hard, exacting evidence. Rao queries, for *whom* are Hindu narratives and rituals important and meaningful? He surmises that "many Indians feel Courtright's book is an example of a more serious issue: Hinduism in Western academia is presented in a manner such that Hindus cannot recognize their own religion". Rao then cited the article by Alan Roland criticizing that the use of psychoanalysis in religious studies leads

> to facile interpretations of the unconscious from textual material, of the equally facile use of primary process symbolization on culturally imbued symbols such as Kali's sword and Krishna's flute, and of increasing certitude and conviction of the rightness of (one's) interpretations in an area that is essentially speculative.[76]

Rao observed that there are a "few Western scholars [who] have begun to express their concerns" but that "such scholars [are] muzzled or ostracized by the powerful and entrenched scholars in the 'Religion in South Asia' group at the American Academy of Religion".

Rao recounted how only two weeks earlier, Wendy Doniger spoke in London on 'Gods, Humans and Animals in the Ramayana,' and in that talk she "regaled her British audience with lurid tales about possible sexual relationships in the epic . . . between Lakshmana and Sita". For context, this is equivalent to regaling a relatively culturally insular audience with lurid tales extrapolated from the Bible about possible sexual relationships between Jesus and the Virgin Mary. Those who know Hindu tradition and texts find the former as baseless, defamatory and as offensive as Catholics would find the latter. One big difference is in the relative powerlessness of the Hindus to prevent such far-fetched fantasies from being spread as *fact* about their religion.

Though Rao is a distinguished university professor, he feels helpless to 'counter the Goliath that is Western academe'. He proposes that Indian-Americans fund India Studies chairs and 'take the initiative to establish our own presses, radio and television stations'. The Western Judeo-Christian traditions as well as increasingly, the Islamic traditions have these structural and economic advantages that enable them to challenge the academia when needed.

Courtright tries to minimize the importance of the emic v/s etic debate, and even claims that he is an 'insider' in a way that Hindu practioners are not, because he claims to have studied more texts than most Hindus. Mercifully, he stops just short of claiming that he knows Hinduism better than Hindus, but does claim in a self-serving way, that he has been told that by Hindus themselves. [77] This is very similar to Marty's and Doniger's claim that white non-Hindu scholars are the best public relations resource for Hinduism, because they can do the job better.

Then Courtright disingenuously recasts the emic/etic debate to conform to Doniger's scurrilous accusation about Hindu 'radicals' wanting to 'control' the study of Hinduism:

> If we say only Hindus can understand Hinduism, only Christians can understand Christianity, only Jews can understand Judaism, only women can understand women, only men can understand men, and so forth, then where does that end? What are we left with?[78]

Hilariously, Courtright next compares himself and his error-ridden Ganesha book to the works of De Toqueville and Myrdal, European 'foreigners' who produced insightful, and deeply respectful, if critically rich, snapshots of America in different historical periods. He seems to be suggesting that just as these masterpieces are a part of American Studies curricula, Indians should make the works by him and Doniger an integral part of any Hinduism Studies curriculum. He implies that this would enable Hindus to better understand Hinduism! He seems to forget the fact that Americans could readily recognize themselves in these portrayals, whereas Hindus find his depictions of Hindu icons and culture unrecognizable and disconnected from reality.

Rao, on the other hand, focuses on improving the self-representation of Hindus and widening the diversity of gazes on Hinduism. For him it is about ensuring real diversity and debate, and challenging the hegemonic control of the West. He asked Indian-Americans to encourage their children to take upper level courses in Indian languages, religions, and the traditional arts and sciences at American universities. "The pervasive pessimistic exoticized depictions of India and Hinduism have been the norm for two hundred years, it is generational ... and a new generation of Hindu scholars who have rejected Hinduphobia will usher in a new tomorrow where Hinduism is treated on par with the same respect as the other world religions."

Thus in the diaspora press, there is a real openness to airing both points of view, and for letting the readership judge what they think of the many issues.

Conclusions: Turning the Issues on End

When American scholars are quoted in major media outlets such as the *New York Times* and the *Washington Post*, they often paint their critics as 'terrorists' without giving them an opportunity to speak for themselves. Hindu-American doctors, scientists, executives and engineers are instantly turned into enemy combatants—guilty without requiring any burden of proof. Scholars whose work has been questioned by Hindu-Americans have published unsubstantiated allegations in professional refereed journals, with titles such as, 'Studying Religion in an Age of Terror'.[79]

Sadly, this cabal of scholars has found a winning device to hold criticism at bay. Every Hindu who protests against the academy from the outside is deemed to be a right-wing dangerous savage. Scholars lump all their Hindu critics into one camp, simply because they are critical of the manner in which Hinduism is represented in many academics' writings. This strategy of labeling your opponent into oblivion is the height of essentializing the 'Other'.

Clearly, mainstream scholars would not feel free to publish similar allegations against 'regular' white Americans simply because they represent a different cultural perspective or dare to examine the work of scholars or seek to debate them. Professors rarely make such assumptions regarding Jewish-Americans who are working to eliminate anti-Semitism or Muslim-Americans critiquing Islamophobia. Sadly, Hinduphobia—either dressed up in academic jargon or nakedly on display with wild accusations of right-wing militancy and terrorism—is still an acceptable stance in America.

Scholars such as Courtright, Kripal, and Doniger deploy a victimhood strategy, akin to the way early American settlers used atrocity literature to isolate the dangerous savage, who is then not entitled to due process that civilized people deserve. Many scholars have reacted to criticism with a volley of self-serving political innuendo, thus positioning themselves as 'victims' and claiming an indignant stand against their 'attackers'. Doniger and Marty have explicitly played the race card, and Rothstein and Vedantam have advanced this scurrilous argument in damaging and gratuitous ways. The scholar-journalist axis drowns out voices that raise the issue of poor scholarship. In so doing, scholars turn valid complaints and arguments on their heads and by evoking powerful American mythic tropes they succeed in derailing the debate.

While some have begun the process, many academics resist honest examinations of Eurocentrism and Hinduphobia. And that has been the great tragedy of this journey which began with the hope of creating space for a greater diversity of voices and for questioning entrenched paradigms and power relations.

APPENDICES

✦

The Uses (and Misuses) Of Psychoanalysis in South Asian Studies: Mysticism and Child Development[1]

BY ALAN ROLAND[2]

Introduction by Prof. Ramesh Rao[3]

India has a long tradition of psychological enquiry, as can be seen by the traditions of yoga, meditation and prayer that focus on inner mental tranquility when dealing with crises, and balancing physical, mental, and emotional health. However, most modern Indian practitioners of psychiatry and scholars of psychology are relatively uninformed about India's philosophical and faith traditions, about mysticism and meditation, the laws of karma, and so on, which engaged both the serious practitioner and the lay Hindu with matters of the mind and of psychological health. Most modern Indian scholars and psychotherapists are uninformed regarding the richness and applicability of their indigenous traditions. Or perhaps they are unwilling to acknowledge the validity of the Dharmic orientation and explanations, for fear of being branded "Hindu nationalists" or "Hindu fundamentalists". There are multiple reasons why India's traditions and knowledge banks have languished, especially since India gained independence. In 1947, rather than unleashing interest in India's native traditions, independence from colonialism, has led to an almost complete marginalization of indigenous traditions and knowledge systems.

Jadunath Sinha's grand tour of India's pursuit of the inner sciences in his three-volume *Indian Psychology* is rarely cited in the works by modern Indian psychologists, or by psychologists studying modern India. India's most well-respected modern Indian psychologists/psychiatrists, Ashis Nandy and Sudhir Kakar, are Freudians or neo-Freudians. They analyze and apply modern theories from within the Indian paradigm—looking at the Western models with Indian eyes. Even so, have they missed the opportunity to develop alternative theories by utilizing the knowledge in the long and serious Indian tradition of seeking an understanding of the human mind and psyche?

Jadunath Sinha's first volume in the *Indian Psychology* series is *Cognition*, the second is *Emotion and Will*, and the third, *Epistemology of Perception*. Sinha was born in 1892. He was of a generation when it was not chic or politically correct to demonize Hindu philosophy, religion, and spirituality. A brilliant graduate of the University of Calcutta, he taught in Colleges at Calcutta, Rajshahi, Dacca, and Meerut. He knew Sanskrit and studied the Indian texts carefully.

Unfortunately, many 'modern' Indian psychologists and psychiatrists are the products of a deracinated, post-independence education system that apes the West and seeks in Western traditions a 'scientific approach' to human travails. Forgotten is the fact that for a dozen centuries prior to Colonialism, Indian commentators and practitioners employed rigorous logical and empirical methods to glean knowledge about the human condition.

Given the fondness of many Western academics to unpack their own and others' texts and iconography from an anthropological, Freudian, Marxist or Feminist perspective, there has been a flood of essays by Indian followers of these 'scientistic' and/or 'new faith' traditions. The result is voluminous work on the purportedly upper-caste, Brahmin manipulation of the gullible but good Indian masses. "Brahmins manipulated society to gather and maintain power, oppress the lower castes and women, and encourage superstition" seems to be foregone conclusion of much of academic social-scientific analyses. It certainly comprises the bulk of the narratives in textbooks written by educators who are guided by publications of South Asian specialists.

It is therefore exciting, to read the work of Prof. Alan Roland, who as a Westerner is better-shielded from attacks from the network of social science academics who vociferously defend their Freudian/Marxist/neo-colonial/post-modern perspective-nexus. He recognizes the power of India's native philosophies— disciplines that for millennia have mined the human condition for profound insights about mental and spiritual health, and psychological and scientific questions.

I am honored to introduce Prof. Alan Roland's essay on issues that continue to consumme significant energy and time. Prof. Roland brings to bear upon these discussions his expert knowledge and experience, gathered over a number of decades. Prof. Roland presented on these matters at the South Asia Conference, University of Wisconsin, Madison on October 11, 2002. He graciously permitted his essay to be published.

Introduction

Psychoanalysis has played a surprisingly major role in South Asian studies, much more so than in other area studies, not to mention many other intellectual disciplines.[4] With but rare exceptions, the application of psychoanalytic theory and at times its reworking, often in conjunction with another discipline in South Asian studies, has resulted from ethnographic and textual methodologies rather than clinical work.[5] To what extent then does psychoanalytic therapy with Indians confirm the conclusions of these studies, or offer a differing viewpoint?[6] Equally important, to what extent do these studies avoid the multiple pitfalls of applied psychoanalysis?

Besides my work as a practising psychoanalyst, I am no stranger to applied psychoanalysis. In an earlier incarnation in this life before becoming involved in clinical psychoanalytic research in India and Japan, I worked for a number of years in the field of psychoanalytic literary criticism and artistic creativity.[7] I am well acquainted with the significant contributions as well as the wondrous temptations, rampant reductionism,[8] and problems of interdisciplinary work that applied psychoanalysis affords.[9]

I found that the pervasive reductionism in psychoanalytic literary criticism more often than not stemmed from the assumption that the work of art is a dream or daydream dressed in aesthetic clothes: that is, aesthetic form in art gives disguised expression to a whole host of unconscious fantasies, which is then seen as the prime mover and meaning of art. This in turn relates to a view of imagery in art, which emphasizes the metaphorical over poetic metaphor and paradox. The former relates much more to primary process emotional expressiveness and unconscious fantasies in art; the latter to higher level integrations of the abstract with the concrete, conveying more universal meanings, which come from an imaginative part of the secondary process (Roland 1978). Imagery in art conveys both simultaneously, with the metaphorical emotionally fueling poetic metaphor and paradox, or the artistic vision. Oddly enough, this problem in psychoanalytic literary criticism is also relevant to the use of psychoanalysis in the study of mystics.

There are two areas I shall delve into. The first is the considerable work on mysticism.[10] The second is important childhood developmental considerations that result in a differently constituted adult relational self from a Northern European/North American one, which I have termed a familial-communal self in contrast to a Western individualized self.

I shall use a two-pronged approach. The first will derive from clinical psychoanalytic experience with Indians, including conversations with other South Asian psychoanalytically oriented therapists. The second will utilize my background in applied psychoanalysis to assess the significant contributions, as well as to draw attention to what I consider temptations of interpretation, overt reductionism, and limited knowledge of psychoanalysis.

Psychoanalysis and Mysticism

In response to a classical Freudian psychoanalytic narrative on mysticism in which spiritual experiences and practices have been viewed as regressive and/or psychopathological,[11] in Hindu studies personified by Masson (1976, 1980), a new Freudian narrative has emerged. Much of it is centered on South Asian studies, particularly but not exclusively on major Hindu spiritual figures. Those who have contributed most directly to this new psychoanalytic perspective are Sudhir Kakar, Jeffrey Kripal, Gananath Obeyesekere, and William Parsons. I would like to address the overall shape of their discourse as well as the particulars.

Almost all are in agreement that there needs to be a seismic shift from what they view as a highly pejorative and reductionistic Freudian psychoanalytic rendering of religious experiences and practices. Kakar (1978, 1991) is the first Freudian psychoanalyst to openly challenge the psychoanalytic establishment to accord the mystic a similar respect to that given the artist in the West. They all agree that religious experiences are valid in and of themselves but all assert that these experiences can at least be partially if not fully explained by psychoanalytic considerations. It is to this inherent tension between the spiritual experience being considered *sui generis* and their psychoanalytic explanations of it that I would like to address this section of the paper. With the exception of Obeyesekere, and to some extent Kripal, they rely on more current Freudian psychoanalytic theorists than classical Freudian theory. Thus Wilfred Bion, Heinz Kohut, Jacques Lacan, Anna Maria Rizzuto, and D.W. Winnicott are cited for a new psychoanalytic rendering of mysticism.

Since I have personal, theoretical, and clinical involvements in the area of mysticism, I shall first briefly state them before critiquing the new Freudian perspective in terms of theoretical orientations and how they actually use their psychoanalytic viewpoints in their analyses of religious experiences. I agree wholeheartedly with Obeyesekere (1981) that the personal views, background, biases, and reactions of researchers can greatly influence their perspective, and should hopefully be stated upfront. Concerning my own personal experience, after encountering the writings of Swami Vivekananda at nineteen, I spent the next three and a half years in the early 1950s immersed in Indian philosophy, with Antioch College work periods at centers and ashrams of the Ramakrishna Order; at a Press run by Theosophists who published the weekly, *Manas*; and at a mountain retreat of Meher Baba, a Sufi, in the Ojai Valley. While on campus, I studied with an Indian professor, M.N. Chatterjee, who was a practising Vedantist, and wrote my senior thesis on Gandhi and the National Movement.

For the next ten plus years I became increasingly involved in the psychoanalytic world through a personal analysis, a psychoanalytically oriented clinical psychology program at Adelphi University, and then through a multi-model Freudian psychoanalytic training institute, the National Psychological Association for Psychoanalysis. In the 1950s and 1960s, the worlds of Freudian psychoanalysis and Indian philosophy and spiritual practices did not mix. In fact, each put the other down. I naturally thought that my earlier immersion in Indian spiritual philosophy was neurotically motivated. It wasn't until a visit to India in 1964 that my interest in the spiritual self became rekindled; and it wasn't until 1977 when my wife and I went to India on our respective research projects that I became involved in meditative practices. In more recent years, similar to some other psychoanalytic colleagues who are mainly involved in Buddhist meditation, I have tried to put together psychoanalysis and spiritual experiences (Roland 1999, 2001; see also Coltart 1992, 1996; Cooper 1998, 1999; Eigen 1998; and Rubin 1996).

As a psychoanalyst, I refer to myself as a multi-model Freudian: that is, one who is knowledgeable about classical Freudian psychoanalysis, as well as about ego psychology, self psychology, object relations theory, and intersubjectivity, with a smattering of Lacan[12] and relational psychoanalysis. From my clinical psychoanalytic research in India, I began working with Hindu patients actively involved in one or another kind of *sadhana*, and in the United States with various patients involved in spiritual practices from a variety of traditions ranging from Hindu to Buddhist to Episcopal Christian to Hassidic

Jewish to Sufi to artists, totaling over fifteen in all, almost half of them being Indian. I have also talked at length with Hindu psychoanalytically or psychodynamically-oriented psychiatrists who are on the spiritual path, and with American psychoanalysts who are Buddhist practitioners of either Zen or Vipassana meditation.[13]

Sudhir Kakar

I would now like to address what I find problematic in the new Freudian psychoanalytic discourse on mysticism before advancing my own perspective. I shall critique Sudhir Kakar first as he has influenced others through writing extensively on the subject of psychoanalysis and mysticism, beginning with his analysis of Swami Vivekananda in *The Inner World*, then on Gandhi in *Intimate Relations*, and finally on Ramakrishna in *The Analyst and the Mystic*. I applaud Kakar for his courage in the Freudian psychoanalytic world for advocating for a radical reconsideration of the mystic.[14] His description of the lives of Vivekananda, Gandhi, and Ramakrishna strike me as being very well done in his gifted style of writing. But what happens when he actually applies his psychoanalytic understanding to these three spiritual figures? His analyses are as fully reductionistic as those of Jeffrey Masson. I shall cite just a few of what could be many examples.

After rendering a solid psychobiographical sketch of Swami Vivekananda in *The Inner World*, and after disavowing the pathographic approach (1978, p.164), Kakar cites the following: "With the advent of adolescence . . . he found he could not always cope with the claims of archaic grandiosity and the anxiety and guilt associated with its breakthrough. Increasingly, he experienced periods of hypomanic excitement; once . . . when he was fifteen . . . Narendra 'spied a large beehive in the cleft of a giant cliff and suddenly his mind was filled with awe and reverence for the Divine Providence. He lost outer consciousness and lay thus in the cart for a long time'." (pp.178–179). Thus, Kakar equates Vivekananda's spiritual experience with archaic grandiosity and hypomanic excitement.

Again, after a good psychobiographic description of Gandhi in *Intimate Relations* and disavowing the pathographic, Kakar reductionistically interprets Gandhi's struggle with celibacy (from his thirties on)—a cornerstone of any fully committed spiritual aspirant in the Hindu and other religious mystic traditions[15]—as essentially related to an unconscious fantasy of maintaining an idealized relationship with the maternal body. "Whereas desexualizing, idealizing, and perceiving only the 'milky' mother in the woman is one part of his defensive bulwark which helped in preserving the illusion of unity with the maternal body intact, the other part consists of efforts at renouncing the gift of sexual desire, abjuring his own masculinity." (1989. p.126); 'with a wished-for feminization defensive in origin'[16] (p.127).

On Ramakrishna in *The Analyst and the Mystic*: "All he yearned for with all his soul, he was to later tell us, was a vision, the personal *darshan* of the Mother. The spiritual thirst, the clinician would observe was embedded in all the signs of a full-fledged depression. There was a great restlessness of the body, sleepless nights, loss of appetite in which eating was reduced to the bare minimum, eyes that filled up often and suddenly with tears." (1991. p.13). "Ramakrishna's longing for the Mother, accompanied by breathlessness of a kind where he feels he is about to die, for instance, is akin to a certain type of asthmatic bodily manifestation of a dammed-up urge for the mother's succor." (p.25). Again, Kakar reductionistically views Ramakrishna's spiritual yearning to a depression and a repressed need for his mother's care. I hope it is obvious from this handful of Kakar's specific analyses of Vivekananda, Gandhi, and Ramakrishna that he continues the very pathologizing and regressive analysis of spiritual aspirations and experiences that he so decries in Masson and other psychoanalysts.

This stems in good part from the second problem in his work, his theoretical understanding of mysticism from a psychoanalytic standpoint. In *The Inner World*, Kakar states: "real knowledge is only attainable through direct primary-process thinking and perception . . ." (p. 107). "In the Hindu ideal, reality is not primarily mediated through the conscious and preconscious perceptions, unconscious defenses, and logical rational thought processes that make up the ego; it emanates from the deeper and phylogenetically older structural layer of personality—the id, the mental representation of the organism's instinctual drives. Reality, according to Hindu belief, can be apprehended or known only through those archaic, unconscious, preverbal processes of sensing and feeling" (p.20).

To what extent primary-process thinking and the id constitute spiritual knowing is highly questionable to say the least. The primary process, perhaps Freud's most original discovery, constitutes certain mechanisms (condensation, displacement, symbol formation, dramatization, and such), symbolic processes essential in dreams, symptoms, and in certain ways in artistic creativity. In Freud's view, they give disguised expression to the instinctual wishes; in later contributions (Deri 1976; Noy 1969; Roland 1972), they also give excellent metaphorical expression to various facets of the self. In *The Inner World* it is Kakar's inaccurate use of Freudian psychoanalytic concepts such as the primary process and the id as a Procrustean Bed to encompass psychological processes involved in spiritual realization that results in his reverting to traditional psychoanalytic reductionism in his analyses of mysticism.

His theoretical understanding of mysticism shifts from the use of the primary process and the id in *The Inner World* to current psychoanalytic relational theories in *The Analyst and the Mystic*. Kakar in this latter work fully accepts what I consider to be the reductionistic psychoanalytic premise that spiritual experiences and motivation are essentially a regression to the preverbal, symbiotic experiences of the mother-child relationship. "The vicissitudes of separation have been, of course, at the heart of psychoanalytic theorizing on mysticism. The yearning to be reunited with a perfect, omnipotent being, the longing for the blissful soothing and nursing associated with the mother of earliest infancy . . . has been consensually deemed the core of mystical motivation" (1991. p.29). Only Kakar puts a more positive spin on this regression than do the classical Freudian analysts, in as much as he sees the mystic as able to effect a deeper regression than that which occurs in psychoanalysis to repair what Kakar deems is the essential depressive core of life; and in Winnicottian terms, the mystic is involved in a creative experiencing through this regression to infancy. Again, it is highly questionable whether spiritual aspirations, practices, and experiences essentially involve regression.

Jeffrey Kripal

Jeffrey Kripal's (1995) *Kali's Child* still swirls around in controversy.[17] In the vortex of this controversy lies a question of enormous importance to the psychoanalytic study of mystics: what is the place of sexuality and sensuality, as well as of psychopathology, in their spiritual aspirations and motivations, practices, and experiences? Kripal, Obeyesekere, and Kakar are all involved in this question. I shall not even attempt to answer this on such a major spiritual figure as Ramakrishna but shall rather draw on my clinical experience with patients deeply involved in one or another *sadhana*, on discussions with other psychoanalytic therapists on the spiritual path, and on my own personal experience.

Before addressing this question, however, I would like to briefly cite what I find positive in Kripal's psychoanalytic approach and what is problematic. Kripal's main thesis is that Ramakrishna tried to alleviate intense homosexual conflicts and experiences—including sexual abuse from his gurus and others, as well as his inclination to sexually abuse his teenage disciples—through his worship of Kali and Tantric practices; and that both structured and constituted his mystic experiences. In the Conclusion, Kripal asserts: "These homoerotic energies, in other words, not only shaped the symbolism of Ramakrishna's mysticism; they were his mysticism. Let me be very clear: without the conflicted energies of the saint's homosexual desires, there would have been no Kali's sword, no unconscious Handmaid, no conflict between the Mother and the Lover, no Child, no Radha, no living *lingam*, no naked Paramahamsa boys, no Jesus state, no love-body, no ecstatically extended feet, no closing and opening doors, no symbolic visions, no *bhava*, and no *samadhi*. In effect there would have been no 'Ramakrishna.' The erotic, then was Ramakrishna." (p.322).

I find it refreshing that Kripal acknowledges the validity of Ramakrishna's spiritual experiences, something missing from the traditional Freudian reading of mysticism. I would certainly agree that Ramakrishna was to a considerable extent a Tantric from memories of reading *The Gospel of Sri Ramakrishna* some fifty years ago. I am not surprised that Vivekananda and other disciples presented him more as a Vedantist given the British colonial/missionary attitudes toward Tantra as the epitome of depravity.

What I find problematic in Kripal's use of psychoanalysis lies in four different areas. First and foremost, he was lured by the great temptress of applied psychoanalysis, the siren of facile interpretations of the unconscious from textual material, of the equally facile use of primary process symbolization on culturally imbued symbols such as Kali's sword and Krishna's flute, and of increasing certitude and conviction of the rightness of his interpretations in an area that is essentially speculative.[18] The siren has lured him onto the shoals of psychoanalytic reductionism as have been so many others in applied psychoanalysis. I and others who have sailed through these straits have had to struggle with her seductiveness.

Parenthetically, I marvel at the ease and assuredness in which Kakar, Kripal, Kurtz, and Obeyesekere interpret unconscious motivation from their textual and ethnographic material. As a practising psychoanalyst,

I often struggle for months to understand the unconscious subtext of what patients are talking about, even with patients freely saying what is on their mind.

I shall cite just one simple example of psychoanalytic reductionism out of very many. Kripal discusses Ramakrishna becoming intensely involved in the worship of Kali after his older brother's death, his brother having been a father figure to him after his father's earlier demise. "It was at this time that Ramakrishna turned to Kali, the divine mother, and sought her 'vision' (*darshana*). He could not eat. He could not sleep . . . He could barely breathe so great was his desire . . . [Kripal then cites Datta] His state at this time was like that of a boy nursing at its mother's breasts. When one looked at Ramakrishna, one immediately thought of an infant who cannot see its mother and so cries '*Ma! Ma!*' and will not be consoled." (pp.61–62).

Kripal then interprets Ramakrishna as regressing to infancy because of having lost a father figure with his brother's death. A psychoanalyst could just as easily interpret that with the death of his older brother, Ramakrishna was now much freer to be completely involved in his intense worship of Kali without interference from his brother, as had previously occurred. Or that confronted with death, from a Rankian perspective, he became even more motivated in his spiritual search; or from a self psychological one, he sought a more enduring self object; or from the standpoint of psychoanalytic literary criticism, Ramakrishna may have drawn upon the emotions of the earliest childhood in the service of spiritual longings for an experience of Kali. Psychoanalytically, these follow from an appreciation of issues of the self, especially a self driven by intense spiritual yearnings, rather than seeing all motivation as deriving from unconscious psychic conflict, in this case, anxiety and depression. However, all of these interpretations remain speculative.

Nevertheless, Kripal always authoritatively asserts the regressive and psychopathological or defensive motivation over the spiritual. This is the second problem in his use of psychoanalysis. Even should he be right on occasion, such a pervasive privileging of unconscious motivation smacks strongly of psychoanalytic reductionism.[19]

The third problem in Kripal's psychoanalytic theorizing is his easily conflating *samadhi*, ecstasy, and other spiritual states and experiences with unconscious dissociated states involving repressed homoerotic feelings. This results from Kripal viewing both spiritual states of heightened consciousness and unconscious conflicts as deriving from a more general unconscious. This he simply defines as "a secret dimension . . . of the human person of which he or she is not aware" (p.43). This does not really encompass psychoanalytic definitions of the unconscious, which usually involve both a repressed, conflictual dimension in which defensive functions predominate, and primary process mechanisms of symbolization, such as in dreams, the two often being interrelated. Nor does it cover spiritual states of consciousness, where those experiencing them are usually quite self-aware. The joining together of spiritual states and unconscious conflicts is a speculative leap on Kripal's part.

The fourth problem in Kripal's use of psychoanalysis is his psychopathologizing the homoerotic, and then facilely equating the homoerotic with homosexuality. Kripal does not seem to understand the psychology of Indian men, especially the homoerotic. Homoerotic feelings in both Indian men and women are far more developed and accepted, with much greater same sex emotional and physical intimacy, and are much less conflicted and laden with anxiety and shame, than in most European-American men. Repeatedly, Kripal privileges unconscious motivation around homoerotic longings or homosexuality over the spiritual.

Gananath Obeyesekere

I would like to address the dimension of Obeyesekere's work that encompasses symbolization. I agree with him that the Western approach to symbolization has been a logocentric one. Even with Freud's seminal formulation of the primary process, the ideal in psychoanalysis has been to put everything into a comprehensible, verbal formulation. Certainly, South Asian cultures such as in India and Sri Lanka may rely a great deal more on imagery in symbolization than language and rational discourse.

From my experience as an artist and from psychoanalytic literary criticism, I greatly appreciate Obeyesekere's (1981, 1990) complex approach to symbolization as relating to both the deep motivation of personal psychobiography and to culturally shared meanings. And then there is the more transcendent dimension of certain cultural symbols, plentiful in South Asia. I question whether this last dimension is basically related to, or a progression from, the deep motivation of psychoanalysis that Obeyesekere posits.

Serious questions must be raised, however, on Obeyesekere's understanding of the primary process, which is so central to his work.

His is basically a classical Freudian view where the primary process is related to psychosexual issues, and functions in a distorting way through various mechanisms (condensation, displacement, symbol formation, dramatization, and such) to give disguised expression to wishes that are forbidden by various cultural norms.

Psychoanalysts now have an enlarged understanding of the primary process that Obeyesekere seems to be unaware of. First, a long-term research project at the New York University Psychoanalytic Research Center in the 1960s revealed that the primary process is not set by ages five or six as Obeyesekere asserts. Rather, there is a progressive organization and structuralization of how the primary process functions throughout adolescence and adulthood.[20]

Even more important is the work of Noy (1969) and Deri (1984). The former posits that the basic function of the primary process in dreams is for the processing and internalization of relational experiences of the previous day into the self. As he, and particularly Deri emphasize, the imagery and mechanisms of the primary process serve not only to give disguised expression to forbidden wishes, but also to give a remarkably accurate metaphorical depiction of multiple facets of the self. The self, of course, would have to be considered as significantly different in South Asians from the self of Euro-Americans. I believe this understanding would add important new dimensions to Obeyesekere's concept of personal and cultural symbols.

Thus, culture would have to be considered not only as symbolizations that help resolve basic psychosexual conflicts and issues, serving at times as culturally constituted defenses and eventually as removed from the basic conflicts; culture must also be considered as oriented around the self and relationships that are central in a given society. Deep motivation is related to the self as well as psychosexual issues in complex ways. To ignore these developments in psychoanalysis is to remain in a pre-1930s understanding of the discipline. Such are the problems of interdisciplinary work.

With regard to mysticism, my strong impression is that there is an independent motivation in certain people to become involved in a spiritual quest and spiritual practices.[21] I doubt very much from patients I have worked with that the primary motivation to embark and stay on a spiritual path is to resolve psychosexual conflicts. However, this does not preclude the presence of all kinds of psychic conflicts and/ or deficits.[22]

Psychoanalytic Therapy with Indians and Other Mystics

A European woman patient who had spent several years in an Indian ashram and has seriously studied astrology before becoming a psychoanalyst, recently remarked in session, "what is most missing in psychoanalysis is reincarnation." She went on to say that we all know that certain patients come into therapy with an inherent make-up regardless of their psychopathology that enables them to make much greater progress than others whose psychopathology is not as serious. Psychoanalysis doesn't take into account where the person is at in their spiritual evolution and what is the nature of their make-up.[23] This, of course, goes beyond issues of psychic conflict and deficit. But I also find that this dimension is largely missing in the psychoanalytic discourse on mystics.

This raises a whole host of questions involving mystics. What is the relationship of psychopathology to the spiritual quest, particularly to spiritual aspirations and motivation, practices, and experiences? Or conversely, to what extent can we relate these various aspects of the spiritual quest to psychic conflict, deficits, developmental stages, or the internal representational world, as is currently done? Then, there is the crucial question of the relationship of sexuality and sensuality to spiritual motivation, practices, and experiences. And finally, to what extent does any of Freudian psychoanalytic theory, as currently constituted, encompass the spiritual quest?

I do not have any definitive answers but shall share my thinking from my work with a number of patients on the spiritual path, from psychoanalytic therapists so oriented, and from my own experiences. Of the sixteen or so patients I have seen over the years who are on a spiritual quest, I can say that two seem decidedly more advanced. One is Shakuntala whom I described in some detail from seeing her in psychoanalytic therapy in 1977–78 and 1980 (Roland 1988), and then followed up with a visit in 1991 (Roland 1996), and have subsequently seen her in 1997 and 1999.

The other is Robert, an American from a white Anglo-Saxon Protestant background, who is the disciple of a Sufi *pir* in India, is now one of the heads of an American *Sufi* group as well as being a designated teacher of *Sufi* meditation, and has been on a *Hajj*.

From my clinical, social, and personal experiences, I doubt very much whether any of the contemporary Freudian theory encompasses the spiritual quest with the possible exception of Bion's concept of 0, the ultimate. Both Kakar (1991) and Parsons (1999) cite Lacan's theory of the Real but according to Paola Mieli, a Lacanian psychoanalyst and recognized Lacanian authority, they have a complete misunderstanding of what the Real means. Further, that although Lacan was interested in mystics, he, himself, never considered himself to be one, only referring to himself as a psychoanalytic mystic in a sarcastic way (personal communication, Paola Mieli).

Conversely, I view the various attempts to link spiritual experiences with various developmental stages as all being highly reductionistic whether it is Freud's primary narcissism of infantile merger with the mother, or a Winnicottian creative experiencing of a transitional space between mother and child, or Rizzuto's god-images from different developmental stages, or Kurtz's concept of later childhood merger with the extended family. These views simply do not take sufficiently into account the existential nature of spiritual experiences. Nor do I think these experiences can be categorized by regression of one sort or another, or to one or another stage of development, or to one or another kind of inner representation of either the mother or father. If anything, clinical experience indicates that spiritual practices and experiences are a strong counterpoint to regression and childhood merger experiences with the mother and with the Hindu extended family.

Where do I think psychoanalysis fruitfully enters the picture with mystics? First and foremost, it is in their relationships with others, often love relationships, but also friends and work relationships, any or all of which can sometimes be truly problematic, and also to their everyday sense of self. In my therapy experience, it is most often in their love relationships, affected by problematic earlier family relationships. Psychoanalytic therapy with those patients who are mystics is often of considerable help in their functioning much better in their relationships while simultaneously freeing them to be more involved on a spiritual path. Mystics, except for the rare ones who live by themselves, are all involved in human relationships.

How then does unconscious motivation, psychopathology, sexuality, and such, enter into the spiritual quest in terms of aspirations and motivations, spiritual practices such as meditation or prayer, and spiritual experiences? These are the areas most addressed by the current psychoanalytic discussion of mysticism. With regard to aspirations and motivation, these can vary considerably.

Some patients have been drawn to meditative practices because of extremely upsetting love relationships. Two Hindu women in psychoanalysis had such distressful love relationships that they were drawn to Vipassana meditation to attain and maintain an inner calm. Psychoanalysis helped each to understand her unconscious motivation in getting involved in an unsuitable relationship but could not initially alleviate her current distress. Once one of them moved on to a more suitable love relationship, she still practised meditation but not on an as intense or daily basis as before. While her initial motivation for meditation was obviously to relieve her emotionally upset state, nevertheless, one can still assert she was inherently inclined in this direction. In contrast, another Hindu woman patient in a long-term, abusive marital relationship was not inclined in any spiritual direction, and coped with the situation entirely through psychoanalytic therapy, which helped considerably.

On the other hand, Shakuntala was having intense spiritual experiences while on a family pilgrimage to a shrine of a goddess by age fourteen or fifteen. There was no particular evidence that her motivation was to alleviate any distress. The decision to embark on a spiritual quest may sometimes result from some of the hard knocks of life, but not always. Even then, the person must be strongly inwardly inclined in this direction for it is still a rare pursuit.

Another patient, a man who was quite schizoid and devoid of friendships and other relationships, used his Zen meditation when he first came to see me in part to remain in his own cut-off world. This changed over a long course of psychoanalytic therapy where he developed many rich relationships; simultaneously his meditation deepened. Further, his meditation enabled him to become more intensely involved in the therapy process. Thus, the motivation for meditation was mixed in the earlier period between psychopathology and spiritual aspirations, becoming more involved in the latter as the therapy progressed.

Or in another telling case, an American woman was drawn to an Indian guru and ashram known for its sexual licentiousness. On one hand, she was unconsciously repeating an early experience of sexual abuse by an uncle; on the other, she was also fulfilling a genuine spiritual yearning. To reduce the whole experience to the psychopathological, or as simply a way of handling psychic conflicts, would be inaccurate and reductionistic. Then, there are the occasional more disturbed cases. An American woman who was deeply involved with a guru and ashram in the United States, was very involved in spiritual practices but was also delusional. She heard voices of her guru telling her to do all kinds of things which were delusional, and in fact often at cross-purposes with the ashram. Together with a genuine spiritual inclination was a psychotic core that probably manifested even more as she became more involved in spiritual practices.

A psychoanalytic discourse on mystics can fruitfully comment on that which has only been minimally discussed, the guru or teacher-disciple relationship. Besides the important teachings that are conveyed by a suitable teacher, there can also be multiple transferences from both the disciple and the teacher, depending on the individual personality. Rubin (1996) has commented on this at length.

In terms of the kind of spiritual practices a given person is drawn to, I would think it is some combination of what tradition is available and even popular—Vipassana, Zen, and Tibetan Buddhism in the United States in recent decades—as well as the spiritual make-up, inclination, and evolution of the person. To ignore these latter factors is to greatly oversimplify the situation. The problem is that it is not so easy or perhaps even possible for the psychoanalyst or psychoanalytically inclined scholar to assess this. For instance, one Hindu psychodynamically-oriented psychiatrist has been drawn to the practice of *raja yoga*, another to bhakti devotional practices. Obviously, both practices were readily available to each. I doubt whether unconscious factors played any significant role in their choice. I would suspect that whatever spiritual experiences they have had is related to their kind of practice, spiritual make-up, and where they are in their spiritual evolution, not to any developmental stage or psychopathology.

To what extent can spiritual practices alleviate emotional problems of whatever sort? My strong impression is that they certainly can have some calming effect, in psychoanalytic therapy to enable a patient to tolerate a greater degree of anxiety in facing difficult inner conflicts or deficits. But they cannot resolve deep-seated psychopathology.

To say then that Hindu men dressing as women in bhakti worship, identifying with Radha in the worship of Krishna, is fundamentally a culturally sanctioned way to resolve or give expression to their bisexuality might apply on occasion to some men, or to some extent to a number of others, but it is not really to the point. It is much more that these men draw on their strong identification with the maternal-feminine for use in a spiritual discipline. It is analogous to the problem in art and psychoanalytic criticism. Is the work of art essentially to give disguised expression to unconscious, infantile fantasies? Or are the unconscious fantasies used by the artist to give emotional power to a broader artistic vision. I strongly believe the latter to be the case. Similarly in bhakti or Tantric practices, I do not see them as essentially there to resolve or handle certain psychic conflicts, but rather to draw upon a whole range of emotion and sexuality to fuel the spiritual endeavor. It is interesting to note that in bhakti devotional practices involving Krishna, the highest spiritual state is that of the emotions and sexuality of a lover, while paradoxically ascetism reigns. And in other spiritual disciplines such as prayer, obviously the person draws on all kinds of inner representations of past emotional relationships with parental figures.

I have so far not seen in any of my mystic patients where problems in their sexuality and love life have changed their spiritual practices; or where they have been drawn to one or another particular spiritual practice out of problems in their sexuality.

Psychoanalysis and Hindu Childrearing

Stanley Kurtz (1992) in *All the Mothers are One* advances the valuable thesis that the Hindu extended family[24] is far more important to the group-oriented make-up of the Hindu psyche than psychoanalytic theorizing on India has realized. His emphasis on the in-law women of the extended family in childrearing is also an important contribution, as is his interesting hypothesis that renunciation may prevail over repression of childhood instinctual needs. I further agree with his views that culture pervades the psyche at all levels, rather than simply shaping a universal psychological template; that one must take into account the Western cultural assumptions of individualism in psychoanalysis that orient it toward a highly individualistic psychology emphasizing individual autonomy; and that psychoanalytic theorizing must be significantly altered for understanding the Hindu psyche as well as the psyches of other non-Western peoples. This includes delineating a different developmental schema than is present in classical Freudian theory and Margaret Mahler's ego psychological theory of separation-individuation (Mahler, Pine, and Bergmann 1965).

Kurtz then makes the astonishing statement that the Hindu mother while physically gratifying her children maintains an emotional distance from them, and is not nearly as empathically or emotionally responsive to her infant, toddler, and young child as an American mother. It is the foundation on which his whole edifice of Hindu childrearing rests. It is an edifice that posits that the Hindu mother by her relative non-responsiveness pushes her child so to speak into the arms of her mother-in-law and sisters-in-law, which thus develops an "ego of the whole"[25] in a process Kurtz terms separation-integration or the *ek-hi* phase of early development—as contrasted to separation-individuation or to a strong maternal symbiotic relationship.[26]

The statement is astonishing because no Hindu or South Asian psychoanalytically-oriented therapist, nor child development person, nor any other Hindu mental health person of any stripe I have talked with, nor other Asian mental health persons would agree to it;[27] nor with the exception of one particular, disturbed mother has it come up in any of my case material of some twenty Hindu patients. Kurtz's theory of early maternal nonresponsiveness is based completely on ethnographic behavioral observations supplemented by mythic analyses, his main methodologies for psychoanalytic theorizing. He clearly doesn't understand the early development of nonverbal emotional and empathic responsiveness and communication that later becomes a hallmark of functioning in Hindu extended family relationships throughout life.[28] Communication in Hindu extended family relationships is always multi-leveled with a strong, conscious orientation to the nonverbal by mood, gesture, and behavior together with the verbal, which can often be ambiguous.

This lack of understanding in Kurtz and other anthropologists also misleads them to conclude that the mother withdraws from her child when she is in the presence of her mother-in-law. They don't realize that the mother is still intimately emotionally connected to her child while observing the proper deferential behavior toward her mother-in-law, something the child realizes in the multi-level communication of Indians. Nor do they realize that a Hindu mother will not overtly praise her child as an American mother does because a) it would be like praising herself because of the we-self; b) it would incur the evil eye or envy of the in-law women; and c) it would build up an egoism that would not only distract the child from the achievement of an "ego of the whole" but also from his spiritual self (atman). Approval and appreciation is nevertheless conveyed nonverbally.[29] **This is not a lack of empathic responsiveness but rather a different mode.**[30]

If Kurtz's *ek-hi* phase of development and his concept of separation-integration is profoundly out of sync with Hindu mothering, then do we have to throw out his important notions of the familial-oriented psyche of Hindus with an ego of the whole, as well as the important role of the in-law women? Not at all. The Hindu mother while normally deeply emotionally connected and empathic to her children (with obvious variations) has herself a we-self and becomes emotionally very much integrated into her in-laws' family, gradually forming close intimacy relationships with her mother-in-law,[31] her husband's sisters especially before they are married, and the sisters-in-law of her husband's brothers. She is therefore very much oriented toward her children becoming an integral part of the extended family, and they identify with her. If she is living in a joint household, since she has other duties besides childrearing such as cooking and taking care of the house, she welcomes the childrearing help from her mother-in-law and sisters-in-law, and is not at all jealous of their relationship with her children (personal communication, B.K. Ramanujam and Nandita Chaudhuri). Although not displaying it before others of the family, she maintains her special relationship with her own children while also being involved with her in-laws' children. *All the mothers are not one*, but the in-law mothers are still very important.

Thus, the prolonged symbiotic tie to the mother for both boys and girls is not so exclusive because of these other emotional ties to the in-law women, as well as at times to the women of the mother's family. Further, the Hindu mother does allow for a separation of inner images of self and other to develop, particularly encourages the development of a private self where all kinds of feelings and fantasies are allowed to be kept to oneself without being intruded upon,[32] and respects her child's idiosyncrasies since she assumes each child comes into this world with the experiences of past lives.

I am not a student of mythology. But if I were to speculate about the benevolent and fierce sides of the goddesses, I would not correlate the former with the mother and the latter with the in-law women of the family as Kurtz does. Rather, I would see these two sides as related to earlier and later childhood. The benevolent goddess is both the mother and in-law women of early childhood when the child receives a great deal of gratification and emotional responsiveness.[33] Whereas the fierce goddess is also both the mother and in-law women from ages four or five on through adolescence when there is a severe crackdown for proper behavior and attitudes in the complex hierarchical relationships of the extended family.[34] The women enforce these values before the men of the family do. The mother, herself, is often more strict about enforcing proper behavior than the in-law women (personal communication, B.K. Ramanujam).

This makes sense psychoanalytically because attitudes toward the fierce goddess are unlike those in Melanie Klein's theory of the split between the good and bad mother, where there are intense paranoid anxieties associated with the latter. In Hinduism, the fierce as well as the benevolent goddess is worshipped and expected to bestow her blessing, whereas Klein's bad mother is avoided or defensively attacked.

Kurtz's notion that psychopathology only occurs when the structure of the joint family with the in-law mothers is not present for the child is oversimplified. Certainly, the dynamics of the extended family is of considerable importance to problems generated in the child, and Indian therapists are well aware of this. What Kurtz leaves out is the idiosyncratically disturbed parent, grandparent, sibling, or whoever that can play a major role in the child's psychopathology. Or as in two cases of Hindu women, mothers who were deeply inwardly conflicted between modernization in the most liberal way for their daughters, and profoundly ingrained traditional attitudes. Life is not so simple when psychopathology is involved.

Finally, there is Kurtz's notion of the Hindu spiritual quest or union with the godhead (*Brahman*) as being correlated with the wholeness of the extended family rather than with the symbiotic mother as in Carstairs and Kakar. I see this as going from one form of reductionism to another. I still view the spiritual path of Hindus as primarily a counterpoint to the strong emotional enmeshments with the tugs and pulls of extended family and other relationships, which then enables the person to function in these relationships with greater equanimity. That the fulfillment of *dharma* in these familial relationships helps the person achieve finer qualities (*sattva*) on the way to spiritual realization does not negate the counterpoint that is present.

REFERENCES

Coltart, N. 'The Practice of Psychoanalysis and Buddhism'. In *Slouching toward Bethlehem,* New York: Guilford Press, (1992), pp.164–175.
——'Buddhism and Psychoanalysis Revisited', in *The Baby and the Bathwater.* New York: International Universities Press, 1996, pp.125–40.
Cooper, P. 'The disavowal of the spirit: Integration and wholeness in Buddhism and psychoanalysis', in *The Couch and the Tree: Dialogues in Psychoanalysis and Buddhism,* ed. A. Molino. New York: North Point Press, 1998, pp.231–46.
——'Buddhist meditation and countertransference: A case study', in *American Journal of Psychoanalysis,* 59:71–86, 1999.

Das, V. 'Masks and faces: An essay on Punjabi kinship', in *Contributions to Indian Sociology*, 10:1–30, 1976.

Deri, S. *Symbolization and Creativity*. New York: International Universities Press, 1984.

Dube, S.C. *Indian Village*. London: Routledge and Kegan Paul, 1955.

Edel, L. 'Hawthorne's symbolism and psychoanalysis', in *Hidden Patterns: Studies in Psychoanalytic Literary Criticism*, eds. Leonard and Eleanor Manheim. New York: Macmillan, 1966.

Eigen, M. *The Pyschoanalytic Mystic*. Binghamton, NY: ESF Publications.

Fromm, E., D.T. Suzuki, and R. DeMartino. *Zen Buddhism and Psychoanalysis*. New York: Harper and Row, 1960.

Grey, A. Oedipus in Hindu dreams. *Contemporary Psychoanalysis*, 9:327–55, 1973,

Hanchette, S. *Coloured Rice: Symbolic Structure in Hindu Family Festivals*. Delhi: Hindustan Publishing Company, 1988.

Horney, K. *Our Inner Conflicts*. New York: W. W. Norton, 1945.

Inden, R. and R. Nicholas. *Kinship in Bengali Culture*. Chicago: University of Chicago Press, 1977.

Kakar, S. *The Inner World: A Psychoanalytic Study of Childhood and Society in India*. Delhi: Oxford University Press, 1978.

——Maternal enthrallment. *Culture and Psyche*, pp. 74-87, Delhi: Oxford University Press, 1997.

——'Observations on "the Oedipal alliance" in a patient with a narcissistic personality disorder', in *Samiksa*, 34:47-53. 1980

——*Shamans, Mystics, and Doctors*. New York: Alfred A. Knopf. 1982

——*Intimate Relations: Exploring Indian Sexuality*. Chicago: University of Chicago Press. 1989

——*The Analyst and the Mystic: Psychoanalytic Reflections on Religion and Mysticism*. New Delhi: Viking by Penguin Books India. 1991

——*Culture and Psyche: Selected Essays*. Delhi: Oxford University Press. 1997

Kapadia, K.M. *Marriage and Family in India*. London: Oxford University Press. 1966

Kelman, H. 'Psychoanalytic thought and Eastern wisdom', in *The History of Psychotherapy*, ed. J. Ehrenwald. New York: Jason Aronson. 1960

Kripal, J. *Kali's Child: The Mystical and the Erotic in the Life and Teachings of Ramakrishna*. Chicago: University of Chicago Press. 1995

Kurtz, S. *All the Mothers are One: Hindu India and the Cultural Reshaping of Psychoanalysis*. New York: Columbia University Press. 1992

Mahler, M., F. Pine, and A. Bergman. *Psychological Birth of the Human Infant*. New York: Basic Books. 1975

Masson, J. M. 'The psychology of the ascetic', in *Journal of Asian Studies*, 35:611-25.

1980. *The Oceanic Feeling: The Origins of Religious Sentiment in Ancient India*. Dordrecht, Holland: D. Reidel. 1976

Milner, M. 1973. 'Some notes on psychoanalytic ideas about mysticism', in *The Suppressed Madness of Sane Men*. London: Tavistock, 1987.

Noy, P. 'A revision of the psychoanalytic theory of the primary process', in *International Journal Psycho-Analysis*, 50:155–178. 1969

Parsons, W.B. *The Enigma of the Oceanic Feeling: Revisioning the Psychoanalytic Theory of Mysticism*. New York: Oxford University Press.

Rizzuto, A. *The Birth of the Living God: A Psychoanalytic Study*. Chicago: Chicago University Press, 1979.

Roland, A. 'Imagery and symbolic expression in dreams and art', *International Journal Psycho-Analysis.*, 53:531–539, 1972

Roland, A. ed. *Psychoanalysis, Creativity, and Literature: A French-American Inquiry*, New York: Columbia University Press, 1978.

——*In Search of Self in India and Japan: Toward a Cross-Cultural Psychology*. Princeton: Princeton University Press, 1988.

——*Cultural Pluralism and Psychoanalysis: The Asian and North American Experience*, New York and London: Routledge, 1996.

Rubin, J. *Psychotherapy and Buddhism: Toward an Integration*, New York: Plenum Press, 1996.

Wolfson, E. and Kripal, J. ed.s. 'The Spiritual Self and Psychopathology: Theoretical Reflections and Clinical Observations', *Psychoanalysis and Psychotherapy*, 16:211–34, 1999.

——'Psychoanalysts and the spiritual quest: Framing a new paradigm', in *The unknown remembered gate: Religious experience and hermeneutical reflection in religious studies*, New York: Seven Bridges Press, 2002.

India and Her Traditions: A Reply to Jeffrey Kripal[35]

By S.N. Balagangadhara[36]

Before addressing this writing to Jeffrey Kripal,[37] I would like to clearly stipulate some of my basic stances so that the discussion does not get derailed into the following issues:

(a) Even though the communication will be directed to Jeffrey Kripal, it is not *ad hominem* but issue-oriented. However, I will eschew making some *kinds* of qualifications that the academics are prone to make, so that any intelligent but layperson can not only follow the discussion but also *evaluate* what is being said.

(b) I do not subscribe to the 'identity politics' popular in US universities, any more than belonging to the community of writers who call themselves 'post-colonial' or as defenders of the 'sub-altern studies'. I find such writings intellectually puerile and pernicious.

(c) In no form or fashion do I want to claim that the location of a person is relevant to *evaluating* what he says. Caste, creed, ethnic origins, cultural location, skin-colour, passport, etc., are no more relevant to this debate than the fact that the 'Jewishness' of Albert Einstein is relevant to evaluating his theory of general (or special) relativity. That is to say, if we can do physics, mathematics, biology, etc., if we can write in illuminating ways about St. Augustine or Martin Luther, I do not see why someone from another culture (whether Western,

African, or American Indian) cannot do the same about
Shankaracharya or Ramakrishna Paramahamsa.

(d) The above stance is not merely a moral one, as far as I am
concerned. It is an *integral part* of what it is to contribute to
human knowledge. In so far as possessing white skin does not
make an individual a scientist only by virtue of this fact, the
same does not disqualify the individual from conducting
scientific research either. It is strictly irrelevant. However, this
does not mean that context is irrelevant to *producing*
knowledge. In more ways than one, an individual's context is
important and, perhaps, in this column I can talk about the
ways in which this is the case. This concerns the production
of knowledge, not its evaluation.

(e) I will be interrogating Jeffrey Kripal with respect to one single
question: has he produced knowledge or not? I do not believe
he has; I believe his stance prevents him from recognizing it;
and I do not believe he knows either of these two realities. I
will try to provide arguments in defense of these charges. This
is my brief.

Dear Jeffrey Kripal,

Many voices will have joined in this debate by the time I get to
publish this. Mine is one such voice. In the course of this
communication, it is possible that I raise my voice now and then to
make some point or another. Let this only draw your attention to
the fact that we are disputing some issues not as disembodied minds
but as human beings; *Menschliches, Allzumenschliches* (Human, All-
too-Human), as Nietzsche put it so beautifully in a title of one of
his contributions.

Your first book raises many issues and your second book even more.
So does Rajiv Malhotra's article. So does your response as well. I want
to take up many of them, but my 'wordiness' (as some people so kindly
characterize my style) will no doubt prevent me from conveying all I
want to say. The issue I want to tackle requires this writing style. So,
please indulge me. In order to set the problem up, I will begin by
sketching some relevant anecdotes.

1. As is the case with most Indians, I learnt English through an Indian
language. I was taught that *puja* was worship, *devas* meant 'gods'
(in the lower case) and so on. It was not clear what exactly 'God'
was, even though I was taught that you write 'God' with a 'big

G' as we used to say. I guess I assumed that 'God' referred to the entity you 'chose': mine, for instance was *Ishwara*. Somehow, I fell in love with this 'erotic ascetic' (as Wendy Doniger titles her book on Shiva): with his abode in the 'cemeteries', with his tendency to be easily provoked to anger; his *veebhoothi*, his snake and, of course, his children Ganesha and Skanda. No doubt, it has something to do with my own name and my short temper (as we say in India) too. One day, I must have been around 14 then, I discovered that *linga* meant phallus (a 'penis' as it was explained to me) and that it was a symbol of male fertility. So, when my sisters and mother went to do *puja* in the nearby temple of Mallikarjuna (another name for Shiva), they actually went to worship a penis. I was terribly, terribly embarrassed by this explanation, and felt it was wrong too, but did not know what to say about it. I still remember running to the temple to see whether the Shiva Linga looked like a penis. I must confess that it did not. However, my insistence on this fact generated jeering laughter from the person who had broken this news to me: "How many have you seen? That is what the penis will look like when you grow old." My sense of wrongness persisted, the embarrassment never left me, especially when Europeans asked me what 'Shiva Linga' stood for. But I did not know what to say.

2. Fast forward to nearly a decade later. I was 24 and on my first trip to Europe. I 'knew' about homosexuality abstractly (i.e. it never occurred to me to visualize it concretely), and had 'no problems with it' (as I used to put it those days). However, I was quite unprepared for the sight of French males kissing each other openly and therefore was incredulously fascinated by the scene when I first came across it in Amsterdam. Anyway, I went back to India having learnt about some of the signs of manifesting homosexual affection. As you will no doubt know, in India, it is a common practice for friends to walk on the streets holding hands and moving them breezily. It is equally common to put your arm across the shoulders of your friend and walk or cycle. In India, I had a friend who had the habit of clasping my hands while walking along with me. After my return from Europe, I could not reciprocate any more: I knew what it could mean. Even though I had no problem doing the same before I went to Europe, after my return, I could not. It was embarrassing; but I could not share this feeling with my friend who had never been to Europe. I could not tell him to stop doing it

either because it would have affected our friendship. So, I tried not to walk next to him when we were together in a group. When two of us were alone and on the streets, I solved this new problem by *constantly* holding a lighted cigarette in the hand he would want to clasp. Instinctively, as it happened many-a-time, he would move to the other side; then, so would my cigarette.

3. Fast forward again. Nearly a quarter century later. Today, I am able to reflect about what embarrassments like the above signified. Now I have begun to fashion the intellectual and conceptual tools needed to interrogate these experiences: not mine alone but those of a culture. What was the nature of wrongness and embarrassment I felt when I discovered that linga 'meant' penis? Why did I feel embarrassed to hold my friend's hand? What sense of 'wrongness' prevented me from telling him what 'embarrassed' me about this simple act of affection between friends?

4. Many readers of the debate that has ensued after Rajiv Malhotra's article are expressing a similar sense of 'wrongness' as well. Probably, most of them do not belong to the Hindu right or to the Hindutva movement. Nor are they expressing an ironed out, prudish 'neo-Vedantic' strain, as you put it. Something else is involved. Before interrogating this experience, let me tell you what happened recently. I asked my brother in India to read the Sulekha column and tell me of his responses. Unprepared for what he was going to encounter, he had the article and the other subsequent responses printed out in order to read them through. The other day, I rang him up to ask what he made of all this. He told me that he could not sleep the whole night after reading Rajiv Malhotra's article. He sat awake the night through, he said, much to his wife's worry, who told him that he was 'foolish' to read all kinds of stuff that upset him. "Why do they write about us like this," he asked, "what *injustice* (*anyaaya*) have we done to the Americans that they write about our *devas* this way?" He feels enraged, ashamed, humiliated and wounded, without knowing what to do about any of these feelings. "I feel like scratching my body incessantly" (a typical Indian expression of helplessness), he said, "they *should not* have written this way. It is wrong. It is *paapa*" (Ganesha is his favorite God. His home is full of pictures of all kinds of Ganeshas: the baby Ganesha, the crawling Ganesha, the dancing Ganesha and, of course, any number of seated ones.) Why do my brother and many others like him on this board

experience feelings like injustice, humiliation, moral wrong and so on? If they are shocked and indignant, which they undoubtedly are, what *kind* of a shock and indignation is it?

5. Surely, Jeffrey Kripal, this is the *first* thing you have to explore when you want to 'understand' a culture different from your own. You say, in your defense, that you have assembled a thick file of correspondence (both positive and negative) from Indians and that you are 'sensitive' to their feelings. You have done well. But this is not an issue about your sensitivity or mine, my friend, but about *cultural sensibilities*. What kind of shock and sense of wrongness does one feel to see Ramakrishna portrayed as a sort of pedophile? (Of course, you do not quite 'say' it in these terms; we will have time to look at your nuances later.) You have the answers ready. I know them; so do the readers. Instead of discussing them in the abstract, let us try and interrogate these experiences themselves, an exercise in 'cultural hermeneutics' as it were.

6. Here is the first striking thing: your purported explanations *trivialize* experiences. When I found out that my mother, my sisters, among all women and all men, were *merely worshipping the penis*, your analyses told me the following: (a) what I was doing was, in fact, 'worshipping' the penis; (b) I was a 'fool' to think that I was doing something else other than this. That is to say, not only did your text make all hitherto acts of worship look foolish, it also insisted that I was being doubly 'foolish' for not knowing this. This is also the case with respect to the claim that Ganesha's love of sweets expresses his appetite for oral sex or that his trunk is a limp penis. How foolish it must seem to cook all those many, many sweet dishes during 'Ganesha Chaturthi'!

7. By virtue of the above, it *transformed* my experience. What does the transformation consist of? Such purported explanations *re-describe experiences by twisting or distorting them*. Before I went to Europe, holding hands *was not* experienced by me as an expression of homosexuality but now it gets distorted to *become* one after my encounter with the European culture. The same is true with respect to the re-description of the linga as penis.

Of course, it is the case that scientific theories 'correct' experiences too: we see a stick appearing bent when immersed in water and see the movement of the sun across the horizon. Our scientific theories tell us that neither is true. In such cases, it is important to note that these theories preserve our experiences the way they are. In fact, the scientific theories explain to us the *necessity* of such appearances. They do not *distort* them, much less *deny* them.

8. These purported explanations *deny our experiences*. Our worship of the linga is *in reality* not a worship of Shiva at all, but a 'subconscious acknowledgement' of some 'repressed' notion of fertility (or whatever else). Whatever we 'experience' is not the said object but something else.

9. What happens when experience is denied by being distorted and trivialized? If those who revere Shiva and Ganesha accept this story of penis, both erect and limp, could they feel the same sense of 'reverence' (or call it what you want) that they once did, and remember it too, without feeling a perfect ass? They cannot. Access to such an experience becomes tainted. That is, these purported explanations *deny access to our own experiences*.

10. Herein lies the root of the sense of wrongness that my brother and many others feel. Who or what is denying access to our own experience? It is not a theory, but a *theorizing of someone else's experience*. Because this point can be easily misunderstood, let me unravel it just a bit.

Much before Freud wrote whatever he did, we had people from other religions coming to India to say the same thing: first from Islam and then from Christianity. They told us (not only them, many Indians in their wake told us that as well!) that we were worshipping the cow, the monkey, the penis, the stone idol and the naked fakir. This is how these people *experienced us and our activities*. Their theologies had prepared them for such an experience much before they came to our part of the world. Of course, they saw only what they expected to see.

The descriptions the missionaries provided, the reports of Christian merchants, the interpretations of the Muslim kings, the developments within Christian theology, etc. were the 'facts' that Freud sought to understand. (To the extent he believed that he was laying the foundation of a 'scientific' theory, to that extent these were the 'facts' he was accounting for.) What did Freud theorize then? He theorized the *European experience* of other cultures and upon a theological elaboration of these experiences.

Consequently, who or what denies us access to our experience? It is the *experience of another culture* (or, the 'theorizing of such an experience'). Though important in its own right, we can safely drop this distinction. Taking it into consideration would make the analysis complex without adding anything of substance. This lies at the root of the feeling of wrongness: *our experiences are being trivialized, denied, distorted and made inaccessible by someone else's experience of the world.* You have the feeling of moral or ethical wrongness because such a situation is neither justified nor justifiable. One is made to think that, apparently, there is only one way of experiencing the world: the 'Western way'.

11. Thus, some among us protest: this situation is morally wrong. "What injustice have we done that you speak of us this way? It is a *paapa*," as my brother put it. Like Rajiv Malhotra, there are others who argue this point of view eloquently and with repeated insistence. But such men and women are easily branded as the RSS, as the Hindutva and, of course, the ever-present threat of being damned as a 'Hindu fundamentalist'. Others, much like the 14-year-old boy that I once was, fall silent because another kind of wrongness is involved as well: *a cognitive wrongness.*

12. Scientific theories, in so far as they explain our experiences, do so without denying or trivializing the latter. But the explanations of the sort you give, and those I heard, do not explain; they merely trivialize, distort and deny what we experience. They do not shed any light on our experiences, but render them opaque and inaccessible. Galileo did not deny that we see the movement of the sun on the horizon or that we see it rise and set. None would have taken him seriously, then or later, if he had done either. Instead, he explained the necessity of this perception, while explaining that the world is not structured this way. Sure, he challenged; but to whom or to what did he address it to? It was to a set of *beliefs* about the world and to the authority that defended those beliefs. He did not tell you or me that we hallucinate every time we see the movement of the Sun; he claimed that the geocentric theory *was false.* This is not what you do do, Jeffrey Kripal. You tell us we have *false* experiences and *not* that we have a false theory about mysticism. How is this accomplished? You trivialize and deny our spiritual experience. And this makes most of us fall silent, making us dumb like the way a boy of 14 could not think of anything to say when he heard that the Shiva Linga was the penis. Not because it struck a chord with him but because he did not know how to counter it. He fell silent because he did not know how to express the sense of cognitive wrongness he felt, a situation that many among of us find ourselves in.

Today, more than three decades later, that boy has grown up. He has studied books, thought about questions and has analyzed relevant experiences. Today, he is able to say what is cognitively wrong: such explanations do the opposite of what scientific theories do. He now knows that these explanations do nothing of the sort they claim; they are merely a way of structuring the experience of a people from another culture. He knows that these *pseudo-*explanations, that is what they are, *sound* fancy; he knows too that many from his culture parrot this exotic product. But since when, he asks himself, are scientific truths decided by means of majority votes? Thus he claims that the *first charge* is true, Jeffrey Kripal: your story is wrong not only morally but also cognitively. That is, you have not produced knowledge. You *could not have* produced it because you have not explained the experience but, instead, provided a trivialized and distorted description of such an experience. You are not even close to capturing (let alone explaining) Indian 'mysticism' or its cultural forms. In fact, you are even blind to seeing it.

13. What an extraordinary thing to say! You have written a book about the mysticism of Ramakrishna and, yet, here I am, suggesting that you are not even able to see it. So, a bit of explanation is in order. It is tricky, so let us take it by stages.

13.1. Let us step back from the psychoanalytical explanations and ask ourselves the following question: *which problem was Freud trying to solve?* Of course, there were many: he wanted to investigate the nature of hysteria; he wanted to figure out the story behind incest fantasies; he wanted to understand slips of the tongue. (I do not mean any of these; what is the underlying problem behind these issues?) Philosophers of science identify it as the 'problem-situation'. What then was Freud's problem-situation? Both the nature of the psychoanalytic practice and the structure (and content) of the psychoanalytical explanations give us ample clues to the direction of an answer. In its blandest form, it is this: "Is one's experience in the world (especially about oneself and the others) veridical (i.e. true)?" If we keep in mind what I have said hitherto and what you implicitly assume, it can be put even more provocatively: *Is the experience of an individual directly accessible to the individual whose experience it is?*

13.2. Freud's answer is known: no, he said, one can access one's own experience *only* through the mediation of another, *in casu*, the psychoanalyst. This is not the only reason why Freud's story appears unbelievable. There is something else of importance as well.

I am sure you will admit that not only the notion of experience but also its existence is of crucial importance to us human beings. We think that experience is valuable and important; it is both the source of and the precondition for most learning. Given its centrality to human existence, one would naturally expect the Western tradition to be bothered about figuring out what this 'experience' is all about. Yet, amazingly enough as it turns out, such is not the case. Despite books and articles in many, many disciplines bearing the title, the nature of 'experience' is hardly studied. More often than not, it is reduced to thoughts, feelings, perceptions, or even physical sensation and action. None of these, either collectively or jointly exhausts experience because one *could experience any or all of them as well.* (One can experience thoughts, feelings, etc.) Thus, what is 'experience'? An important question, but very ill understood.

Such being the case, Freud's observation and his sense of the 'problem-situation' are very valuable indeed. Of course, he hypothesized that the individual experience is not directly accessible to the said individual, and postulated many mechanisms to account for this non-accessibility. We need not take sides on the 'validity' or otherwise of his individual hypotheses here, even though I will return to this issue in another way at the end of this column.

13.3. There is, however, another culture in the world, which has made this 'problem-situation' an absolutely central focus of its inquiry. All the Indian traditions, without any major exception as far as I know, have made experience and its interrogation central to their inquiry. Naturally, they too discovered that experience is not 'veridical'; there are 'things' that prevent us from accessing these experiences. Different traditions named them differently: *maaya, avidya* and *agyana* are the best-known categories in this context. They thought each of these categories was an instance of *paapa* or ignorance and, in fact, removing this has been their central goal:

gyaanoodaya or the 'arising of knowledge' (again, it is called differently by different traditions). The hindrances to knowledge were either 'illusions' (of sorts) or ignorance (of sorts). One could eliminate them, they said, and they developed any number of practical ways of doing so. (The plurality of the Indian traditions is partly a plurality of the ways of removing the veil of ignorance.)

Though ill understood by most Indologists and philosophers, these notions are crucial. Ignorance is not mere absence of information; it is accorded a positive role and is seen as a positive force that actively *hinders* the emergence of knowledge. *Maaya* is not mere illusion; the world exists and impinges upon us too much to make the facile claim of the sort that Patrick Hogan makes in his article on Sulekha. In any case, these traditions believed too that some kind of mediation would be helpful in accessing one's own experience. They called such a mediator *Guru* and suggested that, in most cases, one needed a Guru to achieve enlightenment.

13.4. In other words, Jeffrey Kripal, there exist two rival or competing *practical* traditions that address themselves to the same (or very similar) 'problem-situation'. By virtue of this, they become rival or competing research traditions that provide different answers to the same 'problem-situation'.

13.5. Why did you not look at the Indian traditions this way to understand Kali's child? Why do you speak as though the Tantric 'emphasis on sex' antedates Freud's claims? You say that Tantrism spoke about 'sex' even before Freud, as though you want to compliment the Indian culture for its acuity. Actually, it does not sound complimentary but patronizing. The Indian traditions *challenge* Freud's theories. Why did you not look at the issue in this manner?

It is not as though you are ignorant of the Indian traditions. Even if you are, your mentor Wendy Doniger is supposed to be *the* expert on Hinduism. Why did it not occur either to her or to you that the theories you used were already facing challenges from within the Indian traditions? Here is my simple answer: *you have been blinded to the existence of Indian traditions as alternatives to Freud.*

13.6. This is not all. You do something more in your blindness. You use Freudian explanation to characterize a rival research tradition. Such a move can only yield a caricatured, distorted version of the competitor. When I was young, I remember one of my uncles making fun of my exposition of the Darwinian evolutionary theory with the following riposte, "You might be proud to accept that your ancestors are monkeys. I, however, am not." I felt like a fool again, because I did not know how to respond to my uncle. As I read the research and the controversies later, I discovered that this is one of the most standard ways of ridiculing the evolutionary theory. Who does the ridiculing? Those who belong to the rival research traditions, of course! By caricaturing Galileo's theory, Aristotelians ridiculed it; this is how modern medicine looks at Paracelsus or the medical practices in the Europe of the Middle Ages. That is what you do as well. To use the stories of the Viennese master to understand Kali's child is like using creationism to portray Darwin's theory. You are blind to this distortion as well. So, how could you describe Ramakrishna, when you cannot see him? You cannot; the second charge is obviously not so far-fetched after all.

14. This blindness inherent in your venture must render us blind too whether the 'us' is a Sudhir Kakar or a Sumit Sarkar. It does, *but in a different way and for a different reason*. I suppose you have no problem in accepting the suggestion that theories about cultural worlds have their *roots* in the experiences of such worlds. These theories describe experiences; they reflect on experiences; they problematize such experiences and think through them. In other words, if I want to theorize about the Indian culture, I need to have *access* to an experience of the Indian culture (whether directly or indirectly). These explanations deny such access by acting as a filter between our own experiences and us.

In one sense, all theories act as some kind of a filter: they select some salient aspect of the experience and focus upon it. In the case we are talking about, the situation is not the same. These purported explanations act as a distorting glass. I knew I had such experiences; I saw that others apparently continued to have the experiences I had before (I continued to see adult male friends holding hands, I continued to see people doing puja to the Shiva Linga, etc); I knew too that I had these but was unable to access them *because of these explanations*. That is, these explanations came actively between my own experiences and me, and *actively prevented* me from describing or reflecting on my own experiences. Did I really 'see' the homosexuality of my friend when he held my hands? No. Did I really 'see' the penis when I looked at the Lingam? No, I did not. Our experiences of the world and the explanations that are used are at loggerheads with each other: without speaking about experience, one cannot say what the 'Indian experience' consists of; the (Freudian) stories we reproduce tell us that there is no 'Indian experience' to talk of.

This is the lot and daily life of cultures and peoples colonized by the Western culture. Colonization, as many have pointed out, was not merely a process of occupying lands and extracting revenues. It was not a question of us aping the Western countries and trying to be like them. It was not even about colonizing the imaginations of a people by making them 'dream' that they too will become 'modern', developed and sophisticated. It goes deeper than any of these. It is about denying the peoples and cultures their own experiences; of rendering them aliens to themselves; of actively preventing any description of their own experiences except in terms defined by the colonizers. This is the truth about what the Kakars and the Sarkars of my world sell, no matter how they package it, no matter how they market it.

Of course, there is a very substantial issue here: why do we, Indians, continue to be colonized when the real event ended more than fifty years ago? I will negatively address myself to this issue shortly only to say what the answer *cannot be*. In this process, I can also answer some possible objections, and bring the case to a conclusion.

15. The third charge is that your stance prevents you knowing you are blind. That is to say, why are you blind? Better said, what makes you blind? The answer to this has layers too, and let me peel just a few of them. To do that, I shall have to engage you in your own territory, on your own turf. That is, I want to talk to you about your understanding of your own culture and religion. (Is this not what 'cultural hermeneutics' all about?) Let me, therefore, play the ventriloquist and displace your voice to ask myself a few questions: Is the alienation from our own experience (that I spoke of) any different from what any believer undergoes in the West, when he 'discovers' that God is dead? Is my experience any different from a Westerner losing his belief about God and the mystic? Are our travails anything other than the story of 'modernity' as it plays out in India?

16. *Yes, to all the three questions.* Let me get into an autobiographical mode once again to talk about some of them. I did not quite tell you what happened to me during those decades, when we fast forwarded. Let us rewind a bit and see what happened to the lad between his eighteenth and thirtieth year. You see, he wanted to change the world and became a radical. He left home before he was even twenty, lived in the slums, worked in a quarry, went to the villages and even became a Marxist for a period of time. From an 'orthodox' Brahmana, he had metamorphosed into a fire-breathing 'atheist': India was backward, the Caste System was a curse, Indian traditions were outdated, the 'gods' (though he still wrote it with a 'small g') did not exist (except that they once walked the lands of Europe!). A run-of-the-mill progressive, in other words. In short, the revolution could not come soon enough for him. However, what brought him to Marxism also brought him out of it: the inability of these stories to make sense of his experience. So, he came to Europe, not in search of the Holy Grail (how could he? He was born a Brahmana after all!), but to study the root-cause of the problems of Marxist theory. You see, in those days it was difficult for us to find the books of Hegel, Fichte, Schelling and many other German philosophers in the public libraries. Even as I began to solve my problems with Marx, a new issue was beginning to force itself on me: I had dimly begun to realize that I was an Indian, and that I lived as such in a culture I hardly understood.

17. This realization turned my world upside down; in doing so, however, it helped me regain access to my own experiences. The world that got turned upside down was the one I *thought* I lived in all the time. I had thought until then that I knew Western culture like the back of my hand: it was a shock to discover just how far I was from knowing either. I could hold forth on the notions of 'civil society', 'ought' in ethics, the histories of the Renaissance and the Enlightenment and, why, I could even eat meat and drink wine. None of these, I discovered, meant anything: I had remained an Indian, even if I once thought I was 'modern'. Thus, I reflected on my experiences (fed by reading and yet more reading) until I could begin to grasp the outlines of the question, *what is to be an Indian?* Seventeen years ago, I formulated these reflections as a research project, titling it after a poem from T.S. Eliot that goes like this: " . . . *We shall not cease from exploration*, and the end

of our exploring shall be to arrive where we started and know the place for the first time." I had indeed arrived where I had started from: India, Bangalore, a Brahmana family. I too began to know the place for the first time, because, at last, I could begin to access my own cultural experiences in the way they needed to be accessed. However, the job is not complete and the process not yet over. During all these years, I have been constructing the tools required to gain access to our experiences because I realized too that my individual biography was but the Indian history writ small.

18. That is why I can now say that discovering lingam was called 'penis' did not rob me of my world the same way atheism robs a believer of his world in the Western culture. *It could not.* There are so many reasons why these two processes are not even remotely similar that I cannot hope to mention any of them in the course of this column. Instead, let me recount a story taken from the *Chandogya Upanishad.*

It appears Prajapathi said that he who has found the 'Self' (Atman) and understands it obtains all worlds and all desires. "The Devas and the Asuras both heard these words, and said: 'Well, let us search for that Self by which, if one has searched it out, all worlds and all desires are obtained'. Thus saying Indra from the Devas, Virochana from the Asuras, and both without having communicated with each other, approached Prajapathi . . . They dwelt there as pupils for thirty-two years. Then Prajapathi asked them: 'For what purpose have you both dwelt here?' They both replied: 'A saying of yours is being repeated . . . Now we have both dwelt here because we wish for that Self'". He makes them both look in a pan of water and asks them what they see. They see their own bodies reflected. He makes them dress up and look again into the water pan and asks them what they see. "They said: 'Just as we are, well adorned, with our best clothes and clean, thus we are both there, Sir, well adorned, with our best clothes and clean.' Prajapathi said: "That is the Self, this is the immortal, the fearless, this is the *Brahman*'. They both went away satisfied in their hearts". Prajapathi reflects on their absence of critical thought and thinks that whichever of the two follows this line of thought will 'perish'. The story continues: "Now Virochana, satisfied in his heart, went to the Asuras and preached that doctrine to them, that the self (the body) alone is to be worshipped, that the self (the body) alone is to be served, and that he who worships the self and serves the self, gains both worlds, this and the next".[38] The story further continues about what Indra did, but that is not relevant to me now. What is important are the three *obvious* points in the story:

18.1. Both the asuras and the devas seek enlightenment. Quite obviously, as this story makes clear, this state does not consist of 'believing in' some *deva* or the other for the simple reason that they, the *devas*, thirst after enlightenment too! Further, to reach this state, as it becomes evident when we follow the story further, no 'grace' of any kind of 'God' is required: *one needs to think through*. (The Indian traditions speak of any number of other ways too, but that need not detain us here.) From this it follows that one's enlightenment is the result of one's own effort. It is a *deserved* 'reward' that is in proportion to the effort you put in. Between you and enlightenment, which is the ultimate goal in life, no one or no thing can counteract your efforts.

18.2. Virochana's *insight* that the body requires worshipping because it is the 'Self' is a wrong answer *because* it is superficial. The answer, however, is *not false*. As the story evolves further, the reader appreciates that the asura's answer is superficial because Indra is provided with a 'deeper' answer. An answer is superficial *only relative* to a deeper one but that does not make the former into a false answer. Virochana's insight *appears* as materialistic and as 'atheistic' as they come: yet, the story seems to condone it as a *possible* answer (though wrong and superficial) to *seek enlightenment*. (This answer will not 'help' and that is why it is wrong.) The discovery that all there is to life is the life one has, or the body one has, does not rob an Indian of anything. Very sharply put: in the Indian traditions, 'atheism' (of a particular sort, see below) *can also be a way of reaching enlightenment*. (We are not yet talking about 'Buddhism'!) This claim is not even remotely similar to the shock of 'discovering' (in the Western culture) that 'God is dead'.

You might object that the distinction I have drawn above between the 'wrong' answer and the 'false' one is a quibble about the meaning of words. It is not: there is a cognitive issue involved here. When one has a false answer, one can *know* that it is false and, perhaps, even localize its falsity. To reject a false answer, one does not need the presence of an alternative answer. This is not the case with a wrong answer. One might 'feel' that something is wrong without being able to say what is wrong or even reject the wrong answer. (Look at what I have been saying throughout this communication.) One needs the presence of an alternative and better answer so that one can say what was *wrong* with the 'wrong answer' and reject it.

18.3. What kind of 'atheism' am I talking about? Not the Western atheism: that makes *no sense* to the Indian traditions because of two things. (a) As the story above suggests, the road to 'enlightenment' does not go through Jerusalem. That is, Prajapthi does not tell Indra that he should 'believe' in 'God' in order to be enlightened. (b) Consequently, Indian traditions are not 'theistic' (poly-, heno- or mono- or whatever) the way Judaism, Christianity and Islam are. Consequently, Western forms of 'atheism' do not have the Western kind of a theistic doctrine to oppose, when they come to India.

18.4. The contrast between our asuras and the Devil in the Bible cannot be greater. Even though, in the classical but simple interpretation, the Devil himself is a fallen angel, he does not believe *in God*, but merely *acknowledges* His existence. As the Gospel puts it, "Thou believest that there is one God; thou doest well: the devils also believe, *and tremble*" (James 2: 26; my emphasis.) The Devil makes us *deny* the 'true' God, says the religion that Christianity is. God reveals Himself to save us from the 'clutches' of the Devil, it assures us further. To become an atheist in the West is to lose 'faith' in this revelation. Where is this 'atheism' and where are our traditions? Where is the Devil, and where are our Asuras?

19. Thus, our *asuras* are not like the Devil or his minions in the Bible. Not only do they seek 'enlightenment', as the above story makes it clear, but some of them are also the greatest of the *bhaktas* of our *devatas*. The reason why Rama was born, they say, was to kill Ravana—a supreme bhakta. He deserved to die not in any other way than by being slain by Vishnu himself. To this day, we celebrate the greatest king (an asura) we ever had, and the greatest bhakta who ever lives: Lord Bali (an immortal) on whose head Trivikrama (Vaamana, as he is also called) placed his third foot. Each year, it appears, he ascends from the bottom of the earth to find out how his subjects are faring: the streets are lit as are our houses with their

doors open, so that he may come in and feel welcomed. We call this the festival of lights, the Deepavali. You know all this. Why do I tell it to you then? It is to say that our 'atheisms', our 'asuras', the 'immorality' of our *devas* do not rob us of our traditions the way atheism does rob a believer in the West. *Devatas* may die, be born again, punished, or even remain immortal: our traditions do not suffer from any of these but live on precisely because of these. Consequently, today, *without rejecting any piece of knowledge I have ever learnt*, I can access my traditions and my experience in a very profound way. That is why, Jeffrey Kripal, you would be wrong to say that what I felt when I was fourteen is what the believer feels when he loses his faith in the God of Abraham, Isaac and Jacob. *This is another process altogether.*

When people protest against your portrayal of Ramakrishna, the majority of the Indians are not saying what you think they are. The language they use may sound familiar to your ears; what they say might remind you of your own experience. To see and understand us this way, however, is to understand very little about what makes us different cultures or even what is interesting about this.

20. During the last two decades, I did not merely build the tools to recover my own experiences. I discovered that I could not do this without understanding the Western culture either. My attempts at understanding one could not have begun without trying to understand the other. To know my mother better, it appears, I need to know my mother-in-law as well. So, let us look at how *you* have been treating the latter because we know what you have done with the former. How has psychoanalysis, sociology, psychology, anthropology, or whatever else described what religion is? That is to say, what do they *assume* when they try to explain religion, if they explain it at all? They assume that religion is a human product, if not a human invention. But, Jeffrey Kripal, this assumption denies them *their study object*: a Christian believer sees the Bible as *the word of God* and not just as a book. You cannot explain this belief by appealing to any sets of natural causes unless you begin with the *assumption* that the believer is wrong about his own experience. Of course, you cannot countenance God in your research; however, if you do not, you are not studying religion as the believer experiences it, but its caricatured representation. In other words, your Freud *cannot explain religion*. He explains it as

merely a human product, an assumption for which he has *no grounds*. To formulate simply: atheism is a philosophical option, but this option will *deny* you from doing science. Doing theism, however, will give you theology but not science. To a Christian, the existence or non-existence of Jesus is of great importance, but the answer to the question about the historical Jesus will not tell you anything about his Christ-Nature. If he is not the Christ, Jesus of Nazareth is merely a man, not even 'the Son of God'. But then, of course, you cannot assume that Jesus is the Christ and write a *scientific* tract about it either. Underlying this dilemma is a whole host of other problems. (To write further on this requires a book. I have written one such, which you might care to read.) Therefore, it appears, *by assuming the stance that you do* towards the study of religion, you do 'unto your fellow men what you do unto us as well'. You caricature the experience of the believer in your culture; you caricature the experiences of our entire culture. *It is this that blinds you to what you are doing.*

21. That means your descriptions of our experiences are doubly caricatured. *Firstly*, you tell us that what we 'see' *is not* what we 'see': the linga is not the linga but a penis. As I said earlier, this is what religions like Christianity and Islam had told us. You tell me they are right. This way, you impose your cultural experience upon us and deny our experiences. *Secondly*, you tell us that, even here, what we do is something else: it transpires that we are not 'worshipping' penis or falling in love with Shiva. We do not 'worship' at all (one can only 'worship' either God or the Devil) and Shiva is but an 'erotic ascetic'. The aspect has two *tails that sting*: why does the imagination of Indian culture express itself in such grotesque forms as the penis, the monkey, the stone idol with four arms, and an elephant-headed human? Why is the Western imagination confined to more 'decent' things like visualizing God as the 'father'? Enter Wendy Doniger and her children, who answer these questions in ways known to us all. Is there any wonder people are furious? Are you really that amazed?

22. Let me bring the case to a conclusion: what are you trying to 'understand' when you use your 'hermeneutic' to understand Ramakrishna? How *you* see him? How your culture sees him? Or how *we* see him? What are you theorizing about, *your experience,* your culture's experience, or ours? You insist that how your culture experiences the world is also the only possible experience of the

world (Not explicitly, of course, but, as I have argued, that is what you do). You want to tell us what Ramakrishna's 'mysticism' is *all about* because this is the only way your *theories* allow you to see it. Your theories, your explanations, your assumptions *deny us* what you would not, as a person, dream of denying to us: that we too have an experience, another one perhaps, but one that is as 'valid and legitimate' as any human experience can be.

You end your article with these words: "I at least am ready to laugh again, to exchange gifts, to argue, to apologize, to weep. I always have been." I believe you. But do you know that people from other cultures do so too? We too laugh, exchange gifts, argue, apologize and weep? You know *that* we do it; you *assume* you know what they are because that is what *you* do too. But do you know *how* we do any or all of these things? Does it occur to you that we might do them *differently*? Do you, Jeffrey Kripal, know *how we cry* or even why? I wonder.

Friendly greetings
Balu

The Butterflies Baulked: Public Comments on the Debate

By Yvette C. Rosser

Since 2002, the *RISA Lila* essay has been downloaded over 43,000 times. The steady flow of visitors— almost 1,000 per month for four years—indicates that this is a topic of perennial concern rather than a blog-like momentary burst. A few university professors have assigned several of the essays on Sulekha as required reading for their Comparative Religion or Asian-American Studies classes.

The present book is only a small part of an emerging stream of critiques representing the birth of a new area of Critical Studies researching Hinduphobia in the American academic establishment. It is hoped that encouraging this nascent debate will lead American intellectuals to examine one of the last remnants of prejudicial, colonial era stereotyping still operative in the liberal academy.

Those in control of the 'official' narrative have heretofore rarely admitted that treatments about Indian culture and Hinduism are often exoticized and essentialized. Instead of working against this widely dispersed discrimination, as is the norm in America's usually anti-racist liberal academy, scholars have often closed ranks to defend their subtle and not so subtle biases. Oddly, scholars often defend the essentialisms, because "that's the way Hinduism has always been taught in the West". In order for Indological scholarship to appear 'valid and true', the traditions must somehow be frozen in time. But when the object of this scholarship suddenly talks back, it can be threatening. The butterfly should not baulk. The object must remain compliant. But, as the following collections of quotes will show, the Hindu diaspora is talking back.

The following comments express the collective experiences of a large number of concerned persons. Such on-going testimonials and observations help look at the issues squarely in the face. Dynamic and full of promise to transform old stale paradigms, nonetheless this emergent movement in Hinduism Studies is perceived as a threat to the scholarly status quo. This paranoia blocks opportunities for productive engagement. The responses below represent an outpouring from individuals with concerns about India Studies, South Asian Studies, Indology, Hindu Studies, Religious Studies, and related fields.[39]

On the day of its publication, Prof. Antonio de Nicolas informed the Religions in South Asia scholarly discussion group (RISA-l) that an article named after them had appeared that morning in Sulekha, an online magazine. De Nicolas explained that the article examined the way some scholars of religion 'bathe others in their own cultural waters'. He wrote that it contained some 'very concrete examples', and 'sacred cows are sacrificed'. He requested that his colleagues read the essay and advised RISA-l, as a group, to "develop a policy where both sides of the discussion benefit in the exchange". In his usual wry style de Nicolas wrote: "After all, the *other* is my own possibilities".

Most of the comments on Sulekha were from lay citizens, not from scholars. Many of the contributors, identified only by their user names, wrote just a few lines, while others wrote extensively. One of the first comments was from a man named Peter, "This is a very important article that should be made required reading for all Indians and for those who teach Indic traditions." Bhopali wrote that the essay had "identified the reasons why many 2nd generation Hindus in the US tend to distance themselves from India and Hinduism".

Many of those who posted comments were hopeful that this type of research could lead to positive change, such as Arun Gupta who wrote: "One more step on the way to *purna swarajya!*"[40] Rudra Caitanya expressed the collective feelings of a large number of people when he enthusiastically wrote, "The snowball has started to roll down the slope. It WILL pick up more mass and momentum . . ." He predicted that this giant snowball would eventually overtake RISA and other neo-colonial academicians. He offered his services: "Please let me know if I could be of some help. Grunt work, documentation, anything you need—I volunteer." Another person wrote: "This is a great essay, a true contribution to achieve harmony in the future."

A man named Akskar pointed out the differences he saw in narrations about religion when made by insiders:

Last night, I happened to catch Bill Moyer's show 'Genesis' on PBS. They were discussing the story of Rebecca—how she helped her younger son, Jacob, steal the blessing that his father, Isaac, had intended for the elder son. Apparently this was done so that the covenant that the Biblical God had established with his chosen people would continue. I saw the powerful academic scholarship represented by the panelists [who] grew up in the belief system they were discussing and [still] practice that belief system. They could be objective in discussing the shortcomings of the story, however they were very forgiving because they could connect it to their inner core. They accepted the trickery and deceit because they saw the greater end, they could identify with the story. Obviously, Ms. Wendy and non-Hindus teaching about Hinduism have an academic interest, they don't have a core understanding, and it is really unfortunate that they are shaping the way the religion is being taught and perceived.

He concluded: "Those of us who read this article should try to ensure that it reaches as many people as possible." Another reader named Samartha wrote:

It is now the duty of truly secularist Indians, on both side of the fence—Hindu organizations or Socialist organizations—to bring up such issue and educate the masses in the US and Western world and in the circle of their influence. It is the need of the time and this should not remain one man's fight.

Vikram Masson, co-chairman of an online discussion group called Navya Shastra,[41] contributed an informative comment, quoting Wittgenstein, who famously averred that Freud was "The greatest myth-maker of the twentieth century." Masson continued:

Modern Western scholars have elevated the largely discredited Freudian mythology to the status of a science. This allows them full freedom to superimpose their own versions of this weak mythology upon the stereotypical 'passive Indian'. It is nothing less than 'conceptual colonialism', where previously hegemonic and condescending language has been transmuted into the seemingly neutral, 'scholarly' argot of the academy.

It is precisely the emptiness, indeed the vacuity of their own religious traditions that has lead the West to search for other compensating mythologies. I know several New Yorkers who spent decades sitting on a psychoanalyst's couch, morbidly deconstructing (or reconstructing) Oedipal complexes and infantile fantasies. But none of their recent systems: scientism, psychoanalysis, Marxism, or consumer capitalism has been able to confront what the Buddhist scholar David Loy terms as 'lack'—our abiding sense of impermanence.

The Indic traditions still represent an alternative (threatening?) methodology for confronting our own sense of lack. But the West, with its own ingrained notions of cultural superiority, has rarely acknowledged it ON ITS OWN TERMS. So we are left with their reductive methodologies of denigration, which always seem to come back to sex. Who is really suppressed, I wonder?

Sanjay Garg, expressing similar sentiments as dozens of other contributors, thought that the article was 'very powerful and disturbing'. Even though from the outset he was 'expecting calumny & denigration', he found that examples of RISA scholarship were 'tough' to take and 'anger-provoking'. Garg wrote that "the article's exposé [was] hard hitting in its accuracy [outlining cases] of shoddy scholarship and personal biases". He added: "Chakras as Indian hermeneutics is original, creative and highly amusing".

Garg concluded with an observation that is the exact opposite of Doniger's opinion of the *RISA Lila* essay. Doniger had written to Malhotra in an email that the essay was 'grotesquely ignorant' regarding the 'scholarly approach to Hinduism' and 'hopelessly distorted by . . . strong biases'. In contrast to this Ivory Tower perspective, Garg wrote from a *desi*[42] on the plains point-of-view, that

> *Wendy's Child Syndrome* and *The Myth of the West*[43] are correctly identified as an important new area of study & development. One of its greatest strengths is the sense of meticulous research that underpins the whole article.

Vishal Agarwal[44] opined that the "essay exposes how colonial and racist attitudes, coupled with a subtle hatemongering against Hinduism, Hindus and India, still prevail in Indological studies". He suggested, "A good exercise would be to compare the present day writings of Indologists, and American Scholars of 'Religion in South Asia', with those of Orientalists and Christian Missionaries in early 1900s and 1800s." He surmised that such a study would "demonstrate how old attitudes die-hard", adding, "it is often old wine served in new bottles". Vikram Masson agreed, "Exactly! Whatever happens to be in fashion, Utilitarianism, Hobbes, Deism, Jung, Psychoanalysis . . . indiscriminately used—I hate to say it—as a WEAPON to **wrest away agency from**

Indians and to 'essentialize' the utterly complex Hinduism." [Emphasis added.]

Roopesh Mathur brought up the issue of funding:

The kind of intellectual colonialism described here will continue, until it is challenged by an alternative establishment with [its] own brand of scholarship, and sources of funding. The basic law of business that, 'He who writes the checks gets to call the shots' will ensure that these distorted perspectives continue to persist. If you want to correct a field of academic study and break these cliques, you will have to establish alternative and equally valid scholarly viewpoints.

Mathur pointed out that there is a "wealth of knowledge available in ancient Indian texts and in the huge diversity of Indian society and history" which lends itself to 'exploitation'. As an example, he pointed to the 'psychobabble' produced by Deepak Chopra and various other contemporary writers, concluding that, "they take the knowledge and make it suitable to the Western palate. [...] If you get the blend right, you can make a nice living for yourself." He offered an amusing analogy:

It is very much like Indian restaurants in America: The neighborhood Indian restaurant in a small town is thronged by Americans, who want a little exotic something to spice up their weekends. The Indians who go there know that the food is a pale imitation of the real thing.

He asked: "The real question is, how do you build up alternative viewpoints, with scholarship of a high quality and make it pay for those who make the effort?"

One anonymous contributor using the screen name Guessing, expressed the same consternation and disgust felt by many others:

What's the best way to market pornography? Call it Oriental Research, of course—it pays and is 'respectable' too! I sigh at my own ignorance for so long when I used to believe Katherine Mayo represented the nadir of the gutter mentality. She may have well been the inspector in Gandhiji's famous words, but hey, move over, here's the creature from the gutter itself! And all this muck gets passed off as scholarship!!! A de Sade, alive [today], would have been the biggest name in Indology . . . by its current standards. Arguably, this is worse than physical assault and murder. This is a campaign to destroy the soul before the murder of the body.

A member of the diaspora from Boston, Raj Mohanka, commended the article:

> for bringing together pieces of information to make [the] point— that Indic Traditions are maligned and that a great deal of bias (and bizarre psychosis on the part of Wendy's ... gang) exists out there. The part of the article I welcomed was the proposal for dialogue. Too often people complain, but don't work to solve problems. Rajiv correctly sets an example in the positive direction.

For Mohanka: "The idea of equating 'modernization' with 'westernization' seems antiquated". He added, "After all, many non-Western nations are modern today (Japan, East Asia, a few, small Middle Eastern nations) and they have not lost their culture to become modern." He concluded, that in his opinion:

> What Rajiv has done here is not a 'bombshell'. He is merely pointing out the lack of scholarship among many Americans involved in RISA. This is necessary in order to improve the quality of research for everyone's benefit.

Jonathan Shear, a Professor of Philosophy at Virginia Commonwealth University, wrote the following note:

> I just finished reading your 'Wendy's Children' piece. Whew! As you might expect I've got little suggestions and may disagree with small points here and there. But the overall thrust? Very informative—and it surely looks like it needs to be said! I'm very glad I read it. I especially enjoyed your use of chakras as Indic Hermeneutics, and even incorporated a bit of the notion in a lecture I gave today. What a neat—and to me highly plausible—approach. [Emphasis added]

The RISA-l online discussion group is not the sole electronic portal where scholars of Indology, Hinduism, South Asian Studies, and related subject areas can virtually congregate. The Indology list-serve is another Internet group devoted to the scholarly discussion of the Indian subcontinent. Indology has over 350 members. V.V. Raman, a professor emeritus of Physics and Humanities, wrote to his colleagues on the Indology list:

> By now, many professional/academic Indologists must have heard of, and quite a few might have also read, Mr. Rajiv Malhotra's posting in Sulekha. Whether one agrees or disagrees with his tone and style, it is hard to ignore three aspects of this essay:

(a) It has elicited a groundswell of support from a great many Hindus/ Indians who keep track of current exchanges on matters related to their religion and ethnic roots. The essay has, within a couple of days, elicited more than a hundred enthusiastic accolades.

(b) Unlike some other of Mr. Malhotra's postings, this one is presented as a scholarly paper, end-notes, references and all.

(c) Above all, he does make a valid point which is simply this: Western commentators on Indic traditions ought to be versed not only in the lore and the language via books and manuscripts; they **must also have some sensitivity for the culture** on which they are commenting and which they are trying to interpret, not only for themselves but for **countless readers who may be only vaguely familiar with the very complex and sophisticated culture that the Indic is.**

To me, filtering out all the understandable astonishment and rage at some of the more jarring commentaries on Hindu gods and goddesses, Malhotra's seems to be a fairly reasonable position which, with due respects to him, is not all that original, because it is shared by millions of others: not just practicing Hindus, but some Non-Hindu scholars as well. Indeed, the current collective reaction to some of the more objectionable writings on Hinduism is mild compared to what one might expect elsewhere if corresponding statements were to be made on the prophet and scripture of another major non Judeo-Christian religion.

My own view in this context, which I have repeatedly articulated, is that one cannot, indeed one should not, dissect a living religion as one dissects a dead butterfly, or even a dead religion, for that matter. Talking about Shiva or Sarasvati is not like talking about Zeus or Diana. Shiva and Sarasvati still touch the heart and soul of millions, provoke prayer and prostration, are venerated in places of worship, and celebrated in festivities.

[...]

I for one have often applauded the dedication of Western scholars who elucidate and expound the intricacies of Indic civilization, their compilation of dictionaries and translations of classics, slanted or distorted as they sometimes might be. But when serious academics publish books that are blatantly insulting to the sensibilities of a billion people, and are also frequently distorted, and write in utter ignorance of how the practitioners currently feel about their deeply religious symbols, then somebody should say, 'Stop this nonsense!' I think that is what Mr. Malhotra has done, and in doing so, he is giving voice to millions of his co-religionists.

If professional Indologists are indifferent to or contemptuous of what Mr. Malhotra has unleashed, I fear the situation could get even worse for the whole world of Indological scholarship. Indeed, if we don't wish this episode to degenerate into an uglier Kulturkrieg of even greater proportions, then Indologists would do well to say openly that sometimes they have indeed been insensitive, and that in the future they would be more respectful of the culture about which they write. It would be even nicer if the offending authors offered a formal apology to the Hindu world. Such a gesture is not required of them, but it is likely to initiate a healing process, which, in my view, is sorely needed in the current context. [Emphases added]

The following day Sankrant Sanu[45] posted a message disagreeing with Prof. Raman's comments. He felt that Raman's arguments were based on 'respecting sentiments' and will lead only to more sensitive colonial thinking, not real change. Impassioned, he explained:

Sensitive colonial thinking says: 'These people (/this culture) are savages (/is backward), but we will be hurting their feelings if we say so publicly, so to be political [by] correct, we should be sensitive to that.' Damn political correctness! I am more interested in the truth.

He wrote: "The problem with Wendy, et al, is not lack of sensitivity, but ignorance". Besides, he argued: "Using the 'sensitivity' argument puts us in the same camp as people of certain religions issuing fatwas because their feelings were hurt". [Emphasis added]. Sanu continued: "Hinduism has a much stronger intellectual basis and we should welcome *informed* criticism, sensitive or not, but not half-baked scholarship masquerading as the authoritative account". [Original emphasis].

Sanu proposed an approach to Religious Studies that would require academicians to make 'personal disclosure . . . a key part of such scholarship'. He explained that this practice would recognize that all people approach religion from "a personal point of view and belief system—whether it be atheist, agnostic, 'secular', spiritual, or any . . . of the religious traditions". These belief systems influence scholars 'in a manner that they cannot escape'.

Thus, any notion of objectivity is a myth, and the intellectually honest approach would be a disclosure paragraph in every research paper or publication, of the author's belief system (much like disclosure by financial writers or analysts about stocks they own, *caveat emptor*). Such a disclosure paragraph should include, at the minimum, the belief system of their childhood, significant changes in and influence on the evolution of their belief system, and the current belief system that they practice or subscribe to.

He gave an example of this happening 'in the opposite direction'.

When Prof. Ravi Ravindra wrote *Christ the Yogi,* a remarkable book of real love and insight on John's gospel, there was a lot of pressure from his publisher to add *A Hindu Reflection on the Gospel of John* as the subtitle. Of course, someone of Prof. Ravindra's intellectual integrity was quite happy to detail his own background in the introduction—would Wendy's children do that in all the works they do? The picture that academicians like to paint is of themselves as the bearers of 'scientific' and 'objective' truth. The best approach I believe is one that promotes their self-professed desire for intellectual objectivity, rather than appeals to the 'sensitivity' of the natives.

David Freedholm on Misuse of Literary Theory

David Freedholm responded extensively, observing that, "Rajiv's provocative article ... mentions that Kripal appeals to Gadamer's hermeneutical theory as justification for his 'interpretation' of Ramakrishna's life in *Kali's Child*." Freedholm quoted several paragraphs from *Kali's Child* such as:

[T]he modern study of Ramakrishna extends and radicalizes the history of the texts themselves through the various fusions of horizons ... What, of course, we end up with is radically new visions of who Ramakrishna was and what his life meant that are a bit shocking to someone locked into only one horizon of meaning.

Freedholm pointed out that, "This really is a misunderstanding and misuse of Gadamer's hermeneutics." He explained that Gadamer's

process of interpretation is not the simple and unbridled imposition of the interpreter's 'present life-world and categories' and 'techniques of analysis' upon the horizon of the text ... Gadamer goes on to say that interpretation is the genuine fusion of horizons in which there is no 'presuppositionless' interpretation but also in which the interpreter is open to the meaning of the text and is willing to revise and correct his/her pre-understandings ... Gadamer distinguishes between fruitful and unfruitful pre-understandings and argues that the interpreter must be willing to question him/herself about such pre-understandings.

According to Freedholm, Gadamer is suggesting that acknowledgment of the "temporal, historical, and cultural distance between ourselves and a text can be a 'filtering process'." He concludes, "Kripal failed to take seriously the duty of the interpreter to question his own suppositions and prejudices and to seek the historical, cultural and linguistic horizon of the texts he interpreted." Freedholm concurs with several other critics of *Kali's Child*, that "it is entirely plausible and probable that Kripal's interpretation has far more to do with his own 'life-world and categories' than it does with that of Ramakrishna." Adding, "In any case, I don't think it is possible to appeal to Gadamer as a justification for such a hermeneutical methodology...I think Gadamer and any serious student of hermeneutics would find Kripal's methodology to be seriously flawed."

Psychologists Assess the Chicago School of Hinduphobia

Many professional and academic psychoanalysts are critical of eroticizing non-Western spiritual traditions. For instance, Brant Cortright, an academic psychologist and a follower of Sri Aurobindo, explains how, "Freud made a fundamental blunder due to his own limitations." Cortright wrote:

> Because there are superficial similarities between the ego loss that occurs in schizophrenia or other psychotic states and the ego loss that occurs in the highest mystical experiences of enlightenment, psychology, beginning with Freud, has assumed that they are one and the same. Even some early transpersonal psychologists have made this error by romanticizing childhood and likening the consciousness of an infant to that of a mystic.[46]

This attitude was adopted by many subsequent followers of Freud, who turned it into a truism that denied any legitimacy of spirituality. The mystic's 'oceanic experience' of oneness is simply equated with the 'infantile helplessness' and a 'regression to primary narcissism.'

> Literature produced in the field of Psychology continues to follow this bias, describing spiritual experiences as symptomatic of pathologies, such as borderline psychosis, ego regression, psychotic episodes, or a temporal lobe dysfunction. Marx's attitude against religion has been thoroughly investigated, though in actually, its seeming impact on the enthusiasm of twenty-first century American church-goers is relatively nil, whereas Freud has had a lasting impact on modern perceptions of religion. Scholars have also

looked at Freud's belief that religion was a 'universal obsessional neurosis—and even people who go to church religiously can see that theory in action'.

Freud's negative attitude towards spirituality continues to dramatically taint the way society interprets it. He simplistically dismissed spirituality as pathology, because he couldn't understand the "oceanic feeling". Freud's attitude that dismissed spirituality as narcissistic has influenced generations of Americans. Consequently, visionary or ecstatic episodes must be tranquilized with anti-psychotic medication, protective custody, or other negative consequences. Freudian constructs have inescapably influenced the field of mental health professionals in contemporary Western society.

This approach is diametrical with the Indic perspective. In India, many highly honored saints began their journeys to 'divine realization' with experiences of what in allopathic terms would be called schizophrenic psychotic episodes. Within the Indic worldview there is a supportive environment for these sorts of enhanced spiritual experiences. Those members of society manifesting mystical, alternative states are nurtured and treated with great patience and given more space to manifest their God-intoxication.

For example, Anandamayi Ma "is recognized as a mystic of rare spiritual insight in India". She held together multiple "roles of wife, renunciate, and spiritual guide in a seamless manner".[47] The *Encyclopedia of Religion* wrote that: "Her life pointed out the possibilities for spiritual life that are open for women in the Hindu milieu despite the restrictive norms set for them by the orthodoxy". In the Hindu cultural context there are supportive systems allowing a mystic such as Anandamayi Ma, to spend a few teenage years in complete spiritual distraction, a mad woman, as it were. It has been said, euphemistically, that she turned cartwheels naked for two years. She lived to be eighty-five years old, and is revered throughout India.

However, if she had lived in the West, while in the throes of her Kundalini awakening, family members and the authorities would have tranquilized her, masking her symptoms with a layer of medication to treat some presumed pathology. Instead of allowing her to become one of the greatest women saints of all time, she would have been anesthetized and restrained. Richard Alpert, the controversial scholar who was fired from Harvard's Psychology Department in 1963, and later traveled to India and was given the name Ram Dass by his Guru

Neem Karoli Baba, explained, "in most of the Western religions, the exoteric rituals became available and the esoteric ones became almost completely lost."

Such therapeutic treatments, when applied to the symptoms of mysticism, are meant to put a halt to these perceived pathologies as quickly as possible. Therefore, hospitalization, anti-psychotic medication, and even shock treatments are used to diminish the mystical symptoms. The "recovered" mystics learn to be wary of those "oceanic feelings" that are seen as signs of a pathological condition as opposed to the Hindu view that sees these feelings as possibly divinely induced.

In *Psychotherapy and Spirit,* Brant Cortright described the result of Western psychiatric treatment for mystical experiences wherein "a potentially growthful step of consciousness gets derailed, invalidated, and submerged in a sea of medication and shame, leaving the person unable to integrate the experience".[48] Stuart Sovatsky, who has been an academic psychologist and practitioner of Kundalini Yoga for 25 years, provided the following insights:

> We will never get at Yogic truths beyond the genitals via psychoanalysis, as your use of the chakra system shows—Freud said exactly this when he labeled the furthest stage of maturation he knew of as 'genital primacy' of the 'genital personality'—Wendy, Kripal, et al, miss this point with disastrous results. It is pathetic & disheartening that after reading Sanskrit scriptures for decades, becoming 'world experts', such academics distort the scriptures (and misread lives such as Ramakrishna) using Freudian or other European hermeneutics. Failed monks, such as Kripal (it seems) tend to sexualize monastics to justify their own failure upon the monastic path—Germaine Greer (in *Sex and Destiny*) and Foucault's Vol. 1 of *The History of Sexuality* are the only two Westerners I have read who get it right.

Sovatsky ended his message with a quote from *The World of Ken Wilber* by Roger Walsh, who wrote with a hint of sarcasm, that when looking at spirituality through a psychoanalytical lens,

> [M]ystical experiences have sometimes been interpreted as 'neurotic regressions to union with the breast', ecstatic states viewed as 'narcissistic neurosis,' enlightenment dismissed as 'regression to intrauterine stages,' and meditation seen as 'self-induced catatonia.'[49]

The work of another respected academic scholar of psychology, Prof. Renuka Sharma of the University of Melbourne, was highlighted on the Sulekha comment board. Sharma has been quite critical of Kripal's work and of the Chicago Laboratory School of Indological Studies, in general. She published an extensive critique, "The Foot in the Lap or Kripal's Discontent: A Review of *The Mystical and the Erotic in the Life and Teachings of Ramakrishna* by Jeffrey John Kripal", segments of which were made available on Sulekha.

> Freud as God and Guru of psychoanalysis is now passé in the best of psychoanalytic circles. Feminist deconstructions of Schreber and Dora show just how ahistorical Freud tended to be. The fetishization of Freudian psychoanalysis as a tool of deconstruction outside the clinic has serious epistemological problems written about extensively by clinicians and theoreticians alike. In the absence of clinical records and aligned work the analysis falters.

> To redefine sexuality in the benign horizons of another culture is a welcome undertaking; but to reconfigure the religiosity of that tradition in this exclusive typology is simply bad scholarship. Perhaps the flesh is of little consequence, and human embodiment of insignificant interest to mystics who float past a certain threshold.

Sharma asks, "Must theory assume a perpetual enslavement to sexuality across the board? [...] Or is this an outcome of a modern Chicago academic technology? And that too, gendered in the narrower same-sex, direction?"[50] She chastises those constructs that 'reconfigure the religiosity of tradition in this exclusive typology' and calls it 'simply bad scholarship'. Sharma continues:

> A strange motley of scholars in North America invariably jump to the defense of the author [i.e. Kripal] on rather spurious grounds. Among the reasons advanced are: the inexorability of the connection between 'sexuality and spirituality' (universalized to the Indian subcontinent); the need to use the new-found strategic template of psychoanalysis (which noted Indian social scientists, particularly, Ashis Nandy and Sudhir Kakar, pioneered for psycho-political biographies); and as-it-were constitutional right of the outsider-scholar to interrogate the workings of (an)other's cultural productions. The latter especially is arguably what the professional business of religious studies is all about, even though one of its early founders, the late Ninian Smart, agonized all his life over the chasm that separates the Anglo-American channel from the rest of the world—in uneven world trade relations as much as in the study

of religions and cultures. The (other's) world out there is an open book indeed.

Sharma criticizes this genre of scholarship as a cover for an imperialistic enterprise, whose purpose is to belittle the colonized tradition, or in this case, post-colonized traditions, as being inferior and 'effeminate'. In particular, the imperial venture attacks important cultural icons,

> [T]he veneer of psychoanalysis and symbolic deconstruction . . . are deployed extensively in [Kripal's] work. This kind of reliance on purely psychoanalytic anthropology, again, fails to do justice to the work of postmodern psychoanalysis inspired by Franz Fanon, Wilfred Bion, Foucault, and a whole host of other writers who are careful in their dealings with cultural differences.

> The imperialistic use of some outdated dogmas of psychoanalysis perpetuates a kind of psycho-orientalism that, indeed, Indian feminists such as Tanikar Sarkar, Kumkum Sangari, and Gayatri Spivak argue are a construct of masculinity as a well-known colonial ruse, as is the feminization of poverty and the infantilization of so-called primitive peoples. From Ramakrishna to the 'brown boy, Gandhi', threatening Indian icons stand 'effeminized' and turned into 'intimate enemies', reinforcing the ambiguities and ambivalences of the post-colonial purloined self.

She points out that in some cases, it becomes necessary to locate a scholar's cultural and political positionings. To get a better picture of the theoretical background of the author, Sharma thinks Kripal should be placed 'under the microscope'.

Certain RISA-related scholars have resisted, and often find offensive, the suggestion that they themselves should be psychoanalyzed. This methodology places them in the specimen box where their personal and professional issues can be examined under a magnifying glass. Renuka Sharma proposed that, "the cultural and political positioning of the analyst is as important as is the process of analysis itself." She remarked:

> This growing awareness of the political location of the analyst is brought to general awareness in a number of recent works on the political formations of psychoanalysis in the last twenty years. This opens a new theoretical space from within the practice of psychoanalysis, and it is in this theoretical space that I wish to interrogate Kripal [in the] broader cultural context, and the method of research utilized.

Sharma sees the theoretical space as an opportunity to "interrogate Kripal's attempt in the broader cultural context and [his] method of research". She also feels that the private life of the scholar is crucial to examine when reviewing his/her work. She theorizes how this syndrome worked in Kripal's case:

> Might the tome be actually autobiographical, while the publishers and untutored readers have taken it to be simply about Sri Ramakrishna's life? The question suggests that there may be an intriguing novel game (call it fiction) at work here, where an author seeks to work through his own pains and personal misgivings— about his own uncertain relations to the church, to the other sex, to the Virgin Mary, perhaps also to his mother.

Sharma examines Kripal's motivational trajectory, wherein the story "appropriately begins in a Benedictine monastery, in a small-time Christian town in the U.S. [where Kripal is] haunted by religio-mystico sexuality which was so much, as it were, in the holy air, compounded by the attitude and conduct of the priests towards the altar boys". Sharma points out that Kripal found redemption in 'the assuring images of Teresa of Avila [and] Eckhart'. She continues:

> After some twenty years pass, and while at university, Kripal embarks on the trail of the mystery that takes him to the heartland of modern Indian Tantrism, West Bengal. And Oh Calcutta! There he discovers 'phallus erectus-lingam workshop' under the guise of a tormented sage proclaiming his love for the terrifying goddess Kali, whom Rudolph Otto had showcased for his nebulous category of the numinous 'terror'.

> Here we leap straight into the bed crust with a whole tradition of colonial psychoanalysis which neatly defines 'the Indian personality'—as being homophobic, mother-hating, full of vagina-envy, anally-possessed, and deeply feminized, obsessive compulsive males; and that possibly provides an explanation for the inexplicable presence in India of the largest communities of hijras, sari-clad transvestites, anywhere in the world. So much for the postmodern transference upon subaltern masculinity.

Sharma concludes, after looking at many examples, that Kripal's work is largely a case of projecting his own mental subconscious condition on to his thesis.

> Mutatis mutandis, Kripal is led in part to adduce from his own troubled early life as a boy in Catholic school, that this phenomenon

must be universal across all self-repressive, single-gendered monastic establishments, or cultures wedded closely to renunciatory practices.

Sharma raises a controversial question about the respective stance of the scholars. "One wonders then which culture's homosexuality or homophobia (or alternating phyla-phobia) is precisely at stake here or put on the couch? And who are its accomplices?" She charges some scholars with dubious intentions and agendas—perhaps backed by institutional support.

> In the end, the question is not whether Ramakrishna was homosexual or not—gay rights has rightly halted preoccupation with this closet-hunting attitude—but how one goes about the issues: Why did this question even come up? What motivates one to fly across thousands of miles away from home to probe this matter? Is the agenda controlled from elsewhere or by an over-drive within a particular mode of late (still de-orientalizing) Western scholarship? The probing becomes a cultural habit, a fetish, and soon enough the ill-educated mediawallas parrot these gestations and project them onto other Godmen.

Regarding Kripal's book, Sharma feels that, in the end, the reader is left with "the repetitive gesture of inferred homosexuality, a liberal physicality on the part of the guru fond of holding, touching and placing his foot in the lap of young male disciples". She sees these as 'innocuous culture-specific expressions of affection'. From an Australian perspective, she compares this to someone misinterpreting rituals of 'Australian mateship and victory-scrumming'. Sharma dismisses the case made by Kripal as "hard-pressed to argue that such-and-such effeminate alluding connotations are applicable and should be read into the text . . . given other circumstantial evidence and the sheer weight of inter-textual hermeneutics." She concludes: **"The book under discussion has the well-crafted veneer of scholarship in the fashion of the Chicago History of Religions tradition"**. [Emphasis added]

Don Salmon, another clinical psychologist, joined the discussion and wrote emails in support of the thesis of *RISA Lila,*

> Until the 1970s, when psychiatry withdrew its allegiance to Freud and placed its 'faith' in psychopharmacology, psychoanalysis had little or no respectability within academia. The taking up of psychodynamic thought by clinical psychologists and social workers means very little in terms of the larger academic acceptance of Freudian thinking. Scientific psychology has only a moderate level

of respectability within the larger academic world; clinical psychology would, I think be ranked lower than any particular branch of scientific psychology, and social work—as an academic discipline, still lower.

What seems to have happened . . . is that some time in the 1970s, an obscure corner of academia, now variously known as literary theory, critical theory or postmodernism, began creating an uneasy alliance of Marxist, psychoanalytic and feminist thinking, sprinkled here and there with the more unintelligible aspects of Heideggerian and other phenomenological thinkers. For the most part, as far as I can see, these were individuals inspired by the radical Left of the 1960s, slowly worked their way into various positions of power in various humanities departments.

I had no idea this kind of thought had infiltrated the Religious Studies Departments until I began learning about it through essays on the Infinity Foundation website and through postings to various IF e-groups. I've struggled for over 30 years to understand why the superficial—and to my mind dangerous—misunderstandings of human nature put forth by Freud and his followers gained attention in the first place.

Though virtually nobody that I'm aware of within any branch of psychotherapeutic practice takes the original formulations of Freud seriously, it's quite disturbing to see academics of the stature of someone like Wendy Doniger using such otherwise thoroughly discredited Freudian ideas as a means of interpreting the sacred texts of India. It would be an interesting and I believe quite helpful project to examine closely this misuse of psychoanalytic thought in the study of Hinduism in light of the conclusions that generations of practicing therapists have come to regarding psychoanalysis.

Revolt in Chicago

There was an electronic message from an academic scholar who wished to remain anonymous, because he was one of Wendy's foster children. The former University of Chicago scholar criticized his colleagues' use of psychoanalytic interpretations, because they are 'not qualified psychoanalysts', and they lack 'training in analysis'. The scholar stated that, "If someone from their own culture came before them, they would have no qualifications for analyzing him. Surely analyzing someone from a different culture would be more difficult." Adding that "psychoanalysis has long been rejected by the field of psychology—

it has been out of date for about 40 years—but religion moves slower, and hangs on to it." The scholar concluded:

> As for Wendy, I too was one of her children. But I wouldn't agree with her reductionism, and as a result our time was one of conflict. I did get my degree, but there were lots of roadblocks . . . I hesitate to publicly disagree with my colleagues, but I do disagree with them in many ways.

This scholar opined that, in the early years, as long as the University of Chicago Divinity School defended Eliade's sympathetic 'approach to India, [there] was religious tolerance and respect'. The post-Eliade problems began when the Divinity School at Chicago 'decided to emphasize Area Studies'. Within this genre, scholars' main focus appears to be a competition "to be modern, to out-critique each other, to show that they are less naive and more suspicious, and thus wiser". Ultimately, the trees of dense theories are illusory, as scholars wander myopically through the Indic forests, jotting down parenthetical psychoanalytical notes in their ethnographic/ historiographic journals— conjuring up the spoof about the South Indian pet snakes[51] in the village of Nacirema.[52]

T. Desai, another student at the University of Chicago, shared first-hand experience:

> I would like to relate my own anecdote about Wendy Doniger. This past year, I had the 'pleasure' of taking a class on the Mahabharata taught by her . . . Doniger regularly made comments in class of how the Hindu right in India wants to shove Sanskrit down everyone's throat. **I was amazed to see how she lectured on Indian politics in a Mahabharata class.** I wonder if they also discuss Bush's funding of faith based organizations in Latin classes . . . She even described the meeting between Arjuna and Indra, [son and father] when Indra places him in his lap and caresses his arm, as 'homo erotic'. Doniger also forced the class to use Van Buitenen's translation, which is completely dry and boring, and refers to kshyatrias as 'barons'. I asked her if we could use PC Roy's translation instead, which does not translate things so literally and does a much better job of capturing the spirit of the work. She claimed that Roy's English was too terrible to read. Rajiv is absolutely correct that **all this drivel is drilled into the head of impressionable Indian-American kids (my class was more than half Indian-American)** who then get PhDs and write more such nonsense. [Emphasis added]

The snowball rolls on...

Many observant scholars have remarked that the accumulating pressure on Hindu-American identity formation is currently mobilizing students on many campuses. This growing awareness gives students confidence to stand up and debate. Pressure from the diasporic voices is transforming the field, growing in assertiveness and added awareness of their role in Americans' pluralistic landscape. More effective than any other methodology or strategy, the presence of informed students of Hindu heritage in American classes makes it very difficult for biases to go unchallenged.

Professors are obviously usually very careful with what they say about Christianity in a course on the Old or New Testament, or other Biblical topics in a classroom filled with Christian youths. Muslim students are often taught to counter the nonsense about their traditions in American Social Studies classes—in their religious schools they are often alerted to the problems beforehand. But only in the last few years, have Hindu-American students become more aware of the situation and better informed. They are becoming more able to articulate objections to examples of academic Hinduphobia and offer culturally sensitive correctives. Now that Hindu-Americans have become aware to the ubiquitous problems, much needed change is on the horizon.

A scholar in African American Studies at Princeton University commented:

> Once black students on campus started to talk back based on authentic facts, there was a snowball effect, and the field started to transform. Ditto for feminists, gays, and other groups that had to fight to change their portrayals. So let's shine the light bright and clear.

Hindu Students' Council Petition: 'Against the Book Insulting Lord Ganesha and Hinduism'

Against the Book Insulting Lord Ganesha and Hinduism

To: President James W. Wagner of Emory University,
Governor Sunny Perdue of Georgia,
President George W. Bush of U.S.A,
Prime Minister Atal B. Vajpayee of India,
Members of India's Parliament,
Members US-India Congressional Caucus,
and US Attorney General, Ashcroft.

There is a Book titled: *Ganesa—Lord of Obstacles, Lord of Beginnings* by Professor Paul Courtright, Department of Religion, Emory University, Atlanta, Georgia, USA. First Edition in USA published in 1985 by Oxford University Press, Inc. First Indian Edition, Published in 2001 by Motilal Banarsidass Publishers Private Ltd., with a nude cover picture and insulting interpretations directly from the book.
For nude cover picture of the 2001 edition of the book please visit: http://photos.yahoo.com/hsc_ul

Here are some of the author's vulgar interpretations:

- "Its [Ganesa's] trunk is the displaced phallus, a caricature of Siva's linga. It poses no threat because it is too large, flaccid, and in the wrong place to be useful for sexual purposes." (Page 121)
- "He [Ganesa] remains celibate so as not to compete erotically with his father, a notorious womanizer, either incestuously for his mother or for any other woman for that matter." (Page 110)

- "So Ganesa takes on the attributes of his father but in an inverted form, with an exaggerated limp phallus—ascetic and benign—whereas Siva is a 'hard' (ur-dhvalinga), erotic and destructive." (Page121)
- "Both in his behavior and iconographic form Ganesa resembles in some aspects, the figure of the eunuch...Ganesha is like a eunuch guarding the women of the harem." (Page 111)
- "Although there seems to be no myths or folktales in which Ganesa explicitly performs oral sex; his insatiable appetite for sweets may be interpreted as an effort to satisfy a hunger that seems inappropriate in an otherwise ascetic disposition, a hunger having clear erotic overtones." (Page 111)
- "Ganesa's broken tusk, his guardian's staff, and displaced head can be interpreted as symbols of castration." (page 111)
- "Feeding Ganesa copious quantities of modakas, satisfying his oral/erotic desires, also keeps him from becoming genitally erotic like his father." (Page 113)
- "The perpetual son desiring to remain close to his mother and having an insatiable appetite for sweets evokes associations of oral eroticism. Denied the possibility of reaching the stage of full genital masculine power by the omnipotent force of the father, the son seeks gratification in some acceptable way." (Page 113)

There are plenty of other insidious passages in this book aimed at tarnishing not only the image of Ganesha, but Shiva and Parvati as well: "After Siva has insulted Parvati by calling her Blackie [Kali], she vows to leave him and return to her father's home and then she stations her other son, Viraka—the one Siva had made—at the door way to spy on her husband's extramarital amorous exploits." (Page 105–106).

We believe these are clear-cut examples of hate-crimes inflicted on innocent Hindus who worship Ganesha, Shiva and Parvati.

We the undersigned strongly ask you to take the necessary action to achieve the following:

1) The author and the publisher(s) to give an unequivocal apology to Hindus.
2) The author expunges the above and other offensive passages and revises the book with clarifications and corrections.
3) Publisher(s) to immediately withdraw this book from circulation and the author to stop use of this book in academics.

Sincerely,

Hindu Students' Council—University of Louisiana, Lafayette and written by Devendra Potnis, President HSC-ULL.

Notes

1. Originally posted at: http://alan-roland.sulekha.com/blog/post/2002/11/the-uses-and-misuses-of-psychoanalysis-in-south.htm (Nov. 26, 2002). Printed with author's kind permission. © Copyright Alan Roland 2007.
2. Alan Roland, a practicing psychoanalyst, has worked extensively with Indians and Japanese abroad and in New York City. He is on the faculty of the National Psychological Association for Psychoanalysis. See: *Cultural Pluralism and Psychoanalysis: The Asian and North American Experience*, Routledge, (1996).
3. Ramesh N. Rao, Ph.D., Professor and Chair, Communication Studies and Theatre Department, Longwood University, Farmville, Virginia.
4. Both South Asians and Western South Asian specialists have often been more than receptive to using various aspects of psychoanalytic theory in their thinking. To cite some of the more prominent, among the former are Girindrasekhar Bose, Prakash Desai, Sudhir Kakar, Ashis Nandy, Gananath Obeyesekere, Udayan Patel, B.K. Ramanujam, and A.K. Ramanujan; while the latter include among others, Sarah Caldwell, G.M. Carstairs, Wendy Doniger, Robert Goldman, Christiane Hartnack, Jeffrey Kripal, Stanley Kurtz, Jeffrey Masson, and Ralph Nicholas.
5. This is even true of the considerable opus of Sudhir Kakar (1978, 1982, 1989, 1991, 1995), a psychoanalyst, where case material is just very briefly alluded to in only two places in his first five books. In his last book (1997), *Culture and Psyche*, one chapter is devoted to two case studies. Cases seen in supervision also appear in two journal articles (1979, 1980).
6. Psychoanalytic therapy with patients originated in Calcutta by 1920 through the pioneering explorations of Girindresekar Bose. It eventually spread to other cities such as Ahmedabad, Mumbai, New Delhi, Bangalore, and Chennai. Since 1995, as a result of certain dynamics of social change in the growing urban educated, there is an accelerating demand for counseling and psychotherapy.
7. My essays published in journals in the 1970s and two new papers will be published in *Dreams and Drama: Psychoanalytic Criticism, Creativity, and the Artist*, Continuum International Publishing Company and Wesleyan University Press, November, 2002.
8. "It's a devastation!" averred Lionel Trilling, one of the first critics to use psychoanalysis, in his last years about psychoanalytic criticism (personal communication). Leon Edel, another major critic, despaired over the misuse of psychoanalysis in literary criticism because of conflicting approaches to symbolic expression (Edel 1969).
9. I experienced the difficulties in interdisciplinary work when I collaborated with Gino Rizzo, a noted Pirandello scholar, on Pirandello's *Six Characters in Search of an Author* and *Henry IV* (Roland and Rizzo 1978). We each thought we knew a great deal about the other's field, he about psychoanalysis, I about drama criticism. We found, however, that we were rank neophytes in each other's discipline, a narcissistic challenge if there ever was one. Nevertheless, through collaborative work we were able to interweave Pirandello's changes in dramatic structure and his central metaphors and paradoxes with depth psychoanalytic issues that encompassed both the emotional power of the primary process and broader meanings of the identity struggles of modern humanity.
10. While mysticism is the concept used in the West, Indians I have known who are involved in one or another kind of *sadhana* would more usually refer to it as a spiritual practice or discipline, and the goal as spiritual realization. They very rarely use the word mysticism.
11. The Jungian analytic tradition and neo-Freudian psychoanalysts such as Karen Horney (1945), Erich Fromm (1960), and Harold Kelman (1960), as well as the

Horney group as a whole, departed considerably from the classical Freudian position on mysticism.

12. In spite of being host to the first Lacanian psychoanalysts to visit the United States, and editor of a book that included their papers (Roland 1978), 1 have never really mastered the radically different discourse of Lacanian theory and practice.

13. Indian psychiatrists include Ravi Kapur, B.K. Ramanujam, and Usha Sundaram (now Swami Dharmakeetri); while American psychoanalysts include Marlin Brenner, Paul Cooper, and Jeffrey Rubin.

14. Marion Milner (1987) held up publication of her paper on meditation for some thirteen years, mainly because of the opprobrium she feared she would receive from the psychoanalytic establishment. Similarly, Nina Coltart (1992, 1996) refused to speak about her practice of Vipassana Buddhism before a psychoanalytic audience.

15. Kakar does not mention that Freud, himself, began practicing celibacy in his forties.

16. For a far more insightful psychoanalytic and less reductionistic evaluation of Gandhi's striving for celibacy, see Grey's (1973) analysis of the profound relationship involving sexuality and individuation as it differs between Indian and American men.

17. While Kripal in the preface to his second edition of *Kali's Child* cites considerable support for his book, Swami Tyagananda (2000), a Bengali monk of the Ramakrishna Order, has written a lengthy monograph detailing in *Kali's Child* a persistent pattern of faulty and distorted translations from the Bengali sources. It is an odd coincidence that the two other writers who have used psychoanalysis in their work on Ramakrishna have also been embroiled in controversy. Jeffrey Masson, a Sanskritist turned psychoanalyst who became director of the Freud Archives, was later ostracized from the psychoanalytic movement; while Sudhir Kakar, the well-published psychoanalyst, was asked to leave the Centre for the Study of Developing Societies, the foremost social science/psychological research centre in India.

18. In clinical as in applied psychoanalysis, many interpretations are given. In the former, it makes no difference whether a patient agrees or disagrees with an analyst's interpretation. What is more crucial is whether any change is effected. This testing of the interpretation is not present in applied psychoanalysis.

19. Perhaps Kripal has picked this up from Kakar's work and therefore thinks it is appropriate.

20. This is an example of what I have alluded to above (see footnote 6) about the difficulties of doing interdisciplinary work. One finds oneself more ignorant of the complexities and advances of the other field than one is aware of.

21. Kleinians and other English object relations theorists would assert that aggression must also be included.

22. This relates to the issue of reincarnation which I discuss in the next section.

23. Self psychology is oriented around deficits in the self resulting from deficient self-object familial relationships in childhood and adolescence.

24. As has been reported in the literature (Das 1976; Dube 1955; Hanchette 1988; Inden and Nicholas 1977; Kapadia 1966), the Hindu extended family fluctuates in size in its living arrangements. At times, it is a joint family, especially if the family is well off; at other times it consists of unitary units. But at all times there are frequent and often prolonged visits of extended family members, and the ethos of extended family relationships predominate even in the unitary unit.

25. I have cited this as the experiential we-self, an important part of the familial self (Roland 1988, 1996).

26. I have cited this as the experiential we-self, an important part of the familial self (Roland 1988, 1996).

27. In a monthly discussion group meeting of Asian American Mental Health Professionals from East Asia, South Asia, and Turkey, all cited Kurtz's lack of understanding of the nonverbal, emotional, and empathic mothering in those cultures.

28. In a chapter, "The Influence of Culture on the Self and Self-object Relationships: An Asian-North American Comparison" (Roland 1996, pp. 101-116), I discuss at length differences in issues of esteem, of self-object relationships, and in the modes of empathic attunement as well as the content of what is empathized with.

29. This Western misunderstanding of Indian nonverbal communication occurred in one of the Vedanta centers in the United States when American monks were distressed that the swami, whom they greatly esteemed, never thanked them for the numerous things they did for him. They didn't realize that for the swami to thank them, he would experience it as being insulting to them. In insider, familial relationships such as those in the center, it is assumed that you are appreciative of what is done for you, and this is conveyed nonverbally. You only thank outsiders.

30. Kurtz dismisses my citing empathy in Indian relationships as imposing a Western subjectivity on Hindus. I would suggest that he is simply out-of-touch with one of the most important dimensions of Hindu psychological functioning in extended family relationships. Perhaps he doesn't think in this way because he is completely oriented toward classical psychoanalytic theory and ego psychology, and doesn't seem at all grounded in self psychology, object relations theory, or inter-subjectivity, a major thrust of psychoanalysis over the last several decades.

31. I have had Indian women in therapy bitterly complain when their mother-in-law was not intimately involved with them and their children. Kurtz may have overlooked the complex nature of the mother because he is still psychoanalytically oriented toward classical Freudian theory in terms of the mother being mainly a gratifier or frustrator.

32. Kurtz asserts my concept of the private self is simply a reworking of classical psychoanalytic theory. First of all, this concept has nothing remotely to do with classical theory since Freud never developed the concept of the self. Secondly, this concept was related to me by Anandalakshmi, the dean of child development psychologists in India whose main aim has been to Indianize child development theories. It unlocked for me a great deal about Indian psychological makeup with its sources of individuality, since it is missing in ethnographic descriptions. I find most Westerners, including South Asian specialists, are unaware of this key dimension of the Indian self. Similarly, the private self has been delineated at length by Takeo Doi (1986) in the Japanese term, *ura*, in his dual self theory. The private self manifests itself in psychoanalytic therapy when Hindus and other Asians are able to keep secrets to a far greater extent than most Euro-Americans.

33. One Hindu woman patient who grew up in a joint family until she was five reported that there were fifty different terms of endearment for her.

34. The discussion of the inculcation of hierarchical attitudes and behavior is for the most part missing in Kurtz's work, but it is central to child-rearing in Hindu extended family relationships.

35. http://www.sulekha.com/expressions/column.asp?cid=248359 (September 30, 2002) Many thanks to Prof. Balagangadhara for permission to reprint this article.

36. Prof. S.N. Balagangadhara (Balu) is director of the Research Centre Vergelijkende Cultuurwetenschap (Comparative Science of Cultures) in Ghent University, Belgium. He has authored the acclaimed book, *The Heathen in His Blindness: Asia, the West and the Dynamic of Religion*, on the nature of religion. His central area of inquiry is to develop a description of the Western culture against the background of the Indian culture. Prof. Balagangadhara recently held the co-chair of the Hinduism Unit at the American Academy of Religion (AAR).

37. Readers are also urged to read Jeffery Kripal's posting on Sulekha at http://jeffrey-kripal.sulekha.com/blog/post/2002/09/the-tantric-truth-of-the-matter.htm

38. The translation is taken from Max Müller. *The Upanishads*. In two parts. Reprint edition. New York: Dover Publications, 1962: Part I: pp.134-137.

39. Unless otherwise indicated, the majority of the comments are from the Sulekha website.

40. *purna swarajya*—complete self-rule, total independence.

41. Navya Shastra was created by Hindu-Americans living in Michigan. According to their website, Navya Shastra (Sanskrit for new sacred text) was established as a vehicle to "promote the efforts of Hindu organizations and charities... working to eradicate caste discrimination in India." See: http://www.shastras.org/

42. Native Indian.

43. Garg is referring to another essay by Malhotra, *The Axis of Neocolonialism*, published in July 2002, a few months before *WCS*. That "essay argues that intellectual svaraj (self-rule) is as fundamental to the long term success of a civilization as is svaraj in the political and financial areas." It asks: "whose way of representing knowledge will be in control?" Concluding, "It is the representation system that defines the metaphors and terminology...." See: http://rajivmalhotra.sulekha.com/blog/post/2002/07/the-axis-of-neocolonialism.htm

44. Vishal Agarwal contributed a chapter to Section II of this book.

45. The *Risa Lila* articles brought Sanu into these online discussions. He was soon inspired to write his own critiques such as the one reprinted earlier in this section.

46. Brant Cortright. *Psychotherapy and Spirit: Theory and Practice in Transpersonal Pyschotherapy*, 65.

47. From the *Encyclopedia of Religion*, http://www.bookrags.com/research/nandamay-m-eorl-01/

48. Brant Cortright. *Psychotherapy and Spirit*, 157-158.

49. As per Sovatsky: Roger Walsh in "The World of Ken Wilber," in Assoc Humanistic Psychology Newsletter, May 1982, 4.

50. Renuka Sharma, "The Foot in the Lap or Kripal's Discontent," review of *The Mystical and the Erotic in the Life and Teachings of Ramakrishna*, by Jeffrey John Kripal, in *Sophia* 40, no. 2, Dec. 2001, pp.77-82.

51. Aarati Bachwala, *Cobra Pets In RISA Studies*- http://aarati-bachwala.sulekha.com/blog/post/2003/04/cobra-pets-in-risa-studies.htm

52. Body Ritual among the Nacire.

Endnotes

Chapter 1

1.   Jeffrey Long, Foreword, "Hyperlink to Hinduphobia: Online Hatred, Extremism and Bigotry against Hindus," Hindu American Foundation, 2007, available at www.hafsite.org/hatereport/. Long is referring to the impact of Hinduphobic websites.

2.   See section II of this book for S.N. Balagangadhara's analysis of the problem.

3.   See Conferences announcement at http://chronicle.uchicago.edu/051103/india.shtml.

4.   See Rajiv Malhotra's articles on Peer-Review Cartel at: http://rajivmalhotra.com/index.php?option=com_content&task=view&id=46&Itemid=34. These were originally posted on OutlookIndia.com as part of Malhotra's debate with Prof. Vijay Prashad.

5.   Rajiv Malhotra is the President of Infinity Foundation, Princeton, New Jersey. After graduating from St. Stephen's College, Delhi, in 1971, Rajiv Malhotra arrived in USA to pursue higher studies in Physics and Computer Science. His career in USA spanned the software, telecom and media industries. He worked as a senior executive in several multinational companies, as a management consultant, and as a private entrepreneur. About a decade ago, he decided to leave all for-profit activities. He works full-time with Infinity Foundation, a non-profit organization which he founded in 1995 with his own funds to foster harmony among the diverse cultures of the world. Driven by his vision of respect for the diverse civilizations of the world, many projects of his Foundation strive to upgrade the quality of understanding of Indian civilization in the American media and educational system, as well as among the English language educated Indian elite. The Foundation has already given over 250 grants for research, education and philanthropy, including grants to leading institutions of higher education, specialized research centers, as well as many individual scholars. It organizes conferences and scholarly events in the US and India that challenge Eurocentrism in order to bring out a more balanced worldview. Mr. Malhotra defines himself as a non-Hindutva Hindu, and considers this to be a major factor in his pluralistic worldview. He is an active writer, columnist and speaker on a variety of topics, including the traditions and cultures of India, the Indian diaspora, USA and the West, globalization and East-West relations. Mr. Malhotra served as an Asian-American Commissioner for the State of New Jersey, and as the Chairman of the Education Committee created by the Governor to start an Asian Studies program in schools. He also serves on the Advisory Board of the American Red Cross in New Jersey. Details of the Infinity Foundation's projects may be found at:

http://www.infinityfoundation.com and
http://www.infinityfoundation.com/mandala/indic_mandala_frameset.htm.
Examples of major world events organized by it include the ones described at:
http://www.infinityfoundation.com/indic_colloq/colloq_home.htm.
and http://www.worldcongressps2008.org/event/presenters.aspx His writings are
posted at many webzines, such as:
http://rajivmalhotra.sulekha.com/.

6. Arvind Sharma, "Hindus and Scholars," *Religion in the News* 7, no. 1 (Spring
    2004).

7. For instance, the Hindu American Foundation (HAF) reports that a Christian
    Website called www.blessedquietness.com maintained by Steve Van Nattan, a
    pastor at the House of Prayer in Roane County, Tennessee has the following
    things to say about Hinduism: "The website's Hinduism section is called,
    'Hinduism: The Pig Pen from the East.' It refers to the religion as, 'one of the
    world's most dirty and dignity destroying religions' and also speaks of it as being
    'filthy' and 'sexually perverted.' It uses sexually explicit imagery to assert false
    notions, such as when it states, 'The penis, (particularly if flaccid), may be adored
    as Ganesha's trunk.'" Quoted in "Hyperlink to Hinduphobia: Online Hatred,
    Extremism and Bigotry against Hindus," 16, HAF, 2007.

8. See Richard Drinnon, *Facing West: the Metaphysics of Indian-Hating and Empire-
    Building*; Richard Slotkin, *The Fatal Environment: The Myth of the American
    Frontier in the Age of Industrialization, 1800–1890*; Richard Slotkin, *Regeneration
    through Violence: The Mythology of the American Frontier, 1600–1800*; Richard
    Slotkin, *Gunfighter Nation: The Myth of the American frontier in Twentieth-
    Century America*; Anders Stephanson, *Manifest Destiny*; Reginald Horsman,
    Race and Manifest Destiny.

9. Simon Anholt is the British Government's advisor on Public Diplomacy and
    advises a number of other governments on their branding strategies, in collaboration
    with the United Nations. He first used the phrase 'Nation Branding' in an article
    entitled, "Nation Brands of the 21st Century" in the *Journal of Brand Management*
    5, no. 6 (July, 1998). He is the editor of the quarterly journal, *Place Branding*.
    Anholt is the CEO of Anholt Nation Brands Index, Anholt State Brands Index
    and Anholt City Brands Index, which provide a ranking by brand value of a
    number of cities and countries, based on his Nation Branding Hexagon, a
    theoretical model which explains how places are branded and their brands
    managed (from Wikipedia).

10. Simon Anholt, "Competitive Identity," *Economic Times*, February 5, 2007.

11. *Economic Times*, February 5, 2007.

12. Heather Timmons and Anand Giridharadas, "Arcelor Deal With Mittal Establishes
    New Steel Giant," *New York Times*, June 25, 2006; and Heather Timmons and
    Andrew E. Kramer, "News Analysis: Arcelor's Russian Roulette," *New York
    Times*, May 30, 2006.

Section 1

1. November 19, 2000.

2. January 20, 2007 (emphasis added).

3. "RISA Lila-1: Wendy's Child Syndrome," http://rajivmalhotra.sulekha.com/blog/
    post/2002/09/risa-lila-1-wendy-s-child-syndrome.htm. RISA refers to Religions in
    South Asia, a group within the American Academy of Religion. *Lila* is play,
    commonly referring to the playfulness associated with Lord Krishna, but is used

here in a broader theatrical sense. NOTE: All quotes from Malhotra in this section are from "RISA Lila-1," unless otherwise indicated. Sometimes this article's name is abbreviated as WCS or Wendy's Child Syndrome. "RISA Lila-2," Malhotra's sequel to this article, came out a year after "RISA Lila-1," and is narrated in section III.

4. Such as Michael Witzel, Cynthia Humes, Swami Tyagananda, Antonio de Nicolas, Stuart Sovatsky, and Narasingha Sil, among others.

5. 'Hinduphobia' is a term coined by Rajiv Malhotra, for example, in his article, "Washington Post and Hinduphobia" discussed in section IV.

6. The criticism made in this book does not apply to all Religious Studies scholars working on South Asia. Through the past few years, a number of scholars have encouraged and participated in this on-going analysis of the field. Nor is this criticism intended as a personal attack against any individual. It is hoped that the present book will raise questions about a school of research whose interpretations often lack factual basis in texts or lived traditions. Issues discussed herein may be seen within the overarching framework of Postcolonial Studies.

7. See Richard Drinnon, *Facing West: the Metaphysics of Indian-Hating and Empire-Building*; Richard Slotkin *The Fatal Environment: The Myth of the American Frontier in the Age of Industrialization, 1800–1890*; Richard Slotkin, *Regeneration through Violence: The Mythology of the American Frontier, 1600–1800*; Richard Slotkin, *Gunfighter Nation: The Myth of the American Frontier in Twentieth-Century America*; Anders Stephanson, *Manifest Destiny*; Reginald Horsman, *Race and Manifest Destiny*.

8. The term, "Wendy's Child" was first used in a scholarly forum by Prof. Jack Hawley in a panel at the AAR, in 2001. "Wendy's Children" is used metaphorically and as satire to denote Prof. Wendy Doniger's followers and those who share her attitudes towards Hinduism. Many but not all are also her students. Conversely, not everyone who has a Ph.D. from Prof. Doniger is necessarily a Wendy's Child.

9. Often published in online Indian web-zines, such as: www.sulekha.com.

10. McKim Marriot, "Constructing an Indian Ethnosociology," in *India Through Hindu Categories*. The term "emic" refers to the insider's perspective while "etic" refers to the view of someone outside the given tradition under examination.

11. Malhotra has explained that he has borrowed from his experience, as an industry analyst of power structures, to build a framework about the production of academic knowledge on India. His goal was to "expand the discussion" by making Indian-Americans full participants in the discourse about their culture, rather than passive onlookers.

12. Hostility to alternative points-of-view and close-mindedness goes against the Mission Statement adopted by the AAR in 1995: "Within a context of free inquiry and critical examination, the Academy welcomes all disciplined reflection on religion—both from within and outside of communities of belief and practice—and seeks to enhance its broad public understanding," http://aarweb.org/about/mission.asp. In this context, it is worthy to note that two Professors of Religious Studies were committed to write an item for this book, and though both privately, and rather passionately, agreed with the theories and observations in this book, they both regretfully changed their minds in the end because of possible retaliation or blowback from their more powerful colleagues.

13. Sudhir Kakar, "Reflections on Psychoanalysis, Indian Culture and Mysticism," review of *The Oceanic Feeling: The Origins of Religious Sentiment in Ancient India*, by J.M. Masson.

14. On November 3, 2003, Sunthar Visuvalingam, a noted scholar of Indic traditions, humorously defined the "RISA-L listserv" as "reserved for 'professional

Indologists,' i.e., those who make their living by telling Indians [what] they really are as opposed to who they think they are . . ." http://groups.yahoo.com/group/Abhinavagupta/message/1220.

15. *A Brief History of the American Academy of Religion,* http://aarweb.org/about/history.asp (accessed 10/31/06).

16. Ibid.

17. From the SBL website: "6,000 members from every continent provide a forum to test ideas and advance the understanding of the Bible's role in the public arena," http://www.sbl-site.org/aboutus.aspx.

18. Doniger is Mircea Eliade Professor of History of Religions in the Divinity School, professor in the Department of South Asian Languages and Civilizations, and the Committee on Social Thought, at the University of Chicago.

19. At the 2000 AAR conference, there was a special session in her honor at which each of the presenters spoke eloquently and affectionately about Doniger's accomplishments. Malhotra recalls wryly that among the participants, there was a "noticeable aura of supplication, a certain gushing of cronyism, as if parading to gain patronage in one's career . . . symptoms often operative in large hierarchical networks." As the audience was invited to join in the discussion, Malhotra raised his hand, and when acknowledged, stood up and asked Dr. Doniger, "Since you have psychoanalyzed Hinduism and created a whole new genre of scholarship, do you think it would be a good idea for someone to psychoanalyze you, because an insight into your subconscious would make your work more interesting and understandable?" According to Malhotra's description of the scene in Nashville, there was both tension and uneasy laughter in the room. Doniger replied that, "There was nothing new that any psychoanalyst would find about her, because she has not hidden anything." Malhotra reported that he stood up again, and stated that, "Most clients also tell their psychoanalysts that they have nothing hidden in their mental basement, but such clients are precisely the most interesting persons to psychoanalyze." According to Malhotra, "She laughed, took it well, and replied, 'You got me on this one.'" Malhotra concluded, predicting that in the next several years, "research into her psychology would get done, and that it would become important some day to psychoanalyze many other Western scholars since they also superimpose their personal and cultural conditioning on their research about other peoples."

20. See: http://www.bbc.co.uk/asianlife/tv/network_east_late/biogs/wendy_doniger.shtml.

21. Malhotra uses the term 'franchise' to indicate a mechanism for knowledge distribution, creating lineages or *sampradayas.*

22. *parampara*—a succession of teachers (*gurus*) and disciples (*chelas*), a spiritual lineage.

23. Wendy loves this idea of her children and even grandchildren as a sort of cult: "In a sense you are my past; I worked with you when I was younger. But in a much more important sense you are my future, my living academic Nachlasse, my Doktor-kinder (if I may invert the usual phrase). And as you continue to send me your own students, who become my Doktor-grandchildren (one of whom— Liz Wilson, out of Billy Mahony, out of O'Flaherty—is beginning to send me Doktor-great-grandchildren), you have provided me with a *parampara* more enduring than my own books, let alone my flesh." See: http://divinity.uchicago.edu/research/criterion/autumn2000/mandala_3.html—as cited in WCS on sulekha.com. After the publication of "RISA Lila-1," Dr. Doniger also refers to this metaphor when she sends Malhotra a series of emails (discussed below).

24. Hiriam W. Woodward, *Asian Art in The Walters Art Gallery: A Selection* (Baltimore: The Trustees of The Walters Art Gallery, 1991), 20.

25. Stanley N. Kurtz, *All the Mothers Are One: Hindu India and the Cultural Reshaping of Psychoanalysis.*

26. Prior to the article appearing in 2002, Malhotra had sponsored several conferences, research studies, online discussion groups, academic writings, and round-tables both in the US and India. A good example is the Menla Colloquium on Indic Traditions, co-convened by Malhotra jointly with Robert Thurman, where 45 of the foremost Indologists participated. See other activities of the foundation listed at: www.infinityfoundation.com. This unique perspective of having observed the academy at close hand helped shape some of the compelling arguments in his seminal article.

27. Quoted from "RISA Lila-1."

28. *Journal of the American Academy of Religion* 65, no. 3 (Autumn, 1997): 655-665, as per: http://www.ruf.rice.edu/~kalischi/. Kripal responded in, "Mystical Homoeroticism, Reductionism and the Reality of Censorship: A Response to Gerald Larson," *Journal of the American Academy of Religion* 66, no. 3 (Autumnm, 1998): 627–635. Additionally, Brian A. Hatcher wrote a review, "Kali's Problem Child: Another Look at Jeffrey Kripal's Study of Sri Ramakrishna," *International Journal of Hindu Studies* 3, no.1 (1999).

29. Kripal, Jeffrey J., *Kali's Child: The Mystical and the Erotic in the Life and teachings of Ramakrishna.*

30. Along with numerous other scholars, such as Narasingha Sil, Somnath Bhattacharya, Swami Tyagananda questioned Kripal's grasp of Bengali and his questionable use of original sources, see: http://www.infinityfoundation.com/mandala/s_rv/s_rv_tyaga_kali1_frameset.htm. Through many years of writing rebuttals to critiques of *Kali's Child*, Kripal admitted many mistakes such as errors in translation, but he never retracted his basic assumption that Ramakrishna was a sexually abused homosexual pedophile. For Kripal's version of a history of the discussion, see: http://www.ruf.rice.edu/~kalischi/.

31. Section II presents many such criticisms by both Indian and non-Indian psychologists.

32. While writing "RISA Lila-1," Malhotra notes that he was advised in person, by emails, and via associates, that if he criticized Wendy Doniger he would get personally attacked and blackballed and his foundation's projects would be boycotted. Malhotra writes: "This intimidation is precisely what motivated me, even more enthusiastically, to continue my research into what could be called an 'incestuous cult.' I felt like an investigative reporter who is onto something big. I wondered why they did not take my critical investigations in stride, given their claims of being open-minded? The defensiveness by the *chowkidars* and *sepoys* of the academic fortress has bordered on intimidation." Refer to section III showing RISA's treatment of those who step out of line.

33. Several examples of this will be given in sections III and IV. It is also noteworthy that RISA scholars claimed that Kripal was depressed and regretful about writing the book and that he wished to forget it completely. But Malhotra reported in WCS that in his communication with Kripal, he found just the opposite to be true: "Kripal very much enjoyed the controversy as a way to advance academically. When asked point-blank to produce any evidence of 'threats,' he declined."

34. The complete 130-page response by Swami Tyagananda is posted at: http://www.infinityfoundation.com/mandala/s_rv/s_rv_tyaga_kali1_frameset.htm.

35. Malhotra unsuccessfully asked Kripal to include Swami Tyagananda's critique and then Kripal's rejoinder. "A good example of an outsider's account where an insider is invited to write the final chapter as a response is Father Francis Clooney's recent book, *Hindu God, Christian God*, in which Dr. Parimal Patil

was asked to write a response in the final chapter from the Hindu perspective. Kripal gave all sorts of excuses as to why this had never been done and could not be done by him" (WCS).

36. Swami Tyagananda, "*Kali's Child* Revisited or Didn't Anyone Check the Documentation?" *Evam: Forum on Indian Representations* 1, no. 1–2 (2002): 173–190. Also available online in PDF at: http://www.home.earthlink.net/~tyag/ KCR.pdf.

37. Dr. Sil, a native Bengali, is professor of history at Western Oregon State College and the author of several books, including *Ramakrishna Paramahamsa*, *Ramakrishna Revisited*, and *Swami Vivekananda: A Reassessment*.

38. Narasingha Sil, "Is Ramakrishna a Vedantin, a Tantrika or a Vaishnava?—An Examination," *Asian Studies Review* 21, nos. 2–3 (November 1997): 220. Narasingha Sil's review of *Kali's Child*, "The Question of Ramakrishna's Homosexuality," was published in a Calcutta newspaper, *The Statesman*, on January 31, 1997 and created a furor and a flurry of critiques which caused Jeffrey Kripal to do "little else [for] eight years than think about the discussions and debates [his] work on Sri Ramakrishna . . . generated in India, in the States, and indeed around the world . . ." http://www.ruf.rice.edu/~kalischi/index.html.

39. Kripal, *Kali's Child*, 3. As cited by Tyagananda.

40. Ibid., 2–3.

41. Ibid., 28–29.

42. Swami Tyagananda, "*Kali's Child* Revisited, or Didn't Anyone Check the Documentation?" http://www.home.earthlink.net/~tyag/KCR.pdf, page 18.

43. Kripal, *Kali's Child*, 4–5. As cited by Tyagananda.

44. Kripal, *Kali's Child*, 298–99. As cited by Tyagananda.

45. Tyagananda, *Kali's Child Revisited*, 12.

46. Kripal, *Kali's Child*, 2. As cited by Tyagananda.

47. Tyagananda, *Kali's Child Revisited*, 13.

48. Kripal, *Kali's Child*, 76. As cited by Tyagananda.

49. Ibid., 301.

50. Ibid., 66.

51. Ibid., 65. Note: The word 'vyakulata' can indeed be used for longing, with a slight erotic sense. However, in the context under consideration, it denotes just plain anxiety and longing for someone who is dear.

52. Kripal, *Kali's Child*, 67. As cited by Tyagananda.

53. Kripal, *Kali's Child*, 160. As cited by Tyagananda.

54. Tyagananda, *Kali's Child Revisited*, 18.

55. Ibid., 22.

56. Tyagananda, *Evam*, 207.

57. The intellectual confrontation has even warranted mention in the popular online encyclopedia, Wikipedia, http://en.wikipedia.org/wiki/Jeffrey_J._Kripal# Kali.27s_Child.
    Tyagananda criticized Kripal's translation of Bengali phrases and said that he tended to quote selectively and deceptively from the *Kathamrita* to create evidence for his interpretation. Tyagananda also alleged that Kripal had made at least 191 translation mistakes and/or deceptions. He alleges deliberate ignoring of evidence that contradicts his thesis. Additionally, Tyagananda accused him of having only an elementary knowledge of the Bengali language, and no understanding of Tantra. Since both the translation of Bengali terms and Tantra play an important role in Kripal's argument, this was a serious allegation.

58. Kripal, *Kali's Child*, 57. As cited by Tyagananda.

59. Ibid., xxi–xxii. As cited by Tyagananda.

60. Huston Smith, *Harvard Divinity Bulletin* 30, no.1 (Spring 2001): 2.

61. Tyagananda, *Evam*, 208.

62. Tyagananda, *Kali's Child Revisited*, 3.

63. WCS.

64. There seems to be a rash of public figures suddenly surprised by parental admission of their long-hidden ethnicity, as in the case of George Allen the former senator from Virginia.

65. See: http://www.ruf.rice.edu/~kalischi/secret.html.

66. See Sil's postscript of March 22, 2002, at, http://www.infinityfoundation.com/mandala/s_rv/s_rv_sil_kali_frameset.htm.

67. Recognition of this source of bias became the impetus for Malhotra's continuing interest in *Wendy's Child Syndrome*. Malhotra hypothesizes, "Perhaps, at times, a certain type of psychosis directs the motivations of the practitioners in this academic field and ultimately drives the work of some academic South Asianists—in the form of the topics and questions selected, the data imagined and filtered, and the interpretations given" (WCS).

68. Cited by Malhotra in WCS, based on his conversations with Stuart Sovatsky.

69. See the essays by Alan Roland and Yuvraj Krishna reproduced in the Appendix and section II.

70. Wendy Doniger, "When a Lingam is just a Good Cigar: Psychoanalysis and Hindu Sexual Fantasies," in *Vishnu on Freud's Desk: a Reader in Psychoanalysis and Hinduism*, ed. T. G. Vaidyanathan and Jeffrey Kripal, 290–291. Notwithstanding these concerns, Malhotra discovered during his research that, "scholars within RISA are reticent to challenge Wendy's conclusions, given the political power of her cartel."

71. Ronald Inden, *Imagining India*.

72. John Monaghan and Peter Just, *Social and Cultural Anthropology: A Very Short Introduction*, 27.

73. These trendy interpretations, in fringe publications would not be of worry. However, this is work, written by mainstream scholars that gets adapted and included authoritatively in textbooks, museum displays, and documentaries.

74. Monaghan and Just, *Social and Cultural Anthropology*, 141.

75. Sarah Caldwell, "The Bloodthirsty Tongue and the Self-Feeding Breast: Homosexual Fellatio Fantasy in a South Indian Ritual Tradition," in *Vishnu on Freud's Desk*, ed. T. G. Vaidyanathan and Jeffrey Kripal, 339.

76. Caldwell in Vaidyanathan and Kripal, eds., *Vishnu on Freud's Desk*, 343.

77. Ibid., 350.

78. This point is made by Malhotra in WCS. He wryly points out, "Essentially, this shows the importance of psychoanalyzing these scholars in order to evaluate their work."

79. Sarah Caldwell, *Oh Terrifying Mother: Sexuality, Violence and Worship of the Mother Kali*.

80. Cynthia Humes, review of Caldwell's book, *Journal of the American Academy of Religion* 69, no. 4 (November 2001): 901–02. Note: Page numbers in parenthesis refer to Caldwell's book.

81. Humes writes: "The lack of evidence is noteworthy, for it contrasts sharply with other trenchant psychoanalytic assertions based on detailed, sustained, and well-argued descriptions rooted in recorded male and female experience of the Mutiyettu. For example, Caldwell does convince me that 'by coopting this power in transvestite possession performance, males reclaim the envied feminine procreative power within their own bodies, while denying actual social, sexual, and political power to women' (189). Yet I do not dismiss out of hand homoerotic themes in

Mutiyettu. I find it likely and in keeping with the evidence that the audience consists largely of male Keralites exposed to homoerotic rumor and possible clandestine homosexual activity, as well as unwelcome sexual advances by older female relatives. It would take little to convince me, based on Caldwell's data, that such an audience could experience vicarious attraction to the male transvestite ritualists, especially in reenactment of their own fears of female sexuality and preferred company of men".

82. Rajiv Malhotra, interview.
83. The "personal confession" refers to Caldwell's writings about how she was sexually abused. It may also refer to the role she played in organizing a movement that brought attention to the late Swami Muktananda's alleged sexual relations with women devotees at his ashram.
84. Malhotra concludes, "If scholars don't want to be embarrassed by people publicly quoting their writings and talks, the best policy would be not to utter such embarrassing words in the first place" (WCS).
85. This point is explained in Malhotra's "U-Turn Theory" (See *Evam*, volume 1).
86. Posted on May 5, 1998, at the RISA-L discussion list, which is reserved for exclusive use by academic scholars in their pursuit of 'objective' scholarship.
87. This fear mongering strategy is not dissimilar to the color coded terrorist alerts from the Department of Homeland Security. In this context, using Caldwell's reasoning, the appearance of the Hindu male generates an elevated orange alert, or perhaps saffron.
88. Domestically, it feeds Pat Buchanan's xenophobia against a 'third world invasion' of pure white Christian America.
89. Vaidyanathan and Kripal, eds., *Vishnu on Freud's Desk*, 444.
90. Chicago: University of Chicago Press, 1991.
91. "Reflections on Psychoanalysis, Indian Culture and Mysticism," *Journal of Indian Philosophy* (Springer Netherlands) 10, no. 3 (September, 1982).
92. Ibid.
93. From a comment made by a member of the Hindu-American community, who prefers to remain anonymous.
94. Numerous questions about Paul Courtright are discussed at length in Section II of this book.
95. Paul Courtright, *Ganesa Lord of Obstacles, Lord of Beginnings*, 121.
96. Courtright, *Ganesa*, 110.
97. Ibid., 111.
98. See this anonymous book review on Amazon.com: http://www.amazon.ca/gp/cdp/member-reviews/A2BXVDPCHV6RZN/ref=cm_cr_auth/702-2301183-2120018?ie=UTF8.
99. Malhotra observed, "Multiple scholarly criticisms of such a work [against Christianity], backed by enormous funding from deep-pocket Western foundations and organized religion in the West would bury the book. It is also unlikely that the scholar's career would be enhanced and the scholar rewarded for creatively transcending the bounds of evidence" (WCS).
100. Cited by Malhotra (WCS).
101. Patrick Bresnan, *Awakening: An Introduction to the History of Eastern Thought*, 98–101.
102. Malhotra comments on Dr. Bresnan's one-dimensional interpretation, "It may well be true that many of these strange and terrible things happened in some situations and contexts. The point is that the typical American student [and scholar] uses his/her pre-existing Eurocentric biases as the context for interpretation." He points out that, "Remarkably, scholars have failed to gather

data on how misinformed most Americans are about Indic culture; and especially, on how Hinduphobia harms American society; and significantly, on how Americans' prejudices are correlated with what the mainstream scholars have written and taught."

103. Yvette C. Rosser, "The Clandestine Curriculum in the Classroom," *Education About Asia* 6, no. 3 (2001).

104. See the website maintained by former victims of the church at: http://bishop-accountability.org/priestdb/PriestDBbydiocese.html.

105. Stanley N Kurtz, "Psychoanalytic Approaches to Hindu Child Rearing," in *Vishnu on Freud's Desk*, ed. T.G. Vaidyanathan and Jeffrey Kripal, 199–200.

106. http://www.lalecheleague.org/cbi/bfstats03.html. According the statistics from La Leche League, a larger percentage of Indian women than American women breastfeed their babies. 95% of Indian women breastfeed their babies from the time they are born until 6 months of age, and after six months 43% are still breastfeeding. In the USA, 70% of mothers breastfeed for the first six months and then that number drops to 33%. Therefore if Kurtz's facile and invented methodology is correct, then compared to Indian babies, significantly fewer American babies-about 25% less- even have the chance to bond while nursing and form "western-style, loving, emotional partnerships".

107. Stanley N. Kurtz, *All the Mothers are One: Hindu India and the Cultural Reshaping of Psychoanalysis.* As cited by Malhotra in WCS.

108. Cynthia Humes, review of *All the Mothers are One*, by Stanley Kurtz, *The Journal of Asian Studies* 53, no.1 (February, 1991): 134. As cited by Malhotra, WCS.

109. Kurtz, *All the Mothers are One,* 143. Cynthia Humes brought this and other information to Rajiv's "attention after her review of [a] draft" of this paper.

110. Humes, review *Asian Studies 53.* As cited by Malhotra, WCS.

111. Monaghan and Just, *Social and Cultural Anthropology,* 141.

112. Veena Oldenburg, *Dowry Murder.*

113. See *Hinduism in American Classrooms*: http://www.sulekha.com/column.asp?cid=181242. Malhotra discovered the problem regarding the negative presentation of India's traditions when he saw his own children's World History textbooks in New Jersey. In comparison to the representations about other countries or religions, the descriptions of India and Hinduism were confusing, biased and just plain wrong. This realization sent him on a quest to get to the bottom of the negative representation about Hinduism that is a continuing phenomenon—long past colonialism and the Civil Rights Movement. Many observers have noted that while Western scholars are working to present Islam in a positive light, some scholars seem to be trying to do the *opposite* to Hinduism.

114. For Malhotra this comment foreshadowed the possible production of Hinduphobic scholars with Hindu names. "I have personally seen both kinds of Indian students in Hinduism Studies from Chicago: those who got reprogrammed into neocolonized sepoys, and those who remain loyal to their heritage despite the pressures." He feels that scholars must now address the hermeneutics of power, because there is a concentration of control over the distribution of academic knowledge about Hinduism that is dominated by a cartel of specific scholars at particular institutions.

115. Aditya Adarkar received his PhD from the University of Chicago.

116. In fact, at the WAVES conference that year, there was a paper presented by a scholar from China on Buddhist influence in Chinese Islam.

117. Quoted in another online investigation of the politics of RISA, http://yvette-c-rosser.sulekha.com/blog/post/2003/01/the-groan-final.htm.

118. The posts were removed from the original archive, and were reposted at the following URLs. All quotes from Witzel are from these documents,
    For Jaiminiya Brahmana—http://listserv.liv.ac.uk/cgi-bin/wa?A2=ind9511&L=indology&P=R1031.
    For Manu—http://listserv.liv.ac.uk/cgi-bin/wa?A2=ind9511&L=indology&P=R1167
    For *Rig Veda*—http://listserv.liv.ac.uk/cgi-bin/wa?A2=ind9511&L=indology&P=R1167.

119. He informed Malhotra privately (WCS). Malhotra notes, "Significantly, one cannot defend the criticism of one work of Doniger by showing the greatness of another work by her, nor by psychoanalyzing her critics, nor by disqualifying the critics' pedigrees." With all due respect to Doniger, Malhotra wrote in WCS, he was merely calling attention to the importance of Witzel's analysis, "because it is not universally known, even among Indologists, that the depth of [Doniger's] knowledge of Sanskrit has been called into question by Professor Michael Witzel of Harvard University."

120. Anacolutha—an abrupt change within a sentence to a second construction inconsistent with the first, sometimes used for rhetorical effect, http://www.thefreedictionary.com/anacolutha.

121. <u>See</u>: http://listserv.liv.ac.uk/cgi-bin/wa?A2=ind9511&L=indology&P=R1167; http://listserv.liv.ac.uk/cgi-bin/wa?A2=ind9511&L=indology&O=D&F=P&P=3289.

122. Manu 8.134, on weights, is translated by Doniger as follows: "Six (white) 'mustard seeds' equal one medium-sized 'barley-corn', and three 'barley-corns' make one 'berry'; five 'berries' make a 'bean', sixteen 'beans' a 'gold-piece'. 135 Four 'gold-pieces' equal a 'straw'...." Witzel's criticism of the above translation is as follows: "First logic or common sense: Take 3x5x16x4 (960) barley corns and weigh them... and see whether they equal any blade of straw. Even if you believe, with Herodotos, in gold digging ants and other wonders in India, I haven't seen Indian (rice/barley) straw of that weight . . . But we forget simple philology, the hand-maiden of any translation that is supposedly better than Buehler's in Victorian English and the recent partial one by Derrett, etc. The last straw is : If you check pala in the Petersburg dictionary (PW), or even in its copy, Monier Williams' dict., you see that pala 'straw' is attested only with some lexicographer, who turns out to be Hemacandra (according to the PW, in his Abhidhaanacintaamani 1182), that is, and the word apparently is attested only once). If you check the surrounding words, you find palaala in Manu, Mbh. (and Atharvaveda: palaalii) which mean 'straw'; and palada' (AV) of similar meaning. It is clear that Hemacandra got his truncated (hapax!) word pala from the well known word for straws palaala/ii / palaada' (cf.TURNER 7958)—while pala (Turner 7952!) always meant 'a certain weight/measure' and also 'meat'—Mayrhofer suggests an Indo-European (see: palaava "chaff,grass"), and a Dravidian (Tamil: pul etc.) etymology. Common sense apart, to establish pala 'straw', [Doniger] should at least have searched in texts of similar nature and time level before accepting the meaning of 'straw' in Manu."

123. Malhotra reported in his WCS article that he had received an unsolicited grant request from one of Doniger's students. Malhotra described the proposal as having "the specific purpose of looking for data on such predetermined conclusions as 'Christian persecution in India,' even though everyone knows that a genuine scholar cannot embark upon research with the conclusions already fixed."

124. Professor de Nicolas is emeritus professor of Philosophy at SUNY, Stony Brook.

125. Cited by Malhotra in WCS.

126. *maska lagao*—Hindi, to flatter, literally to "butter up".
127. Wendy Doniger O'Flaherty, *Women, Androgynes and Other Mythical Beasts.*
128. Kazanas, Nicholas. "Indo-European Deities and the Rgveda," *Journal of Indo-European Studies* 29, no. 3–4 (Fall & Winter 2001): 257–293. See note n. 14 on page 283.
129. Wendy Doniger O'Flaherty, *Asceticism and Eroticism in the Mythology of Siva.*
130. Hugh Urban, from the Department of Comparative Studies at Ohio State University, is the author of *Tantra: Sex, Secrecy, Politics and Power.* He has also written humorous fiction poking fun at Tim LaHay's *Left Behind* series and critiques of voter fraud in Ohio.
131. Hugh B. Urban, Ohio State University, "Tantra, American Style: Neo-Orientalism, Globalism, and the Western Appropriation of Tantra" (paper presented at the annual meeting of the American Academy of Religions, Denver, 2001). Abstract: "Tantra has now entered fully into Western scholarship and American popular culture as a whole, becoming a major commercial enterprise, spawning lines of books, videos and spiritual-sensual merchandise. This paper will critically examine the contemporary American appropriation of Tantra, by looking at three key transformations that have occurred during Tantra's complex journey to the West: first, the sexualization and scandalization of Tantra that took place in the Victorian era, with figures like Pierre Bernard, founder of the first Tantrik Order in America; second, the commodification and commercialization of Tantra that occurred in the 1970s and '80s with neo-Tantric gurus like Bhagwan Shree Rajneesh; and finally, the digitalization and globalization of Tantra as it enters the world of the Internet, where we now surf websites like Tantra.com and discover "ecstasy online,"" http://www.aarweb.org.
132. Wendy Doniger O'Flaherty, *Asceticism and Eroticism,* 323–325.
133. Diana L. Eck, *A New Religious America: How a "Christian" Country Has Now Become the Most Religiously Diverse Nation,* 99.
134. Bakker, Hans T. et al., *The Skanda Purana, Volume I.*
135. Doniger O'Flaherty, *Asceticism and Eroticism,* Glossary, 323–325.
136. David White, *Kiss of the Yogini: Tantric Sex in its South Asian Context.* See Wendy Doniger, "Tantric bodies," review of White, *The Times Literary Supplement,* 20th May 2004. http://www.the-tls.co.uk/this_week/story.aspx? story_id=2107312; also saved at Svabhinava, http://groups.yahoo.com/group/Abhinavagupta/message/1888.
137. This synopsis is based on correspondence between Rajiv Malhotra and Jeffrey Lidke, which was posted on the now defunct Yahoo discussion group, Openrisa. Much of this discussion was chronicled in the Abhinavagupta site and is available at: http://www.svabhinava.org/friends/RajivMalhotra/WendyWhite-frame.html.
138. BJP—Bharatiya Janata Party, a Hindu nationalist political party.
139. Ziauddin Sardar, *Postmodernism and the Other: The New Imperialism of Western Culture,* 19–20. Also see: Ziauddin Sardar, "Deconstructing Postmodernism," *Bi-annual Encounters* 5, no. 1 (1999).
140. Per the Malhotra-Lidke debate.
141. Lidke is Chair of the Interfaith Council and Assistant Professor of World Religions, Berry College.
142. Posted on May 28, 2004, at the Internet discussion list, OpenRisa was an online e-group on Yahoogroups.
143. Lidke acknowledged that Malhotra's previous critiques of Indology were "generally worth sound consideration." He expressed interest to seriously discuss Malhotra's criticism of White's book using the online forums.
144. Sitanshu Chakravarti, "Misrepresentation of the Tantras in David White's book:

A flawed methodology instantiated" (paper, presented at the WAVES conference 2004). Also available at http://www.svabhinava.org/HinduCivilization/SitansuChakravarti/default.htm.

145. In making his case Malhotra offered the following analogy: A thousand years from now, some future historian studying 21st century American Christianity could pick a random selection of today's obscure writings that does not reflect mainstream American society or pertain at all to Christianity or relate to one another, but the future historian could combine excerpts from such texts as free-floating elements in a postmodernist bazaar to construct theories about 21st century American Christianity.

146. Jayant Bapat, "Of Yoginis and Tantriksters: Doniger on White's "Tantric Sex"—Reflections in the South Asian context." See: http://www.philosophy.unimelb.edu.au/sophia/bapat.html (accessed January 21, 2007).

147. John R. Dupuche, *Abhinavagupta: The Kula Ritual As Elaborated in Chapter 29 of the Tantraloka.* As cited by Bapat.

148. Bapat, "Of Yoginis."

149. White, *Yogini,* 245. Interestingly Doniger is also not sure if these were metapohorical references or actual practices, but finds the socio-political uses of White's thesis convincing.

150. White, *Yogini,* 159.

151. Ibid., 150.

152. White, *Yogini,* 261.

153. Wendy Doniger, "Tantric bodies," review of *Kiss of the Yogini: Tantric Sex in its South Asian Context,* by David White, *The Times Literary Supplement,* 20 May 2004.

154. It is illuminating to compare the White-Doniger's acceptably dressed up, soft-core "overcoded," essentialization and reduction of Tantra to hardcore colonial psychology's reduction of Vedic Hinduism to an obsession with flatulence discussed in Chapter 12.

155. Doniger, "Tantric bodies."

156. Ibid.

157. Ibid.

158. Jayant Bapat, "Of Yoginis."

159. Wendy Doniger, "Tantric Bodies."

160. White, *Yogini,* 8.

161. Sitanshu Shekar Chakravarti received his M.A from Jadavpur Univ., Calcutta; and his Ph.D. also in Philosophy, from Syracuse Univesrity. He was visiting Professor at the Department of Philosophy, University of Rajasthan, Jaipur, as well as at Visva-Bharati, Santiniketan. His publications include *Hinduism: a Way of Life*; *Modality, Reference and Sense: An Essay in the Philosophy of Language*; *Ethics in the Mahabharata: A Philosophical Inquiry,* Forthcoming. He also has articles relating to Indian as well as Western Philosophy published in the *Notre Dame Journal of Formal Logic, Journal of the Indian Council of Philosophical Research, Prabuddha Bharata,* and *Jadavpur Journal of Philosophy.*

162. Sitanshu Chakravarti, "Misrepresentation of the Tantras."

163. See these books by Madhu Khanna, *Yantra: The Tantric Symbol of Cosmic Unity*; *The Tantric Way: Art, Science, Ritual*; and *The Cosmic Order.*

164. Madhu Khanna, "Paradigms of Female Sexuality in the Hindu World," in *Women of Religion Volume 3,* ed. Durre Ahmed. All quotes from Khanna are from this chapter.

165. Ibid., 241.

166. Ibid., 239–240.

167. White, *Yogini*, 13.
168. As per Malhotra.
169. Professor Saxena is Assistant Professor of English at Nassau Community College, New York.
170. Neela Bhattacharya Saxena, "The Funhouse Mirror of Tantric Studies: A Rejoinder to David Gordon White's 'Kiss of the Yogini,'" *Evam* 4: nos. 1–2 (2006): 358–371. Samvad India Foundation, Delhi.
171. While these online debates are not explicitly cited by Bhattacharya-Saxena it is clear that they informed her thinking.
172. This is a simplified view of the chakra system, and its use here is purely as a device to explain various planes or levels of consciousness from which one may experience something. The chakra system used by Tantrikas for spiritual practice is much more elaborate.
173. *Adhyatma-vidya*: from Sanskrit – adhi = over, above + atman = self + vidya = knowledge from the verbal root vid to know, perceive, learn ... Adhyatma-vidya is the Sanskrit work for 'inner science.' To quote Robert Thurman, "what humans must (do with this inner science is) turn a scientific, systematic attention to the mind, master its energies, ameliorate its qualities, and, if possible, enable it to achieve a permanent endowment of the real happiness all seek." http://is-root.de/wiki/Adhyatmavidya.
174. Sufism in Islam is a small minority of Muslims who do believe in transcendence, but their notion of non-duality is as a temporary epistemology only and not an ontological reality. In Christian history, mystics have always been a small minority with neo-Vedantic worldviews.
175. The Sanskrit dedication reads, "To my parents, without whose bodily fluids, this book would not have been possible"–Sitanshu Chakravarti's translation, in Chakravarti, *Misrepresentations of Tantra*.
176. Harold Coward, *Jung and Eastern Thought*.
177. "RISA Lila-1."
178. A.K. Ramanujan, "Is There an Indian Way of Thinking?" in McKim Marriot's *India through Hindu Categories* (1990).
179. Malhotra has compiled an extensive Bibliography of Critiques of Eurocentrism: http://www.infinityfoundation.com/mandala/h_rs/h_rs_malho_euro_frameset.htm.
180. Dr. Chandrakala Padia, professor of history and director of Women's Studies at Benares Hindu University (BHU) is currently working on a project that is retranslating passages about women from Sanskrit texts, such as the *Rg Veda* and the *Manusmriti*, and showing how they were mistranslated and misinterpreted or partially translated and the correct version is far more sympathetic to females than those based on colonial era translations.
181. See Chapter 18 for trenchant criticism of the intellectual slipperiness of this practice.
182. John Monaghan & Peter Just, *Social & Cultural Anthropology: A Very Short Introduction*, 32.
183. 'Vasanas' are conditionings caused by past karma that bring about certain innate tendencies or desires or personalities in an individual. Carl Jung researched and taught about this using Indian references before mapping it on to Western terminology.
184. Malhotra pointed out one example of Wendy acknowledging the projection of her psychosis onto her scholarship, "She claims that studying Indian culture and enjoying sex are one and the same thing, because Indian religion is *essentially* all about sex." Doniger wrote, "Aldous Huxley once said that an intellectual was someone who had found something more interesting than sex; in Indology, an

intellectual need not make that choice at all . . . Is sex a euphemism for god? Or is god a euphemism for sex? Or both!" See Doniger, "When a lingam is Just a Good Cigar," 279 and 288.

185. *Adhikara*—ability or authorization, rights and responsibilities, Sanskrit term for competence.

186. Dilip Chakrabarti, *Colonial Indology—Sociopolitics of the Ancient Indian Past*, 1.

187. See Sil's posts of May 10, 1998 and March 30, 2001 at: http://www.infinityfoundation.com/mandala/s_rv/s_rv_sil_kali_frameset.htm.

188. Edward Said, "Representing the Colonized: Anthropology's Interlocutors," *Critical Inquiry* 15 (Winter 1989): 217–224.

189. Kripal in *Evam*, 204 argues that, "With Gadamer's 'fusion of horizons' we can see quite easily just why the hermeneutic may in fact legitimately understand the text in ways quite different than those of the original author of culture: in effect, the historian's present life-world and categories provide probes or techniques of analysis that were simply non-existent in the meaning-horizon of the text's past. This present horizon of meaning fusing with the past horizon of the text produces a third, unprecedented space in which new meanings and possibilities of insight can appear. Hence Gadamer can write that the 'meaning of a text goes beyond its author, not only occasionally, but always. Understanding is therefore not merely reproductive but also productive.'[189] . . . [T]he modern study of Ramakrishna extends and radicalizes the history of the texts themselves through the various fusions of horizons that it enacts in its own texts and critical practices (gender studies, psychoanalysis, Marxism, feminism, etc.). What, of course, we end up with is radically new visions of who Ramakrishna was and what his life meant that are a bit shocking to someone locked into only one horizon of meaning (that is one cultural worldview, past or present) but entirely plausible to those who inhabit others . . . Why, then, can Americans such as myself, so deeply inspired by Hindu religious traditions, not think about them with all our religious categories and intellectual practices?"

190. For example, Subhash Kak has written extensively to date the *Rg Veda* and other Indian texts using unambiguous astronomical observations whose dates of occurrence are well established by modern physics.

191. These are just some of the insults that are used against Hindus who question the dominant model. To shut Hindu-Americans up they have also been called trishul-wielding baby-impalers and other such unambiguous taunts.

192. The debate is not a matter of left or right, the issues are complex and the problems not simple. The questions are multihued and the answers are not simplistic black or white.

193. Kripal, *Evam*, 192.

194. *Evam* is a journal in India sponsored by Infinity Foundation, edited by Makarand Paranjape a professor of comparative literature at JNU (Jawaharlal Nehru University).

195. *Evam*, 205.

196. From a Persian word *Sipâhi* meaning "soldier"—a native of India employed as a soldier in the service of the United Kingdom.

197. Hindi for watchman.

198. WCS.

199. See the essays by Sankrant Sanu in this volume and "U.S. Hinduism Studies: A Question of Shoddy Scholarship," by Sankrant Sanu, http://www.beliefnet.com/story/146/story_14684_1.html.

200. Malhotra explains this dilemma, "RISA's internal power structure encourages many *chowkidars* to control entry, and *sepoys* to go out on hit-and-run missions—

in the sense of *ad homines*—against those who question their methods, power structure, or conclusions. When, in 1995, I started to examine the academic scholarship about India, I was told many times that I must first pay homage to the power bosses of this cartel. My initial reason for not patronizing the RISA bosses was to gain an independent perspective, in the same manner as corporate executives bring independent consultants to tell them what the insiders hide. I wanted to hear voices and perspectives that are marginalized by the power structure, as is often the case in any incestuous and corrupt institution. I was repeatedly warned that to be considered legitimate, I must invite the bosses to lead or at least to participate in each activity that I do. Even if they did not accept, the invitation would provide me with 'protection,' or so I was told. However, my entire corporate career had involved fighting many entrenched hegemonies, and the notion of playing along with the flow of power was never appealing. In the computer industry in the 1970s, I enjoyed working for the underdog minicomputer and then the underdog personal computer suppliers, at a time when the mighty IBM mainframe ruled supreme. Subsequently, in the telecom field, once again, I enjoyed working on emerging paradigms that challenged old monolithic behemoths. As a management consultant, I specialized in studying industry structures to find vulnerable spots where new entrepreneurial players could enter and ultimately defeat the old (and inevitably inefficient) *nawabs*. Facilitating change has always appealed to me, especially starting from below. I prefer working with those who challenge the status quo and monopolistic mechanisms. Therefore, the academic field of humanities is not my first encounter with entrenched bureaucracies; the old boys' (and old girls') networks; hostilities against "outsiders" and being at first ignored, on the grounds of being unqualified, and then later, seen as a threat to the incumbents of power. The price of shaking up this neocolonized field of India studies obviously also includes facing insults. I have been studying the anthropological and psychoanalytical methods used by these scholars, and have applied the very same methods to study the scholars themselves. It is fascinating to see them as an exotic, strange and peculiar community. Their attacks against their critics provide further data points for research." (WCS)

201. See the discussion of a recent paper by Russell McCutcheon on how scholars react to diaspora Hindus versus native informants in chapter 23.
202. John Keay, *India: A History*, 425.
203. Cited by Malhotra, WCS.
204. Spivak, Gayatri Chakravorty, "Neocolonialism and the secret agent of knowledge: an interview," *The Oxford Literary Review* 13 (1991): 220–51.
205. Chakrabarti, Dilip, *Colonial Indology – Sociopolitics*, 6–7.
206. NRI = Non-Resident Indian.
207. Throughout this intellectual *lila* of hyphenated identities, Malhotra has played the role of the classic outsider to the academy. His years of engagement, support and sponsorship of western academia, and his on-going studies of the work of American Indologists and professors of South Asian Studies, provide him with a unique perspective. He says he is routinely attacked for "exercising my intellectual freedom to psychoanalyze the scholarship that I have described in the framework of Wendy's Child Syndrome." There are political risks involved when any non-Westerner attempts to psychologically or otherwise deconstruct the work of Western scholars or "their exotic personal lives—exotic trips and other affairs, various pathologies, political connections, and misappropriating ideas from Indian sources"—enough drama for a Hollywood hit. Fortunately, there are many Western scholars, both in RISA and outside, who have distanced themselves from

Eurocentrism, and who go out of their way to help the neo-colonized Indians restore integrity to their religions and knowledge systems.

208. This creates, what Malhotra termed "incestuous inbreeding" that does not readily allow space for alternative opinions.

Section 2

1. Professor Raman is professor of physics (emeritus), University of Rochester. He is a practitioner-scholar of Indian philosophy and traditions and plays an active role as a diaspora intellectual. Often regarded as an elder statesman for the community, his opinions carry considerable weight among the moderate organizations of Indian Americans.

2. Malhotra offered a dialogue proposal, "I am eager to resolve these issues in a friendly and open-hearted spirit that can be as faithful as possible to academic standards of free inquiry and intellectual honesty and to the felt needs of significant segments of the RISA community, whose ideologies and presuppositions I am all too painfully aware of. I subscribe to symmetry between the parties in the true spirit of *samvad* (dialogue). On the other hand, if RISA continues to fight every attempt at dialogue initiated by practitioners of the Indian traditions, without any initiatives from its own side, then it should beware of Swami Tyagananda's warning: 'If contemporary scholars condone sloppy documentation and self-serving translations to support a thesis, then the future of the present scholarship looks bleak to me'" (from *Evam*).

3. He was especially upset due to his young niece's psychological state after reading the insults given by Wendy's Children to various Hindu deities.

4. Christiane Hartnack, *Psychoanalysis in Colonial India.*

5. Two weeks later, on September 30, 2002, Balu also published, "India and Her Traditions: A Reply to Jeffrey Kripal," http://s-n-balagangadhara.sulekha.com/blog/post/2002/09/india-and-her-traditions-a-reply-to-jeffrey-kripal.htm.

6. Professor S.N. Balagangadhara or Balu as he is popularly known, is director of the Research Centre Vergelijkende Cultuurwetenschap (Comparative Science of Cultures) in Ghent University, Belgium. He has authored a seminal book, *The Heathen in His Blindness: Asia, the West and the Dynamic of Religion*, on the nature of religion. His central area of inquiry is to develop a description of the Western culture against the background of the Indian culture. Prof. Balagangadhara held the co-chair of the Hinduism Unit at the American Academy of Religion (AAR) during 2004–2006.

7. Dr. Christiane Hartnack is deputy head of the Department of Cultural Studies at Danube University Krems, Vienna, Austria.

8. Hartnack, *Psychoanalysis in Colonial India.*

9. William B. Parsons, *The Enigma of the Oceanic Feeling: Revisioning the Psychoanalytic Theory of Mysticism.*

10. Ibid.

11. The Indic system also depicts the awakening of the "higher" chakras as a natural potential of human maturation, and not a "diversionary sublimation" (i.e. secondary) or even "channeling" (i.e. artificial) of the energies of the second chakra. The term urdhva-reta is the upward maturation of the life-seed force all the way to the sixth chakra and is considered a natural part of human potential. Thus, psychoanalysis is always reductive, since its maturation system ends with genital puberty of second chakra. Kundalini awakening involving the spine, with

its correlates in Judaic spinal-rocking prayer, Christian "holy ghost" shaking, Quaker "quaking" and numerous other spiritual bodily phenomena world-wide, has no place in psychoanalytic developmental theory, so these phenomena have been pathologized or "primitivized" by psychoanalytic anthropologists.

12. In Appendix-1 of this book, Roland writes: "Psychoanalysis has played a surprisingly major role in South Asian studies, much more so than in other area studies, not to mention many other intellectual disciplines".

13. See Swami Tyaganada's detailed peer review of Kripal's work: http://www.infinityfoundation.com/mandala/s_rv/s_rv_tyaga_kali1_frameset.htm.

14. See Agarwal and Venkat's peer review in this volume (Chapter 17) for numerous examples.

15. Susantha Goonatilake, *Anthropologizing Sri Lanka: A Eurocentric Misadventure.*

16. Gananath Obeyesekere also addressed these issues in *Psychoanalysis in Ethnography: A Forum for Deeper Understanding or Cerebral Colonialism?*

17. Hartnack, *Psychoanalysis in Colonial India,* 69.

18. Sarah Caldwell, "The Bloodthirsty Tongue and the Self-Feeding Breast: Homosexual Fellatio Fantasy in a South Indian Ritual Tradition," in *Vishnu on Freud's Desk,* ed. T. G. Vaidyanathan and Jaffrey Kripal, 343.

19. Ibid., 339.

20. Hartnack, *Psychoanalysis in Colonial India,* 73.

21. Ibid., 69.

22. Caldwell posted the following comment on May 5, 1998, at RISA-l: "In short we need to be careful to examine what 'homosexuality' means in the rhetorical and personal contexts in which it is being used, and the historical and political background of the discussion of masculinity in South Asia, and not to focus exclusively on the personal domain as is common in Europe and America. We need to psychologize public culture as well as the private sphere. Jeff's book, while providing a nuanced and empathetic account of an individual life, invites us to broaden our lens to understand the reception of that life and its distortion in a century of highly contested religious posturing. With the current election of a BJP-led government, such careful analysis is timely and essential."

23. Owen Berkeley-Hill, "The Anal-Erotic Factor in the Religion, Philosophy and Character of the Hindu," *International Journal of Psychoanalysis* 2 (1921): 306–338.

24. Hartnack, *Psychoanalysis in Colonial India,* 69.

25. See Chapter 9 of this book for an explanation of Malhotra's Chakra Hermeneutics model

26. For a similar devastating expert judgment on Freud's penchant for faulty diagnoses, see John F. Kihlstrom, "Is Freud Still Alive? No. Not Really." An updated version of the essay is available at: http://socrates.berkeley.edu/~kihlstrm/freuddead.htm.

27. Thanks to Stuart Sovatsky for this detail about the contemporary application of therapeutic systems derived from psychoanalytical theories.

28. David Friedman, *A Mind of Its Own: A Cultural History of the Penis.*

29. E.M. Thornton, *Freudian Fallacy: An Alternative View of Freudian Theory.*

30. William B. Parsons, *Enigma of the Oceanic Feeling.*

31. Hartnack, *Psychoanalysis in Colonial India,* 76.

32. Ibid.

33. Ibid.

34. Salman Akhtar, *Freud Along the Ganges, Psychoanalytic Reflections on the People and Culture of India.*

35. Frederick Crews, *The Memory Wars: Freud's Legacy in Dispute,* New York Review Books, October 1995.

36. Sometimes Freud is credited with discovering the unconscious mind. However, prior to Freud, William James, America's first psychologist, had already coined the term, not to mention the generations of 'rishis' and sages from India who, millennia ago, spoke of multiple states of consciousness, including various dream states and waking states. William James introduced Freud to American intellectuals in the late 1890s, but commented that Freud was obsessed with the certainty of *his* fixed idea. James cautioned to be more self-critical and not treat classifications as final or absolute. His views on spiritual matters were very different than Freud's. He was the first Western thinker to make a systematic study of the psychology of religion. A Jamesian analysis would lead to entirely different conclusions about Hinduism than Wendy's School has promulgated.

37. See a few instances detailed in section IV.

38. Reprinted with permission from the author Yuvraj Krishan, *Ganesa Unravelling an Enigma*, Appendix II, "Is the Fight Between Siva and Ganesa an Episode of Oedipal Conflict?" Reproduced and adapted from *Spectrum of Indian Culture* (Prof. S.B. Deo Felicitation Volume).

39. Y. Krishan (born 1922) M.A., LL.B. is a scholar of Indology – Indian History, Religion, Philosophy and Art. He has published over 150 research papers on these topics in journals of standing in India and abroad. These also cover the partition of India. He had a long and distinguished record of service under the Government of India – in the Railways, Indian Administrative Service and the Audits & Accounts Department from where he retired as Deputy Comptroller and Auditor General of India in 1980. He was a member of the National Consumer Disputes Redressal Commission from December 1988 to January 1995. He has also published four books *Audit in India's Democracy; The Buddha Image: Its Origin and Development; The Doctrine of Karma in Brahmanical, Buddhist, Jaina Traditions*; and *Understanding Partition*.

40. Seymour Fischer and Roger P. Greenberg, *The Scientific Evolution of Freud's Theories and Therapy*, 173.

41. Sigmund Freud, *The Interpretation of Dreams*, 357. Freud observed: "To represent castration symbolically, the dream work makes use of baldness, hair cutting, falling out of teeth and decapitation." This observation regarding decapitation is supported by two dream episodes on pages 366 and 367.

42. Philip Spratt, *Hindu Culture and Personality*, 126 and 186.

43. Philip Spratt, *Hindu Culture*, 186. Freud in *Interpretation of Dreams*, 367 (fn. 1) says, "A tooth being pulled out by someone else in a dream is as a rule, to be interpreted as castration." Spratt, *Hindu Culture*, 126 says, "The cutting off of the head and the tusk are fairly clear symbols of castration."

44. R.P. Goldman, "Fathers, Sons and Gurus Oedipal conflict in Sanskrit Epics," *Journal of Indian Philosophy* (Dodrecht Holland) 6 (1978): 371–72.

45. A.K. Ramanujan, "The Indian Oedipus," in *Indian Literature: Proceedings of a Seminar*, 129, 130, 135.

46. Ramanujan, ibid., 135.

47. Goldman, ibid., 326, quoting Spratt, *Hindu Culture*, 106.

48. Goldman, ibid., 372.

49. P.B. Courtright, *Ganesa Lord of Obstacles, Lord of Beginnings*, 117.

50. E.R. Leach describes Ganesa as sexually impersonal having a kind of "impersonalised sexuality," cited in Courtright, *Ganesa*, 117.

51. G. Obeyesekere, *The Cult of the Goddess Patni*, 471.

52. Spratt, *Hindu Culture*, 125.

53. R.M. Goldenson, ed. *Longman Dictionary of Psychology and Psychiatry*. See Oedipus Complex.

54. Fischer and Greenberg, *Freud's Theories*, 174.
55. Ibid., 174.
56. Erich Fromm, *Greatness and Limitations of Freud's Thought*, 27–38.
57. Goldenson, ed., *Longman Dictionary of Psychology and Psychiatry*. See Oedipus Complex. According to Kakar and Ross, pages 108, 122–23, 129, 163–64, the Oedipus complex is a child of the western heritage and guilt as a primal danger of love is absent in Islamic and Indian cultures.
58. Goldenson, ed., *Longman Dictionary of Psychology and Psychiatry*.
59. The *Sabdakalpadruma* of Radha Kant Deb, an encyclopedia of Sanskrit published in the 19th century narrates yet another legend. According to this story Ganesa's human head was cut off while he was in the womb of Parvati by a demon Sindūra who entered the womb. So Ganesa was born headless. He cut off the elephant head of a demon Mahesa and appropriated it to his torso and thus became elephant-headed. This legend is attributed to the *Skanda Purāna*, in the *Sabdakalpadruma* but we have not been able to trace it in that Purāna.
60. Carl Jung, *Modern Man in Search of a Soul*, 22.
61. Published on Sulekha.com in December 2002.
62. Bhattacharyya is a member of the International Psychoanalytic Association (since 1961), the Psychoanalytic Society, and the Asiatic Society, Calcutta. He has published over a dozen papers in scientific journals.
63. Vaidyanathan and Kripal, eds., *Vishnu on Freud's desk*. Bhattacharyya wrote that this book "purported to be a reader in psychoanalysis and Hinduism [though] its editors ... were not trained psychoanalysts."
64. Jeffrey Kripal, *Kali's Child*.
65. All quotes, unless otherwise indicated, are from Bhattacharyya's Sulekha.com essay, "Kali's Child: Psychological and Hermeneutical Problems," December 14, 2002, http://prof-somnath-bhattacharyya.sulekha.com/blog/post/2002/12/i-kali-s-child-i-psychological-and-hermeneutical.htm.
66. metonymy—substituting meanings, synaesthesia – co-mingling images
67. One of Kripal's earliest papers was published in a Gay Men's Issues Series (1992), and gay journals received his work with enthusiasm. As cited by Bhattacharyya.
68. Thanks to Professor Wendy Doniger for this phrase from Vienna.
69. Bhattacharyya's Footnote: The terms androgyny and bisexuality, used by some authors, are misleading, because they have specific biological connotations.
70. Bhattacharyya's Footnote: This language issue is important here because what Kripal claims to be doing is a form of "content analysis."
71. See: 'Ramakrishna the Monkey' and 'Mathur's Handmaid,' *Kali's Child*, 103–109. As per Bhattacharyya.
72. Walsh and Vaughan 61–62 (as per Bhattacharyya).
73. He cites, "Katchadourian and Lunde."
74. Jeffrey Kripal, "Textuality, Sexuality and the Future of the Past: A Response to Swami Tyagananda."
75. Kaplan and Sadock, *Comprehensive Textbook of Psychiatry*, 585 (as cited in Bhattacharyya).
76. ... sexualizes ... eroticizes ... and *publicizes*.
77. ... and never look back.
78. There are many forms of catachresis, such as mixing metaphors, confusing words that are almost identical but have different meanings, such as ingenuous and ingenious, or substituting a related word for a concept, much as Bollywood, stands for the entire Indian film making industry, or Hollywood, signifies something more than just a suburb of LA. In a literary context, especially in translation, these devices are often intentionally or inadvertently misused.

79. Bhattacharyya's note: "I am thankful to Richard P. Sloan for the analogy. See his review of "Religion, Faith and Good Health," in *The Telegraph*, Calcutta, 13th May, 2002."

80. For example, in his review of *Kali's Child* in the *Harvard Divinity School Bulletin* 30, no. 1, Huston Smith doubted that "any other book—not even those of early, polemical, poorly informed, and bigoted missionaries—has offended Hindu sensibilities so grossly. And understandably, for despite Kripal's protestations to the contrary . . . *Kali's Child* is colonialism updated." Bhattacharyya also pointed out that "Even [Kripal's] Chicago University colleague, Hugh Urban, who could not but review his book favorably, noted the problems of 'sensationalism,' 'misconception of tantra,' and 'lack of attention to social and historical context.'"

81. In Bhattacharyya's article, he examines the differences in two versions of Kripal's reply to Tyagananda, one published in the *Harvard Divinity School Bulletin*, with a western audience in mind, and one published by *Evam*, in New Delhi, written for an Indian audience. Bhattacharyya was quite incensed about the discrepancies and the sorts of changes found in these two versions of the same essay.

82. McDermott notes that when Professor McDermott teaches her students about New Age appropriations of the Hindu Goddess the "typical initial reaction is outrage and disgust." Rachel Fell McDermott, *Journal of the American Academy of Religion* 68, no.4: 723–727.

83. This article was originally published on Sulekha.com.

84. Reprinted with permission of the author. © Copyright Sankrant Sanu 2007. Sankrant Sanu is a software entrepreneur who lives in Redmond, WA and India. After working for Microsoft for several years, Sankrant left Microsoft in 1999 to co-found Paramark, a software company. A prolific writer on issues to do with India, Sankrant is a strong advocate of India's pluralism. Sankrant counts the University of Texas at Austin and IIT Kanpur as his alumni schools. His interests are varied—from spirituality to skiing, from computers to playing the congas. Most recently he has been involved in volunteering as a teacher at a Hindi school for kids in Redmond, and spending some passionate energy conceiving of a plan for rural education in India.

85. These are hypothetical quotations for the purpose of illustration, not actual quotations from *Encarta*. These quotations are also not the views of the author who neither supports these quotations nor suggests that they be used to depict that religion in question.

86. See previous endnote.

87. Prof. Carl Sagan, distinguished Cornell University astronomer, covered this in the television series "Cosmos" dealing with Astronomy and Scientific exploration, http://www.rediff.com/news/jan/29sagan.htm presents an interview from which this quote is taken.

88. Compare this to Hartnack's rendering of colonial descriptions of Kali in Chapter 13.

89. See, for instance, Rajiv Malhotra's, "RISA Lila-1: Wendy's Child Syndrome," http://www.sulekha.com/column.asp?cid=239156, and associated comments.

90. Yvette Claire Rosser, "Puzzling Dimensions and Theoretical Knots in my Graduate School Research," http://www.infinityfoundation.com/mandala/s_es/s_es_rosse_puzzle_frameset.htm.

91. Yvette Claire Rosser, "Stereotypes in Schooling: Negative Pressures in the American Educational System," http://www.infinityfoundation.com/mandala/s_es/s_es_rosse_school_frameset.htm.

92. This article first appeared in a preliminary and shorter version at: http://www.sulekha.com. Courtright's book is henceforth referred as 'Courtright.'

Reprinted with permission of the authors. © Copyright Vishal Agarwal and Kalavai Venkat 2007.

93. Vishal Agarwal is a Biomedical Materials Engineer with graduate degrees in Materials Engineering and Business Administration. He resides with his wife and children in Minnesota, where he works for a leading biomedical device company. Vishal is an ardent student of religion, archaeology and history of ancient India and has numerous contributions to his credit in peer reviewed publications. He is currently engaged in creating electronic versions of important Hindu scriptures.

94. Kalavai Venkat is a practicing agnostic Hindu with degrees in Business Administration and Physics. He works as a consultant providing solutions to large corporations. He resides with his wife and children in the Bay Area in California. Kalavai's areas of specialization are Tamil literature, historiography and the impact of Abrahamic religions on Indian civilization. He also volunteers as a teacher of Tamil and Hinduism in the Indian community in the Bay Area.

95. Doniger is fond of using pseudoscientific language to make her dismissive, negative and often poorly evidenced opinions on Hinduism sound weightier than they are—claiming for instance that Western feminists who embrace the Hindu Goddess are wrong because, when she compares India to Monotheistic, Male-God cultures, there is "in general **an inverse ratio** between the worship of goddesses and the granting of rights to human women." Doniger does not produce any evidence to substantiate this sweeping statement which she has made, for instance, in the *Washington Post*, January 20, 2007.

96. Doniger for instance is untrained in psychoanalysis, her Sanskrit knowledge has been questioned, and serious questions have been raised over Kripal's training in Bengali (and Doniger's, since she supervised his work), and Courtright's knowledge of Indian texts.

97. Terry Rombeck, "Controversial religious scholar to visit Lawrence," *Lawrence Journal World*, Thursday, March 30, 2006, http://www2.ljworld.com/news/2006/mar/30/controversial_religious_scholar_visit_lawrence/.

98. His book won the 1985 award by the Committee on the History of Religions of the American Council of Learned Societies.

99. Tanmaya Kumar Nanda, "'I am distressed that anyone found my discussion of Ganesha offensive'—Interview with Paul Courtright," *India Abroad*, November 28, 2003.

100. In fact, the petition had already disappeared by the time both the authors had a chance to read it and look at the signatures. This description of the petition is derived from second hand accounts. HSC behaved in a very responsible manner by removing its petition from the Internet promptly.

101. See for instance the article "Scholars of Hinduism Under Attack," by Martin Marty at http://www.beliefnet.com/story/128/story_12899_1.html. A rejoinder to this article titled, "U.S. Hinduism Studies: A Question of Shoddy Scholarship," by Sankrant Sanu is also available at, http://www.beliefnet.com/story/146/story_14684_1.html. In speeches across US University Campuses, Courtright himself has been making similar allegations and has been trying to portray himself as a victim of Hindu fundamentalism, whereas in reality, according to many Hindus, it is "Hindu society that has suffered from his shoddy and perverted 'scholarship.'"

102. Walters Art Gallery, Baltimore. It is also a legitimate question whether the recent offensive transformation of Lord Ganesha into 'Gaynesh' by Australian gay groups, leading to Hindu protests was inspired, at least in part, by Courtright's book which alleges the deity's penchant for oral sex, and his deep similarities with eunuchs. See, http://gaytoday.badpuppy.com/garchive/events/111799ev.htm, for this representation of Ganesha.

103. For example, a contribution in the following volume edited by Romila Thapar (all contributors are from what some non-Marxist scholars call India's, 'Kremlin on River Yamuna,' The Jawaharlal Nehru University, Delhi) summarizes Courtright's psychoanalytic interpretations as an example of 'modern' way of historiographical study of religion in Romila Thapar, ed., *Recent Perspectives of Early Indian History.*

104. Paul Barber Courtright, "Ganesa and the Ganesa Festival in Maharashtra, A Study in Hindu Religious Celebration" (PhD diss., Princeton University, 1974).

105. Vaidyanathan and Kripal, eds., *Vishnu on Freud's Desk.*

106. Yuvraj Krishnan, "Is the Fight between Siva and Ganesa an Episode of Oedipal Conflict?" (reprinted in this volume) in *Ganesa, Unraveling an Enigma.*

107. Evan J. Elkins, "*More than a Cigar,*" available online at, http://www.cigaraficionado.com/Cigar/CA_Profiles/People_Profile/0,2540,52,00.html.

108. For a brief criticism of the extremely shallow and perverse nature of such 'scholarship,' refer to: Rahul Peter Das, *The Origin of the Life of a Human Being,* 9–12.

109. The Sanskrit word 'linga' has numerous meanings, but in the dictionary of these scholars, it has only one, i.e. 'phallus.' Or if we refer to Wendy Doniger's writings, it should be translated only as '*erect* penis'! See for example the following criticism of such tendentious translations in her works: Stefano Piano, "Urdhvaretas: A few Notes on Chastity and Lust in the Mythology of Siva," in *Hindu Masculinities Across the Ages, Updating the Past,* ed. Alessandro Motti, 11–31.

110. She is credited with overseeing the maximum number of doctorates on Indian religions and wields an unparalleled influence in Hinduism Studies in the United States. Her prolific academic progeny has been christened recently as 'Wendy's Children.' Their family saga is discussed in a very insightful manner by Rajiv Malhotra in his essay "Wendy's Child Syndrome" (2002), available online at http://www.sulekha.com/column.asp?cid=239156.

111. Wendy Doniger, "When a lingam is Just a Good Cigar: Psychoanalysis and Hindu Sexual Fantasies," in *The Psychoanalytic Study of Society, Vol. 18: Essays in Honor of Alan Dundes,* ed. L. Bryce Boyer, Ruth M. Boyer, and Stephen M. Sonnenberg, 81.

112. After separation from her husband, she reverted to her maiden name Wendy Doniger.

113. In some reprints of Courtright's book, the error has been corrected mechanically but this corrected sentence "...in which Vyasa dictates the epic to Ganesa" now seems out of context with what follows in the next few sentences. Therefore it is clear that the Doniger had actually intended to say that it was Ganesha who dictated the epic to Vyasa and not the other way round. This is evident from the remaining portion of the sentence that we have quoted above.

114. Courtright, *Ganesa,* viii.

115. Ibid., ix.

116. Ibid., vii.

117. Wendy Doniger O'Flaherty, *Asceticism and Eroticism in the Mythology of Siva,* 1.

118. See her brief autobiographical account, itself a potentially rich mine of 'data' for psychoanalyzing her—Wendy Doniger, "From Great Neck to Swift Hall: Confessions from a Reluctant Historian of Religions," in *The Craft of Religious Studies,* ed. Jon R. Stone, 36–51.

119. Courtright, *Ganesa,* 9.

120. *Brahmavaivarta Purana* 3.44.83 seems to indicate that Ganesha is known in the Vedas as *ekadanta,* by which name the devatas worship him. This seems to be

a reference to mantras such as the one in Taittiriya Aranyaka cited by Courtright.

121. For *Taittiriya Aranyaka*, Book X (= *Mahanarayana Upanishad*), we have used *Mahanarayana Upanisad* edited by Swami Vimalananda (1957), Ramakrishna Math (Madras). In this edition, the Ganesa or Vighneshvara Gayatri occurs as *Taittiriya Aranyaka* X.1.24. The mantra reads—'*tatpurushaaya vidmahe vakratundaaya dhiimahi tanno dantih pracodayaat* '. In several other editions, the mantra occurs at X.1.5.

122. Courtright also notes that the word *hastimukhaaya* occurs in the Maitrayani Samhita of *Yajurveda*. However, he neither gives the address of the mantra in that samhita, not does he attempt to relate it to the corresponding mantra in *Taittiriya Aranyaka* that he discusses a few sentences later.

123. In his Ph.D. thesis (Courtright 1974: 12) however, Courtright has stated correctly that *Rigveda* 2.23.1 refers to Brihaspati.

124. Courtright, *Ganesa*, 9.

125. Popularly known as *Vaidik Padanukrama Kosha*. The concordance does miss out some occurrence of words in the Vedic texts occasionally and therefore we checked the entire original text of the *Taittiriya Brahmana*, but without success.

126. It appears that Courtright actually had *Taittiriya Aranyaka* X.1.5 in mind.

127. Louis Renou, "Note sur les origines védiques de Ganeœa," *Journal Asiatique* 229 (April-June 1937): 271–274.

128. Courtright, *Ganesa*, 61.

129. We have quoted Griffith's translation only because it is the most popular of all translations in European languages. Otherwise we also consulted the translations of Geldner, Velankar, Satavalekar etc., and they were essentially the same.

130. This is not to say that the Vedic literature does not use euphemisms to refer to the phallus. The use of such euphemisms in fact seems quite prevalent in the texts of all religions. One may refer to some examples from the Bible itself, considering that Courtright had a Protestant Christian upbringing. In the Biblical book of Genesis, Abraham orders his servant Eliezer to swear by putting his hand under his (Abraham's) thigh. Jacob, renamed Israel, asks his son Joseph to swear in the same way. In Genesis and Exodus, Jacob's son are said to be born from his thighs. These are all considered euphemisms for swearing by touching the penis in Biblical times.

131. Although Courtright uses the 'mandala-sukta-mantra' scheme in referencing individual mantras of *Rig Veda*, we also crosschecked RV 8.4.1 according to the ashtaka-sukta-mantra scheme. This mantra again did not have any reference to thighs and penises. We do not deny that some mantras in *Rig Veda* might use the thigh euphemistically for genitalia. This particular mantra, however, has no such connotations, and like many other Vedic references provided by Courtright in his book, this one is also dubious or unclear. The only other possibility is that Courtright means *Rig Veda* ashtaka 8, adhyaya 4, sukta 1, mantras 1-23, which is the Vrshakapi hymn. The use of such different and confusing ways of referencing Rigvedic verses in a single book shows that Courtright lacks even a preliminary first hand understanding of this Hindu text and may have relied instead on secondary works without understanding those either.

132. In any case, the Vedic textual references to Ganesha in Vedic texts are now treated in a much better manner in, John A. Grimes, *Ganapati, Song of the Self*; and in Ludo Rocher's contribution, "Ganesa's Rise to Prominence in Sanskrit Literature," in *Ganesh—Studies of an Asian God*, ed. Robert L. Brown.

133. The suspicion is again reinforced by the manner in which Courtright refers to some other Vedic texts. For instance, he cites specific passages from the *Aitareya Brahmana* using the two-fold numbering scheme sometimes (p.9, 125) while

elsewhere he uses the three-fold numbering scheme (Courtright, *Ganesa*, 98). If he had really used a single edition of this text (as listed on p.255 of his book), then he would have more likely used only one numbering scheme. It is well known that different editions and manuscripts of the same Hindu text can number their sections and subsections in different ways. Secondary works of scholarship relying on different editions of these would therefore reproduce these different ways of number specific sections and sub-sections. If Courtright did not use the printed edition of the original text directly, but relied on references to specific passages in the same in secondary works, he is more likely to reproduce the different numbering schemes followed by his secondary authorities. The most charitable explanation would be that Courtright was careless and inconsistent and he derived two different numbering schemes from the colophons of the printed text.

134. In his Ph.D. thesis, however, Courtright seems to have believed in a Dravidian origin for the Deity. Clearly, he changed his views by the time his book was published 11 years later.

135. Courtright, *Ganesa*, 134.

136. Ibid., 18.

137. Courtright makes much of the Pauranic stories of how Ganesha prevents Parashurama from entering Siva and Parvati's room while they are possibly engrossed in love-making, and uses this incident to embark upon a lengthy psycho-analysis on the nature of the Hindu deity. We wonder if the same analysis could be transferred by Courtright now to Nandi!

138. Maurice Winternitz, *A History of Indian Literature* (1907), Volume 1, Translated by S. Ketkar (1962), Calcutta: University of Calcutta, 542–543.

139. P.S. Subrahmanya Sastri, *A History of Sanskrit Literature* (in Tamil), 299. Sastri points out that there are two recensions of *Padma Purana*, and of them, only the later day recension has this Uttarakhanda. See also Ludo Rocher, 1986, *A History of Indian Literature, The Puranas*, Otto Harrassowitz: Wiesbaden, 207. Rocher offers a different arrangement of the 2 recensions, pointing out that the Bengali recension is yet unpublished, and even in Bengal it is the Western recension that is in use. In Rocher's arrangement, the Uttarakhanda figures in both the recensions, but appears with varying number of adhyayas in each of the 4 manuscripts.

    The differences in these 2 scholarly perspectives can be best explained by Winternitz's observation vide *A History of Indian Literature Volume 1*, page 544, that the *Padma Purana* is a loose compilation, with manuscripts from diverse sources, and a lot of research is still to be completed.

140. Numerous Brahmin communities are staunchly Shaivite, e.g., the Dikshitars of Tamil Nadu, or the Naagara Brahmins of Gujarat.

141. Courtright, *Ganesa*, 21.

142. The text was published as Volume No. 26 in the Anandashrama Sanskrit Series (Poona) in 1894 and has since been reprinted. The treatise, attributed to Sage Palakapya, is an extensive compilation, starting with a legendary introduction according to which it was revealed by the Sage to King Romapada of Champa. The king is mentioned as a contemporary of King Dasharatha in the *Ramayana*. Hindu tradition has several other texts devoted specifically to elephants, such as the *Gajashiksha* attributed to Sage Narada, and the *Gajagrahanaprakaara* of Narayana Dikshita. All these have been published well before Courtright published his book.

143. *Ganesa Purana* is divided into two parts—Upasanakhanda and Kridakhanda. The former is now available in an English translation—Greg Bailey (1995),

Ganesapurana, Part I (Upasanakhand), Harrassowitz Verlag: Wiesbaden. We have used this edition, together with an edition of the entire original text. A portion of the Kridakhanda is the Ganesagita, an English translation of which is also available and has been referenced by Courtright.

144. Except in chapter 5, where its use could not have been avoided. Even here, the references are very few and appear to be derived from secondary sources by and large. In addition, we saw one odd reference in chapter 3. Saying that these are merely sectarian Puranas is not an excuse, because all Puranas are sectarian to some extent. For that matter, Courtright has himself used sectarian texts such as the *Devibhagavata Purana* in his book, and numerous Upapuranas such as the *Brhaddharma Purana* in his book. Therefore the relative omission of the *Ganapatya Puranas* is not justified.

145. Courtright, *Ganesa*, 39–40.

146. The only connection he sees between Ganesha and Gajendra is the fact that in some versions of the story, e.g. *Brahmavaivarta Purana* (Ganapati khanda, Chapter XII, verses 12–24) of implantation of the head of an elephant on child-Ganesha, a king of elephants ('Gajendra') is said to be the donor of the head. In the Gajendramoksa story of *Bhagavata Purana*, Lord Vishnu saves a king of elephants (Gajendra) whose foot is caught by an alligator. Now, the word 'Gajendra' is merely a general term merely meaning 'king of elephants' and therefore Courtright's attempt to link the two stories merely on the occurrence of a 'Gajendra' in both is very far-fetched. The two stories have entirely different contexts.

147. This model is discussed in great detail in various publications of Wendy Doniger etc. While the model itself is not necessarily invalid, Courtright's attempt to interpret the Gajendramoksa story in terms of this model is quite strained.

148. Courtright, *Ganesa*, 28.

149. Courtright, *Ganesa*, 95.

150. Ibid., 30–31.

151. Ibid., 41.

152. Ibid., 252.

153. Phyllis Granoff, "Ganesa as Metaphor," in *Ganesh–Studies of an Asian God*, ed. Robert L. Brown, 85-99 (see 95n.).

154. Courtright, *Ganesa*, 18.

155. The edition used by us bears the title *"atha srimudgalapuranam praarambhyate,"* and is published by A.S. Rajadhyaksha for the Nirnayasagara Press, Mumbai in 1976.

156. The possibility that the Mudgala as well as the *Ganesa Puranas* are composite texts with some portions older than the Upanishad and others later than it must also be considered.

157. Courtright, *Ganesa*, 17–18.

158. For a more careful discussion on the dates of *Ganesa Purana* and *Mudgala Purana*, see Anita Raina Thapat, *Understanding Ganapati*, 30–33.

159. Courtright, *Ganesa*, 25–26.

160. Ibid., 26.

161. Ibid., 22.

162. Courtright, *Ganesa*, 29.

163. It is true that living Hinduism also considers them sometimes as sister-brother, or by virtue of their close association in Hindu worship, as a pair wherein Lakshmi is referred to as Ganesa's 'dharmapatni', especially in northern India. This concept, however, is merely an acceptance of their worship as a pair, and by virtue of joint references to them as in the widely prevalent sign 'subha-laabha' on the walls of Hindu homes. In such characterizations, no sexual connotation

of conjugal relationship is implied, and the relationship is 'dharma-maatra' or 'aupacaarika'. We are aware of only one reference occurring in a minor, late text where Lakshmi is referred to as his wife. From the context again it is clear that the relationship is notional, not real. In some parts of Karnataka and Maharashtra, Ganesha is associated strongly with wisdom and knowledge, and Sarasvati is often designated as His dharmapatni. As an illustrative example, we could denote, without any sexual connotations, Wendy Doniger and Robert Goldman as academic 'consorts', because of their excessive employment of Freudian analyses in their writings.

164. cf. Maitrayani Samhita 3.7.5; Kathaka Samhita 24.5; Taittiriya Samhita 3.8.2.4 etc.

165. Courtright, *Ganesa*, 53.

166. cf. Nirukta 7.11.

167. e.g., Manusmriti 1.32.

168. This word is used to denote humans, whereas the word 'Mitra' stands for a Vedic Deity of the same name.

169. This edition has the famous commentary of Shridhar Swami and is published by Motilal Banarsidass. The editor is Jagdish Lal Shastri.

170. This particular section pertains to passages in Chapter III of Courtright's book, but is being included here for the sake of continuity in our description of how Courtright (and his authority Wendy Doniger) routinely misinterpret Pauranic passages in an over-sexualized manner.

171. Courtright, *Ganesa*, 80.

172. Courtright, *Ganesa*, 92.

173. The reconciliatory attitude of the *Kurma Purana* is also evident from the fact that although it is named after an incarnation of Lord Vishnu, it is predominantly Shaivite in flavor. Embedded in the Purana is the beautiful Ishvaragita, which is largely a Shaivite retelling of the Bhagavadgita.

174. Courtright, *Ganesa*, 32.

175. Anand Swarup Gupta, ed., (Varanasi: All India Kashiraj Trust, 1968).

176. Courtright, *Ganesa*, 44–46.

177. e.g. Sringaarashataka of Bhartrhari.

178. In this context, it is to be noted that though the *Vamana Purana* is named after an incarnation of Lord Vishnu, the text glorifies both Lord Vishnu and Lord Shiva in an impartial manner.

179. In fact, Courtright himself cites other versions of the story in which it is Parvati's body-dirt alone which gives birth to Ganesha. These alternate versions would merely support our interpretation that Courtright uses 'sexual fluids' inappropriately in the context of Vamana Purana 28.64 Courtright himself refers to the various meanings of words 'mala' and 'lepa' etc., in pages 54–55 of his book. It is quite clear that Courtright's use of 'sexual fluid' in this context of *Vamana Purana* is derived from the chapter titled "Sexual Fluids," in Wendy Doniger O'Flaherty, *Women, Androgynes, and Other Mythical Beasts*. As a Hindi proverb goes, the disciple sometimes goes much ahead of his teacher in learning and wisdom. Doniger does not cite this particular passage of *Vamana Purana* under the section 'sweat and tears' (pp.39–40) of the chapter "Sexual Fluids," and so her disciple Courtright has indeed made a new 'discovery.'

180. Madhavi Kolhatkar, review of Courtright's book, *Annals of the Bhandarkar Oriental Research Institute* LXXXV: 186–189.

181. Courtright, *Ganesa*, 53.

182. Ibid., 148–149. Courtright refers, only incidentally, to this legend occurring in *Bhagavata Purana* X.8.21. Instead, he dwells on the fact that in a version of the

story by Sant Namadeva, child Krishna stole sweetmeats made by Yashoda for Ganesha. When Yashoda asks him to open his mouth, she sees infinite Ganeshas made of these sweetmeats. The story again reflects the all-pervading nature of Krishna for Vaishnavas, and Courtright rather chooses to suggest that "Ganesha emerges here as a co-trickster with Krishna," and then adds the correct conclusion that "each plays a role to facilitate the revelation to Yashoda that Ganesha and Krishna are embodiments of the whole universe."

183. The episode is taken as an example of how God's mercy is showered even on his four-legged devotees, and not just on human beings, who should therefore make good use of their human birth and seek refuge in God without delay. The belief that God's mercy is available not only to human beings but also to all other living creatures is reiterated in several Hindu scriptures. The traditional recitation of *Rig Veda* is often closed with the words "May both the bipeds and the quadrupeds attain welfare."

184. Courtright, *Ganesa*, 39–40.

185. Ibid., 40.

186. In fact, the Monier-Williams Sanskrit dictionary apparently uses this very verse to support its translation of *madacyut* into 'elephant in rut.'

187. On page 29, Courtright states correctly that, "ichor, a thick sap like secretion oozing from the elephant's temples during the season of mating, is a pervasive symbol of elixir of erotic desire that intoxicates the bees buzzing around it so that they foolishly cast aside and disregard all risks."

188. David Shulman, "Remaking a Purana," in *Purana Perennis*, ed. Wendy Doniger, 129.

189. Translation David Shulman, "Remaking a Purana," page 130, reproduced here because it conveys the emotion in the verses very nicely. Shulman is another of Wendy Doniger's cohorts, but this should not deter us from accepting what is good in his works.

190. The story of the previous life of alligator comes later in the Purana, not in chapters 2–3 in the 8th 'skandha' of the text, as Courtright seeks to convey.

191. Courtright, *Ganesa*, 40.

192. Ibid., 37–38.

193. The story, found in the *Brahmavaivarta Purana*, is summarized by Courtright, *Ganesa*, 34–35.

194. Courtright, *Ganesa*, 37. This reference given by Courtright is wrong and should read instead *Devibhagavata Purana* 9.40.13–25. The text used by us is edited by Radheyamohan Pandeya in Samvat 2019 (=1962), and is published by Pandit-Pustakalaya (Kasi = Varanasi). The edition used by Courtright (as listed in the bibliography) was printed from Varanasi in 1960. Courtright does not give the name of the editor or the publisher. According to a bibliography (P. Flamm et al, eds., 1992, *Epic and Puranic Bibliography*, Otto Harrassowitz: Wiesbaden, vol. 1, pp. 361–362, item nos. 2003–2005), our edition is identical to Courtright's edition as far as the Sanskrit text is concerned. However, our edition does not have a Hindi commentary whereas Courtright's edition has one. We plan on consulting this in the future for additional verification. In any case, the text is not explicit at all on incest, as Courtright makes it out to be.

195. Note that he puts the words "in the manner of a mere beast" in double quotes, implying that this is a direct quote from the text, or at least a close paraphrase. We will show later that these words are perhaps taken without attribution from an earlier book by Wendy Doniger.

196. A notable exception of course is the version in the *Kurma Purana* that we have discussed earlier in this review.

197. The text in our edition from Varanasi is somewhat corrupt and therefore we have also taken help from an English translation by Swami Vijnanananda, 2nd edition, reprint published by Munshiram Manoharlal: Delhi in 1977.
198. According to *Kaalikaa Upapurana*, her mother was Virani, a wife of Daksha. She is, however, not mentioned in the relevant portion of the *Devibhagavata Purana*. According to the *Mahabhagavata Upapurana*, her mother's name was Prasuuti. The *Vishnu Purana* concurs with *Kaalikaa Purana* in stating that Daksha's wife was Asikni, the daughter of Prajapati Virana (hence her name could also be 'Virani').
199. So we do concede here that the garland played the same role as 'paarijaata' flower in the Indra-Durvasa story. What we are objecting here too is the unnecessary insertion (and the unjustified inclusion of this episode in his narrative as a consequence) of the 'paarijaata' flower by Courtright in this context when the more reasonable choice of Jasmine leads to the same result (although less smoothly).
200. One could also explore another line of thought—the word 'pashu' has a technical meaning in the Pashupata philosophy, and some texts (e.g., Purvabhaaga of the Vaayaviiya Samhita of the *Siva Purana*) related the Pashupatavrata in close proximity to the story of Daksha. In the Pashupata school, Siva is Pashupati. However, we decided not to bring together irrelevant and disjointed facts together by free-association in the manner of Courtright.
201. This interpretation is supported by the slightly different and expanded version of the same story occurring in the *Mahabhagavata Upapurana*, a text that is different from the (Vaishnava) *Bhagavata Purana* and the *Devibhagavata Purana*. In this *Upapurana*, the Devi appears for Daksha's grand sacrifice in the form resembling that of Ma Kali. Daksha is infuriated and embarrassed at his daughter's horrific form, and says that she has also become uncouth in the company of her husband Shiva. The Devi realizes that Daksha, her father, who had worshipped her in the past in the form of Kali, and her begged her to take birth in his own home, is not her devotee any longer and worships her external form more than her internal essence. The Devi then destroys her body, which was born of Daksha, because she will not tolerate insult to Shiva and also in order to crush Daksha's pride based on the outer form of the human body.
202. Vedic texts sometimes hint at androgynous procreation of Daksha Prajapati's children. The dominant theme in the Puranas, however, does not attribute androgyny to Daksha, who is said to marry Brahma's daughters etc., and procreates through them. There is also the recurring tale of Prajapati lusting after his daughter, but this Prajapati is basically different from our Daksha Prajapati and the tale as such has no connection with the one we are discussing in this section. For a good description of Daksha in the Vedic literature, see J. Bruce Long, "Daksa, Divine Embodiment of Creative Skill," *History of Religions* 17, no. 1 (August 1977): 29–60.
203. She is uniformly held as an embodiment of an ideal wife in the Hindu tradition, because she chooses to relinquish her life rather than stand her father's insults directed at her husband.
204. Courtright, *Ganesa*, 37.
205. See the online article "Kali's Child Revisited or didn't anyone check the documentation," by Swami Tyagananda available at http://www.infinityfoundation.com/ECITkalichildframeset.htm. The book has many highly questionable and inane translations, mainly used to imply or allege inappropriate sexual desire and behavior. For instance, 'tribhanga' is translated as 'cocked-hips.'
206. Wendy Doniger, *Hindu Myths*, 250–251.
207. But, Courtright does not mention the book of Doniger as the source of these words. In fact, he inserts the commentary 'to his daughter Sati' in Doniger's

translation, thereby inventing an incestuous rape! If Doniger's translation was not kinky enough, Courtright kinks it even more. Interestingly also, both Doniger and Courtright use the *same* edition of the text, *Devibhagavata Purana* (Varanasi, 1960), according to the bibliography section of their respective books.

208. Courtright, *Ganesa*, 140–141.
209. Courtright also cites the text but interprets such versions as indications of Ganesha's moral ambivalence, 120.
210. John Grimes, trans., *Ganapati*, 49.
211. Courtright, *Ganesa*, 65.
212. Ibid., vii.
213. Ibid., 67, 110.
214. Ibid., 7.
215. Ibid., 113.
216. Ibid., 156.
217. Courtright, *Ganesa*, 120.
218. Even in the *Vamana Purana* 28.72 where Ganesha is described as creating obstacles for gods and others, the description could be seen in the light of the how the gods themselves had just tried to prevent Shiva and Parvati from begetting a child.
219. Refer Thapat (1997), chapter 3, for a more rigorous and balanced treatment of the dual nature of Ganesha. She argues that the original name of Vinayaka was 'one without a superior' (pp.84 sqq.) and cites examples from Puranas wherein a distinction is maintained between malevolent Vinayaks and the benevolent Vinayaka Ganesha.
220. Courtright, *Ganesa*, viii.
221. Ibid., 136.
222. Courtright, *Ganesa*, 134–135.
223. For a historically more sound analysis of the transformation of Ganesha from the *Kalpasutras* to the Puranas, refer A.K. Narain's contribution (pp.19–48), referenced in 115–139 in Robert L. Brown, *Ganesa, Studies of an Asian God.*
224. Courtright, *Ganesa*, 57.
225. Ibid., 49.
226. Unfortunately, psychoanalyst Sudhir Kakar uses this dubious, non-attested tale for constructing his own theories, and attributes it to the *Varaha Purana* as well. He does not give its address in the Purana text, and his version is only slightly different from the one cited by Courtright. See Sudhir Kakar, *The Essential Writings of Sudhir Kakar*, 49. This is a classic example of how a lie when repeated a hundred times comes to be taken as axiomatic truth.
227. Courtright, *Ganesa*, 109.
228. Thapat, *Understanding Ganapti*, 125–126 mentions various conflicting textual traditions regarding the relative seniority of Ganesa and Skanda. Since the issue is not settled, and evidence from tradition is mutually contradictory, Courtright should not have proceeded rashly with his one-sided psycho-analysis that relies only on one of the versions.
229. Kolhatkar, 2004.
230. This section of our review deals primarily with Chapter III of Courtright's book.
231. Courtright, *Ganesa*, 17–18.
232. Yuvraj Krishan, *Ganesa Unraveling*, 205–207.
233. Parashurama's father.
234. Courtright, *Ganesa*, 103.
235. Ibid., 7.
236. Ibid., 4.

237. Ibid., 11.
238. Ibid., 95.
239. Robert Goldman is another academic consort of Wendy Doniger who relies on Freudian analysis of Hindus and their sacred texts.
240. Courtright, *Ganesa*, 116–117.
241. Courtright, *Ganesa*, 159. Even these generalizations are invalid in view of the data available from various Ganapatya minor Upanishads, and the *Mudgala Purana*—texts that are practically ignored by Courtright.
242. For this aspect of the deity see, Saligrama Krishna Ramachandra Rao, *Ganesa-kosha*, 70–131.
243. Ibid., 90–93. In addition, *Vinayakar Akaval*, a Tamil devotional work (before 1400 CE?) sees Ganesha not as an external deity but rather as an internal *devata* in the *muulaadhaara*.
244. Courtright, *Ganesa*, 121.
245. This is an important detail, because Courtright cites numerous passages from the Puranas describing the sexuality of Airavata. If Airavata is intimidated by Ganesha, then the latter's trunk should be considered more potent than Airavata's per Courtright's 'methodology'. Earlier, we had cited other passages from *Ganesa Purana*, which depict Ganesha showering water with his trunk over Brahma's head.
246. Courtright, *Ganesa*, 74–90.
247. *Brahmavaivarta Purana*, Ganapatikhanda, 44.88.
248. Courtright, *Ganesa*, 109.
249. See the online review at http://vishalagarwal.voiceofdharma.org/freud.html.
250. Courtright, *Ganesa*, 110.
251. Ibid.
252. Courtright, *Ganesa*, 49. Ironically, on page 134, Courtright himself says of Dubois, "He was never excessively generous of his appraisal of Hindu religious practices." Anyone who is familiar with the writings of Dubois can easily see his contempt and hatred for anything Hindu.
253. Courtright, *Ganesa*, 124.
254. A 'jati' or community that served in the armed forces for centuries. In the years following the collapse of the Peshwa regime, following the rout and subsequent liquidation of the Marattha forces, the Mahars lost the main source of their livelihood. As has been the case with many an Indian martial jati, this collapse of economic institution led to their loss of prominence in the society, and they soon ended up as untouchables.
255. The tale rather has socio-political implications, as correctly stated by Anita Raina Thapat, *Understanding Ganapati*, 225.
256. Courtright, *Ganesa*, 111.
257. Ibid.
258. The reader may note that the discipline of Anthropology itself has been accused of perpetuating colonial and racist prejudices in a new garb and there does seem to be some merit in this accusation. However, a discussion on this topic is beyond the scope of the present review.
259. Courtright, *Ganesa*, 111–112.
260. Ibid.
261. Contrary to how Courtright sees things, the Hindu tradition regards the *modaka* as a symbol of Mahabuddhi or Supreme Wisdom (Skanda Purana, Avanti Khanda 36.1). This explanation is quite consistent with Ganesha's general association with wisdom and intellect in the Hindu tradition, a detailed description of which is beyond the scope of this review.

262. Courtright, *Ganesa*, 113–114.
263. Ibid., 81.
264. Ibid.
265. Courtright, *Ganesa*, vii.
266. Ibid., 121.
267. Cited by Courtright himself in this context.
268. Courtright, *Ganesa*, 101.
269. Ariel Glucklich, "The Royal Scepter ('Danda') as Legal Punishment and Sacred Symbol," *History of Religions* 28, no. 2 (Nov. 1988): 97–122. See also, M. A. Mehendale, "Nirukta Notes IV: Yaska's Etymology of Danda," *Journal of the American Oriental Society* 80, No. 2 (Apr-Jun 1960): 112–115.
270. As far as the Vedic tradition is concerned, the whole of north India north of Narmada river, is dominated by Brahmins following Shukla *Yajurveda* in its Madhyandina Shakha. Followers of Kanva Shakha of Shukla *Yajurveda* are found in significant numbers in several other parts of India such as Orissa and Maharashtra. Both these Shakhas employ the Paraskara Grihyasutra as their principal ritual text for domestic rites. Amongst the commentaries of this text are: Paraskara Mantrabhashya of Murari Mishra, Bhashya of Halayudha, Bhashya of Harihara, Bhashya of Jayarama, Bhashya of Gadaadhara, Vivarana of Karka, Bhashya of Vishveshara, Prakaashika of Vishvanatha, etc.
271. This is text 2.2.12 in the edition used by us. See the footnote below for details of this edition by Bakre. In fact, Courtright seems to have made another typing error here because Oldenberg's edition that Courtright has used also gives the address of this text as 2.2.12 and not 2.2.14.
272. Hermann Oldenberg, trans., *The Grihya Sutras: Rules of Vedic Domestic Ceremonies Part I* 309.
273. Mahadeva Ganghadhar Bakre, ed., *Grihya-Sutra by Paraskar with Five Commentaries of Karka Upadhyaya, Jayaram, Harihar, Gadadhar and Vishvanath*, 197–206.
274. See for instance Raj Bali Pandey, *Hindu Samskaras, Socio-Religious Study of the Hindu Sacraments*, 134–135.
275. Harihara on Paraskara Grihyasutra 2.2.14 cites *"diirghasatram vaa esha upaiti yo brahmacharyamupaiti."*
276. Jan Gonda, "A note on the Vedic Student's Staff," *Journal of the Oriental Institute* (Baroda) 14, nos. 3–4 (March-June 1965): 262–272.
277. Courtright, Paul Barber, "Ganesa Festival," 26.
278. For a more reasonable account of the wives of Ganesha, see Lawrence Cohen, "The Wives of Ganesa," in *Ganesa, Studies of an Asian God*, ed. Robert L. Brown (Albany: SUNY Press, 1991), 115–139.
279. Courtright, *Ganesa*, 124.
280. Chapter 7.11 of the *Mudgala Purana* is especially relevant in this respect, with Siddhi and Buddhi described as manifestations of Lakshmi. The chapter has numerous verses jointly addressed to Vishnu and Ganesha, and the former is said to be born of the latter. Courtright has perhaps missed a golden opportunity here to discuss potential sexual relationships.
281. Alladi Mahadeva Sastri, ed., *Parasurama Kalpasutra* (Baroda: Gaekwad Oriental Series 23–24, 1923).
282. Courtright, *Ganesa*, 124.
283. The theme of 'ardhanaariisvara' is quite recurring in the Hindu traditions, and occurs in regions far and wide. For example, Silappadikaram, a Tamil epic compiled around 170 CE, speaks of "the dance of the Lord who had Uma as His part" vide verses starting 28:67 and "the One with Uma as His other half" vide

verses starting 28:100 This concept of 'arddhanaarishvara' had metaphysical meaning for the Hindus, and the tradition never read anything sexual perversion into it.

284. Courtright says (pages 219–220) that the Tantric modes of worship of the deity are not followed to any significant extent today. This, however, cannot be a potential excuse for ignoring these texts in the present study. After all, has Courtright not cited all kinds of obscure, non-verifiable regional myths, and has he not used sectarian Puranas that have no considerable following?

285. Ibid., 155.

286. Ibid., 155–156.

287. A few years ago (November 14, 2003), Wendy Doniger flew across the Atlantic and gave a lecture titled "Indian Variants of the Myth of the Woman Who Pretended To Be Herself" at the SOAS in London. We have received two eyewitness accounts in a written manner, and a tape recording of the same. The attendees tell us that the lecture was full of who raped whom, who lusted with whom and so on. Here is an unedited paragraph from a participant—"she referred to the Ramayana as mythology and to Rama as a mythical figure who had no historical basis. She talked about his humiliation of Sita by subjecting her to fire and doubting her a second time. She linked the fire incident to the "terrible" custom of sati inferring that it was Sita who started off this tradition. She talked of the traditional belief in Hindu embryology where the foetus is aware of all its previous births but at the moment of being born in this life, loses all this knowledge. "This is why Indian babies cry," she added. This was accompanied by laughter from the audience and also by wry faces and grimaces made William Dalrymple, the so-called independent moderator. She talked about Sita and Lakshman's supposed lust for each other and Rama's jealousy that Lakshman might take his place beside Sita on the marrige bed. She talked about the innumerable examples of minor gods guarding the entrance to the bedchambers of Hindu gods copulating. She went on to give a long and garbled account about Vishnu raping several females etc . . ."

288. Alice Getty, *Ganesa: A Monograph on the Elephant-faced God*.

289. In any case, the designation of Ganesa as a demon does not hold good for Thailand, Kampuchea and Vietnam although it was true for Indonesia in the past. For this, see Robert L. Brown, "Ganesa in Southeast Asian Art, Indian Connections and Indigenous Developments," in *Ganesh*, ed. Robert Brown, 171–234.

290. Census data consistently indicates that after 1951 (no data for the state as such is available before then) the Muslim component of Maharashtra's population has always been above 7%. In fact, in 1981, a few years before Courtright's book was written, it was 9.25%. See A P Joshi et al., *Religious Demography of India*, 78.

291. Amarendra Gadgil, *Sri Ganesa-kosha* (In Marathi).

292. Courtright, *Ganesa*, 209.

293. Gadgil, *Sri Ganesa-kosha*, 2.43.

294. However, the *Mudgala Purana* version does mention that they emerged from the dirt in Vishnu's ears, as does *Ganesa Purana* (Upasana Khanda, 16.11).

295. Courtright, *Ganesa*, 218.

296. See Thapat, *Understanding Ganapati*, 35–36. The author considers various views and then assigns the text to 10th and 11th century. She rejects the late dates of various scholars on the grounds that this text does not mention Smarta Ganapatyas who became prominent before 15th century. Using this argument of silence, she concludes that at least the portion of the text dealing with the Ganapatyas dates between 10th and 11th century, even though the rest of the text might belong to a different (later) period. The most recent detailed study by Vidyashankar

Sundaresan, "Conflicting Hagiographies and History: The Place of Sankaravijaya texts in Advaita Tradition," *International Journal of Hindu Studies* 4, no.2 (August 2000): 109–184, demonstrates that the text is a very late forgery, and is from the pen of Anantaanandagiri, not Advaita tiikaakaara Anandagiri. Courtright, however, ignores the entire controversy on this matter.

297. Fortunately, the book has an appendix providing a translation of the *Ganapati Atharvasiras Upanishad.*
298. A good contemporary treatment of the major shrines to the deity is by John Grimes, *Ganapati, Song of the Self.*
299. Courtright, *Ganesa*, 246.
300. Courtright, Paul Barber, "Ganesa Festival."
301. Ibid., iii.
302. Ibid., vii.
303. RISA (Religions in South Asia).
304. Paul B. Courtright, http://www.sandiego.edu/theo/risa-l/archive/msg07297.html. The archives of this list have now gone underground, and a copy of the original posting on this list is available with the authors.
305. Doniger, in her Foreword to *Kali's Child* writes ". . . it was full of sex and humor and playful writing, and I found myself smiling often and laughing almost as often as I read it . . . When I took chapters of it to the beach last summer, people offered to trade me their novels . . . for a chance to read it, so evident was my pleasure for it."
306. Works such as Courtright's clearly help fuel anti-Hindu hatred and contempt, especially from Fundamantalist Christians, an important American constituency. For instance, the Hindu American Foundation (HAF) reports that a Christian Website called, www.blessedquietness.com, maintained by Steve Van Nattan, a pastor at the House of Prayer in Roane County, Tennessee has the following things to say about Hinduism: "The website's Hinduism section is called, 'Hinduism: The Pig Pen from the East.' It refers to the religion as, 'one of the world's most dirty and dignity destroying religions' and also speaks of it as being 'filthy' and 'sexually perverted.' It uses sexually explicit imagery to assert false notions, such as when it states, 'The penis, (particularly if flaccid), may be adored as Ganesha's trunk.'" Quoted in "Hyperlink to Hinduphobia: Online Hatred, Extremeism and Bigotry against Hindus," 16, HAF, 2007.

Section 3

1. Richard Slotkin, *Gunfighter Nation*, 10.
2. Numerous historians have written about this topic, staring with Frederick Jackson Turner in 1893, and Henry Nash Smith's groundbreaking work on American studies *The Virgin Land*. Some key historians who have explored this myth in a balanced and unflinching way include Richard Drinnon, *Facing West: the Metaphysics of Indian Hating and Empire Building*; and Reginald Horsman, *Race and Manifest Destiny: The Origins of American Racial Anglo-Saxonism.* Richard Slotkin is the pre-eminent historian of the American myth, with his three volume exposition, which includes *Regeneration through Violence: The Mythology of the American Frontier 1600–1860*; *The Fatal Environment: The Myth of the Frontier in the age of Industrialization 1800–1890*; *Gunfighter Nation: The Myth of the Frontier in 20th Century America.*
3. The wilderness was both a threat and opportunity. Henry Nash Smith's seminal book, titled, *Virgin Land*, is one of the most thoughtful and detailed studies of

America's cultural history. One of the very important ideas of America, he explains, has been the tremendous opportunity offered by a "vacant" continent— an unspoiled Eden for God's chosen people. This sense of righteous authority over lands whose inhabitants were deemed to not have any rights became a core ingredient in shaping the American Myth.

4. Reginald Horsman, *Race and Manifest Destiny*, 210.
5. Brands, H.W. *Andrew Jackson: His Life and Times*, 170; and Richard Slotkin, *Regeneration through Violence*, 97.
6. Reginald Horsman, *Race and Manifest Destiny*, 191.
7. Edwin Fussel, *Frontier: American Literature and the American West*.
8. Based on the stories found in works of famous American writers like James Paulding, author of *Westward Ho*, they became a rallying cry for frontier America in the 1800s. Other writers using this device include Timothy Flint.
9. See Drinnon, *Facing West*, 126–127 and 156–157 for examples of such changes of heart in genteel White conscience keepers confronted with atrocity data.
10. Brands, H.W. *Andrew Jackson: His Life and Times*. Westminster, MD, USA: Doubleday Publishing, 2005, 107.
11. Slotkin, *Regeneration Through Violence*, 97.
12. Drinnon, *Facing West*, 483n.
13. John Quincy Adams, quoted in Drinnon, *Facing West*, 111.
14. Ibid., 111.
15. Incidentally, this imbalance of documenting and portraying victims on the Native American side remains unchanged, despite the continuing efforts of many scholars. Indeed to this day all over America there are many memorials and annual commemorations for whites killed in "battle" with the Indians, but few indeed for countless the Native American patriots who were killed fighting for their lands and way of life.
16. Ibid., 127.
17. Arvind Sharma, "Hindus and Scholars," *Religion in the News* 7, no.1 (Spring 2004).
18. The ADL or Anti-defamation League has been "Fighting Anti-Semitism, Bigotry and Extremism" in the USA for over 90 years. See these web sites: http://www.adl.org/ and http://antidefamationleague.us/.
19. For example, see: The Council on Islamic Education (CIE), founded in 1990 http://www.cie.org/.
20. A "seat" represents a cultural presence, embracing the idea that there is a reserved space where the particular culture is given consideration. Awareness of the existence of the newly integrated ethnic entity lends a presence that requires respect. Though there may be biased individuals, who hold on to stereotypes, such attitudes must not be allowed in government or education.
21. Rajiv Malhotra, "RISA Lila-2: Limp Scholarship and Demonology," November 17, 2003, http://rajivmalhotra.sulekha.com/blog/post/2003/11/risa-lila-2-limp-scholarship-and-demonology.htm (often abbreviated RL-2).
22. Malhotra, "RISA Lila-2."
23. Yvette Rosser, "Stereotypes in Schooling: Negative Pressures in the American Educational System on Hindu Identity Formation," http://www.mssu.edu/projectsouthasia/tsa/VIN1/Rosser.htm.
24. The HSC (Hindu Students Council) includes both first and second generation Hindu-American students.
25. See Chapter 17 in this book for a detailed review of Courtright's work and the numerous problems with it.

26. On October 28, 2003, three weeks after the petition was brought to his attention, Malhotra received a one-line email from Paul Courtright accusing him of generating the petition. Courtright asked him what he intended to do, given that his efforts had 'lead' to the petition. But in fact, Malhotra had learned about the petition only after it had appeared and had refused to sign it because he had strong reservations about its emotional focus. So Malhotra immediately sent Courtright a reply hoping to re-focus attention on the academic issues: "Dear Paul, First of all, YOU started this—when you wrote [the book] you started a dialog with the Hindus, even though at that time it might have seemed liked a monolog. Please note that freedom of speech works both ways nowadays. Sustaining an asymmetry of power/privilege is no longer as easy as it once was. [...] First you must stop the 'blame' habit. [...] Think of this as the native informants talking back, using the age of interactivity as in so many other fields. You could also consider ENGAGING your opponents and taking your chances. I am no expert or public relations advisor and you know best what to do. Personally, I don't support banning books in print, but I do feel that controversial issues must be debated in a balanced way in the open." Malhotra compared Courtright's situation to Kripal's and explained that he had urged Kripal to include an unedited rejoinder by Swami Tyagananda as a final chapter of the book, so as to balance out the perspectives. Though Kripal had decided against it, Courtright was urged to select a Ganesha scholar-practitioner to write a rejoinder and thereby "start a new era in 'interactive' scholarship." Malhotra offered the example of Francis Clooney, whose book *Hindu God, Christian God*, included a final discussant chapter by Parimal Patil.

27. "I disagree with the petitioners' stance that the issue is about 'feelings' being hurt —such a petition can and is dismissed easily as being irrelevant to objective scholarship. The petition is facile in its lack of critical analysis. However, my problem with many scholars is entirely different. It is about their works' lack of authenticity and objectivity—a charge that they are not responding to, because they prefer to construct a false *purva-paksha27* that is easier for them to deal with. The issue of non-authenticity takes us deep into questioning the 'critical theories' that are the very foundation of liberal arts. I want PROOF that these 'theories' are valid and especially in the Indian context. Just because they are widely quoted does not make them valid scientifically, as popularity simply means that they have the power of distribution channels on their side—which comes with money and institutional control. So the burden of proof of the validity of the 'theories' should be on the shoulders of those who wish to use them. Nobody in Religious Studies to the best of my knowledge has proven these 'theories', and, instead, they merely quote others who quote others. It's all about having established a brand name for oneself, or learning to use someone else's . . . It is this shallowness and lack of scientific objectivity that is the crux of my criticism and not 'feelings' —but these scholars have not even acknowledged the true nature of the complaint, which is disingenuous on their part. Freudianism, as a theory for such purposes, has been rejected by psychology departments in the West, but it has become the 'export' product to mis-educate those third worlders who are in awe of the West. [Alan] Roland27 and others have gone far to explain, based on their empirical data, that such 'theories' do not work in explaining Indian culture. In the same manner, I wish to openly challenge much of postmodernism, western feminism, and many other sociological and anthropological constructs—in fact, Wendy's entire 'tool-box'" [Emphases added]. Malhotra's email dated October 31, 2003. *Purva paksha* is a technique of correctly understanding the opponent's position in order to respond.

28. For an example of an earlier criticism of Courtright's book, see: Yuvraj Krishan, "Is the Fight Between Siva and Ganesa and Episode of Oedipal Conflict?" in *Spectrum of Indian Culture*. Reprinted in Section II of this book.

29. Malhotra repeatedly challenged Courtright to restore the debate to the ideas and evidence rather than about 'hurt feelings': "If you feel [that your theoretical approach is on] a solid scholarly basis, then why be afraid of criticism? Why not give *your* theory as a rejoinder—write an article on Sulekha—and let the chips fall where they may." (RL-2)

30. In a private email to a selection of Western scholars who he hoped would be interested in dialogue, Malhotra wrote, "The diaspora is now highly aware of AAR/RISA—suspicious, and getting mobilized rapidly. Their kids are getting bolder about raising their hands [in class] to question the items selected for depiction in a one-sided manner...If left to itself things will deteriorate, and there may well be someone who will file a lawsuit on hate speech or something similar. This must be avoided by proactive positive thinking. It would take leadership skills replacing career politics as the driver...The diaspora activists are not one or even a small number of groups. In classical Indian fashion, it is highly decentralized and there are more such self-styled activists popping up all the time...I have made the same offer many times before to the academy: I am available to participate in win-win deals that consider the views of all sides. I have repeatedly clarified that the intellectual debates I seek would expand the discourse rather than collapse it—i.e., my position would have exactly the opposite effect than censorship."

31. She wrote, "I urge you to contact the petitioners and offer your opinion that their behavior is unwarranted, and that their petition lacks credibility. It would also be helpful to remind them that it is 'never' acceptable to threaten someone physical harm for what they have expressed 'or' to continue to circulate a petition containing such threats. Never." After emailing her back the same day with an offer to facilitate a dialogue, she responded, "Thanks. The generators of the petition should also consider the legality of what they are doing when they circulate documents that contain direct threats against an individual. I could be wrong, but I think it is illegal to directly threaten someone's life, as some of the signatories have done—? Someone circulating those threats might be opening themselves up to prosecution under the law." In an email response to a second scholar requesting his intervention, Malhotra wrote, "Please note that I have tried many times to set up AAR-Diaspora dialog mechanisms but there has been no reciprocity. All I get back are more insults . . . My own interests are in theories and methods as they get applied to Indic traditions. Regarding death threats, you must find out who made these and get them to stop. But at the same time, I would advise against blowing things out of proportion, as 'victimhood' has been tried many times before but does not deal with issues. It's best to be balanced and not lose perspective." The scholar replied, backing down somewhat from the blame game, but remaining focused on the threats as the *only* issue. She wrote, "Re: victims: I hate victim stuff. I am not playing victim re: the death threats. I am simply saying that 20+ statements about Paul's being hanged, burned, and shot with his address publicized on the same petition is a serious issue, and it undermines the credibility of ALL the signers." Another Western scholar of Hinduism Studies commented to Malhotra off-line: "I think it's great you are making the effort to elevate the discourse." In another email, she wrote that the petition was in her opinion, "appropriately interpreted as a cyber attack." But later she also accepted that scholars must not remain so aloof from the diaspora, concurring "that better means of communication need to be put in place."

32. On October 31, 2003.
33. A diaspora leader bluntly conveyed to him the petitioners' anger and resentment.
34. Dr. Alex Alexander is a retired physician who came from India to the US in the early sixties and served in the US federal government. He often posts comments and essays on the Sulekha website.
35. Posted on the Abhinavagupta Yahoo e-group, on October 30, 2003. Dr Sunthar Vishvalingam is a scholar of Abhinavagupta and also runs a popular scholarly web site that brings together both academic and non-academic voices. See: http://www.svabhinava.org/index.php. Malhotra summed up his role in an email to Dr Sunthar Vishvalingam: "I was unhappy about the petition's sole emphasis on 'feelings' and also about the abusive comments added later. At the request of several scholars, I engaged in private efforts to try to diffuse the 'threatening' situation, working simultaneously with both sides. While working with the Hindu students' group to pull back the petition, I was forthright about criticizing the methodologies of RISA scholarship. Through the years, I had made numerous but unsuccessful attempts to get the academy to engage in serious dialogue on these important issues."
36. Hindu American Foundation, "Much Ado About Lord Ganesha: The Fraud and Why it Happened," Available on the Foundation's website at http://www.hinduamericanfoundation.org/campaigns_emory_full.htm.
37. Hindu American Foundation, "Hyperlink to Hinduphobia: Online Hatred, Extremism and Bigotry against Hindus," 16 (2007), available at, www.hafsite.org/hatereport/.
38. It is noteworthy that the academics and Emory University in particular did not take the initiative on this issue.
39. At the meeting between the Concerned Community and Emory's Dean on February 18, 2004, a copy of the Briefing Book was distributed to the attendees. The Briefing Book included "a collection of the community's presentations at the meeting and allied supporting references. This material was submitted "to help enhance and clarify the understanding of concerns of the citizens and help pave the way to better relations between Emory University and the constituencies it serves."
40. For more examples of the "Negative Pressures in the American Educational System on Hindu Identity Formation," see: http://www.mssu.edu/projectsouthasia/tsa/VIN1/Rosser.htm.
41. From the Concerned Community's Briefing Book.
42. Ramesh Rao, "Hindu God must Indeed be Heathen," *India Abroad*, November 28, 2003, http://www.rameshnrao.com/religion-philosophy-hindu-god-must-indeed-be-heathen.html.
43. Reprinted in Section II of this volume.
44. On February 18, 2004 by members of the concerned community who met with him.
45. The Concerned Community team included Subash Razdan, Narayanan Komerath, Ramesh Rao, Shree Vinekar, Kamala Kant Vijai, Ram Sidhaye, Dhiru Shah, and M.P. Rama. The Emory panel included Peter Wakefield, Robert Paul, Marion Creekmore, Joyce Burkhalter Flueckiger, Deepika Petraglia-Bahri, Rakesh Ranjan, and P.V.N. Rao (from the minutes of the meeting).
46. As per the minutes of the February 18, 2004 meeting.
47. These included essays by Sanu, Malhotra, Bansi Pandit, Venkat and Agarwal questioning Courtright's scholarship; also essays by noted psychologists such as John F. Kihlstrom, "Is Freud Still Alive? No. Not Really," in *Hilgard's Introduction to Psychology*, 13th Ed.

48. John F. Kihlstrom, "Is Freud Still Alive? No. Not Really." An updated version of the essay is available at http://socrates.berkeley.edu/~kihlstrm/freuddead.htm.

49. Kihlstrom, "Is Freud Still Alive?"

50. From the Concerned Community's Briefing Book.

51. Professor and Chair of the Department of Communication Studies and Theatre at Longwood University in Farmville Virginia.

52. From the Minutes of the February 18, 2004 meeting compiled by the Concerned Community.

53. Incidentally, after the meeting, the young Dr. Bahri was promoted to Director of Emory's South Asia Program, thereby serving as an Indian face to deal with the diaspora and its potential donors.

54. This is a significant problem. While Indian Universities do offer degrees in Indian Philosophy, they do not teach Religion as an academic discipline, so unlike say, China, which has many institutes studying Confucian thought, India has no "home team" specializing in its many religions.

55. From a discussion with members of the Concerned Community.

56. Ramesh Rao, "Hindu God must Indeed be Heathen." See: http://www.rameshnrao.com/religion-philosophy-hindu-god-must-indeed-be-heathen.html.

57. Minutes of the February 18, 2004 meeting.

58. "RISA Lila-2" explained it thus: "Many RISA scholars have defended this state of scholarship by [saying] 'of course, all theories are relative and not scientific', as if that solves the problem. Subjectivity and relativism merely compel us to take the inquiry further: this is where 'the role of power in distribution channels and controls' and hence the adoption of standardized theories or lenses, become important. The asymmetry of power is a relevant topic for discussion—but Religious Studies avoids it, particularly in the context of modern Westernized Hindus. No longer can one claim the irrelevance of emic and etic, because the power asymmetry in the case of (neo) colonized religions determines who is licensed to say whatever is said using whichever lens—and reproduce more of their own kind as graduate students dependant on them" (RL-2).

59. The academy plays a role in legitimizing and channeling knowledge about India to the media and educational system as a form of what Malhotra calls "gate-keeping." It must be noted, in spite of all of their claims of sensitivity and being tuned in to the discourse on India, American academicians in Hinduism Studies have never lobbied to end the denigration of Hinduism in the media, in school classrooms, and in mainstream and Evangelical churches. It has been seen, at times, that some scholars have embraced the critics of Hinduism as activists in Hinduphobic causes. Malhotra issued an appeal to the scholars, pointing out that the "Hinduism Unit of AAR has a unique opportunity to be open about allowing participation—which means not using asymmetric power to block off dissent as 'unqualified.'"

60. Author and therapist, http://home.jps.net/~stuartcs/.

61. Father Clooney is a Jesuit priest presently on the faculty of Harvard Divinity School.

62. Malhotra is troubled by the implications of Clooney's comment that scholars in the field prefer to "stay out of each other's way." Malhotra summarized, "If we understand this remark correctly, the attitude seems to be: You have your opinion and I have mine, so let us 'ignore' each other and keep publishing and building our resumes without any rigorous attempts to separate opinion and fantasy from fact."

63. Dr. Goonátilake is a noted Sri Lankan Buddhist scholar. His books include *Anthropologizing Sri Lanka*, University of Indiana Press, Bloomington.

64. Dr. Cleo Kearns got her PhD from Cambridge University and is author of the book, *T.S. Eliot and Indic Traditions,* Cambridge University Press.
65. David Freedholm, email November 18, 2003.
66. AAR scholars' website on Islam: http://groups.colgate.edu/aarislam/response.htm.
67. http://www.arches.uga.edu/~godlas/#islam.
68. A violent and hard-line Marxist movement in India.
69. RISA-list (or RISA-l) is an online discussion list meant for RISA members. Only those deemed to be 'proper scholars' as certified by the RISA establishment are allowed to post on it. However, the posts were available for the public to read, *until* these embarrassing events caused the RISA management to close the list to the public, and take it underground.
70. November 1, 2003.
71. Narasingha P. Sil attended the Presidency College and Calcutta University. He obtained his doctoral degree in English history from University of Oregon. He is presently Professor of History at Western Oregon University, http://www.parabaas.com/rabindranath/articles/RT_authors.html. Posted on November 1, 2003.
72. William Harman is Head of Philosophy & Religion Department at the University of Tennessee. He teaches "Indian religions, Goddess Traditions, and Introduction to Religions." He has a Ph.D. from the University of Chicago, http://www.utc.edu/Departments/phildept/staff/william_harman.php.
73. November 2, 2003.
74. Retired English Professor Emeritus, Tufts University, M.A. the University of Florida, Ph.D. University of California, Berkeley. In 1971–72, he was a Fulbright lecturer at New Delhi University. He returned to India in 1978–79 (as a Whiting Fellow); in 1981 on a Ford Foundation Grant, and in 1986–87 as a Fulbright Research Fellow. His primary focus is modern Indian literature.
75. An ironic aspect of Perry's posts on RISA are his almost incoherent grammatical structures, especially considering that his area of expertise is literature.
76. On RISA list, November 2, 2003.
77. Ramdas Lamb, Department of Religion, University of Hawaii (Ph.D. 1991, University of California at Santa Barbara). Methodology in religious studies, Mysticism, Indian Religions (especially Ram Bhakti, Untouchable, and monastic traditions), interface of religion and contemporary society, and fieldwork studies. He is currently working on a documentary film on the Ramnamis, their practices, and their social programs (see www.ramnam.net). From http://www.hawaii.edu/religion/FAC-DOC.HTM.
78. November 2, 2003.
79. Lance E. Nelson, Department of Theology and Religious Studies, University of San Diego: Fields: Indian Philosophy, Hindu Religious History, Western Religious Thought.
80. Narasingha P. Sil wrote in an email on November 12, 2003: "Depicting Ganesha as a naked toddler in the fashion of Gopala is neither popular nor meaningful . . . Similarly, the picture of an angry Ganesha is not culturally popular . . . Ganesha is an adorable deity who is a harbinger of success (Sidhdhidata) and he is a happy god, much like the Maitreya (Laughing Buddha) of China. Advancing or hazarding erotic guesses for a naked Ganesha makes a mockery of one of the most popular folk gods of India."
81. Joanna Kirkpatrick is a social and cultural anthropologist. Now retired from Bennington College, where she taught for almost thirty years, she continues research and writing on popular arts and conveyance arts worldwide, with special focus on South Asia.

82. Deepak Sarma, Assistant Professor of Hinduism, Case Western Reserve University, Cleveland, Ohio (Ph.D. Philosophy of Religions, University of Chicago). Fields: South Asian religious and philosophical traditions, especially Hinduism. Vedanta and Indian Philosophy, Madhva School of Vedanta, Method and theory in the study of religion, Comparative philosophy of religion.

83. On RISA-list on November 3, 2003.

84. Gene R. Thursby, Associate Professor, Department of Religion, University of Florida at Gainesville. (Ph.D. Duke University) Fields: Religions of India, New Religious Movements, Spirituality and Health.

85. November 3, 2003.

86. Kathleen M. Erndl is an associate professor at Florida State University and teaches in the field of South Asian religions, especially Hinduism, as well as gender and religion, comparative studies, and Sanskrit (Ph.D. '87, University of Wisconsin, South Asian Language and Literature: Religions of South Asia).

87. November 3, 2003.

88. Patrick Olivelle has been the Chair of the Department of Asian Studies at the University of Texas at Austin since 1994, where he is the Professor of Sanskrit and Indian Religions. Prior to coming to Texas, Olivelle taught in the Department of Religious Studies at Indiana University, Bloomington, from 1974 to 1991, where he was the Department Chair 1984–90, http://asnic.utexas.edu/asnic/olivelle/index.htm.

89. November 3, 2003–RISA-l.

90. *Shabash* is Hindi for "bravo."

91. November 3, 2003.

92. Olivelle and Humes seem to blindly maintain that the peer-review process is itself above review—even when serious problems are subsequently pointed out. Indeed this should bring attention to the lopsided nature of the much lauded, peer-to-peer exercise, and its robustness and rigor should be periodically assessed to ensure that it does not deteriorate into a mutual admiration society.

93. November 4, 2003.

94. RISA-list, November 4, 2003.

95. Email to Malhotra, November 5, 2003.

96. John Grimes, who at the time of the Courtright controversy was teaching Religious Studies at Michigan State University, is an authority on Ganesha, *Ganapati: Song of the Self.* Grimes' work on Ganesha, elicited the opposite types of responses than did Courtright's. (Excerpt of review on Amazon.com: I have never yet read a book on a Hindu deity written by a westerner that so captures the simple faith of the average Hindu while simultaneously providing such a wealth of information to the reader.) Grimes has an M.A. & Ph.D. in Indian Religion and Philosophy, with a specialty in Advaita Vedanta from the University of Madras and a B.A. in Religious Studies from the University of California at Santa Barbara.

97. He compared Ray Bradbury's bleak future to the *Kali Yuga*, evoking a similarity in attitude, "The yuga known as Kali has just become blacker! By the by, I am curious if those who are considering boycotting Motilal are going to dispose of all their personal copies of Motilal's books??? Fahrenheit 451 anyone?" (Posting on RISA-l, November 5, 2003)

98. Arun Gupta, November 17, 2003, on Sulekha.com.

99. "RISA Lila-2."

100. See: "Secularism, Colonialism, and the Indian Intellectuals," http://www.india-forum.com/forums/index.php?showtopic=556,Secularism. De Roover wrote that "Nehruvian secularism" is adhered to by India's intellectuals and despite the

"upsurge . . . of intercommunity conflict" they stubbornly adhere "to the value of secularism . . . in spite of [its] spectacular failure. This adherence seems based in dogmatism, rather than in rational, critical or scientific argument."

101. See also: "The Vacuity of Secularism, On the Indian Debate and Its Western Origins," http://colonial.consciousness.googlepages.com/vaucityofsecularism.

102. On RISA-l, November 5.

103. "RISA Lila-2" notes that Zydenbos's witch-hunting case against De Roover relied on the charge that De Roover had posted a message on the Indian Civilization yahoo e-group – yet another demonized Diaspora e-group. However, De Roover responded that he was "not even been a member of that yahoo e-group."

104. See this article about academic labels, written in 2000, "Puzzling Dimensions and Theoretical Knots in my Graduate School Research," by Yvette Rosser: http://www.infinityfoundation.com/mandala/s_es/s_es_rosse_puzzle.htm.

105. November 5, 2003.

106. All too familiar words during the 'Red Scare'; now fully operative during the 'Saffron Scare.'

107. "RISA Lila-2."

108. Sankrant Sanu, Comment posted on Sulekha.com, November 23, 2003.

109. "RISA Lila-2."

110. Madhu Kishwar, "When Religions claim Superiority," April 18, 2004, http://madhu-kishwar.sulekha.com/blog/post/2005/04/when-religions-claim-superiority.htm.

111. See for instance, Amy Braverman, "The Interpretation of Gods," *The University of Chicago Magazine*, December 2004. A discussion of this article appears in section IV.

112. These included numerous scholars such as V.V. Raman, T.S. Rukmani, Purushottama Bilimoria, Chakravarthi Ram-Prasad, Vasudha Narayanan, Antonio de Nicolas, Jack Hawley, Mary McGee, Edwin Bryant, Cynthia Humes, Laurie Patton, Lance Nelson, Mary Hicks, and Robert Thurman.

113. In this segment, all quotes are taken from email correspondence between Rajiv Malhotra and Wendy Doniger, and others such as Satya Prabhakar.

114. Jeffrey Kripal, "The Tantric Truth of the Matter," http://jeffrey-kripal.sulekha.com/blog/post/2002/09/the-tantric-truth-of-the-matter.htm (September 20, 2002).

115. "The Insider/Outsider Academic Game," http://rajivmalhotra.sulekha.com/blog/post/2002/10/the-insider-outsider-academic-game.htm (October 25, 2002).

116. Malhotra wrote, "Dear Wendy and Jeffrey, I know we have differences on many issues, on how best to interpret Indic traditions. But Satya's invitation is an important one, and I hope that both of you, or at least one of you, will accept it. What matters is having a dialogue in which the community being studied gets to participate directly. Otherwise, we feel treated like subalterns with no voice. I have put my positions on the table very openly. As a retired businessman, I know that everything is negotiable and I am open to modifying my views based on your arguments. At least we must start the process, even though we will probably never agree on everything. Let's keep this professional, and stick to the issues. I await your response." He continued, "Therefore, I make this sincere offer to include your perspective. It means we each can have perspectives that the other disagrees with strongly, but that we must interact across the boundary. A dialog is better than two monologs. [...] In the long run, we could be breaking new ground for this discipline. It might be an important contribution towards the secure and respectful integration of Hindus into American culture without losing their distinctiveness or self-esteem."

117. Wendy Doniger, "A Fire in the Mind," Book Review in the *New York Times*, March 2, 1992.

118. Stephen and Robin Larsen, letter to the editor, *New York Times*, March 22, 1992.
119. Stephen and Robin Larsen, letter to the editor, *New York Times*, March 22, 1992.
120. See for instance, observations by Sam Keen, Janelle Balnicke, the Larsens, in the *New York Times*, March 22, 1992.
121. Janelle Balnicke, Letter to the Editor, *New York Times*, March 22, 1992.
122. Doniger claimed, "I have learned most of what I know about Hinduism from Hindus, beginning with Rajendra Hazra in Calcutta back in 1963, when I was working on Puranas, and continuing with conversations with A.K. Ramanujan for precious decades in Chicago, conversations deeply reflected in every one of my books during that period, and culminating with the co-authorship of my most recent book with Sudhir Kakar, JUST THIS YEAR, another Hindu who has had a profound influence on me."
123. The following passages are excerpted from Malhotra's forthcoming book on the American Frontier mindset and how that mindset influences contemporary attitudes towards Indian culture. It is based on discussions with him. See also chapter 18 of this book.
124. Brands, H.W, *Andrew Jackson: His Life and Times*, 309–310.
125. Ibid., 490.
126. Doniger claims that she does not recognize her own work when seen through Malhotra's critical lens. This is ironic phrasing since Hindus often complain that they cannot recognize their own religion in some of the narratives about Hinduism written by Doniger and other Eurocentric scholars.
127. In answer to that question, please see the essay by Sankrant Sanu in this volume to highlight the sensationalism with which Doniger often portrays Hinduism.
128. Malhotra told Doniger, "You are entitled to your crude and rude remarks because that is in line with your reputation." After she accused him of being an ignorant, mean-spirited racist, he replied, "I still wish you well, because probably you are a decent human being, just too full of yourself and ignorant without knowing it." He concluded sarcastically, telling Doniger that she was said to be "the kind of person who would joke about all this fun being poked at you," and that "this would start a meaningful dialogue and also some fun in the process." Ever persistent, he closed asking Doniger what she thought of the "idea of chakras as epistemological levels and as hermeneutics . . ." and again expressed disappointment that his "proposed *samvad* was aborted." And in case she changed her mind, he would "be glad to argue each point, one by one –let arguments speak and not pedigrees or degrees." That same evening, Wendy Doniger sent her last reply to Malhotra's "Request for *samvad*." Perhaps realizing that her attack on Malhotra was both impolitic and crude (even for someone with her inclination for *ad hominem* attacks), she wrote, backpedaling from her egregious and insulting tone, "I do take it as a joke, as you know from my response to you at the AAR and the tone of my note to you now, with all the jackals and mouse-turds." She concluded defiantly, like a mother protecting her young, "Jeff Kripal has been tormented by your attacks, and I don't think that that is fun at all." Actually, Kripal's trouble began four years earlier, when Professor N. Sil wrote several articles critical of *Kali's Child* in the *Calcutta Statesman*.
129. Brown wrote, "Rajiv Malhotra, who seems to be behind this attack, has been behind the open attack of several scholars in the past several years. I have personally been witness to the verbally violent interrogation and **attack of scholars by individuals acting 'on his request'** at the past two AAR annual meetings, and have heard by word of mouth of other incidents at other major academic conferences (such as the Tantra conference in Flagstaff, AZ)" [Emphasis added] (November 4, 2003).

This *ad hominem* attack was particularly egregious, as Malhotra was prevented from posting on the RISA online list and was therefore unable to defend himself against such unsubstantiated attacks. In a note to Deepak Sarma, the moderator of the RISA list, Malhotra cited Brown for violating RISA's official rule that "no personal attacks or flaming will be tolerated." Sarma had recently received his Ph.D. from Wendy Doniger at U Chicago and was dependent on her political support to get a job and eventually tenure. He should have excused himself from moderating a discussion criticizing her work, in order to avoid a conflict-of-interest. Instead, Sarma allowed all sorts of biased personality assassination messages to pass, and seemed only to interrupt the flow of messages when they dealt with the content/context of academic research.

Malhotra raised an important point: "I request you to please let me know in particular what rights individuals have, who are not allowed to become members of your list, to be able to respond when they are attacked on the list. This is a serious matter of fair due process that cannot wait, as the list management's complicity makes it a party to slander and libel by allowing such items to get posted with impunity." Malhotra contrasted the current character assassination on RISA to the more cautious, interactive approach he took when writing his critiques of the works of RISA related scholars: "Please note that when I criticized Doniger, Kripal, Caldwell and Courtright, EACH OF THEM RECEIVED AN ADVANCE DRAFT WITH A REQUEST TO COMMENT. Courtright did comment and pointed out errors, which I corrected via private email exchanges. **Doniger refused to engage with me other than if I became the native informant and she the scholar (very explicitly using those words in an email I have saved).** Kripal stated that he would write a separate response, which he did, and Sulekha was very open about posting everything anyone had to say. Caldwell wanted to have an email exchange that could be published; this went through several dozen iterations of private email and was posted ONLY AFTER BOTH SIDES AGREED THAT THE DRAFT ACCURATELY REPRESENTED THE SITUATION. I have saved all the emails from the above set of private interactions. The point is that I have acted with reciprocity in my criticisms and now it is the turn of the scholars to give me a fair chance to speak my side on these matters on their forums [Original emphasis in CAPS.]

It turned out that neither Malhotra nor any representatives from his organization had attended the Flagstaff conference in question. Some RISA members were disturbed by these baseless attacks. Balagangadhara condemned Brown's attack because it offered "No proof, no evidence, but a free-for-all accusation directed against an individual, who is in no position to defend himself." Brown's key point was that he had seen individuals at conferences wearing the Infinity Foundation badge. This proved, to him: (i) that whatever these individuals did or said in any capacity, anywhere, had to be requested by Malhotra; and (ii) whatever any other individuals did or said (such as the petitioners) which was critical of scholars must also be caused by Malhotra. He called this Mr. Malhotra's 'authority.' Brown lacked a basic understanding of institutions, as Malhotra pointed out, "Infinity Foundation is an institution just like College X. Just as a conference attendee with a badge saying "College X" may not be deemed to be acting on behalf of another colleague from College X, so also the advisors and scholars who work with any foundation are diverse, autonomous and independent and speak for themselves. Anyone who has attended our foundation's events or worked on its projects would attest to this autonomy. In fact, our foundation lacks full-time in-house scholars. It is classified as a "non-operating foundation," meaning one that gives grants to third parties but does not perform much work in-house. (This is the same classification as Ford, Fulbright and most other foundations, except that ours is tiny by comparison)." Malhotra categorically stated, "Infinity Foundation has not had any affiliation with the students involved in the petition or the HSC (the organization that put up the petition)." Referring to Western civilization's medieval judicial system's guilt-by-association approach to witches, he noted, "To prove our innocence, the Inquisitors demand that we show that we have no relationship with the Devil." This episode was an example of how RISA's mainstream scholars often rely upon flimsy or manufactured 'evidence'. That this remained unopposed by those in authority casts reasonable doubt on the peer-review process.

Prof. Balagangadhara sent the following message to Sarma (November 5, 2003): "If he [Stephen Brown] has [proof], he should 'name' the individuals, who have acted thus in 'the past two AAR meetings,' and specify the 'times' (it must have happened at least twice), where and when Rajiv Malhotra made this request. If he cannot, he is indulging in libel. He claims to have 'heard by word of mouth of other incidents.' This is plain defamation of character.' Balu also wrote privately to Stephen Brown and received illogical responses.

The behavior of RISA justifies the use of the witch hunt analogy. Given the diversity of independent Hindu voices involved in this controversy, Brown's charge that "all these authors and many dozen others over the past two years are working *solely* at Malhotra's request" was a crude reductionist attempt to lump all Hindu voices together. Brown's failure to recognize the depth and breadth of diversity within the growing Hindu-American community typifies the overall RISA reaction to Hindu-Americans' engagement with academia.

130. On the RISA listserv, Pincince announced, "Activities and pursuits of the 'Infinity Foundation . . . [consist of] numerous exciting essays, such as those by Prof./Dr. de Nicolas, Director of the 'Biocultural Research Institute' in Florida, David Frawley, Subhash Kak, Koenraad Elst . . ." The last few names are a 'code' that RISA scholars well understand. Frawley is a white American Hindu—i.e. a white apostate who has crossed over to the savages—and whose appreciative writings on Hinduism are mocked by academic scholars; Kak is a pro-Hindu academic; and Elst is an alleged Hindutva, i.e. 'fascist,' scholar. Thus in picking these few names out from the many found on the foundation's website (including scholars like Doniger, Hawley and Witzel who, unlike Frawley, Elst, etc., have received funds and travel grants from the foundation), Pincince was playing the game of selective guilt-by-association. A site search of the foundation shows, however, that, for instance, Frawley's name comes up only in the bibliographies of some other authors' essays. Pincince's syllogisms were flawed, because, using his logic, any academic journal whose articles include bibliographical references to some author X would have to be condemned as being 'linked' to X.

Many other far-fetched conspiracy theories were circulated in a gleeful game of connect-the-dots including imagining non-existing dots. In another flight of fancy, Pincince's convoluted reasoning led him to conclude that because "the anti-Courtright petition" appeared on the same on-line petition site where a previous petition against Prof. Thapar's appointment to the US Library of Congress had appeared, somehow the two petitions were both linked to Malhotra. However, the website is an independent organization, which specializes in hosting petitions by *anyone* and on *any* issue, and hosts thousands of unrelated petitions, from *Saving the Whales* to protesting US Congressional politics. Neither Malhotra nor the Infinity Foundation participated in the well-documented online discussions about Thapar's appointment.

Pincince's demonization campaign blundered on as he placed all the contemporary political problems of India at the doorstep of Hinduism, attacking Hindus as being inherently anti-Muslim and fearful of the Western scholars' gaze. Echoing Caldwell's attempts to psychoanalyze Hindu society to defend Kripal (see section I), Pincince wrote, "So, I would imagine the issue is related less to Ganesa's state of affairs (e.g. 'limp,' 'flaccid') and more a part of a larger campaign for the 'self-defense of 'Hinduism' in the face of 'attack' by Western scholars (the new colonial gaze) and problematic Muslims (the feared 'other')."

However, Pincince was on a roll and not so easily deterred by facts. In the process, he failed to do even rudimentary homework before making his numerous allegations. For instance, he claimed that the anti-Courtright petition was posted by a student at the Univ. of Louisiana at Lafayette, where, he claimed, Prof. Kak teaches. Actually, Prof. Kak teaches at Louisiana State University, Baton Rouge, 50 miles away from Lafayette, and was forced to explain in a letter that he had nothing to do with the petition.

131. A downloadable report (approx. 100 pages) on Infinity's programs at the University of Hawaii is available at, http://www.infinityfoundation.com/haw.htm.
132. Yvette Rosser, a long-time member of H-ASIA, took Miriam Sharma's suggestion and looked at the Infinity Foundation website (www.infinityfoundation.com). She reported, "There are articles by a very diverse group of scholars . . . June McDaniel . . . Rod Moag and Arvind Sharma. There were a large number of fascinating essays, including several by well known social activists and commentators, Madhu Kishwar and Ashis Nandy. I also saw essays by two JNU professors, Makarand Paranjape and Kapil Kapoor. Of particular interest, in light of . . . the on-going critique of the political orientation of Hindus in and out of India, see the essay by Ruth Vanita, "Whatever Happened to the Hindu Left?" available at: http://www.infinityfoundation.com/mandala/s_es/s_es_vanit_left_frameset.htm. I didn't find any links to deviate types . . . "
133. One wonders if the reverse application Wendy's toolbox might some day be used to psychoanalyze scholars like Miriam Sharma, who is carrying the White Woman's Burden into South Asian Studies (Dr. Sharma's last name comes from her husband who is from India).
134. John Stratton (a.k.a. Jack) Hawley is Professor of Religion and Chair of the Department Barnard College, Columbia University. He is a prominent RISA leader and supporter of Doniger, Kripal and others who often stereotype Hinduism using Eurocentric lenses.
135. Hawley's email on November 27, 2003, 7:10 PM.
136. November 29, 2003.
137. Hawley's email on November 29, 2003, 7:17 PM.
138. December 01, 2003 8:53 AM.
139. Madhu Kishwar, "When Religions claim Superiority," April 18, 2004, http://madhu-kishwar.sulekha.com/blog/post/2005/04/when-religions-claim-superiority.htm.
140. Ibid.
141. Ibid.
142. "RISA Lila-2."
143. Dr. Ram-Prasad Chakravarthi, Senior Lecturer in Religious Studies and Director of Postgraduate Research, Lancaster University, England.
144. November 5, 2003.
145. Malhotra, "RISA Lila-2."
146. A similar point was made by Cleo Kerns.

147. Chakravarthi: "Deeply reactionary apologetics is not something confined to elements of the Hindu community (in America, or in India itself), as the well-explored literature on fundamentalism, evangelism and their relationship with political conservatism has shown. The difference is that there has not been either the critical mass or the structural opportunity for Hindus of that 'right-wing' cast . . . to develop programs and forums comparable to Christian fundamentalism in America. Now, I would guess that practically every Western member of the list would be deeply resistant to such fundamentalisms—but I am suggesting that the analytic understanding of reactionary and/or fundamental Christian politics be extended to Hindutva in the West."

148. David Freedholm, "Thoughts on the Courtright controversy," email sent November 18, 2003.

149. November 4, 2003.

150. Anantanand Rambachan was born in Trinidad and received his Ph.D. from the University of Leeds, publishing *Accomplishing the Accomplished: The Vedas as a Source of Valid Knowledge in Sankara* and *The Limits of Scripture: Vivekananda's Reinterpretation of the Vedas* and numerous articles and books on various facets of Advaita Vedanta and Hinduism, including its dialogue with Christianity. His scholarly interests include the contemporary encounter among religious traditions, Hinduism in the modern period, and the Hindu tradition outside of India. Rambachan has been Professor of Religion, Philosophy and Asian Studies at St. Olaf College in Northfield, MN since 1985.

151. November 6, 2003.

152. Also see Agarwal and Venkat for a different take on this issue.

153. Pratap Kumar has studied in India for his undergraduate and postgraduate levels and received his Ph.D. from the University of California, Santa Barbara, USA. He is the author of *The Goddess Lakshmi: The Divine Consort in South Indian Vaishnava Tradition* (Scholars Press, 1997), *Hindus in South Africa* (University of Durban-Westville, 2000) and has, together with Knut Jacobsen, edited the volume *on South Asians in the Diaspora* (E.J. Brill, 2004). He is also the Series Editor for the Numen Book Series of the International Association for the History of Religions. He is a Professor and Director of the School of Religion and Theology at the University of KwaZulu Natal, South Africa.

154. The Indian Marxist depiction of Hinduism as being a dominant religion, because of its position in India, must be reexamined and not parroted blindly in the American context.

155. Email, November 18, 2003.

156. Ashok Aklujkar: professor of Asian Studies at University of British Columbia, Canada, with a major research interest in Philosophy of language and grammar in the Sanskrit tradition.

157. Email, November 24, 2003.

158. Sushil Mittal, associate professor of Religion, and Director of the Mahatma Gandhi Institute for Global Nonviolence at James Madison University.

159. Email, November 17, 2003.

160. See, www.barnard.columbia.edu/religion/hinduismhere/index.html.

161. William Butler Yeats, "The Second Coming."

162. Russell T. McCutcheon, professor and chair of the Department of Religious Studies, 212 Manly Hall, at the University of Alabama, Tuscaloosa.

163. Russell T. McCutcheon, "'It's a Lie. There is NO Truth in it! It's a Sin!': On the Limits of the Humanistic Study of Religion and the Costs of Saving Others from Themselves," *Journal of the American Academy of Religion* 74, no.3 (September 2006): 720–750.

164. Robert A. Orsi, "Fair Game," Bulletin of the Council of Societies for the Study of Religion 33, no. 3–4: 87–89.

165. Wilfred Cantwell Smith, "The Comparative Study of Religion: Wither and Why?" in *The History of Religions: Essays in Methodology* 31–58, ed. Mircea Eliade and Joseph Kitagawa, Chicago: University of Chicago Press, 42.

166. Jose Ignacio Cabezon, "The Discipline and Its Others: The Dialectic of Alterity in the Study of Religion," *Journal of the American Academy of Religion* 74, no.1 (2006): 21–38.

167. Paul Courtright, "Studying Religion in an Age of Terror," *Religious Studies News* 19, no.4: 19.

168. Martin Marty, "Scholars of Hinduism under Attack," available at Beliefnet.com. See a detailed review in Section IV.

Section 4

1. Shankar Vedantam, "Wrath Over a Hindu God; U.S. Scholars' Writings Draw Threats From Faithful," *Washington Post*, April 10, 2004, p. A–01.

2. Email to Shanker Vedantam, quoted in Rajiv Malhotra, "Washington Post and Hinduphobia," April 20, 2004, http://rajivmalhotra.sulekha.com/blog/post/2004/04/washington-post-and-hinduphobia.htm.

3. Vedantam, "Wrath."

4. Chitra Raman to the *Post* April 22, 2006. The *Post* refused to acknowledge or publish this brief rebuttal, but we were able to obtain a copy.

5. Rajiv Malhotra, "10 Challenges to Washington Post," April 26, 2004, http://rajivmalhotra.sulekha.com/blog/post/2004/04/ten-challenges-to-washington-post.htm.

6. For more information on this situation, see: Manu Bhagavan, "James Laine, Shivaji and Freedom Of Speech," http://www.countercurrents.org/comm-bhagwan300304.htm (March 30, 2004).

7. Vedantam, "Wrath."

8. What the community asked for was that "Academicians having a demonstrated bias against and disrespect of the Hindu ethos should therefore not teach [introductory] Hindu religion courses at Emory". They quoted Prof. Antonio de Nicolas, "A scholar (teacher) who does not know how to present other cultures by their own criteria should not be allowed to teach those cultures".—from the Concerned Community's Briefing Book, a copy of which was also provided to authorities at Emory University.

9. Letter to Shankar Vedantam, quoted in Rajiv Malhotra, "Washington Post and Hinduphobia."

10. Malhotra, "Washington Post and Hinduphobia."

11. See Shankar Vedantam, April 23, 2004, http://team-sulekha.sulekha.com/blog/post/2004/04/in-response-to-rajiv-malhotra-s-column.htm. Vedantam wrote: "[Malhotra] fails to mention that critics are quoted throughout the story, and given prominent space to present their views. My notes on the story ran to more than 50,000 words. The finished article, which was unusually long, was about 1,900 words . . . No one I interviewed was quoted in entirety. The point is not whether every person and every opinion is quoted, but whether the article presented multiple viewpoints fairly. Most readers felt the story was balanced and comprehensive."

12. Vedantam, "Wrath."

13. Never did this gentleman, in the course of the past few years of lively discussions about psychoanalysis in India, ever contribute a comment to challenge or critique one of the many articles written by his fellow Indian-Americans.
14. Rajiv Malhotra, "10 Challenges."
15. Beloo Mehra in the IndianDiaspora e-group, quoted in an email by Mehra, April 16, 2004.
16. Jeffrey Long, email, April 20, 2004.
17. Lucinda Hopkins, email, April, 2004.
18. See Shankar Vedantam, "In Response To Rajiv Malhotra's Column," April 23 2004, http://team-sulekha.sulekha.com/blog/post/2004/04/in-response-to-rajiv-malhotra-s-column.htm.
19. Malhotra wrote in his rejoinder: "Mr. Vedantam labels the Hindu voices in ways to brand them with pejorative associations. He refers to Mr. Sanu as a "Hindu activist" and McGill's Prof. Arvind Sharma as a "practicing Hindu," in an article that is lavishly sprinkled with terms such as Hindutva, militancy, violence, threats, and so forth. This is guilt-by-association and every journalist knows what that means. He also includes Doniger's *ad hominem* attacks calling me "ignorant" of her writings, without any basis or verification. On the other hand, he fails to use comparable labeling of the side he supports. He fails to tag Vijay Prashad as a communist activist even though this is well-known publicly, based on Mr. Prashad's own writings. He fails to explain the Christian fundamentalist beliefs or the parochial backgrounds of important protagonists in this matter. This is inconsistent and is an asymmetric labeling of the voices involved" (Malhotra, Ten Challenges).
20. Rajiv Malhotra, "Ten Challenges" and "Washington Post and Hinduphobia."
21. Shankar Vedantam, "In Response."
22. Instead of listing only to one side, he might have shown both fringes—some people sincerely believed that perhaps partisans of Courtright posted the threats to derail the debate.
23. The biblical stories are often treated as literal—its many versions have to be "reconciled." No such pressure to literalize or to reconcile various stories exists within Hinduism, nor do meanings derive exclusively from the stories.
24. A recent Google search resulted in 1,130,000 hits for the term Islamophobia. Most of the first few dozen sites are maintained by groups devoted to upgrading the American understanding of Islam, such as the Forum Against Islamophobia and Racism (FAIR), Islamawareness.net, and Islamophobia.org. There are also sites featuring commentators, such as Daniel Pipes, who discuss the term Islamophobia from different perspectives. Though the analyses of Islamophobia may vary, at least there is the recognition that there is an issue of discomfort about religious difference. It is being discussed, not ignored. Amazon.com lists 12 books when one searches "Islamopbobia" in the title. See: http://www.amazon.com/gp/search/ref=sr_adv_b/?search-alias=stripbooks&field-keywords=&author=&select-author=field-author-like&title=islamophobia&select-title=field-title&subject=&select-subject=field-subject&field-publisher=&field-isbn=&node=&field-binding=&field-age=&field-language=&field-dateop=before&field-datemod=0&field-dateyear=2009&chooser-sort=rank%21%2Bsalesrank&mysubmitbutton1.x=32&mysubmitbutton1.y=9 (Accessed on January 8, 2006). But no book titles with "Hinduphobia show up. A Google search on Hinduphobia produces only 1700 sites and many of these take the reader to articles by or pertaining to Malhotra. Wikipedia has a large amount written on Islamophobia but no section on Hinduphobia. (There is a section on "anti-Hindu" which is based to a considerable extent on the writings of Malhotra and others who have been inspired to take up this issue very recently).

25. In 1978 the editors of 26 religious magazines voted Marty and Billy Graham as the two people having the most influence on religion in the United States. See Kerry Temple, "Martin Marty: Faith's Familiar Face," *U.Chicago Magazine*, August 1998.

26. Cited in Kerry Temple, "Martin Marty: Faith's Familiar Face" *U.Chicago Magazine*, August 1998.

27. Marin E. Marty, "Scholars of Hinduism Under Attack," http://www.beliefnet.com/story/128/story_12899_1.html.

28. Ibid.

29. Philip Hensher, "Stop me if you've heard this one before" *The Independent*, (UK newspaper), February 8, 2006, http://comment.independent.co.uk/columnists_a_l/philip_hensher/article343896.ece.

30. Alan Watkins, the famous British Political commentator notes that, "Eggs were sometimes chucked at political meetings in the pre-1914 era, perhaps the golden age of egg-throwing. But they were hardly seen after 1945, partly because there was food rationing till 1954 and they were too scarce to waste. They returned briefly to political fashion in the 1970 election campaign, when Harold Wilson toured the country and occasionally found himself bespattered by an egg." See: Alan Watkins, "Mr Prescott's bad temper was Mr Blair's lucky strike," *The Independent*, (UK newspaper), 20 May 2001, http://comment.independent.co.uk/columnists_m_z/alan_watkins/article245032.ece.

31. Alan Watkins: "Mr Prescott's bad temper was Mr. Blair's lucky strike" *The Independent*, (UK newspaper), 20 May, 2001.

32. William Hague, quoted in Alan Watkins: "Mr Prescott's bad temper was Mr Blair's lucky strike."

33. See Editorial in the *Oxford Student*: "Egg throwing not celebration enough," 29th April, 2004, http://www.oxfordstudent.com/tt2004wk1/Editorial/egg_throwing_not_celebration_enough. In fact, throwing eggs, tradition or not, can be medically dangerous if it hits the victim.

34. Marin E. Marty, "Scholars of Hinduism."

35. Alex Alexander, "Response to Martin Marty," posted May 15, 2004, http://www.beliefnet.com/story/128/story_12899_1.html.

36. Marin E. Marty, "Scholars of Hinduism."

37. Ibid.

38. Ibid.

39. Alex Alexander, "Response to Martin Marty."

40. Arvind Sharma, "Hindus and Scholars," *Religion in the News* 7, no. 1 (Spring 2004).

41. This article originally appeared on Beliefnet in June of 2004 http://www.beliefnet.com/story/146/story_14684_1.html.

42. Marty does not in fact use the word "lately"—this appears to have been inserted by the editors of Beliefnet in their blurb to Marty's article to qualify his broad claims, and Sanu generously accepts this clarification.

43. Richard Slotkin, *Regeneration Through Violence: The Mythology of the American Frontier, 1600–1860*, 95.

44. Ibid., 96–97.

45. Ibid., 63.

46. Richard Slotkin, *Gunfighter Nation: The Myth of the American frontier in Twentieth-Century America*, 15.

47. Richard Drinnon, *Facing West*, 101.

48.	Moreover, in the Laine controversy it was orthodox Hindus and their institutions who were the victims, and the dispute was about ethnic pride and not Hinduism. But these hard facts are glossed over. As in the *Washington Post* and the University of Chicago articles, the incident is used to demonstrate the violent nature of all Hindus who scrutinize scholarship.
49.	See the chapter 8 in section I for details on this controversy.
50.	I had sent my letter by express US Postal Service., and after two weeks, had heard back neither from Mr. Sulzberger nor the Ombudsman, Mr Okrent.
51.	The incident occurred when Doniger was a guest of William Dalrymple at the University of London's School of Oriental and African Studies, in November 2003. She was presenting a "lecture on the Hindu Ramayana text." According to a report by Professor Ramesh Rao published in *India Today* (November, 2003), the title of her talk was, "Gods, Humans and Animals in the Ramayana." An irate man in the audience threw an egg that hit the wall behind Doniger.
52.	When using the word diaspora in the context of the Hindu diaspora, the small case d is used to differentiate between the physical dispersal of a people or groups such as Hindus and the historical and symbolic Diaspora in the Jewish tradition. The word is used in a generic sense, with due respect to its symbolic importance.
53.	These quotes, taken from an on-line article, "The Benign Face of Modern Hatred," at http://www.hinduhumanrights.org/articles/hatred.htm, accuse Doniger of "attempting to hide the fact that she has been sprung for her insulting and racist behaviour."
54.	Regarding the feminine as sacred, one must note that a majority of Hindu men worship the Goddess whereas in the Abrahamic religions this is largely taboo and even those Americans who break ranks to worship the Goddess tend to be mainly women.
55.	Trisha Pasricha, http://www.hinduismtoday.com/archives/2004/4–6/18–27_mythbusters.shtml.
56.	Teaching South Asia, Volume I, No. 1, Winter 2001: http://www.mssu.edu/projectsouthasia/tsa/VIN1/Rosser.htm.
57	See these testimonials from Hindu-American youths: http://www.thevedicfoundation.org/Textbook_Reform_Initiative/youth_stories.html. Some examples from the website:
"I will never forget an incident I had in class with my teacher in middle school. There had been a bee flying inside the room and instead of killing it, I had suggested that we set it free outside. My teacher glared at me and said, "What's the matter, are you afraid we are killing your uncle? If that's the case, we should set him free." Comments like this from people I admired, such as teachers, embarrassed me and forced me to stay silent. I could not argue because I did not know where to start. [...]Instruction I receive in school on Hinduism often mentioned that Hindus pray to many gods, cows, and even snakes. I was taught that Hinduism is polytheistic. This is incorrect, yet it is often repeated to make our religion look ridiculous and backward."
From another student:
"In my 5th grade class my teacher was totally against me being Hindu and made my daily life miserable. At the beginning of the school year she asked the class if any of us were vegetarians. Not wanting to be a spectacle, I did not raise my hand and then she said, "Good, because I don't like vegetarians." My stomach sank as I could not believe any one could ever say something so mean. The year went on and she made other comments like that.
Then we had a class project to do in which you had to chose to eat a piece of fish or not. Being vegetarian I could never think of eating fish, so I had to tell

my teacher. It was very difficult as she gave me a very hard time about this. In front of the class for 5 minutes she tried to get me to eat fish, knowing that it was against my religion."

58. David White, *Kiss of the Yogini: Tantric Sex in its South Asian Contexts*.

59. Professor of Biblical and Constructive Theology.

60. For frequently asked questions about Professor Ted Jennings book, see: www.ctschicago.edu/pdf/Jennings_fact_sheet_6-3-03.pdf.

61. Homosexuality and Heresy: Liberal Theology Loses its Mind, http://www.baptist2baptist.net/Issues/Marriage/MohlerJul202004.asp.

62. See the Malhotra-Prashad debate on Outlook India at: http://www.outlookindia.com/full.asp?fodname=20040115&fname=rajiv2&sid=1 Or at: http://www.outlookindia.com/author.asp?name=Rajiv+Malhotra.
In case that archive is unavailable the articles by both sides were also posted at the following yahoo e-group: http://groups.yahoo.com/group/Dharmvhba-FOIL-Dialog/messages (Requires membership in Yahoogroups).

63. Znet, http://www.zmag.org.

64. For information about the alleged abuses of the Coca-Cola corporation in India see: http://www.indiaresource.org/campaigns/coke/2004/risingstruggles.html.

65. The letter to the editors in the *University of Chicago Magazine*, February 2005, Volume 97, Issue 3, were published under the title, ". . . but in all the shouting, no one's listening", available at: http://magazine.uchicago.edu/0502/issue/letters.shtml.

66. Volney P. Gay is professor of Religion, professor of Psychiatry, and professor of Anthropology at Vanderbilt University and director of the Center for the Study of Religion and Culture. He is also on the Editorial Board of *The Journal of Ritual Studies, Journal of Applied Psychoanalytic Studies*, and *Journal of the American Academy of Religion*. He is a faculty member of the St. Louis Psychoanalytic Institute, from which he graduated in 1990. He was certified in Adult Psychoanalysis in 1990 by the American Psychoanalytic Association and was made a Training and Supervising Analyst in December, 1994. From: http://www.vanderbilt.edu/gradschool/religion/faculty/facultypages/gay.html.

67. Professor Ramesh N. Rao- Chair, Communication Studies and Theatre Department, Longwood University, Farmville, Virginia.

68. Ramesh Rao, "Hindu God, Must Indeed Be Heathen," *India Abroad*, November 28, 2003.

69. Tanmaya Kumar Nanda, "'I am distressed that anyone found my discussion of Ganesha offensive'—Interview with Paul Courtright," *India Abroad*, November 28, 2003.

70. Rao, "Hindu God must Indeed be Heathen."

71. Nanda. "I am Distressed . . ."

72. Ibid.

73. Quoted in Rao, "Hindu God must Indeed be Heathen."

74. Email to Malhotra cited in section III.

75. Letter to the Concerned Community from Joyce Flueckiger.

76. Alan Roland, "The Uses (and Misuses) Of Psychoanalysis in South Asian Studies: Mysticism and Child Development," http://www.sulekha.com/expressions/column.asp?cid-270005 [This article is reprinted in an appendix to this volume].

77. Nanda, "I am Distressed."

78. Ibid.

79. Paul Courtright, *Religious Studies News*.

Bibliography

Adriaensen, R., Hans Bakker and H. Isaacson, eds. *The Skanda Purana, Volume I.* Groningen: Egbert Forsten, 1998.

Akhtar, Salman. *Freud Along the Ganges, Psychoanalytic Reflections on the People and Culture of India.* New York: Other Press, 2005.

Atmajnanananda, Swami. "Scandals, Cover-ups and Other Imagined Occurrences in the Life of Ramakrishna: An Examination of Jeffery Kripal's Kali's Child," *International Journal of Hindu Studies* 1, no.2 (1997): 401-20.

Austin, James H. *Zen and the Brain.* Boston: MIT Press, 1998.

Bakre, Mahadeva Ganghadhar, ed. *Grihya-Sutra by Paraskar with Five Commentaries of Karka Upadhyaya, Jayaram, Harihar, Gadadhar and Vishvanath.* New Delhi: Munshiram Manoharlal Publishers, 1982.

Balagangadhara, S.N. *The Heathen in His Blindness: Asia, the West and the Dynamic of Religion.* Volume 64 of the Studies in the History of Religions (Numen Bookseries), edited by E.J. Brill. Leiden/New York/Koln: Brill, 1994.

Boss, Medard. *A Psychiatrist Discovers India.* London: Oswald Wolff, 1965.

Berkeley-Hill, Owen. "The Anal-Erotic Factor in the Religion, Philosophy and Character of the Hindu." *International Journal of Psychoanalysis* 2 (1921): 306-38.

Brands, H.W. *Andrew Jackson: His Life and Times.* Westminster, MD, USA: Doubleday Publishing, 2005.

Bresnan, Patrick. *Awakening: An Introduction to the History of Eastern Thought.* Upper Saddle River, NJ: Prentice Hall, 2001.

Brown, Robert L. "Ganesa in Southeast Asian Art, Indian Connections and Indigenous Developments." In *Ganesh: Studies of an Asian God*, edited by Robert Brown, 171-234. Albany: SUNY Press, 1991.

Cabezon, Jose Ignacio. "The Discipline and Its Others: The Dialectic of Alterity in the Study of Religion." *Journal of the American Academy of Religion* 74, no.1 (March 2006): 21-38.

Caldwell, Sarah. *Oh Terrifying Mother: Sexuality, Violence and Worship of the Mother Kali.* New Delhi: Oxford University Press, 1999.

——"The Bloodthirsty Tongue and the Self-Feeding Breast: Homosexual Fellatio Fantasy in a South Indian Ritual Tradition." In *Vishnu on Freud's*

Desk, edited by T.G. Vaidyanathan and Jeffrey Kripal, 339-366. New Delhi: Oxford University Press, 1999.

Chakrabarti, Dilip. *Colonial Indology – Sociopolitics of the Ancient Indian Past.* New Delhi: Munshiram Manoharlal, 1997.

Chakravarti, Sitanshu. "Misrepresentation of the Tantras in David White's book:

A Flawed Methodology Instantiated." Paper presented at the WAVES conference 2004.

——*Hinduism: a Way of Life.* New Delhi: Motilal Banarsidass, 1991.

——*Modality, Reference and Sense: An Essay in the Philosophy of Language.* New Delhi: Munshiram, Manoharlal, 2001.

Chetanananda, Swami. *They Lived with God.* Vedanta Society of St. Louis, 1989.

Clooney, Francis. *Hindu God, Christian God: How Reason helps Break Down the Boundaries between Religions.* Oxford: Oxford University Press, 2001.

Cortright, Brant. *Psychotherapy and Spirit: Theory and Practice in Transpersonal Pyschotherapy.* Albany: SUNY Press, 1997.

Courtright, Paul. *Ganesa Lord of Obstacles, Lord of Beginnings.* New York: Oxford University Press, 1985.

——. "Ganesa and the Ganesa Festival in Maharashtra, A Study in Hindu Religious Celebration." PhD diss., Princeton University, 1974.

—— "Studying Religion in an Age of Terror." *Religious Studies News* 19, no.4: 19.

Coward, Harold. *Jung and Eastern Thought.* Albany: State University of New York Press, 1985.

Crews, Frederick. *The Memory Wars: Freud's Legacy in Dispute.* New York: Review Books, 1995.

Das, Rahul Peter. *The Origin of the Life of a Human Being.* New Delhi: Motilal Banarsidass, 2003.

Das, Upendrakumar. *Shastramulak Bharatiya Shaktisadhana.* Viswabharati, 2nd Edition, B.E. 1391.

Diagnostic and Statistical Manual of Mental Disorders (DSM) IV. Washington: The American Psychiatric Association, 1994.

Doniger, Wendy. *Asceticism and Eroticism in the Mythology of Œiva.* New York: Oxford University Press, 1973.

——,ed. *The Critical Study of Sacred Texts.* Berkeley: Graduate Theological Union, Religious Studies Series, 1979.

——*Dreams, Illusion, and Other Realities.* Chicago: University of Chicago Press, 1984.

——"From Great Neck to Swift Hall: Confessions from a Reluctant Historian of Religions." In *The Craft of Religious Studies*, edited by Jon R. Stone, 36-51. New York: St. Martin's Press Inc., 1998.

——*Hindu Myths: A Sourcebook, translated from the Sanskrit.* Harmondsworth: Penguin Classics, 1975.

——*The Origins of Evil in Hindu Mythology.* Berkeley: University of California Press, 1976.

——*Other Peoples' Myths: The Cave of Echoes.* New York: Macmillan, 1988.

——, ed. *Purana Perennis: Reciprocity and Transformation in Hindu and Jaina Texts.* Albany: SUNY Press, 1993.

——*The Rig Veda: An Anthology, 108 Hymns Translated from the Sanskrit.* Harmondsworth: Penguin Classics, 1981.

——*Tales of Sex and Violence: Folklore, Sacrifice, and Danger in the Jaiminiya Brahmana.* Chicago: University of Chicago Press, 1985.

——"Tantric Bodies." Review of *Kiss of the Yogini: Tantric Sex in its South Asian Contexts,* by David White. The *New York Times* Literary Supplement, May 20, 2004.

——*Textual Sources for the Study of Hinduism.* Manchester: Manchester University Press; 1988.

——"When a Lingam is just a Good Cigar: Psychoanalysis and Hindu Sexual Fantasies." In *Vishnu on Freud's Desk,* edited by Jeffrey Kripal and T.G. Vaidyanathan, 379-303. New Delhi: Oxford University Press, 1999; In *The psychoanalytic study of society, Vol. 18: Essays in honor of Alan Dundes,* edited by L. Bryce Boyer, Ruth M. Boyer, Stephen M. Sonnenberg, 81-103. Hillsdale, US: Analytic Press, Inc.

——*Women, Androgynes, and Other Mythical Beasts.* Chicago: University of Chicago Press, 1980.

Doniger, Wendy, Carmel Berkson, and George Michell. *Elephanta, the Cave of Śiva.* Photographs by Carmel Berkson. Princeton: Princeton University Press, 1983; New Delhi: Oxford University Press, 1987.

Drinnon, Richard. *Facing West: the Metaphysics of Indian-Hating and Empire-Building.* Norman, OK: University of Oklahoma Press, 1998.

Dupuche, John R. *Abhinavagupta: The Kula Ritual As Elaborated in Chapter 29 of the Tantraloka.* Delhi: Motilal Banarasidass, 2003.

Eck, Diana L. *A New Religious America: How a "Christian" Country Has Now Become the Most Religiously Diverse Nation.* San Francisco: Harper San Francisco, 2001.

Eilberg-Schwartz, Howard and Wendy Doniger, eds. *Off with Her Head! The Denial of Women's Identity in Myth, Religion, and Culture.* Berkeley: University of California Press, 1995.

Erickson, E. H. *Life History and the Historical Moment,* New York: Norton, 1975. In *Theories of Personality,* 4th ed., edited by Hall, Lindzey and Campbell, 213. New York: John Wiley, 1998.

Fenichel, Otto. *The Psychoanalytic Theory of Neurosis.* New York: W.W. Norton & Co., 1972.

Fischer, Seymour, and Roger P. Greenberg. *The Scientific Evolution of Freud's Theories and Therapy.* New York: Basic Books, 1978.

Friedman, David. *A Mind of Its Own: A Cultural History of the Penis.* New York: Free Press, 2001.

Freud, Sigmund. *The Interpretation of Dreams.* Translated by James Strachey. London: George Allen and Unwin, 1971 (4th impression).

Fromm, Eric. *The Art of Loving.* New York: Harper and Row, 1956.

——*Greatness and Limitations of Freud's Thought.* London: Jonathan Cape, 1980.

Fussel, Edwin. *Frontier: American Literature and the American West.* Princeton: Princeton University Press, 1965.

Gadgil, Amarendra. *Sri Ganesa-kosha.* Pune: Ganesa-kosha Prakaasan Mandala, 1968 (In Marathi).

Getty, Alice. *Ganesa: A Monograph on the Elephant-faced God.* Oxford: Oxford University Press, 1936.

Goldenson, R.M., ed. *Longman Dictionary of Psychology and Psychiatry.* New York: Longman, 1988.

Goldman, R.P. "Fathers, Sons and Gurus Oedipal conflict in Sanskrit Epics." *Journal of Indian Philosophy* 6 (1978): 325-92.

Gonda, Jan. "A Note on the Vedic Student's Staff." *Journal of the Oriental Institute* (Baroda) 14, nos. 3-4 (March-June 1965): 262-72.

Goonatilake, Susantha. *Anthropologizing Sri Lanka: A Eurocentric Misadventure.* Bloomington: Indiana University Press, 2001.

Glucklich, Ariel. "The Royal Scepter ('Danda') as Legal Punishment and Sacred Symbol." *History of Religions* 28, no. 2 (November 1988): 97-122.

Granoff, Phyllis. "Ganesa as Metaphor." In *Ganesh- Studies of an Asian God,* edited by Robert L. Brown , 85-99. New York: SUNY Press, 1991.

Grimes, John. *Ganapati: Song of the Self.* Albany: SUNY Press, 1995.

Gupta, Anand Swarup, ed. *Vamana Purana.* Varanasi: All India Kashiraj Trust, 1968.

Gupta, Mahendranath 'M', Sri, Sri Sri Ramakrishna Kathamrita, 17th Ed. Kathamrita Bhavan, 1356 B.E.

Harlan, Lindsey. "Perfection and Devotion: Sati Tradition in Rajasthan." In *Sati, the Blessing and the Curse,* edited by J.S.Hawley, 79-90. New York: Oxford University Press, 1994.

Harlan, Lindsey, and Paul Courtright, eds. *From the Margins of Hindu Marriage: Essays on Gender, Religion and Culture.* New York: Oxford, 1995.

Hartnack, Christiane. *Psychoanalysis in Colonial India.* Delhi: Oxford University Press, 2001.

Hatcher, Brian A. "Kali's Problem Child: Another Look at Jeffrey Kripal's Study of Sri Ramakrishna." *International Journal of Hindu Studies* 3, no.1 (1999).

Hawley, John S., ed. *Sati, the Blessing and the Curse: The Burning of Wives in India.* New York: Oxford University Press, 1994.

Hawley, John S. and Donna Marie Wulff, eds. *Devi: Goddesses of India,* Berkeley: University of California Press, 1996.

Horsman, Reginald. *Race and Manifest Destiny: The Origins of American Racial Anglo-Saxonism.* Cambridge, Massachusetts: Harvard University Press, 1981.

Humes, Cynthia. Review of *All the Mothers are One,* by Stanley Kurtz. *The Journal of Asian Studies* 53, no.1 (February, 1991): 256-58.

——Review of *Oh Terrifying Mother: Sexuality, Violence and Worship of the Mother Kali,* by Sarah Caldwell. *Journal of the American Academy of Religion* 69, no. 4 (November, 2001): 901-02.

Inden, Ronald. *Imagining India.* Bloomington: Indiana University Press, 2001.

Joshi, A.P., M.D. Srinivas, and J.K. Bajaj. *Religious Demography of India.* Chennai: Centre for Policy Studies, 2003.

Jung, Carl. *Modern Man in Search of a Soul.* San Diego:Harvest Books, 1955.

Katchadourian, H.A. and D.T. Lunde. *Fundamentals of Human Sexuality,* 2nd Ed. New York : Holt, Rinehart and Winston, 1975.

Kakar, Sudhir. *The Analyst and the Mystic: Psychoanalytic Reflections on Religion and Mysticism.* Chicago: University of Chicago Press, 1992.

——New York: Viking, 1991.

——*The Essential Writings of Sudhir Kakar.* New Delhi: Oxford University Press, 2001.

——"Reflections on Psychoanalysis, Indian Culture and Mysticism." Review of *The Oceanic Feeling: The Origins of Religious Sentiment in Ancient India,* by J.M. Masson. *Journal of Indian Philosophy* (Springer, Netherlands) 10, no. 3 (September, 1982): 130-31.

Kakar, Sudhir, and John M. Ross. *Tales of Love, Sex and Danger.* Delhi: Oxford University Press, 1986.

Kaplan and Sadock. *Comprehensive Textbook of Psychiatry,* 7th Ed., Vol. 1. Philadelphia: Lippincott Williams and Wilkins, 2000.

Kazanas, Nicholas. "Indo-European Deities and the Rgveda." *Journal of Indo-European Studies* 29, nos. 3-4 (Fall & Winter 2001): 257-93.

Keay, John. *India: A History.* New York: Grove Press, 2000.

Khanna, Madhu. "Paradigms of Female Sexuality in the Hindu World." In *Women of Religion.* Vol. 5, edited by Durre Ahmed, 219-252. Lahore: Heinrich Boll Foundation, South Asia Office, 2000.

Kihlstrom, John F. "Is Freud Still Alive? No. Not Really." In *Hilgard's Introduction to Psychology,* 13th edition., by R. Atkinson, R.C. Atkinson, E.E. Smith, D.J. Bem, & S. Nolen-Hoeksema. New York: Harcourt Brace Jovanovich, 2000.

Kolhatkar, Madhavi. Review of Courtright's book, in *Annals of the Bhandarkar Oriental Research Institute,* Vol. LXXXV (2004): 186-89.

Kripal, Jeffrey J. *Kali's Child: The Mystical and the Erotic in the Life and teachings of Ramakrishna.* 2nd ed. Chicago: University of Chicago Press, 1998.

——"Mystical Homoeroticism, Reductionism and the Reality of Censorship: A Response to Gerald Larson." *Journal of the American Academy of Religion* 66, no. 3 (Autumn 1998): 627-35.

——"Ramakrishna's Foot: Mystical Homoeroticism in the Kathamrita." In *Religion, Homosexuality, and Literature*, edited by Michael L. Stemmeler and José Ignacio Cabezón. Las Colinas, TX: Monument Press, 1992.

——"Secret Talk: Sexual Identity and Politics of Scholarship." *Harvard Divinity School Bulletin* 30, no.1 (March 2001).

——"Textuality, Sexuality and the Future of the Past: A Response to Swami Tyagananda." *Harvard Divinity School Bulletin* 30, no.1 (March 2001).

Krishan, Yuvraj. *Ganesa Unravelling an Enigma*. Delhi: Motilal Banarsidass Publishers, 1999.

——"Is the Fight between Siva and Ganesa and Episode of Oedipal Conflict?" In *Spectrum of Indian Culture* (Prof. S.B. Deo Felicitation Volume), edited by C. Margabandhu and K.S. Ramachandran. Delhi: Agam Kala Prakashan, 1996.

Kurtz, Stanley N. *All the Mothers Are One: Hindu India and the Cultural Reshaping of Psychoanalysis*. New York: Columbia University Press, 1992.

——"Psychoanalytic Approaches to Hindu Child Rearing." In *Vishnu on Freud's Desk,* edited by T.G. Vaidyanathan and Jaffrey Kripal, 339-366. New Delhi: Oxford University Press, 1999.

Larson, Gerald J. "Polymorphic Sexuality, Homoeroticism and the Study of Religion." *Journal of the American Academy of Religion* 65, no.3 (Autumn, 1997): 655-65.

Marriott, McKim. "Constructing an Indian Ethnosociology." In *India Through Hindu Categories*, edited by McKim Marriott, 1-39. New Delhi: Sage Publications, 1990.

Maslow, Abraham. *Toward A Psychology of Being*, 2nd ed. New York: Van Nostrand Reinhold Company, 1968.

Masson, J.M. "Sex and Yoga: Psychoanalysis and the Indian Religious Experience." *Journal of Indian Philosophy* 2 (1974): 307-20.

Masters, W. H. and V.E Johnson. *Human Sexual Inadequacy*. Boston: Little Brown, 1970.

McCutcheon, Russell T. "'It's a Lie. There is NO Truth in it! It's a Sin!'": On the Limits of the Humanistic Study of Religion and the Costs of Saving Others from Themselves." *Journal of the American Academy of Religion* 74, no. 3 (September 2006): 720-50.

Mehendale, M.A. "Nirukta Notes IV: Yaska's Etymology of Danda." *Journal of the American Oriental Society* 80, no. 2 (April-June 1960): 112-15.

Meissner, W.W. *Psychoanalysis and Religious Experience*. New Haven: Yale University Press, 1984.

Monaghan, John, and Peter Just. *Social & Cultural Anthropology: A Very Short Introduction*. New York: Oxford University Press, 2000.

Müller, Max, trans. *The Upanishads*. Reprint, New York: Dover Publications, 1962.

Nanda, Tanmaya Kumar. "'I am distressed that anyone found my discussion of Ganesha offensive'—Interview with Paul Courtright." *India Abroad*, November 28, 2003.

Narain, Dhirendra. *Hindu Character*. Bombay: University of Bombay, 1957.

Nikhilananda, Swami, trans. *The Gospel of Sri Ramakrishna*, 3rd impression. Mylapore: Sri Ramakrishna Math, 1970.

Obeyesekere, Gananath. *The Cult of the Goddess Patni*. Chicago: University of Chicago Press, 1984.

O'Flaherty, Wendy Doniger, and J. Duncan M. Derret, eds. *The Concept of Duty in South Asia*. London: School of Oriental and African Studies; Delhi: Vikas Publishing Company, 1978.

——, ed. *Karma and Rebirth in Classical Indian Traditions*. Berkeley: University of California Press; Delhi, Motilal Banarsidass, 1980.

Oldenberg, Hermann, trans. *The Grihya Sutras: Rules of Vedic Domestic Ceremonies Part I*. Sacred Books of the East Series Volume XXIX. Delhi: Motilal Banarsidass, 1964; 1886.

Oldenburg, Veena. *Dowry Murder*. New York: Oxford University Press, 2002.

Ormiston, Gayle L., and Alan D. Schrift. *The Hermeneutic Tradition: From Ast to Ricoeur*. State University of New York Press, 1990.

Pandey, Raj Bali. *Hindu Samskaras, Socio-Religious Study of the Hindu Sacraments*. New Delhi: Motilal Banarsidass, 1969.

Parsons, William B. *The Enigma of the Oceanic Feeling: Revisioning the Psychoanalytic Theory of Mysticism*. Oxford: Oxford University Press: 1999.

Piano, Stefano. "Urdhvaretas: A few Notes on Chastity and Lust in the Mythology of Siva." In *Hindu Masculinities Across the Ages, Updating the Past*, edited by Alessandro Motti. Turin, Italy: L' Harmattan Italia, 2002.

Ramanujan, A.K. "The Indian Oedipus." In *Indian Literature. Proceedings of a Seminar*, edited by A. Poddar. Simla. Simla: Indian Institute of Advanced Study, 1972.

—— "Is There an Indian Way of Thinking?" In *India Through Hindu Categories*, edited by McKim Marriott, 41-58. London: Sage Publications, 1990.

Rao, Ramesh. "Hindu God must Indeed be Heathen." *India Abroad*, November 28, 2003.

Rao, Saligrama Krishna Ramachandra. *Ganesa-kosha*. Bangalore: Kalpataru Research Academy, 1992.

Renou, Louis. "Note sur les origines védiques de Ganeœa." *Journal Asiatique* 229 (April-June 1937).

Roland, Alan Ramakrishna. "Mystical, Erotic, or Both?" *Journal of Religion and Health* 37, no.1 (Spring 1998).

—— "The Spiritual Self and Psychopathology: Theoretical Reflections and Clinical Observations." Paper presented at the Indian Institute of Advanced Studies, Simla, July 1997.

Rocher, Ludo. *The Puranas*. Vol. 2 of *A History of Indian Literature*, 3rd fasc. Wiesbaden: Otto Harrassowitz, 1986.

Rosser, Yvette C. "The Clandestine Curriculum in the Classroom." *Education About Asia* 6, no. 3 (2001).

Roy, Parama. *Indian Traffic: Identities in Question in Colonial and Postcolonial India*. Berkeley: University of California Press, 1998.

Rubin, Zick. *Liking and Loving: An Invitation to Social Psychology*. New York: Holt Reinhart and Winston, 1973.

—— "Measurement of Romantic Love." *Journal of Personality and Social Psychology* 16, (1970): 265-73.

Said, Edward. "Representing the Colonized: Anthropology's Interlocutors." *Critical Inquiry* 15, (1989): 217-24.

Saradananda, Swami. *Sri Ramakrishna: The Great Master*, 7th impression. Translated by Swami Jagadananda. Madras: Sri Ramakrishna Math.

—— Saradananda, Swami, Sri Sri Ramakrishna Lilaprasanga, Udbodhan Karyalaya, 1396 B.E.

Sardar, Ziauddin. "Deconstructing Postmodernism." *Bi-annual Encounters* 5, no. 1 (1999).

—— *Postmodernism and the Other: The New Imperialism of Western Culture*. London: Pluto Press, 1998.

Sarkar, Sumit. "The Kathamrita as a Text: Towards an Understanding of Ramakrishna Paramahamsa." In *Occasional Papers on History and Society XXII*. New Delhi: Nehru Memorial Museum and Library, 1985.

Sastri, Alladi Mahadeva,ed. *Parasurama Kalpasutra*. Baroda: Gaekwad Oriental Series 23-24, 1923.

Saxena, Neela Bhattacharya. "The Funhouse Mirror of Tantric Studies: A Rejoinder to David Gordon White's 'Kiss of the Yogini.'" *Evam: Forum on Indian Representations* (Samvad India Foundation, Delhi) 4, no. 1-2 (2006): 358-71.

Sharma, Arvind. "Hindus and Scholars." *Religion in the News* 7, no. 1 (Spring 2004).

Sharma, Renuka. "The Foot in the Lap or Kripal's Discontent." Review of *The Mystical and the Erotic in the Life and Teachings of Ramakrishna* by Jeffrey John Kripal. *Sophia* 40, no. 2 (Dec. 2001).

Shulman, David. "Remaking a Purana." In *Purana Perennis*, edited by Wendy Doniger. Albany: SUNY Press, 1993.

Sil, Narasingha. "The Question of Ramakrishna's Homosexuality." Review of *Kali's Child: The Mystical and the Erotic in the Life and teachings of Ramakrishna* by Jeffrey Kripal. *The Statesman* (January 31, 1997).

—— "Is Ramakrishna a Vedantin, a Tantrika or a Vaishnava?—An Examination." *Asian Studies Review* 21, nos. 2-3 (November, 1997).

——*Ramakrishna Revisited: A New Biography*. Lanham: University Press of America, 1998.

—— *Swami Vivekananda: A Reassessment*. London: Associated University Presses, 1997.

Slotkin, Richard. *The Fatal Environment: The Myth of the American Frontier in the Age of Industrialization, 1800-1890*. Middletown, CT: Wesleyan University Press, 1986.

—— *Gunfighter Nation: The Myth of the American frontier in Twentieth-Century America*. Norman, OK: University of Oklahoma Press, 1998.

—— *Regeneration Through Violence: The Mythology of the American frontier, 1600-1800*. Middletown, CT: Wesleyan University Press, 1973.

Smith, Henry Nash. *Virgin Land: The American West as Symbol and Myth*. Cambridge, MA: Harvard University Press, 1950.

Smith, Huston. *Harvard Divinity Bulletin* 30, no.1 (Spring 2001): 2.

Smith, Wilfred Cantwell. "The Comparative Study of Religion: Wither and Why?" In *The History of Religions: Essays in Methodology*, edited by Mircea Eliade and Joseph Kitagawa, 31-58. Chicago: University of Chicago Press.

Spivak, Gayatri Chakravorty. "Neocolonialism and the Secret Agent of Knowledge: An Interview." *The Oxford Literary Review* 13 (1991): 220-51.

Spratt, Philip. *Hindu Culture and Personality*. Bombay: Manaktalas, 1966.

Staal, Frits. *Rituals and Mantras*. Delhi: Motilal Banarasidass, 1996.

Stemmeler, L. and Jose Ignacio Cabezon. *Religion, Homosexuality, and Literature*. Vol. 3 of *Gay Men's Issues in Religious Studies Series* 3, 31-74. Las Colinas, Texas: Monument Press, 1992.

Stephanson, Anders. *Manifest Destiny*. New York: Hill and Wang, 1995.

Sundaresan, Vidyashankar. "Conflicting Hagiographies and History: The Place of Sankaravijaya texts in Advaita Tradition." *International Journal of Hindu Studies* 4, no.2 (August 2000): 109-84.

Thapar, Romila, ed. *Recent Perspectives of Early Indian History*. Popular Prakashan: Bombay, 1995.

Thapat, Anita Raina. *Understanding Ganapati*. New Delhi: Manohar, 1997.

Thornton, E.M. *Freudian Fallacy: An Alternative View of Freudian Theory*. New York: Double Day, 1984.

Tyagananda, Swami. "*Kali's Child* Revisited or Didn't Anyone Check the Documentation?" *Evam: Forum on Indian Representations* 1, nos. 1-2 (2002):173-90.

Urban, Hugh. "Tantra, American Style: Neo-Orientalism, Globalization and the Western Appropriation of Tantra." Paper, presented at the Conference of the American Academy of Religion, Denver, 2001.

—— Review of *Kali's Child* by Jeffrey Kripal. *The Journal of Religion* 78, no.2 (April 1998): 318-20.

——*Tantra: Sex, Secrecy, Politics and Power*. Berkeley and Los Angeles: University of California Press, 2003.

Vaidyanathan, T.G. and Jeffrey Kripal, ed. *Vishnu on Freud's Desk*. New Delhi: Oxford University Press, 1999.

Walsh, Roger and Frances Vaughan. *Paths Beyond Ego*. New York: Tarcher/ Putnam, 1993.

White, David. *Kiss of the Yogini: Tantric Sex in its South Asian Context*. Chicago: The University of Chicago Press, 2003.

Winternitz, Maurice. *A History of Indian Literature* (1907), Volume 1. Translated by S. Ketkar. Calcutta: University of Calcutta, 1962.

Woodward, Hiriam W. *Asian Art in The Walters Art Gallery: A Selection*. Baltimore: The Trustees of the Walters Art Gallery, 1991.

Zaleski, Philip, ed. *Best Spiritual Writing 2000*. San Francisco: Harper, 2000.

Acknowledgements

This book has been several years in the making. When Rajiv Malhotra's 'RISA Lila-1' essay appeared on the web-magazine *Sulekha.com*, it unleashed remarkable intellectual ferment on both online and academic forums. In addition to various reader comments (the article has attracted over 45,000 hits), numerous scholars from around the world posted responses. Some of the authors and readers involved came together and developed the idea for a book with a collection of articles/comments on the subject. These included S.N. Balagangadhara, Arjun Bhagat, Sankrant Sanu, Sanjay Garg and Krishnan Ramaswamy, among others. *Sulekha* was very interested in facilitating this. Meanwhile, Prof. VV Raman was very helpful in rewriting the entire 'RISA- Lila-1' article in simpler language, because there was interest among many readers to serialize it for Indian newspapers. None of these initial efforts proceeded to fruition, because the individuals involved were preoccupied with other projects and the ripple effect on *Sulekha* and other forums was exploding too rapidly. 'RISA Lila-1' (and its follow-up, 'RISA Lila-2') had tapped into a groundswell of intellectual and cultural dissatisfaction with the status quo.

Then, in 2005, Malhotra started to work with Pandita Indrani Rampersad to compile a collection of these writings into a reference book, because the scattered writings were being used by some colleges as reading materials on courses dealing with diaspora, immigration, Hinduism, American Studies, etc. Jay Patel also helped compile the materials and began work on a series of cartoons. This later provided the basis for Yvette Rosser to turn them into some of the scripts used in the cartoons included in this book with the excellent artwork and penmanship of Viraj Circar. Unfortunately, Rampersad suffered some health setbacks and the project had to be shelved. In 2006 Yvette Rosser revived the project, and Krishnan Ramaswamy joined the effort a couple of months later. Later Antonio de Nicolas and Aditi Banerjee joined him on the editorial team. All three editors had been following and participating in the on-line debate from the very beginning.

Thus the present volume is the culmination of efforts by many individuals over nearly five years. We thank each of them, particularly Yvette Rosser, who provided valuable editorial input and advice on various parts of the book. The book would not achieve its purpose without the help and participation of each of the authors of its various chapters. We also thank the readers who posted several thousand comments on various web discussions lists where academic Hinduphobia, became one of the most hotly discussed topics. Indeed, many of the comments were articles in their own right. If all the materials published online on this debate were compiled it would take several thousand pages. The present volume is an attempt to highlight the key writings that serve to convey the main issues debated in the voices of the principal parties involved.

The editors also wish to thank Shamanthaka Subramanian, Rahul Sinha, James Abro and Ashok Malik for their able help in copy-editing and proofing this book, and Sanjana Roy Choudhury of Rupa & Co. for her meticulousness as an editor. Dhruv Kaji reviewed early drafts of the book and provided numerous insights. We thank Shruti for her able help in all creative aspects of the book from cover design to commenting on the content and argumentation in the book. We are grateful to the generous support and encouragement of Sashi Kejriwal in making this book possible. And finally we wish to acknowledge the pioneering role played by Rajiv Malhotra and Infinity Foundation in opening up and nurturing this area of research.

The debate is far from over, and we invite readers to participate at www.invadingthesacred.com

Index